Digesting Metabolism

Artificial Land in Japan 1954–2202

4	Preface and Acknowledgments

12	**0 Excavating Artificial Land**

42	**1 Rebuilding Building**
54	Maximum Dwelling: Yosizaka House, 1954–81
70	Transitional Type: Harumi Apartments and Metabolism, 1956–97
104	Avant-Garde Real Estate: Sakaide Artificial Land Platform, 1963–

130	**2 The Metabolist-Industrial Complex**
148	Symbolic Planning: Motomachi Apartments, 1968–
176	Megastructured: Ashiyahama Seaside Town, 1972–
194	Solutionism: Stratiform Structure Module, 1973–
220	Artificial Land Without Architects: Sawada Mansion, 1971–

246	**3 Open Systems**
266	Anti-Speculative Speculation: NEXT21, 1989–
286	Helping DIY: Flex Court Yoshida, 1994–
300	From Promise to Performance: Tsunane Cooperative House, 1996–
316	Concrete Timber: Kugahara House, 1998–2202

336	**4 Neo Edo**

352	Appendix: Mottainai Metabolism—A New Artificial Land

360	Index
367	Image Credits

Preface and Acknowledgments

This book would not have been written had I not moved to Hong Kong at the beginning of the millennium. My preconceptions of the metropolis were permeated by images of Kowloon Walled City, an occupiable sponge of illegal buildings that had captured the imaginations of so many people who, like me, never visited it. Already demolished by the time of my arrival, the Walled City was nevertheless still a phantom, fragmentary presence throughout Hong Kong, echoed in countless facades similarly self-organized into patterns of air conditioners, hanging laundry, and DIY balconies that expanded the spaces of tiny apartments, in hidden restaurants and factories that hummed far above streets overlaid with rhizomes of skybridges, stairs, and escalators. Hong Kong made real those "fantasies" of three-dimensional urbanism that Western academia insisted didn't work. Here they did. The compelling shock of an urban architecture so dense and open to appropriation and adaptation triggered my curiosity in how such a reality is, if not entirely designed by architects, at least enabled by them. Metabolism, the 1960s Japanese avant-garde of which I was at that time only dimly aware, seemed to be one movement that had attempted to implement such a reality. As I became more familiar with the Metabolists, it became clear that their fascination with the concept of artificial land bore out my intuition.

Kowloon Walled City,
Hong Kong, 1990

Like the "investigations in collective form" begun in 1958 by Fumihiko Maki, who soon afterward became a member of the Metabolists, my initial research was enabled by a grant from the Graham Foundation for Advanced Studies in the Fine Arts.[1] Thanks to this support, I made my first study trip to Japan in 2010, travelling from Hiroshima to Osaka, Sakaide, Kofu, and Tokyo to observe firsthand how Metabolism's capsules and megastructures were faring. By that point, it had become clear that I was far from alone in my interest in the group's legacy, with the appearance of Zhongjie Lin's *Kenzo Tange and the Metabolist Movement* and, on the horizon in 2011, the Mori Art Museum's retrospective exhibition and catalog, *Metabolism—The City of the Future,* as well as Rem Koolhaas and Hans Ulrich Obrist's oral history, *Project Japan.* I benefitted hugely from this timing, both through being able to draw on all of this impressive research to help my own, and finding myself free to tell the story of a strand of Metabolism that has been obscured if not ignored in that scholarship.

I do not speak or read Japanese, which is partly why my early idea of a Metabolist post-occupancy study, inspired by Stewart Brand's *How Buildings Learn: What Happens After They're Built*, was later adjusted due to the difficulties of privacy requirements, interview arrangements, and translations in the context of Japanese housing.[2] But I also came to realize that post-occupancy studies are themselves limiting, and that a more synthetic and speculative history needed to be written for the architect's toolbox.

Despite my linguistic shortcomings, much of the following relies on Japanese primary sources and original interviews translated by my invaluable research assistant Riyo Namigata, helped by her partner Shohei Kawanaka. Without Namigata's help, my content would be much diminished.

Early on, I was pointed to key sources for this content by Hajime Yatsuka, perhaps the foremost historian of Metabolism, who also introduced me to Namigata so that I could read them. Throughout this project, Yatsuka's great generosity in all matters Metabolist has been an enormous help and an education, for which I thank him.

For the final stretch of work, I am also greatly indebted to Thomas Daniell for addressing my shortcomings in English. He has been an ideal copy editor, combining a critical fluency in both Japanese language and architecture. He has helped me become a better writer.

Tomoyo Nakamura has also been a major help in the last key stages. She has been equally skilled with Rhino modelling, translation, and the often challenging task of image permissions.

Among the many other people who have helped this book in various ways, I would particularly like to thank Tadatoshi Asano, Ken Awazu, Toshiaki Ban, Shinichi Chikazumi, Masaya Fujimoto, Ariel Genadt, John Habraken, Shizuo Harada, Florian Idenburg, Osamu Ishiyama, Lok Jansen, Tetsuro Kagaya, Yukie Kamiya, Fumihiko Maki, Kazunobu Minami, Mark Mulligan, Koichiro Okamura, Makiko Otaka, Larry Rosensweig, Jun Sato, Hiroe and Kazuko Sawada, Mutsuko Smith, Adam Staniland, Yositika Utida, Nader Vossoughian, and Masakuni Yosizaka. I would also like to single out Jacob Moore, who along with Thomas Daniell and Hajime Yatsuka, was a first reader providing criticism that led to great improvements in precision and tone.

At Hatje Cantz, my publisher, I am grateful for the help and fortitude of Claire Cichy, Adam Jackman, and Thomas Lemaître. Thank you.

Institutionally and beyond, I thank the Architectural Institute of Japan, the Fondation Le Corbusier, the City of Gotemba, the Hiroshima Housing Authority and Municipal Archives, the Mechanical Social Systems Foundation, the National Archives of Modern Architecture, Osaka Gas, and the Urban Renaissance Agency. For financial support, I am deeply grateful to the Graham Foundation, as well as the New York State Council on the Arts and the Takenaka Corporation.

But above all, this book has been made possible by my wife Alice Chung. In addition to being my graphic designer, she has been extraordinarily patient in giving space and time to this extraordinarily long and intense project. I dedicate this book to her and our daughter Ise, my two travelling companions.

Casey Mack
Brooklyn, 2022

---

[1] Maki's Graham-funded research led in part to the publication of his book *Investigations in Collective Form* (St. Louis, MO: School of Architecture, Washington University in St. Louis, 1964).

[2] See Stewart Brand, *How Buildings Learn: What Happens After They're Built* (New York: Penguin, 1994).

An enlightening term: "artificial building sites."
—Le Corbusier, *The Radiant City*[1]

Le Corbusier, perspective of Fort l'Empereur, Algiers, 1931

0
Excavating
Artificial Land

... unhappily as in a thousand student projects (from the time of Le Corbusier's Algiers project onwards), the romance of the idea of "each man building his own house" on man-made platforms stands unsupported by a demonstration of how it is to be done.

—Peter Smithson, "Reflections on Kenzo Tange's Tokyo Bay Plan," 1964[2]

Like the ancient challenge of squaring the circle, since the early twentieth century architects have been working on horizontalizing the vertical. With the increasing ease of high-rise construction came the loss of old freedoms provided by floors on, or close to, the ground, thereby connected to life in the street or garden, and requiring little or no structural engineering for their support. Features such as balconies and high-speed elevators can be seen as compensations for this loss of freedom in tall buildings. One of the grandest visions of this compensatory ambition is Le Corbusier's Fort l'Empereur proposal for Algiers, from 1931, best known through a perspective drawing that shows a horizontalized verticality described by the architect as *terrain artificiel*, or "artificial land." Fort l'Empereur is a building conceived as a building site, as layered planes of empty plots able to accommodate freestanding houses of all variety, the layers forming an infrastructure that is a critique of both greenfield development and uniform mass housing. Departing from that unbuilt progenitor, this book is a response to Peter Smithson's complaint about Kenzo Tange's Tokyo Bay housing, part of his unbuilt A Plan for Tokyo, 1960 proposal. It explores built demonstrations of how "man-made platforms" of artificial-land housing have

Kenzo Tange, A Plan for Tokyo, 1960, view of housing

13

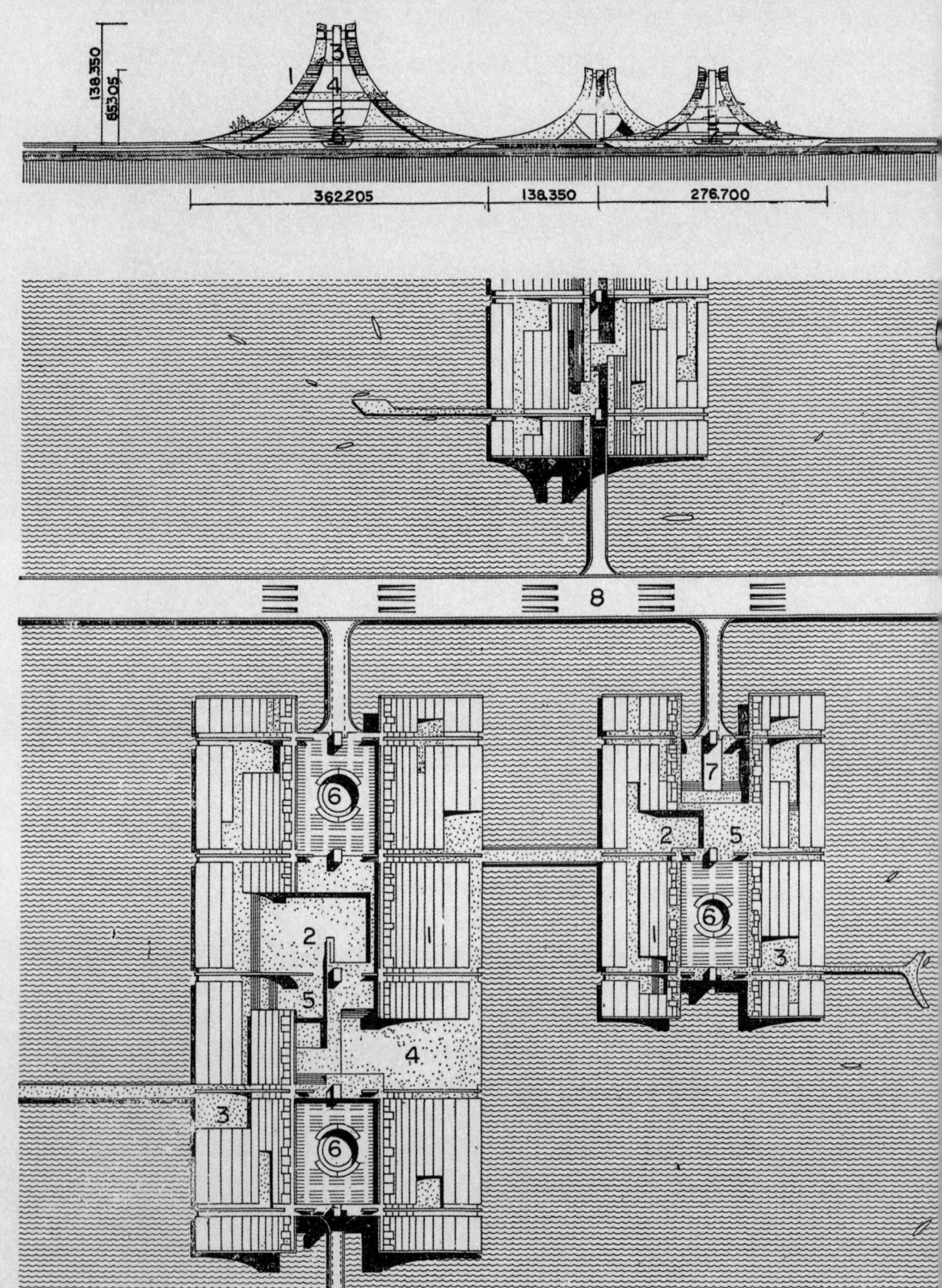

0 EXCAVATING ARTIFICIAL LAND

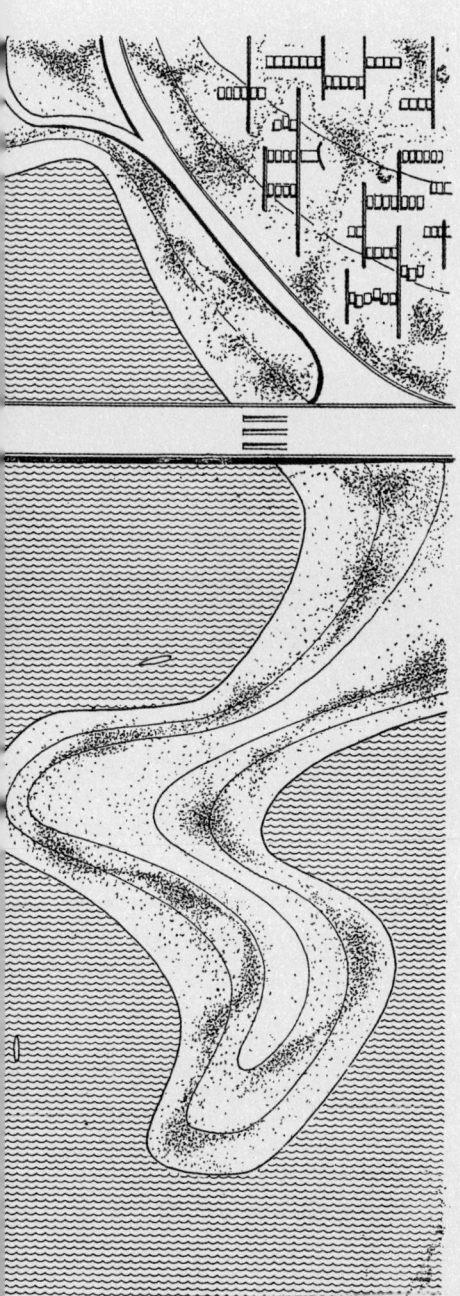

1. residential space
2. public facilities & public square
3. square & kindergarten, etc.
4. school
5. shopping center
6. parking space
7. monorail station
8. highway

Kenzo Tange, A Plan for Tokyo, 1960, typical housing plans and sections. Note assortment of apartments on "man-made platforms" in area 1.

been done—or at least interpreted—in a nation that has pursued such infrastructure with particular zeal.

While this introduction will spend some time in Japan, its main objective is to examine the origins of artificial land elsewhere, as well as the issues and sensibilities that form the global context of the concept. At the outset, it must be stated that artificial land is the most famous architectural concept barely anyone has heard of, buried by "megastructure," the term that it inspired. It's familiar in form, if not name, from Architectural History 101: from Fort l'Empereur, to Yona Friedman's Ville Spatiale (1958–2020), Tange and his students' proposals for Boston Harbor (1959) and Tokyo Bay (1961), Constant Nieuwenhuys's New Babylon (1959–1974), and SITE's Highrise of Homes (1981), to name only a few of the most prominent examples. It connects manifestoes as ideologically diverse as John Habraken's *Supports* (1961) and Rem Koolhaas's *Delirious New York* (1978), and building types from core-and-shell office towers to sites-and-services self-help housing. The advertising slogan for the nineteen floors of New York's Starrett-Lehigh Building (1931) exemplifies the concept's topological implications: "Every floor a first floor," achieved due to huge elevators able to deliver trucks from the street to any one of its vast levels. Since Smithson's complaint, artificial land has, it's safe to say, inspired many thousands more student projects. Smithson, an architect who spent his career interpreting the manifestations of modernism, understood the concept's allure as presented in Le Corbusier's drawing: a harmony between infrastructure and individual, density and spaciousness, modern and vernacular. To link such apparently opposed conditions is the essence of the concept's romantic appeal.

Despite its graphic prominence in architectural history, artificial land is undoubtedly a phrase and concept that creates confusion. It has appeared at different times and places as "artificial sites," "man-made ground," and of course "man-made platforms," which seem to cumulatively drain it of specificity. On the other hand, several audiences to whom I have presented aspects of this research were expecting to hear about landscape urbanism or land reclamation, which though not unrelated, are not essential to the idea of artificial land. But most significantly, the concept's components of a durable, flexible frame for an infill of variable dwellings sounds like the

top: Yona Friedman, Ville Spatiale, c. 1958

center: Kenzo Tange MIT studio, Community for 25,000 over Boston Bay, 1959

bottom: Constant Nieuwenhuys, View of New Babylonian Sectors, 1971. Watercolor and pencil on photomontage.

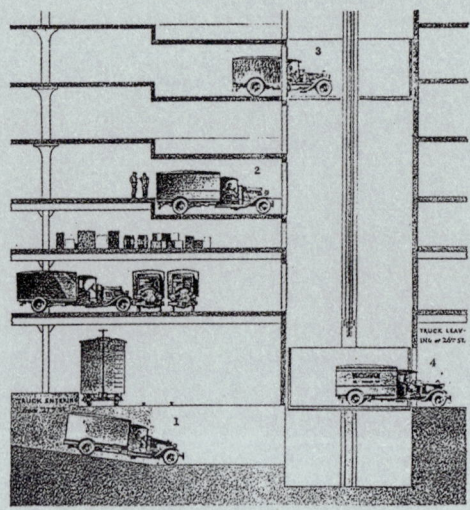

0 EXCAVATING ARTIFICIAL LAND

definition of megastructure, the well-known term introduced in Fumihiko Maki's *Investigations in Collective Form* in 1964, defined there as "a large frame in which all the functions of a city or part of a city are housed."[3] The rise and fall of the megastructure movement in academia and practice was memorialized by historian Reyner Banham's *Megastructure: Urban Futures of the Recent Past* in 1976. As Banham writes, echoing Maki, a megastructure is "a permanent and dominating frame containing subordinate and transient accommodations," with Fort l'Empereur presented by Banham as the "most general ancestor" of all megastructures. No mention is made of Fort l'Empereur's designation by its designer as artificial land.[4]

This book exposes a history and the potentials of artificial land that have been lost, forgotten, or hidden—an obscuring aided by Maki and Banham. Megastructure and artificial land are like two circles of a Venn diagram that significantly but incompletely overlap. A fuller unpacking of their relationship is at the end of chapter 1, but for now it may be stated that artificial land is:

1. A concept not reducible to housing, but most significant for housing, which includes aspects of countryside and city, combining "sun, space, and greenery" with vertical density.
2. A skeleton frame whose floors or platforms simulate terrestrial building sites on which one may build freely. The infill of homes built on these sites, together with the skeleton, produce the overall exterior appearance.
3. A temporal and indeterminate strategy by design, open to change and allowing the creation of homes for specific residents, often making a critique of standardized and commodified housing.
4. Not necessarily large.
5. A productive metaphor and ethic as much as a type. Any skeleton-frame building could be called artificial land, depending on how it is used.

top left: SITE, Highrise of Homes project, 1981

top right: Starrett-Lehigh diagram, "Every floor a first floor," 1931

bottom: Filip Dujardin, Untitled #6, 2013

Suffice it to say at this time that the rejection of commodified housing and the possibility of being small are outside Maki and Banham's definition of megastructure. It should also be noted that these points derive from the eleven case studies that are the focus of this book, in which they sometimes manifest more as aspirations than as realities.

But point five needs further clarification now, as it highlights another source of confusion: artificial land's obscurity is connected to its reliance on the skeleton frame, which makes the concept appear both everywhere and nowhere due to its reliance on the world's most ubiquitous modern building system.

To clarify this haziness, a useful comparison might be made with the fascination of Japanese intellectuals for public plazas, or *hiroba*, in the period after World War II. A type of space considered to be lacking in Japan at that time, the Western-style plaza was seen as a necessity for Japan's new democratic society. The dearth of such spaces for public gatherings and exchanges of opinion led to the appearance of the notion of *hirobaka suru*, translatable as "to plaza-ize": the attitude and act of appropriating spaces such as "Buddhist temples, riverbanks, bridges, and street corners" to perform as plazas.[5] Similarly, for *jinko tochi*, Japanese for "artificial land," there is what can be called *jinko tochika suru*: "to artificial land-ize." This is an interpretation with a similarly democratic spirit, sometimes applied to the most banal of skeleton-frame buildings, assigning them a new dimension of freedom.

Operationally, *jinko tochika suru* indicates a spectrum of examples from the romantic to the realist. At its most romantic is the *Delirious New York* "theorem" of the skyscraper, found in a 1909 cartoon that shows the type's "ideal performance," wherein stacked "virgin sites" support country houses in the middle of the city.[6] At its most realistic, it appears in the common activities of renovation and interior design that characterize industrial lofts in any post-industrial city. Or, somewhere precariously in between, there is the Torre David, the half-finished office high-rise in Caracas appropriated by squatters who converted it into apartments as they were able. While the external expression of different homes may be the ideal of artificial land—the exact opposite of Koolhaas's notion of "lobotomized" skyscrapers that conceal their various interiors behind uniform facades—*jinko tochika suru* remains an inherent potential of any skeleton frame, however it may be clad.[7] If megastructure is a state of size, artificial land is often a state of mind.

As Samuel R. Delany has observed, there "are very few 'ideas' in science fiction. The resonance between an idea and a landscape is what it's all about."[8] This is also true of architecture, and artificial land is one such idea. The projects surveyed in the

top: A.B. Walker, "All the comforts of the country with none of its disadvantages," 1909

bottom: Squatters in the Torre David, c. 2012

"BUY A COZY COTTAGE IN OUR STEEL CONSTRUCTED CHOICE LOTS, LESS THAN A MILE ABOVE BROADWAY. ONLY TEN MINUTES BY ELEVATOR. ALL THE COMFORTS OF THE COUNTRY WITH NONE OF ITS DISADVANTAGES."—*Celestial Real Estate Company.*

following chapters are examples of its resonance in Japan, a place that has for decades found it applicable to ongoing problems and desires. Provoked by war, economics, and earthquakes, the nation has made artificial land in order to enhance its actual land: the layers—be they geological, constructed, or a combination of the two—whose uppermost surfaces are described by topographic maps and property lines, from individual plots to national borders.

Hypothesis

When I started this project, in 2009, it was almost fifty years after the 1960 launch of Metabolism, which seemed like an excellent time to commence a study of a movement predicated on notions of time. The Metabolists—comprising architects Kiyonori Kikutake, Kisho Kurokawa, Fumihiko Maki, and Masato Otaka; editor and historian Noboru Kawazoe; graphic designer Kiyoshi Awazu; and industrial designer Kenji Ekuan—appeared on the global scene thanks to Tange's leadership, with the help of his close colleague, the architect Takashi Asada. They made the "wager" that their designs could anticipate and adapt to the needs of the future, so their work comprised experiments that required time for verification.[9] While the movement cannot be reduced to this wager, it's now a testable hypothesis. How successful have they been?

Feeling that architects frequently claim the status of experiment for designs whose results are rarely known or communicated, I began my research with a decision about a movement largely famous for what it failed to build. Despite the slew of Metabolist-related publications in the last decade, they have rarely engaged the movement's designs in any detail, even where built examples exist, whereas my idea was to investigate only built work through some form of post-occupancy evaluation, which of course requires the presence of occupants. Initially I thought that this survey would assess the performances of established Metabolist types, such as capsules, megastructures, and "group form" clusters. But as my research proceeded, "artificial land" kept appearing in original texts by the Metabolists to such a degree that it was clearly a distinct type or idea, not just a synonym for megastructure. While I realized the phrase originated with Le Corbusier, it seemed to have an independent Japanese history, which was confirmed in 2010 when I learned of the Artificial Land Committee organized in Tokyo in 1962, which included the Metabolists Maki and Otaka.

Artificial land receives insufficient attention in histories of Metabolism, but more importantly, it speaks to what I find most vital about the movement, historically and for the present: its engagement with flexibility in housing. My focus shifted toward finding the concept's role in the movement and beyond, leading to the small collection of projects here, which tend to be exceptions rather than the models their architects wanted them to be. As such, they are often tinged with a sense of failure.

Given this focus, readers will find very little here about capsules or widely published projects such as Kikutake's 1958 Sky House, a design that has historically overshadowed parts of what follows.[10] Speaking about overshadowing, architect, historian, and Tange Lab graduate Hajime Yatsuka suggests there's an "Archigram" Metabolism and a "Team 10" Metabolism.[11] Like their Western counterparts, the "Archigram" Metabolism is far more widely recognized than the "Team 10" version due to its pop sci-fi imagery, as seen especially in the work of Kurokawa, whose 1972 Nakagin Capsule Tower is the most emblematic project of the movement, and of its alleged failure to change over time as planned. The artificial land projects presented here have a lineage much closer to the Team 10 side of the family, represented particularly by Otaka. Like Team 10, of which Peter Smithson was a key member, this branch is fascinated by innovations developed from a search for modern vernaculars, or vernaculars made modern, and far more concerned with the prosaics of dwelling than anything necessarily high-tech.

Despite this basic if impure distinction in the group—Kurokawa attended the 1962 Team 10 meeting at Royaumont in France—artificial land was a key idea for all of the Metabolists, to a greater or lesser extent. Without artificial land's influence, we would not have the group's operative critic Noboru Kawazoe calling for the introduction of a "time factor into city planning."[12] Nor would we have Tange, at Tokyo's 1960 World Design Conference, the venue of Metabolism's debut, famously calling for an architecture strategically combining "shorter" and "longer cycles" of obsolescence, the de facto essence of the movement.[13] The Metabolists didn't just repeat the Western avant-garde tradition of claiming a zeitgeist by declaring their time had now arrived, but rather opened themselves to engaging the uncertainties of times yet to come, with the combination of longer and shorter life cycles promising an architecture adaptable

24　　　　　　　　　　　　　　　　　　　　　　0　EXCAVATING ARTIFICIAL LAND

to Japan's breathtaking postwar growth, a growth notably fueled by changes in Japanese housing and its technologies.

It's easy to take Tange's two cycles as inspiring but naïve. Banham attributes Metabolism's success precisely to the "mind-numbing simplicity" of the idea.[14] Yet little has been written, at least in English, about the complexities that have spread from this apparently simple and clichéd strategy over the following sixty-odd years. While there are common clichéd observations of Japanese modern architecture, such as its fusion of Western and local traditions or its blurring of distinctions between inside and outside, to be aware of these clichés is not necessarily to understand their material impact and value, positive or otherwise.

Housing Metabolism

Today, neoliberal housing practices have exacerbated inequity most everywhere, Japan very much included.[15] The vast majority of housing is created for maximum exchange value, to be sold or rented within a globalized market in which financial speculation has led to increasingly risk-averse and fast-tracked products. The Congrès Internationaux d'Architecture Moderne (CIAM), the Western lobbying organization for modern architecture, stated in its 1933 *Charter of Athens* that "after more than a century of subjection to the brutal games of speculation, [the home] must become a humane undertaking."[16] Unfortunately, these brutal games still persist almost a century later, and there remains a need to create humane housing that meets a diversity of requirements, from cost, to location, to number of bedrooms, to supportive communities, to list some of the most common. My hope in examining the projects that follow is to offer some approaches to these requirements through designs that engage flexibility, found across a spectrum of housing forms and methods of supply, from vast blocks of public "minimum dwelling" rentals, to self-builds, to small private owner-occupied collectives, to designs selected from an online menu.

Flexibility often gets a bad rap in architecture, at least academically.[17] The ability to physically resize, redivide, and reprogram a space or site is seen as a breach in the architect's obligation to define relationships, and as a path to sterility. What's usually promoted instead is what architect Herman Hertzberger calls "polyvalency": architecture that, to again quote Smithson, "leaves itself open to—even suggests—interpretation,

Kisho Kurakawa, Nakagin Capsule Tower, 1972 (2017)

without itself being changed."[18] Polyvalent form, an approach that maintains the architect's traditional position of control, suggests a belief that any activity can happen anywhere in a static design, and happen well. While there are examples such as Mies van der Rohe using his bathroom as a bedroom, polyvalency won't always be a successful approach.[19] Instead, the need for a flexibility of changeable or moveable parts is made clear by the architect Moshe Safdie, whose Habitat project in Montreal, built in 1967, exceeds Algiers in its inspiration for both students and professionals. In 2013, Safdie reflected, "Flexibility is critical. If I had known that, I would have designed more flexibility into Habitat—holes you can knock out or something."[20] We can rightly envy Habitat, rigid or not, when comparing it with the vast majority of urban housing built today for any income bracket, all constructed with the widespread and pliant reality of flat-slab skeletons infilled with drywall. As we will see, though, this reality is almost alright. The projects ahead also show that flexibility and polyvalency are not necessarily mutually exclusive.[21]

    In the last few decades, parametric design has risen to a position of dominance, wherein software algorithms are used to link and integrate multiple and often conflicting requirements into a tailored whole, resulting in a design process more responsive to data than ever before. This has led to an explosion of inventive and complicated buildings whose design processes, smoothly translated into fabrication, enable a tremendous rationalization of variation in space. Less clear, however, is parametric design's value in enabling the rationalization of variation in time, driven by the changing needs of a given project. Contrary to the productivism common in parametric work, which often seems to aim at generating as much variation as possible as an end in itself, this book examines flexibility not solely in terms of how variation may occur in housing, but also when, and most critically, with whom.

Arcades des Anglais, Algiers waterfront (1929)

Algiers to Tokyo

Before leaving for Japan, we need to return in more detail to the genesis of artificial land in Le Corbusier's work, seen particularly with Fort l'Empereur. While the Japanese designs surveyed here both extend and question its implications through their own innovations, Fort l'Empereur is certainly their "most general ancestor."

Artificial land's birth is connected to one of the main areas of experimentation and excitement in the skeleton frame's early development, found in the reinforced-concrete buildings of American factories in the early 1900s, an architecture of continuous floor space. Well-documented as an inspiration for European modernism, spatially and structurally, these buildings were designed to facilitate changes in machinery and organization by means of few columns, strong floors, high ceilings, and ample daylight.[22] Digging into trade publications of the time, such as those of the Atlas Portland Cement Company, then a major concrete manufacturer, the material is described as "artificial stone," the name under which Portland cement—concrete's critical ingredient—was patented in 1824. Le Corbusier appears to have known this phrase, and it's a short step from a stack of airy floor plates made of artificial stone to their becoming artificial land.[23]

While central to Le Corbusier's work since the 1915 Dom-ino House, the skeleton frame is not presented as artificial land until Algiers, the city that provoked its first explicit application. There he labored from 1931 to 1942 as self-appointed master planner for what was then the colonial capital of French Algeria. On the Algiers waterfront, he found the Arcades des Anglais, a boulevard viaduct running along the harbor edge that joined an expansion of the harbor to the urban fabric. Built in the 1860s, the vast Arcades extended into the mountainous topography rising up from the harbor to create what the historian Antillio Petruccioli calls "a new base for the city."[24] But the Arcades weren't only a massive piece of infrastructure under the city, since the city was also within the infrastructure: the viaduct's huge arches had become occupied by piecemeal housing constructed by local fishermen. This transportation infrastructure merged with an unintended infrastructure for housing had a clear impact on Le Corbusier, who drew multiple sketches of the Arcades and their infill. One of the sketches, reproduced in his 1933 book *The Radiant City*, directly acknowledges it as a precedent for his Algerian work, along with Giacomo Matté-Trucco's 1923 Lingotto Fiat factory.[25] The fact that such an extensive

Le Corbusier, sketch of fishermen's dwellings within the Arcades, c. 1931

28 0 EXCAVATING ARTIFICIAL LAND

infrastructural element already existed in Algiers made the scale of the Fort l'Empereur design seem reasonable, and offered proof that such an intervention could support the vernacular life of the city.

Le Corbusier once remarked "it is always life that is right and the architect who is wrong."[26] The prototypes of the Arcades and the flexible factory suggest a rapport with this sentiment: the mass-housing architect could be a designer of infrastructure consciously planned for multiple forms of occupation, accommodating demographic, stylistic, and other differences. In describing the perspective drawing of Fort l'Empereur, the keystone of his initial master plan, located above the city on slopes deemed by others as too difficult to develop, he writes in *The Radiant City* that:

> Here are "artificial sites," vertical garden cities. Everything has been gathered here: space, sun, view; means of immediate communication, both vertical and horizontal; water, gas, etc. thriftily supplied; ideally simple sanitation—sewers, garbage pails, etc. The architectural aspect is stunning! The most absolute diversity, within unity. Every architect will build his villa as he likes; what does it matter to the whole if a Moorish-style villa flanks another in Louis XVIth or in Italian Renaissance?[27]

One of the most influential drawings in modern architecture, the perspective is paradoxically very distant from the functionalist dwellings of modernism. The drawing's dissonance is due to an assortment of Moorish villas abutting ones in Corbusian style on the massive floors, a plurality that suggests cultural integration, not merely stylistic indifference or colonial novelty, even if that may have been the architect's feeling. For as we will soon see, the drawing's hybrid styles and tectonics seem to have had a particular appeal in Japan where, as in Le Corbusier's description, architects played a central role in artificial land's development. In practice, the concept will only rarely be "architecture without architects" with "each man building his own house."

Though the naked frame is utterly familiar in Le Corbusier's work through his extensive exploration of the free plan's compositional liberty in space, artificial land uses the free plan as a financial opportunity in time. The rationale was that the modernization and expansion of Algiers' transportation and housing infrastructure would be financed by the sale of the layered sites built by the government, then sold to individuals who could build houses as they pleased. Artificial land was thereby a strategy for filling the city's coffers

AL 3056
A
GASPILLAGE PARADOXE
URBANISTIQUE DES
CITÉS JARDINS
ROUTES
CANALISATIONS
TRANSPORTS COMMUN
PRIVÉS
ENTRETIEN
TEMPS PERDU =
TONNEAU DES DANAIDES = DEFICIT DES VILLES = IMPOTS
LES TRAVAUX URBAINS SONT UNE SOURCE DE DEFICIT
UN LOGIS=
PLAFOND ÉTANCHE
PLANCHER
PLANCHER FONDÉ
1. m²
REVIENT à 450. frs
14132
FONDATION LE CORBUSIER

AL 3057
B
CRÉATION
DU TERRAIN
AMENAGÉ
EN CITÉS JARDINS
VERTICALES
AUTOSTRADE
GARAGES
ASCENSEURS COMMUNICATION VERTICALE
PILOTIS
SERVICES COMMUNS
TEMPS GAGNÉ =
CAISSE MUNICIPALE
TECHNIQUE MODERNE = INSONORISATION, AIR EXACT.
LES TRAVAUX URBAINS SONT UNE VASTE ENTREPRISE BÉNÉFICITAIRE.
UN LOGIS=
PLAFOND ÉTANCHE
PLANCHER
PLANCHER FONDÉ
1. m²
REVIENT à 320. frs
L'AUTOSTRADE ÉTANT PAYÉE
14133
FONDATION LE CORBUSIER

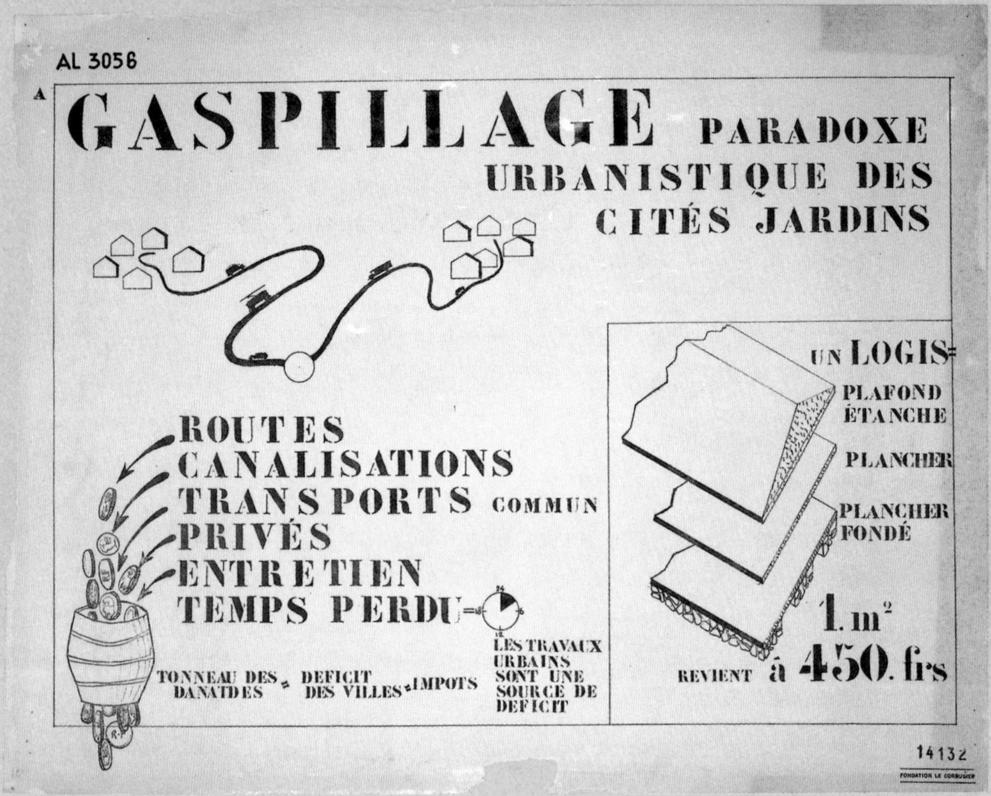

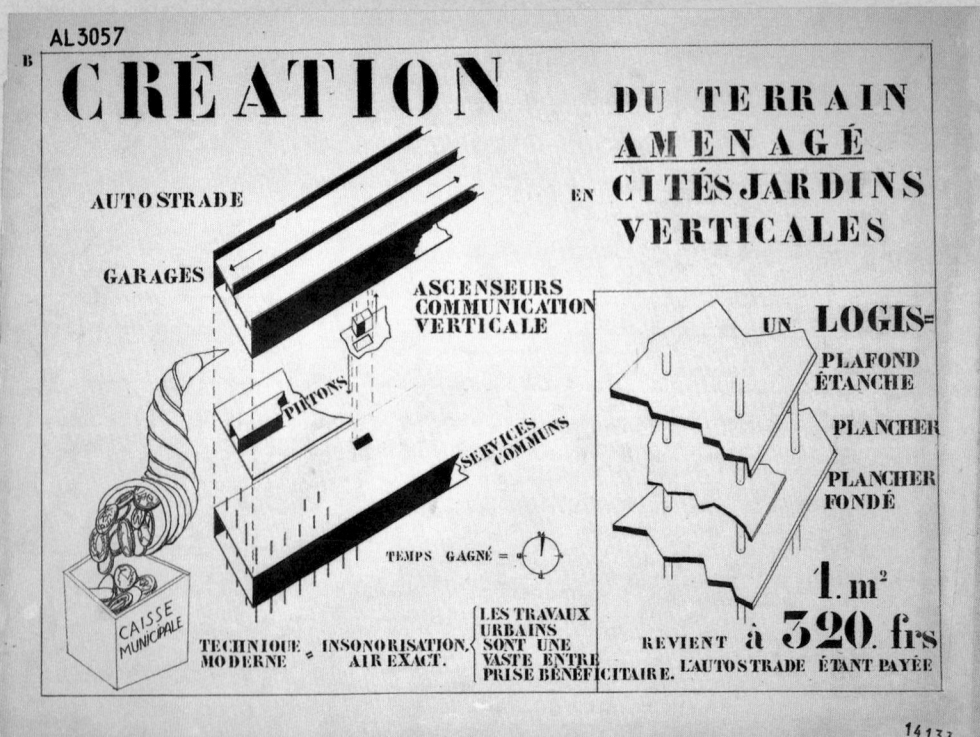

through reduced public investment, since the government was only fronting the cost for housing services and structural support on a challenging topography, not the actual houses or apartments. This made for an incredible merger of top-down and bottom-up activity.[28]

In two diagrams, Le Corbusier juxtaposes Fort l'Empereur with what he considered to be the undesirable option of a decentralized Garden City built from scratch, wherein new freestanding homes entail the wasteful expense of new dispersed road infrastructure.[29] Instead, his scheme offers a "vertical Garden City" supporting freestanding homes within the structure of artificial land that may be read as compensation for the desirability of the horizontal Garden City's sunlight, spaciousness, and proximity to nature, but made more cost-effective through being verticalized, densified, and part of the existing city. Despite his criticism of the Garden City model, proposed by the self-taught English planner Ebenezer Howard and first published in 1898 in *To-morrow: A Peaceful Path to Real Reform*, Le Corbusier turned the health benefits of nature advocated by Howard into his own objective and mantra—"sun, space, and greenery" as the "essential joys."[30] Artificial land is a vehicle for providing these resources, and a transformation of Howard's influential approach, at that time a huge inspiration to architects and planners around the world.[31]

Ample light and air are goals common to the reformist agenda of modernist housing, but other aspects of Howard's concept engage domestic diversity in a way that is specific to Le Corbusier's interpretation. Howard's new cities were to provide plots with site infrastructure such as roads and sanitation already in place, and he encouraged "the fullest measure of individual taste and preference" in how housing might be built on the plots.[32] With regard to the issue of control raised by this arrangement, Howard writes that for the Garden City:

> The very question at issue is [...] *what those things are* which the community can do better than the individual; and when we seek for an answer to this question we find two directly conflicting views—the view of the socialist, who says: Every phase of wealth-production and distribution can be best performed by the community; and the view of the individualist, who contends these things are best left to the individual. But probably the true answer is to be found at neither extreme, is only to be gained by experiment, and will differ in different communities and at different periods.[33]

top: Le Corbusier, "Waste: urban paradox of Garden Cities," 1931

bottom: Le Corbusier, "Creation: sites converted into vertical Garden Cities," 1931

AL 3059
ECHELLE 1:1000
N
1:500
PREMIERE
DEUXIEME ETAGE
14134

GARDERIE D'ENFANTS
RAMPE (SERVICE SANTÉ 17e ETAGE SUD)
TOUR D'ASCÉNSEURS
CHEMINÉE DE VENTILATION
MUR BRISE-VENT (THÉÂTRE)
GYMNASE
VESTIAIRES ET TERRASSE SUPÉRIEURE
RUES INTÉRIEURES
SERVICES COMMUNS DE RAVITAILLEMENT
LOGGIAS BRISE-SOLEIL
ESCALIER DE SECOURS
TERRAIN ARTIFICIEL (MACHINERIES)
LES PILOTIS

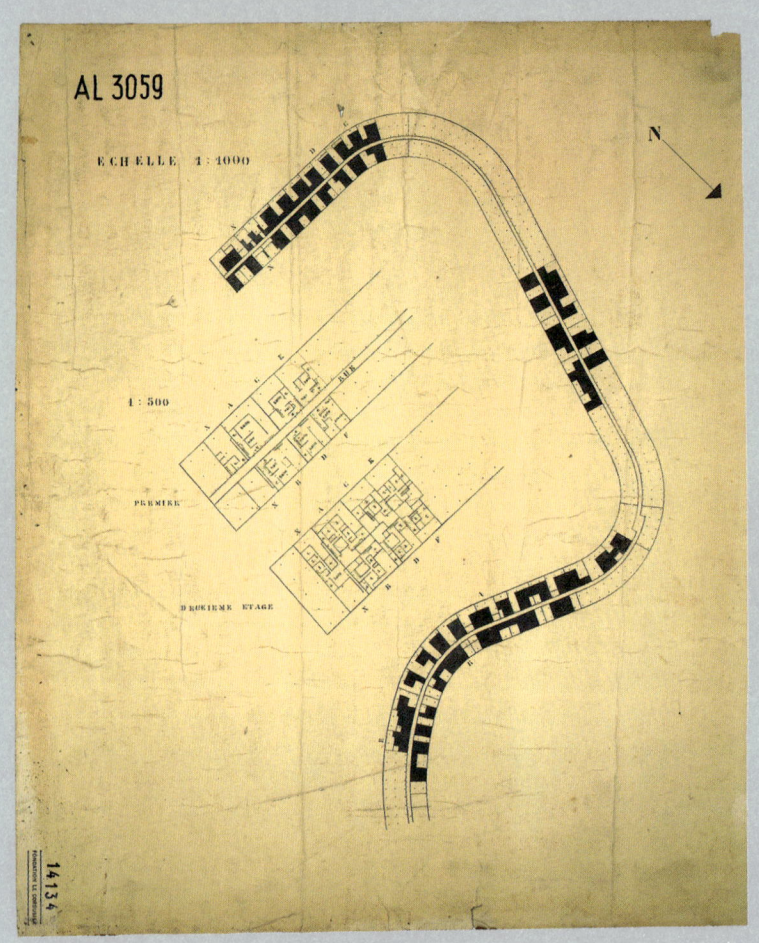

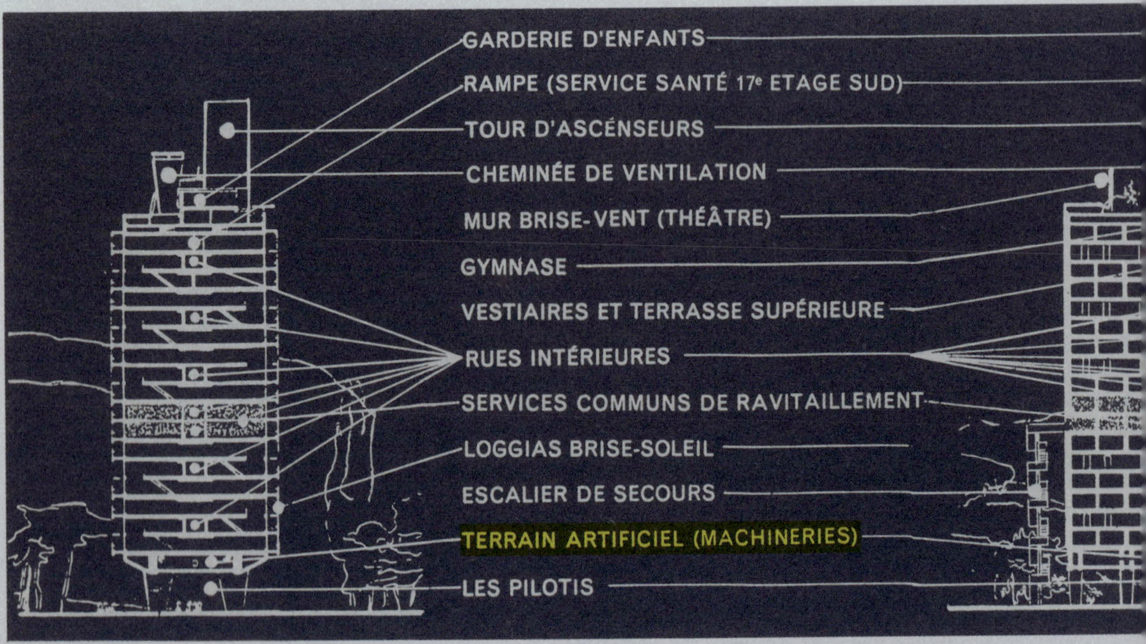

Though a dynamic combination of these views characterizes much development—the gridiron of the 1811 Commissioners' Plan for Manhattan is a prime example—Fort l'Empereur's innovation is the three-dimensionalization of such city planning within the body of a building. As we will see, the negotiation of control between individual and communal or managerial bodies is a major theme in the Japanese experiments that follow.

Turning to design specifics, Fort l'Empereur amplified possibilities for what could be built upon its layers. The plot size one could buy was variable, thanks to pilotis allowing barrier-free subdivision, and the floor-to-ceiling height of each level was to be 4.5 meters. This height was seen as optimal for allowing daylight deep into the plan, and also the insertion of mezzanines at 2.2 meters, a configuration apparently inspired by a truckdriver café in Paris that Le Corbusier lunched at—another example of vernacular influence in the proposal.[34] The 2.2-meter height was considered perfect for more private functions, while 4.5 meters would accommodate more social ones. The resulting loose fit, both in plan and section, recalibrates the relationship between load-bearing structure and infill units, a disconnect that expands the spectrum of how plots could be occupied. *The Radiant City* advocates making the 4.5-meter height a new building code.[35]

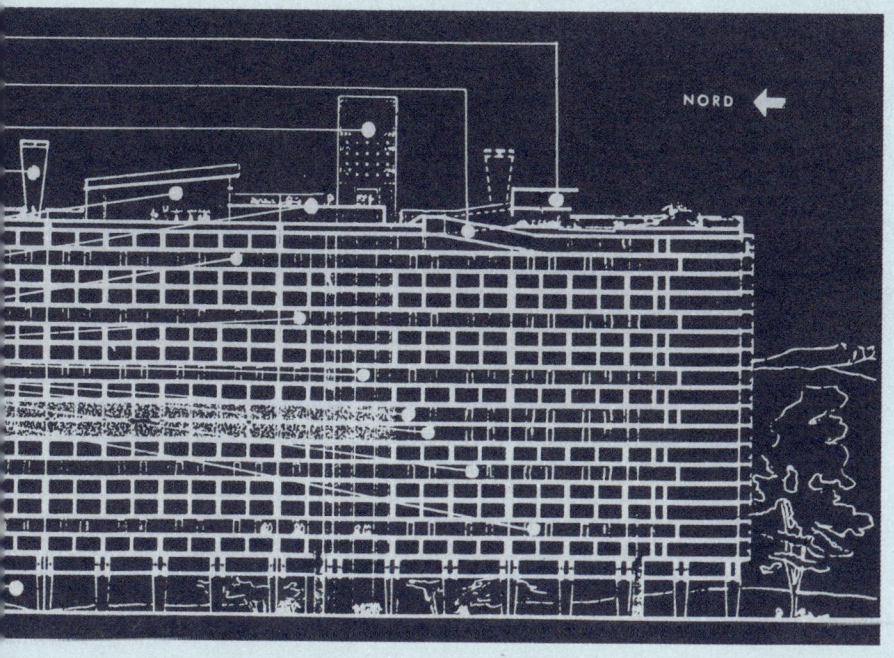

top: Le Corbusier, variable plot sizes of Fort l'Empereur, 1931

bottom: Le Corbusier, Unité d'Habitation Marseilles, 1952. Note hollow base as *terrain artificiel* for plumbing and other building services.

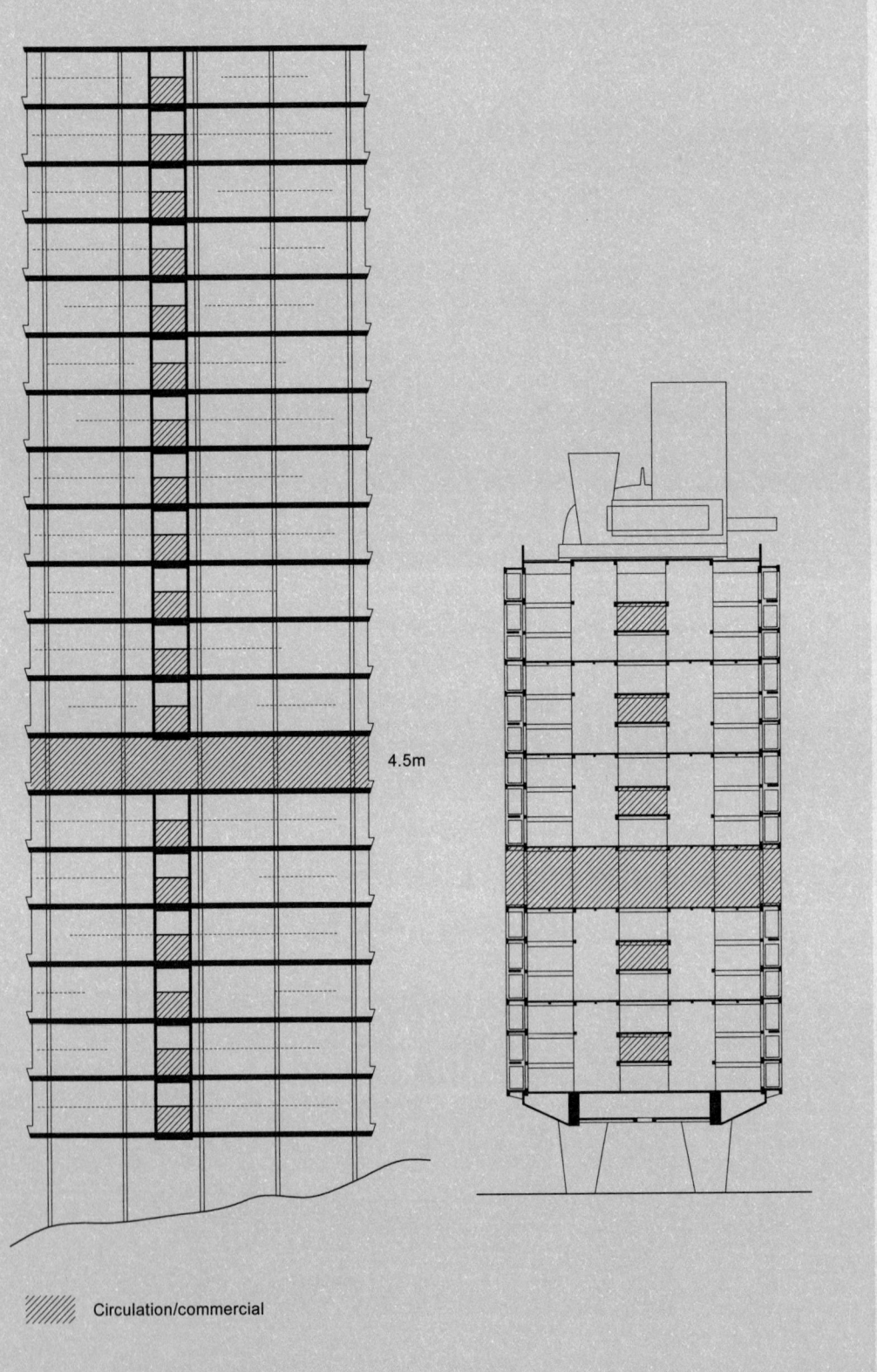

Circulation/commercial

left: Comparison of skeletons
for Fort l'Empereur, 1931,
and Unité d'Habitation
Marseilles, 1952

above: Unité d'Habitation
Marseilles steel structure

Fort l'Empereur's social imagination may seem like a grand exception in Le Corbusier's work, as Banham writes in *Megastructure*, but this is not the case.[36] Turning to the Unité d'Habitation Marseilles, completed in 1952, its polychromatic facades and mid-level shopping street clearly reference the mid-level roadway and patchwork of villa facades presented in 1931. Furthermore, original documentation of the Unité shows the plinth on which all the superstructure rests referred to as *terrain artificiel*, and Le Corbusier will continue to use the term for his Unité projects into the 1960s.

Taken at face value, artificial land now refers to the role of the plinth as a giant plenum for distributing building services. But operationally, Marseilles' artificial land is throughout its fabric. As the architect Edward R. Ford has pointed out, despite a widespread impression that it is mostly a cast-in-place concrete building, only about half of it uses this method.[37] Much of the remaining structure is steel and wood. These materials are used for prefabricated flooring and partition components, unlike the fully unitized apartments implied by Le Corbusier's famous photo of a hand slipping an apartment "bottle" into a structural "bottle rack." Instead, the small-scale components are fitted into cast-in-place racks running between cast-in-place floors at every third level. Reduced to this monolithic structure, the triplex voids of the Unité's section are striking: it's a more radical version of Fort l'Empereur itself. While Le Corbusier is still operating as master architect, designing all the units top-down, he built a structural system with the potential, under other circumstances, to be occupied quite differently.

Takamasa Yosizaka, an architect mostly known, if at all, for his tiny Japan Pavilion in Venice, fully understood this potential. After World War II, Japan was on a voracious hunt for ideas for its reconstruction, a hunt impressive in breadth and depth. In the early 1950s, Yosizaka, a young veteran of two years' work in Le Corbusier's atelier, and briefly involved in overseeing the construction of Marseilles, arrived back in Japan with artificial land in mind as a solution to the nation's enormous housing emergency.

Long Tail

Finally, obvious as it may be at this point, over the long period covered by this study—from 1954 to a speculation about 2202—a network of architects has expanded well beyond the official group of Metabolists. The people and projects that compose these links could be described as the movement's "long tail."[38] A kind of probability graph used to

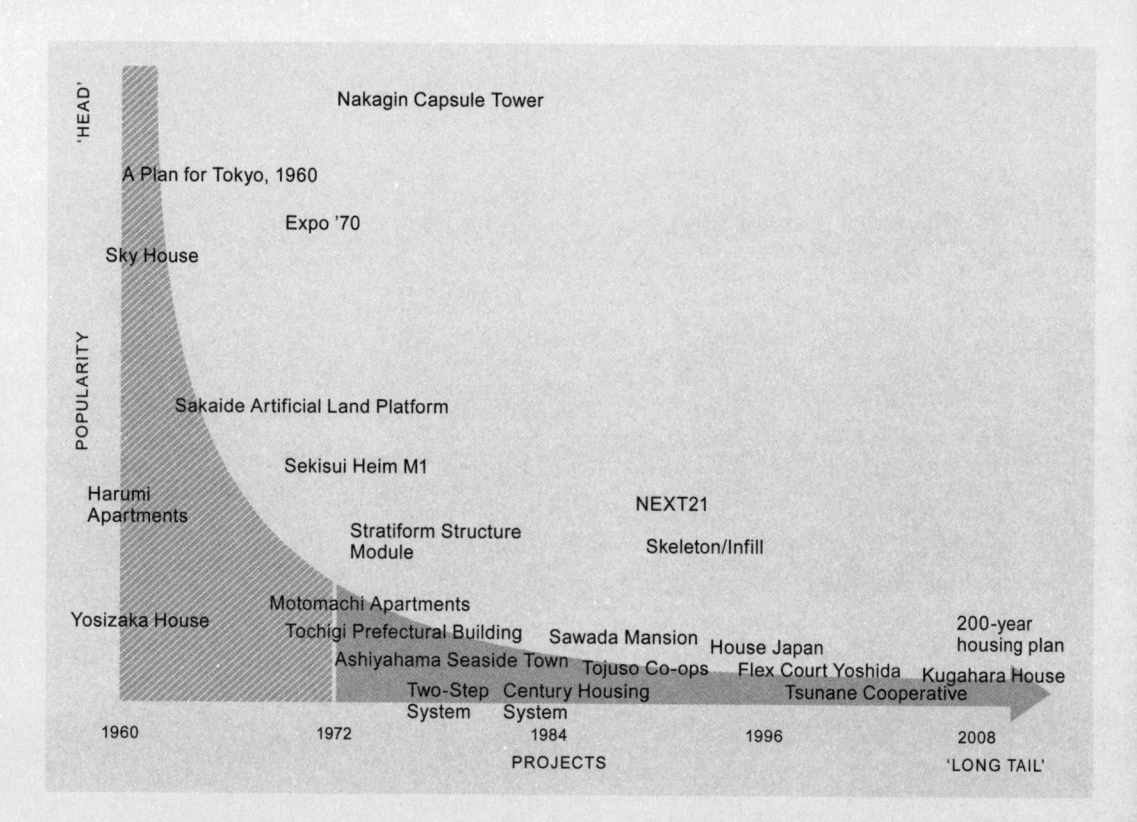

```
'HEAD'
                    Nakagin Capsule Tower


         A Plan for Tokyo, 1960
                    Expo '70
    Sky House

POPULARITY

         Sakaide Artificial Land Platform

              Sekisui Heim M1
                                           NEXT21
    Harumi
    Apartments        Stratiform Structure
                      Module                Skeleton/Infill
                                                                    200-year
    Yosizaka House  Motomachi Apartments                             housing plan
               Tochigi Prefectural Building  Sawada Mansion  House Japan
                 Ashiyahama Seaside Town  Tojuso Co-ops  Flex Court Yoshida  Kugahara House
                    Two-Step   Century Housing              Tsunane Cooperative
                    System     System
    1960            1972             1984              1996        2008
                              PROJECTS                             'LONG TAIL'
```

measure phenomena such as popularity over time, a long tail is the asymptotic "tailing off" from a "head" of high concentration over a shorter period, to a tail of a lower concentration distributed over an extended period. A long tail is larger in quantity than the population that is apparently dominant, but in fact only more visible. As we will see, the tail here has done much of the digesting of Metabolism from aspiration into practice, an activity in which little-known architects and engineers, opaque government ministries, and giant design-build contractors have undertaken important roles behind the scenes. Many of these actors, such as MOC and MITI, go by acronyms, which permeate this book.

    With this perspective, I'm not overly concerned with exact designations, such as whether or not Tange or Arata Isozaki were official Metabolists. Rather, I'm much more interested in de facto membership encompassing a history that a focus on such categories could never reveal. I'm more interested in what Metabolism could be than what it was. For unlike other architectural "-isms" such as Purism, Brutalism, Deconstructivism, or Parametricism, Metabolism contains a premise that still needs testing.

Metabolism's Long Tail. This diagram is partial and focused on work discussed in this book. It is also not entirely scientific.

37

1. Le Corbusier, *The Radiant City*, trans. Eleanor Levieux et al. [1933] (New York: Orion Press, 1967), 55.
2. Peter Smithson, "Reflections on Kenzo Tange's Tokyo Bay Plan," *Architectural Design* 34 (October 1964): 480.
3. Fumihiko Maki and Masato Ohtaka, "Collective Form—Three Paradigms," in Maki, *Investigations in Collective Form* [1964] (St. Louis, MO: School of Architecture, Washington University in St. Louis, 2004), 6.
4. Reyner Banham, *Megastructure: Urban Futures of the Recent Past* (New York: Harper & Row, 1976), 7–9.
5. The phrase *hirobaka suru* was coined by the architectural historian and critic Teiji Itoh. See Jordan Sand, *Tokyo Vernacular: Common Spaces, Local Histories, Found Objects* (Los Angeles: University of California Press, 2013), 45. The translation of *hirobaka suru* that I am using differs from Sand's.
6. Rem Koolhaas, *Delirious New York: A Retroactive Manifesto for Manhattan* [1978] (New York: The Monacelli Press, 1994), 82–83.
7. Koolhaas, *Delirious*, 100.
8. Samuel R. Delany, "Letter to a Critic," *The Jewel-Hinged Jaw* (New York: Berkley Windhover Books, 1977), 11.
9. I am indebted to Hajime Yatsuka for the characterization of Metabolist planning as a "wager." See Yatsuka, "Masato Otaka's Housing Complex in Saka-ide," *OASE* 57 (2001): 122.
10. See page 69n18 of this book for a discussion of the Sky House relative to the work of Takamasa Yosizaka on which Kikutake draws.
11. See Hajime Yatsuka, "Capsule or 'Move-net:' Philosophical Differences," chap. 13-2 in "Metabolism Nexus" (unpublished manuscript, 2012), PDF file. English translation by Riyo Namigata of Hajime Yatsuka, *Metabolism Nexus* [in Japanese] (Tokyo: Ohmsha, 2011). Tange Lab was Tange's student laboratory at the University of Tokyo, which ran from 1946 to 1974. Architectural education in Japan is typically organized in a lab structure, where, like schools within a school, students work under a selected head professor, often over multiple years or the course of a degree program, with the professor establishing research and design themes.
12. Noboru Kawazoe, "The City of the Future," *Zodiac* 9 (1961): 100. It should be noted, in order to indicate Kawazoe's status as "operative critic," that this phenomenon of partisan criticism was identified and attacked by the architectural historian Manfredo Tafuri, who considered a key culprit to be the historian and editor Bruno Zevi, *Zodiac*'s founder. As Tafuri wrote, operative criticism or history is "analysis of architecture [...] programmatically distorted and finalized." See Carla Keyvanian, "Manfredo Tafuri: From the Critique of Ideology to Microhistories," *Design Issues* 16 (Spring 2000): 4.
13. Kenzo Tange, "Technology and Humanity," *The Japan Architect* (October 1960): 12.
14. Banham, *Megastructure*, 47.
15. This is not to say that neoliberal policies have been the same or occurred at the same time in different nations. For an analysis of Japan's situation, discussing the shrinking access to home ownership as well as low-income rentals, see Yosuke Hirayama, "Neoliberalism and Low-Income Housing in Japan," *LHI Journal* 4, no. 1 (January 2013): 15–22.
16. CIAM, "Charter of Athens: Tenets," in *Programmes and Manifestoes on 20th-Century Architecture*, ed. Ulrich Conrads (London: Lund Humphries, 1970), 143.
17. I have often heard its rejection by fellow critics at reviews for housing studios. Writing in 2021, during a pandemic that has forced many to combine home, office, and school, this attitude may be changing.
18. See Herman Hertzberger, "Flexibility and Polyvalency," *Forum* 16, no. 3 (1962): 115–118; and Alison and Peter Smithson, *Without Rhetoric: An Architectural Aesthetic 1955–1972* (Cambridge, MA: The MIT Press, 1974), 69. Italics in original.
19. See Franz Schulze, *Mies van der Rohe: A Critical Biography* (Chicago: The University of Chicago Press, 1985), 95.
20. Moshe Safdie, "Habitat '67," *CLOG: Brutalism*, ed. Kyle May et al. (2013): 76.
21. While I see polyvalency as a type of programmatic flexibility, opposed to a spatial flexibility designed for physical transformation, I am keeping to Hertzberger's classification cited above.
22. The best history of this period is Reyner Banham's *A Concrete Atlantis: U.S. Industrial Buildings and European Modern Architecture* (Cambridge, MA: The MIT Press, 1986), which, from the perspective of this introduction, can be read as a prequel to *Megastructure*.
23. Portland cement, the binding agent holding together the aggregates in concrete, was patented as "Artificial Stone" in England by Joseph Aspdin. For the continued use of his term more generally for concrete in the early twentieth century, see for example, The Atlas Portland Cement Company, *Reinforced Concrete in Factory Construction* (New York: The Atlas Portland Cement Company, 1907), 20. Banham notes in *A Concrete Atlantis* that Atlas was one company purported to be purveying the factory photos and publications that would be influential on European modernists such as Le Corbusier and Walter Gropius. See Banham, *A Concrete Atlantis*, 195. Other companies at the time, like the Lehigh Portland Cement Company, also referred to their product as "artificial stone" in, for example, Maurice M. Sloan, *The Concrete Country House and Its Construction* (Philadelphia: The Association of American Portland Cement Manufacturers, 1912), 139.

Whether or not Le Corbusier knew of these exact publications is uncertain. However, he mentions a youthful revelation on the benefits of "artificial cement" in *The Radiant City* to segue to his introduction of "artificial sites," the chosen translation of *terrain artificiel* by one of the book's translators, Eleanor Levieux. See Le Corbusier, *The Radiant City*, 53–55.

24 Antillio Petruccioli, "Algiers: The Colonial City," *The City in the Islamic World* 1, ed. Salma Khadra Jayyusi et al. (Leiden; Boston, MA: Brill, 2008), 996.
25 Le Corbusier, *The Radiant City*, 241.
26 Quoted in Philippe Boudon, *Lived-in Architecture: Le Corbusier's Pessac Revisited* [1969] (Cambridge, MA: The MIT Press, 1979), 2.
27 Le Corbusier, *The Radiant City*, 247.
28 Le Corbusier, *The Radiant City*, 247.
29 Le Corbusier, *The Radiant City*, 228–229.
30 The necessity of these qualities appears throughout Howard's writing, but never with Le Corbusier's zeal. Indeed, in the 1964 and 1967 republication of *The Radiant City*, "soleil, espace, verdure" appears on the book's cover like a bold subtitle. For a detailed analysis of Howard and the Garden City's influence on Le Corbusier, see Robert Fishman, *Urban Utopias in the Twentieth Century* (Cambridge, MA: The MIT Press, 1982).
31 It should be noted that the Garden City and artificial land share a similar propensity to cause confusion or be misinterpreted. Fishman writes that the Garden City was often shorn of Howard's cooperative social objectives, and seen as no more than a garden suburb. See *Urban Utopias*, 178.
32 Ebenezer Howard, *Garden Cities of To-Morrow* [1898] (Cambridge, MA: The MIT Press, 1970), 54.
33 Howard, *Garden Cities*, 90. Italics in original.
34 See Willy Boesiger and Hans Girsberger, eds., *Le Corbusier 1910–65* (New York: Praeger, 1967), 25.
35 See Le Corbusier, *The Radiant City*, 55.
36 Banham, *Megastructure*, 8.
37 Edward R. Ford, *The Details of Modern Architecture, Volume 2: 1928 to 1988* (Cambridge, MA: The MIT Press, 1998), 183.
38 The term "long tail" was coined in 2004 by former *Wired* editor-in-chief Chris Anderson to describe the business model of companies such as Amazon and Netflix relative to the pursuit of "megahit" movies, songs, etc. See Chris Anderson, "The Long Tail," *Wired*, October 1, 2004, https://www.wired.com/2004/10/tail/.

Dramatis Personae

Le Corbusier	1887–1965
Wajiro Kon	1888–1973
Kunio Maekawa	1905–1986
Kenzo Tange	1913–2005
Takamasa Yosizaka	1917–1980
Masato Otaka	1923–2010
Yositika Utida	1925–2021
Noboru Kawazoe	1926–2015
Toshihiko Kimura	1926–2009
John Habraken	1928–
Kiyonori Kikutake	1928–2011
Fumihiko Maki	1928–

General Notes

Japanese names are given in Western order. Spellings of some personal names vary in sources. In general, the spellings used reflect the author's reliance on the conventions of major archives and publications, and architects' business cards. Macrons have not been used, except when quoting or citing sources that include macrons, or in transliterating sources in endnotes. Words that were transliterated from English into phonetic Japanese have been restored to their English form.

Project start dates denote the year design work began, while end dates are the year of demolition.

For all project photography, dates given in parentheses are for photos taken after the date of primary construction, and typically taken by the author.

The red used in some drawings indicates short-lived or changeable components, typically infill, in contrast to more durable and fixed components drawn in black, typically load-bearing skeleton frames. Drawings with this red/black categorization were produced by the author.

Acronyms/Abbreviations

AIJ:	Architectural Institute of Japan
ALC:	Artificial Land Committee
ASTM:	Ashiyahama Shin'nittetsu Takenaka Matsushita
BCJ:	Building Center of Japan
CHS:	Century Housing System
CIAM:	Congrès Internationaux d'Architecture Moderne
CLT:	Cross-Laminated Timber
Docomomo:	International Committee for Documents and Conservation of Buildings, Sites, and Neighborhoods of the Modern Movement
FAR:	Floor Area Ratio
GHLC:	Government Housing Loan Corporation
HHA:	Hiroshima Housing Authority
JHC:	Japan Housing Corporation
LR:	Land Readjustment
MITI:	Ministry of International Trade and Industry
MLIT:	Ministry of Land, Infrastructure, Transport and Tourism
MOC:	Ministry of Construction
MOE:	Ministry of the Environment
nLDK:	number of bedrooms + Living + Dining + Kitchen
NOHS:	Nikkenkei Open Housing System
PAU:	Prefabrication, Art and Architecture, Urbanism
SAR:	Stichting Architecten Research (Foundation for Architects' Research)
SI:	Skeleton/Infill
SMC:	Sound Material-Cycle
SRC:	Steel-Reinforced Concrete
Tojuso:	Association of People Who Wish to Create Their Own Urban Apartment Buildings With Their Own Hands
TSHS:	Two-Step Housing System
WoDeCo:	World Design Conference

HOKKAIDO

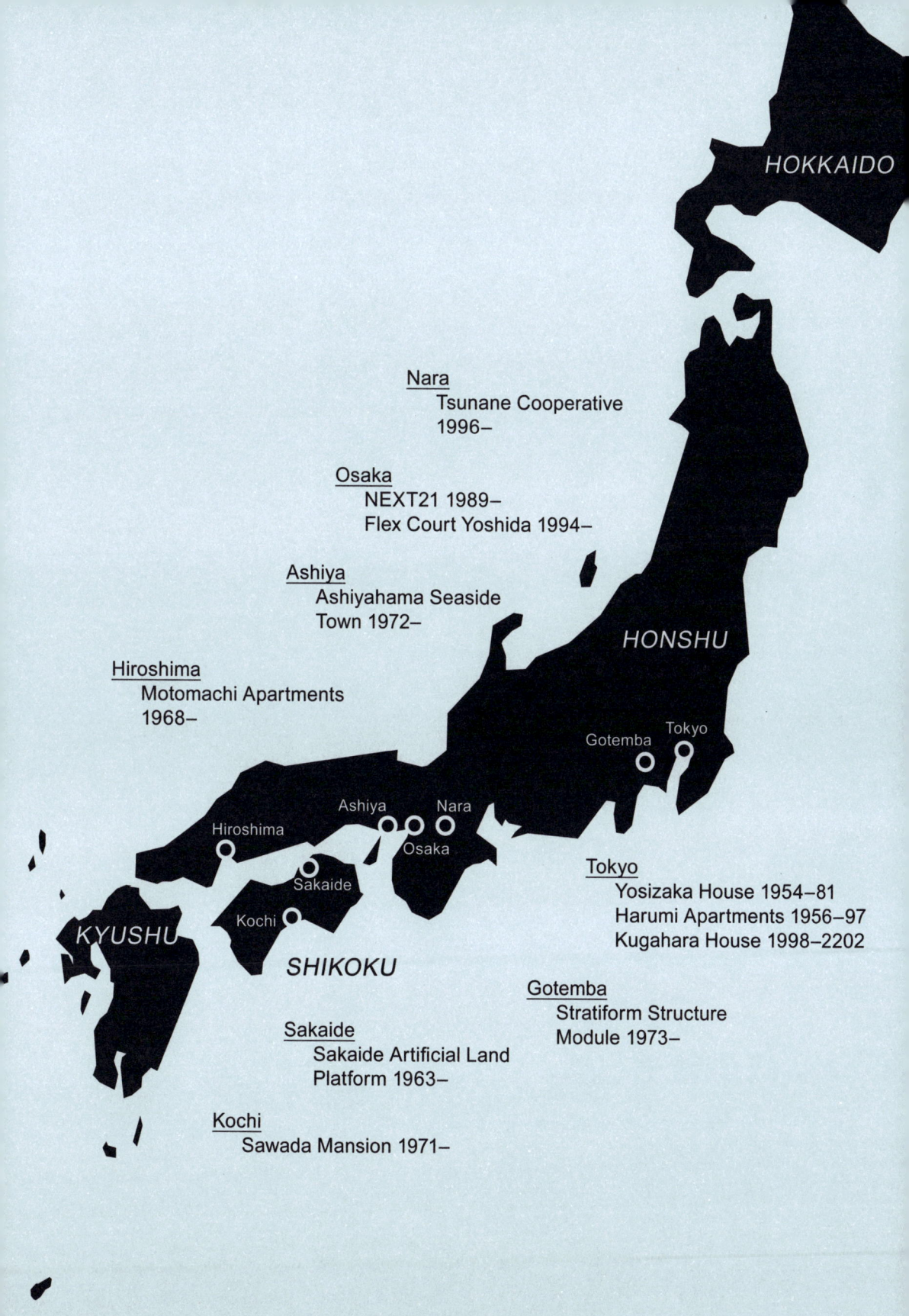

Nara
Tsunane Cooperative
1996–

Osaka
NEXT21 1989–
Flex Court Yoshida 1994–

Ashiya
Ashiyahama Seaside
Town 1972–

HONSHU

Hiroshima
Motomachi Apartments
1968–

Gotemba   Tokyo

Hiroshima

Ashiya Nara
Sakaide Osaka
Kochi

KYUSHU

Tokyo
Yosizaka House 1954–81
Harumi Apartments 1956–97
Kugahara House 1998–2202

SHIKOKU

Gotemba
Stratiform Structure
Module 1973–

Sakaide
Sakaide Artificial Land
Platform 1963–

Kochi
Sawada Mansion 1971–

41

1
Rebuilding
Building

We should not admire poverty, but should admire the state of mind that emerges only from poverty.

—Wajiro Kon, 1946[1]

When Takamasa Yosizaka returned to Tokyo in 1945 from military service in Korea, he did what many Japanese did at the time: he built a shack. Located on the former site of his parents' house in Tokyo's Shinjuku ward, Yosizaka's "barrack," to use the usual term for post-disaster shelter in Japan, was soon joined by four others that were built by friends in a similar fashion—little more than roofs and furniture turned into buildings. So began their barrack lifestyle.

    The house of Yosizaka's parents, where he lived for many years, was one of an estimated 2.1 million that were destroyed by firebombs from American air raids. During the war, around 55,000 more were demolished to make firebreaks, and with returning military personnel exacerbating the shortage that already existed before the war, Japan needed approximately 4.2 million new houses.[2]

    In the five years following Japan's surrender to the Allied Powers in September 1945, Tokyo's population grew from 2.78 to 5.39 million.[3] Sheer necessity led to a period known, according to Metabolist Noboru Kawazoe, as "an era of self-construction," which was an incredible building boom that was mostly without government oversight, and mostly illegal.[4] Working with whatever materials could be found, but mostly wood, on their

Tokyo after American firebombing, 1945

43

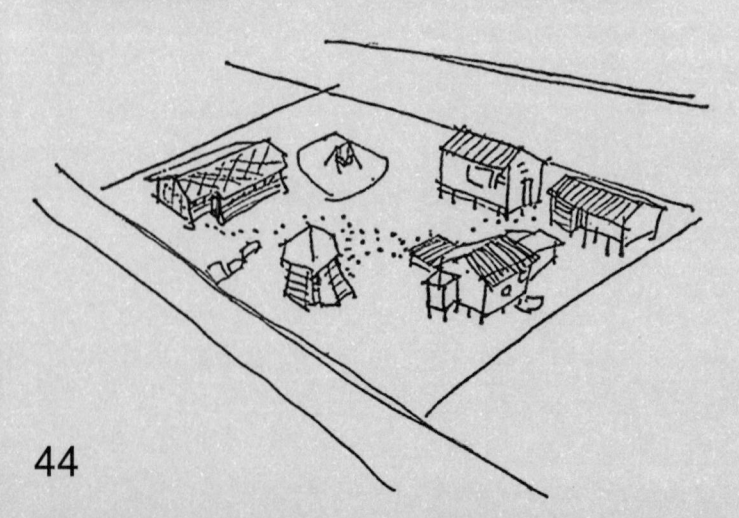

top: Yokohama after the Great Kanto Earthquake, 1923

center: Takamasa Yosizaka's barrack, c. 1945

bottom: Takamasa Yosizaka, sketch of barracks on plot in Shinjuku, c. 1945

1 REBUILDING BUILDING

own or with the help of *daiku* (Japan's traditional carpenters, who were both builders and designers), people quickly rebuilt large areas of the city in an improvised form.

Improvisation was nothing new. Immediately after the war's end, the Japanese government seemed intent on repeating the fundamental errors made following the Great Kanto Earthquake of 1923, which also devastated a large part of Tokyo. The destruction was largely due to fires triggered by the quake in a city mostly built of wood, and in the aftermath enforcement of building laws was suspended in the interest of speeding recovery. But the stated deadline for vacating the illegal private buildings that resulted, again mostly built of wood, was never upheld. Therefore, the city of crowded and flammable structures produced in the 1920s was again perfectly combustible for the firebombings two decades later. Likewise, after 1945 the government did little detailed urban planning, and what it did plan was rarely enacted, let alone enforced.[5] Wood construction did have one advantage in these disasters: it did not leave much to clean up before rebuilding could begin.

Hajime Yatsuka distills the challenge of postwar reconstruction into "a fundamental choice: build urgently needed housing in as great a number as possible or [...] build the foundations of a long-term vision for cities."[6] By and large, the former path was chosen. But Yosizaka, along with other architects and engineers, refused to see housing and urban planning as mutually exclusive. After the Great Kanto Earthquake, new national building laws developed by the architect-engineer Toshikata Sano introduced the "vision of a concrete Japan," a reconstructed urban landscape of fireproof buildings engineered for seismic resistance.[7] This vision, realized before the war in only piecemeal fashion amid the seas of wood construction, was revived after the war through writing, policy making, and design. A new inspiration for this vision was artificial land, a concept introduced by Yosizaka and inspired by his work with Le Corbusier, presented as one way to resolve the country's rebuilding dilemma. As an approach able to combine the short- and long-term, the planned and unplanned, artificial land offered reconciliation. Instead of accepting reconstruction by whatever means necessary, Yosizaka and others sought to rebuild the building process, using concrete to reconceptualize housing. In a culture where the one- or two-story wooden house was still the norm, what relationship could tradition have to much taller and much-needed mass housing?

Lifeology

Yosizaka's work on this question would not begin in earnest until the mid-1950s. In the meantime, in 1946 he began teaching architecture at Waseda University's Faculty of Engineering, from which he had graduated in 1941. One prominent professor at the university was Wajiro Kon, who had been teaching there since 1912 and had also been one of Yosizaka's teachers. Kon was an architect and set designer with an anthropological and artistic drive to document and interpret that influenced Yosizaka's entire career, and was directly connected to his life in the barracks.

Right after the Great Kanto Earthquake, Kon became fascinated by the improvised, ad hoc shelters that were appearing throughout Tokyo, and set out to record them in sketches and photographs. Kon had experience in documenting vernacular peasant housing—known as *minka*, "houses of the people"—through field surveys that he had been conducting with others since 1917.[8] The particular vernacular of disaster housing was an extension of this research. Similar to *minka*, such housing resulted from a constructive mindset that had to be resourceful, inventive, and open to collaboration. Shortly after he began his barrack documentation, Kon shifted from observer to participant, forming with several artist friends the Barrack Decoration Society, who gave themselves the mandate to paint facades and murals to enliven various humble structures such as temporary bars and coffee houses. As cosmetic as this action may have been, it was another step in the city's revival.

When Yosizaka was living in his shack, it was impossible for him not to reflect on Kon's studies. In 1939, he had investigated villages and *minka* on Waseda University field trips under Kon's supervision.[9] For teacher as for student, the primitive houses and barracks, while not equivalent in economic terms, were direct responses to local conditions, with variations of form provoked by the situations and abilities of particular people. It was the relationships between situation, construction, and mode of inhabitation, revealed through what Kon called *seikatsu-gaku*—"lifeology," the study of everyday life through close observation—that made such structures important.[10] Lifeology was for Kon a wide field, encompassing everything from clothing to food, but in architectural terms he saw it as manifesting in the idea of architecture as a "container" shaped by everyday activities.[11] When Yosizaka described his own barrack as being "like the shell of a creature,"

Wajiro Kon, sketches of barracks after the Great Kanto Earthquake, 1923

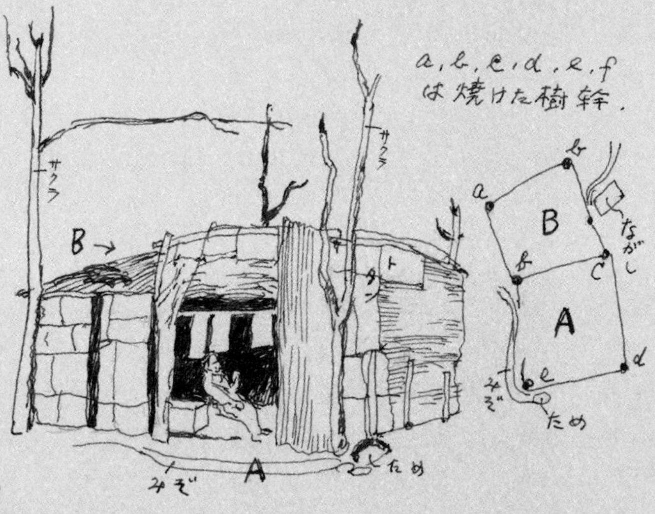
a, b, c, d, e, f
は焼けた樹幹.
サクラ
サクラ
B →
トタン
ながし
B
A
ため
みぞ
A
ため

トタン
トタン
トタン
ござ
なわ

焼けた材木
石
トタン
手拭
トタン
たきもの

看板画工
看板画工
布
うすべり
みぞ

he perfectly expressed this organic concept of his professor, seeing the house's internal organs—the objects embodying his own lifestyle—as giving shape to the envelope that contained them.[12]

The "close fit" in this description brings to mind the Western modernist maxim of "form follows function." Japanese architects did closely follow Western modernists' theories and practices, but the sensibility that drove Kon's studies of *minka* and barracks placed him far away from functionalist obsessions with type and standardization. While the maxim may be no less true for him than it was for his Western counterparts, it was true in a different way: the insights he gained through fieldwork blew open and multiplied the ways a given function might be performed, thereby multiplying the possible architectural containers. Indeed, after the war, Kon was explicitly opposed to the modernist commitment to making standardized housing for the masses, believing that architects should instead observe and discuss directly with the people being designed for. This was the only way to arrive at designs that best served their actual ways of living.[13]

Search for a Standard

But Kon's bottom-up thinking was out of step with the government initiatives then emerging. The government saw standardized apartments for lower- and middle-income families as essential for speedy reconstruction and future growth, and for the safe replacement of the self-built barracks. This search for a new standard drew on the development of the "minimum dwelling" in Europe in the aftermath of World War I, a project aimed at codifying standards for minimum but adequate amounts of space, daylight, fresh air, privacy, and other factors deemed necessary for healthy living.

In Japan, these considerations led to the 2DK floor plan, a modest design that swept the country as the national model for dwelling.[14] Initially averaging about 40 square meters, the 2DK was the most typical example of the nDK system, later known as the nLDK system, in which "n" is the number of bedrooms, "D" is dining room, "K" is kitchen, and "L" is living room. The main innovation of the 2DK, thanks to architect and planner Uzo Nishiyama, was the separation of areas assigned to eating and sleeping. In 1941, Nishiyama pioneered the idea that separating these would avoid conflicts of use and problems of hygiene. Historically, Japanese houses had been programmatically flexible, with rooms generally lacking fixed functions. In the postwar context of democracy introduced by the Allied occupation that started in 1945, Nishiyama's idea was seen as liberating for the housewife, who would no longer need to constantly convert the usage of a room from sleeping to dining and back again. It was also seen as enhancing privacy, increasingly regarded as a democratic right, allowing an individual's personal development, particularly a child's, with less parental scrutiny.[15] Now sleeping and living would take place in two rooms floored with tatami mats, while dining and food preparation would happen in a room with wooden floorboards, using tables and chairs as in the West. Separating these two zones would be traditional fusuma sliding screens.

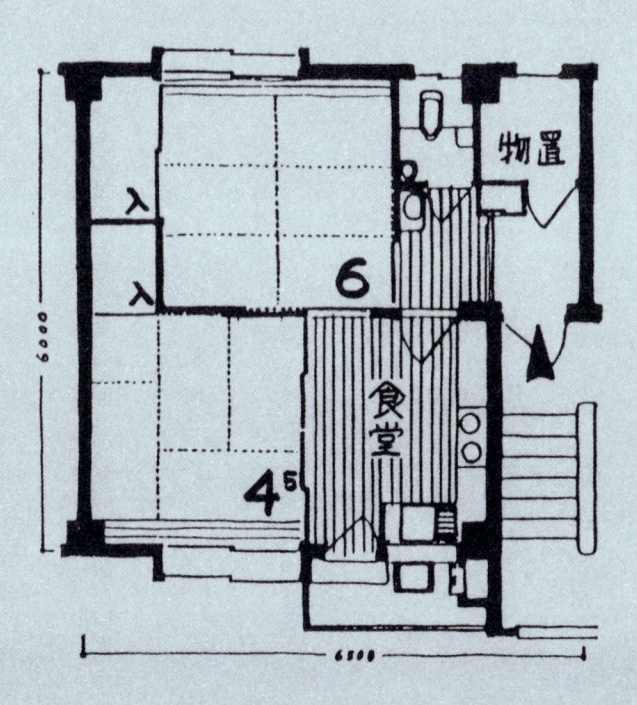

Nishiyama had been researching apartment standardization since the 1930s, and was deeply influenced by the scientific method of Berlin architect Alexander Klein, an innovator in diagramming movement paths as a way to judge efficiency in his designs for minimum dwellings. Klein's diagrams demonstrate his belief that it was preferable to have plans free of intersecting movement paths—for example, the path between a bedroom and bathroom should not intersect the path between the kitchen and dining room. This ambition to make frictionless floorplans inspired

"51C" 2DK plan, 1951

49

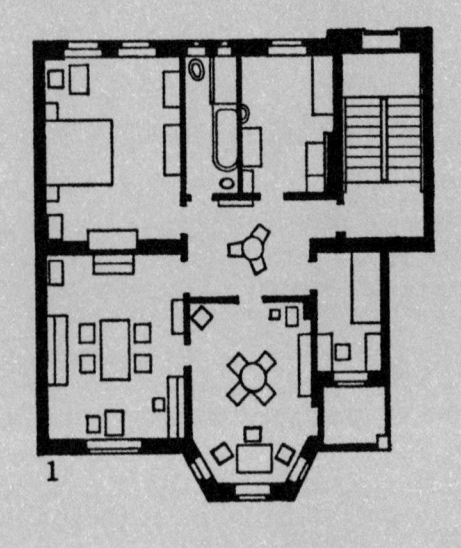

A. Bad Example

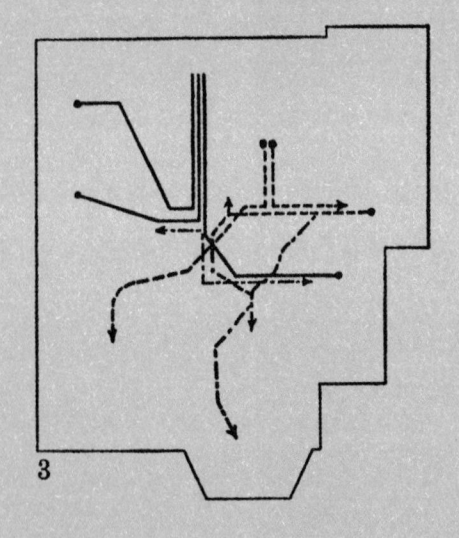

B. Good Example

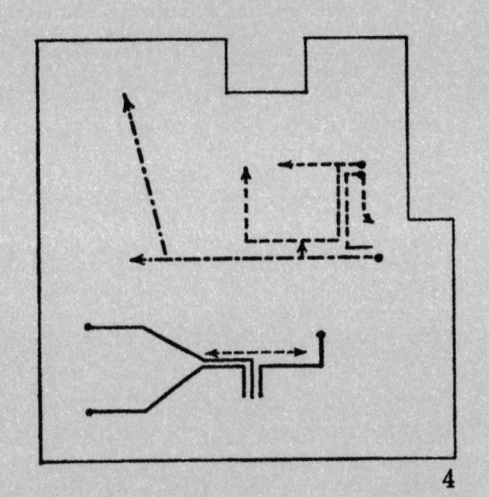

50   1 REBUILDING BUILDING

the 2DK's separations, in which an occupant of one of the "private" tatami rooms would not need to pass through the other tatami room to access the "public" space of dining room, kitchen, and bathroom.

    Kon found such thinking to be pure functionalist abstraction, wherein abstraction served to average individual particulars into a single simplified form predicated on economic construction.[16] Indeed, in 1951 the 2DK was formalized as model "51C" by Shigebumi Suzuki and others in the lab of Yasumi Yoshitake at the University of Tokyo, and adopted soon after for general use by the Japan Housing Corporation (JHC).[17] Established in 1955, the JHC was a public organization funded by private corporate investors, and is the most famous entity in Japan's postwar mass-housing history. Distinct from Japan's publicly-funded housing, the JHC's developments became iconic, with the corporation popularizing not just the 2DK, but also *danchi*, or "group land," the term for new towns of Western-inspired mass housing filled with 2DKs that were to proliferate on the nation's urban peripheries.

Le Corbusier Sensei

The poles of Nishiyama and Kon articulate the conflict that arose within Yosizaka when he confronted the housing crisis: on the one hand, there was his belief in Kon's idea of the need to understand individual lifestyles prior to the act of domestic design; on the other, there was his support of Nishiyama's agenda of achieving social progress through the expedient of standardized housing for rebuilding from wartime destruction.[18] Around the time he started to teach, Yosizaka began to develop what he called *jukyo-gaku* (dwelling studies), which were basically an extension of Kon's lifestyle studies. Attracted by Le Corbusier's innovative housing designs, Yosizaka, a French speaker who had lived in Geneva as a youth, successfully applied for a French government grant that allowed him to join the architect's Paris atelier in 1950, with the intention of exploring dwelling further.[19]

    He had thought that working with Le Corbusier would be an opportunity to pursue his anthropological interests. However, he found that his new employer was much more of a top-down formalist, emphasizing fine proportions rather than engaging with diverse lifestyles. That said, while Le Corbusier's designs may have been acts of lifestyle imposition, they did envision his own unique idea of lifestyle, boldly conveyed through forms that deeply impressed Yosizaka.[20]

Alexander Klein, "Functional Housing for Frictionless Living," 1928

His responsibilities at the atelier included work on the High Court at Chandigarh, the Maisons Jaoul in Paris, as well as the Unités in Marseilles and Nantes-Rezé. For three weeks in 1951, he supervised construction in Marseilles. Over the days spent with the massive structural base of the Unité, labeled *terrain artificiel* in the construction drawings, Yosizaka felt a twinge of disappointment over the monotony of the apartments it supported.[21] Was repetition the only way to make such a project affordable? He thought that the Marseilles structure could, in his own hands, enable a combination of the freedom of individual lifestyles with the collective responsibility of mass housing and urbanism. Perhaps Kon's diverse "containers shaped by everyday life" could occupy the building's rack instead of Le Corbusier's standardized "bottles." Returning to Tokyo in 1952, in an experimental and somewhat reckless mood, the city seemed to him to be a laboratory.

Takamasa Yosizaka (far left) at the Unité d'Habitation Marseilles, 1951

1. Wajiro Kon, quoted in Izumi Kuroishi, *Kon Wajirō: A Quest for the Architecture as a Container of Everyday Life* (PhD diss., University of Pennsylvania, 1998), 115.
2. These estimates were made by Japan's Ministry of Construction soon after the country surrendered. See Ishida Yorifusa, "Japanese Cities and Planning in the Reconstruction Period: 1945–55," in *Rebuilding Urban Japan After 1945*, eds. Carola Hein, Jeffry M. Diefendorf, Ishida Yorifusa (New York: Pallgrave Macmillan, 2003), 22–23.
3. See Ichikawa Hiroo, "Reconstructing Tokyo: The Attempt to Transform a Metropolis," in *Rebuilding*, 54.
4. Noboru Kawazoe, *Contemporary Japanese Architecture* (Tokyo: The Japan Foundation, 1973), 38.
5. See Yorifusa, "Japanese Cities," in particular 42–43.
6. See Hajime Yatsuka, "Bitterness and Glory: Iconoclast in Hiroshima," chap. 4-2 in "Metabolism Nexus" (unpublished manuscript, 2012), PDF file. English translation by Riyo Namigata of Hajime Yatsuka, *Metabolism Nexus* [in Japanese] (Tokyo: Ohmsha, 2011).
7. Gregory Clancey, *Earthquake Nation: The Cultural Politics of Japanese Seismicity, 1868–1930* (Berkeley: University of California Press, 2006), 213.
8. These early surveys on traditional farmhouses were conducted with a group of experts known as the Hakubōkai, or "White Birch Society," under the auspices of the Ministry of Agriculture and Commerce. In 1918, Kon was sent to colonial Korea to perform similar rural surveys. See Izumi Kuroishi and Masamitu Ogihara, *Kon Wajiro Retrospective* (Tokyo: Seigensha, 2011), 53.
9. Yosizaka also participated in surveys in Northern China, Manchuria, and Mongolia in 1941. Hajime Yatsuka writes that this investigation unavoidably was done with the support of the Japanese military. Yatsuka, email to the author, September 7, 2018.
10. Lifeology, introduced in the early 1930s, is an extension of Kon's better-known "modernology," the term he applied to his activities from 1925 to 1930. See Kuroishi, *Kon Wajirō*, 128 and 185–186. Conceived as an archaeology of the present, modernology has been noted by architectural historian and maverick architect Terunobu Fujimori as an inspiration for Atelier Bow-Wow's "behaviorology." See Fujimori, "The Origins of Atelier Bow-Wow's Gaze" in *The Architectures of Atelier Bow-Wow: Behaviorology* (New York: Rizzoli, 2010), 122–129. In 1975, Yosizaka became the chairman of the Japan Lifeology Society, founded in 1972 to continue and unify Kon's legacy, a post also occupied by Noboru Kawazoe. For extensive discussion of modernology and lifeology (under the name *seikatsu-gaku*), see Kuroishi, *Kon Wajirō*, chaps. 4–5.
11. Kuroishi, *Kon Wajirō*, 223.
12. Takamasa Yosizaka, *Aru jūkyo: Hitotsu no kokoromi* [About a house: one experiment] (Tokyo: Sagami Shobo, 1960), 47. Translation by Riyo Namigata. *Aru jūkyo* is Yosizaka's chronicle of the origins of his artificial-land house and its first five years of inhabitation.
13. Kuroishi, *Kon Wajirō*, 236.
14. See Jordan Sand, *House and Home in Modern Japan: Architecture, Domestic Space, and Bourgeois Culture, 1880–1930* (Cambridge, MA: Harvard University Asian Center, 2003), 375.
15. For an excellent discussion of gender roles, privacy, and space planning in postwar apartment design, see Ann Waswo, *Housing in Postwar Japan: A Social History* (London: RoutledgeCurzon, 2002), in particular 62–85, on which I have drawn here.
16. Kuroishi, *Kon Wajirō*, 236.
17. See Jordan Sand, *Tokyo Vernacular: Common Spaces, Local Histories, Found Objects* (Berkeley: University of California Press, 2013), 66. While the nLDK system and the 2DK were developed by Suzuki and the Yoshitake Lab, they were based on Nishiyama's idea of separating eating and sleeping. Consequently, Nishiyama is often credited as their creator.
18. Nishiyama and Kon should not be seen as totally antithetical: the younger Nishiyama acknowledged a major debt to Kon's field surveys and pursuit of lifeology. See Hiroshi Nakabayashi, "Uzo Nishiyama's Planning methodology based on investigations of common people's lives," *International Planning History Society Proceedings* 18, no. 1 (Oct. 2018): 1128–1137, https://doi.org/10.7480/iphs.2018.1.2757.
19. Yosizaka spent two extended periods in Switzerland with his parents due to his father's work, and attended high school in Geneva. He would go on to translate a number of Le Corbusier's books from French into Japanese, beginning with *Le Modulor* (Tokyo: Bijutsu Shuppan-Sha, 1953).
20. Shunsuke Kurakata, *Yoshizaka Takamasa Le Corbusier* (Tokyo: Ohkokusha, 2005), 81.
21. See Takamasa Yosizaka, "Jūkyo wa kō to shūdan no rieki kyōkaisen" [The home is the boundary between the individual and group's profit: one proposal to solve the housing shortage], *Kokusai kenchiku* 21, no. 1 (January 1954): 67. Translation by Riyo Namigata.

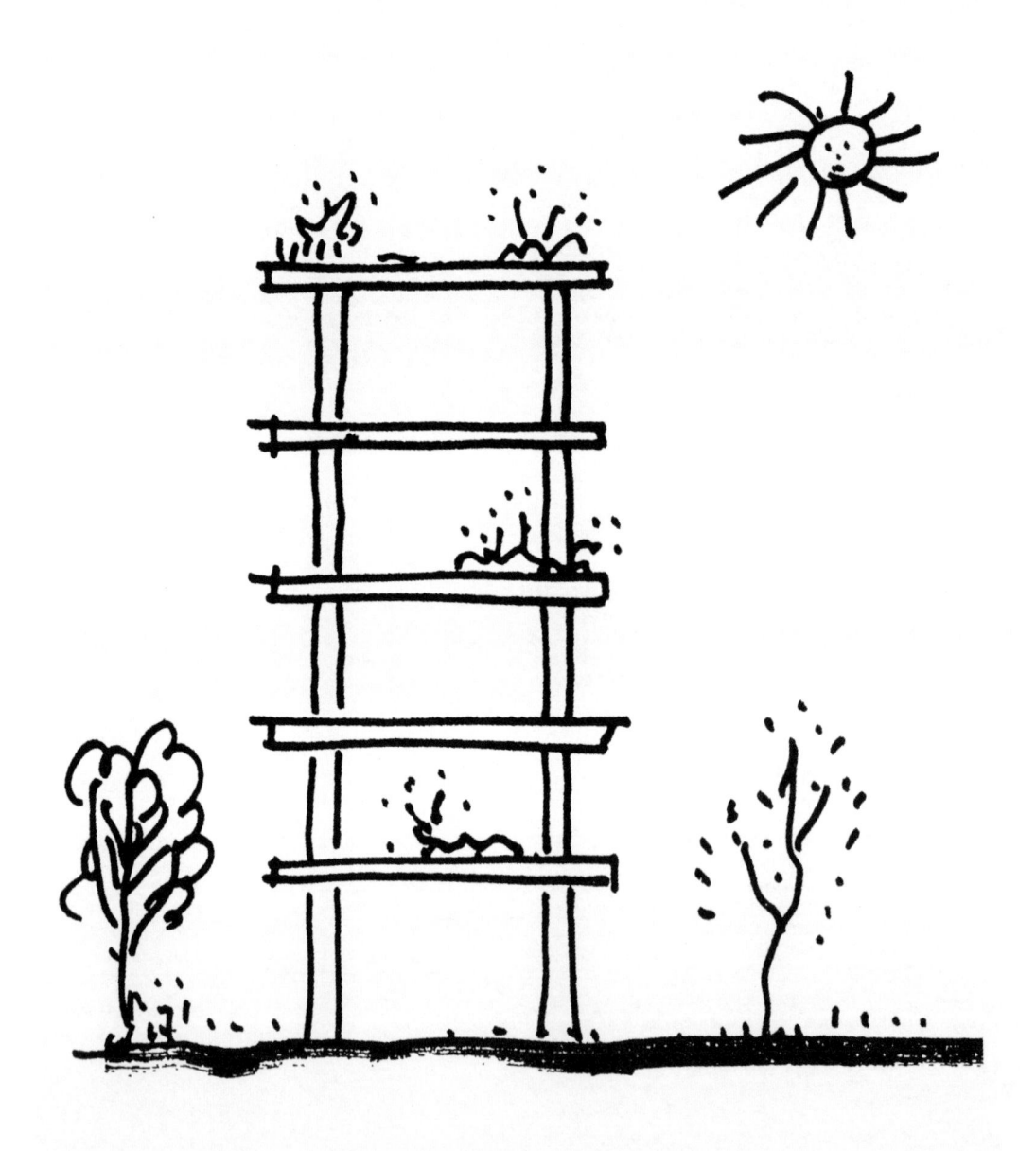

Maximum Dwelling:
Yosizaka House, 1954–81

As luck would have it, the sky space above Tokyo is very little occupied.

—Takamasa Yosizaka, 1954[1]

Takamasa Yosizaka, artificial land sketch, 1954

A Japanese pro-democracy slogan of the early 1950s was "Architecture of the People, for the People," and Yosizaka perhaps saw artificial land as the slogan's realization.[2] The housing crisis had persisted throughout his years in Paris, and in 1954 he debuted his new thinking on the problem. In the essay "The Home is the Boundary between the Individual and Group's Profit: One Proposal to Solve the Housing Shortage," published in the journal *Kokusai kenchiku*, he addressed the topic through a critique of CIAM. The organization was a main inspiration for the public housing ideology then emerging in Japan, which Yosizaka felt was overly infatuated with mass production. While CIAM's principles of "light, space, and greenery" were important, he felt its faith in standardization had caused an imbalance between group profit and individual freedom. His essay proposed instead that:

> It is not necessary to make all the fine details of the home with our current budget for public housing. What we need to do is to make land. This land, however, does not need to be earth. A land that can provide the electricity, gas, water supply, and sewage required for modern technology could be a land made of concrete. We should make land that is suitable for housing, and that can make effective use of what little city space we have by being able to be layered. We do not need any more than this. If we think of this instead of providing all the small amenities in the homes, it does not seem impossible. All we need to do is loan the land. The people can then rent a piece of this land, set with all its facilities, and build their own homes as they want, wherever they want.[3]

Though derivative of Le Corbusier's declaration of artificial land in *The Radiant City*, Yosizaka's call addresses specific Japanese realities, to which the concept promised to be uniquely responsive.[4] Most immediately, his experience with the barracks in Tokyo offered the example of a vast city partly remade from the bottom up. Why not help expand this process into the sky?

The variation and self-reliance of the barrack lifestyle was an inspiration, but Yosizaka was not proposing a vertical slum. Instead he took the responsiveness of the barracks and formalized it—that is, made it legal and safe—through a creative approach to the Government Housing Loan Corporation (GHLC).[5] Founded in 1950, the GHLC was established to provide low-interest loans of public money to individuals for the private construction of single-family homes, a method of supply that ultimately led to the creation of far more dwellings than were made by the public rental housing system or the JHC.[6] Indeed, the government overwhelmingly promoted single-family home ownership ahead of any other form of housing.[7] The loans incentivized improved construction through more favorable terms: loans for wooden houses needed to be repaid in fifteen years, while fireproof ones could be repaid in thirty.[8] Loans could not be used to acquire land however, which applicants needed to secure first in order to be approved for a loan. This was a major obstacle. Addressing the land problem specifically in terms of the GHLC, Yosizaka writes further in his essay that:

> To build a home—this costs money. It is possible to build a home with the salary of approximately one year of work. If more money is required, [people] should receive the help of the Housing Loan Corporation. Because they will be building a home on a piece of land with the facilities already in place for the floor and the roof, there should be less burden placed on the Housing Loan Corporation as compared to today.[9]

Within the cramped, horizontal density of Japanese cities, terrestrial land was increasingly expensive and difficult to acquire, and the ongoing search for affordable sites contributed to urban sprawl. Vertically layered land would provide new sites in the heart of the city, thereby helping more people to receive GHLC assistance and further relieve the housing crisis.

Artificial Land as Housing Studies

Yosizaka considered it unnecessary, not to mention undesirable, for the government to make "all the fine details of the home." Rather than a framework for mass uniformity, artificial land was a literal test bed for his housing studies, a concept that allowed the unfolding of lifestyles in all their architectural specificity. This diversity could be aided by the design-build services of *daiku*, who could be hired by a household that had leased a plot, as well as by a spate of new GHLC-provoked publications that were filled with single-family house plans ready for construction. The key feature that made specificity possible was home ownership, albeit on leased concrete land, which allowed a freedom of design opposing the rented 2DK minimum dwelling.

Through home ownership as an alternative to rental public housing, Yosizaka suggests the "maximum" dwelling. This is not maximum in the sense of biggest or fanciest, but rather the dwelling maximally suited to a given household within the limits of its members' needs, tastes, and budget, in an attempt to escape the minimum dwelling's constriction of lifestyle to a statistical average.

While the minimum dwelling delivered, for a nominally reduced rent, the lowest acceptable level of amenity as determined by the state, Yosizaka's maximum dwelling offered the greatest possible amenity in relation to budget—including sweat equity—as determined by individuals.[10]

Yosizaka, in a 1955 article in *Shinkenchiku*, imagined the progressive completion of the home "alongside the progression of the lifestyle in the home."[11] This possibility was all too often stymied by the 2DK, which many Japanese couples found too small, an experience exacerbated for many parents as their children grew.[12] Why not build an apartment that's bigger but cheaper due to being less refined? An irony of minimum dwellings is their increased cost compared to larger ones: since a greater number of small units fit within a given building envelope, construction costs rise due to the need for more partition walls, mechanical systems, fixtures, and so on.[13] These increased expenses then get passed on to renters as higher rents per square meter, despite an overall lower rental cost for such predetermined units. Artificial land would allow decisions about how much space was needed and the size of the loan that could be justified, with fixtures and other fit-out variables to be added by individuals based on whether they were urgently needed, possible to add later, or simply unnecessary.[14]

Infrastructure

The maximum dwelling may seem to overemphasize individualism. But such a dwelling would sit on artificial land built and owned by a public agency, thereby guaranteeing profits for wider society through urban planning: widening streets, making new parks, and modernizing community services. While Fort l'Empereur also integrated public services through new transportation, its sites were properties for sale. It is important to note that the principle of renting municipal land for private construction was a basic component of Howard's Garden City, in which increases in land value could be used by a municipality to fund public improvements.[15] While lacking Howard's public dimension, private landlords renting land on which others own houses is still a phenomenon in Japan, so this dichotomy in Yosizaka's proposal is not unusual. Yosizaka's land in Shinjuku was in fact rented from a family friend.[16]

Yosizaka believed artificial land could allow the earth's surface to mostly return to nature, with shopping streets, nurseries, schools, and bathhouses on midair platforms allowing one to "lead a life similar to the primitive ages," an era apparently quite desirable.[17] Despite this vision, Yosizaka hardly produced any grand images of his thinking, unlike Kikutake, Tange, and others who soon followed him into Tokyo's sky.[18] But to get a sense of possible scale, he calculated that ten layers within Tokyo's Yamanote Line loop—the central train circuit just outside of which his house stood—could accommodate about ten million people, allowing spacing for adequate sunlight and natural ventilation.[19] This would be a height of residential construction that did not exist in Japan at the time. Significantly, the Yamanote Line is roughly coterminous with the "wooden house belt," the greatest concentration of flammable barrack buildings in the city, a legacy of the era of self-construction that has partly survived into the early twenty-first century. Having chosen this area, the calculations suggest a massive act of urban renewal, thereby improving living quality and access to public transportation, as well as reducing the chances of fire. Yosizaka encouraged home builders to use concrete block.

Embryo

At the time he was writing, right next to his barrack Yosizaka was also building a new home that would be a practical test of his theory. He first erected a concrete frame, with formwork made from salvaged US Army lumber, and indeed financed by a loan from the GHLC. Then he waited. Over the following year, his two layers of concrete ground were fit only for parties and sleeping on summer nights. After a period of saving up funds, he made his experiment habitable by infilling it with concrete block walls, and then inserting windows and doors.[20]

He was the first to admit it was an imperfect experiment: his slice of artificial land was ultimately paid for out of his own pocket rather than rented from a public agency.[21] Furthermore, it's unclear what the estimated rent payments would be for a resident after having calculated the cost of constructing, say, a ten-story skeleton, as well as the total monthly cost once this fee was added to a likely mortgage from the GHLC. The idea's financial aspects remain murky.

Peter Smithson apparently didn't know of Yosizaka's house, or else thought it was too small to count as a demonstration. Though tiny, it may be evaluated in terms of its implications for larger infrastructure. That Yosizaka saw the house as a prototypical unit of a larger organization is unclear from any archival information, but its L-shaped profile suggests the possibility of aggregation in a series of row houses. The larger footprint of the first floor suggests continuous street level commercial space. Reading the frame in an overly literal way is not without problems, especially if it is seen as the base of a ten-story structure and the consequent requirements for vertical circulation. But if we take the exterior stairs to be a shared street entry, then the second-floor terrace appears to be the rear of the structure, a semi-private space that could belong to individual residents or be used communally.[22] A row-house condition with a distinct front and rear is reinforced by Yosizaka's decision to cantilever floor slabs in the house's longitudinal dimension. As with its predecessor the Dom-ino House, which was also proposed in the context of postwar reconstruction after World War I, this cantilevering allows a free facade uninterrupted by columns. The cantilevered zones can be either enclosed or left open as balconies, providing a flexible armature for a public or semi-public face that could be built out to represent various kinds of people, perhaps facing a street and the semi-private rear terrace.

above: Yosizaka House, concrete frame, 1954

right: Frame infilled with concrete block walls, windows, and doors, 1955

MAXIMUM DWELLING: YOSIZAKA HOUSE, 1954–81

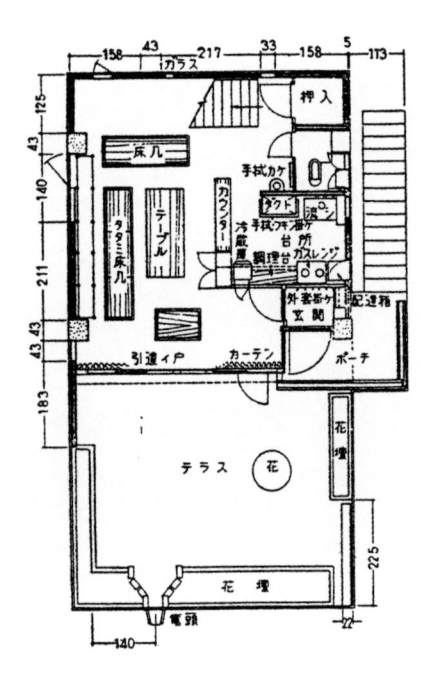

2nd floor

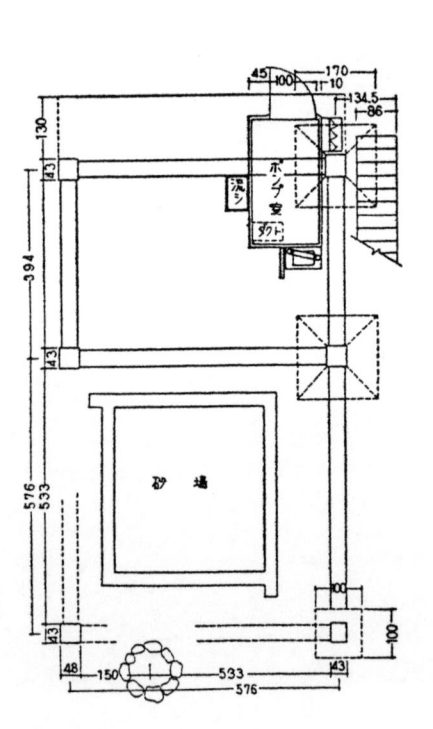

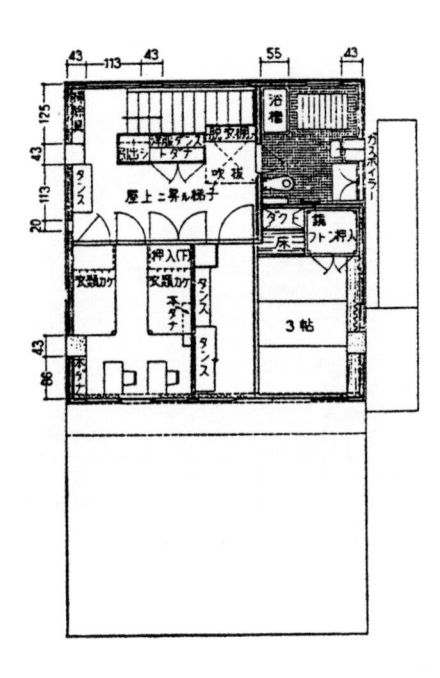

3rd floor

1st floor

1 REBUILDING BUILDING

East

North

The house's terrestrial plot was without walls or fences. When it came to actually placing his home on the hypothetically public artificial plots above, Yosizaka built to the edges of the slabs and thereby enclosed the maximum volume. Totaling about 66 square meters for both the second and third floors, the house was considerably larger than a 40-square-meter 2DK apartment. The second floor was primarily open, serving as combined kitchen, eating, and living area opening onto the terrace. Above were two bedrooms, one for Yosizaka and his wife, and one for their children. Overall, the planning suggests a mixture of Japanese and Western elements, with the bedrooms, bathroom, and hallway upstairs reminiscent of Klein's "frictionless" approach, whereas the second floor is ready for the social exchanges and banter of entertaining in a more loosely defined space. One cultural issue with which the architect struggled was the boundary of where to take shoes off.

As Shunsuke Kurakata has observed, Yosizaka acted as both architect and client for the house. The client's questionable taste—seen in the dowdy masonry, a collection of antique bells hung from the ceiling, and an inlaid plaque with the Latin proverb "Be bold to grasp happiness"—was enabled by artificial land's indifference to style.[23] The pressures and opportunities of being both occupant and architect later manifested due to a leak in the roof. After bitter complaining by his wife and children—his son Masakuni has said that growing up in the house was like living in a swimming pool—Yosizaka solved the problem in perfect artificial land fashion: he plugged the leak by adding a fourth floor.[24] This capacity to grow is shown in an inhabited section drawing from 1973, showing the new attic over the original roof and the first-floor space partly enclosed as a library. Earlier, in a small book on his

Yosizaka House, plans and elevations

MAXIMUM DWELLING: YOSIZAKA HOUSE, 1954–81

61

62 1 REBUILDING BUILDING

house that Yosizaka wrote in 1960, he made a drawing of the additions made to his childhood home that had stood on the site, recording the multiple changes to the traditional timber structure in response to changes in his family's lives.[25] Above all, his home on artificial land demonstrated his desire to attain the same adaptive ability in a modern, vertical form, not from a theoretical perspective, but inspired by his own experience.

Yosizaka House, third floor, children's room (top left); second floor, living area (bottom left); and third floor, parents' room (above)

MAXIMUM DWELLING: YOSIZAKA HOUSE, 1954–81

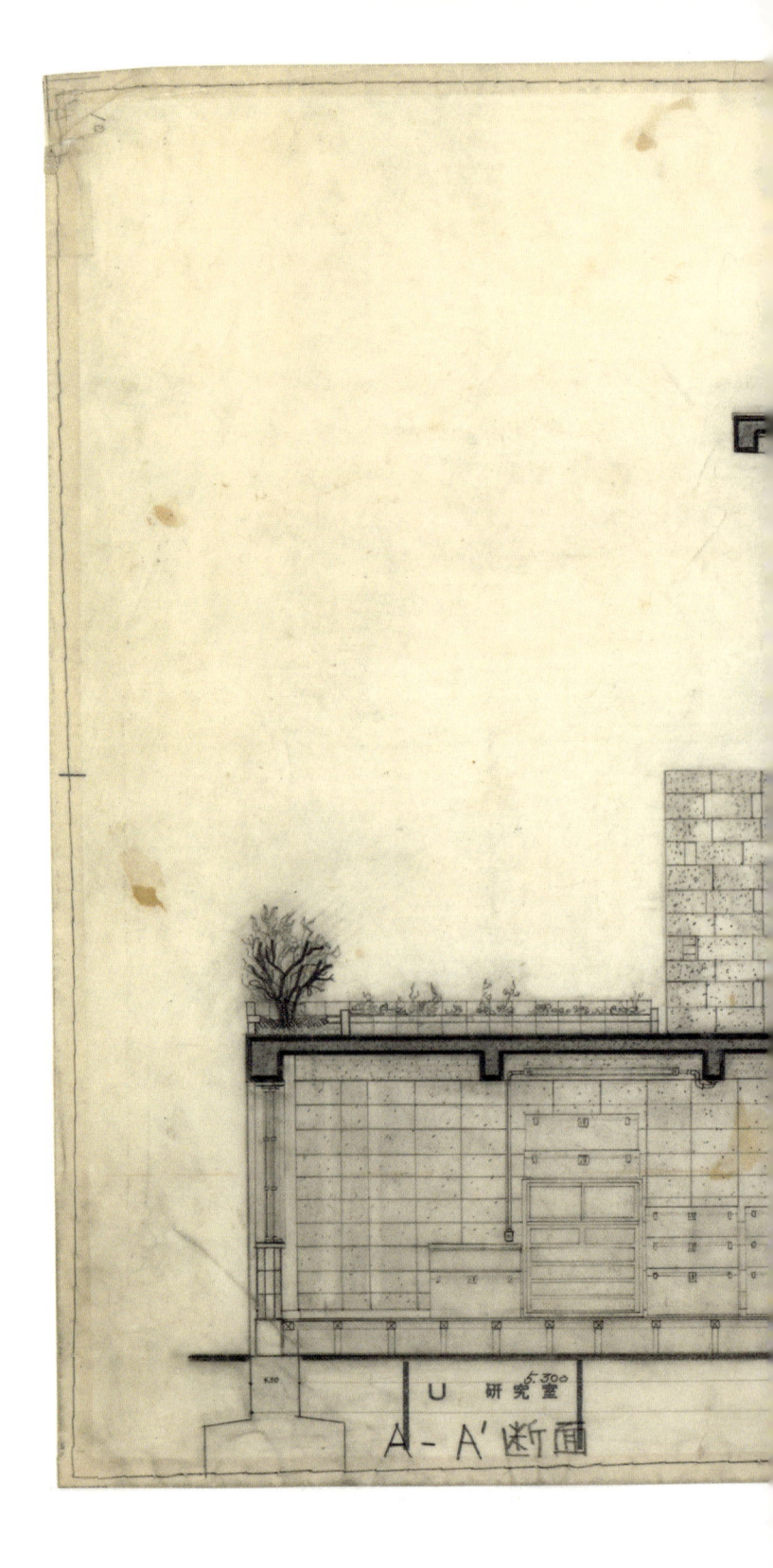

Masamitsu Yosizaka, Yosizaka House section, 1973. From right to left on the second floor: Takamasa's wife, Fukiko; Takamasa; second son Masamitsu; oldest daughter Takako; oldest son Masakuni; and Masakuni's wife, Teruko.

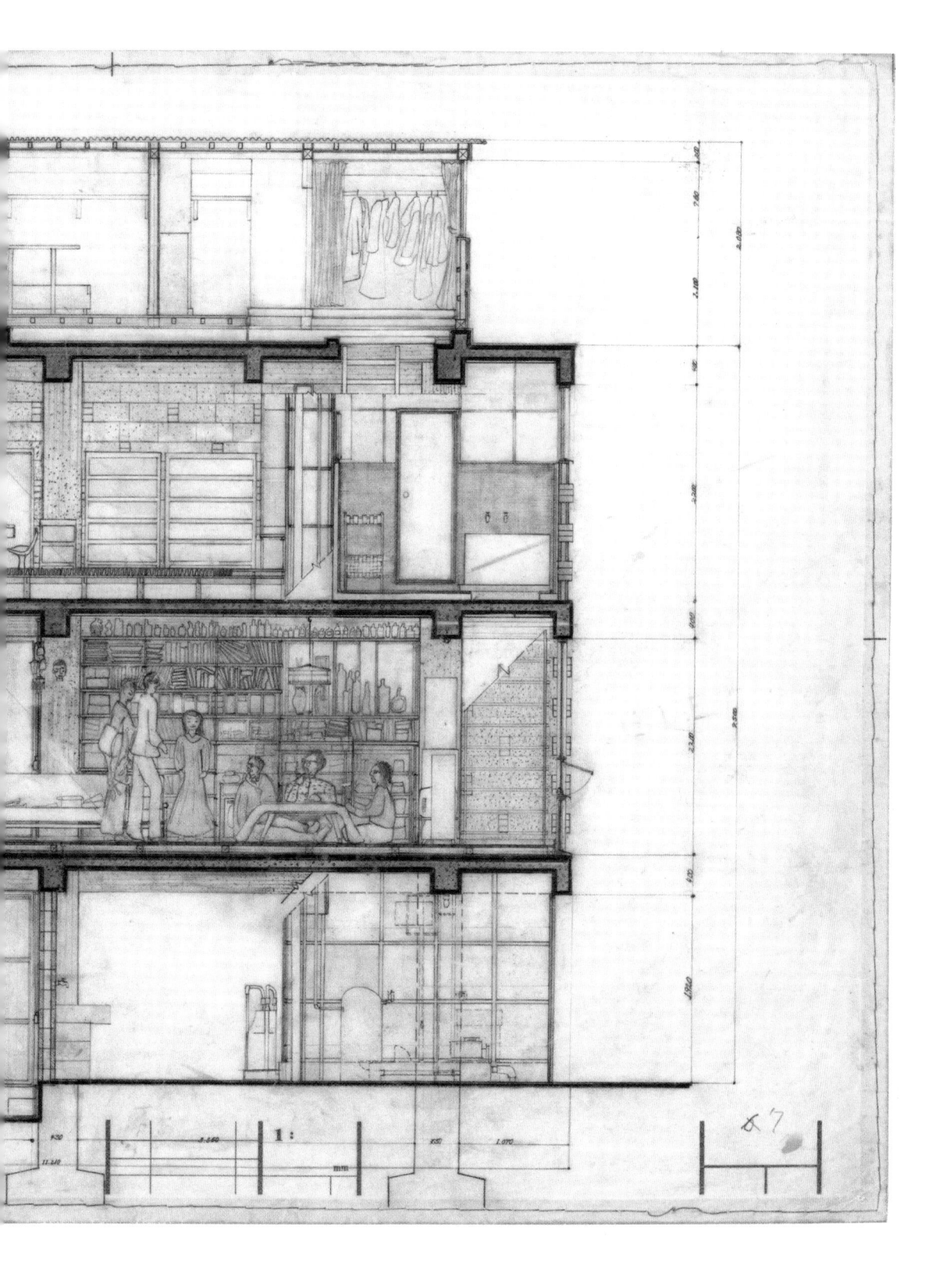

MAXIMUM DWELLING: YOSIZAKA HOUSE, 1954–81

Reaction

In November 1955, Le Corbusier visited the house during his first and only trip to Japan. After the tour, he told Yosizaka, "Only you could live here."[26] Perhaps not intended as a compliment, Yosizaka may have regarded it as the highest he could have hoped for: his home on artificial land fit him like the shell of a creature. He lived in the house until his death in 1980, and it was torn down the following year.

Returning to the large scale of Yosizaka's hoped-for solution as a general plan, the strategy left him open to criticism, particularly through his reliance on the help of the GHLC. With full employment and membership in the professional class, he was hardly one of the neediest members of Japanese society, and his relative affluence was exactly what the GHLC actively catered to, with the government believing that helping those with money would be a more effective policy for rebuilding and new growth than helping those without.[27] Going further, Motoo Miyazaki would charge the GHLC with attempting to give the impression that it was ending the housing shortage, whereas in reality it was only giving low-cost loans from public funds to those who could already help themselves, asserting that "one-third to one-half" of GHLC applicants "want to build houses of over 18 *tsubo*, a luxury in the eyes of those suffering from house-famine."[28] The *tsubo*, a traditional measure of area, is approximately 3.3 square meters, so Yosizaka's house was 20 *tsubo*.

The critic Akira Ushimi directly attacked the concept of artificial land in *Kokusai kenchiku,* several months after Yosizaka's essay there. Ushimi charged that, if the proposal was to achieve its claim to respect the need for adequate sunlight, each layer of land could be no more than 10 meters deep, a dimension that merely reproduced the "framework for a high-rise building."[29] Accurate as this criticism may be for those lacking imagination, based on the evidence of Yosizaka's house, he clearly had no issue with artificial land as a conventional framework—so long as occupants could freely build within it. But Ushimi's observation highlights the persistent problem with the concept's identity that has no doubt contributed to its obscurity, its name creating the expectation of something that looks like an artificial mountain, plateau, or forest. Ushimi continues, "Just think, a framework of a high-rise building, wherein each individual's personal fillings are stuffed in a scattered mess like the doorless clothing chests in the dressing rooms of bathhouses from a former age!" Here we find a particularly ironic criticism: Tokyo already looked like a doorless clothing chest, with houses high and low draped with drying laundry, as they still are in the early twenty-first century.

More damning is Ushimi's belief, reinforced by Miyazaki's criticisms of the GHLC, that Yosizaka's formulation of artificial land could never help the working poor. Unable to afford the GHLC's required down payment, renting an apartment would be their only option. Instead of architecture, only decoration and furniture would allow them to express their individuality, which would remain hidden inside.[30] And why should artificial land be complicit with the meagerness of the existing public-housing budget? Recognizing that many cities were suffering from serious land shortages, Ushimi did see artificial land's potential value. But he suggested that, instead of sacrificing the public-housing budget to make artificial land, it should have a new dedicated budget. Rental public housing could then be built on these new layers, a rejection of Yosizaka's reliance on a home that could be built with one year of middle-class salary or the help of the GHLC as any kind of solution.[31] Indeed, artificial land as infrastructure for the rental minimum dwelling was on the very near horizon.

Le Corbusier visiting Yosizaka
at his house in 1955

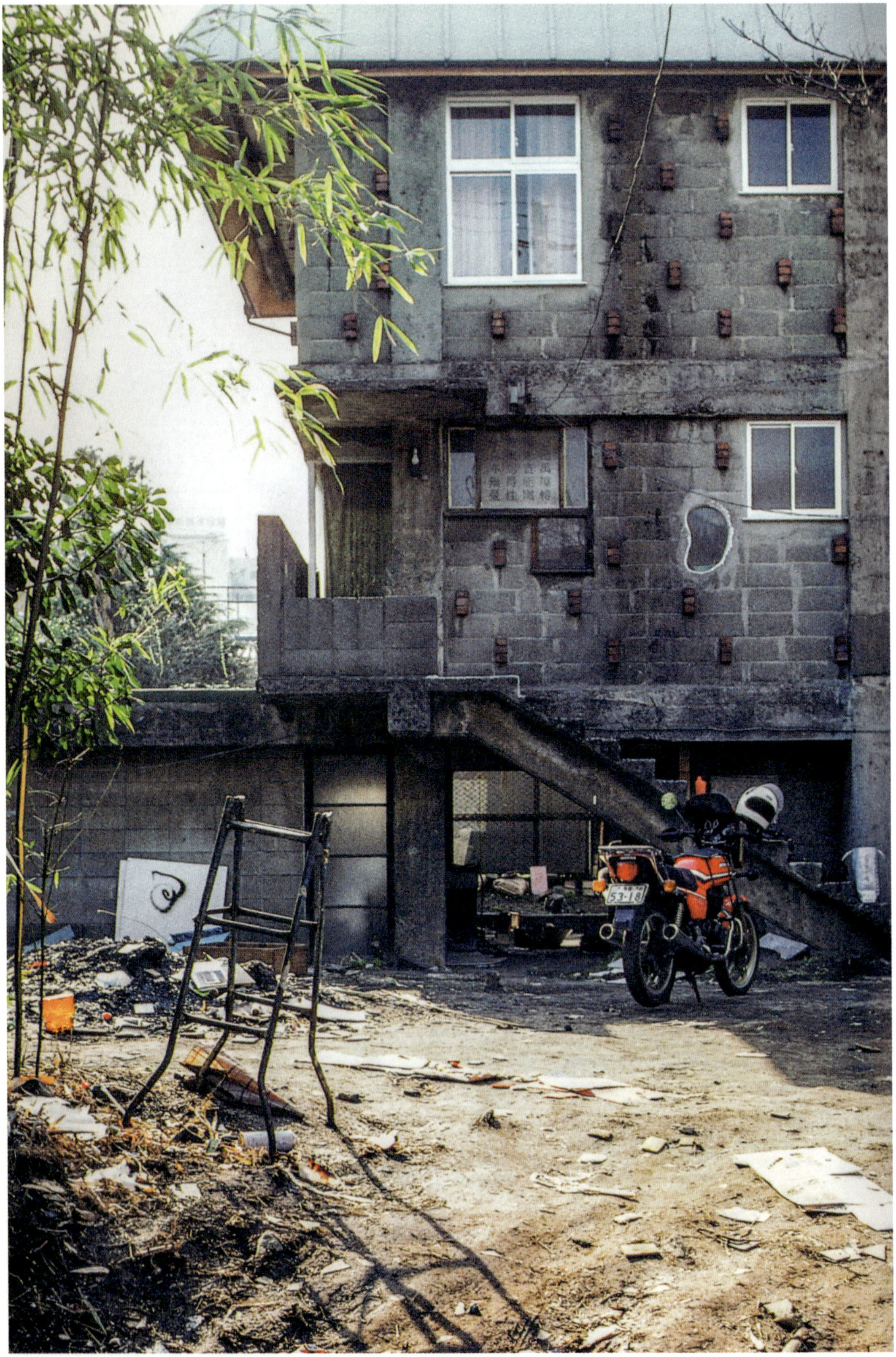
53-18

1. Takamasa Yosizaka, "Jūkyo wa kō to shūdan no rieki kyōkaisen" [The home is the boundary between the individual and group's profit: one proposal to solve the housing shortage], *Kokusai kenchiku* 21, no. 1 (January 1954): 67. Translation by Riyo Namigata.
2. Noboru Kawazoe, *Contemporary Japanese Architecture* (Tokyo: The Japan Foundation, 1973), 36.
3. Yosizaka, "Jūkyo," 67.
4. See page 29 in this book's introduction for the passage from *The Radiant City* on which Yosizaka drew, or Le Corbusier, *The Radiant City* [1933], trans. Eleanor Levieux et al. (New York: Orion Press, 1967), 247.
5. The Government Housing Loan Corporation is occasionally given in English as the Housing Financing Corporation, or similar.
6. Ann Waswo, *Housing in Postwar Japan: A Social History* (London: RoutledgeCurzon, 2002), 58.
7. See Yosuke Hirayama and Richard Ronald, "Introduction: Does the Housing System Matter?," in *Housing and Social Transition in Japan*, eds. Yosuke Hirayama and Richard Ronald [2007] (New York: Routledge, 2012), 2–3.
8. Waswo, *Housing in Postwar Japan*, 50.
9. Yosizaka, "Jūkyo," 67.
10. The conflict between minimum and maximum housing has a parallel in the thinking of the architect John F. C. Turner. Based on his experiences with self-help housing in Peru from the late 1950s to mid-1960s, Turner noticed a phenomenon he called the "supportive shack" versus the "oppressive house." While the squatter residents of a shack did not have security of tenure, they could build what they actually needed and could afford, as opposed to the imposition of standards and rents that could make the "step up" to a minimum dwelling unaffordable, rendering its pretense to improvement meaningless. See John F. C. Turner, *Housing by People: Towards Autonomy in Building Environments* [1976] (New York: Marion Boyars, 1991), 54–59.
11. Takamasa Yosizaka, *Aru jūkyo: Hitotsu no kokoromi* [About a house: one experiment] (Tokyo: Sagami Shobo, 1960), 94. Translation by Riyo Namigata.
12. Waswo, *Housing in Postwar Japan*, 71.
13. Karel Teige discusses this irony in his book *The Minimum Dwelling* [1932] (Cambridge, MA: The MIT Press, 2002), 234–237.
14. This flexible situation should be compared with the phenomenon of the kitchen in much new residential construction, which is often demolished soon after a residence sells, resulting in a huge amount of waste.
15. See Ebenezer Howard, *Garden Cities of To-Morrow* [1898] (Cambridge, MA: The MIT Press, 1970), 59.
16. Shizuo Harada, email to the author recounting a conversation with Takamasa's son, Masakuni Yosizaka, September 15, 2016.
17. Takamasa Yosizaka, quoted in Shunsuke Kurakata, *Yoshizaka Takamasa Le Corbusier* (Tokyo: Ohkokusha, 2005), 85.
18. Yosizaka does make one very amateur sketch of a supposedly artificial-land cityscape in *Aru jūkyo*, 88–89. On the scale of ambitious houses, Kiyonori Kikutake became famous for his 1958 Sky House, a design strongly indebted to Yosizaka's 1956 Ura House. Yosizaka also considered the Ura House to be an example of artificial land. While the Sky House could merit inclusion in this study, it has been extensively covered elsewhere, to the detriment of Yosizaka's contribution to Metabolism being acknowledged. For excellent documentation of the Sky House's evolution over fifty years, see "Sky House," in *The Japan Architect* 73 (Spring 2009), 18–27.
19. Yosizaka, "Jūkyo," 64–67.
20. It does seem that much of the house's construction was done by Yosizaka, with help from Waseda University students. Shokan Endo was one such student, and later the vice president of Kikutake's office. Endo in conversation with the author, May 15, 2014.
21. Yosizaka, *Aru jūkyo*, 56.
22. Floor numbering here and in the rest of the book follows the Japanese convention of the floor at ground level being designated as the first floor.
23. Kurakata, *Yoshizaka*, 86–90.
24. Masakuni Yosizaka in conversation with the author, May 15, 2014. Regarding the leak solution, Osamu Ishiyama in conversation with the author, May 13, 2014.
25. See Yosizaka, *Aru jūkyo*, 42.
26. Kurakata, *Yoshizaka*, 86–90. Le Corbusier was in Japan for his National Museum of Western Art project in Tokyo, for which Yosizaka was the local architect, along with Kunio Maekawa and Junzo Sakakura.
27. Waswo, *Housing in Postwar Japan*, 53.
28. Motoo Miyazaki, "Character of Housing Financing Corporation," *Shinkenchiku* 31, no. 9 (September 1956): 55.
29. Akira Ushimi, "Yoshizaka-shi no jinkō tochi-ron wo hihan suru" [Criticizing the artificial ground theory of Yosizaka], *Kokusai kenchiku* 21, no. 4 (April 1954): 8. Translation by Riyo Namigata.
30. Ushimi, "Yoshizaka-shi," 8.
31. Ushimi, "Yoshizaka-shi," 8.

Yosizaka House in 1981, shortly before demolition

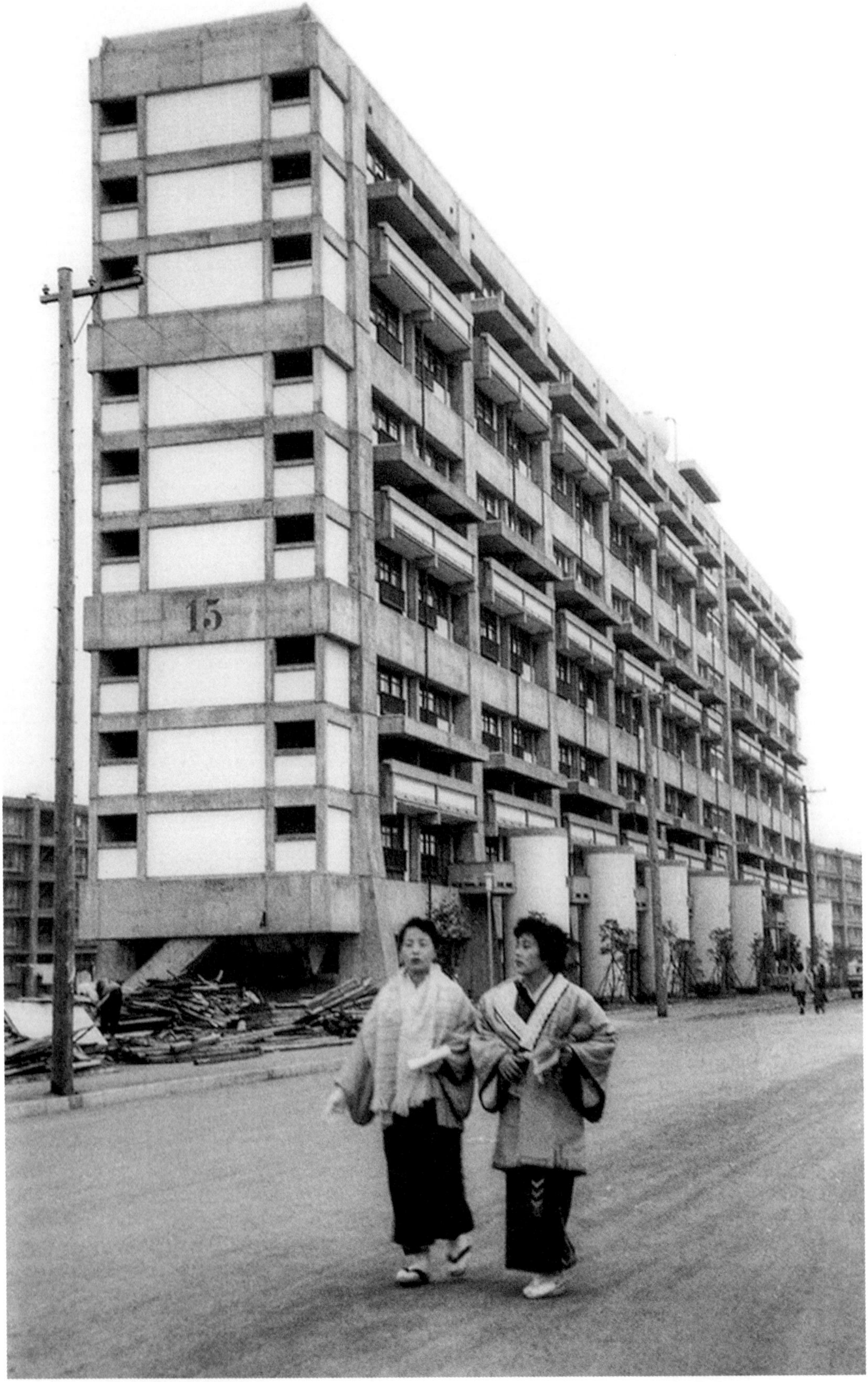
15

Transitional Type: Harumi Apartments and Metabolism, 1956–97

...modern and contemporary Japanese architecture is distinguished by one particular aspect: the fact that it is at one and the same time utopian and concrete.

—Marco Pompili[1]

In a 1959 review of Kunio Maekawa's Harumi Apartments, completed in 1958, Noboru Kawazoe wrote that "when a city is built of flimsy materials and can be easily rebuilt, no one feels much responsibility for the planning of the city."[2] Harumi—made of concrete, one of the least flimsy of materials—was instead a demonstration of long-term planning. Located on Harumi Island in Tokyo Bay, it was a slab of housing ten stories tall, reaching the 31-meter height limit that then capped the Japanese skyline. While Harumi is often regarded as the "Eastern equivalent" of Le Corbusier's Unité in Marseilles, both designs are closely related to Moisei Ginzburg and Ignatii Milinis's Narkomfin Communal House, completed in 1930 in Moscow.[3] It may be this Constructivist prototype that influenced Harumi's introduction of a new interpretation of artificial land, quite different from Yosizaka's maximum dwelling. Finished just before Metabolism's debut, Harumi provided architects with an essential inspiration, one easily visited in Tokyo Bay, that soon-to-be notorious site of unbuilt visions.

Experiment

Harumi's owner and operator was the JHC, the great disseminator of the 2DK apartment, led by former international banker Hisaakira Kano. Harumi was the first realized project of this new public-private organization, as well as the country's first residential high-rise.

The JHC modeled its housing mission on the Dojunkai (a neologism for Association for Equal Profit), a government agency founded in 1924, in the aftermath of the Great Kanto Earthquake. With an intensity unsurpassed in recorded history in Japan up until the 2011 Tohoku earthquake,

Kunio Maekawa, Harumi Apartments, 1958 (left) and 1959 (following)

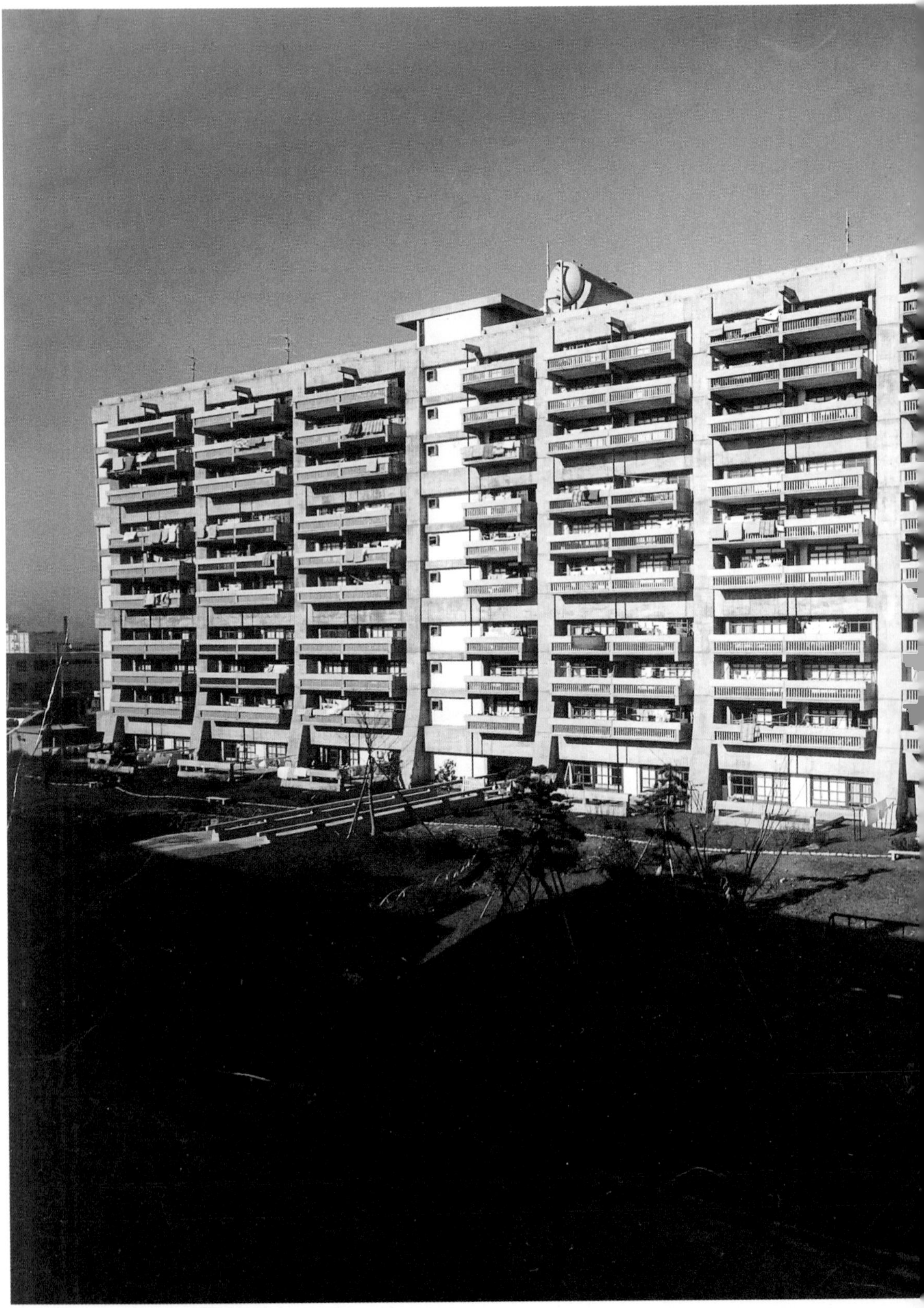

TRANSITIONAL TYPE: HARUMI APARTMENTS AND METABOLISM, 1956–97

the Great Kanto Earthquake demonstrated the resilience of Tokyo's concrete buildings compared to timber ones, particularly in resisting fire. Concrete was therefore fundamental to the Dojunkai mission of providing disaster-resistant housing. The organization's first director was Yoshikazu Utida, an architect and engineer trained under Toshikata Sano, the father of Japanese seismic engineering. Another aspect of the organization's mission was to introduce Western innovations for supplying gas, water, and electricity. Combining these services with traditional interior design, the Dojunkai introduced to Japan a new hybrid prototype for living.

Kano also wanted a new prototype. The JHC was bound by its charter to create housing of "incombustible construction" for a "medium income group" to either rent or buy on installment plans.[4] The huge influx of people moving to Tokyo and other major cities was prolonging the housing shortage—in 1958, the shortage nationally was 2.3 million units—so the JHC needed a design model able to increase urban density.[5] Although land prices were then low enough to make high-rise construction uneconomical, developing such a typology was considered prudent, as costs would inevitably rise.[6] Harumi Island was a perfect test site: a land reclamation project built in 1929, intended as the location for Japan's cancelled 1940 International Exposition, its prominence in Tokyo Bay, with a short commute to the city center, made it highly attractive.

Major- and Minor-Structure

Maekawa received the commission in 1956. Known prior to the war as the "people's architect" due to his focus on progressive architecture for common needs, he was also a protégé of Le Corbusier, working with him from 1928 to 1930. Twelve years older than Yosizaka, Maekawa reflected in 1953 on his twenty years of struggle to "delete" the confining seismic shear walls that had become ubiquitous in Japanese concrete construction, searching instead "to create more elastic space and economical structure."[7]

With Harumi, this search for elastic space was immediately confronted by the limitations of the site and budget. Though the site was perfect for marketing, it was not for ordinary engineering. The JHC's brief called for 169 2DK units, with the budget allowing only two elevators. Maekawa was faced with the challenge of supporting this unavoidably heavy load on the island's soft soil, with stable bedrock far below the surface. Toshihiko Kimura, an engineer within Maekawa's office, was particularly concerned about 60 percent of the construction budget being devoted to structure, a "decisive influence upon whether the building would be a success or a failure."[8] The engineering necessary for resisting earthquakes, support on spongy soil, and providing quality apartments all had to be done on a shoestring budget.

Kimura collaborated with the engineer Fugaku Yokoyama on the design of the structure, using a material system typical in Japan for seismic design called SRC (steel-reinforced concrete). More durable than the rebar-reinforced concrete structures elsewhere in the world, SRC entails first making self-supporting steel lattices, then encasing them in concrete to form a rigid frame. This approach required skilled welding, which was expensive. In response, Harumi's structural concept arose from an attempt to minimize welding and the driving of costly piles, resulting in a massive gridded frame with voids measuring 12 meters wide by 9 meters high. Decreasing the number of primary columns and beams by using fewer, larger ones caused direct savings in both the SRC and the foundations.

But the scale of the frame led to more than reduced costs, as it allowed Maekawa's desired flexibility. Lightweight concrete frames inserted within the larger frame would support the apartments themselves, together defining what Kimura called "major-structure" and "minor-structure." The major-structure would be permanent infrastructure for resisting gravity and earthquakes, while the inserted minor-structure could be changed over time, providing elastic spaces. Each void defined by the big frame would initially accommodate two apartments in width and three in height. Maekawa foresaw the small apartments expanding and recombining to adapt to rising living standards, a transition from austerity to affluence enabled by the structure.[9]

A contrasting example of temporal design is the *khrushchevka* apartment building type, introduced in the USSR in the mid-1950s by its namesake, Nikita Khrushchev. Yokoyama travelled to the USSR in 1961 to study the system of large panel concrete construction used in this housing, wherein all elements are load-bearing structure, from the exterior shell to the interior partition walls. But the *khrushchevka*'s rigidity was not considered suitable for Japan's domestic future. Despite its chunky concrete, Harumi offered a far suppler approach.

top: Toshihiko Kimura (left) and Kunio Maekawa, Brussels, 1958

bottom: Steel frame for Harumi's SRC

TRANSITIONAL TYPE: HARUMI APARTMENTS AND METABOLISM, 1956–97

76   1   REBUILDING BUILDING

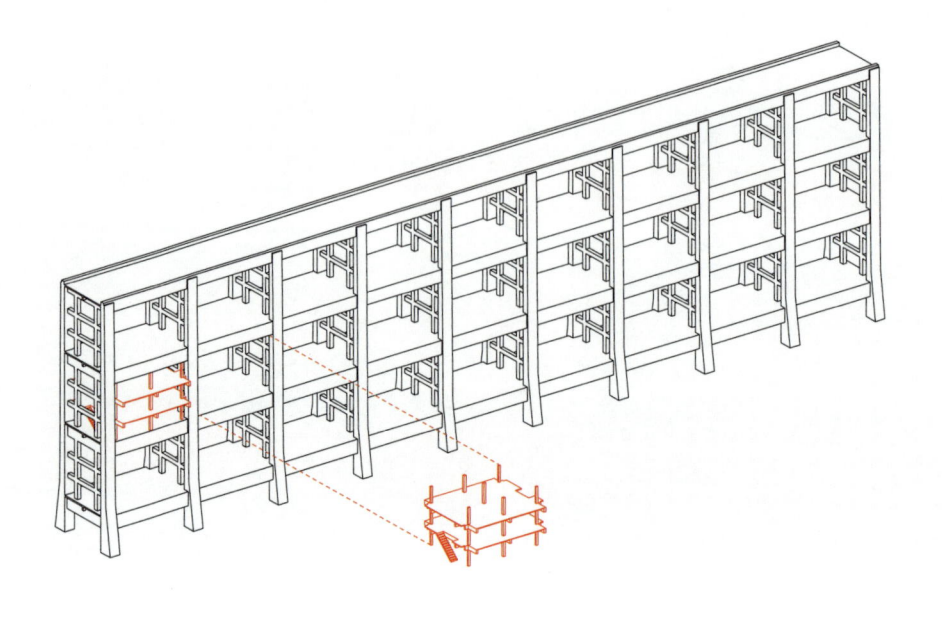

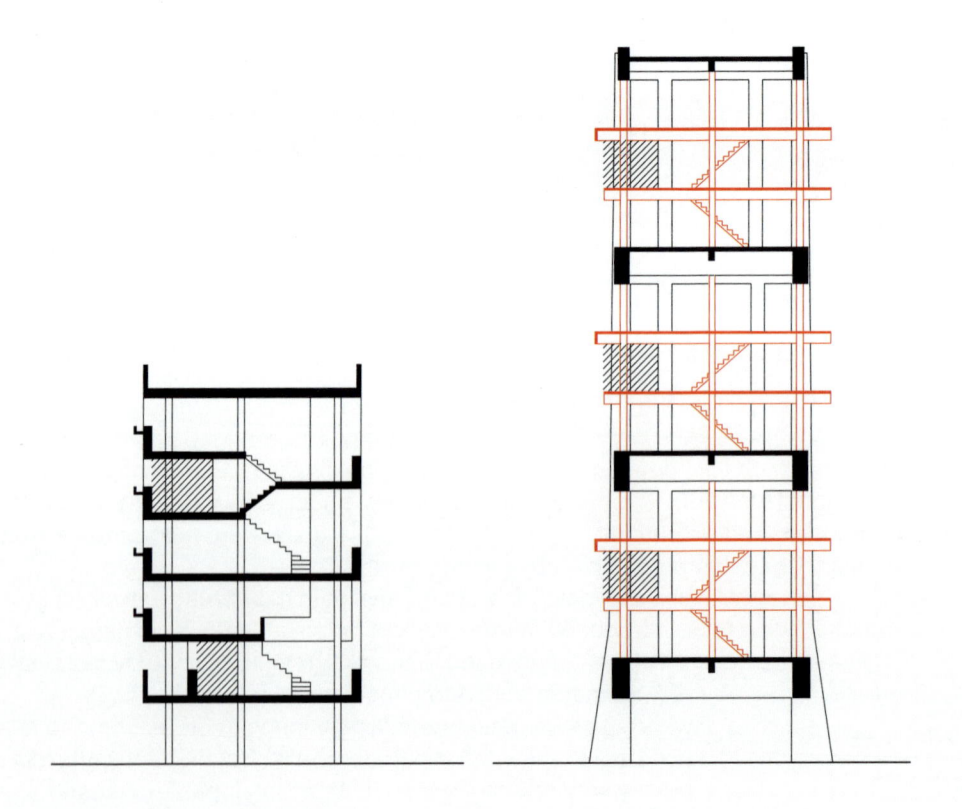

Familiarization

There is, however, likely to have been a direct Soviet influence on Harumi. Maekawa had visited the Marseilles Unité with Kenzo Tange while it was under construction in 1951, but as has been well-documented, Le Corbusier's skip-floor corridors for the Unités were inspired by Soviet experiments.[10] A prime example is the Narkomfin Communal House, and at one point Le Corbusier returned to Paris from a Moscow trip to oversee his Centrosoyuz project with a copy of Narkomfin's blueprints, which we can imagine landing on Maekawa's drafting table.[11] At the time, Maekawa was part of the Centrosoyuz design team.

Harumi and Narkomfin are both slabs with skip-floor corridors, in which stairs serving apartments are collected on corridors shared by two or more floors. Unlike Marseilles, which is also skip-floor, they are both time-based in concept, predicated on ideas of gradual social transformation. In 1929, Moisei Ginzburg wrote about Narkomfin that, "it is absolutely necessary to incorporate certain features that … stimulate the transition to a socially superior mode of life, *stimulate but not dictate*."[12] He classified Narkomfin as a "transitional type."[13] The ethno-archaeologist Victor Buchli describes this stimulating environment at Narkomfin as "accommodating pre-existing bourgeois living patterns … in such a way as to ease an individual's transition towards fully socialized life," achieved through the "edifying effects of architecture on its inhabitants."[14] It was a machine for converting bourgeois residents living in units with private kitchens into—hopefully—proper comrades living in kitchen-free units using only the complex's communal dining hall. This metamorphosis was to be achieved partly through the skip-floor system, where contact and exposure in the shared corridors between the social classes in different unit types would induce conversion toward correct communist lifestyles.

Harumi's corridor design was partly rationalized by the project's two elevators being able to make fewer stops. But the corridors were also seen as social spaces to "chat and admire the view" from heights previously unavailable in a Japanese home.[15] Apartments were accessed either directly off the corridor or by stairs to units above and below.

Led by project architect Masato Otaka—like Kawazoe, soon to be a Metabolist—Maekawa's team tested multiple apartment plans during the schematic design phase. They rejected some types as suited only to "urban intellectuals," and deemed others organized around a double-loaded corridor, like the Unités, as too dark and cramped for their frame's smaller width.[16] Eventually the plans were resolved with reference to the square *noka* and rectangular *machiya*, the wooden farmhouse and townhouse types of pre-modern Japan. Otaka emphasized this inspiration in a 1957 article on the project.[17]

Through either eliminating kitchens or lodging vernacular house forms in the sky, both Narkomfin and Harumi are transitional types that acted to familiarize the strange: on the one hand, collectivization, and on the other, Western high-rise living.[18] But while Narkomfin sought to eliminate the old, Harumi strove to preserve it. Recalling the juxtaposition of Fort l'Empereur's sweeping modern infrastructure containing Moorish villas, Harumi's minor-structural interpretations of *noka* and *machiya* indicate the central role that vernacular architecture played in the "Debate on Tradition." Instigated by Kawazoe in 1956 from his editorial position at *Shinkenchiku*—the prominent publication better known internationally through its English-language edition, *The Japan Architect*—this debate

top: Major- and minor-structure

bottom: Comparative sections of Narkomfin and Harumi

town house

farm house

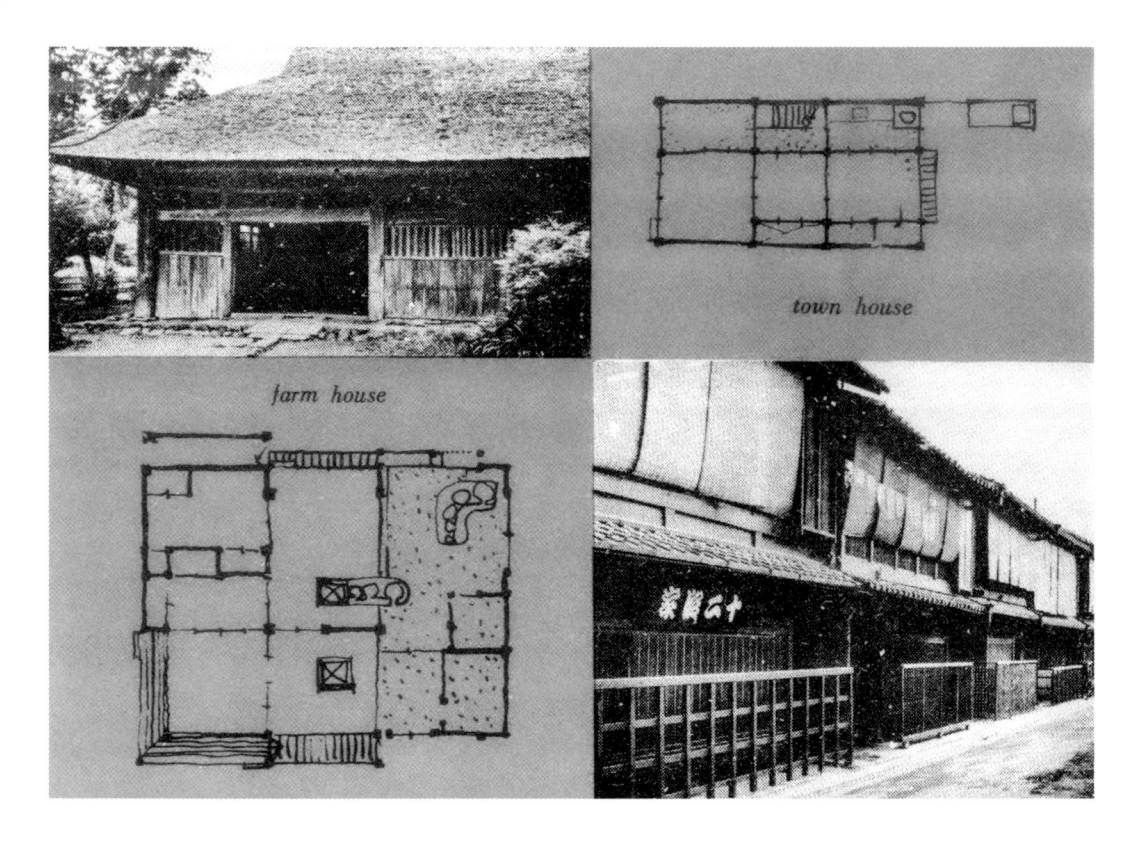

revived a call for "Japanese spirit with Western knowledge," an objective dating back to the acceleration of Western influences in the late nineteenth century.[19]

In the postwar context, the question animating some architectural thinkers had shifted from how to combine Western modernity with tradition to asking which tradition. Historic institutional architecture had been corrupted by its association with Japanese nationalism, and folk types appeared to be an antidote. This reorientation was given momentum by the national Law for the Protection of Cultural Properties, passed in 1955, which moved beyond preservation of only high-culture monuments to include *minka* such as *machiya* and *noka*.[20] In this light, Harumi was an incubator, with a fire- and earthquake-proof frame that Kawazoe called a "manmade rock" protecting a wooden *minka* past for future revitalization.[21] As the architectural historian Teiji Itoh has written, *minka* planning was based on primary and secondary posts, with the secondary ones being the nonstructural system for flexible internal partitioning.[22] The minor-structure partakes in this past model's openness to modification, aspiring to nativize concrete as a new version of wood, an obsessive pursuit that permeated Metabolist work in the 1960s.

Signs of Life

As a result of its experimental nature, rents at Harumi were high. The first occupants were professional and upper middle-class, with many "urban intellectuals" it appears, including doctors, lawyers, playwrights, painters, university professors, photographers, and secretaries of Diet members, encompassing various types of households, from single to multigenerational.[23]

above: Harumi's *minka* inspiration, 1957

right: Plans for 2DK unit type A (top) and type B (bottom)

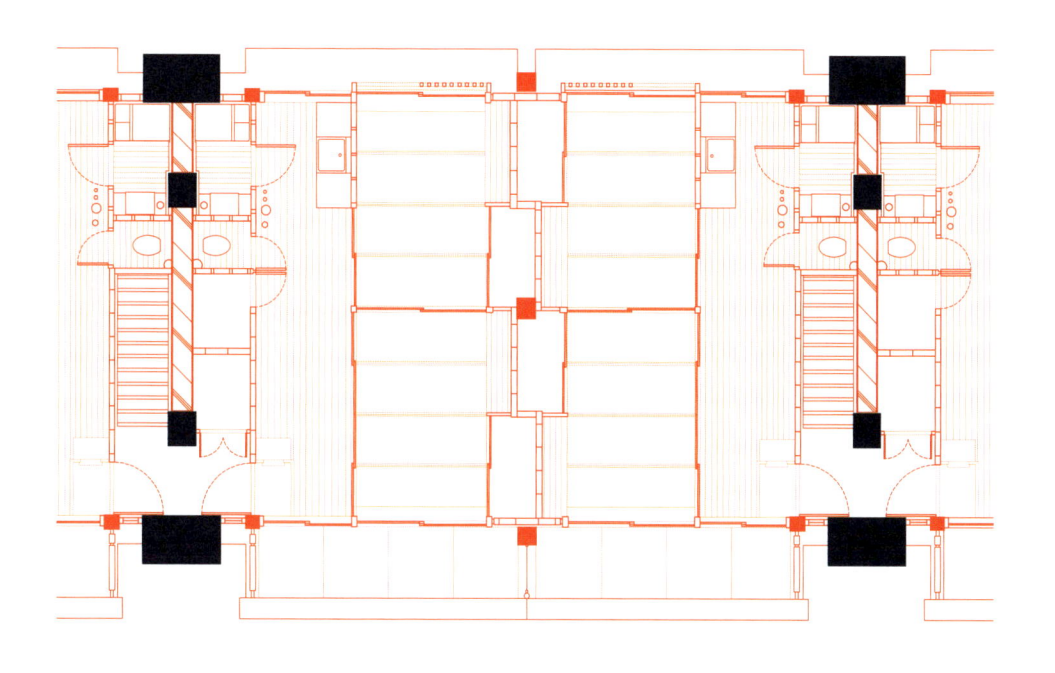

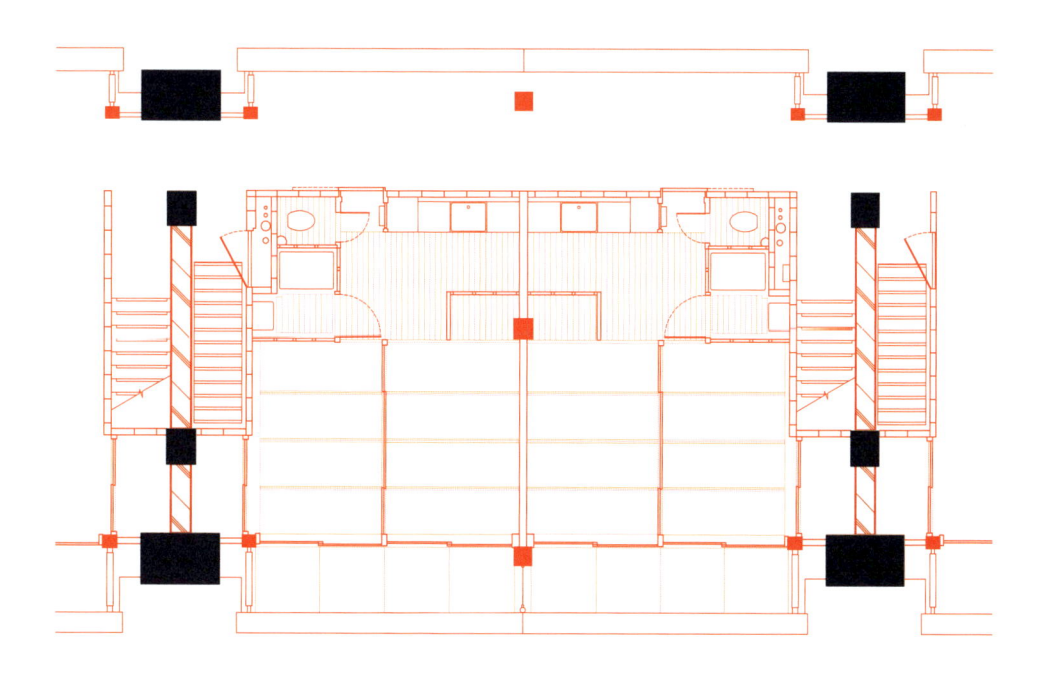

TRANSITIONAL TYPE: HARUMI APARTMENTS AND METABOLISM, 1956–97

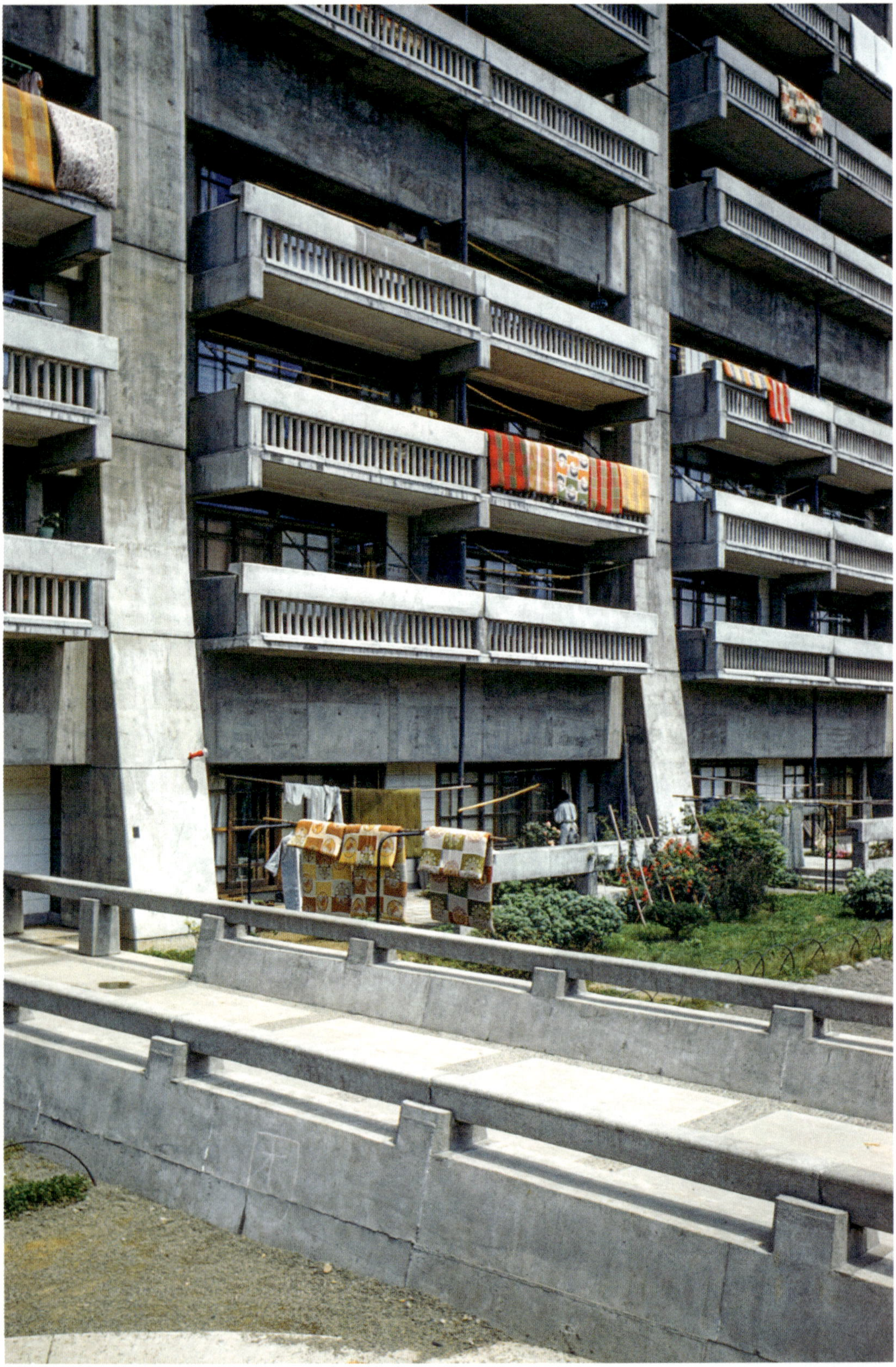

Once occupied, one of the most contested aspects of tradition appeared on Harumi's facades in the form of drying laundry. The motley patchworks of drying laundry throughout Japanese cityscapes were the topic of a 1956 article by Tange in the *Sankei Newspaper*, where he complained that it spoiled the facades of apartment buildings.[24] Yet Kawazoe, Tange's sparring partner throughout the tradition debate, saw this practice at Harumi as showing the building's strength, writing, "It seems to me [...] drying diapers are a sign of life and energy," and that an "apartment house should be able to withstand these manifestations of human life. If it cannot, it is a weak building."[25]

But resident participation and significant variations in unit types were absent at Harumi, the opposite of what Yosizaka had proposed in 1954. The project was controlled top-down, with all units designed for a speculative population of renters, and artificial land used for the purposes of economic construction and long-term renovation planning by management—not the ludic opportunity of "each man building his own house." The transitional type soon will become the model for important large-scale developments to follow, an approach to artificial land that will be the favored strategy of government, that is far easier to implement than indeterminate maximum dwellings. However, the transitional approach remains radical in its foresight and long-term investment, even though Harumi's adaptability seems never to have been acknowledged by Kano. Though pleased with his prototype, the ex-banker referred to the design as only a "considerable savings in steel and concrete."[26]

Harumi Apartments,
south facade (left) and
north facade (above), 1961

Harumi Apartments, type-A unit

Metabolism's DNA

Not long after Harumi's completion, Otaka was approached by Kawazoe and asked to join what would become the Metabolists. The movement made its debut in Tokyo in May 1960 at the World Design Conference, known as WoDeCo, an event modelled on the International Design Conference at Aspen, Colorado, which started in 1951. Like Aspen, WoDeCo was intended to cross multiple design disciplines, and it would be the first such international design event ever held in Japan. After initial contact with Aspen's organizers in 1956, thanks to the designers Isamu Kenmochi and Sori Yanagi, preparatory planning for a 1958 event in Japan was initiated by none other than Kano, with the financial support of Japan's Ministry of International Trade and Industry (MITI). Despite Aspen soon leaving the initiative, the Japanese were committed to its realization. The executive committee for the event was chaired by Junzo Sakakura—another graduate of Le Corbusier's atelier and a leading architect—with direction of the conference programming assigned to Tange, due to his professional and academic prominence.[27]

For Tange, well-versed in the ways of the Western avant-garde, WoDeCo was an excellent opportunity to construct a movement. He saw the event's potential for presenting a new brand of architecture, both global and distinctly Japanese, and engaging urban-architectural policy-making in the vein of CIAM and its offshoot, Team 10.[28] It was a chance to invite leading Western designers, such as Louis Kahn, Jean Prouvé, Paul Rudolph, and Team 10's prime movers, Alison and Peter Smithson. These were some of the figures that the Japanese took as inspiration and desired as competition.

Tange left Japan in 1959 to teach for a year at the Massachusetts Institute of Technology (MIT). He charged his trusted associate Takashi Asada, deputy director of Tange's research and design lab at the University of Tokyo, to assemble a team of daring designers able to invent a movement. Asada enlisted Kawazoe, just fired from his editorship of *Shinkenchiku*, to help in this task.[29]

The architects found were somewhat diverse in age and experience, bringing different skills and achievements. Otaka was the oldest at thirty-seven, and well-known for his role in realizing Harumi; Fumihiko Maki brought international prestige with his Harvard degree, teaching at Washington University in St. Louis, and a Graham Foundation Fellowship; Kiyonori Kikutake's recently completed home in Tokyo, Sky House, was a sensation; Kisho Kurokawa, at twenty-six the youngest, was a promising graduate of the Tange Lab then researching prefabrication in the Soviet Union. The group was rounded out by Kawazoe, as well as the industrial designer Kenji Ekuan, soon to create the iconic Kikkoman soy sauce bottle, and Kiyoshi Awazu, a self-taught graphic designer known for his poster designs.

Kawazoe's role in the Debate on Tradition has been described as similar to the making of propaganda, and this was a skill he now brought to his new assignment.[30] A movement needs a name, and he proposed *shinchintaisha*—"regeneration," or to replace the old with the new, a term taken from the Japanese edition of Friedrich Engels's *Dialectics of Nature*. It was also the term used in Japanese biology for "metabolism," the name suggested by Kikutake after consulting an English-Japanese dictionary.[31] Metabolism had a far more global appeal. It also helped to synthesize and inspire the work of the group as they prepared for the conference.

Despite the group's diversity and the variety of projects they presented at WoDeCo, all their ideas revolved around temporality. While Western modernism took replacing the old with the new as a basic premise, Metabolism saw replacement as an ongoing process. It was the first architectural movement to thematize obsolescence in cyclical time, unlike the linear time of Western architecture, as exemplified by the controlled decline of a building in Albert Speer's "theory of ruin value."[32]

Time's creative role in design was expressed most powerfully at the conference in Tange's keynote speech. Entitled "Technology and Humanity," it was an essential statement of Metabolism's temporal agenda. Tange observed that:

> Even our dwellings cease to be serviceable after five or ten years.
> Short-lived items are becoming more and more short-lived,
> and the cycle of change is shrinking at a corresponding rate.
> On the other hand, the accumulation of capital has made it possible
> to build in large-scale operations. Reformations of natural topography,
> dams, harbors, and highways are of a size and scope that involve
> long cycles of time, and these are the manmade works that tend to
> decide the overall system of the age....
> The two tendencies—toward shorter cycles and toward longer
> cycles—are both necessary to modern life and to humanity itself.[33]

Seen architecturally, these tendencies appear to be a sublimation of artificial land, a distillation of the combined durations of major- and minor-structure into a generally applicable temporal concept, one able to reconcile, according to Tange, such conflicts as "order versus freedom" and "system versus spontaneity."[34]

The combination presented in the speech was illustrated through work by one of Tange's student teams at MIT, from where he'd just returned, to whom he had set the assignment to design a "New Community on the Sea" that could house 25,000 people on Boston Harbor. With the harbor acting as a surrogate Tokyo Bay,

世界デザイン会議 1960年5月
World Design Conference, 1960 May

P. ルドルフ、L. カーン
P. Rudolph, L. Kahn

Y. ヌミ、E. ハーロー、黒川紀章、剣持勇、
C. Y. Numi, E. Harlor, Kisho Kurokawa, Isamu Kenmochi,
C. Orbach, Kiyoshi Seike

白井、田中、永井、宇野
Shirai, Tanaka, Nagai, Uno, Yamashiro

Kenji Ekuan

Fumihiko Maki

Koji Kamiya

1 REBUILDING BUILDING

Kiyonori Kikutake, M. Yamasaki

Tsune Sesoko, Kenzo Tange, Jane Drew

Images from WoDeCo, 1960, shown during a symposium for the 2011 show *Metabolism— The City of the Future*, Mori Art Museum, Tokyo

TRANSITIONAL TYPE: HARUMI APARTMENTS AND METABOLISM, 1956–97

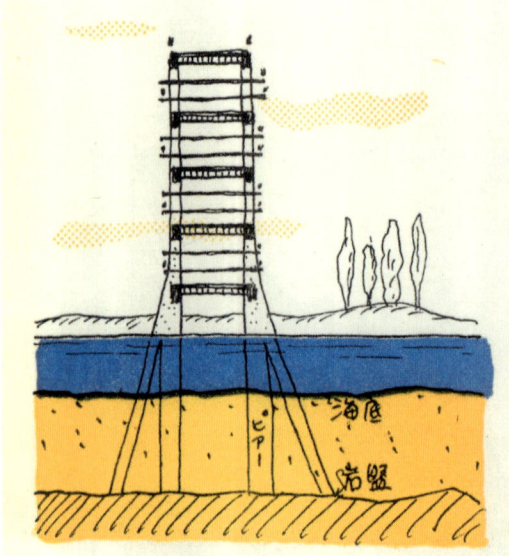

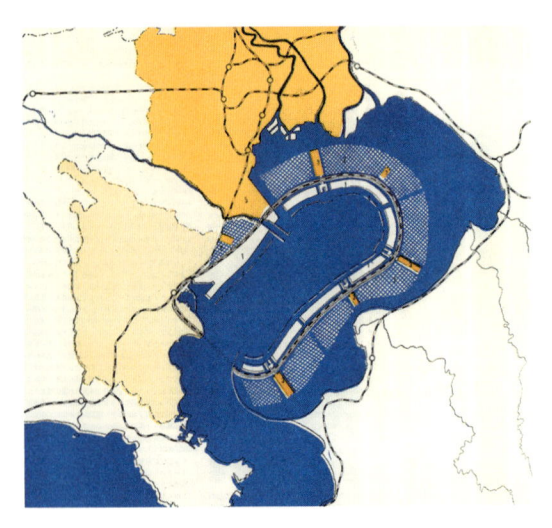

Tange was able to research strategies for Tokyo's expansion.³⁵ The bay had already been used by others as a site on which to imagine vast developments: in 1958, Kano made a proposal for occupying it that envisioned an enormous axis of reclaimed land, starting at Harumi Island and terminating at a new international airport far south at Futtsusu; and in 1959, Otaka published a proposal in the journal *Kenchiku bunka* that treated the Harumi Apartments as a repeatable module, grouping copies in pinwheel clusters that formed a belt along the waterfront.³⁶ Otaka took Harumi as the replicable model it was intended to be. The MIT project drew on Harumi too, with its giant A-frames also described as "major-structure" composed of voids three floors high, imagined to contain changeable housing "left up to individual tastes."³⁷

While Tange was never officially a member of the group, it's been said that "Without Tange, no Metabolism."³⁸ True as this is, without artificial land, there would hardly be the avant-garde Tange we know. Though his portfolio can't at all be reduced to this one concept, it is a key concept in the projects that cemented

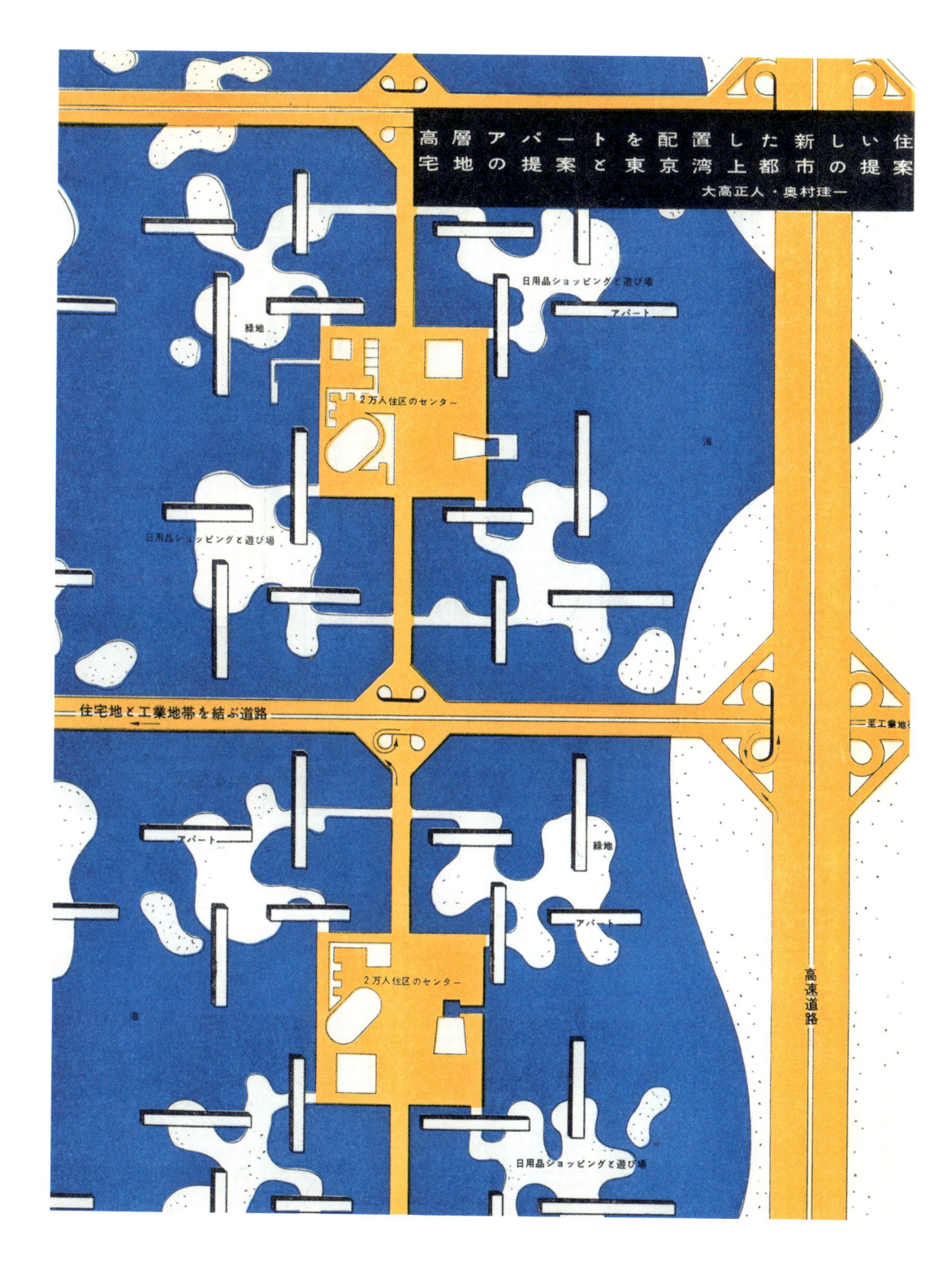

Masato Otaka, Tokyo Bay
proposal, 1959

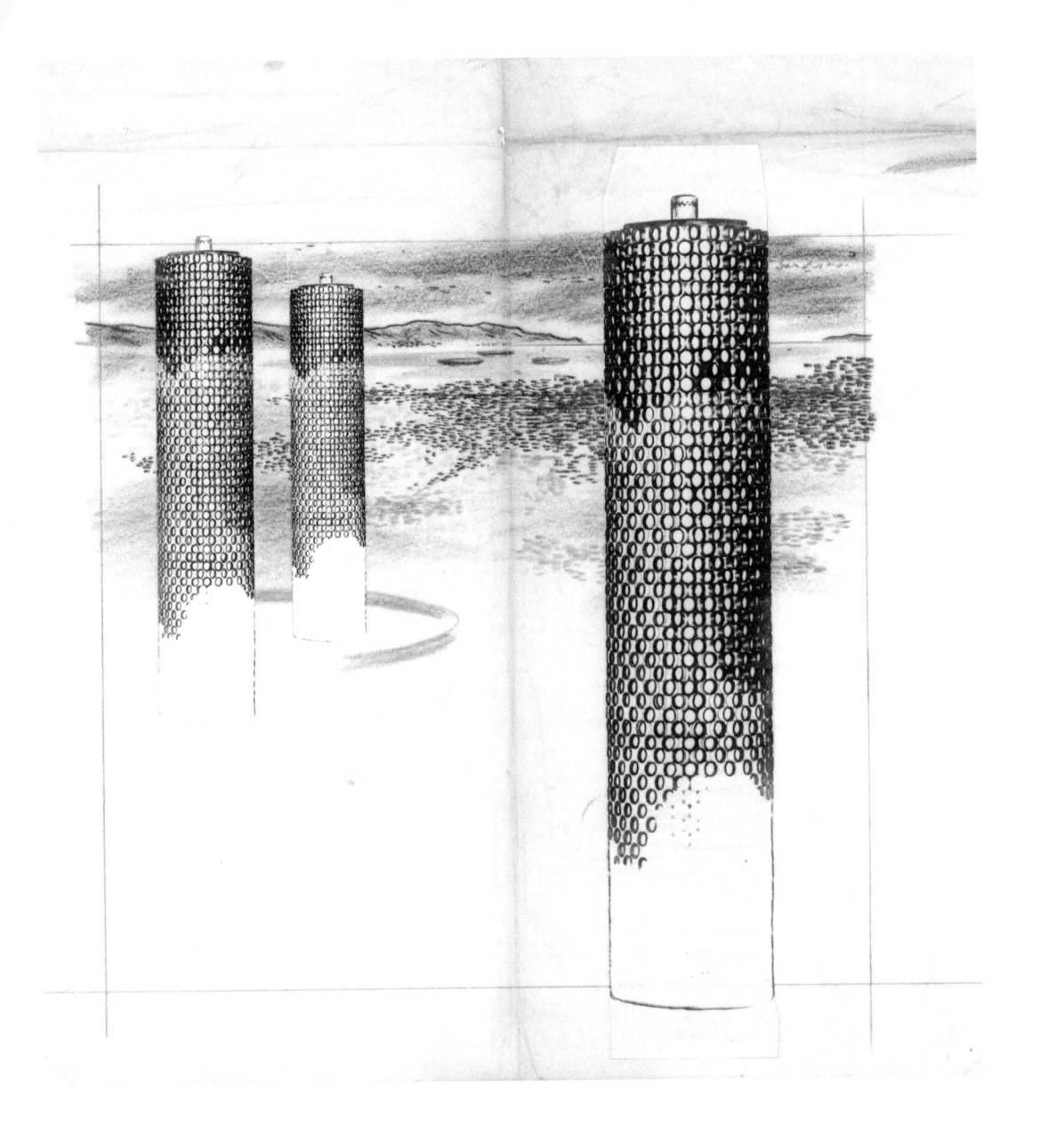

above: Kiyonori Kikutake,
Tower-Shaped Community
proposal, 1958

right: Kisho Kurokawa,
Agricultural City proposal, 1960

his international fame and position as Metabolism's spiritual guide. The major highlight of this prominence was the debut of his A Plan for Tokyo, 1960, the culmination of the MIT research being applied to Tokyo Bay. The artificial land housing of A Plan for Tokyo is what Peter Smithson found to be its most successful yet frustrating component, and one that was to have a significant influence on later projects.

In the meantime, the temporal dualism of artificial land permeated the work presented by the Metabolists at WoDeCo, as recorded in *Metabolism/1960: The Proposals for New Urbanism*, a small, manifesto-like book, written in Japanese and English, and sold at the conference. The concept makes its first appearance in the book in Kikutake's "Ocean City" essay. There he argues that "artificial land should be planned as a wall," as demonstrated in his Tower-Shaped Community proposal that shifts the site of changeable units onto a fixed vertical core, in an early instance of plug-in capsule architecture.[39] In this counterintuitive interpretation, we see the eagerness of designers to make artificial land their own, which makes it less odd to hear Kurokawa describe his 1972 Nakagin Capsule Tower, Metabolism's greatest icon, as an "artificial-land base" in *The Japan Architect* over a decade later.[40]

But Kurokawa's Agricultural City represented the theme at WoDeCo in its more typically horizontal form. Conceived as a gridiron of streets elevated high over farmland, with the grid supplying services such as water and electricity—now established as basic necessities for artificial land—the city's residents live in the "basic housing unit" of "mushroom-shaped" houses. While lifting buildings above the ground is a common trope in modernism that often seems merely formalist, Kurokawa lifts his scheme as a disaster-prevention strategy: the proposal was to be located in Kanie in Aichi Prefecture, location of the architect's hometown, which had been heavily damaged by the Ise Bay Typhoon in 1959.[41]

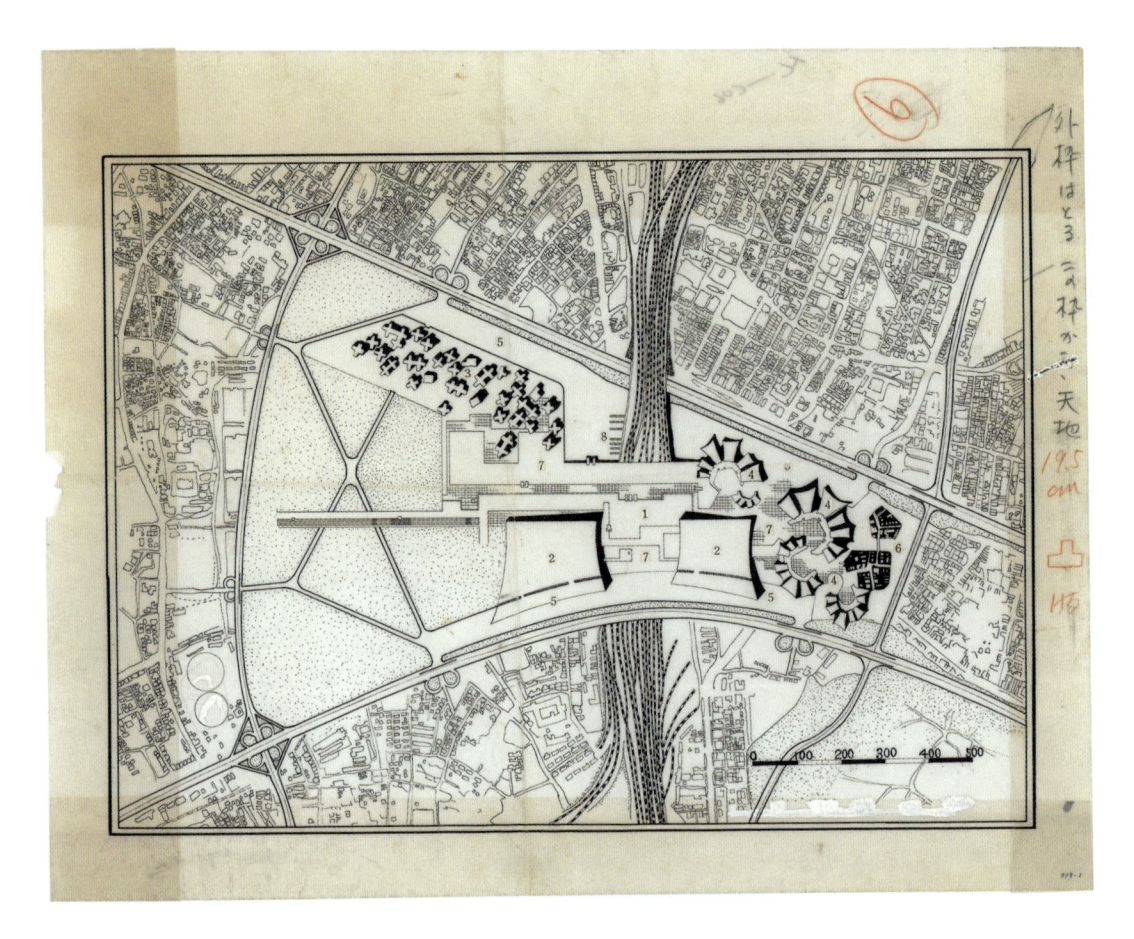

Lastly, artificial land supports the schemes in Maki and Otaka's "Toward Group Form," the first major airing of the "group form" concept for which Maki is known. Group form's inspiration lies in the aggregation of small repetitive buildings found in much vernacular architecture, and seen by Maki on his travels around the Mediterranean in the late 1950s. In such an urban architecture, there is a reciprocal relationship between the solids of buildings and the voids of exterior spaces between them. With this vision of aggregation, the two architects attacked the perpetuation of architecture as "the image of a single structure, complete in itself."[42] Open-ended and incomplete, group form instead proposed an arithmetical architecture formed by clusters of units, able to produce a new scale of urban images that would be inherently flexible, retaining the same basic identity if pieces were added or subtracted. This was illustrated with a design for theaters and other performance spaces arrayed like flower petals around a plaza: despite some petals being absent, there was still a strong identity, leading the architects to the idea of "master form" instead of a static master plan that may never be completed.[43] Zooming out from these group form clusters, part of Maki and Otaka's proposal for Tokyo's new Shinjuku Station area, we see that all of the scattered and packed elements are supported by a massive artificial plateau. Taking multiple forms, artificial land was Metabolism's conceptual DNA.

Fumihiko Maki and Masato Otaka, Shinjuku Station proposal, 1960

Repairing the Rift

The definition of "Metabolism" presented in the *Metabolism/1960* book was vague and poetic, described as a "denotation of vitality."[44] As such, it acted as an umbrella for architects with quite different fascinations, from sci-fi to old villages. Yet, right after the conference, Kawazoe became active in articulating a more precise meaning for the name. At the time, none other than Maekawa felt that Metabolism meant only the exchange of the old with the new, amounting to no more than "letting things take their course."[45] Countering Maekawa's impression, Kawazoe's writings later in the 1960s make it clear that he saw Metabolism's task as making positive societal change through rejecting anything laissez-faire. This activist stance had in fact already been announced in the *Metabolism/1960* book, wherein the group—presumably in Kawazoe's words—called for the "active metabolic development of our society."[46] His thinking was aided by what he calls in a 2005 interview in Rem Koolhaas and Hans Ulrich Obrist's book *Project Japan* "our own particular brand of Marxism."[47] Indeed, the historian Yasufumi Nakamori writes that Kawazoe considered the application of Marxist ideas to architecture to be a huge challenge until he encountered the use of metabolism by Marx and Engels, which suggested a possible way.[48]

Kawazoe was not alone in his postwar discovery of Marx—or perhaps rediscovery. As John Dower writes in *Embracing Defeat*, Marxism's postwar rise in Japan was the restarting of an "interrupted critical tradition" that had been repressed since the late 1920s.[49] Antiwar communists freed from jail now appeared as heroes, and Marxist analyses provided a framework for critiquing imperialist aggression. This gave rise to a culture of "revolutionary optimism" bolstered by the Allied occupation's imposition of democracy, which was seen, much to the surprise of the Americans, as a positive step towards a future socialist society.[50] Largely an academic phenomenon, this resurgence was strong at Kawazoe's *alma mater*, Waseda University, which Kikutake and, of course, Yosizaka also attended.[51] While there, Kawazoe was an organizer of the school's Communist Party, making for an early training in propaganda.

All of this calls for a better understanding of Marx's metabolism and how it may illuminate Kawazoe's Marxism. John Bellamy Foster's *Marx's Ecology*, published in 2000, helps investigate this relationship through its recovery of the ecological basis of Marx's thinking. As Foster writes, the concept of metabolism has been in use since the mid-nineteenth century as a term for the ways in which organisms take matter and energy from their surrounding environment and convert them into the "building blocks of growth."[52] First coined in 1815, its basis in biology was established by the biologist Theodor Schwann in 1839, who described the "metabolic phenomena" of cells as those that are "liable to occasion or to suffer change," using the term to refer to the internal dynamics of an organism.[53] Over the century, the term increasingly became associated with energetics, referring to the processes controlling external and internal energy transfers between organisms and their environments. This energetic aspect is brought to the fore in Marx's use of the concept which, as Foster points out, is very indebted to the work of German chemist Justus von Liebig.

For Marx, the significance of Liebig lies in his description of the dangerous separation between agricultural areas and cities, which were reaching unprecedented levels of size and density. A pioneer in the study of the nutrients that provide soil fertility, Liebig was responding to an era in which soil degradation was a poorly understood problem with international impact. Declining fertility due to overfarming, connected to the rise of urban populations, had created crises in the 1820s and '30s, precipitating a worldwide hunt by the United States and England for bat and bird guano as replacement fertilizers for previous sources that were no longer sufficient.[54] Though Liebig invented artificial fertilizers to mitigate this problem, his later writings became increasingly critical of capitalist agriculture's "robbery" of the soil that demanded ever-expanding networks of resources to maintain its productivity, driven by the increasing distances between countryside and city due to industrial development. These distances meant that the soil no longer received the nutrients necessary for maintaining its productivity and health, the main source of those missing nutrients being human excrement. Indeed, Liebig asserted in his 1865 *Letters on the Subject of the Utilization of the Municipal Sewage* that if the nutrient-rich excrement of city dwellers was returned to each farmer in proportion to the nutrients they consumed, that "the productiveness of his land might be maintained almost unimpaired for ages to come."[55]

Marx was deeply influenced by these writings, which presented metabolism as a cycle of nutrient inputs and outputs, exchanges (or the lack thereof) that he then used as the basis for his own critique of capitalism's exploitation of nature. Marx's innovation was to broaden the term to include what Foster describes as a "specific ecological meaning and a wider social meaning."[56] While this social meaning is partly manifested in the

(from left) Kiyonori Kikutake, Takashi Asada, Noboru Kawazoe, and Kisho Kurokawa on a recuperative holiday following the WoDeCo conference. Asada notes:
– WoDeCo has ended. I don't know how it happened, but I have somehow found myself the leader of the Metabolism group.
– Following the international conference, the designers seem exhausted and lethargic.
– I intended to take them to Toyohashi, where I have friends, so I could show them the reality of the social situation... while the Mikawa development... is quietly underway, and have them think about global problems.
– Maki and Otaka did not join us.
– We stayed at the Gamagori Hotel.

above: Metabolism's symbol or *mon*, designed by Kiyoshi Awazu

92   1 REBUILDING BUILDING

relationships of city dwellers to rural farmers, it is also found in Marx's definition of metabolism as labor. Understood as labor, metabolism describes the way that nature's materials are worked and processed by humans, with Volume 1 of *Capital*, published in 1867, stating that labor is "the universal condition for the metabolic interaction between man and nature, the everlasting nature-imposed condition of human existence."[57] For Marx, to answer the metabolic question of how humans should work the earth, particularly for farming, had the same urgency as the need to eat.

This ecological agenda borne by metabolism was expanded in the unfinished Volume 3 of *Capital*, published by Engels in 1894 after Marx's death in 1883. There, in a statement that summarizes the influence of Liebig as well as the notion of metabolism as labor, Marx writes of the "irreparable rift in the interdependent process of social metabolism, a metabolism prescribed by the natural laws of life itself."[58] The "irreparable rift" that Marx describes has been condensed by Foster into "metabolic rift," the "material estrangement of human beings within capitalist society from the natural conditions which [form] the basis for their existence."[59] It captures the alienation from nature that contributes to its exploitative treatment as a free and limitless resource serving capitalism's demand for continuous growth.

Returning to Kawazoe, we learn from *Project Japan* that he had been rereading *Capital* all his adult life (a fact that Koolhaas and Obrist do not explore further).[60] It seems that forty years before Foster, an awareness of the "metabolic rift" is at the core of Kawazoe's concept of Metabolist architecture. The goal of the movement, at least for him, is to repair the metabolic rift. In his 1969 article "Metabolism," he writes that, "contemporary cultural form...is directed toward schism."[61]

Repair of this schism or rift had been further fleshed out in a 1961 essay titled "The City of the Future." There he writes that the "development of the city must be pushed forward in unison with the metabolism of civilization and of nature. Or rather, the development of the city should be one which will accelerate the latter towards a higher and superior direction."[62] The construction of nature and city had to be conscious and coordinated. Elsewhere in the piece he develops in more detail the joining of city and nature, suggesting, as in Yosizaka's idea for the Yamanote Line, that the entire population of Tokyo could be accommodated in an area only twice the size of Setagaya Ward. This would liberate tremendous amounts of open space, if everyone lived in a replica of Harumi. The massive piers of the design would merge the social and ecological by allowing vegetation to run under the buildings, now connected by elevated roads, thereby rewilding the city's ground plane as nature made public property, with towers in fields or forests, rather than in manicured parks.[63] Artificial land, if correctly implemented, would be a way to regenerate natural land.

Kawazoe was particularly taken by "The Trinity Formula" chapter in Volume 3 of *Capital*.[64] This trinity comprises capital, land, and labor, and one passage stands out in particular. Marx writes:

> Just as the savage must wrestle with nature to satisfy his needs, to maintain and reproduce his life, so must civilized man, and he must do so in all forms of society and under all possible modes of production. This realm of natural necessity expands with his development, because his needs do too; but the productive forces to satisfy these expand at the same time. Freedom, in this sphere, can consist only in this, that socialized man, the associated producers, *govern the human metabolism with nature in a rational way*, bringing it under their collective control instead of being

dominated by it as a blind power; accomplishing it with the least expenditure of energy and in conditions most worthy and appropriate for their human nature. But this always remains a realm of necessity. The true realm of freedom, the development of human powers as an end in itself, begins beyond it, though it can only flourish with this realm of necessity as its basis. The reduction of the working day is the basic prerequisite.[65]

We should reflect that calls to shorten the work day can be found throughout the history of modernism, appearing in the writings of Le Corbusier, Marcel Breuer, Buckminster Fuller, and no doubt others—a call quite absent from leading architects in the early twenty-first century. Increased free time would allow a cultural flourishing, and for Kawazoe, referring explicitly to Marx's call, it would lead to the expansion beyond the weekend of what he calls the "'Sunday carpenter' of the Do-it-yourself persuasion." Recalling the *minka* and barrack builders that had inspired Kawazoe's Waseda professors Kon and Yosizaka, such Sunday carpenters would have "their own freedom of expression" in building their dwellings, a freedom enabled by stacked plots of artificial land.[66]

It's important to note that Marx doesn't present "human metabolism" as inherently good: seen in terms of its damage to humans and nature, it's often irrational in its methods and objectives, and with a tendency toward domination. To return to Liebig's example, the ways in which humans were metabolizing soil through capitalist agriculture was paradoxically imperiling food production. Similarly, well before Metabolism's 1960 debut, Japanese cities were already metabolizing in terms of the vast labor of reconstruction, work that was also not rationalized in the interests of democratic and lasting human freedom—to give but one example, freedom from pollution.

While Kawazoe's stance of Marxist Metabolism was not necessarily shared by all his fellow Metabolists, his position is the most progressive version of their objectives, and one that complicates their relationship to the "super creative bureaucracy and [...] activist state" celebrated in *Project Japan*.[67] As we will see, the 1960s was a period of significant activism by Japanese people against the state. Opposed to Maekawa's impression of a passive "going with the flow," Kawazoe's particular brand of Metabolism appears to have been an active question: how, through architecture, can human metabolism within nature occur in a rational way? Only by working to answer this could architects contribute to the repair of the metabolic rift.

Creative Destruction

Harumi was demolished in 1997, thirty-nine years after its completion. With the removal of height limits in 1970, thanks in part to the arrival of more sophisticated high-rise engineering, Maekawa's design was suddenly and drastically underbuilt. While it had been planned as transitional, able to change together with the fortunes of Japanese society, the economic growth that accelerated in the 1960s totally surpassed the most optimistic projections: the "National Income Doubling Plan" introduced by Prime Minister Hayato Ikeda in 1961 called for a doubling of personal incomes in ten years, which was achieved in only seven.[68] By 1997, Japan was in the "Lost Decade" of economic stagnation following the crash from the 1980s high of the "bubble economy"—another period of tremendous growth. But even amid comparative stagnation, the rise in land prices since 1958 was enormous, with the value of land in Tokyo rising about 200 percent over the 1980s alone.[69] As a result, Harumi was destroyed by money rather than earthquake or fire.

Harumi Apartments,
variability test, 1997

TRANSITIONAL TYPE: HARUMI APARTMENTS AND METABOLISM, 1956–97

1. 住戸内の可変

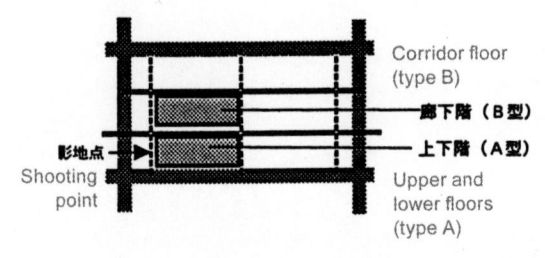

住戸内木部の解体
A型、B型、計2戸

＊A型は下階でも可

Variability in a house
– Demolition of the wooden part of the house
– Type A and type B, two houses in total

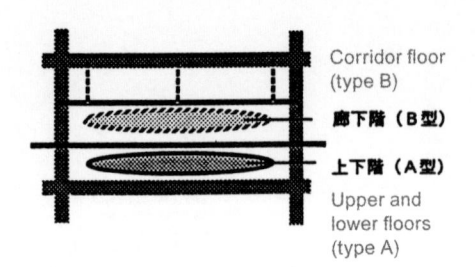

Corridor floor (type B)
廊下階（B型）
上下階（A型）
影地点 / Shooting point
Upper and lower floors (type A)

2. 2戸1の可変

戸境コンクリートブロックの解体

Variability in houses on the same floor
– Demolition of concrete block wall between houses

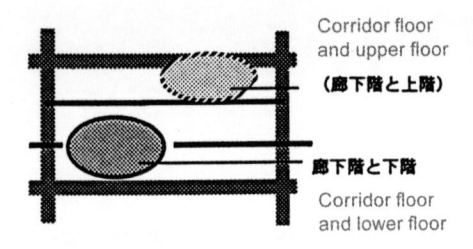

Corridor floor (type B)
廊下階（B型）
上下階（A型）
Upper and lower floors (type A)

3. 上下階の可変

マイナーＲＣ（一部スラブ・柱梁）の解体
廊下コンクリートブロックの解体

Variability in houses on the upper and lower floors
– Demolition of minor reinforced concrete structure (a part of the slab, column, and beam)
– Demolition of concrete block corridor

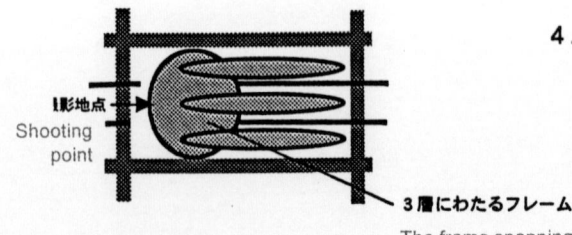

Corridor floor and upper floor
（廊下階と上階）
廊下階と下階
Corridor floor and lower floor

4. フレーム内の可変

全てのマイナーＲＣの解体

Variability in a frame structure
– Demolition of all minor reinforced concrete structure

影地点 / Shooting point
3層にわたるフレーム
The frame spanning three floors

1 REBUILDING BUILDING

But before demolition, the Housing and Urban Development Corporation, an entity created by a JHC merger in 1981, conducted what it called, in an internal report, a "variability test." After decades of lying dormant, one bay of major-structure was methodically excavated, its minor-structure incrementally removed by a special team working like a rationalist Gordon Matta-Clark to create phantom suggestions of lofts, duplexes, and sky gardens that had never existed. Momentarily and crudely simulating the dream of the transitional type made real, the minor-structure's removal implied a spacious domesticity not to be found in Japanese housing in 1958. As Kawazoe wrote in his 1959 review of the project, housing "must be strong enough architecturally to allow people to live as they wish. Indeed, it should provide them additional means for freedom and for aggressive, dynamic living." But here, artificial land's freedom would be only a brief and simulated performance.

In Hachioji, on the western edge of Tokyo, there is a testing facility run by the Urban Renaissance Agency—the JHC's current incarnation. Strewn with the remnants of various experiments devoted to the improvement of their housing, from seismic tests to investigations of rooftop vegetation, the facility also has a museum, the Housing Apartment History Hall. Kawazoe had complained that the absence of "potential ruins" like Harumi showed Japan's cultural poverty— it lacked architecture capable of inspiring a continuity of quality, even in a state of decay that returned it to bare bones. While financial calculations denied Harumi the chance to become a ruin, preserved in the museum are a number of relics: a staircase, the building directory, a stretch of corridor, and a complete apartment interior. In a reversal of Metabolist planning, supposedly short-lived components survive while the major-structure has disappeared.

left: Variability test diagram

above: Recreation of Harumi type-A apartment, Urban Renaissance Agency (2010)

TRANSITIONAL TYPE: HARUMI APARTMENTS AND METABOLISM, 1956–97

晴海団地高層アパート 案内図

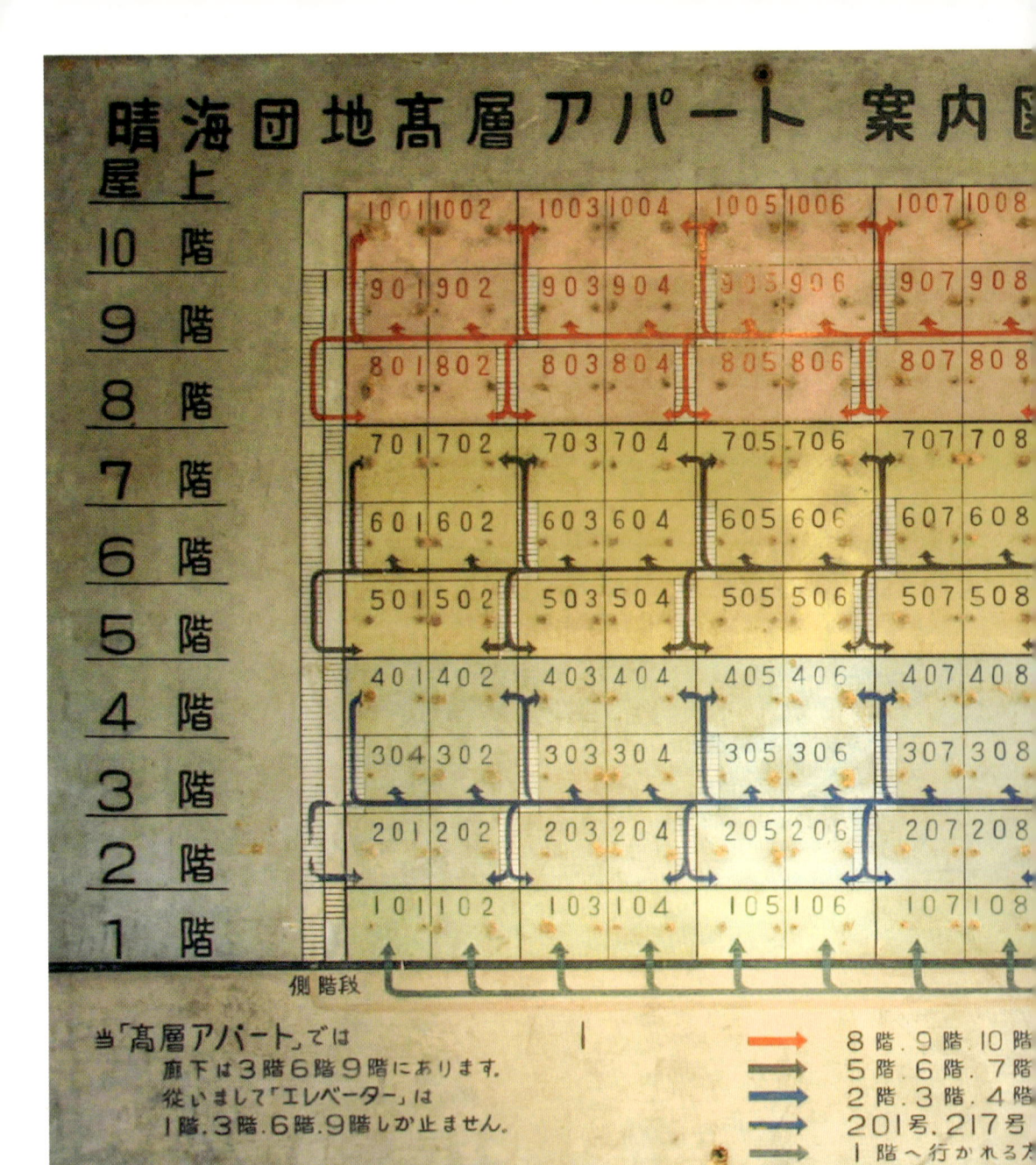

当「高層アパート」では
廊下は3階6階9階にあります。
従いまして「エレベーター」は
1階.3階.6階.9階しか止まません。

→ 8階.9階.10階
→ 5階.6階.7階
→ 2階.3階.4階
→ 201号.217号
→ 1階へ行かれる方

Salvaged building directory, Urban Renaissance Agency (2010)

following: Salvaged spiral stair entry (left) and *trompe l'oeil* corridor (right), Urban Renaissance Agency (2010)

1 REBUILDING BUILDING

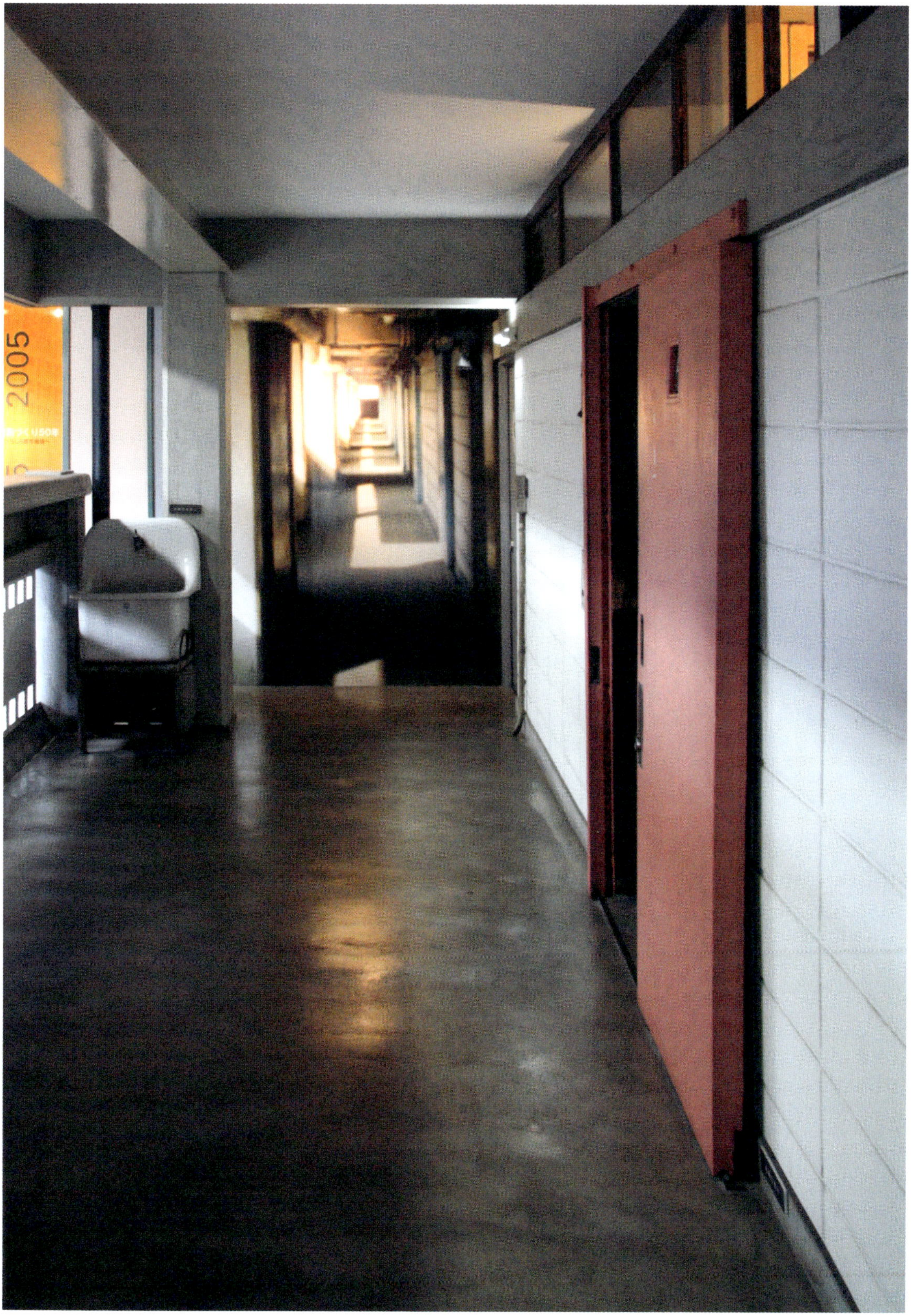
2005

1. Marco Pompili, *Dojunkai Apartments: Tokyo 1924–1934* (Rome: Editrice Librerie Dedalo, 2001), 17.
2. Noboru Kawazoe, "A Step Toward the Future," *The Japan Architect* 34 (March 1959): 25.
3. For comparison of Harumi and Marseilles, see Roger Sherwood, *Modern Housing Prototypes* (Cambridge, MA: Harvard University Press, 1978), 126.
4. Hisaakira Kano, "Public Housing in Japan," *Annals of Public and Cooperative Economics* 30, issue 1 (January 1959): 77. Kano's article is an abridged version of a lecture delivered in February 1958.
5. Kano, "Public," 76.
6. Manabu Hatsumi, "Kōsōka no yume—Harumi kōsō apāto" [The dream of high-rises: Harumi high-rise apartments], *Nihon ni okeru shūgo jūtaku keikaku no henkan* [Transition of mass housing planning in Japan], ed. Mitsuo Takada (Tokyo: Foundation for the Promotion of The Open University of Japan, 1998), 51. Translation by Riyo Namigata.
7. Noboru Kawazoe, *Contemporary Japanese Architecture* (Tokyo: The Japan Foundation, 1973), 58.
8. Toshihiko Kimura, "On Construction Design," *Shinkenchiku* (January 1957): 22.
9. See Hatsumi, "Kōsōka," 52.
10. See, for example, Jean-Louis Cohen, *Le Corbusier and the Mystique of the USSR* [1987] (Princeton, NJ: Princeton University Press, 1992), 122–124.
11. The blueprints are in the archive of the Fondation Le Corbusier. See Cohen, *Le Corbusier,* 123.
12. Moisei Ginzburg, quoted in Anatole Kopp, *Town and Revolution: Soviet Architecture and City Planning 1917–1935* [1967] (London: Thames and Hudson, 1970), 141. Italics in original.
13. Moisei Ginzburg, *Dwelling: Five Years' Work on the Problem of the Habitation* [1934] (London: Fontanka Publications/Ginzburg Design, 2017), 82.
14. Victor Buchli, *An Archaeology of Socialism* (New York: Berg, 2000), 67.
15. Ichiro Kawahara and Masato Otaka, "Toward the New Living Space," *Shinkenchiku* (January 1957): 24.
16. Kunio Maekawa, "Floor Plans in the Harumi Apartments," *The Japan Architect* 34 (March 1959): 27.
17. See Kawahara and Otaka, "Toward," 24–25.
18. I am indebted here to the Russian formalist critic Victor Shklovsky's concept of "defamiliarization," coined in 1917, in which the familiar is made strange in order to transform or reawaken our perception of it. See "Defamiliarization," accessed March 23, 2020, https://en.wikipedia.org/wiki/Defamiliarization.
19. See Zhongjie Lin, *Kenzo Tange and the Metabolist Movement: Urban Utopias of Modern Japan* (New York: Routledge, 2010), 39.
20. See Cherie Wendelken, "Aesthetics and Reconstruction: Japanese Architectural Culture in the 1950s," in *Rebuilding Urban Japan After 1945*, eds. Carola Hein, Jeffry M. Diefendorf, Yorifusa Ishida (New York: Pallgrave Macmillan, 2003), 201–203.
21. Kawazoe, "A Step," 26.
22. Teiji Itoh, *Traditional Domestic Architecture of Japan*, trans. Richard L. Gage (New York: Weatherhill, 1972), 43.
23. See Hatsumi, "Kōsōka," 53.
24. See Kawazoe, "A Step," 25.
25. Kawazoe, "A Step," 25.
26. Kano, "Public," 80.
27. For a detailed chronology of WoDeCo's planning and events, see Rem Koolhaas and Hans Ulrich Obrist, *Project Japan: Metabolism Talks...* (Cologne: Taschen, 2011), 174–204.
28. Tange participated in the 1951 CIAM meeting at Hoddesdon, England, as well as the final meeting in 1959 at Otterlo, the Netherlands, where he presented Kikutake's Tower-Shaped Community and Marine City projects. CIAM dissolved after this meeting, and the avant-garde's leadership passed to the younger CIAM members who formed Team 10. Through the 1960s and into the '70s, Kurokawa, Maki, and Tange would attend or be invited to a number of Team 10 gatherings throughout Europe. See "Team 10 Meetings," accessed April 9, 2019, http://www.team10online.org/index.html.
29. Kawazoe was asked to resign due to a critical essay on the architect Togo Murano, a close friend of *Shinkenchiku*'s owner.
30. See Yasufumi Nakamori, "Kawazoe Noboru: Architecture Journal *Shinkenchiku* and *dentō ronsō* (the Tradition Discourse): as a Breach to a Japanese Tragedy," in *Metabolism—The City of the Future: Dreams and Visions of Reconstruction in Postwar and Present-Day Japan*, ed. Mami Hirose et al. (Tokyo: Mori Art Museum, 2011), 242.
31. I am reliant here on the recollection of events in Koolhaas and Obrist, *Project Japan*, 234. It should be noted that different recollections exist elsewhere. Zhongjie Lin's account gives credit for the name more exclusively to Kawazoe. See Lin, *Kenzo Tange*, 22.
32. For a discussion of Speer's "theory of ruin value," see Stephen Cairns and Jane M. Jacobs, *Buildings Must Die: A Perverse View of Architecture* (Cambridge, MA: The MIT Press, 2014), 174.
33. Kenzo Tange, "Technology and Humanity," *The Japan Architect* (October 1960): 12.
34. Tange, "Technology and Humanity," 12.
35. The use of the Boston Harbor assignment to develop ideas for Tokyo Bay is mentioned by Seng Kuan. See Kuan, "Visions of Tokyo Bay," in *Kiyonori Kikutake: Between Land and Sea*, ed. Ken Tadashi Oshima (Zurich: Lars Müller Publishers, 2016), 32–33.

36. See Keiichi Okumura and Masato Otaka, "Kōsō apāto wo haichi shita atarashii jūtakuchi no teian to Tōkyō-wanjo toshi no teian" [The new residential area with high-rise apartments and the proposal for Tokyo Bay], *Kenchiku bunka* 14, no. 2 (February 1959): 39–42. Translation by Riyo Namigata.
37. Kenzo Tange, "A Building and a Project," *The Japan Architect* (October 1960): 16.
38. See Koolhaas and Obrist, *Project Japan*, 12.
39. Kiyonori Kikutake, "Ocean City," in *Metabolism/1960: The Proposals for New Urbanism* [1960] (Tokyo: Echelle-1, 2011), 17.
40. Kisho Kurokawa, "Challenge to the Capsule," *The Japan Architect* (October 1972): 25.
41. Regarding the typhoon as the impetus for the design, see *Metabolism—The City of the Future*, 58.
42. Fumihiko Maki and Masato Ohtaka, "Toward Group Form," in *Metabolism/1960*, 59. It should be noted that Otaka's thesis at the University of Tokyo, completed in the late 1940s, was entitled *On Grouped Architecture*. See Yoshiyuki Yamana, "New Forms of Community: Visions of Collective Housing Pursued by Otaka Masato and Otani Sachio," in *Metabolism—The City of the Future*, 272.
43. Maki and Ohtaka, "Toward Group Form," 59.
44. *Metabolism/1960*, 5.
45. See Noboru Kawazoe, "The Thirty Years of Metabolists," *Thesis, Wissenschaftliche Zeitschrift der Bauhaus-Universität Weimar* 6 (1997): 148. This essay was first published in *Approach* 116 (1991).
46. See *Metabolism/1960*, 5.
47. See Koolhaas and Obrist, *Project Japan*, 229.
48. Nakamori, "Kawazoe Noboru," 243.
49. See John Dower, *Embracing Defeat: Japan in the Wake of World War II* (New York: W. W. Norton, 1999), 185.
50. See Dower, *Embracing Defeat*, 234–236.
51. Kikutake graduated in 1950 and Kawazoe in 1953. Kawazoe had Yosizaka as a lecturer in material technology.
52. John Bellamy Foster, *Marx's Ecology: Materialism and Nature* (New York: Monthly Review Press, 2000), 160.
53. See Francis C. Bing, "History of the Word 'Metabolism,'" *Journal of the History of Medicine and Allied Arts* 26, no. 2 (April 1971): 161. Note that Bing is a key source cited by Foster in his description of metabolism's origins. See Foster, *Marx's Ecology*, 159–163.
54. Foster, *Marx's Ecology*, 150–51.
55. Liebig, quoted in Foster, *Marx's Ecology*, 154. Liebig's general claim was based on analysis of London's Thames River, and later, Friedrich Engels would quote Liebig on this topic explicitly in terms of London. See Friedrich Engels, *The Housing Question* [1872] (Moscow: Progress Publishers, 1975), 92. This same metabolic rift will later be noted by Ebenezer Howard, who saw the ease of town sewage being used as country fertilizer as a benefit of his Garden City concept, a concept that returns us to one of the main influences on Le Corbusier's idea of artificial land. See Ebenezer Howard, *Garden Cities of To-Morrow* [1898] (Cambridge, MA: The MIT Press, 1970), 60–62.
56. Foster, *Marx's Ecology*, 158.
57. Marx quoted in Foster, *Marx's Ecology*, 157.
58. Marx quoted in Foster, *Marx's Ecology*, 155.
59. Foster, *Marx's Ecology*, 155, 163.
60. See Koolhaas and Obrist, *Project Japan*, 229.
61. Noboru Kawazoe, "Metabolism," *The Japan Architect* 44 (December 1969): 102.
62. Noboru Kawazoe, "The City of the Future," *Zodiac*, no. 9 (1961): 101.
63. Kawazoe, "City," 104–105. Tokyo's Setagaya ward totals about 58 square kilometers, compared to metropolitan Tokyo's overall size of around 2,188.
64. See Koolhaas and Obrist, *Project Japan*, 233.
65. Karl Marx, *Capital: Volume III* [1894], trans. David Fernbach (London: Penguin, 1991), 959. Italics added.
66. Kawazoe, "City," 106–107. Wakisangyo, a maker of home-improvement tools, was using "Sunday carpenter" in its advertising at least as early as 1963. The company may be the source of Kawazoe's expression. See "From household hardware to do-it-yourself, and towards the age of DIY," accessed July 23, 2020, http://www.waki-diy.co.jp/about/start_diy/.
67. Koolhaas and Obrist, *Project Japan*, back cover.
68. See "Hayato Ikeda," https://en.wikipedia.org/wiki/Hayato_Ikeda, accessed April 13, 2019.
69. Yukio Noguchi, "Land Prices and House Prices in Japan," in *Housing Markets in the United States and Japan*, ed. Yukio Noguchi and James Poterba (Chicago: University of Chicago Press, 1994), 14.

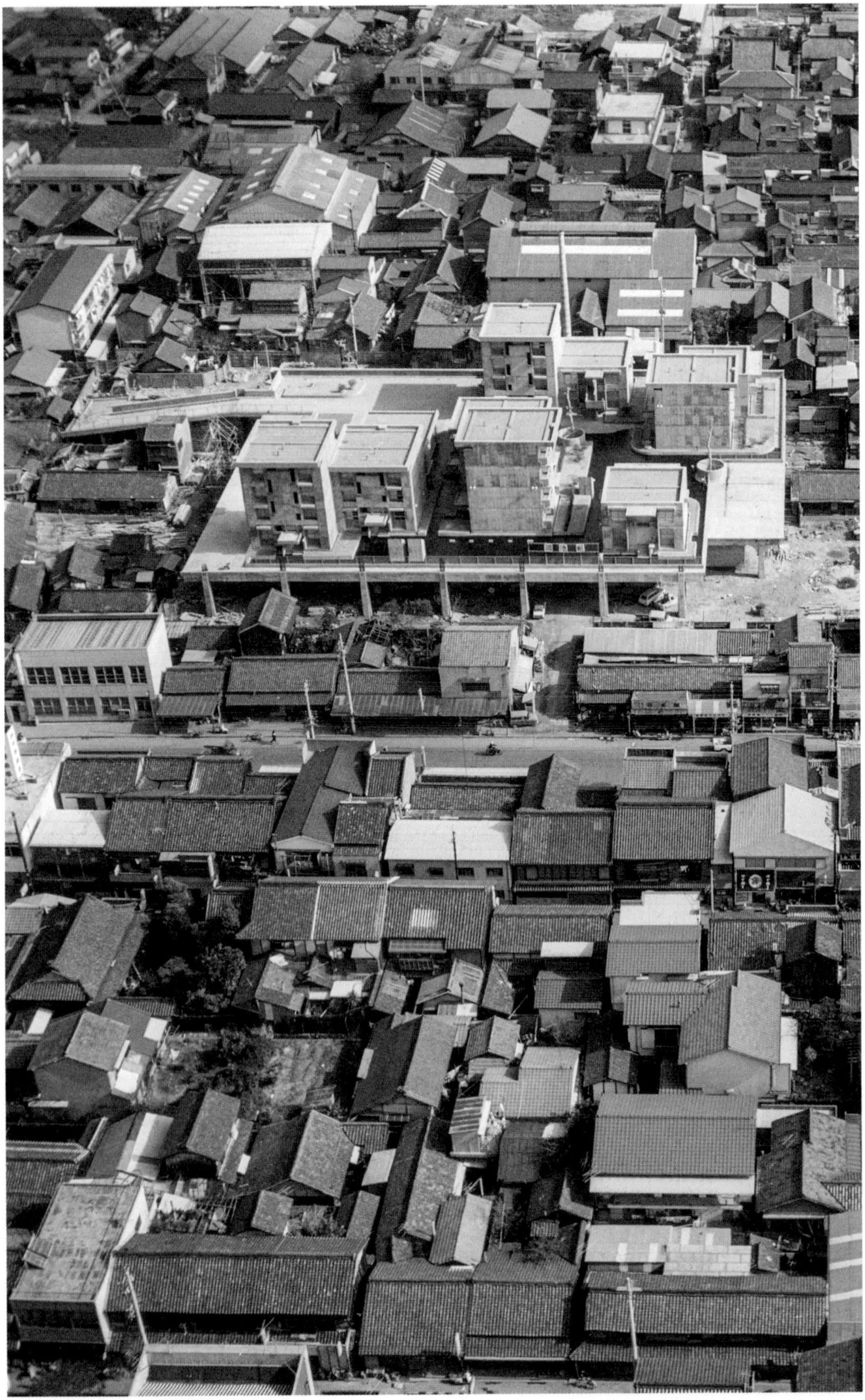

Avant-Garde Real Estate:
Sakaide Artificial Land Platform, 1963–

In 1900, architect Cass Gilbert declared a skyscraper to be a "machine that makes the land pay."[1] Its enormously profitable multiplication of the ground, enabled by the same construction systems that would soon stimulate the experiments of modernist architects, comes to manifest a merging of avant-garde speculation and real-estate speculation. The architectural historian Manfredo Tafuri suggests this link in what he calls the modern intellectual's tendency toward "capitalist science."[2]

Prospecting for new forms for real-estate development, led or adumbrated by adventurous architecture, is what might be called avant-garde real estate, capitalist or otherwise. It is often not architect-branded condominiums, though it can be. Avant-garde real estate is instead predicated on feedback between massing and regulations that allow for new configurations of ownership and use, joining innovative buildings and innovative zoning. A prime example is the relationship between tower and plaza at Mies van der Rohe's 1959 Seagram Building, the direct inspiration for "incentive zoning" in New York City's Zoning Resolution adopted in 1961. The new regulation stated that for every square foot of public plaza built on a project's site, 10 square feet could be added to the gross floor area allowable by Floor Area Ratio (FAR), which controls the maximum floor area that may be built relative to the size of a given site.[3] Thanks to Mies's fascination with the scenography of setting his tower back from Park Avenue to produce the plaza, his composition of solid and void led to the codification of a method for profit maximization through creating privately owned public space.[4]

Masato Otaka, Sakaide Artificial Land Platform, Phase 1, 1968

following: Sakaide with all phases completed, 1986

1 REBUILDING BUILDING

AVANT-GARDE REAL ESTATE: SAKAIDE ARTIFICIAL LAND PLATFORM, 1963–

Right of Support, Right of Passage

Another historic example of avant-garde real estate is Fort l'Empereur, a project that is a logical extrapolation of what could be called artificial real estate. Generally speaking, until France's introduction of the Code Napoléon in 1804, to own real estate was to own soil, inclusive of any structure built on it. From ancient Roman property law came the terrestrial plot conceived as the base of an endless column extending up into the air as well as down into the ground, horizontally separated from its neighbors by the walls of this extrusion.[5] Only with the Code Napoléon did the practice of sectional ownership or condominium-ization appear, as a legal right to own real estate above the ground surface, thereby fragmenting the historical extrusion by introducing real estate defined by both vertical and horizontal borders. Artificial real estate arose from making the relationship to soil both distant and abstract. The Code Napoléon went on to have a global impact as its statutes were disseminated, first through introduction in areas colonized by France, and later through European expansion into other parts of the world. It made its way to Japan in the late nineteenth century.[6]

The complexities unleashed by the code's legalization of horizontal property borders were still troublesome in the early twentieth century, as well-described in a 1930 article from *The Yale Law Journal*, titled "Division into Horizontal Strata of the Landspace Above the Surface." The author, Stuart S. Ball, reasons that, as the vertical borders cutting land into separate properties are essentially arbitrary, it is no less arbitrary to cut land horizontally, leading him to conclude that the "real 'land' in law is three-dimensional space, containing solid matter treated as realty because of more or less permanent occupancy of a defined space."[7] However, aerial plots have problems with height and gravity. Previously, earthbound real estate naturally provided all owners with access to their own property, as well as complete structural independence from their neighbors. A building could be freely destroyed and rebuilt, simply because all property touched *terra firma*. But once property is in the air, these were no longer givens: lower levels structurally support upper levels, and space must be reserved for vertical access. This reliance of above on below was the source of innumerable legal headaches. For owners above the earth's surface, the situation demanded what Ball refers to as "right of support" and "right of passage."[8] Only with these rights in place could artificial real estate enjoy the same status as the earthbound. For the aerial plot, he theorizes, "If the space be truly owned, logic does not demand that ownership be affected by destruction of the building."[9]

Wealth from the Air

But how to preserve the aerial plot's support and access from destruction? The answer is to not make a building, but to make artificial land: provide support and passage to plots in the sky with disaster-resistant structures duplicating the soil's constructive potential. In Tokyo in 1962, soon after the passing of New York's new zoning laws, this approach was studied by the Artificial Land Committee (ALC). Sponsored by the Ministry of Construction (MOC) and the Architectural Institute of Japan (AIJ), the ALC was chaired by Takashi Asada. Committee members included Metabolists Maki and Otaka, structural engineer Kimura, urban planner Hidemitsu Kawakami, economist Akira Tamura, and architect Yositika Utida, whose influential father Yoshikazu had been the director of the Dojunkai and president of the AIJ.[10]

The committee's work, presented in a report released in May 1963, saw artificial land as "The Creation of the Foundation of Urban Activities."[11]

It positioned the concept as a tool for major economic development, and revealed direct inspiration from New York. In particular, New York's 1961 resolution had introduced "Transferable Development Rights," better known as "air rights,"whereby air space above an underbuilt site can be leased or sold to others to develop.[12] While Le Corbusier's Villes-Pilotis (1915) or El Lissitzky's horizontal skyscrapers (1924) may be seen as forerunners, the practice began in New York in the early 1900s in the decking placed above the railyard for the new Grand Central Terminal.[13] Once covered, development rights over the yard were sold to help fund the new station. Grand Central's engineer William J. Wilgus, in an echo of Cass Gilbert, called this "taking wealth from the air."[14] Likewise, the strategic use of platforms offering plots for private construction over transportation infrastructure is at the center of the ALC's investigation, making for another interpretation of artificial land different from Yosizaka's.

Artificial Land Readjustment

In his introduction to the report, Hidemitsu Kawakami describes artificial land as an installation to be deployed wherever the use of natural land proves difficult, thereby offering it to the entirety of the seismically challenged nation. Furthering the "vision of a concrete Japan" that emerged after the 1923 earthquake, the dynamics of the ground would be countered by replacing the ground itself.[15] Writing that, "Only once the topography and ground quality is stabilized will it be possible to talk of permanent defense mechanisms against natural disasters," the report's authors focused on new land above the fragmented surfaces of urban Japan.[16]

Under the Allied occupation, large property owners, such as landlords of rental apartments and farms, were divested of their holdings in 1947, and forced in many cases to subdivide and sell their land to their tenants. Property taxes were simultaneously raised, compelling many existing and new property owners to further subdivide and sell portions of their land in affordable yet increasingly tiny parcels.[17] This dynamic persists today, making for slow negotiation with a multitude of small landowners in order to assemble plots large enough for public improvements such as wider streets, parking lots, train lines, or green areas.

The work of the ALC aimed to overcome the obstructions due to this fragmentary ownership, in an extension of "Land Readjustment" (LR), the main planning tool used by the Japanese government since 1919. Known as the "mother of urban plans," LR is a form of eminent domain for assembling private land for public projects. Most frequently used for street widening, LR legalized government claims to a percentage of a property owner's land with only limited compensation.[18] The ALC brought LR into three dimensions, with artificial land poised to be the new mother of urban plans.

Similar to the model of Grand Central Terminal and LR, the ALC proposed that public agencies could acquire private land, layer it, and then sell the new concrete plots above to finance public improvements below.[19] The existing ground and its new platform roof would be a vast infrastructural plenum, rationalized and updated with the latest technologies for transportation and other public amenities. This continuous space could not be implemented through the development of solitary high-rises on small sites, and Akira Tamura believed that layered land could make its greatest contribution to the national economy through the rationalization that such spaces allowed. Urban Japan's new foundations would have the added benefit of not requiring the cost of excavation, since the existing ground would become in effect a basement floor.[20]

1940

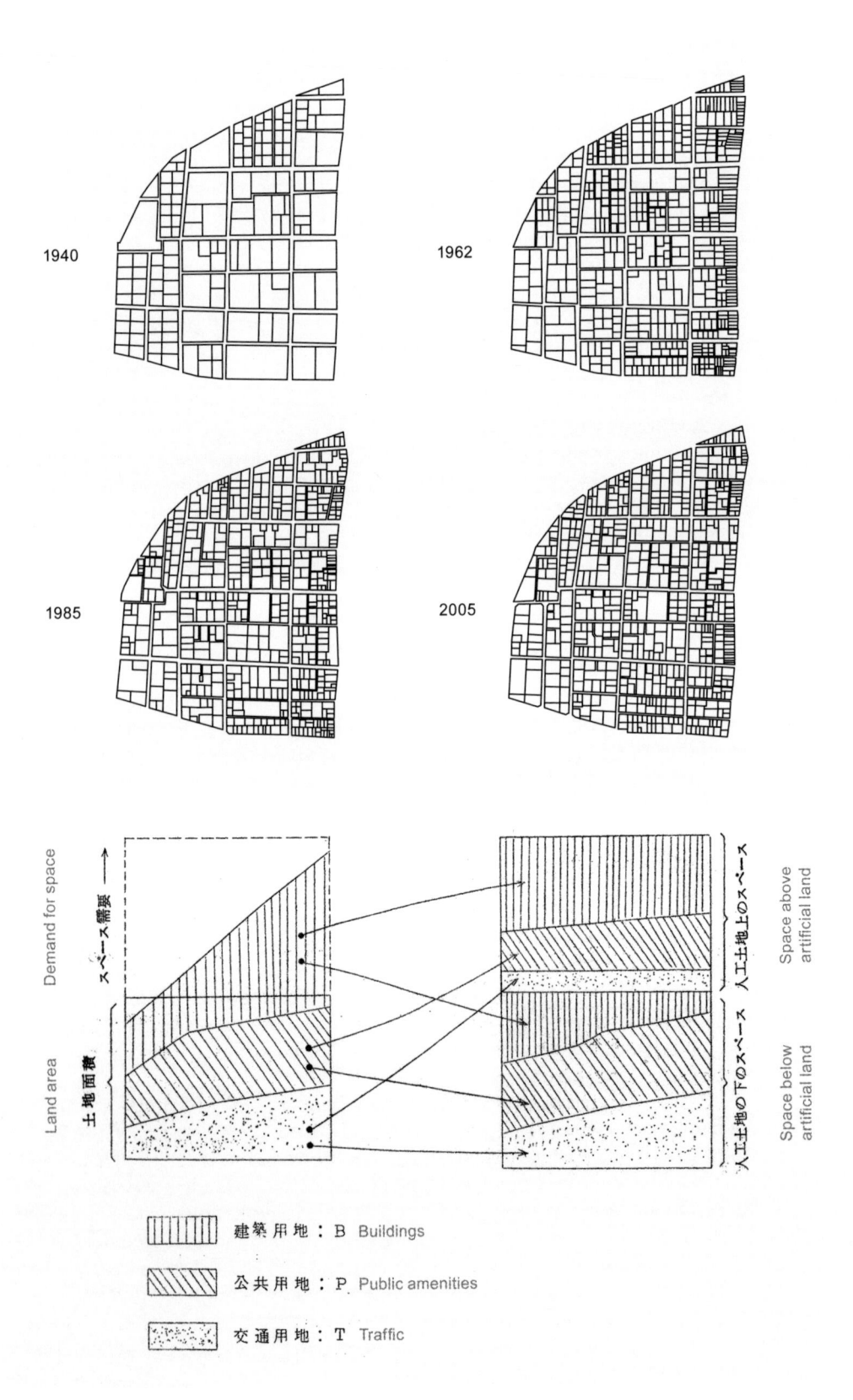

1962

1985

2005

	建築用地：B Buildings
	公共用地：P Public amenities
	交通用地：T Traffic

Demand for space スペース需要

Land area 土地面積

人工土地上のスペース Space above artificial land

人工土地の下のスペース Space below artificial land

110　　　　　　　　　　　　　　　　　　　　　　　　　　　1　REBUILDING BUILDING

Cushions

Toshihiko Kimura, author of the report's chapter on structural design, describes these new platforms as "cushion structures" able to absorb various kinds of loads.[21] But design of such cushions entailed a basic structural conflict: the platforms required long beam spans in order to reduce the number of columns that would otherwise impede traffic in the "basement," which had to be reconciled with the desire for freely sized and located buildings on top of the platforms, a situation that could easily lead to problematic beam deflections and seismic instability.[22] Aerial plots, for the most efficient transfer of loads, would ideally have a regular array of columns below them, whereas roads and railways would ideally have no columns at all. Fewer columns meant much deeper (and more expensive) beams.

The conflict between these competing freedoms highlights the question of "rights of support." In effect, the committee was speculating on speculation. If the government was now in the business of making elevated building sites, how much could and would private development build on them?[23] How flexible could or should they be? The question of flexibility became more complicated, as the committee saw that realization of a universal cushion was impossible. Instead there would be a differentiation of design requirements in every case, varying dependent on regional characteristics, with new aerial layers necessarily adapting to factors of budget, location, and relationship to the natural geology supporting them. If widely applied, there would be a diversity of artificial lands comparable to nature's own variety.

Maki and Otaka's chapter of the report presented design studies, including one proposal by Otaka for a massive redevelopment in the Otemachi district of Tokyo. The scheme looks like office towers over parking garages seen throughout the world. While this generic quality suggests a universality, the platforms that Otaka designed for the city of Sakaide, presented in the report at a very early stage, show in their as-built form the specific opportunities offered by the ALC's concept for public programs both below and on artificial land.

Incremental Infrastructure

Sakaide is a small coastal city on the Seto Inland Sea, in Kagawa Prefecture on Shikoku Island. In the early 1960s, its sea-salt industry was in decline, and a dilapidated residential area occupied by salt workers had emerged near the train station. With the city needing new public housing and new industries, an agreement was made in 1964 with Kagawa's governor, Masanori Kaneko, to establish an artificial-land pilot project in the block containing the slum area. Asada, a man always with a diversity of projects and connections, had been working on the development of tourism in Kagawa and was a friend of the governor. Kaneko believed in modern culture's role in reinvigorating his prefecture, having brought Tange and Isamu Noguchi to the area to make important contributions, and now Otaka to carry out the platform commission.[24]

The project was built in four phases that accumulated into an aggregate of platforms covering more than one hectare. Elevated between 5.3 and 9 meters above the existing ground, the concrete waffle slabs of the platforms support two- to four-story concrete apartment buildings, with commercial space and public parking below. Access to the second ground is by a vehicular ramp and multiple stairways, with large perforations allowing trees to pop through from big planters in the parking lot.

top: Progressive subdivision of Setagaya, Tokyo

bottom: Artificial Land Committee, "The Creation of the Foundation of Urban Activities," 1963

6-13 断面図・人工土地

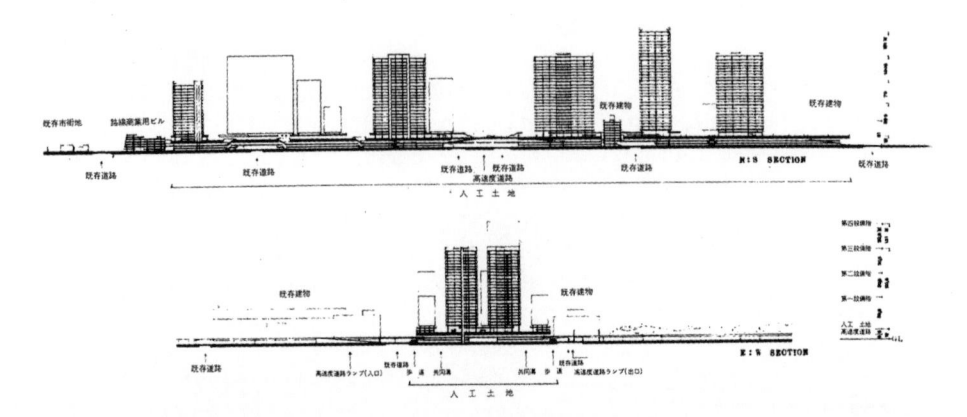

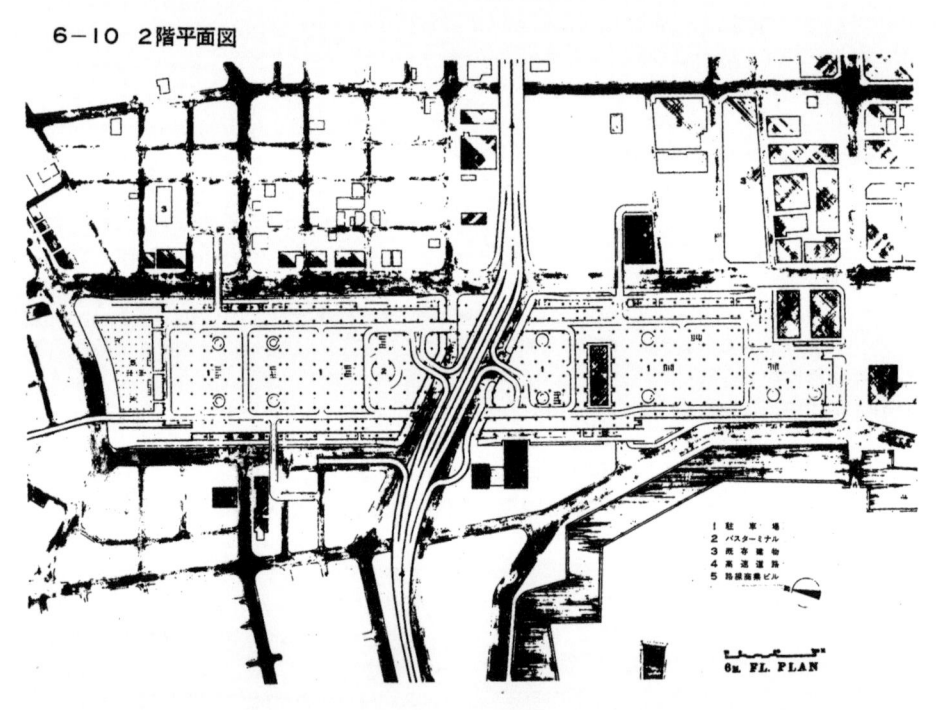

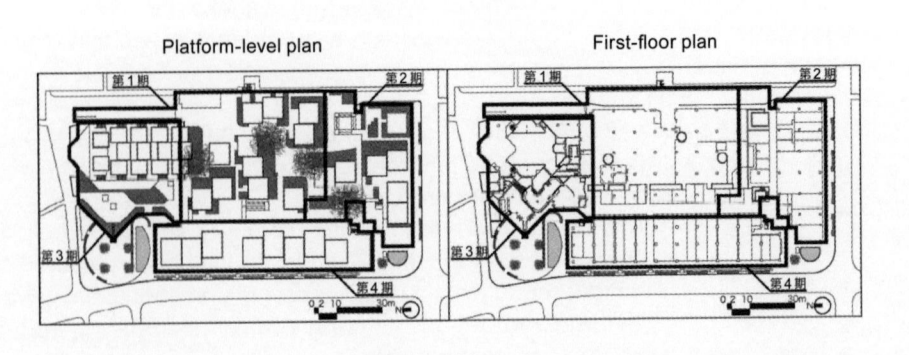

6-10 2階平面図

Platform-level plan　　　　First-floor plan

1　REBUILDING BUILDING

Different land prices and stakeholders associated with the inner and outer areas of the block drove the phasing, with greatly varying degrees of complexity in negotiations between owners and Sakaide City. For Phase 1's platform on the interior of the block, the city simply bought the property and built 56 new rental apartments, all designed by Otaka's office, and competed in 1968. But the properties of Phases 2 and 4 along commercial streets consumed so much time and money that Phase 3's civic hall was completed in 1973, ahead of Phase 2's completion in 1974. Phase 4, with the main street frontage, would not be completed until 1986—not a rapid speed for a project born in the period of rapid growth.

Unable to afford outright purchase, the city agreed with the landowners in Phases 2 and 4 to rent their air rights at 20 percent of the cost of their land over a period of seventy years, and also to adjust their property boundaries to allow for wider sidewalks. Having rented, the city built housing on the new platforms hovering over the businesses below, accommodated in rebuilt spaces. After seventy years, the city and owners would renegotiate the roof rights, or the owners would be required to buy the housing above them.[25] While this arrangement is different from the initial ALC air-rights model of government purchasing land and then selling artificial land above it, the platforms did enable the city to make housing in a location where it could not have afforded to otherwise, with a high degree of architectural autonomy given above and below. Otaka did not believe he needed to design everything, and so as a way to stimulate business and diversify the frontage, the replaced shops were given to local architects.

top left and center left: Masato Otaka, Otemachi proposal, sections and plan, 1963

bottom left: Sakaide, phasing diagram

above: Masato Otaka with model of Sakaide, 1963

AVANT-GARDE REAL ESTATE: SAKAIDE ARTIFICIAL LAND PLATFORM, 1963–

113

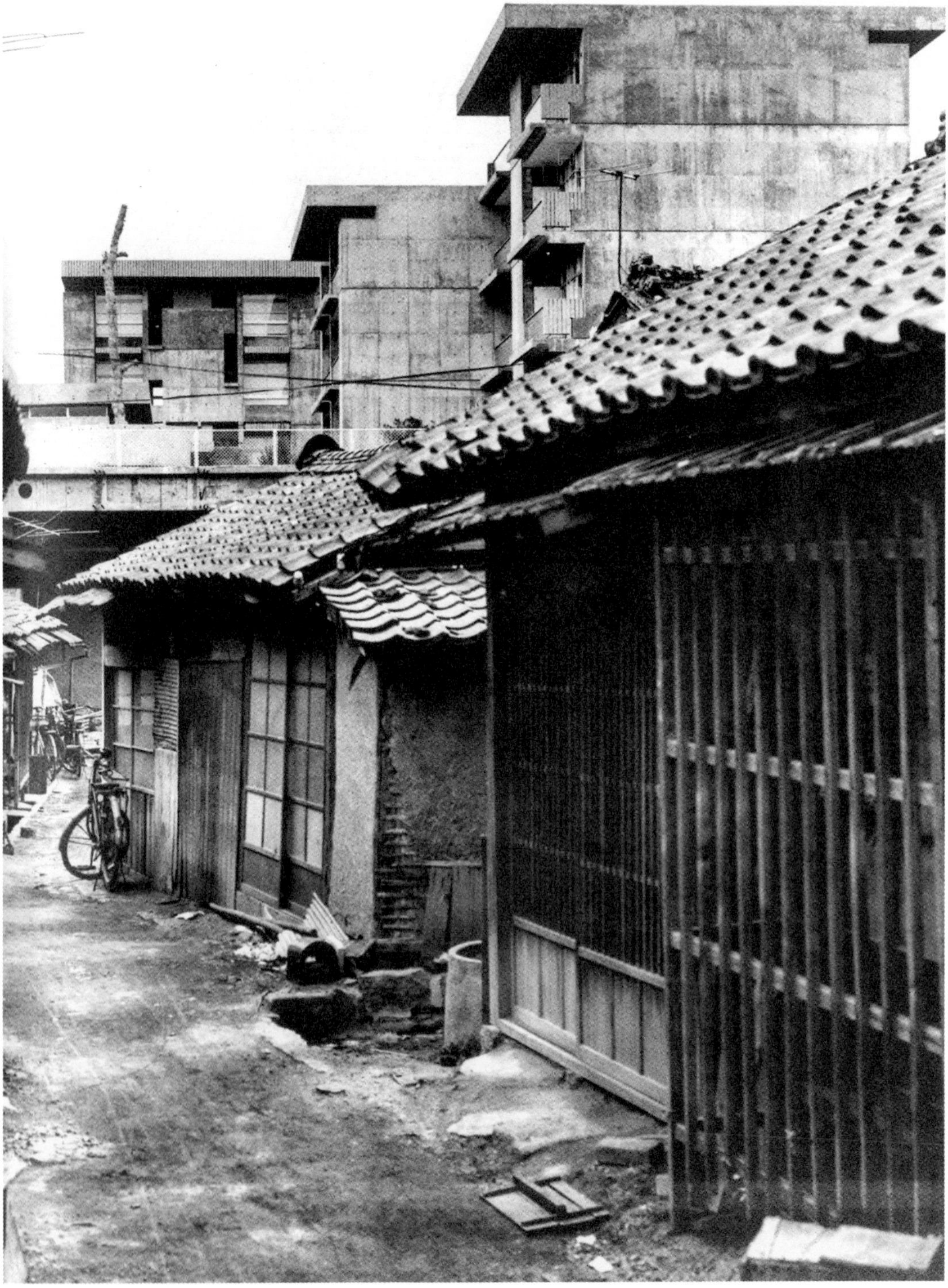

Futureproofing

Masaya Fujimoto, Sakaide's project architect from Otaka's office, states that the design aimed at "organically knitting together private and public enterprise," a description that belies the ownership conflicts the development experienced.[26] Despite this challenge, Otaka and the city were committed to the design facilitating two cycles of change, with the platforms made structurally independent of the housing to allow for new configurations of architecture and possibly ownership. The platforms, to be useful in perpetuity, needed to simulate as faithfully as possible the freedoms of the earth-bound building site, and Sakaide's attempt to achieve this makes it in technical terms one of the most extreme examples of avant-garde real estate ever created. Extrapolating from the transitional concept inaugurated by Harumi, the platforms anticipate extensive new construction and program, not just bigger apartments.

Speaking to the uncertainties that Metabolism's two cycles of change sought to engage, Kawazoe stated in 1961, "we are not to specify in detail how the city of the future must be."[27] Yasuke Hachinohe, Sakaide's project engineer from the Shigeru Aoki Lab, had the challenge of converting such Metabolist rhetoric into reality, an effort showing that openness to future uses will in practice require quite specific details. In a memo that reads like a structural manifesto for the ALC's vision of artificial land, Hachinohe expressed his hope that the Phase 1 platform would "meet the various changes inherent in a dynamically growing city" through the following requirements:

1. Maximum freedom in placement [of housing on the platform] to create variety and richness in apartment exterior spaces.
2. Allowances must be made for the possibility of adding four-story apartment buildings in areas left vacant in the present plan.
3. Provide for the possibility of dismantling the present buildings (if the foundation beams of the buildings on the platform and platform's own beams are one, dismantling becomes impossible).
4. Provide for the possibility of future extensions raising the heights of all the apartment buildings to four stories.
5. To increase the freedom of use on the ground level by reducing the number of columns to a minimum.[28]

Additionally, the platform could support heavy trucks and 40 centimeters of soil across its entire surface. Notably, in objective one, the components to be freely placed are no longer merely partition walls, as in typical free-plan design, but entire four-story buildings. Objectives one and five define the conflict between beams and columns that Kimura identified as artificial land's structural contradiction, with Hachinohe's response to the problem being to overbuild the foundation pilings, columns, and waffle slab to take loads in excess of the initial construction. Ultimately, however, such flexibility was limited to a gridded zone inset from the platform edges. It was planned such that new buildings on the platform could be as tall as seven stories, if placed directly over the column locations that defined the zone.[29]

The square grid of the waffle slab, with columns spaced at 9.18 meters, gives the platform better seismic stability and avoids strict directionality, supporting the group-form clusters of apartments that produce a variety of outdoor spaces. Otaka saw this quality as essential for relieving the standardization in apartment design forced by the low budget.[30] Even so, in order to maintain balance in the overall structure so as to avoid

New land above old:
Sakaide Phase 1, 1968

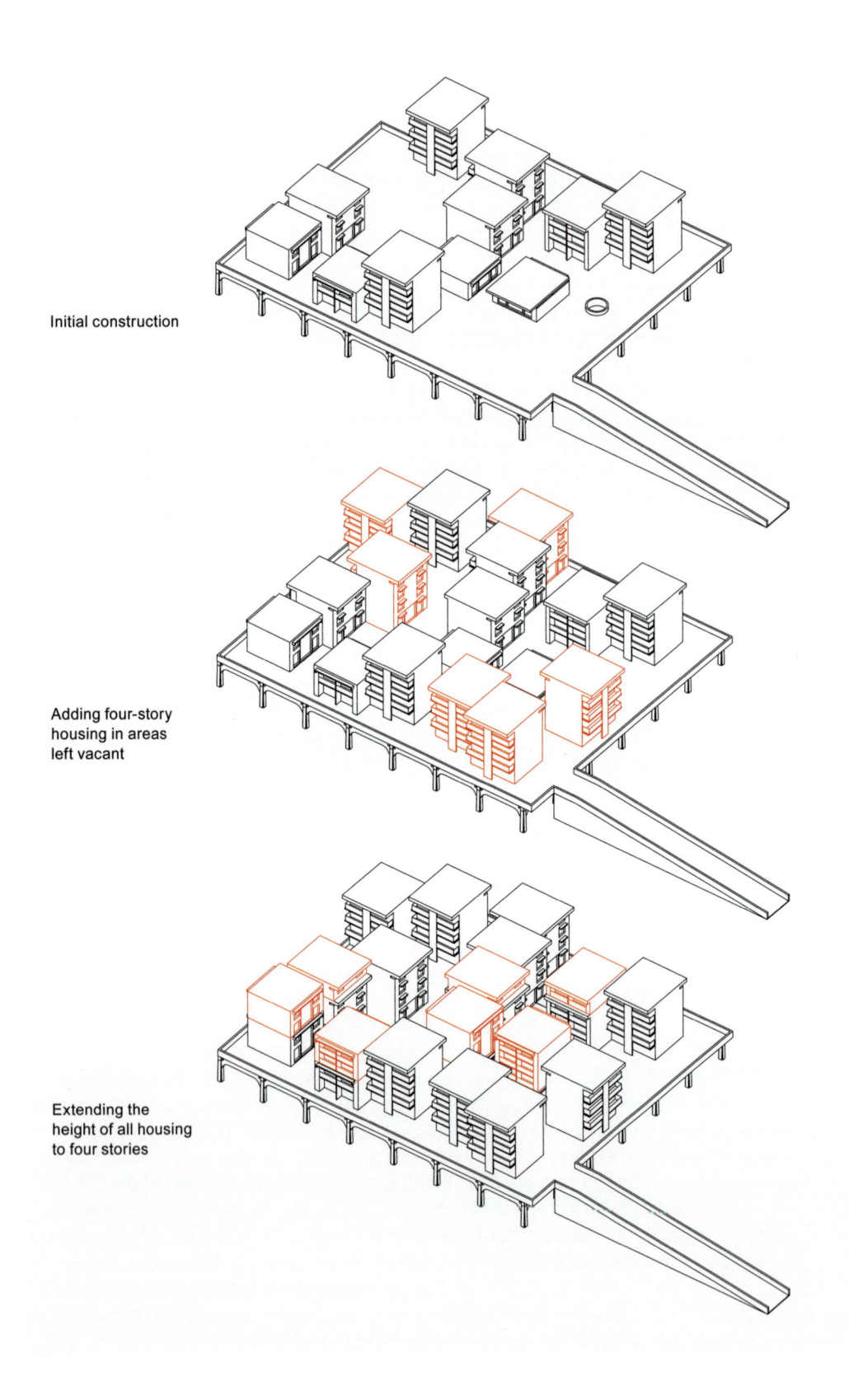

Initial construction

Adding four-story housing in areas left vacant

Extending the height of all housing to four stories

116   1   REBUILDING BUILDING

destructive torsion in an earthquake, the positioning of building volumes is limited to being either centered on a bay or half-bay of the column grid.[31] Under the platform, an X-Y grid of sleeves passing through its beams allows the re-routing of electrical and plumbing services for anticipated changes above.

Through the creation of these capacities, so unlike those of today's fitness-obsessed parametric architecture, the platform has a heftiness that is far from optimized.[32] Flexibility, the bane of optimization, will rarely be the cheapest short-term option. But Sakaide City made a long-term investment for civic durability, treating flexibility like insurance—something else into which people put large amounts of money that may never be used.

While the Aoki Lab worked to simulate land physically, a second and less visible challenge was obtaining a legal definition of the platforms as land, distinct from real estate such as a building, or a part of one. Surprisingly, the ALC did not have a lawyer to help draft a legal definition for the concept, and *jinko tochi* has never been legally defined by the city of Sakaide or elsewhere. Instead, government documents on the project normalize the platforms through referring to them not as *tochi* (land), but as *jiban* (foundations). And while the platforms were approved as refuge floors for fire egress—a designation previously reserved for ground level—the denial of their status as land resulted in their heights and areas being added together with the buildings on top when calculating the project's FAR compliance.[33] Despite their avant-gardism in engineering and their contribution to introducing air rights to Japanese development, the platforms did not lead to a new form of zoning specific to artificial land.

Urban Temperatures

As of the early twenty-first century, Sakaide is a city that has experienced less dynamic growth than Otaka's design anticipated. The city seems to embody what housing researcher Yosuke Hirayama calls "cold places," the many small cities and regions of Japan that have been left behind by the economy, with development ever-more focused on the "hot places," in particular Tokyo.[34] While this is no more than my personal impression of a tiny area of Sakaide from a visit in 2010, the shops along the perimeter of the platforms and nearby looked shuttered or empty. On top of the platforms, none of the housing had been torn down and transformed into more spacious living, as imagined, and some of the units were abandoned. A faded coat of dusty pink and blue paint indicated some attempt at softening the concrete, a quality better achieved through the profusion of multiple small gardens, ubiquitous drying laundry, air conditioners, and in at least one case, the infill of a balcony with the found capsule-architecture of a fiberglass bathroom pod. Together, these manifested Metabolism's shorter cycle of change combined with the longer, achieved through the most banal activities and elements of everyday reality.

The larger issue with Otaka's experiment, however, is not a lack of dynamic growth that leaves the flexibility of the platforms without justification. It's rather the stubborn complexity of existing property rights that artificial land was unable to truly simplify, at least on a tight budget. Negotiating these rights is still slow even with a big budget, but much more possible. Turning to Tokyo, the famous developer Minoru Mori spent seventeen years assembling the necessary plots for the site of his Roppongi Hills, a luxury mixed-use project completed in 2003 that Mori calls a "vertical garden city." Mori, who was a major collector of Le Corbusier's artworks, describes Roppongi Hills as "manmade raised ground levels," on which he and his team

Sakaide Phase 1 scenarios for a "dynamically growing city"

B-B elevation. Scale: 1/400.

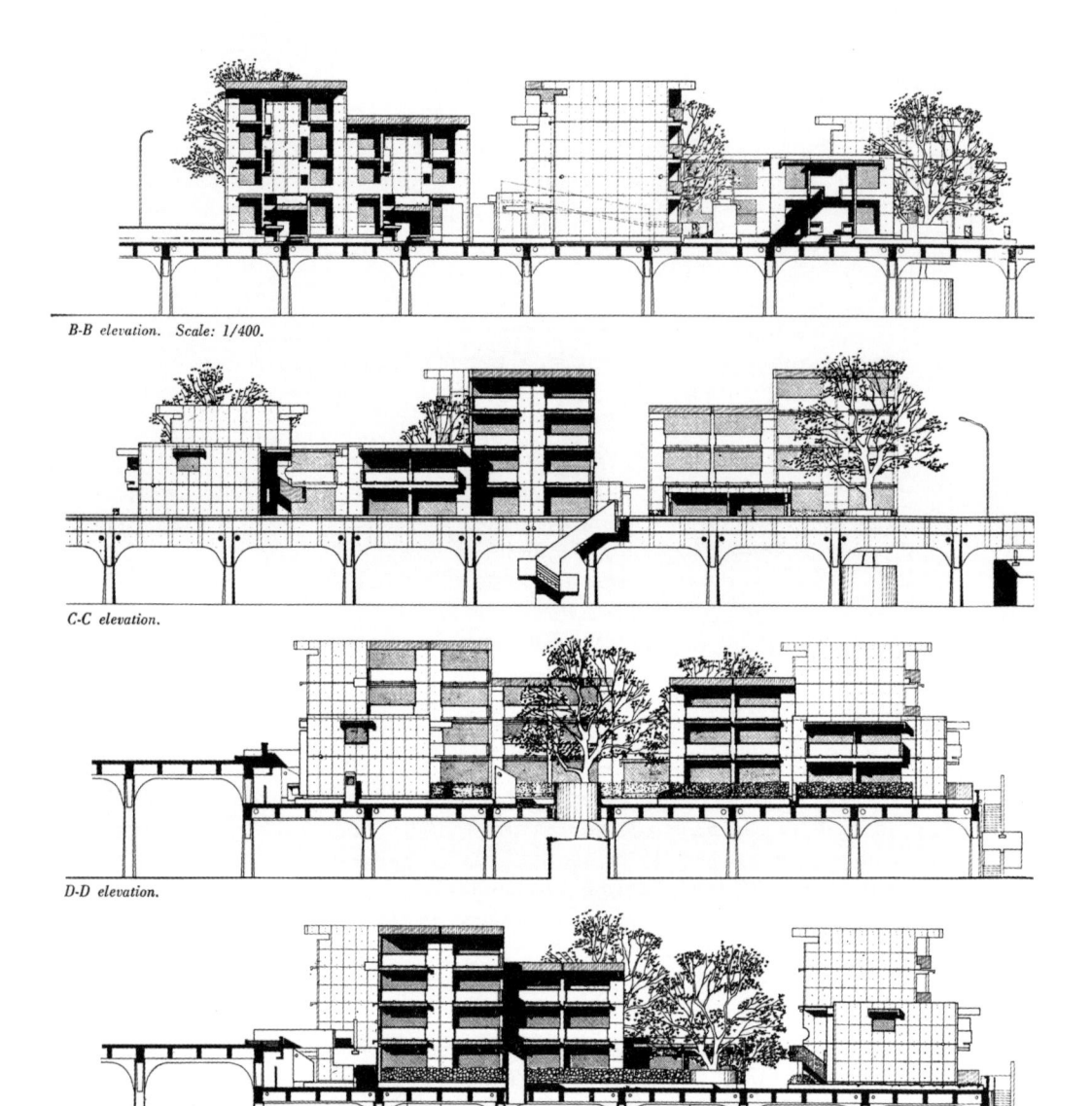

C-C elevation.

D-D elevation.

E-E elevation.

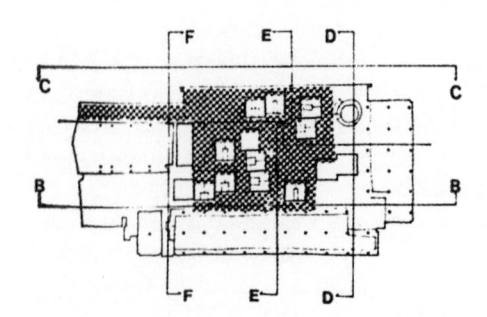

118   1   REBUILDING BUILDING

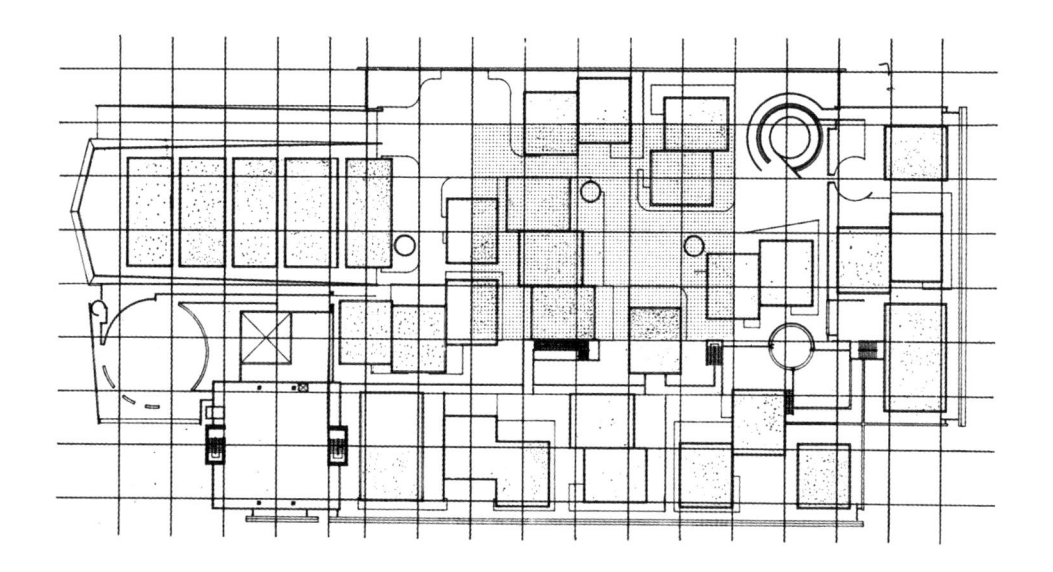

"placed different elements."[35] While they may be free of Mori's rhetoric, indebted to *The Radiant City* and perhaps to Metabolism, innumerable other projects—such as Manhattan's Hudson Yards or Pacific Place in Hong Kong—show that in hot places, Sakaide's general type is pervasive.

Rebranding

In 2003, the year Roppongi Hills was completed, Sakaide was selected by Docomomo as worthy of conservation, suggesting a freezing of the design, no less ironic than Harumi's demolition in terms of Metabolism's agenda of anticipating change.[36] While Sakaide became better known following the spate of events around Metabolism's fiftieth anniversary in 2010—including a vast show at the Mori Art Museum at Roppongi Hills in 2011—its fame is nothing compared to Hillside Terrace in Tokyo, Fumihiko Maki's group-form paragon. Not an artificial land project, Hillside has had a major impact on its affluent Daikanyama neighborhood, sparking a proliferation of artful boutique buildings influenced by Maki's formal language. Despite these differences, Sakaide is basically Otaka's version of Hillside, with both being mixed-use incremental projects completed in phases over the same approximate decades. Also like Sakaide in relation to Hillside, Otaka is a little-known architect compared to Maki, despite their important collaborations.

Maki was by far Metabolism's most cosmopolitan member, thanks to his elite education and work experience in America, as well as travels through Southeast Asia, India, the Middle East, and Europe to study urban form.[37] He distanced himself from Metabolism soon after the group's debut. In 2010, despite having been a member of the ALC, he declined to talk

left: Sakaide elevations and sections

above: Sakaide structural grid. Note hatched zone for additional loading in the future.

AVANT-GARDE REAL ESTATE: SAKAIDE ARTIFICIAL LAND PLATFORM, 1963–

Compositional Form   Mega-Structure   Group Form

about artificial land beyond saying that it was an "idea initiated by Masato Otaka, not by me."[38] What's revealing here is Maki's focus on conceptual provenance, given extra significance due to the fact that "megastructure," an idea attributed to him, may be the most well-known architectural meme ever created. In 1964, one year after the release of the ALC report, Maki published *Investigations in Collective Form*, in which megastructure was first defined. With this small book, the obscuring of artificial land's social imagination began.

A collection of essays and projects, the book's most influential piece is "Collective Form—Three Paradigms," cowritten with Otaka. Oriented toward designers, the essay defines three approaches: compositional form, megastructure, and group form, articulating these organizational strategies for the designer's toolbox. Compositional form, exemplified in the plans of temples and government buildings such as Chandigarh and Brasília, is characterized as a technique based on the programmatic definition of separate building blocks that are then brought into an overall layout. The approach is seen as useful and familiar, but ultimately too static. The bulk of the essay turns to further elaborating the idea of group form introduced at WoDeCo, and to explicating megastructure—a term that did not exist at the time of the 1960 debut despite having become almost synonymous with Metabolism. The new term is defined, with language referencing artificial land, as:

> A large frame in which all the functions of a city or part of a city are housed. It has been made possible by present day technology. In a sense, it is a *manmade feature of the landscape.* It is like the great hill on which Italian towns were built.[39]

above: "Collective Form— Three Paradigms"

right: Sakaide Phase 1 public parking (2010). Note sleeves through beams for relocating services above.

1 REBUILDING BUILDING

AVANT-GARDE REAL ESTATE: SAKAIDE ARTIFICIAL LAND PLATFORM, 1963–

1 REBUILDING BUILDING

The authors go on to claim that megastructures hold "great promise" for environmental engineering, multipurpose usage accommodated by the flexible frame, and infrastructure as a publicly owned investment delivering "three-dimensional land use."[40] These promises are familiar now as the ambitions for artificial land so far presented.

We can deduce the likely genealogy of the word megastructure: artificial land at Harumi gives birth to Kimura's "major-structure," a coinage Maki and especially Otaka were intimate with, which then becomes crossed with the geographer Jean Gottmann's idea of "megalopolis" to first appear in "Collective Form" as "mega-structure," with the hyphenation signaling a debt to Kimura.[41] Gottmann's megalopolis—his term for the dense aggregation of city, suburb, and countryside through transportation networks challenging geographical identities—first appeared in a journal article in 1957, then in 1961 as a book, *Megalopolis: The Urbanized Northeastern Seaboard of the United States*.[42] The geographer's observations captured the imagination of the urban sociologist Eiichi Isomura, who met Gottmann while both were at Harvard in 1957. Isomura brought megalopolitan thought back to Japan, where it had a major impact on planning discourse. Tange would start to use the term, at the latest, by 1964.[43] Otaka and Maki clearly shared in this enthusiasm.

Megastructure sounds like exciting science fiction. In comparison, artificial land sounds as interesting as processed cheese. Francis C. Bing, in his medical history of metabolism's etymology, notes how the word was adopted partly due to its ready conversion from noun, to verb, adverb, and adjective, as compared to its ungainly competitor "metamorphosis."[44] Artificial land has the same problem, but far worse. "Megastructural" and "megastructuralism" work quite well, while "artificial landism" is a dud.

left: Eastern edge of Sakaide Phase 1 (2010)

above: Sakaide, commercial space under Phases 1 and 4 (2010)

AVANT-GARDE REAL ESTATE: SAKAIDE ARTIFICIAL LAND PLATFORM, 1963–

1 REBUILDING BUILDING

The new name was a way to own an important concept and escape Le Corbusier's long shadow. By 1966, the success of this rebranding was such that the architectural historian Sigfried Giedion had added megastructure to the updated edition of his canonical *Space, Time and Architecture*, proclaiming that "Urbanism has become the organization of horizontal levels below and above the ground," illustrated by Tange's A Plan for Tokyo, 1960 and Maki's K-Project, from 1964, earlier published in *Investigations in Collective Form*.[45] In 1976, Reyner Banham devoted an entire book to the subject, *Megastructure: Urban Futures of the Recent Past*, a critical review of the global "mega" phenomenon that heavily relies on the definition in "Collective Form." As previously noted, in his introduction Banham calls Fort l'Empereur the "most general ancestor" of all megastructures, with no mention of Le Corbusier's designation of artificial land. While the older term appears several times in Banham's book, it does so in passing, appearing to be a synonym for megastructure, free of history.[46]

To what degree were Otaka and Maki accomplices in this marketing endeavor? It's revealing that *Space, Time and Architecture* calls Maki "one of the word-makers" of his generation, while Otaka makes no appearance in the text whatsoever.[47] Certainly Maki, with his global web of connections ready to broadcast new ideas, was well prepared to gain from a good neologism. Otaka, who never built outside Japan, seems provincial in comparison. This suggests the new term was coined by Maki, especially in combination with Maki's disinterest in discussing its predecessor.[48]

Otaka's deep commitment to artificial land as a strategy for his nation's future reinforces this perspective. It's notable that, in English-language articles after "Collective Form," he still uses the older term instead of megastructure. That Otaka uses artificial land indicates that the two terms don't always have the same meaning. Turning to the French word *terrain*, it and "land" connote the context of both property ownership and construction sites. The translation of *terrain artificiel* into Japanese by Yosizaka retains the association with property as *jinko tochi*. Megastructure, however, contains no such engagement with ownership and rights. It therefore makes perfect sense that the definition of megastructure in "Collective Form" characterizes it as a "landscape" rather than land, with landscape's picturesque associations divorced from innovations in public and private property. Over a brief interval, the new term jettisoned the most controversial and complex aspects of artificial land in favor of technical flexibility and large-scale engineering. As a key example of this, the 1965 reprint of "Collective Form" in Gygöry Kepes's *Structure in Art and in Science* actually omits the original sentences regarding megastructure's possibilities for public ownership.[49] Jettisoned too by the new term was any real attention to what should be its essential reason for being: flexibility of occupation. Minor-structure was therefore, like artificial land, also lost.

But for those designers committed to rebuilding building—Yosizaka, Maekawa, Kimura, Otaka—the layers of construction existed as much for their social responsibility and potential as for physically holding buildings together. Their enthusiasm for a newly democratic Japan, released from the oppression of feudal structures and militarized nationalism, drove them to pursue the disaster-resistant and publicly owned artificial land that would possess the ability to fulfill, eventually if not immediately, a diversity of lifestyle desires. By the time of Banham's book, however, awareness of this specific housing content outside of Japan,

top: Seam between Sakaide Phases 1 and 4

bottom: Sakaide Phase 1 (2010)

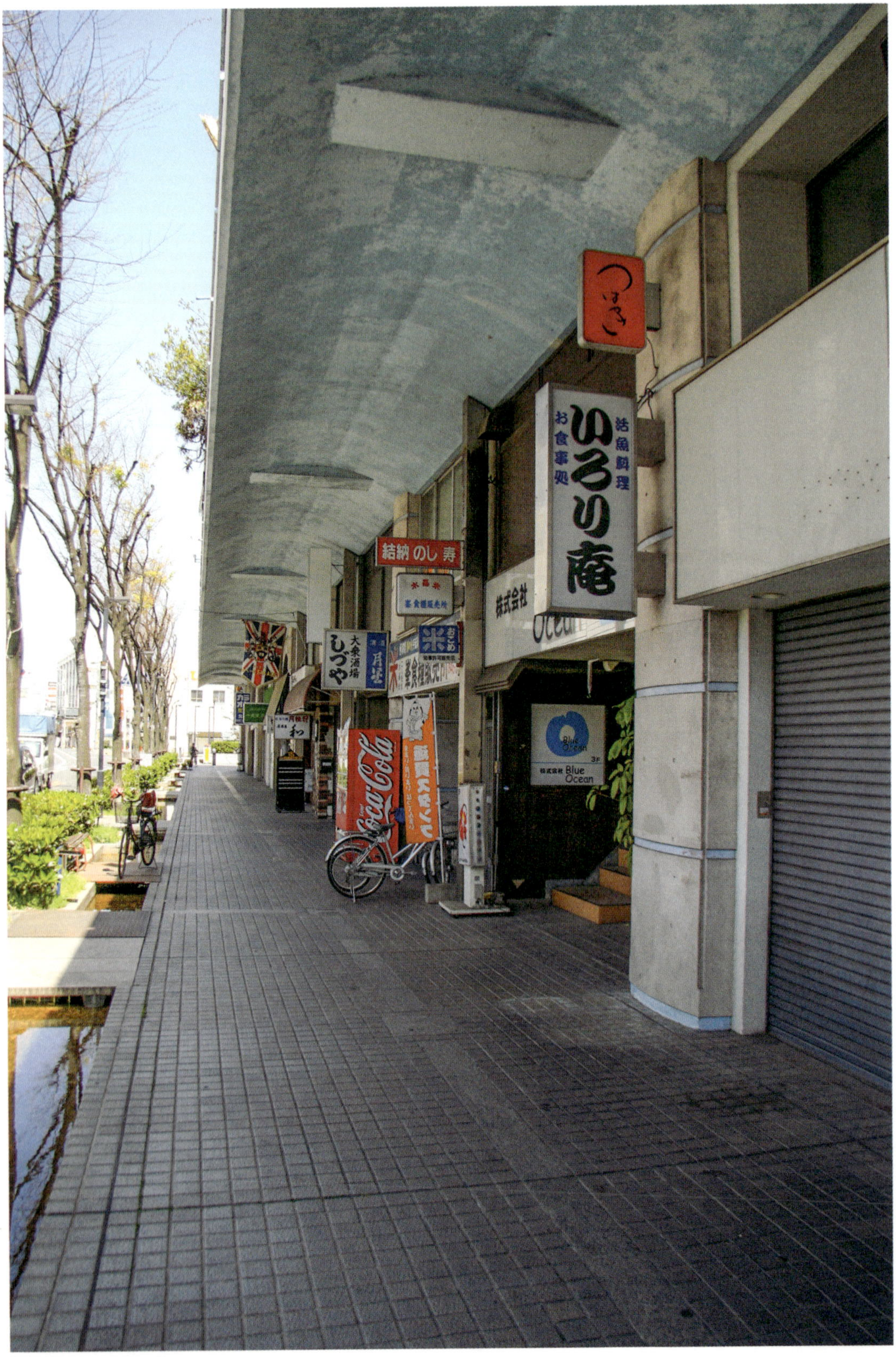
活魚料理
お食事処
いろり庵
結納 のし 寿
大衆酒場
しづや
株式会社
Blue Ocean
3F
Coca-Cola

if there had been any awareness of it all, was buried under spectacular designs inspired by megastructure.

As a case in point, the architectural historian Robin Middleton, quoted by Banham, writes that "Sakaide is no more a megacity model than any other housing scheme built on a first floor slab."[50] This is a strange comment, implying a desire for Metabolism to be only in pursuit of futuristic forms rather than struggling with strategies extrapolated from Grand Central Terminal. On the other hand, the "housing scheme built on a first floor slab" is the tower-on-podium model that is a very successful megacity model, as demonstrated by Roppongi Hills. Instead, Sakaide's relative failure lies elsewhere, beyond Middleton's disappointment, and aside from artificial land not being a magic wand able to make property-right complexities disappear. Unlike its typological relatives that are products of privatized global investment, and often directed at the global elite, Sakaide is unfortunately quite rare in being a publicly owned platform topped with public housing—another kind of infrastructure. Public ownership is no guarantee of satisfying public needs, but this condition opens Otaka's design to forms of inclusion and change that are not to be found at Roppongi Hills. Successful or not, Sakaide was conceived as a machine to make the land pay benefits to the public.[51]

1 Quoted in Carol Willis, *Form Follows Finance: Skyscrapers and Skylines in New York and Chicago* (New York: Princeton Architectural Press, 1995), 19. Gilbert was notably the architect of the Woolworth Building in Manhattan, completed in 1912, which was the tallest building in the world for almost two decades.

2 Manfredo Tafuri, *Architecture and Utopia: Design and Capitalist Development* [1973], trans. Barbara Luigia La Penta (Cambridge, MA: The MIT Press, 1976), 63.

3 See City Planning Commission, *The City of New York: Zoning Maps and Resolution* (New York: City Planning Commission, 1961), 126.

4 Preceding Seagram, a prime example of avant-garde real estate is the series of sculptural skyscraper studies drawn by Hugh Ferriss, that gave inspiring interpretation to the setback requirements in New York City's 1916 Zoning Resolution. See Ferriss, *The Metropolis of Tomorrow* [1929] (New York: Princeton Architectural Press, 1986), 72–82. For further history on the stimulus provided by Seagram to incentive zoning, see Phyllis Lambert, *Building Seagram* (New Haven, CT: Yale University Press, 2013), 194–196.

5 This is expressed in the famous legal phrase *cuius est solum, eius est usque ad coelum et ad inferos*, Latin for "whoever owns the soil, it is theirs up to Heaven and down to Hell." See "Air rights," Wikipedia, accessed May 7, 2019, https://en.wikipedia.org/wiki/Air_rights. Note that property is defined as the legal rights that apply to an owner of real estate.

For a brief discussion of the Code Napoléon's introduction and impact, see Donna S. Bennett, *Condominium Homeownership in the United States: A Selected Annotated Bibliography of Legal Sources* (2010), 2–3. https://works.bepress.com/donna_bennett/4/.

6 The Meiji government hired foreign experts to help with numerous tasks for the nation's modernization, including French legal scholars such as Gustave Émile Boissonade de Fontarabie, who, starting in the 1870s, helped draft Japan's civil code based on the Code Napoléon. See "Gustave Boissonade," Wikipedia, accessed April 7, 2020, https://en.wikipedia.org/wiki/Gustave_Boissonade.

7 Stuart S. Ball, "Division into Horizontal Strata of the Landspace Above the Surface," *The Yale Law Journal* 39, no. 5 (March 1930): 626.

8 Ball quotes these terms from the case of a Mr. Justice Davies. See Ball, "Division," 626.

9 Ball, "Division," 619.

10 Other members of the committee included Kou Irie, Tsuneyoshi Oniwa, and Ichiro Ueda. While at the University of Tokyo, the planner Kawakami had studied the American superblock, a type immediately relevant to the ALC. See Hajime Yatsuka, "Research Committee on High-rise Buildings: The First Step toward a City in the Air," chap. 6-3 in "Metabolism Nexus" (unpublished manuscript, 2012), PDF file. English translation by Riyo Namigata of Hajime Yatsuka, *Metabolism Nexus* [in Japanese] (Tokyo: Ohmsha, 2011).

11 See Hidemitsu Kawakami, "Jinkō tochi no teigi/shurui/ritchi" [Artificial land—definitions/categories/locations], in *Jinkō tochi—seiritsu jōken, kōka oyobi keikaku* [Artificial land—conditions for its formation, effects, and planning] (Tokyo: Architectural Institute of Japan, 1963), 1. Translation by Riyo Namigata.

Street edge of Sakaide
Phase 4 (2010)

12 Hajime Yatsuka writes of Asada and Kawakami's knowledge of New York zoning innovations, such as FAR and air rights, yet other members of the committee certainly knew of these practices as well. The AIJ was researching these topics in general at the time for an update of Japanese regulations, and the ALC research is a subset of this work. See Yatsuka, "Nexus," chap. 6-3.
13 The *Villes-Pilotis* proposal envisioned cities built on platforms covering municipal infrastructure. Typologically identical to the ALC's investigation, the proposal is another branch in Le Corbusier's development of the idea of artificial land. Despite its possible influence on the ALC, I'm hesitant to emphasize this project in the face of the ALC's obvious interest in New York zoning. It's feasible that Le Corbusier's design was in fact inspired by Grand Central Terminal's deck or Harvey Wiley Corbett's 1910 "City of Tomorrow" proposal for Manhattan, making all influences lead back to New York. See the section on the *Villes-Pilotis* in Le Corbusier, *Toward an Architecture* [1923], trans. John Goodman (Los Angeles: Getty Research Institute, 2007), 126–127.
14 William J. Wilgus, quoted in "William J. Wilgus," Wikipedia, accessed May 8, 2019, https://en.wikipedia.org/wiki/William_J._Wilgus.
15 Regarding this "vision" from 1923, see Gregory Clancey, *Earthquake Nation: The Cultural Politics of Japanese Seismicity, 1868–1930* (Berkeley: University of California Press, 2006), 213.
16 See Kawakami, "Artificial Land," 1.
17 See Yatsuka, "Nexus," chap. 3-4 on this topic, as well as Masato Otaka, "The Theory and Background of Artificial Land," *The Japan Architect* (August 1968): 27.
18 See Yorifusa Ishida, "Japanese Cities and Planning in the Reconstruction Period: 1945–55," in *Rebuilding Urban Japan After 1945*, eds. Carola Hein, Jeffry M. Diefendorf, Yorifusa Ishida (New York: Pallgrave Macmillan, 2003), 30.
19 See Otaka, "Theory," 28–30.
20 See Akira Tamura, "Jinkō tochi no keizai kōka" [The economic effects of artificial land], in *Jinkō tochi*, 36. Translation by Riyo Namigata.
21 See Toshihiko Kimura, "Jinkō tochi keikakuan no kōzōhōshin ni tsuite" [Structural principles for the artificial land plan] in *Jinkō tochi*, 28. Translation by Riyo Namigata.
22 Kimura, "Jinkō tochi keikakuan," 29.
23 While height limits and FARs would allow some estimation of size and weight for construction on the platforms, these constraints could of course catastrophically change, as with Harumi. Height limits were in fact lifted in a limited area of Tokyo in 1963. See Yatsuka, "Nexus," chap. 6-3.
24 Kaneko was responsible for commissioning Tange to design the 1958 Kagawa Prefectural Government Hall and 1964 Kagawa Prefectural Gymnasium, both in Takamatsu. The governor introduced Noguchi to the area in 1957 to help revitalize its stone industry. See Masayo Duus, *The Life of Isamu Noguchi: Journey Without Borders* [2000], trans. Peter Duus (Princeton, NJ: Princeton University Press, 2004), 311–312.
25 The source for this and other detailed aspects of negotiation are from Hikaru Kinoshita and Hiroaki Kondou, "Sakaide jinkō tochi ni okeru kaihatsu shuhō ni kan suru kenkyū" [A study on the development method of Sakaide artificial ground], in *Nihon toshi keikaku gakkai toshi keikaku ronbunshū* [Journal of the City Planning Institute of Japan], no. 43-3 (October 2008): 477. Translation by Riyo Namigata.
26 Masaya Fujimoto, "The Purpose of the Sakaide Manmade Land," *The Japan Architect* (March 1965): 69.
27 Noboru Kawazoe, "The City of the Future," *Zodiac*, no. 9 (1961): 99.
28 Yasuke Hachinohe, "Memo on the Structure of the Artificial Land Project," *The Japan Architect* (August 1968): 31.
29 Hachinohe, "Memo," 32.
30 Fujimoto, "Purpose," 74.
31 This limitation was related by Masaya Fujimoto in conversation with the author, April 23, 2010.
32 As a case in point, architect Patrik Schumacher writes that "Just like natural systems, parametricist compositions are so highly integrated that they cannot be easily decomposed into independent subsystems." Putting aside the role of decomposition in natural systems, the kind of integration Schumacher embraces is precisely the opposite of Sakaide and artificial land at large. See Schumacher, "Parametricism as Style—Parametricist Manifesto" (2008), https://www.patrikschumacher.com/Texts/Parametricism%20as%20Style.htm. Note that I do not mean here a dismissal of parametric design per se, just its more rigid manifestations.
33 See Kinoshita and Kondou, "Sakaide jinkō tochi," 479.
34 See Yosuke Hirayama, "The Changing Context of Home Ownership in Japan" (2004): 4, https://www.housingauthority.gov.hk/hdw/ihc/pdf/hayh.pdf.
35 Minoru Mori, *Mori Building: The Making of Vertical Garden Cities* (New York: Penguin Books, 2012), 3. The TV Asahi Headquarters (2003) at Roppongi Hills was designed by Fumihiko Maki.
36 Docomomo is an international "watchdog" organization devoted to documenting and conserving the legacy of modern architecture. Regarding Sakaide's selection by the group—which does not constitute protected status—see *DOCOMOMO Japan: The 100 Selections* issue of *The Japan Architect*, no. 57 (Spring 2005): 154.
37 See Fumihiko Maki, *Nurturing Dreams: Collected Essays on Architecture and the City*, ed. Mark Mulligan (Cambridge, MA: The MIT Press, 2008), chap. 1.

38 Fumihiko Maki, email to the author, March 11, 2010.
39 Fumihiko Maki and Masato Ohtaka, "Collective Form—Three Paradigms," in Maki, *Investigations in Collective Form* [1964] (St. Louis, MO: School of Architecture, Washington University in St. Louis, 2004), 6. Italics added.
40 Maki and Ohtaka, "Collective," 9.
41 In other parts of the essay, the hyphen is absent.
42 See Jean Gottmann, *Megalopolis: The Urbanized Northeastern Seaboard of the United States* (New York: The Twentieth Century Fund, 1961).
43 See Jeffrey E. Hanes, "From Megalopolis to Megaroporisu," *Journal of Urban History* 19, no. 2 (1993) and Yatsuka, "Nexus," chap. 14-2.
44 See Francis C. Bing, "History of the Word 'Metabolism,'" *Journal of the History of Medicine and Allied Arts* 26, no. 2 (April 1971): 176.
45 Sigfried Giedion, *Space, Time and Architecture: The Growth of a New Tradition* [1941] (Cambridge, MA: Harvard University Press, 1982), 862.
46 See this book's introduction, page 19, for first mention of this elision, found in Reyner Banham, *Megastructure: Urban Futures of the Recent Past* (New York: Harper & Row, 1976), 7. See *Megastructure*, 52–53, for mentions of artificial land and ground where a reader could take the expressions as Banham's own turn of phrase.
47 Giedion, *Space,* 863. Despite Otaka being absent from *Space, Time and Architecture*, Giedion had an interest in his work, having sent him an enthusiastic letter supporting his development of prefabricated architecture, discussed in the following chapter. This letter was displayed in the Mori Art Museum's *Metabolism—The City of the Future* exhibition in 2011.
48 Furthering Otaka's relative absence in architectural history, he is not mentioned as a coauthor in the reprinting of "Collective Form" in Maki's *Nurturing Dreams* (2008). Otaka may have had a relatively minor role in the essay's actual writing, and been more of a sounding board for Maki. However, Otaka it seems did not particularly resist his own erasure from high-profile architecture culture. Over his final decades, he increasingly withdrew from any interest in publicity, and refused an interview with Koolhaas and Obrist for *Project Japan*.
49 See Fumihiko Maki and Masato Ohtaka, "Some Thoughts on Collective Form," in *Structure in Art and in Science*, ed. Gygöry Kepes (New York: George Braziller, 1965), 119. The enumerated "promises" of megastructure here should be compared with the corresponding list in Maki and Ohtaka, "Collective," 9.
50 Robin Middleton, quoted in Banham, *Megastructure*, 207.
51 This is not to discount the public benefits that private upmarket developments can contribute, through green spaces and other amenities, as well as tax revenue. But those are not their primary reasons for being. Such developments are often major vehicles of displacement for low-income people and increased income inequality.

2
The Metabolist-
Industrial Complex

Small as Japan was, she was laden with plan upon plan—construction plans, regional plans, municipal plans, plans for the reorganization of industrial areas. This year, however, within the space of the first four months of the calendar year, the vague, somber shadow of something heretofore unknown had begun to fall across all of these plans. On the face of it, it seemed merely a matter of the perennial conflict with nature having become somewhat intensified, but once the data had been viewed in perspective, one sensed that the beginnings of a still faint mosaic was emerging, something sinister, its outline still no more than a pale shadow.

—Sakyo Komatsu, *Japan Sinks*, 1973[1]

A collaborator with Noboru Kawazoe on the development of themes for Expo '70 in Osaka, Asia's first World's Fair, science-fiction author Sakyo Komatsu became critical of Japanese government bureaucracy after his seeing its suppression of potential expo content.[2] By the early 1970s, government ministries had indeed laden the country with plan upon plan. But who did these plans best serve?

While Japan's standard of living did generally improve over the 1960s, a key failing in the boom caused by the 1961 Income Doubling Plan is how little the government spent on improved living conditions for the majority of the population, particularly for housing and related infrastructure, despite a national housing crisis.[3] This reality helps explain the government's preference for low-interest mortgages for privately built houses rather than the construction of public housing. But even so, these government loans, which were part of Yosizaka's 1954 proposal, accounted for only 15 percent of all Japanese housing constructed between 1945 and 1973. Public housing was only 8 percent, and the public-private JHC was a mere 4 percent. In contrast, about 65 percent of housing constructed during this period was entirely private, which led to major problems that continue to beset the country in the early twenty-first century.[4]

ASTM, Ashiyahama Seaside Town, unit types, 1973

131

As the historian Ann Waswo has noted, the JHC succeeded in developing industrialized domestic components, such as unitized kitchens, that were adopted by private developers who then chose to ignore the JHC's attention to quality architecture and urban design, as demonstrated at Harumi.[5] Despite the intention for them to be widely replicated models integrating all scales of design, publicly supported endeavors such as Harumi and Sakaide remained exceptional, with unfortunately only their mass-produced equipment becoming widespread.

The Developmental State

Indeed, what the government did spend money on was extreme industrialization. Well before Ikeda's 1961 plan, the groundwork for the heavy industry that engendered the 1960s boom was laid by the Enterprises Rationalization Promotion Law of 1952. The law committed central and local governments to building new infrastructure—"ports, highways, railroads, electric power grids, gas mains, and industrial parks"—all at public expense and for the support of selected private industries.[6] This mobilization, led by the national government's powerful MITI and MOC, had the objective of total rationalization: first, of the delivery of imported raw materials, then their processing, and finally the deployment of finished products to create the country's vast new wealth.[7]

If the language here sounds military, that's no mistake: MITI grew out of the Munitions Ministry that controlled aircraft manufacturing and other industrial logistics during the war, and MOC was the successor to the War Reconstruction Institute, tasked with triage-like urban planning in immediate response to American bombings.[8] In their postwar roles, MOC controlled all building regulations and approvals while also initiating its own infrastructure projects. As for MITI, among its multiple activities was controlling the licensing of foreign patents, such as for transistors, thereby enabling it to assign rights for particular technologies to companies in industries it wanted to nurture. The political scientist Chalmers Johnson saw this role of MITI as fundamental to Japan's postwar rise, as described in his 1982 book *MITI and the Japanese Miracle*.[9]

This miracle was enabled by the close cooperation of the elected government, these ministries, and the private industries they selected for strategic support, a triad that built upon strategic coordination during the war. Together, these three actors created what Johnson famously described as a "developmental state."[10] As Johnson wrote, the developmental state is an approach typically found in economically

Fig. 6. Rough boundary of Japan Megalopolis overlapping of factors.

Takashi Doi, Tokaido Megalopolis, 1968

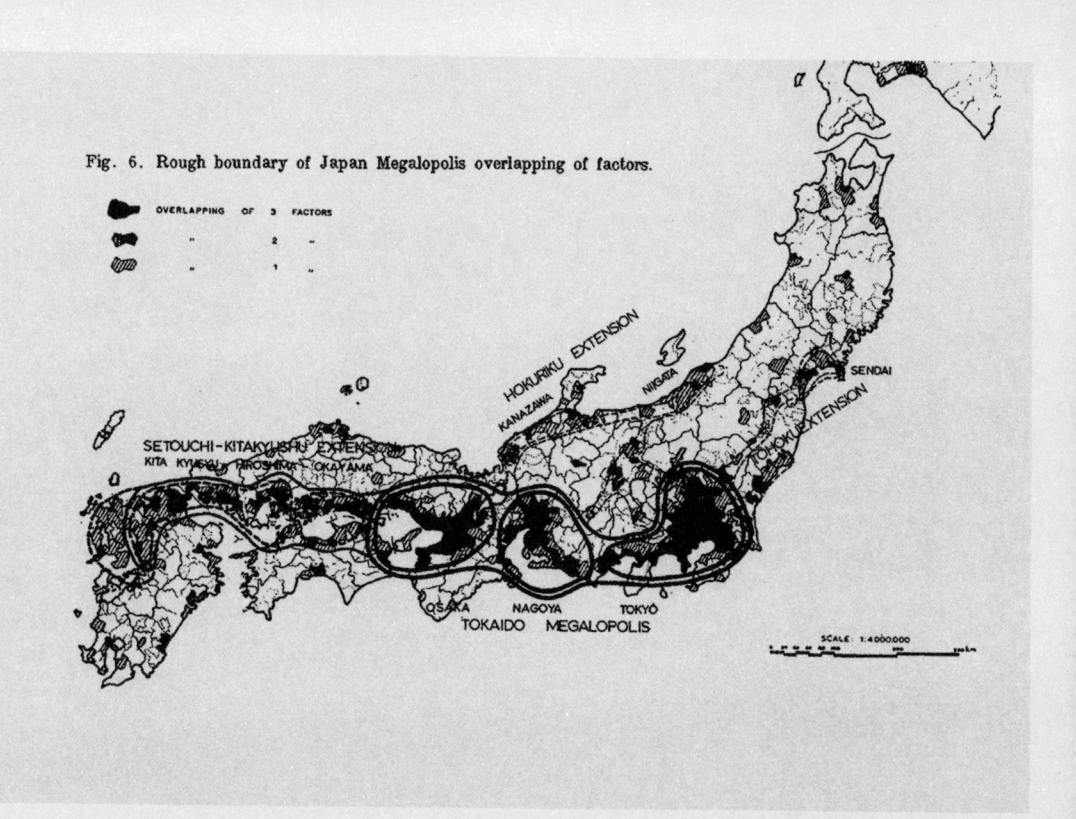

undeveloped nations, adopted as a strategy to catch up to competition, using a "plan-rational" system that he distinguishes from a "market-rational" system, as in America. Unlike a market-rational system, plan-rationality is based on a state's operation under shared, overarching goals, prioritizing outcomes over procedures. For the objective-oriented developmental state, huge bureaucracies undertake detailed planning that elsewhere would be considered hugely inefficient and opposed to a free-market vision. Despite this intense drive to clarify and support national economic objectives, the developmental state should not to be confused with the planned economy of a communist state that aims for total control of all sectors of the economy. Instead, the developmental approach simply ignores any sector considered non-strategic. Two areas considered less strategic in Japan were housing and the environment.

Conflicts

The nation's postwar mobilization resulted in the emergence of megalopolitan Japan, a continuous network of urbanization linking Tokyo, Nagoya, Osaka, and beyond to form a logistical web of "agglomeration efficiency" serving industry.

2 THE METABOLIST-INDUSTRIAL COMPLEX

Also known as the "Pacific Belt," or what Tange and others called the "Tokaido Megalopolis," the cities of this coastal network had historically been linked by the Tokaido Road, the "main street" of Japan dating from the seventeenth century, now adapted for trucks and trains.[11]

By 1964, the year of the Tokyo Olympics (also Asia's first), the number of new residents added annually to Tokyo surpassed one million, thereby changing the city's territorial definition. Land Readjustment, and its new three-dimensional version tested in Sakaide, were too slow to boost new residential densities in established urban areas that could fight sprawl's consumption of land driven by such population growth in the Pacific Belt.[12] Instead, development expanded into greenfield sites that were comparatively inexpensive and free of ownership conflicts, with the late 1950s to the late '60s being the era of *danchi*—the often remote housing estates pioneered in Japan by the JHC, two of the most famous being Senri New Town in northern Osaka and Tama New Town in western Tokyo.[13] Thanks to Japan's extensive railway system, *danchi* on the urban peripheries gave rise to a new commuter class, mostly males travelling from their homes on the fringes to their workplaces in the city centers, often leaving wives and children stranded at home in what effectively were bed towns. Though the JHC's *danchi* strived to be mixed-use, self-sufficient new communities, the preexisting city centers remained dominant as locales of paid work.

While the JHC was still a role model, private developers were far more inspired by its push into low-cost countryside than its thoughtful community design, in addition to their attraction to its mass-produced kitchens. Urban geographer André Sorensen notes, in his invaluable *The Making of Urban Japan*, that far more common than the JHC's integrated planning was "unserviced development," wherein residents of privately built new housing could find themselves without such basic provisions as parks, schools, sidewalks, and even sewage systems.[14]

Residents could also find themselves living dangerously close to toxic factories and other polluted sites. With planning dominated by the logistics of industry, zoning was ignored in the interests of achieving whatever agglomerations of functions would best serve industry. As a result, environmental and human causalities soon appeared, seen in rising cases of chronic asthma and mercury poisoning, and by the early 1960s, there were mounting protests by residents against pollution and the building of new industrial parks.[15] One of the most infamous polluters was Showa Yokkaichi Oil,

top: Senri New Town, Osaka, 1960s

bottom: 1966 photo in Yokkaichi, from a series by the photographer Kenji Higuchi on the impact of the Showa Yokkaichi Oil refinery

whose refinery in the city of Yokkaichi was built on landfill under the auspices of MITI, opening in 1963.[16] Otaka specifically called out Yokkaichi as an example of the lethal dangers of rushed modernization, a phenomenon of which he considered Metabolism to be a part.[17]

Jean Gottmann suggests in *Megalopolis* that "growing pains" such as pollution are intrinsic to the "endless process of civilization."[18] Yet such pains cannot be accepted as inevitable when caused by an unjust lack of planning, and grassroots demands for environmental regulation escalated during the 1960s. These demands resulted in the passage of the New City Planning Law in 1968, the first national planning revision since 1919. The main goal of the law was to fight sprawl with controls on the processes by which rural land could be urbanized, selecting certain areas for urbanization and protecting others. It also required proper residential infrastructure to be constructed prior to, or in parallel with, new housing.[19] The early 1970s saw earnest attempts at the new plan's implementation as well as the election of Prime Minister Kakuei Tanaka.

Known as the "the computerized bulldozer" for his love of technocratic construction projects, Tanaka was a politician emblematic of the developmental state: like Prime Minister Ikeda before him, he had been the head minister of MITI. Taking office in 1972, Tanaka made Japan's casualties of growth central to his agenda—an objective that may be contrasted with Ikeda's statement that, "it makes no difference to me if five or ten small businessmen are forced to commit suicide" due to the country's industrialization.[20] In Tanaka's bestselling 1972 book, *Building a New Japan: A Plan for Remodeling the Japanese Archipelago*, he asserts that, despite the country's industrial strength, "various contradictions have surfaced amidst the affluence," including "inflation, pollution, urban overcrowding, rural depopulation and stagnation, educational disorders, and the generation gap."

Kakuei Tanaka, *Building A New Japan: A Plan for Remodeling the Japanese Archipelago*, 1972

He concludes, "Of all these problems [...] our lack of accumulated social overhead capital must be promptly rectified since it is now acting as a brake on national economic growth and the improvement of Japanese life."[21] Social overhead capital, defined as publicly funded infrastructure such as roads and electrical utilities—necessary preconditions for the growth of economic activity—had been funded by public money under the Enterprises Law of 1952. But this occurred in a lopsided way, oriented to industry rather than supposedly nonstrategic housing infrastructure.[22] Now such infrastructure needed to be created—and regulated—for the population's health.

Livingry

Chalmers Johnson believes that, in the United States, the closest analog to MITI "is not the Department of Commerce but the Department of Defense," for only the Department of Defense has a similar mission to closely collaborate with private industry in the development of technologies vital to national interests.[23] If we extend this comparison, a primary "defense contractor" for MITI is the Takenaka Corporation, the vast design-build company central to three of the four projects in this chapter. Able to commit extensive resources to research and design as well as construction, Takenaka played a major role in the new task of defending Japan from itself.

With its origins in seventeenth-century shrine carpentry, the Osaka-based company was incorporated in 1899 as a modern contractor using Western technologies. In 1921, it hired two young designers from the Bunriha—Japan's first modernist collective, complete with its own manifesto—helping to establish the corporation's reputation for progressive design.[24] Indeed, Kiyonori Kikutake worked at Takenaka from 1950 to '52, and Maki, who is related to the Takenaka family through marriage, received its design support for *Investigations in Collective Form*.[25] The company became a major force, both making and being made by the country's tremendous growth, eventually known as a member of the "Big Five" of similarly comprehensive contractors. Others also had their origins in carpentry guilds, such as the Shimizu Corporation, who built the Harumi Apartments and Tange's Yoyogi National Stadium. Known as *zenekon*, a portmanteau word for "general contractors," these corporations still dominate complex and large-scale projects in Japan in the early twenty-first century.[26]

The architect Arata Isozaki has remarked that the early 1970s was a period of major transition: plentiful work for small cutting-edge offices dried up thanks to *zenekon* coming to monopolize design as well as construction.[27] This monopolization was given a huge boost by the many *zenekon* building Expo '70, located on a massive site selected by MITI on Osaka's periphery, adjacent to Senri New Town. The expo was a record-setting event, attracting 64 million visitors, with its planning led by Tange, and some of the Metabolists contributing designs for pavilions and other elements. Yet the expo is often seen as the movement's "swan song," with its commercialization—displayed by pavilions for Mitsubishi, Toshiba, and Pepsi, among other major makers of consumer products—tainting Metabolism with a loss of progressive objectives to corporate advertising.[28] Combined with a shift in the orientation of young architects toward single-family house designs, such as those by Kazuo Shinohara, and the 1973 OAPEC oil embargo that virtually halted the country's economy, Metabolism looked dead.[29] Following these events, Tange and Kurokawa found their major commissions in the Middle East and Africa, outside a Japan that seemed no longer interested in or able to afford Metabolist visions.[30]

While this narrative applies to Tange and Kurokawa, it ignores the fact that *zenekon*, or at least Takenaka, didn't simply take commissions that might previously have gone to a Metabolist. Takenaka also embraced Metabolist ideas. In the late 1960s and early '70s respectively, the corporation would start to build relationships with Otaka and Kikutake—established advocates for artificial land—on projects for mass housing as called for in the 1968 Plan, working with these architects on and off into the 1980s. Just as certain industries were selected by the developmental state for nurturing, Metabolism and its belief in artificial land were nurtured as well, the MOC-supported ALC being an example, as well as MITI's support of WoDeCo and Expo '70. Thanks to these ministries and Takenaka, Metabolism's ambitions were being built in the 1970s on a larger scale than ever before, just when the movement is seen as dying.

Japan's steel industry, having rapidly advanced through wartime shipbuilding and then through promotion by MITI, enabled the products of these collaborations between Takenaka and the Metabolists. Such a transfer of sophisticated techniques from military manufacturing to housing construction has a precedent in wartime America, where the inventor-engineer Buckminster Fuller proposed that the country's armaments industry convert from making weaponry to what he called "livingry." For Fuller, this conversion would shift the fast, strong, and lightweight methods of making aircraft into making houses that were

Kisho Kurokawa, Toshiba IHI Pavilion, Expo '70, Osaka

similar to planes in their logistical coordination of resources and performance, made in factories and thereby avoiding the inefficiency and imprecision of on-site construction.[31] Fuller pursued this goal in his Wichita House, developed from 1944 to '46, that was built in a military airplane factory in Kansas. In the face of a global housing crisis, he saw livingry as armaments for waging domesticity, to be produced with the "velocity of total war."[32]

    The acceleration of Japan's steel industry in turn accelerated the creation of a new livingry of artificial land, technically far more advanced than cast-in-place concrete, and striving to correct the damage caused by the emphasis on economic metrics during the income-doubling period. This new industrialization underscores the loss of Yosizaka's model that was open to DIY resident-builders and local *daiku* for the creation of individualized homes. Building was moving into the precise and controlled space of the factory. Deployed for housing projects much bigger than previously, underwritten by the most influential of ministries, and built if not also designed by a giant *zenekon*, this new livingry expresses a facet of the Japanese developmental state as a "Metabolist-industrial complex."[33]

139

Like America's "military-industrial complex," so named by US President Dwight D. Eisenhower in 1961 to warn of the danger of private arms makers influencing government policy, the Metabolist-industrial complex at times offered solutions that depended on the perpetuation of problems from which it profited. While opportunities arose for artificial land to address problems such as unserviced sprawl, it was also used to facilitate new levels of consumerism and a continuing quest for cheap land that could make sprawl worse. The Metabolist concept of cyclical replacement could easily legitimize the wastage of planned obsolescence that encouraged disposing of last season's model, further opening the rift between humans and the environment rather than closing it.

1   Sakyo Komatsu, *Japan Sinks* [1973] (Tokyo: Kodansha, 1995), 61. A science-fiction novel describing Japan's disappearance due to massive earthquakes, from which the passage quoted here shows the Minister of Construction telling the Prime Minister (both fictionalized) that the country will need to start increasing its budget for natural disasters.
2   See William O. Gardner, "The 1970 Osaka Expo and/as Science Fiction," *Review of Japanese Culture and Society* 28 (2011): 38.
3   See André Sorensen, *The Making of Urban Japan: Cities and Planning from Edo to the Twenty-First Century* (New York: Routledge, 2002), 183–184. Sorensen's book is the best of which I'm aware (at least in English) for a critical charting of the nation's urban development.

Buckminster Fuller, Wichita House, 1946

4. See Ann Waswo, *Housing in Postwar Japan: A Social History* (London: RoutledgeCurzon, 2002), 57–58.
5. This diffusion of domestic equipment developed for the JHC happened with other products as well, such as compact water heaters. See Waswo, *Housing*, 74–75.
6. See Chalmers Johnson, *MITI and the Japanese Miracle: The Growth of Industrial Policy, 1925–1975* (Stanford: Stanford University Press, 1982), 217–218.
7. See Johnson, *MITI*, 218. It's important to note that the majority of Japan's new wealth was not, as is often thought, based on exports. The domestic market was a far larger percentage of the GNP, with Johnson writing that national demand is in fact what drove the economy from the mid-1950s to mid-1970s. See Johnson, *MITI*, 15–16.
8. Regarding MITI's origins, see Johnson, *MITI*, 169. For MOC, see *Metabolism—The City of the Future: Dreams and Visions of Reconstruction in Postwar and Present-Day Japan*, ed. Mami Hirose et al. (Tokyo: Mori Art Museum, 2011), 28.
9. See Johnson, *MITI*, in particular 17 and 199.
10. See Johnson, *MITI*, 17–22.
11. For further discussion of the origins of the Tokaido Megalopolis in the Tokaido Road, see Jeffrey E. Hanes, "From Megalopolis to Megaroporisu," *Journal of Urban History* 19, no. 2 (1993): 59–61.
12. See Sorensen, *Making*, 184. Note that Sorensen refers here to only Land Readjustment, not the related work of the ALC.
13. As mentioned on page 51 of this book, these developments were inspired by Western mass-housing models driven by extreme standardization. Against this direction, Otaka worked for the JHC in the late 1960s to create a schematic plan for Tama that used the existing hilly topography, preserving these and other natural features. However, the JHC rejected the plan due to the varying site conditions that would make standardization difficult, and instead undertook extensive grading. See *PAU: Uniting Architecture and Society—The Approach of OTAKA Masato* (Tokyo: National Archives of Modern Architecture, 2016), 46.
14. See Sorensen, *Making*, 200–207.
15. See Sorensen, *Making*, 200–207.
16. See "Yokkaichi asthma," last modified May 15, 2020, https://en.wikipedia.org/wiki/Yokkaichi_asthma.
17. See Masaya Fujimoto, "Architect Otaka Masato's Messages for the Next Generation of Youths," trans. Gen Machida, in *PAU: Uniting Architecture and Society—The Approach of OTAKA Masato* (Tokyo: National Archives of Modern Architecture, 2016), 4.
18. Jean Gottmann, *Megalopolis: The Urbanized Northeastern Seaboard of the United States* (New York: The Twentieth Century Fund, 1961), 15.
19. Sorensen, *Making*, 213–214.
20. This statement, made to the Japanese Diet in 1952, led to Ikeda's forced resignation as minister of MITI. See Johnson, *MITI*, 202.
21. Kakuei Tanaka, *Building a New Japan: A Plan for Remodeling the Japanese Archipelago* [1972] (Tokyo: The Simul Press, 1973), 18. Bureaucrat Atsushi Shimokobe, a graduate of Tange Lab, relates that Tanaka's book was largely a compilation of speeches written by a MITI official and a journalist and did not necessarily reflect Tanaka's own views. See Rem Koolhaas and Hans Ulrich Obrist, *Project Japan: Metabolism Talks…* (Cologne: Taschen, 2011), 649. Nonetheless—and more importantly—the views expressed were reflective of MITI objectives and real major problems.
22. The concept of social overhead capital is associated with development economics, particularly with the work of Albert O. Hirschman. See "Strategy of Unbalanced Growth," last modified June 4, 2019, https://en.wikipedia.org/w/index.php?title=Strategy_of_unbalanced_growth&action=history.
23. Johnson, *MITI*, 21.
24. Regarding the early history of Takenaka's hiring practices after its 1899 incorporation, see Dana Buntrock, *Japanese Architecture as a Collaborative Process: Opportunities in a Flexible Construction Culture* (New York: Spon Press, 2001), 20. For discussion of the Bunriha's origins, see Jonathan M. Reynolds, *Maekawa Kunio and the Emergence of Japanese Modernist Architecture* (Los Angeles: University of California Press, 2001), 21–23.
25. Takenaka's design department is credited with assisting Maki on several speculative projects in the book's appendix. See Fumihiko Maki, *Investigations in Collective Form* [1964] (St. Louis, MO: School of Architecture, Washington University in St. Louis, 2004), 39. Maki's marriage into the Takenaka family: Yositika Utida, in conversation with the author, April 23, 2010.
26. The other three members of the Big Five are Kajima, Obayashi, and Taisei. In the bubble era, Kumagai Gumi came to be included too, making for a "Big Six." See Fumio Hasegawa, *Built by Japan: Competitive Strategies of the Japanese Construction Industry* (New York: John Wiley & Sons, 1988), 4.
27. Arata Isozaki, *Inside Architecture—A Challenge to Japanese Society*, DVD, directed by Tomomi Ishiyama (P(h)ony Pictures, 2015).
28. Kurokawa in fact designed the Toshiba pavilion, as well as the Takara Beautilion pavilion for Takara, a cosmetics maker. Regarding the expo as "swan song," see for example Zhongjie Lin, *Kenzo Tange and the Metabolist Movement: Urban Utopias of Modern Japan* (New York: Routledge, 2010), back cover.
29. Regarding this contemporaneous shift toward Shinohara, one driven in part by the availability of commissions for small houses, see Thomas Daniell, *An Anatomy of Influence* (London: AA Publications, 2018), 29.
30. This narrative is advanced in various parts of Koolhaas and Obrist, *Project Japan*, for example page 14.
31. Buckminster Fuller, *Ideas and Integrities: A Spontaneous Autobiographical Disclosure* [1963] (New York: Collier, 1974), 196 and 247.
32. Fuller, *Ideas*, 195.
33. Johnson notes that some in Japan in fact refer to its political-business organization as the "bureaucratic-industrial complex." See Johnson, *MITI*, 21.

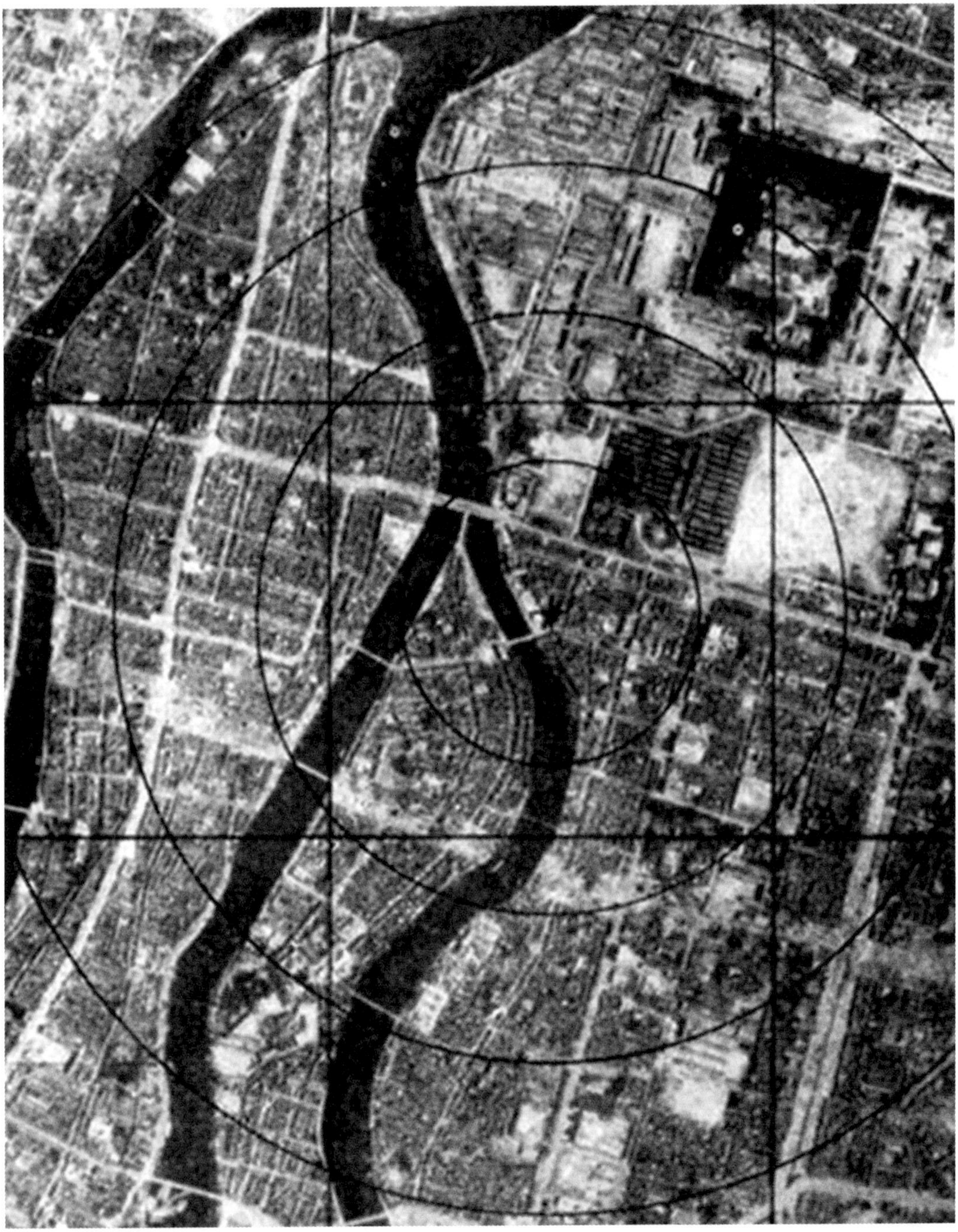

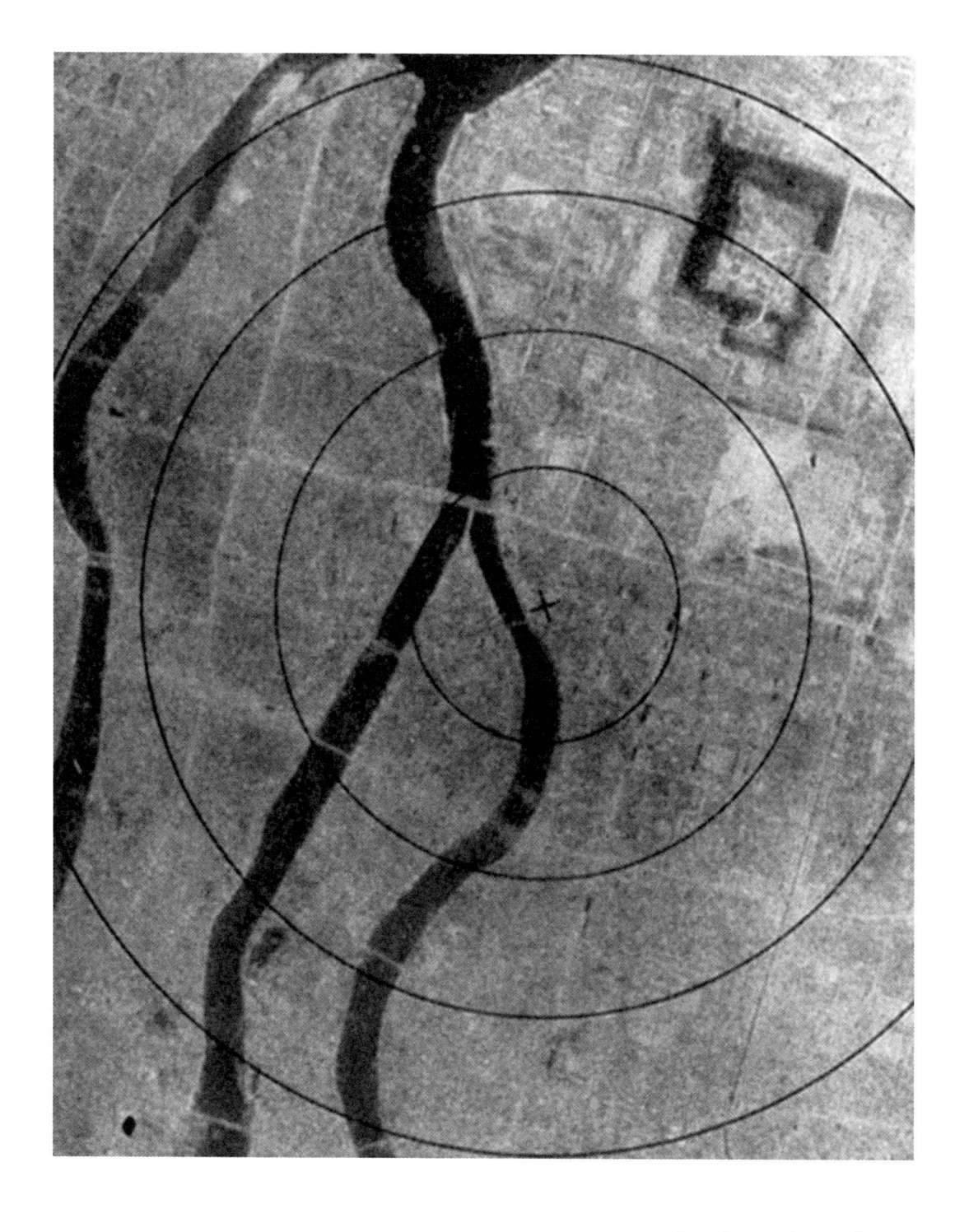

Ground zero and surrounding area in Hiroshima before (left) and after bombing on August 6, 1945 (above), with 1,000-foot circles

following: The "A-Bomb Slum," 1973

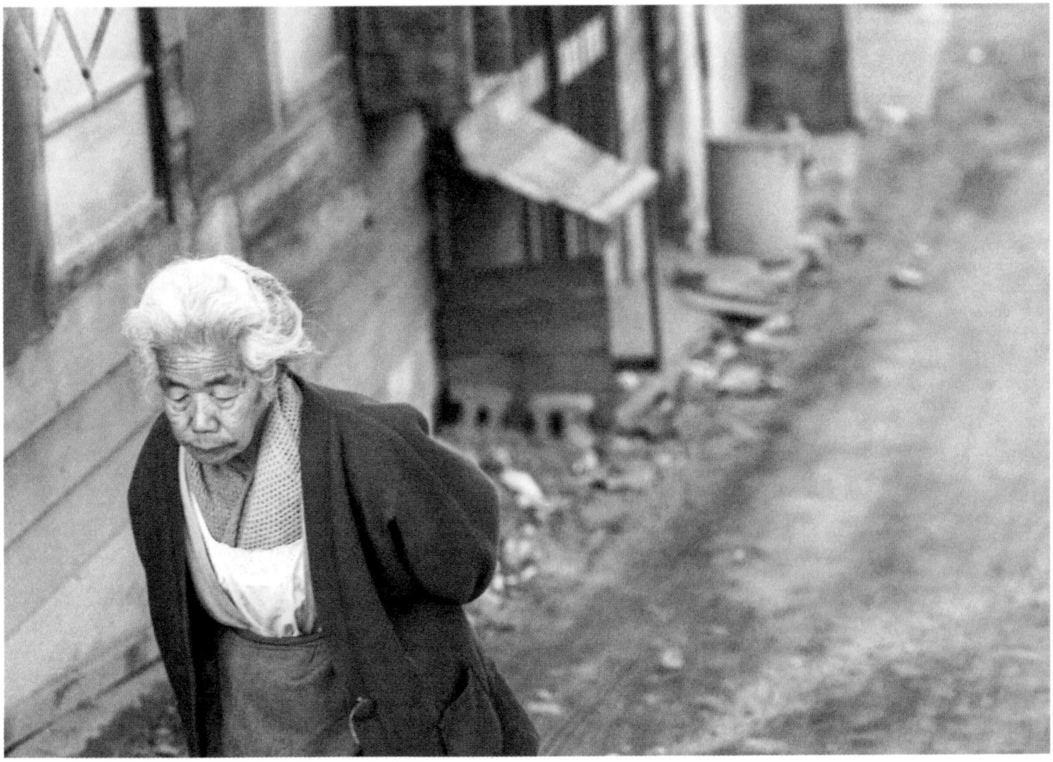

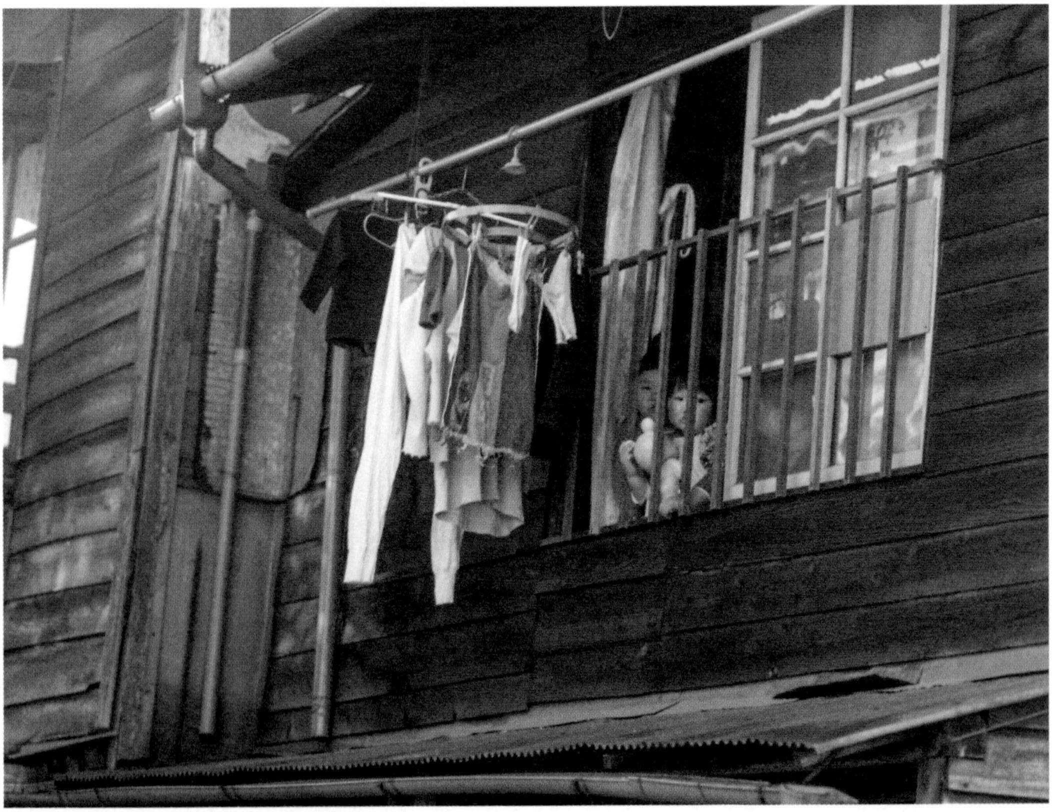

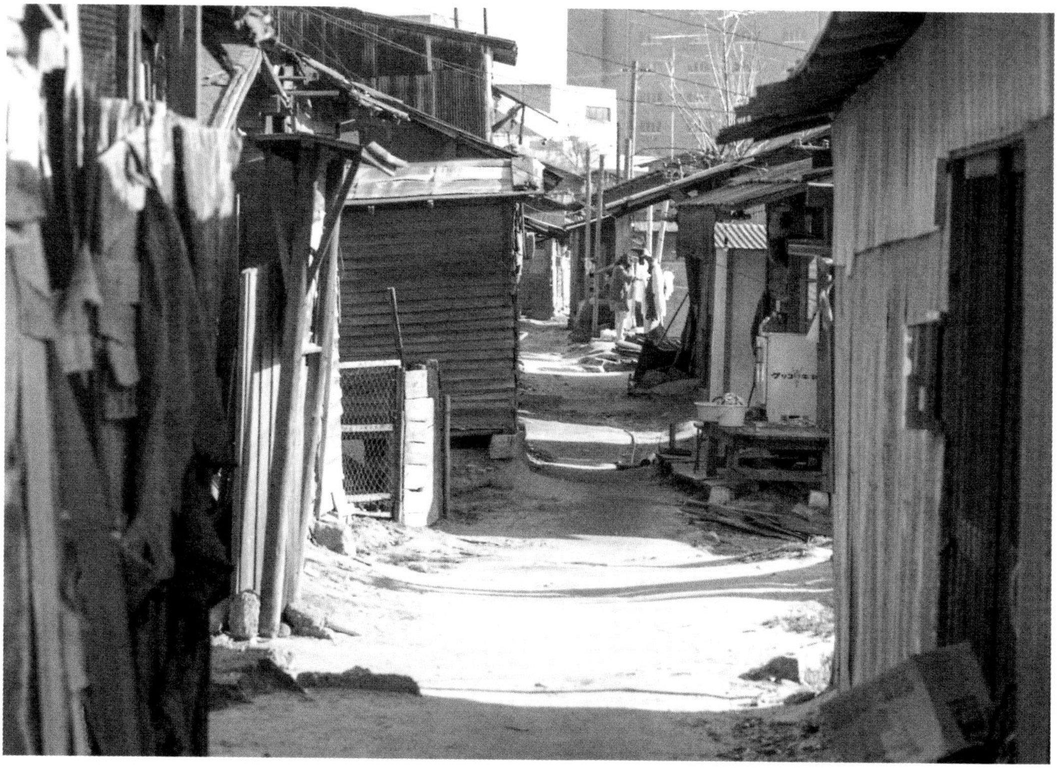

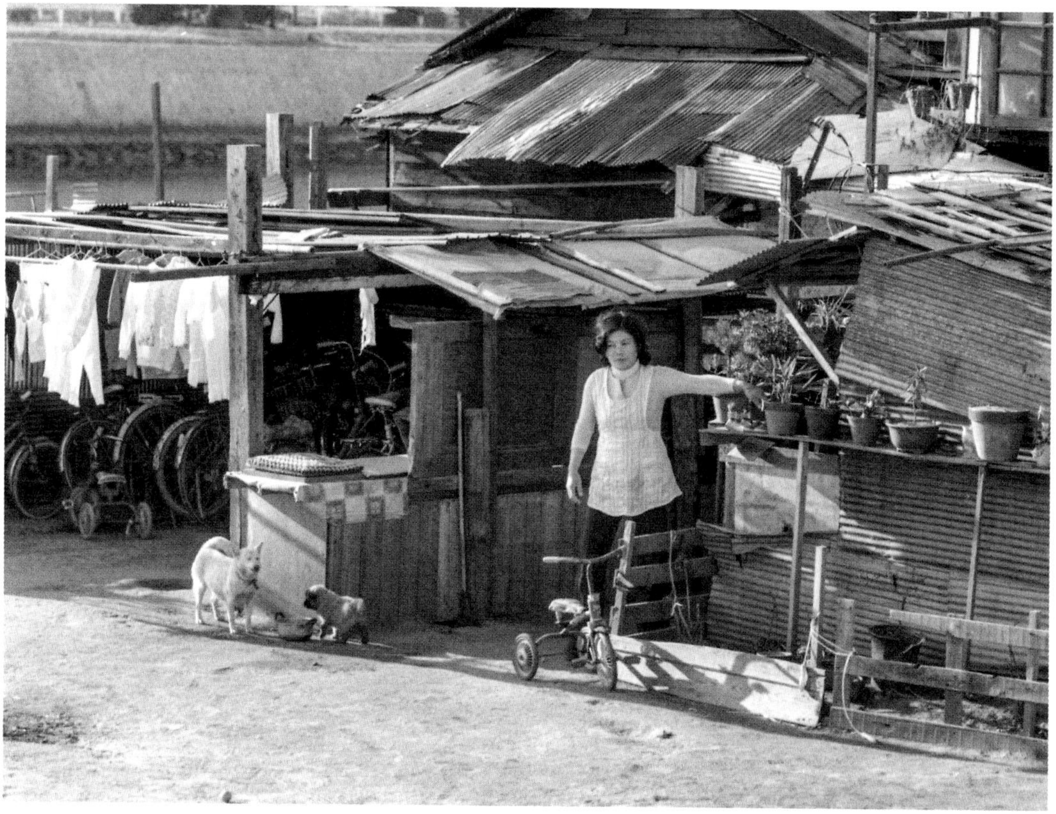

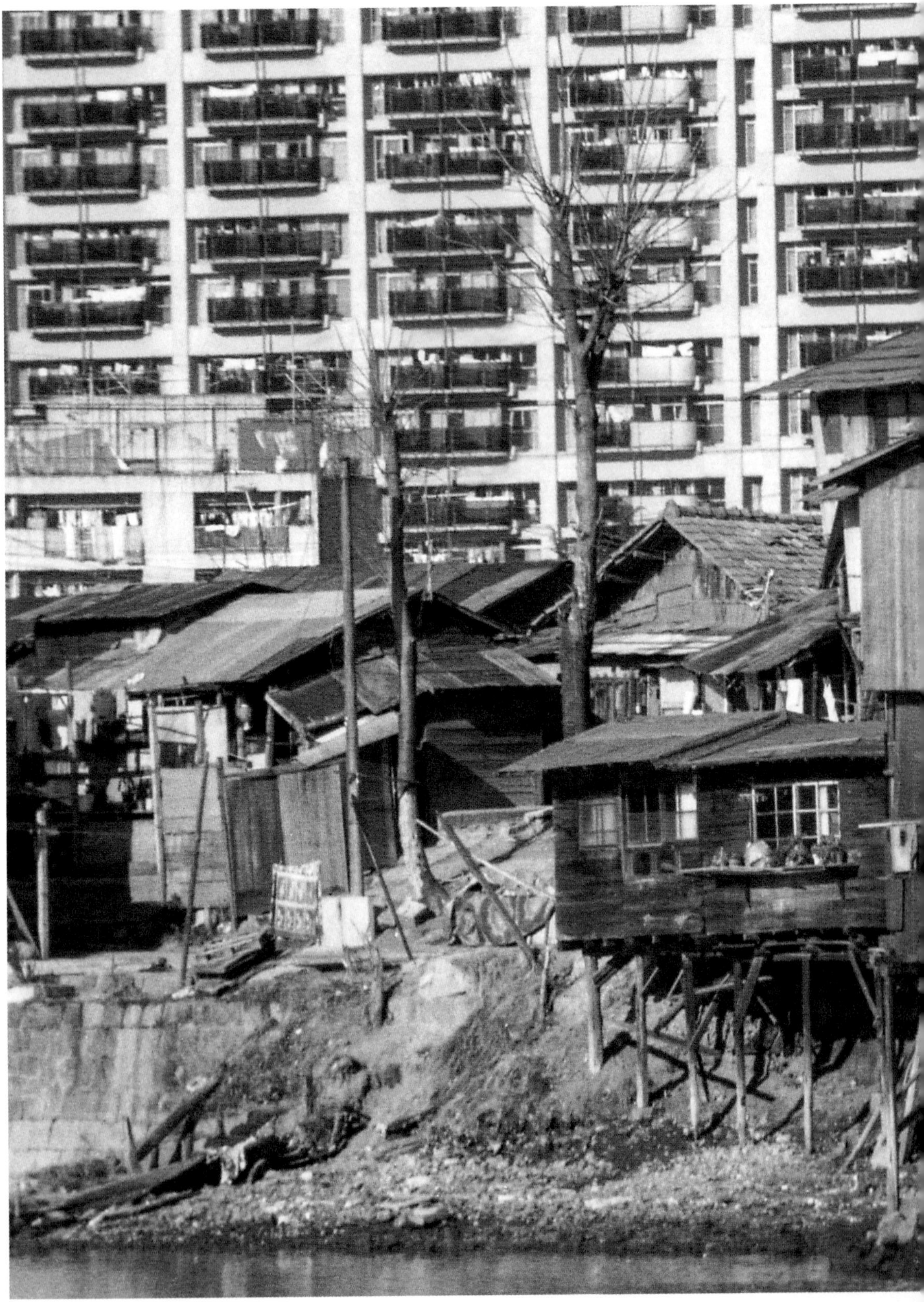

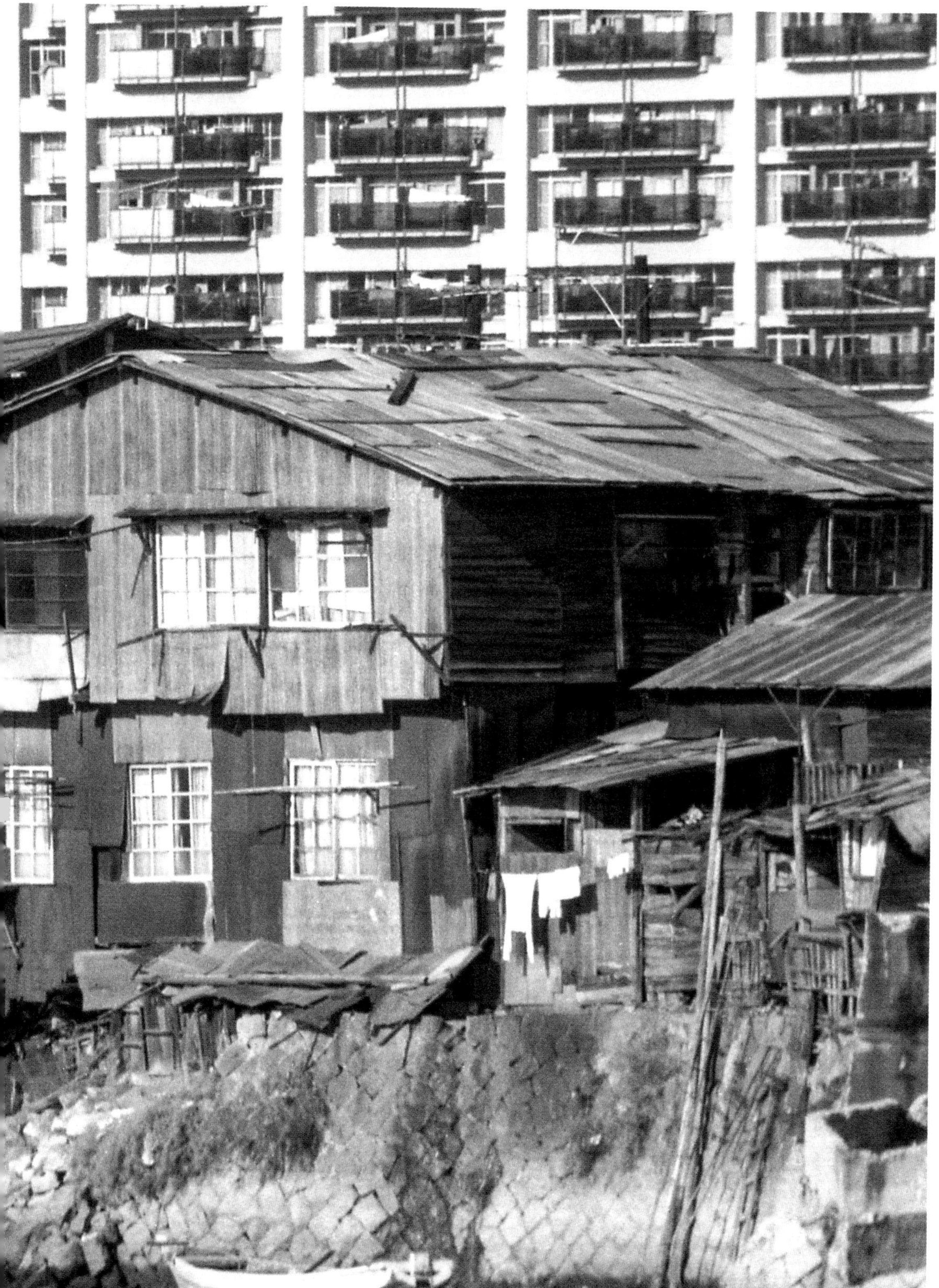

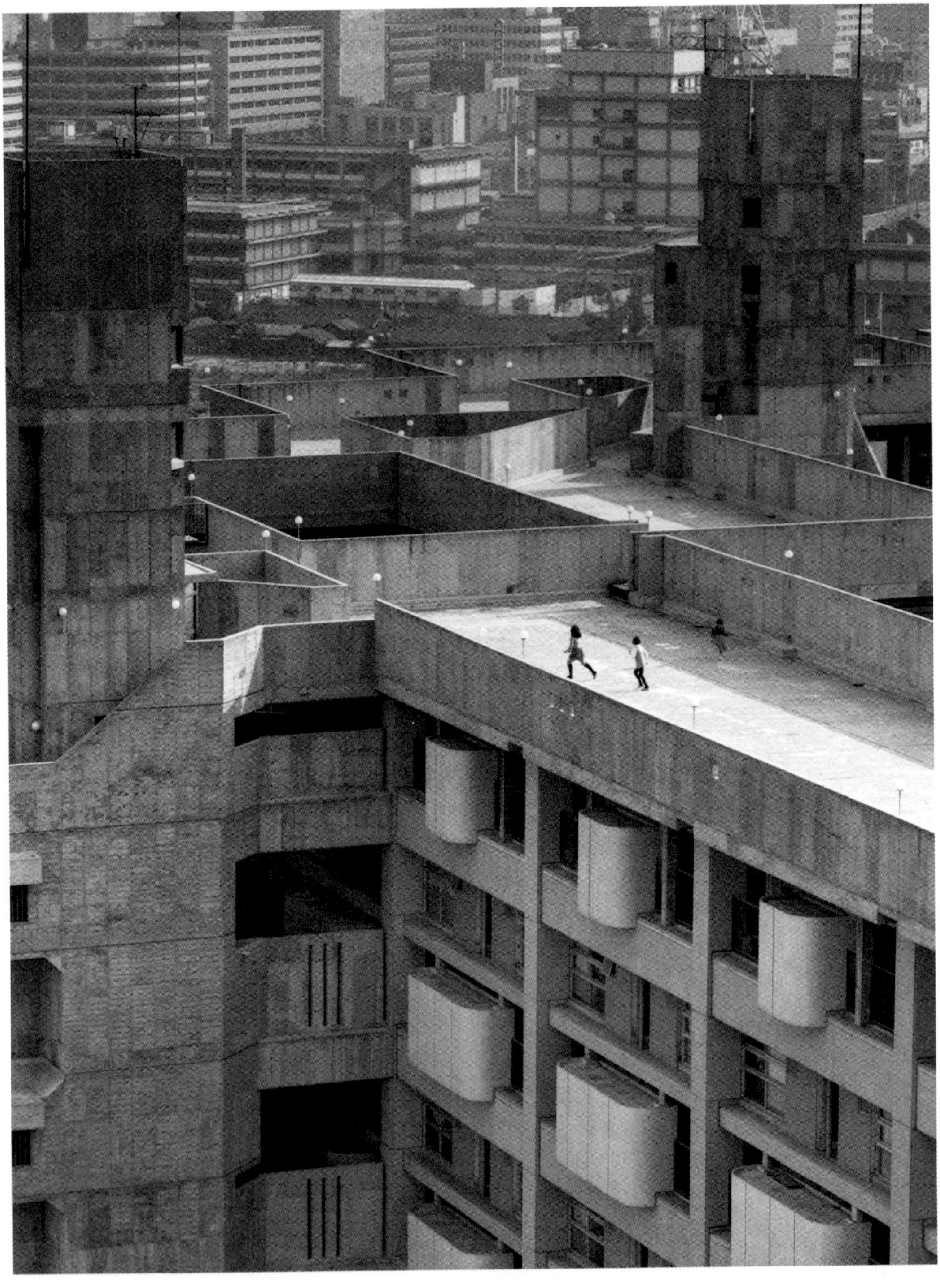

Symbolic Planning:
Motomachi Apartments, 1968–

Into the 1970s, around 3,000 people were living in shacks in an area of Hiroshima that had been close to the hypocenter of the American atom bomb detonation on August 6, 1945. Known as the "A-Bomb Slum," this remnant of the era of self-construction was home to many *hibakusha*, the "explosion-suffering people," as survivors of the bomb are known. Many were also Korean, brought from their colonized nation to Japan and forced into wartime labor.[1]

In 1968, work began on rehousing the slum's residents in new high-rise housing, the Motomachi Apartments and the smaller Chojuen Apartments, both designed by Masato Otaka. Motomachi in particular is a response to challenges that were both typical and unique in postwar reconstruction.[2] It is a masterpiece of Otaka's career, and one of the most successful realizations of Metabolism on its own terms. It is also one of the movement's most ignored projects, barely known at all outside Japan.[3]

At the time of Motomachi's completion in 1978, the project was Japan's tallest housing development ever built. Ranging in height from eight to twenty stories, group-form clusters contain 2,945 apartments (in addition to the 1,554 units completed earlier at Chojuen), and define a central area with schools, a shopping center, a hospital, a public bath, park, and playgrounds—many of the features so often lacking in new housing of that era. All of this was delivered through Otaka's strongest ever use of PAU (an acronym for Prefabrication, Art and Architecture, and Urbanism), the guiding methodology that he invented at the founding of his office.

PAU was a manifestation of Otaka's desire to interrelate designing, making, and living through a reconceived modularity across scales. This interrelation is expressed by his statement,

Masato Otaka,
Motomachi Apartments,
Hiroshima, 1972

following: Motomachi (2013)

2 THE METABOLIST-INDUSTRIAL COMPLEX

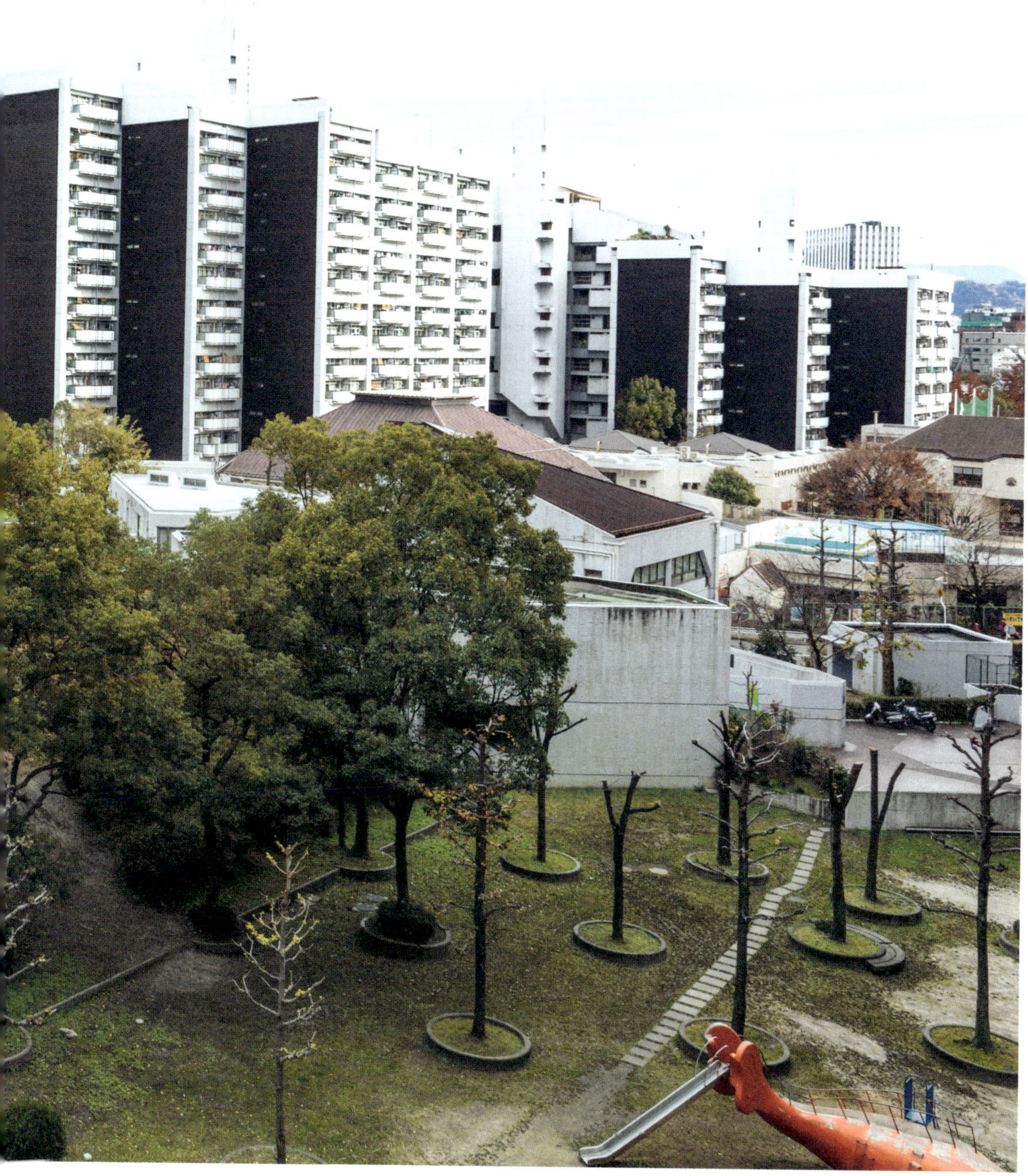

Motomachi, 1972

following: Motomachi
and Chojuen Apartments
Master Plan

"Quality should be the quality of parts as well as that of architecture. The quality of architecture should also be the quality of environment."[4] Masaya Fujimoto, a long-time staff member of Otaka's office and one of the project architects for Motomachi and Chojuen, notes that PAU was always a "symbol for creating a new environment for living" as much as a practical approach.[5] But the Hiroshima projects were an intense engagement with factory production, and resulted in a city within the city. With Chojuen constructed by Takenaka, and Motomachi by another large *zenekon*, Kumagai Gumi, the high level of industrialized systematization in Otaka's pixel-like designs makes them paradigms of Metabolist livingry.

Buckminster Fuller's livingry was universal, intended to be deployed anywhere. Metabolism too is often seen as universalist, with a taste for endlessly additive building systems indifferent to location. As the architectural historian Cherie Wendelken writes, voicing an opinion shared by other critics, "Metabolist projects do not seem to acknowledge any siting in a local or national landscape, nor do they address any historical context."[6] Numerous Metabolist proposals are indeed connected loosely at best to a site's specificity: Tange saw the 1959 Boston Harbor project's location as incidental; no discernable boundaries contain the expansion or orientation of Arata Isozaki's City in the Air, from 1961, despite being nominally sited in Tokyo; Kisho Kurokawa's Helix City, also from 1961, similarly spreads in an apparently aimless pattern. Perhaps because all of these projects are unbuilt speculations, they were driven mostly by their own internal logics.[7]

But in the case of Motomachi, its massing is highly site-specific. It addresses its historical context as an implicit rebuke to the notion of *tabula rasa* in a city center that had in fact been mostly erased. Otaka's livingry creates within the site what can be interpreted as a symbolic response to an unprecedented horror, and makes a place in which to live a better life. These two things don't go together easily.

City of Peace

Immediately after the war's end, Hiroshima struggled to obtain reconstruction funds from the national government, which was wary of acknowledging the city's particular status. The fear was that doing so would open the door to similar financial claims from any war-damaged city. Only after Hiroshima had launched the idea of transforming itself into an "International City of Peace" did it gain national and international support for lasting reconstruction work—achieved through the creation of a narrative wherein the atom bomb became a vehicle of peace, swiftly ending the war. This view was promoted by the American military occupiers, who censored any Japanese coverage of the bombing that could contradict their moral high ground, which was maintained by presenting Hiroshima as no more than an "important Japanese Army base," free of civilians, and the bomb itself as similar to a very large quantity of TNT, free of radiation.[8] The peace concept was partly based on a desire to bolster the city's tourism, turning it into a kind of pilgrimage site.[9] In 1949, Tange won the competition for the master plan of the Hiroshima Peace Memorial Park, with his design establishing a grand north-south axis passing near ground zero of the blast. The plan inaugurated the design of Hiroshima's new identity.

Starting in the south at the Peace Memorial Museum, completed in 1955 and designed by Tange as a modern interpretation of an ancient Japanese granary to store relics and present displays about the bombing, the axis acts as a sightline toward the north.[10] It passes through the parabolic arch of the Cenotaph for the Atomic Bomb Victims, also designed by Tange, and onward to the "A-Bomb Dome,"

基町・長寿園団地 綜合計画図

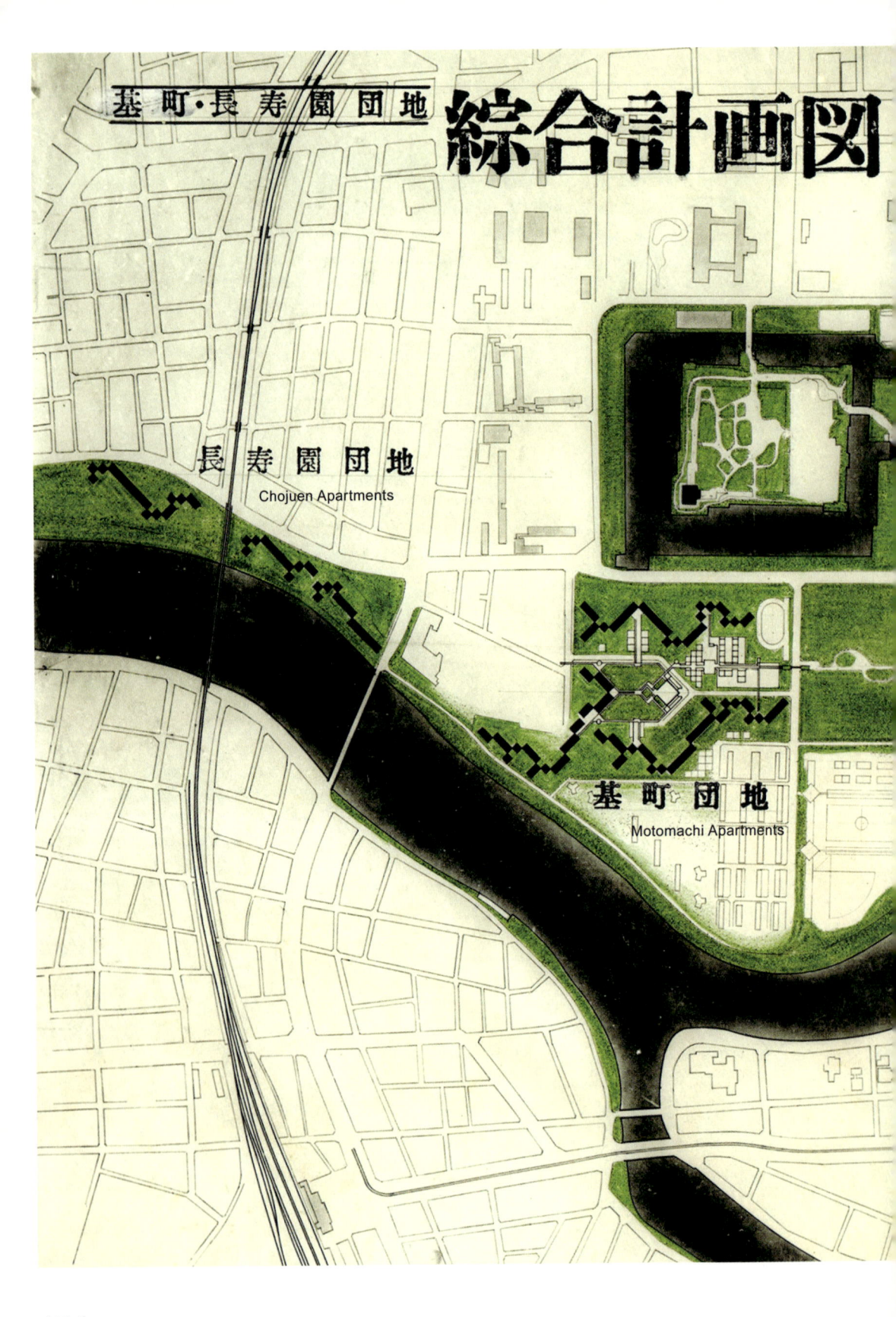

長寿園団地
Chojuen Apartments

基町団地
Motomachi Apartments

SYMBOLIC PLANNING: MOTOMACHI APARTMENTS, 1968–

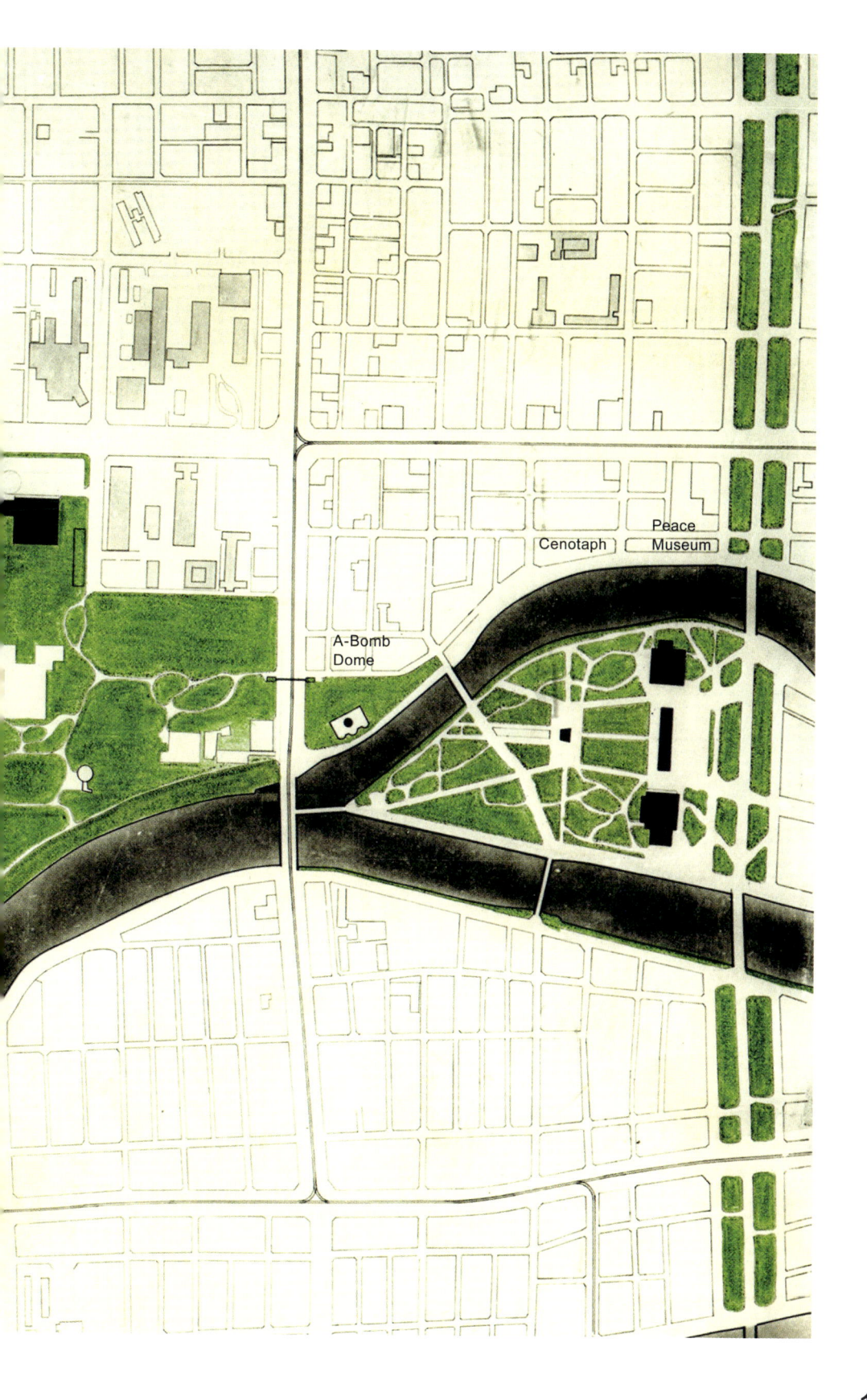

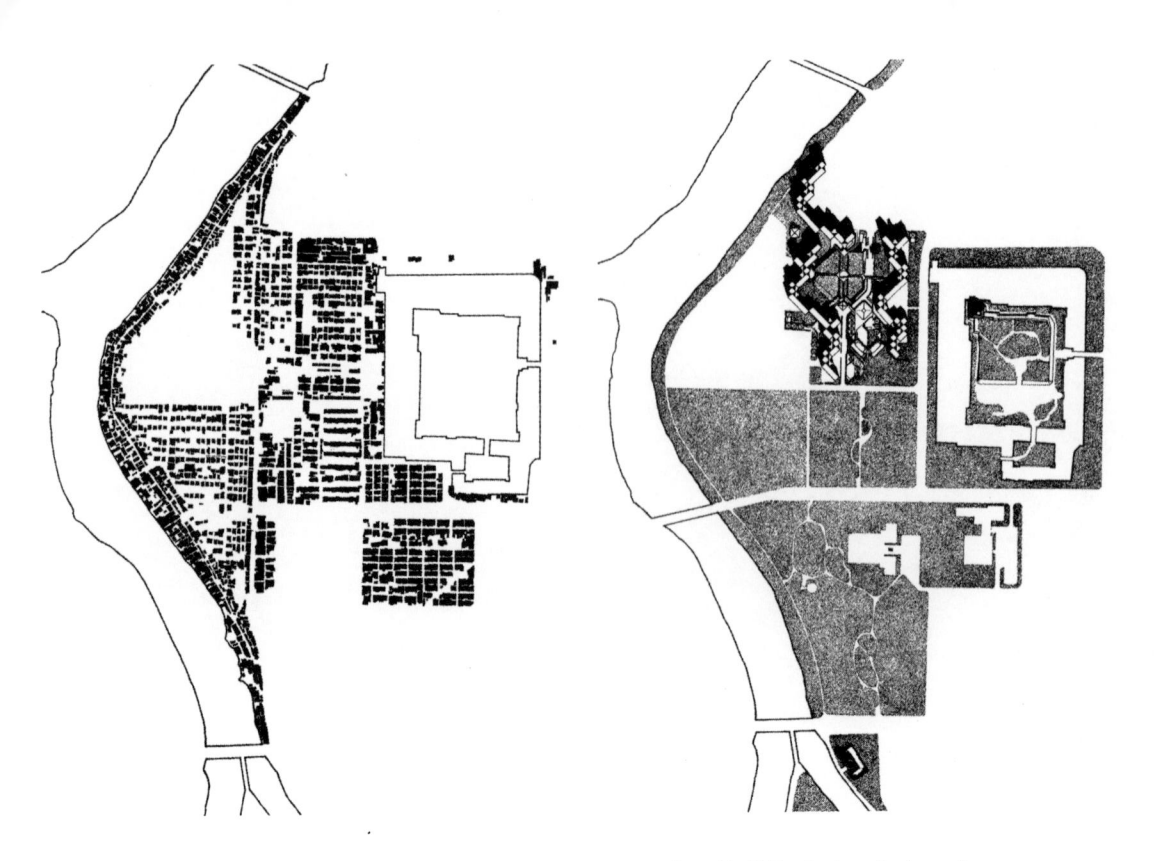

the shell of the Hiroshima Prefectural Industrial Promotion Hall that stood almost directly below the hypocenter, a preserved ruin left as a reminder of the bomb's devastation. In 1950, Tange extended the axis further north to form the spine of a new public park in the Motomachi district, between the grounds of Hiroshima Castle to the east, and the bank of the Ota River to the west.

    With the enormous loss of dwellings due to the bombing, as well as the influx of people returning from the war, Hiroshima was, like other Japanese cities at the time, experiencing a desperate housing shortage. The Motomachi district had had numerous military facilities, and as it was public property, the government was able to quickly build temporary housing there between 1946 and 1948. Illegal self-built shacks soon spread between this housing and the riverbank, forming the A-Bomb Slum, which reached a peak size of over 1,000 buildings around 1970.[11] After the slum emerged, it became clear that relocating it to make way for Tange's park was untenable. Finally, in 1968 the approximately 32-hectare area was selected for comprehensive residential redevelopment that would include the new park. The project was led by the city government, which hired Takashi Asada for assistance, who in turn brought in Otaka, who ultimately was given the commission for new housing and related facilities for the area. The commission was broken into two main portions: Chojuen, the northernmost part, on a narrow site directly along the river, and Motomachi, adjacent to the castle. By using a high-rise approach, Otaka freed the ground to reconcile the creation of park space with the rehousing of all the slum's residents.

above: "3,000 slums"—site before project (left) and "3,000-unit high-rise housing and 20-hectare citizens' park— proposed scheme" (right) [quoted from notes on drawings]

right: Motomachi and Chojuen, 1976

SYMBOLIC PLANNING: MOTOMACHI APARTMENTS, 1968–

2 THE METABOLIST-INDUSTRIAL COMPLEX

Technology Transfer

Turning to previous collaborators for the structural design, Otaka worked with Shigeru Aoki on Motomachi, and Toshihiko Kimura on Chojuen. For both, Otaka returned to the precedent of Harumi in order to further develop the design of a transitional type. Fujimoto, in a report on the two projects from 1973, states that "we conceived of […] a main, permanent frame that will not alter with passing time, and a subframe consisting of the housing units that can be altered to suit the changing needs and living patterns of the dwellers."[12] Future transformation was now part of the official agenda in a way it had not been for Maekawa in 1958. Similar to Harumi, in both portions all the vertical and horizontal loads are taken by major-structure moment frames, which form large voids, two apartments in width and two in height. Apartments are also organized in a skip-floor system, with 2DK type-A units on the single-loaded corridor levels, and 3K type-B units above, served by stairs branching from the corridors. Unlike Harumi, all of the major-structure is welded steel, clad in precast concrete fireproofing.

According to Fujimoto, the project's steel design was derived from technology developed at the Kure Naval Arsenal. Located in the city of Kure in Hiroshima Prefecture, this shipyard was famous for having built the *Yamato*, the lead battleship of the Imperial Japanese Navy, launched in 1940. The prowess of the builders there was such that, after the war, their methods were shared with various steel companies in order to boost their capabilities, a demonstration of the developmental state's activities: steel had been selected by the government as an industry to be nurtured in the national interest. The *Yamato*, the pinnacle of Japanese imperialist engineering and construction, can be seen as an artifact whose techniques were inherited by Otaka's designs, which mark the demise of that imperialism.

In the late 1960s, the Kure area was still home to many expert welders who were instrumental in rationalizing the major-structure, enabling the type of sophisticated factory production that became the P in PAU. As one example, the large box-columns, which were located so as to define the overall 9.9 by 9.9-meter planning module, needed to support sections of varying height. The resulting variation in loading required different strengths and thicknesses of steel plate. Potential complications from this were addressed through a naval technique of insetting the different thicknesses inside the hollow columns, thereby maintaining a uniform exterior dimension to ease connections with beams and other elements.[13] In the factory, custom-built automatic welding machines were used to fuse the plates together. In the field, wide-flange beams were welded directly to the box-columns without intermediary gusset plates, allowing a 30 percent reduction in cost.[14]

Like the aircraft that inspired Fuller, ships were highly rationalized, and arguably a much better model for architecture than planes. Otaka's design was not just rationalized, but also highly standardized, as exemplified by the uniform box-columns, and the fact that apartments located on corners do not take advantage of their location through additional windows on the side elevation, the usual move in high-rise apartments.[15] For reasons of cost control, and perhaps social equality, the units remained as identical as possible.

Motomachi under construction, 1972. Note steel major-structure prior to fireproofing.

2 THE METABOLIST-INDUSTRIAL COMPLEX

Memorial axis, 1988

Massing and Memory

Internally, the frame design held the potential for future variations in the apartments. But looking at Motomachi, variation is also important for the massing of the frames. Responsiveness to site differences was made possible by the square plan modules, which are small in size relative to the vast site, thereby allowing them to be aggregated into bundled slender towers, or stretches of slabs, lower in height near the castle and to the south, rising to the north and along the bend in the river. The modules loosely frame the central facilities, with the group-form method breaking the project into smaller zones of program and identity. Overall, the layered planes step back in what's known as *ganko* (flying geese) formation, a type of plan organization made iconic by the seventeenth-century Katsura Imperial Villa in Kyoto, a native exemplar of group form.[16]

In 1965, historian Teiji Itoh identified architects working in a new relationship to traditional Japanese column planning. Looking to projects such as Kikutake's Sky House and Tange's Yamanashi Press and Broadcasting Center (then under construction), Itoh asserted that such designs created spatial order across the scales of architecture and city, achieved by "setting symbolic grids with specific patterns, and generating [...] space by implementing [...] components on them," a method he called "symbolic planning."[17] Motomachi seems to be another example of the idea, with its column-like tower "components" placed on an implied planning grid set at forty-five degrees to Tange's north-south axis. The components are massed in an open form that allows the axis to enter the center of the park area that is bracketed by the housing, making Otaka's project its northern anchor, aligned with the A-Bomb Dome and the Peace Museum which anchors the south, a memorial ensemble clearly visible in a large site plan. Though not part of the pedestrian experience at the level of the plaza between the museum and the cenotaph, Motomachi is visible from within the museum. In turn, the rising form of the housing is capped with linked roof gardens, originally open to the public as well as the residents, from which one can look south along the axis.[18] While the museum houses relics of the dead, Motomachi houses the living, and the axis thereby articulates the city's transformation from death to rebirth. Described by Fujimoto as the "finale" to Hiroshima's reconstruction, Motomachi is a monument to this conclusion that looks toward the future.[19]

The rotation of the implied grid is not essential to this symbolic alignment. But along with the *ganko* stepping, it allows the square modules to be packed efficiently into the site in a way that gives each apartment either a southeast or southwest exposure, providing good sunlight and shade over the seasons. This regularity is unexpected from a site plan that at first glance seems disordered—and would not have been possible with a perimeter scheme set orthogonal to Tange's axis, which would have resulted in large numbers of apartments facing either east or west. To make best use of his two orientations, Otaka reuses the apartment planning from Harumi, with the south-oriented areas containing the main living spaces, and service spaces toward the north, connected to the corridors.

Katsura's *ganko* plan was also environmental in intent, with the multiple exposures of its stepped rooms providing better daylighting as well as cross ventilation. Perhaps with this prototype in mind, Otaka and Maki write in "Collective Form" that the geometry of a group-form element is "meaningless" unless derived from "environmental needs."[20] But the orientation of Motomachi's units corresponds to a symbolic interpretation of the project in a way that expands the definition of

top: Katsura Imperial Villa, *ganko* plan

bottom: Motomachi, typical plans

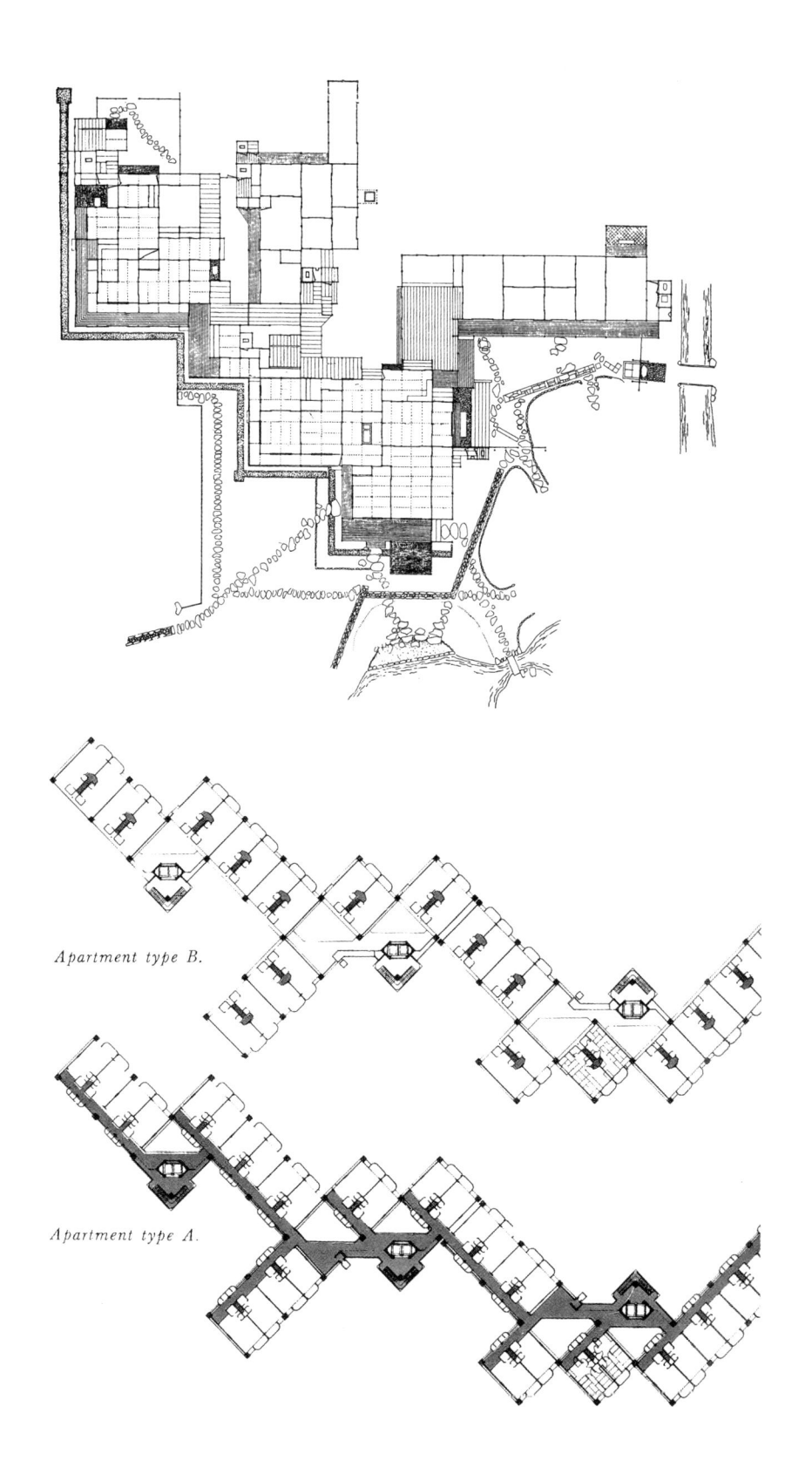

Apartment type B.

Apartment type A.

SYMBOLIC PLANNING: MOTOMACHI APARTMENTS, 1968–

164   2 THE METABOLIST-INDUSTRIAL COMPLEX

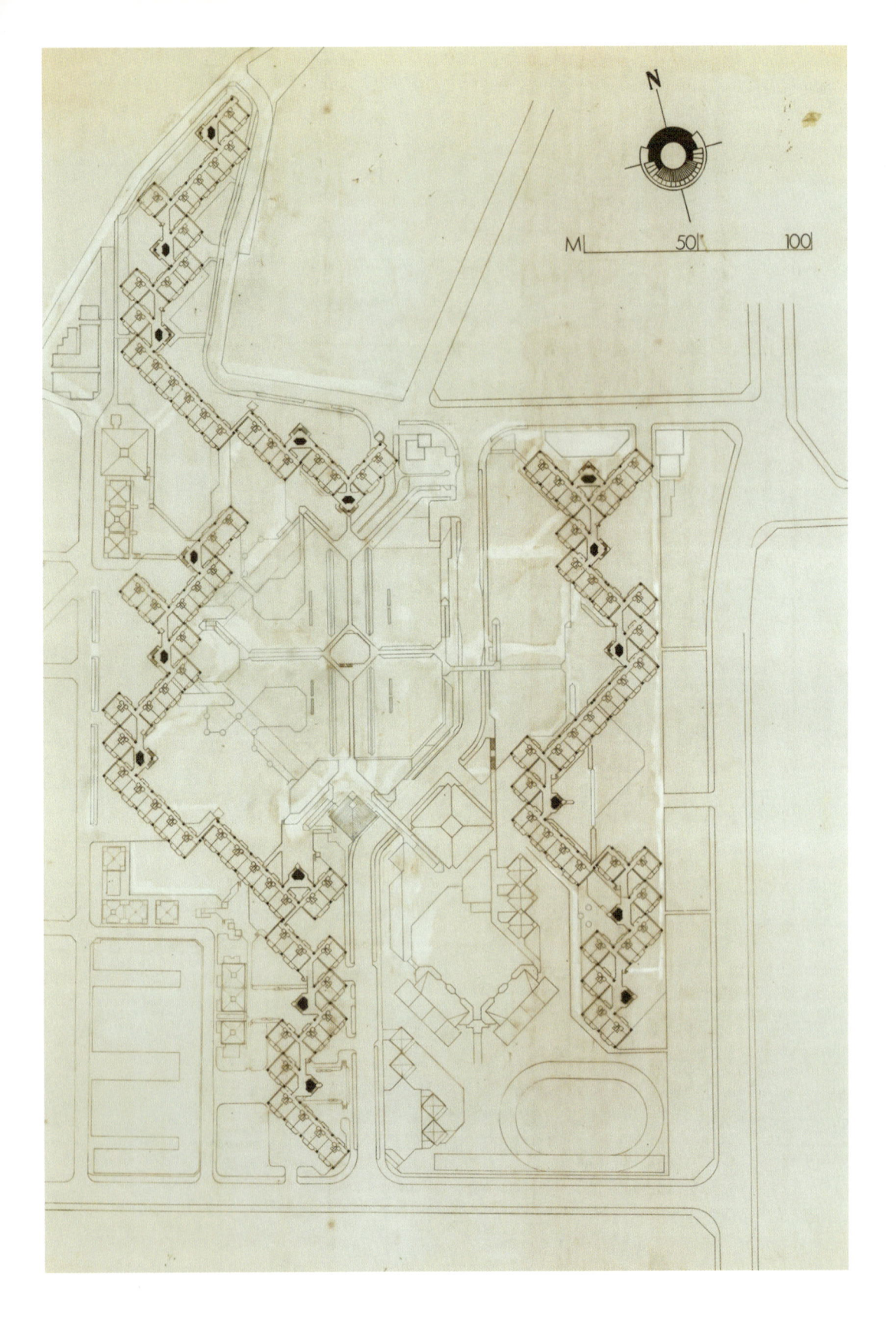

environmental beyond the bioclimatic to include the historical context. By orienting all of the apartments in a southerly direction, they all face into the core of the city's destruction and rebuilding, a thematization of view direction consistent with Tange's sightline axis aimed at the A-Bomb Dome.[21]

Vertical Neighborhoods

Fujimoto writes that Motomachi "is not an apartment building; it is a multilevel street, which must be designed so as to produce a mass resulting from ordered public spaces."[22] The architect Adam Staniland has documented this order, showing how Motomachi's plan is subdivided into zones formed by groupings of the square tower modules, with each zone corresponding to a residents' association. With seventeen in total, each served by its own elevator and stair core, the associations take responsibility for cleaning, informal policing, and tending to a section of roof garden, now limited to residents only.[23] There is thus a direct relation between group form and the form of groups.

The effectiveness of these associations may be partly due to the initial residents. In his 1957 essay on Harumi, Otaka wrote that the project's aspiration was to create a "spirit of cooperation" inspired by the "downtown apartments where people live frugally with an open heart." Unlike Harumi, though, many of Motomachi's residents were not a speculative population, as they had previously lived together. With many coming from the A-Bomb Slum, it seems they brought with them the ethos Otaka admired, having acted collectively in the slum to organize things such as fire protection, cleaning, and cram schools for their children.[24] This spirit seems to have helped make the

left: Motomachi, site plan

above: 60th Anniversary of the Bombing of Hiroshima, 2005. Note Motomachi roofscape in background.

SYMBOLIC PLANNING: MOTOMACHI APARTMENTS, 1968–

165

project's "streets in the sky" successful as safe and sociable spaces, contradicting the negative assessments of this type of shared gallery circulation as implemented in housing in the West, such as Pruitt-Igoe and Robin Hood Gardens.[25]

Also studied by Staniland, some corridor areas at Motomachi are extensions of the apartment interiors. This phenomenon of extension is enhanced by exterior storage closets, designed by Otaka, and prefigured by the appropriation of public space in Japan's residential streets located on the ground, where plants, seating, and other items act to expand the space of a home beyond its walls.[26] Artificial streets, as at Fort l'Empereur, Marseilles, and Harumi, are typically part of artificial land.[27]

Transition

Today, some of the older residents of the project worry that the cohesion of the vertical neighborhoods is weakening. The apartments have become popular with Chinese, apparently often students, and alliances and customs are changing.[28] While these changes might be welcomed, a challenging transformation for this project and for the rest of Japan is the aging of the population. As of 2017, almost 28 percent of the country was over 65, and by 2060 it's projected to be close to 40 percent, the consequence of a declining birth rate and among the world's longest average life spans: 87.1 years for women and 81 years for men.[29] Since its completion, Motomachi has always housed a significant proportion of elderly people, and now almost half of the residents are elderly.[30]

above: Motomachi resident associations

right and following: Motomachi (2010)

SYMBOLIC PLANNING: MOTOMACHI APARTMENTS, 1968–

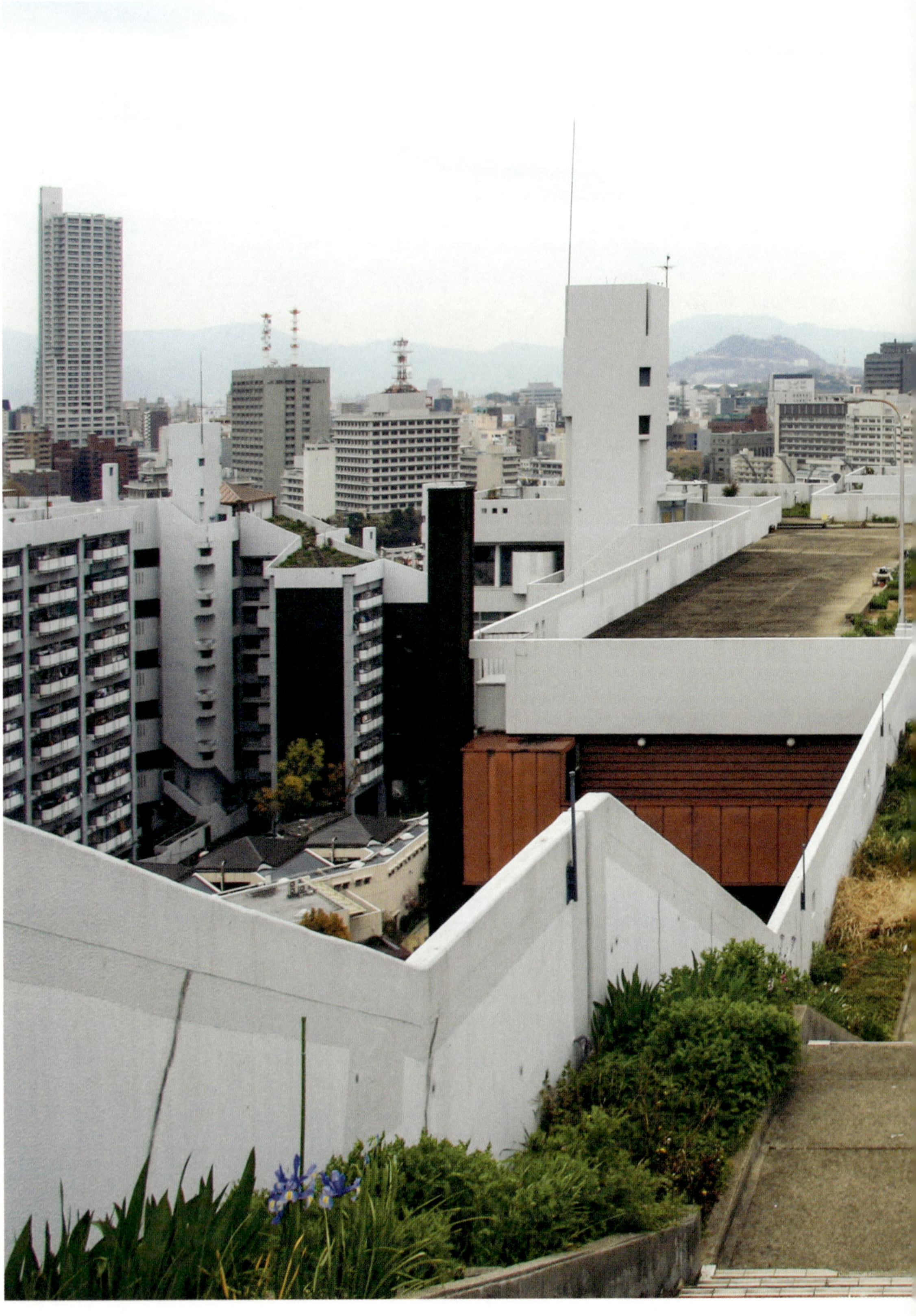

SYMBOLIC PLANNING: MOTOMACHI APARTMENTS, 1968–

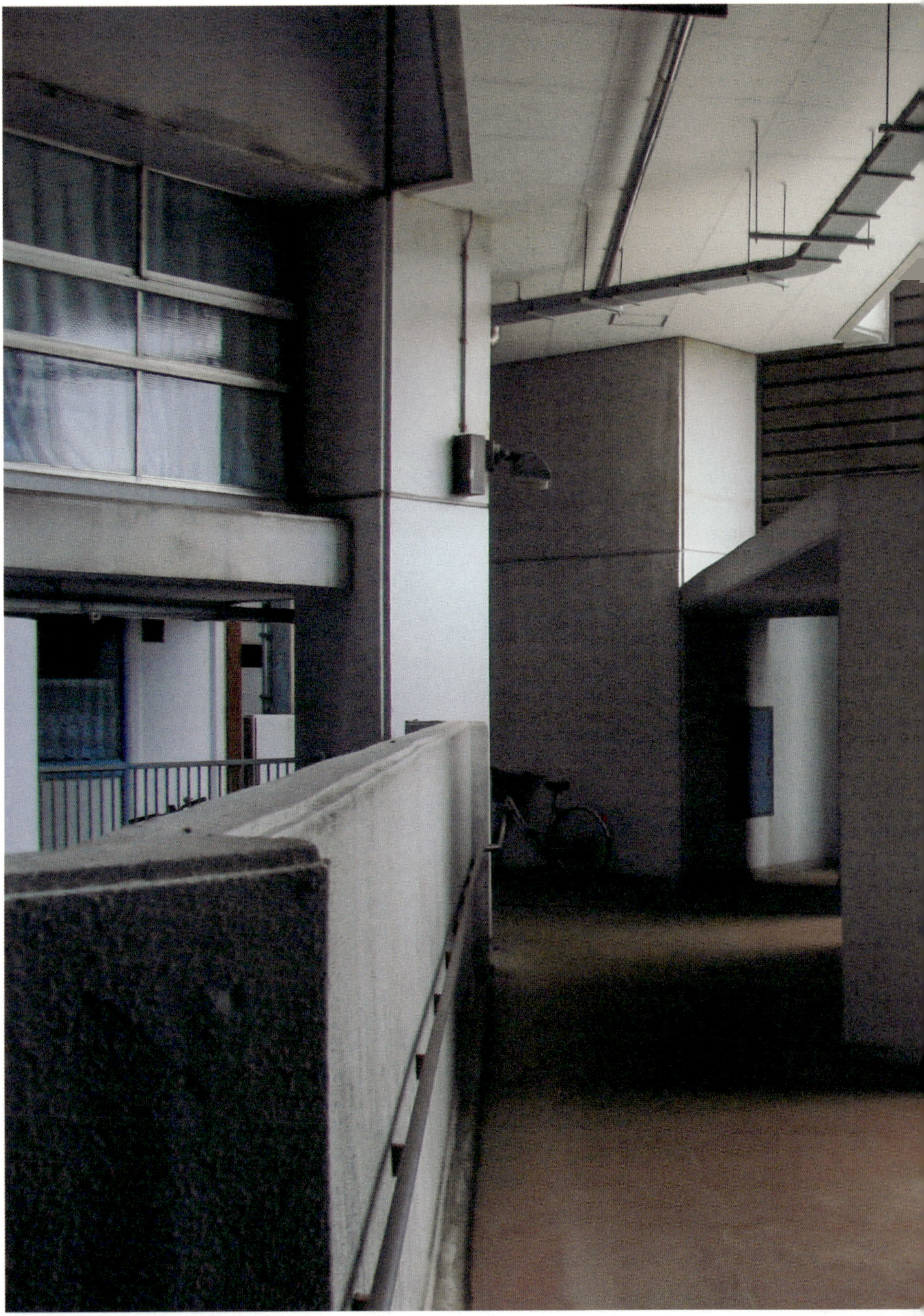

SYMBOLIC PLANNING: MOTOMACHI APARTMENTS, 1968–

2DK 結合前　　　　　　　　　　　　　　　　　　　　結合後

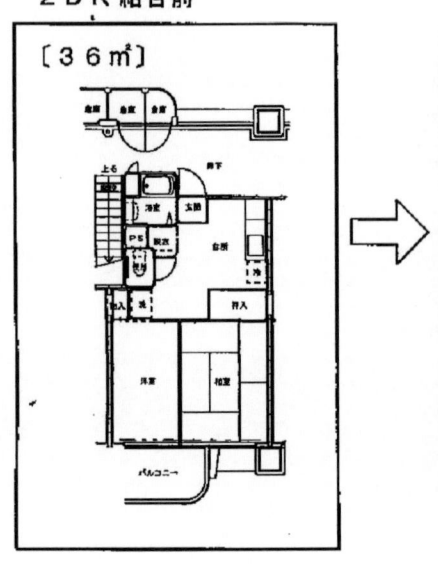

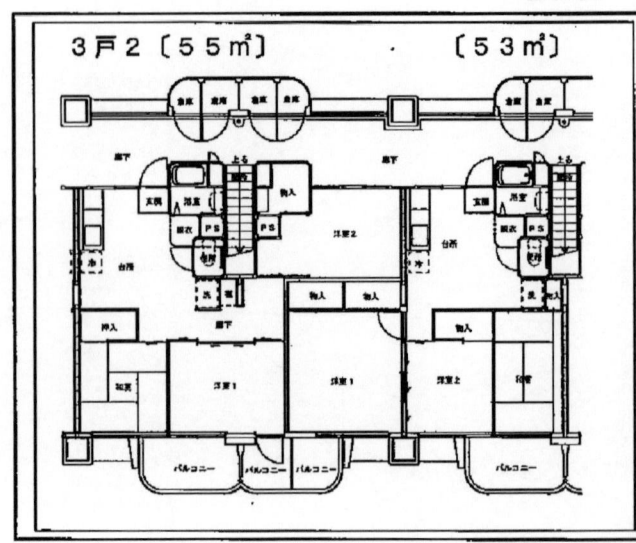

[36㎡]　　　　　　　　　　3戸2 [55㎡]　　　　[53㎡]

3K 結合前　　　　　　　　　　　　　　　　　　　結合後

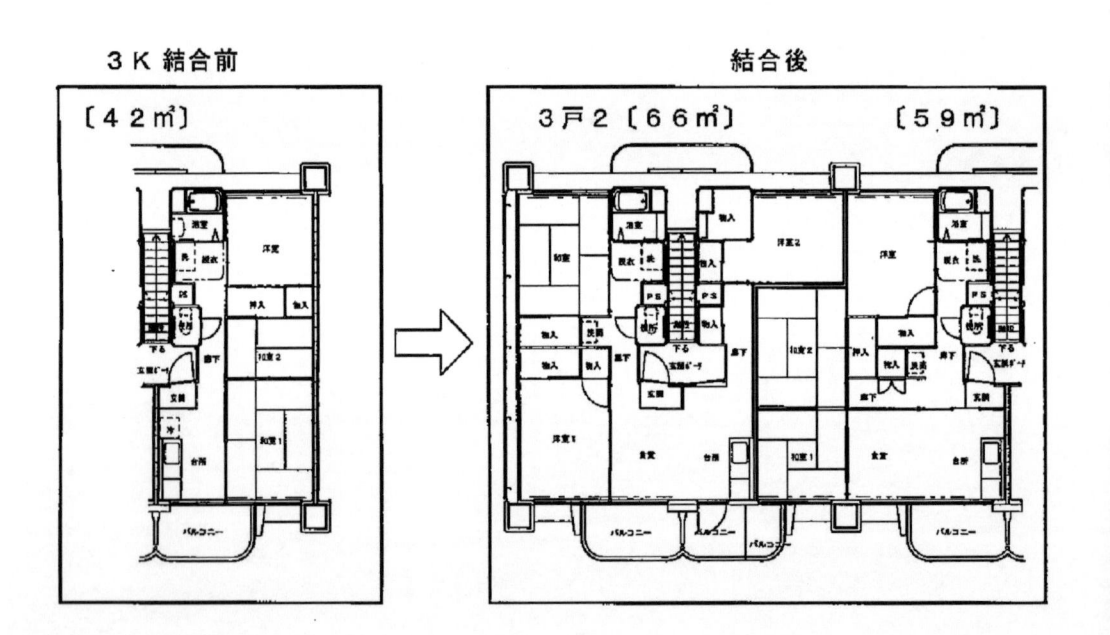

[42㎡]　　　　　　　　　　3戸2 [66㎡]　　　　[59㎡]

2　THE METABOLIST-INDUSTRIAL COMPLEX

2戸1 [72㎡]

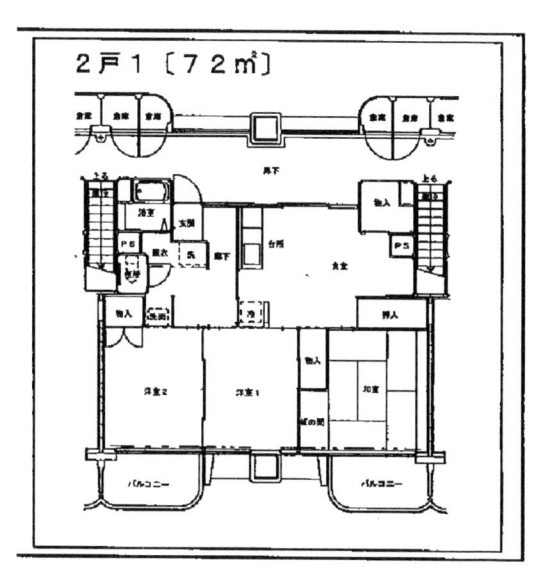

This demographic has difficulty with the stairs needed to access half of the units. Despite the skip-floor system providing flexibility within the double-height bays of the frame and more sociable corridors, it of course relies on able stair-climbers, who have been decreasing in number. Competition for corridor-level apartments is strong, and elderly residents are now required to have a note from their physician in order to receive priority for these units.[31]

Fuller believed that livingry should be on a rental basis, so as to better control systematic renovation with updated technology.[32] In a similarly top-down fashion, the Hiroshima Housing Authority (HHA), owner and operator of the project, initiated a comprehensive renovation of Motomachi in 2000.[33] Hiroshima's younger citizens see the housing as outdated, and the HHA hopes to make it appealing to new generations, and to better help the elderly. The work spans from removing asbestos, to updating bathrooms and kitchens, to minor-structure alterations that produce bigger units—just as Otaka intended—with the original 36- and 42-square-meter sizes now ranging from 53 to 72. While each square module of major-structure originally contained two units, there are now units that extend through more than one module, or that have partly combined with the other unit within a module. Completion of the entire renovation is slated for 2022, with the next renovation anticipated to occur around 2050.

The HHA has found these changes to be more difficult to make than expected. Socially, one initial issue was negotiations with residents over being relocated within the housing to allow the work to be undertaken, particularly for unit expansions. Technically, much of the original infill construction was precast concrete, used for fabricating elements such as bathrooms and the storage closets. In earlier phases of the construction, the bathrooms were installed and then fixed in place by site-cast concrete floor slabs, making apartments difficult to renovate. Fujimoto notes that this sequence was improved in subsequent phases, rationalized so that precast parts came in after the floor was poured, simplifying installation and easing renovation, a change that improved what should be called the design's metabolism.[34]

Through the use of steel-framed modules, PAU brought to Hiroshima a system for variations in space that has enabled variations in time. Though imperfectly and modestly, the apartment changes indicate the validity of transitional planning, though this can only really be substantiated by the quality of life to be found now at Motomachi. Located in a city that cannot be disassociated from a history of death and rebirth, transformation defines Otaka's design as both symbol and ongoing operation.

Apartment metabolism: planned expansion of original Motomachi units, c. 2000

following: Renovated Motomachi unit (2010)

SYMBOLIC PLANNING: MOTOMACHI APARTMENTS, 1968–

173

1. See Yuki Tanaka, "Photographer Fukushima Kikujiro—Confronting Images of Atomic Bomb Survivors," *The Asia-Pacific Journal* 9, issue 43, no. 4 (October 24, 2011), https://apjjf.org/2011/9/43/Yuki-Tanaka/3623/article.html. Masaya Fujimoto mentions the area containing 4,000 households, indicating a population much larger than 3,000 people. However, it's unclear how this number of households was split between those in the area who were squatting and those legally living in government-constructed barracks, both of which were cleared for Otaka's design. See Masaya Fujimoto, "Two Apartment Settlements in Hiroshima," *The Japan Architect* (August 1973): 34. It should also be noted that *hibakusha* and Koreans were targets of discrimination, and some residents of the slum were both.

2. The claim to uniqueness could be challenged in the face of Nagasaki's bombing. Yet Hiroshima's political elite insisted on their city's unique status as the first to be bombed in order to position it as a "peace city," which proved to be an effective strategy in gaining support for reconstruction, as discussed later in this section. For an excellent analysis of Hiroshima's postwar positioning, see Ran Zwigenberg, *Hiroshima: The Origins of Global Memory Culture* (Cambridge: Cambridge University Press, 2014), 23–64.

3. Motomachi, as well as Chojuen, make no appearance in Zhongjie Lin's *Kenzo Tange and the Metabolist Movement* (2010), nor in Rem Koolhaas and Hans Ulrich Obrist's *Project Japan* (2011). They are also absent from all major surveys of modern housing by Western authors of which I am aware.

4. Masato Otaka, in Takashi Minohara, Hiroshi Matsukuma, Naoto Nakashima, *Ōtaka Masato no shigoto* [The work of Masato Otaka] (Tokyo: X-Knowledge, 2014), 166. Translation by Tomoyo Nakamura.

5. Masaya Fujimoto, "Architect Otaka Masato's Messages for the Next Generation of Youths," in *PAU: Uniting Architecture and Society—The Approach of OTAKA Masato* (Tokyo: National Archives of Modern Architecture, 2016), 4.

6. Cherie Wendelken, "Putting Metabolism Back in Place: The Making of a Radically Decontextualized Architecture in Japan," in *Anxious Modernisms*, eds. Sarah Williams Goldhagen and Réjean Legault (Cambridge, MA: The MIT Press, 2001), 280.

7. Logics coming from site considerations can be found, but they're generic. For example, Isozaki's City in the Air was a rejection of Tokyo's seemingly incurable chaos on the ground, seen through his interest in designing architecture lofted above the nation's 31-meter height limit.

8. Regarding Hiroshima's adoption of the peace narrative, see Zwigenberg, *Hiroshima*, 34, and Robert Jay Lifton, *Death in Life: Survivors of Hiroshima* [1968] (Chapel Hill: The University of North Carolina Press, 1991), 271. The characterizations of Hiroshima as a purely military target and the atomic bomb as a very large conventional explosive were made by US President Harry S. Truman. See "August 6, 1945: Statement by the President Announcing the Use of the A-Bomb at Hiroshima," https://millercenter.org/the-presidency/presidential-speeches/august-6-1945-statement-president-announcing-use-bomb.

9. See Zwigenberg, *Hiroshima*, 42.
10. Granary reference: see Hajime Yatsuka, "The Social Ambition of the Architect and the Rising Nation," in *Kenzō Tange: Architecture for the World*, eds. Seng Kuan and Yukio Lippit (Zurich: Lars Müller Publishers, 2012), 47. As discussed on page 323 of this book, this granary reference is also an Ise Shrine reference.
11. See Yoshifumi Fukushima, "Redevelopment of the Motomachi district," (1995) https://www.hiroshimapeacemedia.jp/?p=27437.
12. Fujimoto, "Two Apartment Settlements," 40.
13. This technique may have been borrowed from hull construction where, aside from structural requirements, plate thicknesses were varied for armoring. See Janusz Skulski and Stefan Draminski, *Battleships Yamato and Musashi* (London, New York: Bloomsbury, 2017), 85–86.
14. Masaya Fujimoto, in conversation with the author, April 23, 2010.
15. On some elevations, very small clerestory windows do appear.
16. The *ganko* formation at the villa is discussed by Arata Isozaki in his essay "The Diagonal Strategy: Katsura as envisioned by 'Enshu's taste'," in *Katsura Imperial Villa*, ed. Virginia Ponciroli [2005] (London: Phaidon Press, 2011), 19.
17. Teiji Itoh, "Dai-ni dentōron no taidō" [Signs of a second dispute over tradition], *Kenchiku bunka* 20, no. 22 (April 1965): 81. Translation by Riyo Namigata.
18. A pedestrian's difficulty perceiving the axis passing beyond the dome to Motomachi is due in part to street-level visual continuity being obstructed by several buildings. One of these was the Hiroshima Municipal Stadium, home to the Hiroshima Toyo Carp baseball team until the stadium was demolished in 2012. However, in a testament to the memorial continuity of the axis even with obstructions, the stadium field was reported to be haunted by ghosts of the bombing's victims after dark, as was related by a local guide to Peter Eisenman upon attending a Carp home game with Arata Isozaki, sometime in the late 1970s or early '80s. See Thomas Daniell, *An Anatomy of Influence* (London: AA Publications, 2018), 64.
19. Fujimoto, "Two Apartment Settlements," 33.
20. Fumihiko Maki and Masato Ohtaka, "Collective Form—Three Paradigms," in Maki, *Investigations in Collective Form* [1964] (St. Louis, MO: School of Architecture, Washington University in St. Louis, 2004), 14.
21. While Otaka's attention to southerly orientation of the apartments may seem normal for good residential planning, such planning is absent or inconsistent in numerous other relevant housing designs, from Tange's housing over Tokyo Bay, to Senri New Town, Sakaide, Sachio Otani's Kawaramachi Housing (1972), and ASTM's Ashiyahama Seaside Town (1979). This is not to say that these projects give no consideration to solar planning, but rather that they use different concepts of beneficial orientation and massing.
22. Fujimoto, "Two Apartment Settlements," 40.
23. Paul Adam Staniland, "What Does it Mean to Build a Street in the Sky in Japan?" (B.Arch diss., University of Glasgow, 2007), 10.
24. See Tanaka, "Photographer Fukushima Kikujiro." Numerous fires occurred in the area over the years of its existence.
25. Pruitt-Igoe in St. Louis, Missouri, USA, designed by Minoru Yamasaki and opened in 1954, began to be demolished in 1972. While the project is often seen as the exemplar of failed modernist good intentions—in features such as its gallery corridors meant to double as play spaces, and so on—its failure significantly lies in deterioration due to long-deferred maintenance as a consequence of economic changes, rather than in its architectural concepts. See *The Pruitt-Igoe Myth*, directed by Chad Freidrichs (Unicorn Stencil, 2011), http://www.pruitt-igoe.com. Robin Hood Gardens in London, designed by Alison and Peter Smithson and opened in 1972, began to be demolished in 2017 after much controversy over its architectural merits, including its similar "streets in the sky" corridors. The project was also arguably a victim of deferred maintenance, strategically in the interest of redevelopment for an area of London now far more valuable than it was in the 1970s.
26. Staniland, "What Does it Mean," 39.
27. My photos here of Motomachi in 2010 certainly don't show any street-like liveliness whatsoever. Photo opportunities arose only on a tour led by the HHA, who had selected our itinerary through a section of the giant project, then partly under renovation. Regarding "artificial streets," Le Corbusier famously labeled the corridors in his Unités as "interior streets."
28. See Staniland, "What Does it Mean," 64–65. As of 2013, no official demographic information was available from the HHA on the development's residents, as communicated by Sachiko Komatsu (International Relations Division, Citizens Affairs Bureau, The City of Hiroshima) in an email exchange with the author, April 22, 2013.
29. See *Statistical Handbook of Japan 2018*, http://www.stat.go.jp/english/data/handbook/pdf/2018all.pdf#page=23. In a 2015 comparison of elderly populations, meaning people 65 or older, the percentage of total population for the USA was 14.6 compared to Japan's 26.6.
30. Staniland, "What Does it Mean," 65.
31. Sachiko Komatsu, in conversation with the author, April 8, 2010.
32. See Buckminster Fuller, *Ideas and Integrities: A Spontaneous Autobiographical Disclosure* [1963] (New York: Collier, 1974), 299.
33. A more limited renovation was already underway at Chojuen, having started in 1992. It was completed in 2013.
34. Fujimoto, "Two Apartment Settlements," 39.

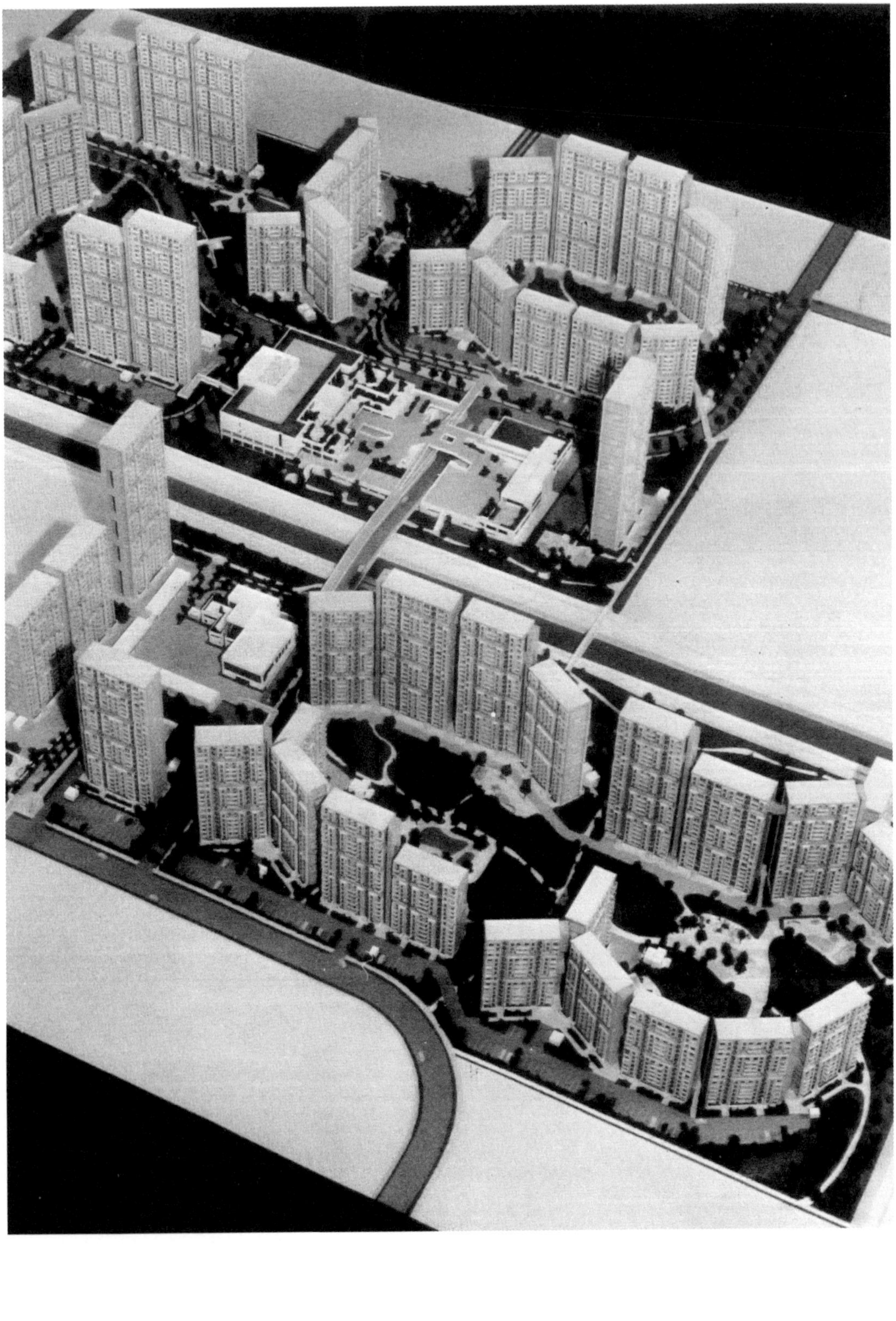

Megastructured: Ashiyahama Seaside Town, 1972–

In *The Language of Post-Modern Architecture*, critic Charles Jencks writes that "Modern Architecture died in St. Louis, Missouri on July 15, 1972 at 3:32 pm"— the moment at which the vast Pruitt-Igoe housing was dynamited.[1] In Japan, on January 1, 1973, the ASTM design team submitted its proposal for the "Competition for the Ashiyahama High-Rise Housing Complex using Industrialized Construction Methods." ASTM stands for Ashiyahama Shin'nittetsu Takenaka Matsushita, and this team, led by Takenaka, is an emblematic formation of the Metabolist-industrial complex, with Shin'nittetsu being the Nippon Steel Corporation, and Matsushita better known outside Japan as Panasonic. On the coast of Ashiya City in Hyogo Prefecture, near Kobe, modern architecture was alive and well.[2]

To Jencks's announcement of the death of modern architecture can be added another death usually placed around the same time: that of Metabolism. With deteriorating integrity identified in its consumerist designs for Expo '70, the movement's death knell is considered to be the 1973 OAPEC oil embargo. The embargo—a punishment of pro-Israel nations by Arab oil producers—was a massive blow to Japan's limited natural resources for energy and construction materials, and is also seen as marking the end of the era of rapid growth. A 1973 article in the *Asahi Shimbun*, one of Japan's major newspapers, reported that Tange was at the time suffering from a lack of domestic commissions, and had as a result turned to the Middle East for new clients. This pivot is ascribed to Tange having been shut out of new work in Japan by the *zenekon*.[3] Apparently "too big to fail" within the recession caused by the embargo, the *zenekon* had increased in prominence and capability since Expo '70, and had come to monopolize large new projects.[4] However, as noted, Takenaka was then also actively

Ashiyahama model, c.1973

following: ASTM, Ashiyahama Seaside Town, Ashiya, 1979 (2010)

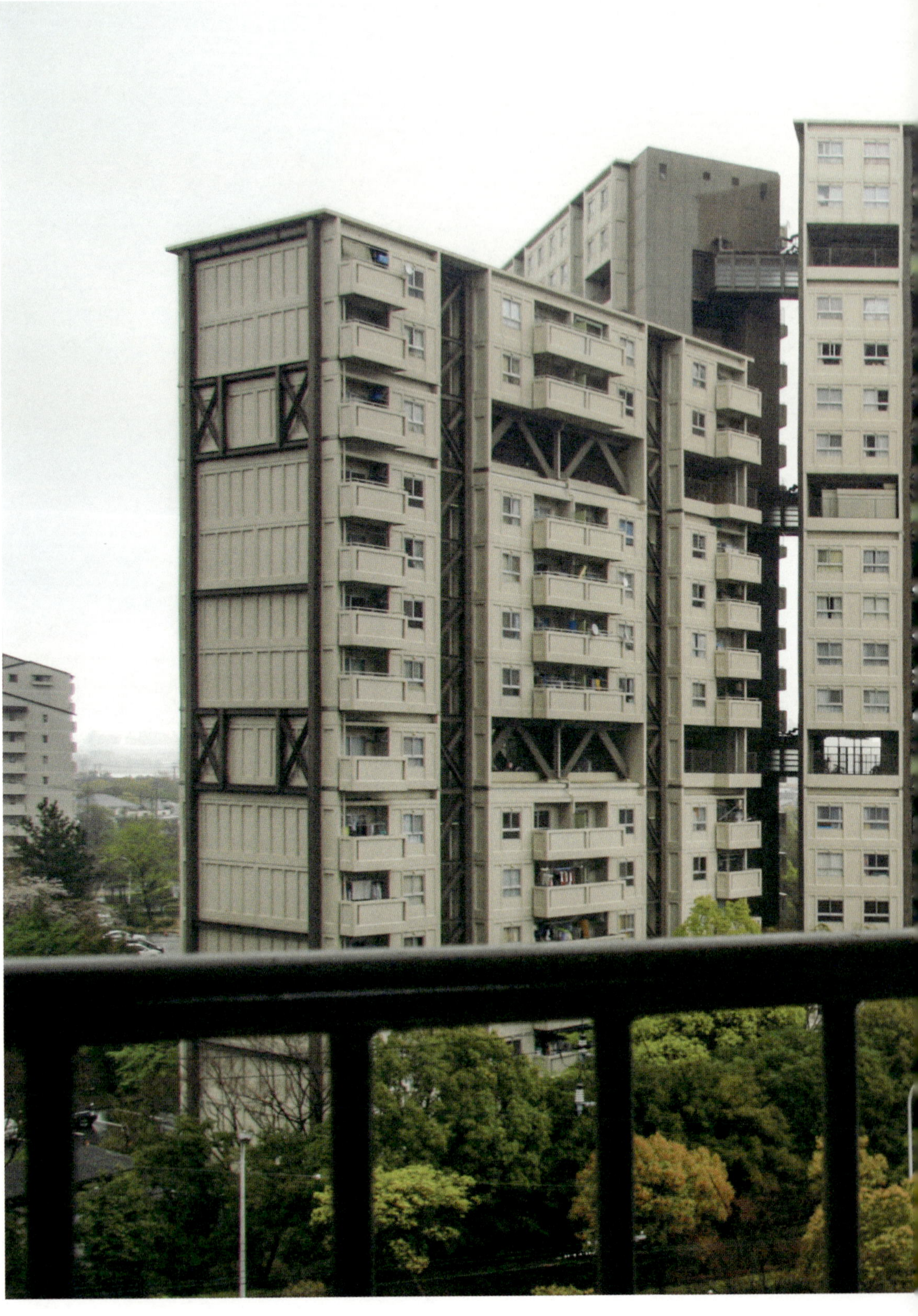

MEGASTRUCTURED: ASHIYAHAMA SEASIDE TOWN, 1972–

absorbing Metabolist principles, thereby problematizing the idea of the movement's death. This death would be plausible only if we insisted that Metabolism had to be designed by the original Metabolists.

In addition to the ASTM design's similarity to Arata Isozaki's Joint Core System (1960), we find Metabolists closely entwined with supporting the team's proposal. Takenaka had been the main contractor for Otaka's Chojuen Apartments, and Otaka was a prominent member of the Ashiyahama jury, along with Yositika Utida, his colleague from the Artificial Land Committee. Maki informally consulted with ASTM during the competition phase on issues ranging from site planning to shipping logistics.[5]

Completed in 1979, Ashiyahama is a close descendant of the major-structure lineage from Harumi to Chojuen and Motomachi. Yet it obstructs the realization of a transitional type as developed by its predecessors, even as it may appear to be the type's apotheosis. Through this failure, it illuminates the difference between artificial land and megastructure. Perhaps the most megastructural housing ever built, its design problems were anticipated in theory: as Maki and Otaka wrote in their definition of megastructure, "If the megaform becomes rapidly obsolete, as well it might, especially in those schemes that do not allow for two kinds of change cycle, it will be a great weight about the neck of urban society."[6] At Ashiyahama, that urban society is the people who live in it.

Demonstration Project

The competition was initiated by MOC, and as suggested by "Industrialized Construction Methods" in the name, it was committed to finding advanced techniques for delivering quality housing in quantity. In 1971, MOC had in fact announced a quest for "quality-" over "quantity-oriented" design, with the goal of providing "one room per person" in housing nationwide. The previous target, from 1961, of "one housing unit per household" had been met, mostly thanks to the 2DK.[7] Achieving both quality and quantity was the ideal.

The Building Center of Japan (BCJ), a branch of MOC, was responsible for running the competition. Founded in 1965, BCJ's mission was to research and evaluate building techniques for directing new codes and policies.[8] Such research was a main part of the Ashiyahama agenda, along with demonstration of the 1968 Plan's requirement for integrated residential services as well as new seismic codes for high-rise construction. High-rise living was seen as a key way to provide "social overhead capital," the absence of which was seen by Prime Minister Tanaka as impairing Japan's health.[9]

The site on which the competitors had to work was empty, and in fact was new. Approximately 20 hectares, bisected by the Miya River, it was a land reclamation project that had been completed in 1969. The twenty-two participating teams were required to provide 3,400 units, about two-thirds of which would be rental, and the rest privately owned.

System Building

ASTM began work on its proposal in May of 1972. The massing that developed was composed of fifty-two apartment towers, ranging from fourteen to twenty-nine stories, split between the two halves of the site, and grouped into clusters framing abundant parks and shared facilities such as schools and a shopping area. A waste-treatment plant and incinerator were

top: Arata Isozaki, Joint Core System proposal, Tokyo, 1960

bottom: Ashiyahama site plan, zoned by owner/operator

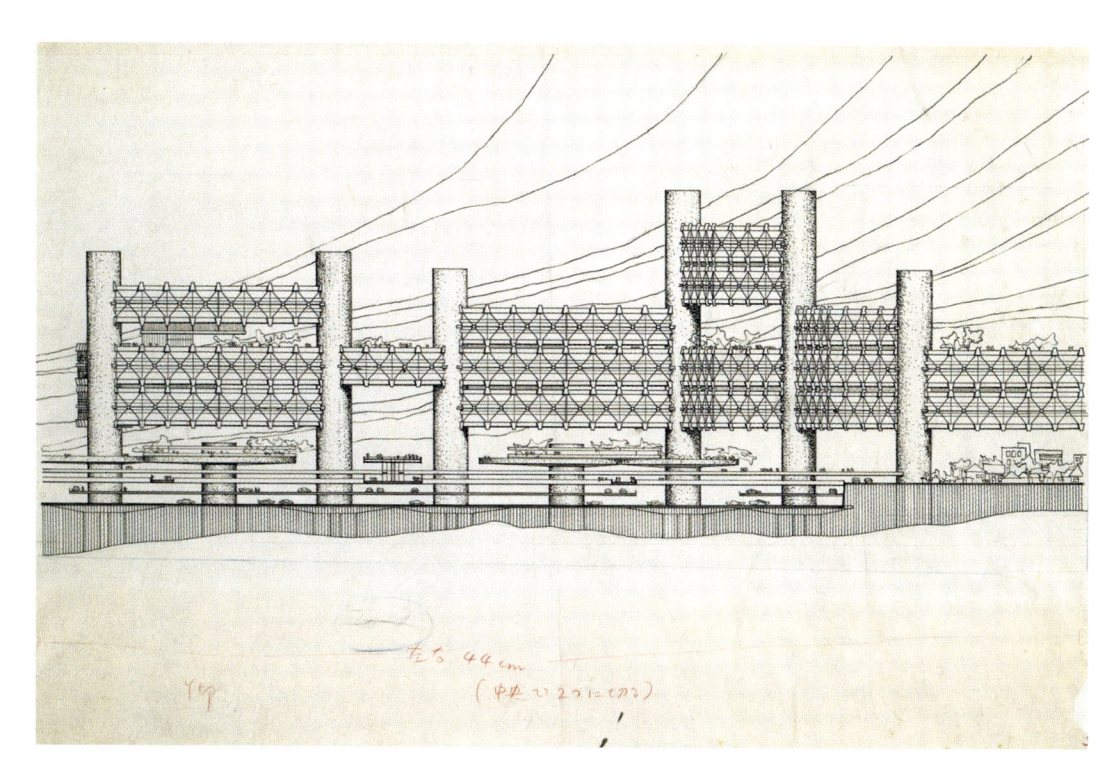

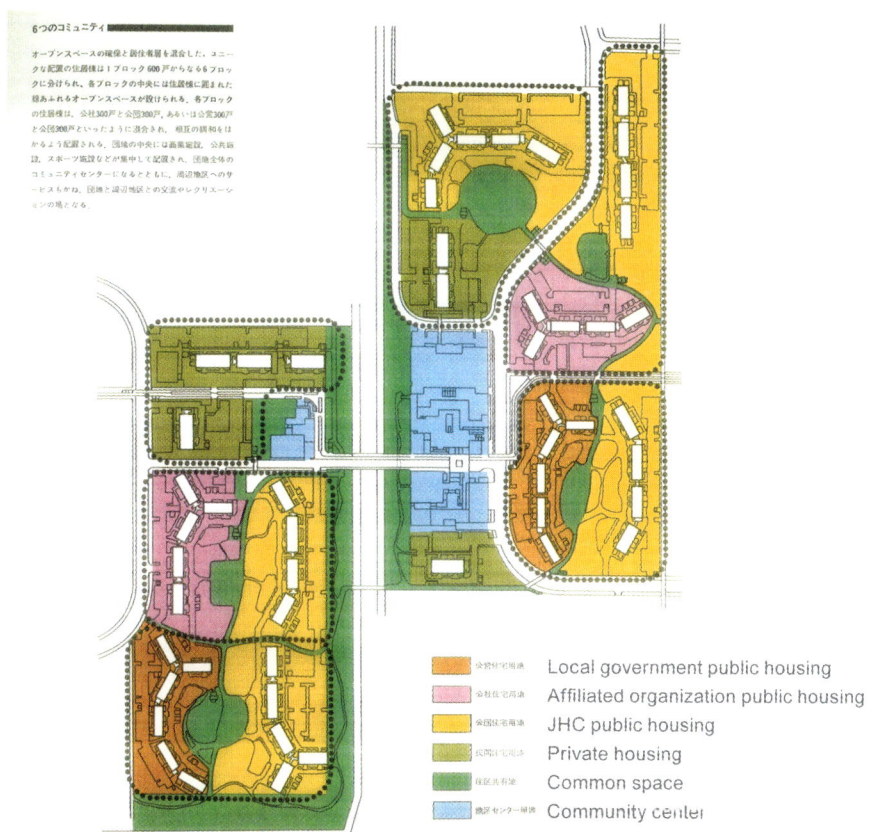

	Local government public housing
	Affiliated organization public housing
	JHC public housing
	Private housing
	Common space
	Community center

MEGASTRUCTURED: ASHIYAHAMA SEASIDE TOWN, 1972–

プレイルーム
(Play room)

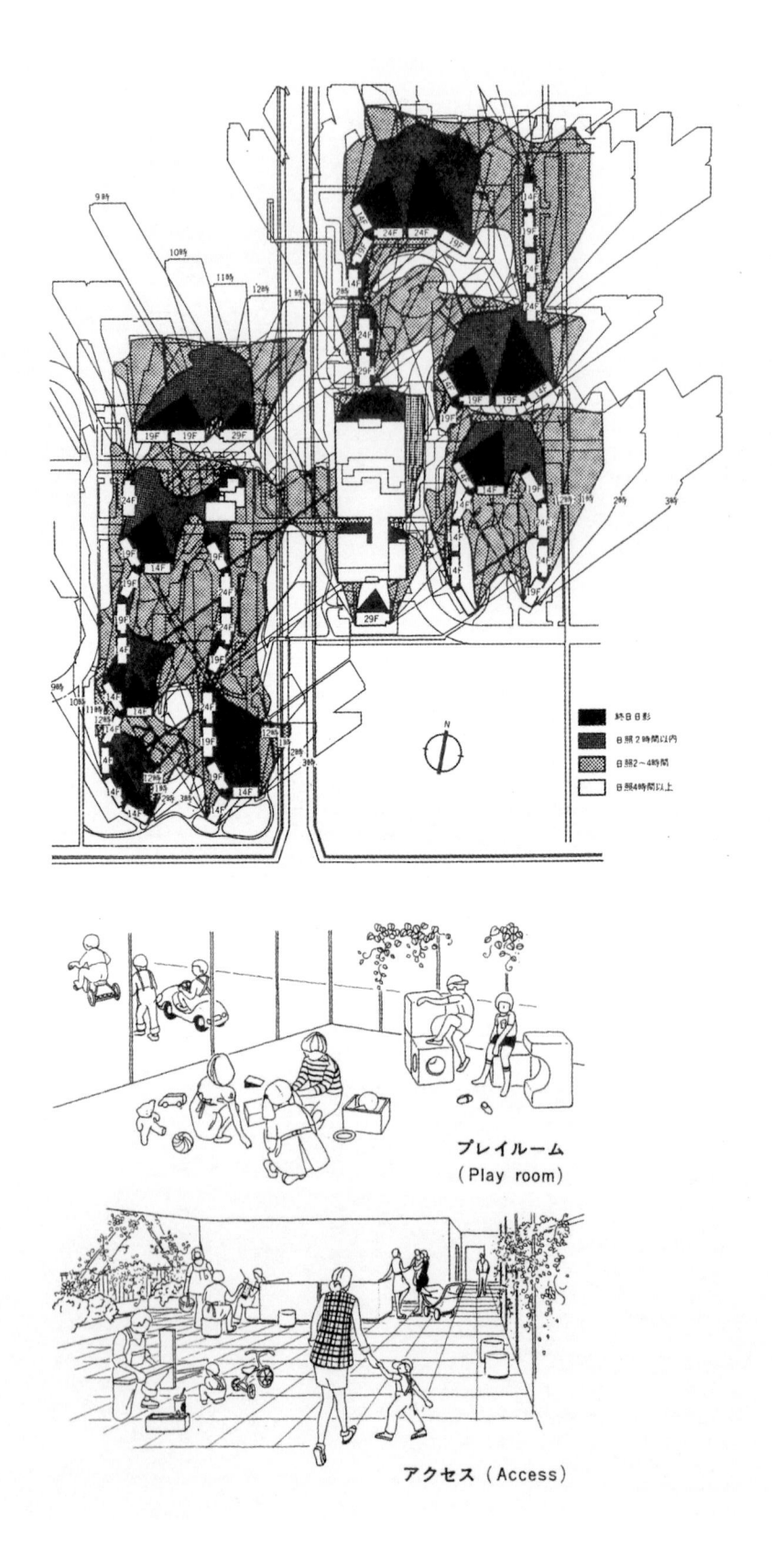

アクセス (Access)

2 THE METABOLIST-INDUSTRIAL COMPLEX

also included. The clusters were assigned to four different operators for the apartments: Hyogo Municipality, Hyogo Prefectural Housing Corporation, JHC, and ASTM itself. Regulations stemming from the 1968 Plan aimed to control the overshadowing of existing buildings by new, an injustice or simple carelessness that the team worked to avoid. Diagrams in the submission show that great attention was paid to the massing's solar impact on itself as well, with seasonal shadow plans and shading masks demonstrating each tower's "sunshine rights," allowing a prescribed minimum of daily sun.[10]

Tadatoshi Asano, the former director of Takenaka's housing division who led the ASTM team, says he had been a close follower of Otaka's community planning, especially his work in Hiroshima.[11] ASTM's major-structure approach is indicative of this, but with a typical frame so big that its steel-truss columns and beams contain the corridors and stairs for accessing units.[12] The frame defines voids four-stories high, infilled by precast concrete apartments stacked and bolted to the steel. Elevators stop only at every fifth level, with people then walking through the structure, going either up or down as many as two flights of stairs to get to their apartments. It may be the most ambitious skip system ever built.

The beam corridors were to play a key role, through providing sky gardens to cure pathologies associated with high-rise living, such as lack of community spaces and play areas, mothers isolated from friends and the outside world, and anxiety over escape routes in the event of disaster. Occurring at the elevator floors, and so distributed up the height of each tower, the sky gardens link to secondary means of egress within a given tower, and often to multiple adjoining towers,

left: Sunshine plan (top) and sky garden activities (bottom)

above: Redundant emergency egress

following: Apartment life-cycle planning

MEGASTRUCTURED: ASHIYAHAMA SEASIDE TOWN, 1972–

Private Space
プライベート スペース

独身
Single

夫婦＋子供(6−19才)
Couple + child
(6–19 yrs old)

18 app.

住戸計画

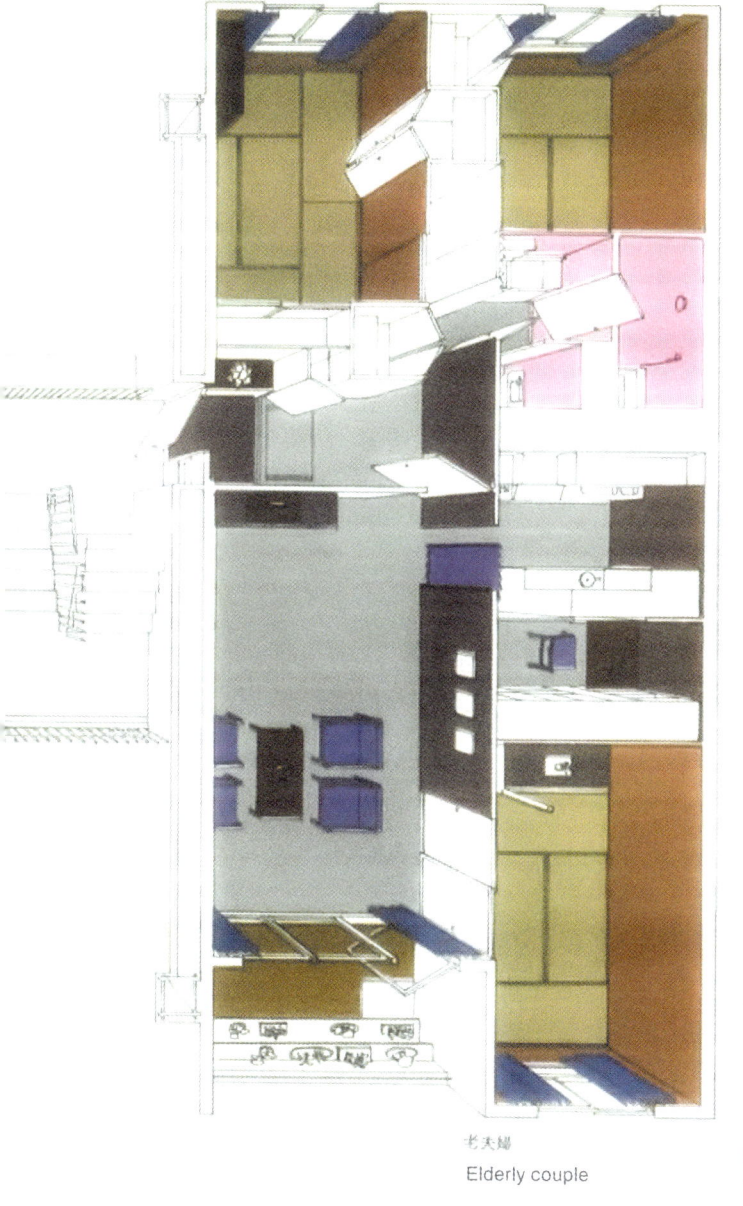

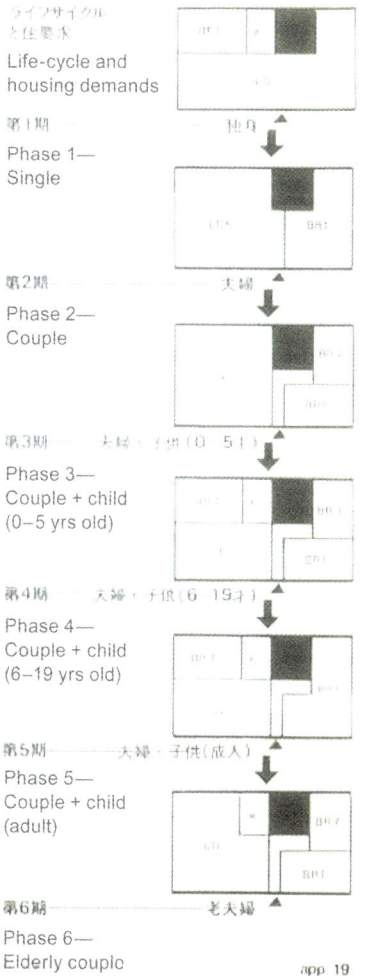

住居棟は、空中公園の設置を可能にした純鉄骨構造とPCa板による新しい架構体を採用することにより、柱・梁のない広々とした自由なスペースが得られる。住居は2LDK～3LDK(67㎡～110㎡)、2住戸1階段、1床4戸形式で各戸が独立しているため、プライバシーが守られ居室もよく、日照・通風も十分で物理的にも快適な環境であり、またライフサイクルに合わせて自由に間仕切りができるよう、移動可能な間仕切壁を採用して家族構成の変化に対応している。住居棟はエレベーターコアで2棟がつながり、さらに連絡デッキひびの橋とつらなっている。かしこらに快適な生活環境を創出し、かつ可能ならしめ、公民共同によるトータル管理共同の設置を図り、各自の床・柱・壁・階段で区画を割って配当の空き容器として利用できるように計画している。

Elderly couple

Life-cycle and housing demands

Phase 1—
Single

Phase 2—
Couple

Phase 3—
Couple + child
(0–5 yrs old)

Phase 4—
Couple + child
(6–19 yrs old)

Phase 5—
Couple + child
(adult)

Phase 6—
Elderly couple

MEGASTRUCTURED: ASHIYAHAMA SEASIDE TOWN, 1972–

thereby creating ample means of escape. Other representations submitted to the jury make clear that each giant frame, beyond just the sky gardens, was seen as an occupiable trellis, with model photos and section diagrams showing vegetation spilling over and climbing up the steelwork. One rendering shows the towers totally obscured by trees in one of the parks, suggesting that the mature plantings would hide the relentless trusses.

Though hardly noticeable, the dimensions of the trusswork do vary. With most units ranging from about 51 to 83 square meters (as seen in the plan diagram on page 130), depths and widths of the frames differ between towers to accommodate the varied apartments, assembled from large precast panels for slabs, envelope, and demising walls. Interior partition walls were specified to be moveable gypsum panels, a strategy allowing both for greater freedom in the design process and the capacity to better accommodate lifestyle changes, with the team stating that the "plan allows variation within standardization."[13] They drew detailed scenarios for how they imagined these changes might play out, with a diagram of a unit showing shifting subdivisions marking transitions from single, to couple, to couple with children, to elderly empty-nesters. Servicing every unit would be "equipment cores" by Matsushita. Combining all HVAC and plumbing, including bathrooms and kitchens designed in detail to integrate numerous Matsushita products, the cores would come as one tidy plug-in package.

Everything in the submission was extremely detailed. Once a winning team had been selected, construction of its design was to be swiftly begun, so logistical considerations were critical. As one example, the precast apartments would be made in an onsite factory simultaneous with the construction of the steel frame, and the factory design was part of the submission as well. Methods were also specified for the future replacement of the equipment cores and the fabric covering the gypsum panels.[14]

This level of planning seemed essential for success, with all of the project's systems forming a tightly integrated whole. As ASTM stated, the "use of prefabrication and industrialization systems makes it possible to offer quality housing in a shorter construction period and at reduced costs."[15] We should note that this statement is a pure expression of the holy grail of modernist housing ideology: overcoming the Good Fast Cheap triangle. Though known by different names, the Good Fast Cheap triangle posits that for any project you can only achieve two out of three conditions: you can be cheap and fast, but the project won't be good; you can be cheap and good, but it won't be fast; you can be good and fast, but it won't be cheap. To pursue all three is the everyday utopianism of design, and rarely successful.[16]

ASTM was announced the competition winner in August of 1973. In an interview with Yositika Utida in 2010, I asked about his experience on the jury and why the design was selected. His answer was simple: "Takenaka!"[17] Such was the power of the *zenekon*'s reputation at the time. While the start of construction was not until March 1976, due to much complex negotiation with the prefecture and the four operators, once begun the enormous project was indeed swiftly completed, with its advance covered almost daily in newspapers.[18] On March 15, 1979, the first people moved in.

top and bottom left: Ashiyahama structure as occupiable trellis

bottom right: Utopian ambition of mass housing

MEGASTRUCTURED: ASHIYAHAMA SEASIDE TOWN, 1972–

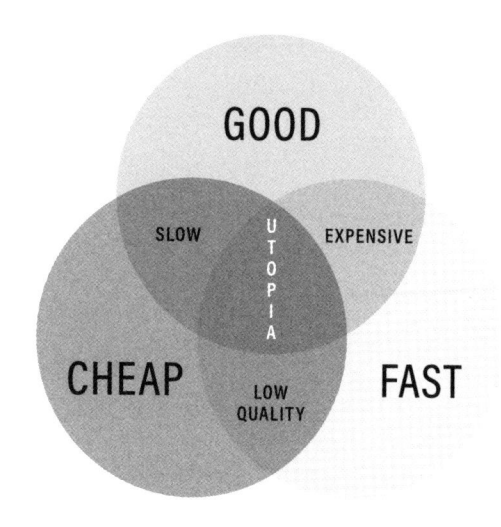

軀体構法

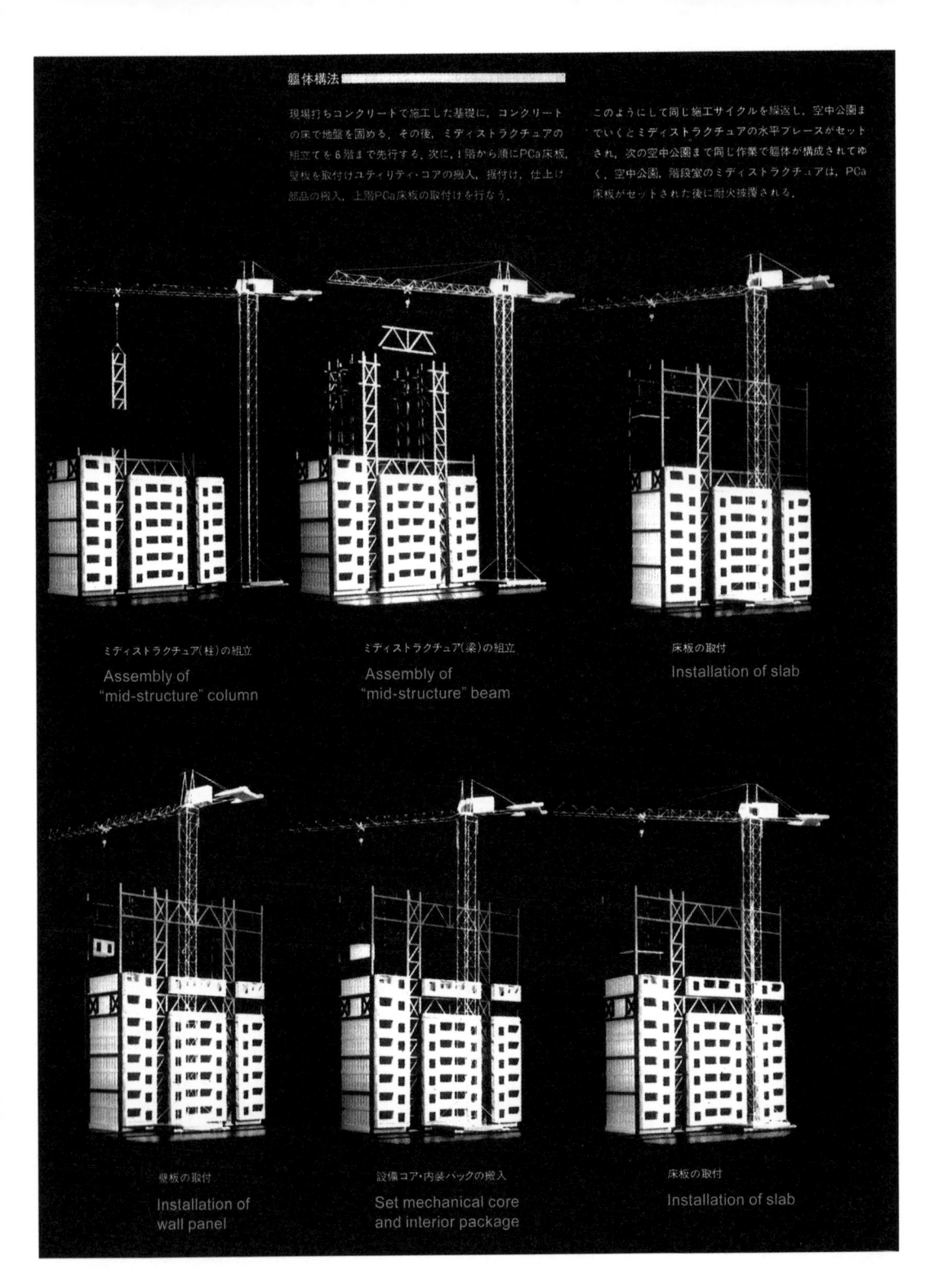

現場打ちコンクリートで施工した基礎に、コンクリートの床で地盤を固める。その後、ミディストラクチュアの組立てを6階まで先行する。次に、1階から順にPCa床板、壁板を取付けユティリティ・コアの搬入、据付け、仕上げ部品の搬入、上階PCa床板の取付けを行なう。

このようにして同じ施工サイクルを繰返し、空中公園までいくとミディストラクチュアの水平ブレースがセットされ、次の空中公園まで同じ作業で軀体が構成されてゆく。空中公園、階段室のミディストラクチュアは、PCa床板がセットされた後に耐火被覆される。

ミディストラクチュア(柱)の組立
Assembly of "mid-structure" column

ミディストラクチュア(梁)の組立
Assembly of "mid-structure" beam

床板の取付
Installation of slab

壁板の取付
Installation of wall panel

設備コア・内装パックの搬入
Set mechanical core and interior package

床板の取付
Installation of slab

188　　　　2　THE METABOLIST-INDUSTRIAL COMPLEX

System for System's Sake

> The first resident, Tomo-san, says he felt a bottomless anxiety that night as he watched the massive silhouette of the ultra high-rise soaring above his eleventh-story window and the nightscape on the beautiful Rokko mountains glittering like jewels.
>
> This was not, of course, an experience unique to Tomo-san. All the residents shook with the anxiety of the twenty-first century that no one had ever set foot in.[19]

Capturing the mood of the initial dwellers, Sanae Satoh's firsthand history *Future City on the Sea* describes how the residents' emotions were not caused by bewilderment over Ashiyahama's futuristic appearance. Rather, they were a result of finding themselves perched in a high-rise without running water, and with malfunctioning vacuum tubes for garbage.

These problems were soon fixed, but other inherent problems of the massive frames may be unfixable. From the start, the skip system caused considerable stress for residents moving in, and their moving companies. Now, decades on, the much more urgent problem caused by the extreme skip-floor is the relatively tiny number of units that are accessible without stairs. Only one unit is on the sky garden level of every tower—the only levels served by elevators without requiring stairs—and this quantity is wholly inadequate for Ashiyahama's increasingly elderly population. The design worsens the access issue already seen at Motomachi and Chojuen. While ASTM's designers had considered life-cycle changes inside the units, changes which Asano believes have been quite extensive in those that are privately owned, they didn't consider this issue outside the apartment walls.[20]

Major reprogramming of the sky-gardens with apartments, where units would collide with diagonal bracing and threaten the horizontal circulation, is hardly an option. Asano admits that these levels are the most obvious shortcoming in the design. Once built, they proved far too windy for any significant plantings, and the budget didn't allow sufficient space for attractive play areas.[21] Surveys in 1980, 1988, and 2006 found that over half of the residents almost never use them, with the most typical usage appearing to be bicycle parking.[22]

According to Asano, keeping the project on budget was the most excruciating part of his work. The multitasking of systems was one way to reduce costs, but it was not without risks. An example of this danger was demonstrated by the 1995 Kobe earthquake, which shocked the engineering community and terrified Ashiyahama's residents, causing numerous truss members within stair-core trusses to crack at ground level. This was especially disturbing given the confidence placed in Takenaka.[23] While the cracks were repaired by welding on massive buckling plates for reinforcing, engineers involved in assessing the damage were uncertain as to what went wrong. However, one likely theory, merging issues of architecture and engineering, was that the absence of diagonal bracing in order to allow stair access at the base of the column trusses created a critical weakness, a so-called "soft story" liable to deformation.[24]

When asked about his thoughts on the project in 2010, Utida declared it to be a "system for system's sake; not for the occupants."[25] More specifically, Ashiyahama is the Metabolist-industrial complex for the sake of the Metabolist-industrial complex, and this self-serving aspect raises the issue of control through design that further distinguishes megastructure from artificial land. While the difference can be unclear, as at Harumi and

Construction sequence

Motomachi, Ashiyahama crosses a threshold into megastructure through its lack of indeterminacy in the overall definition of apartments, particularly in terms of access. Like the Nakagin Capsule Tower, which is also limited in its adaptive capacity due to its units' construction by structure and vertical circulation, Ashiyahama ignores the obvious: thanks to gravity, extensive horizontal planes are readily traversed, built upon, subdivided, renovated, and occupied. Harumi and Motomachi respect this ease of the horizontal, allowing for Motomachi's extensive reconfigurations. In contrast, Ashiyahama's near-total reliance on stairs that serve and confine small floor plates makes it a frozen monument to Metabolism's goal of two cycles of change. The giant trusses holding the notionally changeable apartments make it clear that providing for these cycles is no guarantee of quality if they can't deliver the adaptations that residents really need.

Distributing Decisions

The architect John Habraken, in his essay "Lives of Systems," contrasts the logistics of small concrete blocks with big precast panels. He writes that "The most successful element will be the one that dictates least the distributions that can be made by those who use it," upholding the near infinite number of configurations available to those building with blocks.[26] For our purposes, here onward, this statement defines a vernacular ethic. It is not a complete definition of vernacular design, but it speaks to Metabolist objectives and their development.

Applied to Ashiyahama, Habraken's observation illuminates the problems with the large panels of the apartments as well as the infrastructure of trusses: there is only one way to use the panels, and only one (problematic) location for apartment access relative to circulation. Habraken's belief in small blocks instead of large panels is a commitment to the distributed action enabled by small-scale components, ones also readily available to any builder, from expert or amateur. Turning to the suburban American house made of 2x4s, he notes that "What is worth our attention is not that in many cases the developer puts down rows of exactly similar houses but that variety appears when the inhabitants take over, exploiting the true potential of the vernacular."[27] The wood-frame construction material used by the professional builder can also be used by the homeowner after a trip to the lumberyard, while for Ashiyahama, no such vernacular potential exists beyond the limited shifting of gypsum walls.

While using a house to criticize a high-rise may seem inappropriate, the combination of these types is of course the objective of artificial land at its romantic core. To Habraken's point, the squatters at Torre David in Caracas built their variety of high-rise homes with hollow bricks, the same wieldy and ubiquitous construction material with which houses are built in the ground-level *barrios*.[28] Such actions by occupants are hardly possible with large panels of precast concrete.

Habraken writes that the elimination of distributed "decision-making" is the real danger of factory production, not homogeneity per se.[29] As with Ashiyahama's panels and frames, decisions centralized in the design office and factory easily preclude decisions on possible adaptations at the site, both during construction and over the life of a project. Individual agency is lost. Ashiyahama's big or megastructural elements, all tightly integrated, dictate the ways in which components may be distributed, highlighting that the question of integration—how building systems connect, intersect, overlap, merge, and nest—is essentially a question of a design's metabolism, or life cycle.

Truss-beam corridor (2010)

MEGASTRUCTURED: ASHIYAHAMA SEASIDE TOWN, 1972–

2   THE METABOLIST-INDUSTRIAL COMPLEX

This reality is not specific to Metabolism the movement. While ASTM's integrated approach did improve speeds and lower costs, it has become an obstruction to the quality of living that was the goal of MOC policy. In contrast, artificial land is not anti-system, but an approach enabling the possibility of major decisions by residents. By 1973, the year of ASTM's submission, Yosizaka had added the attic to his house, and on the open ground floor, the library.

1. Charles Jencks, *The Language of Post-Modern Architecture* (New York: Rizzoli, 1977), 9. Jencks's suggestion of Pruitt-Igoe's failure due to its modern design is a fundamental part of the project's mythology, as examined in *The Pruitt-Igoe Myth*. See comment on page 175n25 of this book.
2. For comparison, Pruitt-Igoe contained 2,870 apartments while Ashiyahama has 3,400.
3. See Kayoko Ota, "The Architects who Caught the Global Wave," trans. Julian Worrall, in *Metabolism—The City of the Future: Dreams and Visions of Reconstruction in Postwar and Present-Day Japan,* ed. Mami Hirose et al. (Tokyo: Mori Art Museum, 2011), 302.
4. Ota, "Global Wave," 302.
5. Maki's advising: Tadatoshi Asano, email exchange with the author, December 28, 2014.
6. Fumihiko Maki and Masato Ohtaka, "Collective Form—Three Paradigms," in Maki, *Investigations in Collective Form* [1964] (St. Louis, MO: School of Architecture, Washington University in St. Louis, 2004), 8.
7. See *A Quick Look at Housing in Japan*, eds. The Building Center of Japan et al. (Tokyo: The Building Center of Japan, 2014), 26.
8. See "History," The Building Center of Japan, accessed July 24, 2019, https://www.bcj.or.jp/en/about/history/.
9. See Kakuei Tanaka, *Building a New Japan: A Plan for Remodeling the Japanese Archipelago* [1972] (Tokyo: The Simul Press, 1973), 188–199.
10. For more of an introduction to "sunshine rights," see André Sorensen, *The Making of Urban Japan: Cities and Planning from Edo to the Twenty-First Century* (New York: Routledge, 2002), 254.
11. Asano, December 28, 2014.
12. As of my visit in 2010, Ashiyahama's circulation was publicly accessible and one could freely wander the project at any level.
13. "Ashiyahama Housing Complex," *Approach* (Autumn 1973): 38. Founded in 1964, the quarterly journal *Approach* is published by Takenaka.
14. The team's submission is reprinted in *Kōgyōko shuhō ni yoru Ashiyahama kōsō jūtaku project teian kyōgi* [Competition for Ashiyahama high-rise project using industrialized construction techniques], ed. The Building Center of Japan (Tokyo: Kogyo Chosakai Publishing, Inc., 1974), 725–760.
15. "Ashiyahama Housing Complex," 38.
16. An excellent example of this modernist objective is "Build better, cheaper, and faster," a slogan stating explicitly the ideology of East Germany's postwar building program for housing, a program completely reliant on prefabricated concrete panels. The country achieved speed and low cost, but quality is debatable. See Reinier de Graaf, *Four Walls and a Roof: The Complex Nature of a Simple Profession* (Cambridge, MA: Harvard University Press, 2017), 35.
17. Yositika Utida, in conversation with the author, April 23, 2010.
18. Utida, April 23, 2010.
19. Sanae Satoh, *Umi ni tatta mirai toshi—Ashiyahama no chōkōsō* [Future city on the sea: Ashiyahama super high-rise] (Tokyo: Mainichi Shimbun-sha, 1980), 15–16. Translation by Riyo Namigata.
20. Asano, December 28, 2014.
21. Asano, December 28, 2014.
22. Asano, December 28, 2014. These surveys were focused on the use of Ashiyahama's public spaces only.
23. Michel Bruneau et al., "Seismic Design of Steel Buildings: Lessons from the 1995 Hyogo-ken Nanbu Earthquake," *Canadian Journal of Civil Engineering* 23 (1996): 746.
24. Bruneau, "Seismic Design," 750.
25. Utida, April 23, 2010.
26. N. J. Habraken, "Lives of Systems," in *Transformations of the Site* (Cambridge, MA: Atwater Press, 1983), 173.
27. Habraken, "Lives," 172.
28. See *Torre David: Informal Vertical Communities*, eds. Alfredo Brillembourg and Hubert Klumpner (Zürich: Lars Müller Publishers, 2013), 208–209. Squatting started at the complex in 2007. In 2014, the squatters were evicted by the government.
29. Habraken, "Lives," 176–177.

top: Typical front door to an apartment (2010)

bottom: Northeast view (2010)

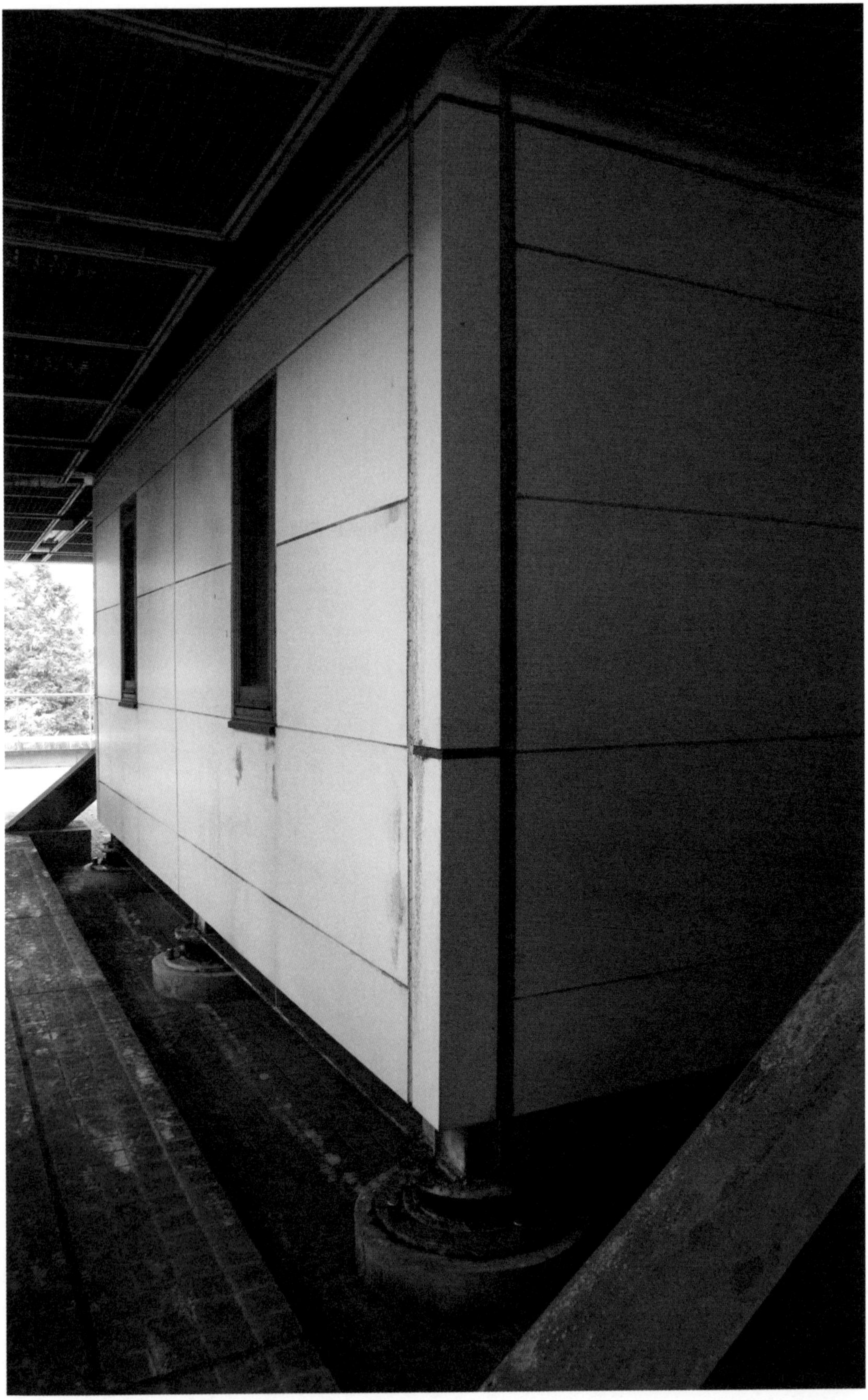

Solutionism: Stratiform Structure Module, 1973–

A rendering of the Stratiform Structure Module from 1977 shows a giant space-frame shooting out of a dense city, carrying platforms laden with trees and freestanding Mediterranean-style houses, evoking a futuristic suburban idyll serviced by an integrated monorail and highway. While some imagination is required to see Harumi as artificial land, Stratiform requires none.

    In 1973, one year after Kakuei Tanaka's election, Kiyonori Kikutake began working with a team to develop Stratiform. Sponsored by MITI, the ministry delegated supervision to its subsidiary, the sinisterly named Mechanical Social Systems Foundation. Financing was from organized gambling—a practice common in Japanese ministries during the 1960s and '70s, and in this case from betting on motorcycle races.[1] Kikutake had additional support from Yositika Utida, who had been appointed project chairman, and testing and construction support from the ubiquitous Takenaka Corporation. The team's goal was a new healthy habitat for the average Japanese, as called for by Tanaka, with Stratiform planned as a swiftly deployable infrastructure for housing. As admirable as this objective was, the design shows the costs as well as the benefits of a "solutionist" approach to problems, thereby illuminating one of architecture's most common, if least acknowledged, methods.

Kiyonori Kikutake, Stratiform Structure Module, Gotemba, 1982 (2014). Note base-isolation pads under infill unit.

following: Stratiform rendering, 1977

Building a New Japan as Brief

Ashiyahama's goals also fit with the national agenda of Tanaka, but the prime minister had a direct influence on Stratiform. Indeed, the content of Tanaka's 1972 book *Building a New Japan*, his manifesto for "remodeling" the entire nation in order to undo the environmental damage of the Pacific Belt's industrialization,

195

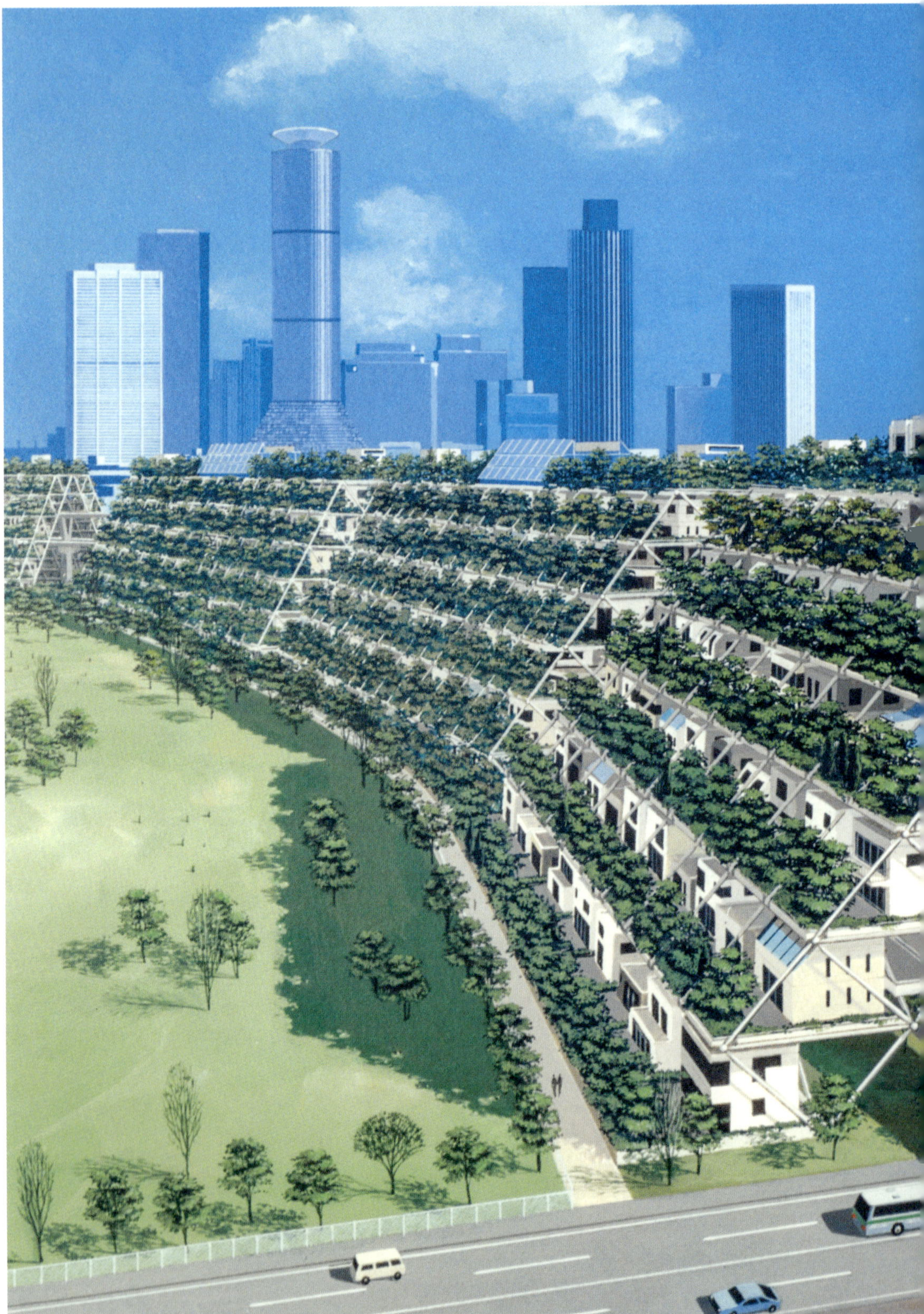

SOLUTIONISM: STRATIFORM STRUCTURE MODULE, 1973–

can be read as Stratiform's design brief. Published just before his election on July 6, 1972, by August the book had sold 800,000 copies, making its attack on the megalopolis and the dynamics of centralization versus decentralization subjects of popular debate. These dynamics underly discussions on Japanese development still today.

That *Building a New Japan* provides Stratiform's de facto brief is given credence by the book repeating policies already advanced by MITI, for which Tanaka was appointed minister in 1971.[2] The book, apparently written by MITI speechwriters, built on aspects of the 1968 Plan's fight against sprawl and pollution by proposing a radical decentralization of industry and population out of the Pacific Belt megalopolis, not just the improvement of conditions found there.[3] In his introduction, Tanaka summarized these and his other key issues in a five-point manifesto. First, he called for a "new national land program" to set development policies for all Japan; second, both new and existing cities needed "three-dimensionalizing," especially in housing, to make way for proper public amenities; third, "focal" cities needed to be created, either through remodeling existing ones or building on new sites, which would allow for a dispersal to underpopulated regions, to be served by new highways and Shinkansen service; fourth, new zoning should prioritize public interest over private; and fifth, capital resources for the remodeling should be secured through new government incentives given to private investment.[4]

Too dense and too expensive, having pulled millions of Japanese into its urbanized web, the Tokaido Megalopolis left behind a hinterland of shrinking villages and small cities often not strategically useful to its industries, aside from supplying a flow of young workers.[5] Tanaka believed these ills could be corrected through dramatically expanding mass transit. In his words, or those of MITI speechwriters, such "pump-priming social overhead capital" would allow abandoned areas to be revitalized.[6] It would also allow the rational planning of the new focal cities receiving redistributed industries. Better connectivity would make the megalopolis less attractive, allowing it to be progressively decongested and outfitted with the proper living environments it needed. Tanaka noted that "overcrowding and underpopulation are two sides of the same coin," and his policies aimed to solve them "simultaneously."[7]

This emphasis on transit is joined in Stratiform by the Prime Minister's belief in the average Japanese person's "life-long dream of owning a house."[8] As he describes, "People with modest savings lament not being able to build their own homes, but it is not the house which is beyond their means. It is the lot on which to build which is the problem."[9] This was abundantly true. In response to high land prices in central urban areas, both private and public developers looked for increasingly distant railway stations close to cheap forest and farm areas where they could build new housing. Development was often driven more by prices than planning. Even when there was responsible planning, as with JHC projects, it wasn't enough. A 1970 survey by the corporation revealed dissatisfaction with the situation, indicating that 76 percent of *danchi* residents wanted to move elsewhere, with "remote, expensive, and cramped" being the most common complaints.[10]

Shizuo Harada, a project architect for Stratiform from Kikutake's office, defines its goal specifically as the creation of a suburban lifestyle without the painful commuting, often two hours one way.[11] The project would allow greater urban proximity by being located over transit routes, straddling them with A-frame legs to offer "inexpensive artificial land" for homebuilding, putting to work the unused airspace in Tokyo and other existing or new urban centers.[12] Once again, artificial land was given an ambitious mission.

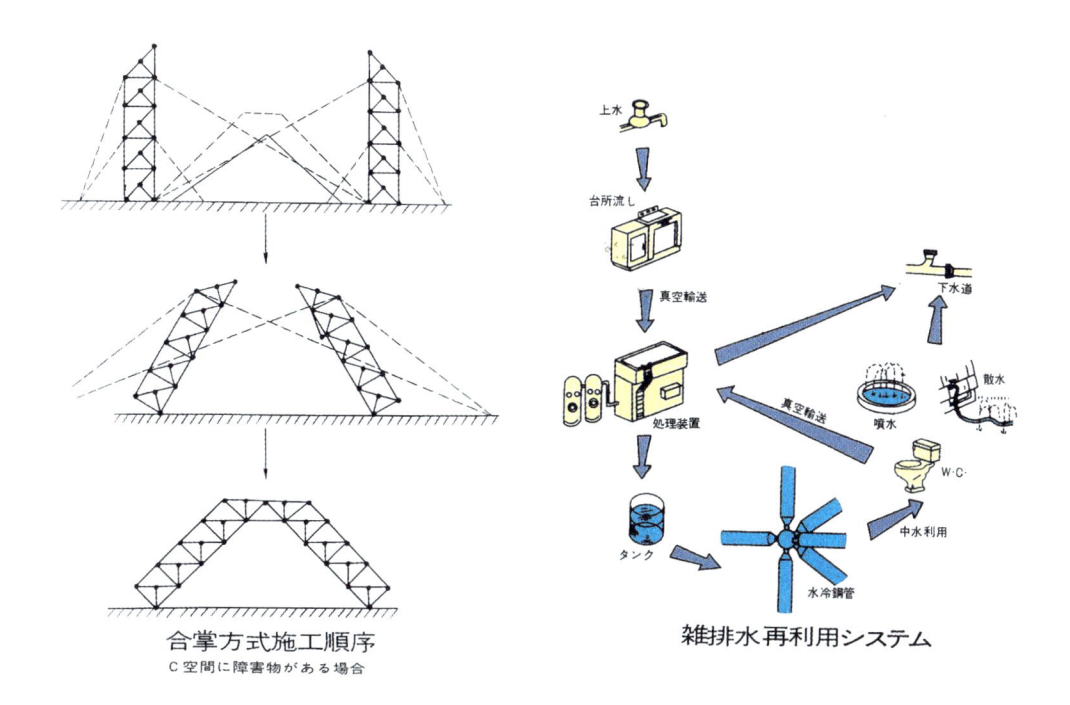

A-frame

Decking over transit routes can of course be done without A-frames, but the research hypothesized that this geometry had a practical advantage: they could be constructed by gradually tilting the two sides inward above existing train tracks or highways, like a drawbridge, until they touched at the peak and were bolted together, with transportation running uninterrupted below during this process.[13] Such rapid deployment would be possible due to Stratiform's use of steel, which dispensed with the slowness and weight of site-cast concrete. Instead, Stratiform was new land with minimum mass, made in a factory and sent wherever needed.

The steel frame would be made from hollow tubes that could also serve as pipes for potable, gray, and waste water, resulting in a structural plumbing network that indicates clear ecological thinking. Serving also to cool the structure in the event of a fire, the water network and the seismic resistance of the triangular frame responded to Tanaka's call for new levels of disaster safety.

Precast concrete planks, comprising U-shaped troughs capped with pavers, would be bolted onto the frames. These hollow planks formed Stratiform's housing plots, their removable tops allowing them to be used like raised access floors for data and HVAC management. Instigated by the needs of IBM's early mainframe computers in the 1950s, access floors allow underfloor cabling and ducts to be rerouted by simply removing large floor tiles elevated on small pedestals over a continuous plenum. By the early 1970s, this flexible system had become a common feature of new corporate offices.[14] Technology transfers were basic to MITI's operation, and this feature is one architectural example of such crosspollination. The Stratiform team's genius was to use this flexibility for domestic plumbing.

Lowering of Stratiform frame over mass transit (left) and gray water recycling system (right)

SOLUTIONISM: STRATIFORM STRUCTURE MODULE, 1973–

In multistory housing, water-related spaces such as bathrooms and kitchens are typically aligned vertically in order to simplify the placement of pipes. This rigidity was avoided due to Stratiform's access floors, which allowed branch plumbing to run horizontally, with appropriate slopes in multiple directions and lengths. Wet services could therefore be freely located, thereby liberating the apartment layouts. Sakaide had explored a similar approach with the grid of sleeves passing through the beams on the underside of its Phase 1 platform. However, by changing the location from the ceiling cavity to the underfloor cavity, Stratiform's approach allowed the floor to be "dug up" as if it were land. Indeed, the design team imagined some floor tiles being removed and the voids below filled with dirt and plantings. It was the most realistic artificial land yet, a breakthrough that would be adopted in many projects that followed.[15]

Thanks to this innovation and the frame's two zones of scale—provided by the huge central space and the more compartmentalized levels within the frame—Stratiform was presented as highly adaptable. Flexibility was a strategy for preserving the resources embodied in its construction far into the future, and the team imagined many scenarios in addition to housing, such as schools, automated hospitals, waste treatment facilities, sports centers, department stores, supermarkets, factories, cattle grazing, bus terminals, and yacht storage.[16] In short, anything that might be needed anywhere.

Mass Customization

Despite presenting itself as all things for all sites, Stratiform's key objective was inexpensive residential plots, emphasized by the quaint, pitched roof houses that infill the spaceframe in many representations. This juxtaposition of modern and vernacular is reminiscent of Le Corbusier's combination of skeleton frame and Moorish villas, and as at Algiers, it would be a mistake to see Kikutake's images as merely fanciful. By the early 1970s, factory production of single-family homes had emerged in Japan with a level of commercial success far greater than that of any housing ever designed by a Metabolist. The brilliance of the Stratiform team was to piggyback on this existing industry, appropriating it as a ready-made design-build system for supplying Stratiform's suburban infill. Also vitally important was the industry's sophisticated sales system, with showrooms and networks of contractors throughout the country. This made the seeming fantasy of Stratiform highly pragmatic. According to Harada, the design team spent little time thinking about housing in any detail, since they took it for granted that prefab houses would "complete" their design.[17]

Despite the products of the prefab industry often being relatively conventional in appearance, they were part of the Metabolist-industrial complex. Starting in 1963, its fledgling companies received the support of MOC and MITI in promoting prefab to consumers. Misawa Homes, one of the largest prefab builders, also developed a concept with a distinctly Metabolist pedigree. Founded in 1962, the company was awarded in 1967 the contract for expanding the living quarters for Japan's Antarctic base, a base designed and prefabricated around 1955 by a Takenaka team led by none other than Takashi Asada, Tange's close associate. Presaging capsule architecture, it was totally modularized and designed to allow rapid transport and easy assembly by its scientist inhabitants while wearing mittens. Through the contract, Misawa inherited an advanced panelized system ripe for other uses.[18] The base's system indeed influenced their

top: Stratiform access floor as artificial land

bottom: Takenaka, Antarctic research station, 1957

床概念図

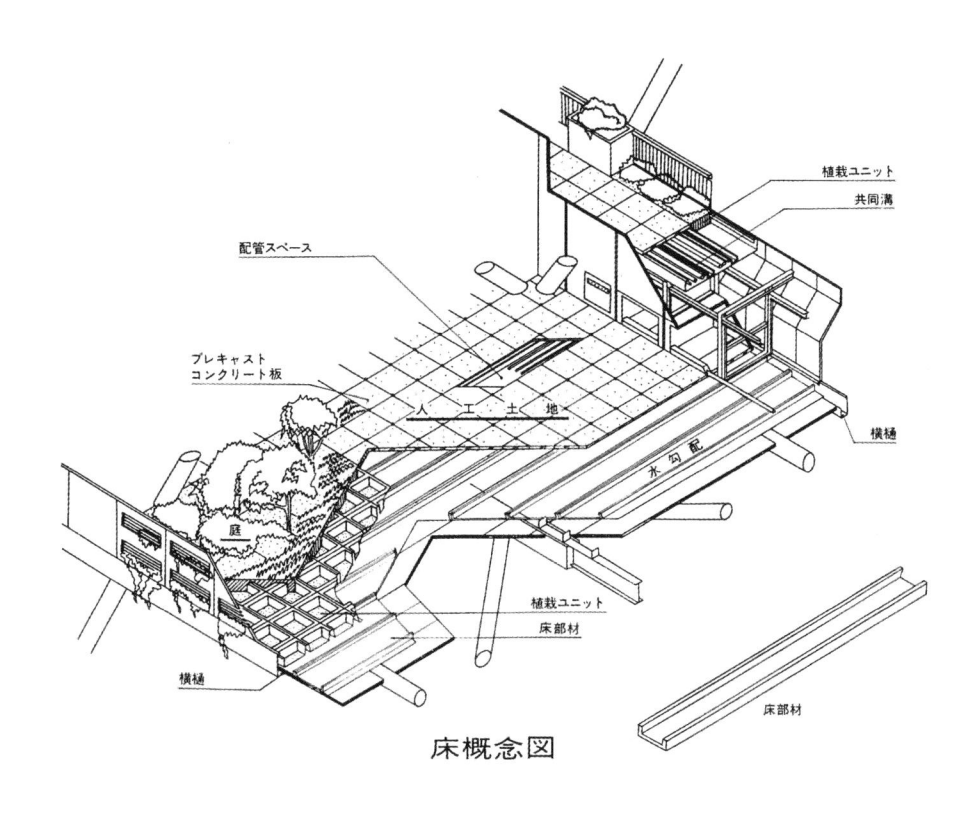

SOLUTIONISM: STRATIFORM STRUCTURE MODULE, 1973–

2 THE METABOLIST-INDUSTRIAL COMPLEX

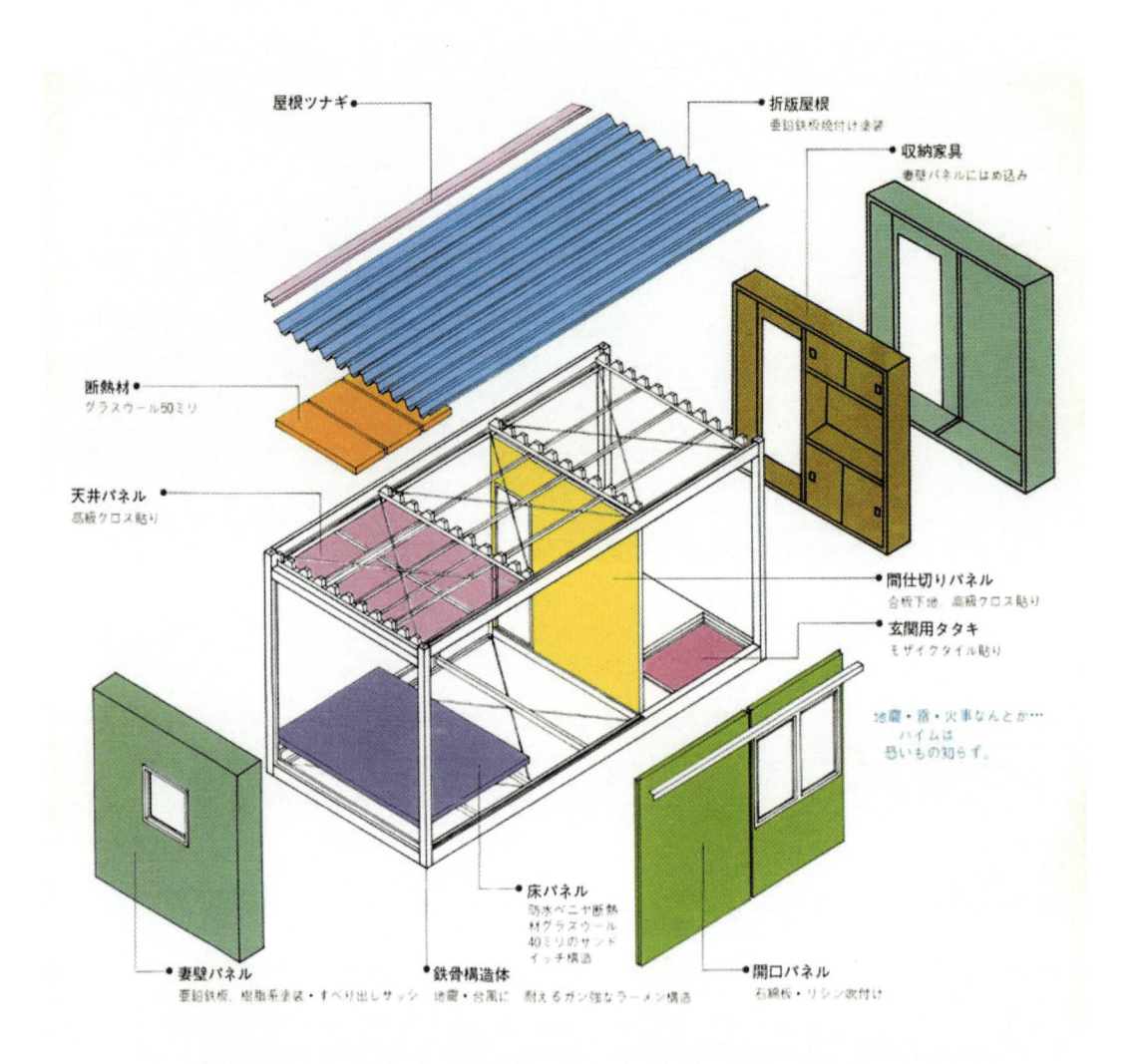

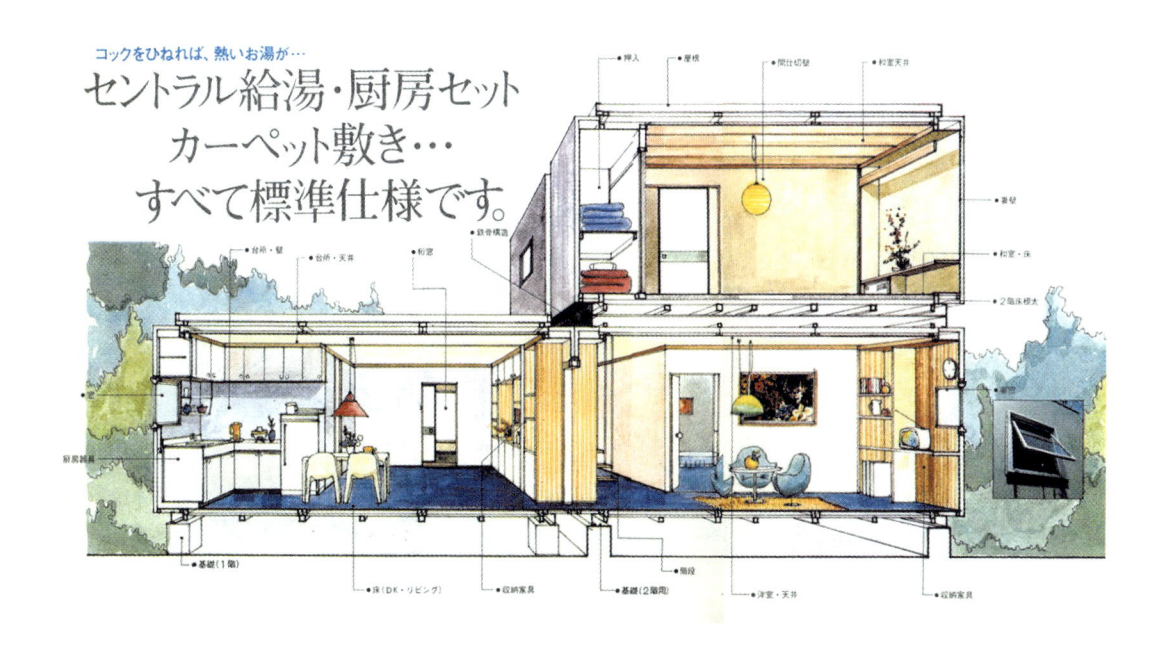

development of panelized homes, with factory assembly and modular coordination being primary ingredients for cost reduction, a strategy that helped Misawa gain the top market share by 1971.[19]

Misawa is an example of a prefab company that had always made homes. Some companies had moved into prefab home-building from other fields with relevant know-how and products, such as Toyota and Panasonic. Toyota Home, for example, was able to apply or adapt aspects of automotive technology.[20]

Another example of such transfer, and also of Metabolist relation, is the Sekisui Chemical Company, a plastics maker that saw home-building as offering outlets for many things it had already developed, such as bathtubs. In 1970, it launched the Sekisui Heim M1, Japan's most famous prefab home.[21] Designed by Katsuhiko Ohno, a graduate of Utida's architectural lab at the University of Tokyo, it was a flexible system comprising modular "box-units" that allowed home buyers to customize their houses. By the early 1970s, Sekisui was constructing approximately 40,000 boxes per year, with seven to eight boxes being sufficient for a three-bedroom house.[22]

In addition to support from MOC and MITI, the prefab industry had significant help to sell such large quantities. Single-family home ownership had been state-promoted by the GHLC since its founding in 1950, and after 1962 it also approved mortgages for factory-built dwellings.[23] In the late 1960s, as construction of rental housing declined, the "life-long dream" of owning a home was given a further boost by private companies that provided loans to their employees.[24] The home dream was also

Katsuhiko Ohno, Sekisui Heim M1 "box-units," c. 1970

SOLUTIONISM: STRATIFORM STRUCTURE MODULE, 1973–

203

greatly encouraged by vast marketing campaigns by the prefab industry, comparable in impact to those for cars. This focus on the freestanding home was further amplified by Kazuo Shinohara and the work of "New Wave" architects, such as Tadao Ando and Toyo Ito, whose hermetic houses were then being prominently featured in architectural journals.[25] While Shinohara critiqued Metabolism for its apparent dismissal of the house as an arena for serious architecture, this was an argument within the avant-garde. Everywhere else in Japan, the house was already serious business, if not usually designed to the avant-garde's taste.[26]

In 1973, the year Stratiform's development started, Manfredo Tafuri noted the alignment between artificial land and the demands of capitalist growth. Describing Fort l'Empereur, he writes that the design obediently accommodates "the exigencies of the continual technological revolution […] dictated by a dynamic capitalism in expansion," where the home can be "substituted at any change of individual necessity—at any change of necessity induced by the renewal of models and residential standards dictated by production."[27] Yet this seems to be a more apt description of Stratiform than Fort l'Empereur. Like a supermarket for houses, its plots would be an accommodating shelving system, perfect for displaying a stream of products designed for rapid consumption. In 1966, so-called "show villages" had appeared in Japan, large expo-like displays of prefab houses and domestic appliances from various manufacturers, shown in at least one instance on giant tiered shelves.[28] Stratiform turned the show village into urban infrastructure.

Higashikata Unit Laboratory, Store System Show, Tokyo, 1973

following: Sachio Otani, Kawaramachi Housing, Kawasaki, 1972

204

2 THE METABOLIST-INDUSTRIAL COMPLEX

Silver Bullet?

With the team's piggybacking on the successful prefab industry, it might appear puzzling that the radically pragmatic design never went further than two very modest examples built in Toyama and Gotemba. The design's realism—from its connection to specific aspects of government policy to its engagement of industry and current events—supports scholarship asserting that the Metabolists were not merely utopian. As Hajime Yatsuka has written, the group anchored "their proposals in the realities of society, hoping to reshape it."[29]

But at this point, with a knowledge of how diverse the Metabolists were as a group, it is dualistic to confine the movement to being either utopian or realist. This is especially so because between utopianism and realism another approach exists: "solutionism." This may be the most appropriate characterization for much of Metabolism, built or not, and certainly for the livingry of Stratiform.

The urban designer Michael Dobbins writes that when a "problem-driven" approach is dominated by the "solution-driven," a "big idea may be so seductive, may get so imageable so fast that people are swept up in the process, potentially disastrous if the voice of reason or plain old common sense doesn't stand up."[30] Rather than engaging layers of subtle investigation and stakeholder interests in order to fully define a project's problems and then make appropriate res ponses to them, solutionism jumps to a sales pitch promoted with convincing images. "Beware of the solution in search of a problem," Dobbins warns, and behold the A-frame, bolstered by the ancient authority of a pyramid—and in Japan, by Mount Fuji.[31]

Stratiform was also bolstered by an avant-garde lineage of hollow mountains before it, giving typological gravitas to the A-frame as a solution. For Stratiform and its predecessors, the type offered a confident section, integrating structural stability with a tidy relationship between public and private, large and small. This lineage in Japan includes Sachio Otani's 1972 Kawaramachi Housing, as well as Tange's Tokyo Bay housing contained in his 1960 Plan. In America, Paul Rudoph proposed transit-straddling A-frames for his Lower Manhattan Expressway plan in 1972, and in 1971, Welton Beckett completed his Contemporary Resort for Disney World, an A-frame hotel with a monorail train running through it. Going back further, we find the ziggurat apartment buildings and hotels by Henri Sauvage for early twentieth-century Paris, containing in their middles swimming pools and garages.

Looking at the Rue des Amiraux Apartments by Sauvage, completed in 1925, it appears that the reality of the A-frame was problematic from the beginning. While the setbacks of the profile were meant to improve access to light and air, their provision is confounded by the communal swimming pool in the central void—the ample space that's always part of the type's attraction, and usually part of its problems. Fantastic as the building's combination of form and program is, exposure to an enclosed pool's humidity and odors conflicts with the environmental needs of apartments. These two zones are separated, leaving most apartments with only a single exposure and no borrowed space from the cavern-like pool. Despite numerous later proposals, the design never became the replicated type Sauvage wanted—at least in Paris.[32]

Of course, Stratiform's goal was also to be replicated, even mass produced. But it also suffered from conflicts of use like those in the Amiraux Apartments, and worse. Regardless of the program that the Stratiform team imagined in the central void, it would be largely without daylight, let alone direct sunlight, precisely at the time that sunshine rights had become part of the building code,

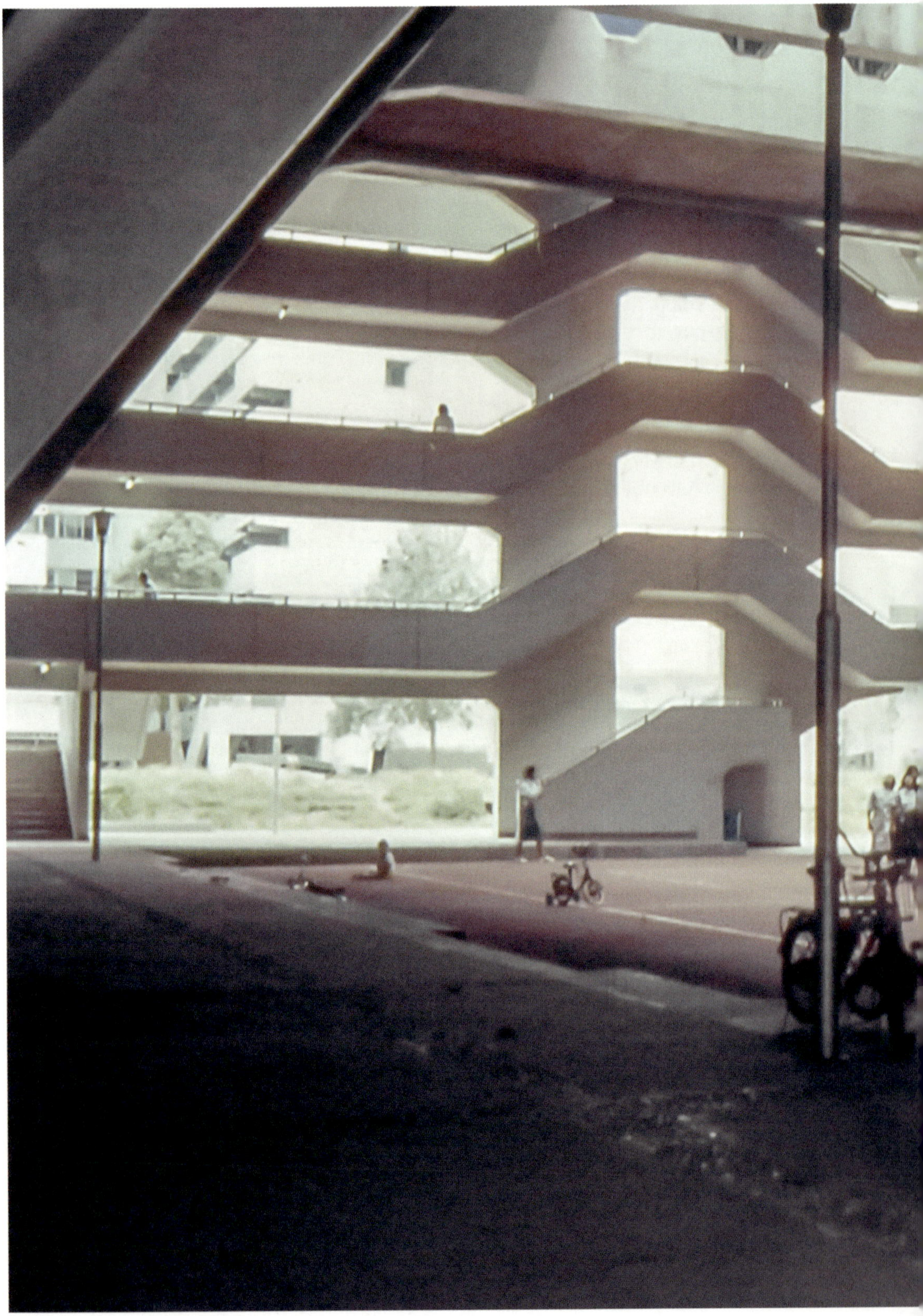

SOLUTIONISM: STRATIFORM STRUCTURE MODULE, 1973–

in response to popular demand.[33] While not an artificial-land project, a view into the void of Otani's Kawaramachi Housing gives a good idea of how such a space might feel. In effect, Stratiform's void acted as an extremely large double-loaded corridor. Long the bane of progressive architects due to its reduced natural light and ventilation for the apartments served, a double-loaded configuration had been rejected at Harumi, Motomachi, and Ashiyahama for good reasons. Stratiform would also seem to contain exhaust from the cars and trains running through it, in a country afflicted with airborne pollution that, like sunlight, was a major political issue.[34]

In the face of Stratiform's questionable levels of light and air—urban issues that provoked the 1968 Plan and Tanaka's policies in the first place—we are left with a proposal whose solutionism resides in stating a problem in overwhelmingly structural and logistical terms. As the team wrote, "it is necessary to develop a city infrastructure that can be constructed quickly and inexpensively."[35] Like Buckminster Fuller's insistence on geodesic domes for all locations and situations, the Stratiform team saw the A-frame as a silver bullet for economically engineering new land. Yet it ignored critical, if less visible, issues of habitation.

But along with its apparent indifference to the conflict between homes and fumes, the structural form did have significant issues with regard to the efficient use of a site. Unlike an extruded tower, as Stratiform's pyramid grows in height, so grows the footprint of its base.[36] From a real-estate perspective, this made Stratiform very inefficient, posing no competition to extrudable "mansions," the term for the high-rise condos booming in the early 1970s due to zoning changes and better seismic engineering.[37]

If Stratiform is, then, solutionist architecture, that may be because it was responding to policies for a solutionist city. Yatsuka writes that *Building a New Japan* oversimplified the problems of Japanese development through "equating urban concentration with evil, and decentralization with good," with the power of these "catchphrases" polarizing public debate and obscuring other possibilities.[38] Ironically, the hoped-for decentralization into new regional cities, thanks to new rail lines and highways, backfired: speculation in areas to be served by the planned transportation led to the second major rise in land prices since the end of the war, causing between 1972 and 1973 a 30% rise in prices nationwide. Sprawl was only magnified, as affordable land for housing continued to be sought further and further away from existing urban centers.[39] Interpreted at its most cynical, Stratiform would be perfect for these exurban areas, offering platforms for quick colonization.

Stratiform's ignorance of regulations and their politicization suggests a disdain for bureaucracy endemic to the solutionist belief that smart design can sidestep politics. As a case in point, Harada, Kikutake's project architect, believes that the death knell for the project was caused by rivalry between MITI and MOC. Despite in principle having complimentary roles, with MOC controlling regulations for buildings and MITI promoting the manufacture of building components, the two had long competed fiercely.[40] One of the specific sites the team considered was above the tracks of the Japanese National Railways' Yotsuya Station in central Tokyo, and MOC was particularly involved with land use around railway sites.[41] It would not change its regulations to accommodate the MITI design, there or anywhere else over transportation.[42] After this experience, Harada characterized the Mechanical Social Systems Foundation, the MITI subsidiary overseeing the project, as "very good at research; very bad at implementation."[43]

top: Paul Rudolph, Lower Manhattan Expressway proposal, 1972

bottom: Henri Sauvage, Rue des Amiraux Apartments, Paris, 1925

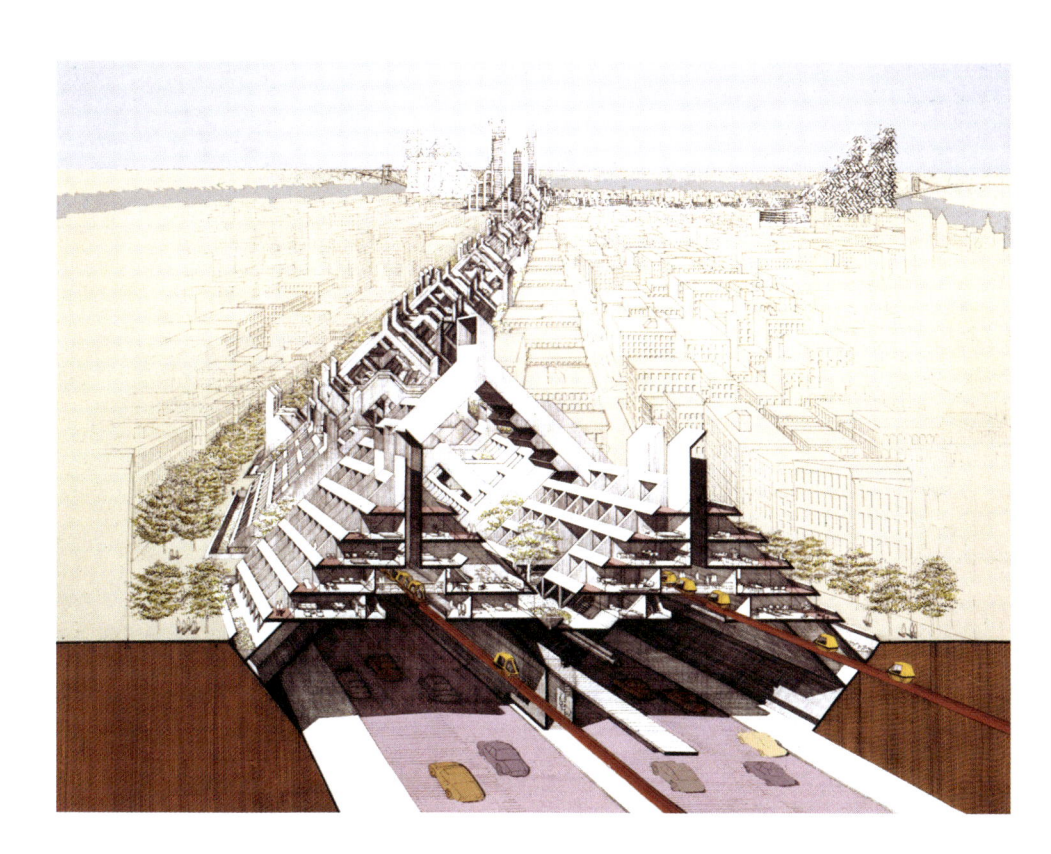

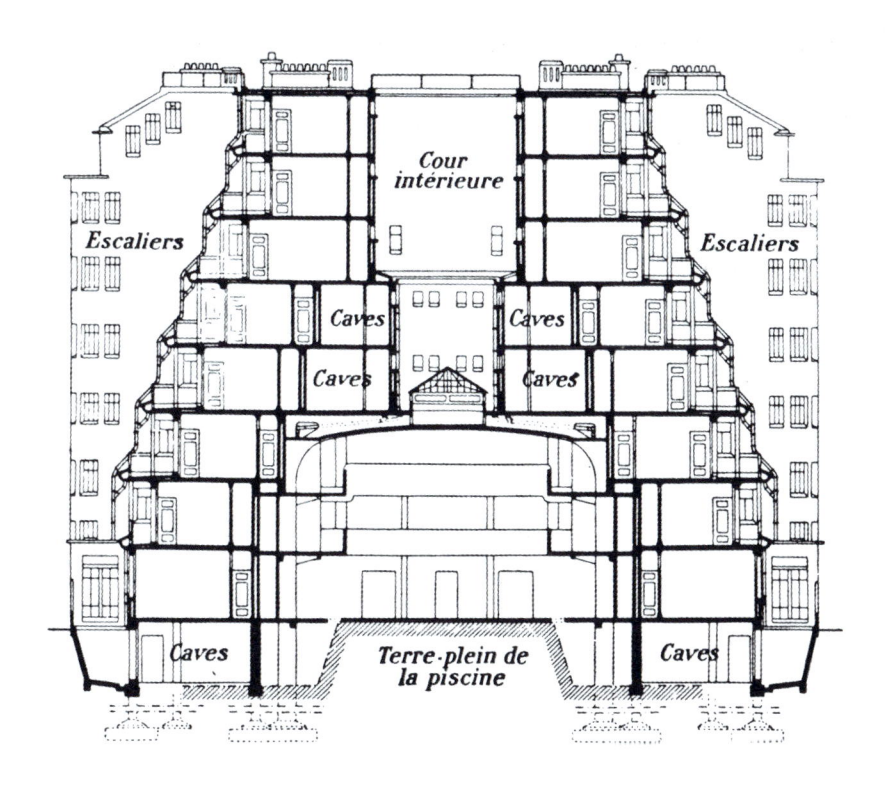

SOLUTIONISM: STRATIFORM STRUCTURE MODULE, 1973–

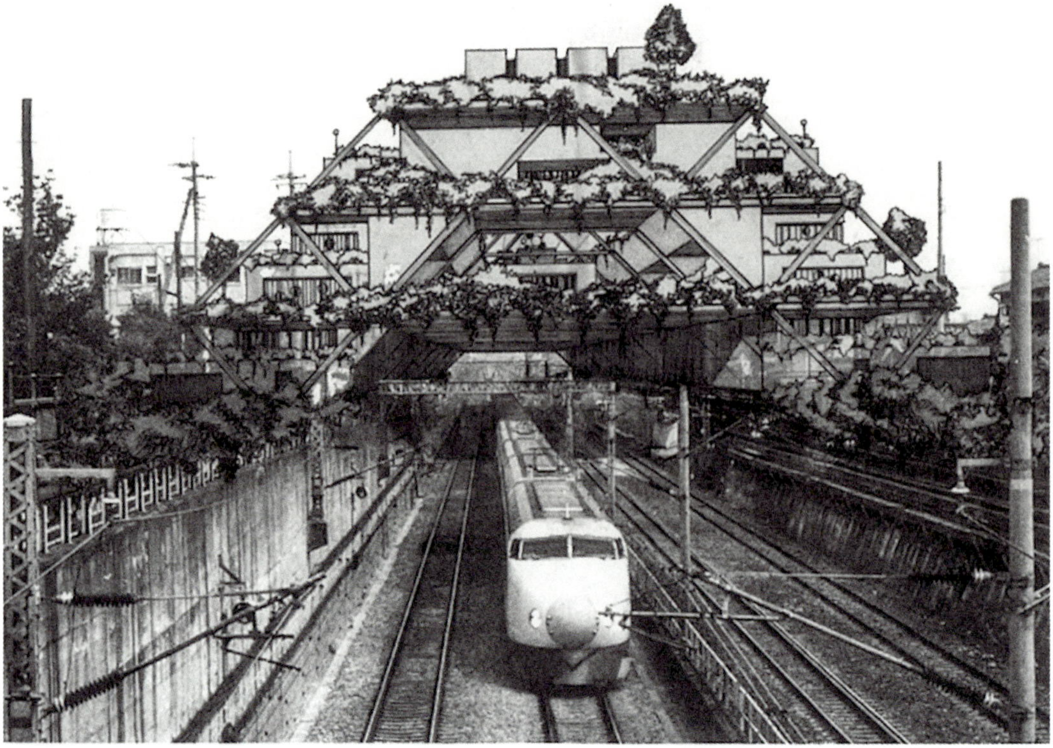

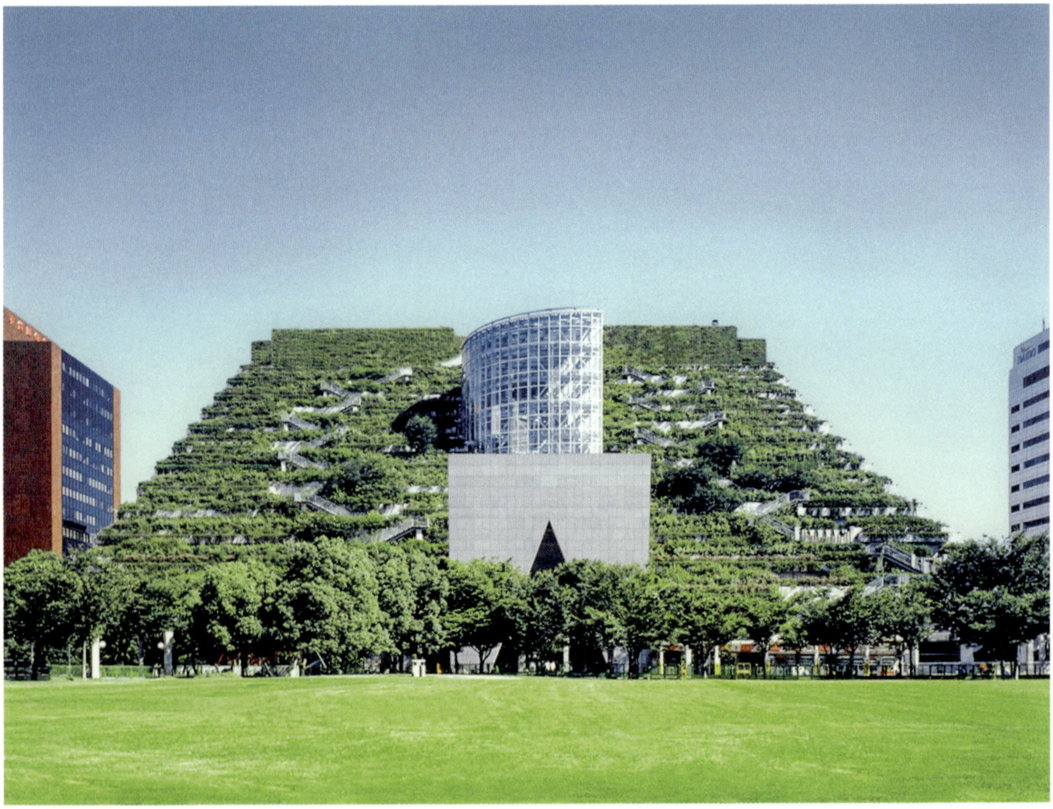

From Gotemba to 3/11

The best approximation of Stratiform's implementation is the full-scale prototype in Gotemba, built in 1982. Constructed by Takenaka, the project is located in a government-owned park, closed to the public, on the outskirts of the city. Due to local zoning, it's composed of only two layers of land, separated by only the height of a single story, and the ball-jointed spaceframe has been replaced by more basic rectangular tubes.[44] It has been essentially abandoned since the late 1980s. Standing on its layers, you can see Mount Fuji in the distance, just as in some of Kikutake's renderings. Between this formal affinity, substantial avant-garde lineage, and diagrammatic boldness of section, the A-frame solution was understandably exciting for its designers.

In May 2014, I visited the project together with a Gotemba city official and my research assistant. Stepping onto the pyramid's lowest layer, we entered one of the infill structures. The lock had recently been picked, because the city had lost the key. We found ourselves in a dusty meeting room with wall-to-wall carpet redolent of ancient cigarette smoke. Hung with various representations of how and where Stratiforms could be deployed, the centerpiece of the room was a large-scale model of the design represented in all its glory, complete with tennis courts. Leaning on a wall was a presentation board that, aside from announcing Stratiform's concept, states that between 1973 and 1988 the cost for the research project was twenty million US dollars.

With no Stratiform ever delivering a suburban idyll over a train track or highway, it's fair to ask what MITI got for its money. According to Harada, many of the technologies developed through the research migrated into other projects, and Stratiform's role as a node hosting various investigations may actually be more important than making an inexpensive A-frame. To a certain extent, the design offered a compelling narrative to inspire a team making discoveries for future buildings that might not be A-frames. Seen from this perspective of technological development and dissemination, the A-frame offered a clear and convenient diagram to explore.

Several examples of this developmental influence are conspicuous. One is ACROS Fukuoka Prefectural International Hall (1994), designed by Emilio Ambasz and built by Takenaka. A set of massive stepping terraces that resembles the Hanging Gardens of Babylon, Harada asserts that it is a direct application of the greening systems first tried in Gotemba in 1984, where various armatures of wire mesh and planters were deployed to turn the A-frame into a pile of shrubs and vines.[45] Other examples are found in the later work of Utida. Although he apparently had little involvement with Stratiform, his subsequent research extended the use of access floors and a pragmatic reliance on the open market for providing infill elements within a structural frame. But the most important technology tested in Gotemba was seismic base isolation, which later became standard practice in earthquake-prone regions. At the time an emerging approach, base isolation entails placing special pads between a structure and its foundation, allowing a degree of horizontal motion between the two. As a result, the destructive tremors of an earthquake are mostly absorbed in the foundation while the structure atop remains relatively stable. In Gotemba, such pads were tested under the infill houses on the frame. Tadatoshi Asano, the former Takenaka housing director, notes that by the 1990s base isolation had made high-rise residential construction much more flexible.[46]

top: Kiyonori Kikutake, Stratiform study, 1977

bottom: Emilio Ambasz, ACROS Prefectural International Hall, Fukuoka, 1994

following: Stratiform prototype in Gotemba (2014)

SOLUTIONISM: STRATIFORM STRUCTURE MODULE, 1973–

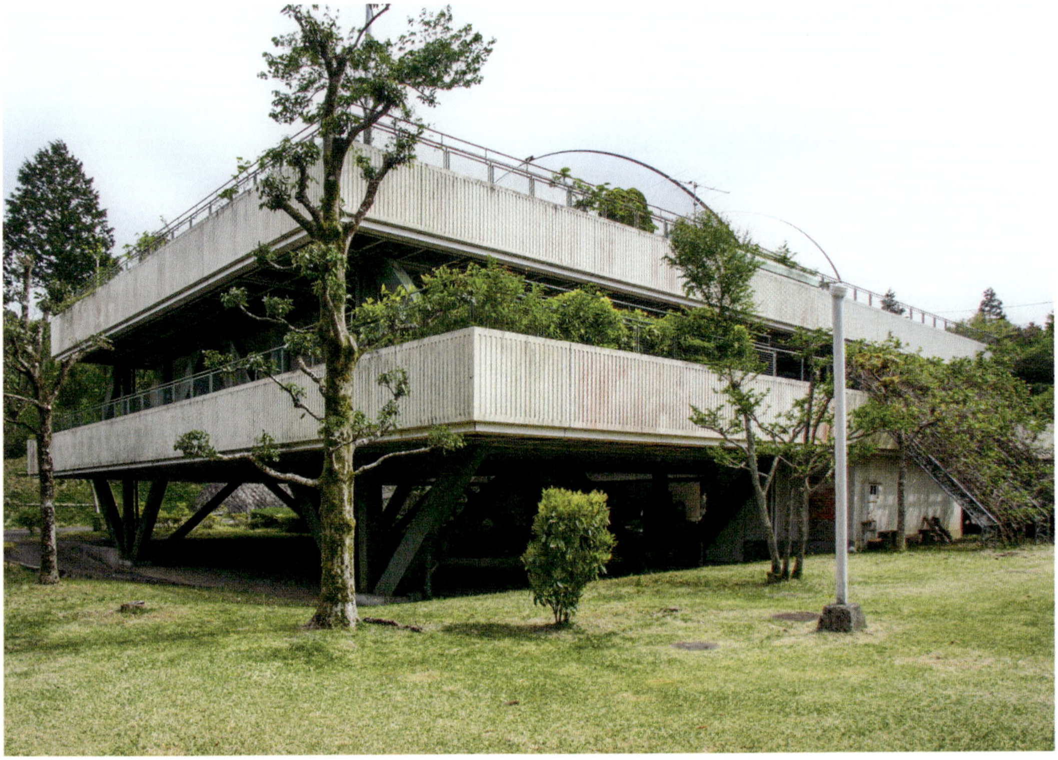

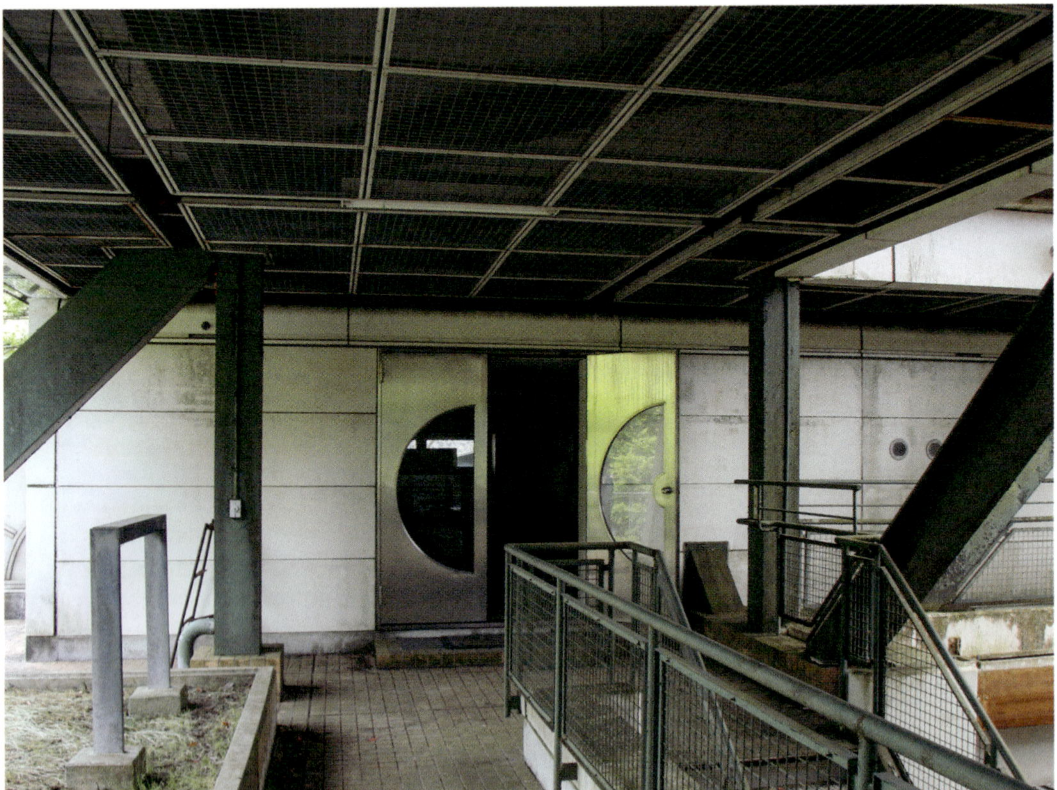

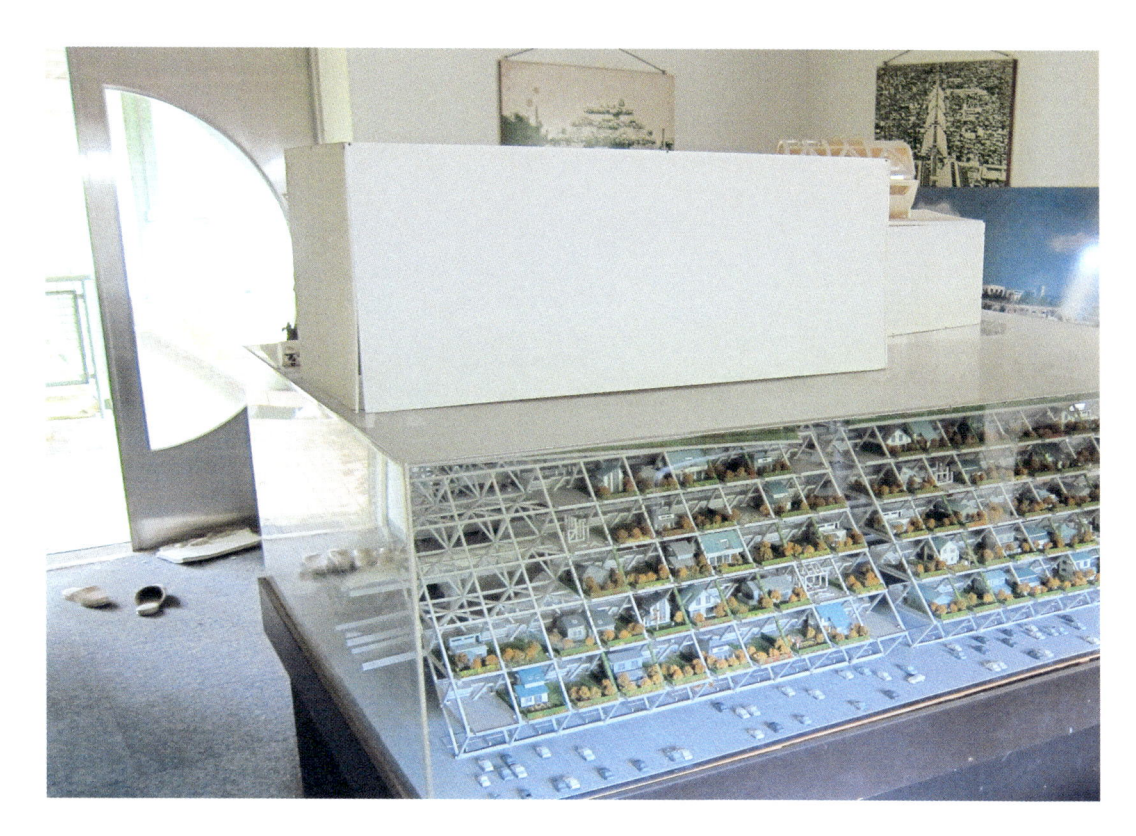

SOLUTIONISM: STRATIFORM STRUCTURE MODULE, 1973–

213

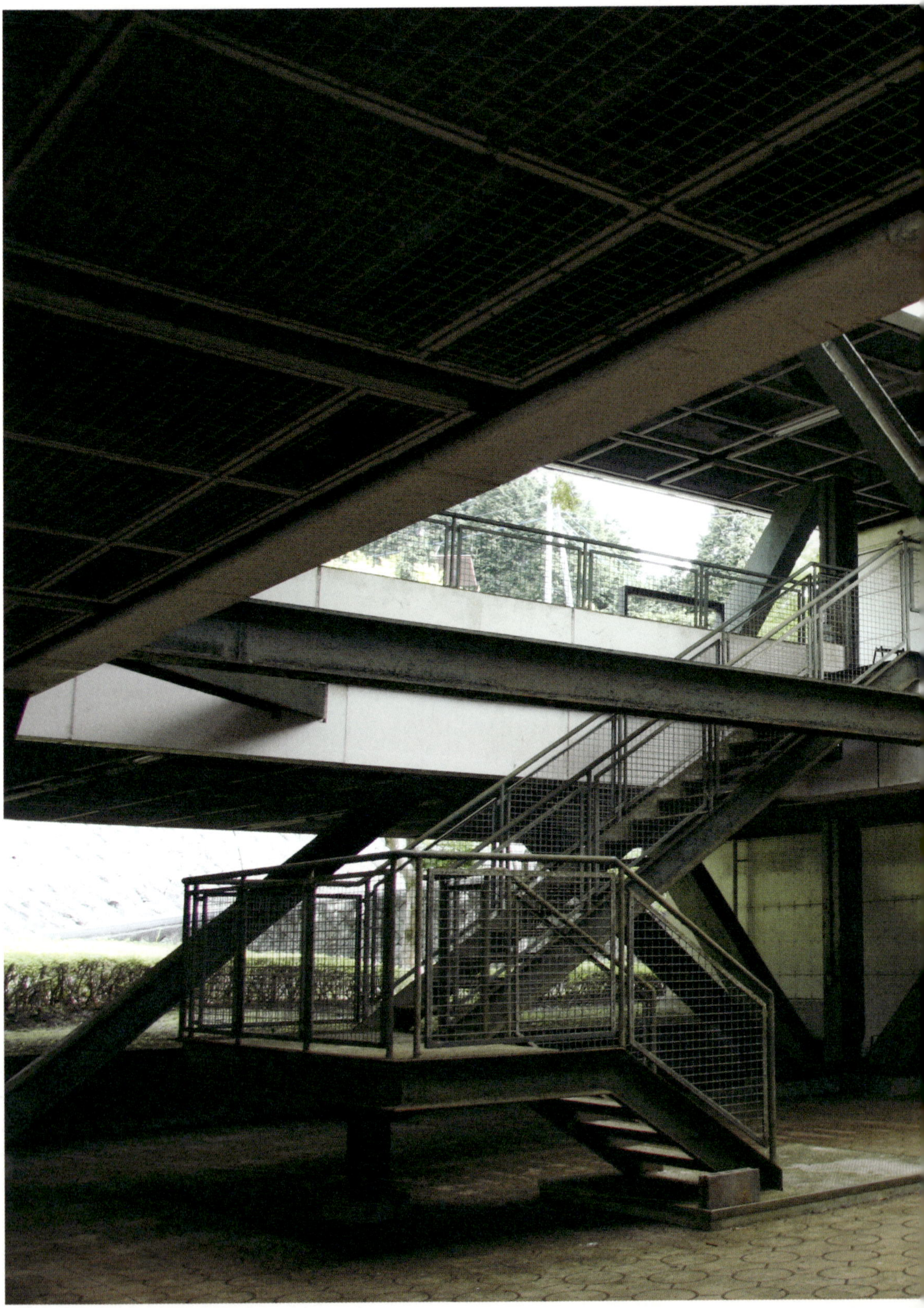

SOLUTIONISM: STRATIFORM STRUCTURE MODULE, 1973–

2 THE METABOLIST-INDUSTRIAL COMPLEX

SOLUTIONISM: STRATIFORM STRUCTURE MODULE, 1973–

Despite Stratiform's solutionism, it's perfectly plausible that situations exist for which it is appropriate. One such situation might be the areas destroyed on March 11, 2011 by the Tohoku earthquake and tsunami. During my interview with Harada, I asked how long he worked on Stratiform, and he replied, "I still am!"[47] With his office, founded after leaving Kikutake, he has been working to convince officials in Miyagi Prefecture and Rikuzentakata City to use a Stratiform approach for an integrated reconstruction of public infrastructure and private buildings. One of the most contentious aspects of reconstruction is the approach to new sea walls, as those proposed by the government would completely sever the local towns and cities from the water—the ocean may be a threat to the residents, but it is also their livelihood. Harada imagines that the spaceframe of Stratiform could straddle these walls, creating continuity between land and ocean, while providing refuge on its raised levels in the event of flooding. Though the spaceframe had threatened to let vehicular pollution enter the simulated suburbia, here its porosity could let tsunami water simply flow underneath. Sometimes the solution may find the problem.

1. Shizuo Harada, in conversation with the author, May 15, 2014. Alex Kerr further confirms this source of income for Japanese ministries in general, noting that gambling proceeds provide "pocket money" free of scrutiny from the Ministry of Finance. See Kerr, *Dogs and Demons: Tales from the Dark Side of Japan* (New York: Hill and Wang, 2001), 156.
2. Regarding connection between the book's policies and pre-existing MITI policies, see André Sorensen, *The Making of Urban Japan: Cities and Planning from Edo to the Twenty-First Century* (New York: Routledge, 2002), 229.
3. On MITI speechwriters, see Rem Koolhaas and Hans Ulrich Obrist, *Project Japan: Metabolism Talks…* (Cologne: Taschen, 2011), 649.
4. Kakuei Tanaka, *Building a New Japan: A Plan for Remodeling the Japanese Archipelago* [1972] (Tokyo: The Simul Press, 1973), 3–5.
5. This was not always the case. Some provincial cities, such as Minamata and Yokkaichi, were major sites for polluting industries.
6. Tanaka, *Building*, 77.
7. Tanaka, *Building*, 20.
8. Tanaka, *Building*, 51.
9. Tanaka, *Building*, 200.
10. See Ann Waswo, *Housing in Postwar Japan: A Social History* (New York: Routledge, 2002), 79.
11. Harada, May 15, 2014.
12. *The Stratiform Structure Module* (Tokyo: The Mechanical Social Systems Foundation, 1990), 2–3.
13. The recent Hudson Yards project in Manhattan built its platform over active train tracks with a completely different approach. See "Hudson Yards Platform Construction Video," accessed August 27, 2019, https://www.youtube.com/watch?v=XbRxT50jjUo.
14. See "History," Irvine Access Floors, accessed August 28, 2019, http://www.irvineaccessfloors.com/about-us/history/, and Iñaki Ábalos and Juan Herreros, *Tower and Office: From Modernist Theory to Contemporary Practice* [1992] (Cambridge, MA: The MIT Press, 2003), 150–151.
15. Access floors appeared in the Stratiform research at latest by 1977.
16. *The Stratiform*, 9–10.
17. Harada, May 15, 2014.
18. See Saikaku Toyokawa, "Cold Climate Housing Research and the Syowa Station Building in Antarctica: Asada Takashi and the Beginnings of Capsule Architecture," in *Metabolism—The City of the Future: Dreams and Visions of Reconstruction in Postwar and Present-Day Japan*, ed. Mami Hirose et al. (Tokyo: Mori Art Museum, 2011), 236–239.
19. See "History of Misawa Homes Group," accessed August 27, 2019, https://www.misawa.co.jp/en/info/history.html.
20. As of 2016, Toyota Home controls Misawa as a subsidiary.
21. The M1 was recognized for its significance in 2005 by Docomomo Japan. See *DOCOMOMO Japan: The 100 Selections* issue of *The Japan Architect*, no. 57 (Spring, 2005): 137.
22. See Michael Franklin Ross, *Beyond Metabolism: The New Japanese Architecture* (New York: McGraw-Hill, 1978), 65.
23. See Yositika Utida, *The Construction and Culture of Architecture Today: A View from Japan* (Tokyo: Ichigaya Publsihing, 2002), 25.
24. See Waswo, *Housing*, 93.
25. Many of the architects considered "New Wave" were in *A New Wave of Japanese Architecture*, a 1978 exhibition and catalog organized by the Institute for Architecture and Urban Studies in New York. There is overlap, however, between this cohort and Metabolism through Arata Isozaki and Fumihiko Maki's inclusion in the New Wave camp. See *A New Wave of Japanese Architecture*, ed. Kenneth Frampton (New York: The Institute for Architecture and Urban Studies, 1978).

26. Regarding Shinohara's lack of faith in Metabolism's urban-scale orientation that ignored house design, see Toyo Ito's 1975 essay, "We ask Kiyonori Kikutake, 'Teach Us to Outgrow Our Madness'," translated and reprinted by Thomas Daniell in his *An Anatomy of Influence* (London: AA Publications, 2018), 100–101.
27. Manfredo Tafuri, *Architecture and Utopia: Design and Capitalist Development* [1973], trans. Barbara Luigia La Penta (Cambridge, MA: The MIT Press, 1976), 132.
28. See James Barlow and Ritsuko Ozaki, "Building Mass Customized Housing through Innovation in the Production System: Lessons from Japan," *Environment and Planning A* 37 (2005): 15. Barlow and Ozaki note that as of 2000, there were 405 show villages nationally.
29. See Hajime Yatsuka, "Beyond Architecture and Design," chap. 14-1 in "Metabolism Nexus" (unpublished manuscript, 2012), PDF file. English translation by Riyo Namigata of Hajime Yatsuka, *Metabolism Nexus* [in Japanese] (Tokyo: Ohmsha, 2011).
30. Michael Dobbins, *Urban Design and People* (Hoboken, NJ: John Wiley & Sons, 2009), 183. I was introduced to Dobbins through Evgeny Morozov, *To Save Everything, Click Here: The Folly of Technological Solutionism* (New York: Public Affairs, 2013), 5–6.
31. Dobbins, *Urban*, 182.
32. See Maurice Culot and Lise Grenier, eds., *Henri Sauvage 1873–1932* (Brussels: Archives d'Architecture Moderne, 1978), 23.
33. Regarding sunshine rights, see Sorensen, *Making*, 254.
34. Asthma was especially a problem, as noted in this chapter's introduction, most notoriously caused by oil refineries in the city of Yokkaichi. See page 135 of this book and "Yokkaichi asthma," last modified May 15, 2020, http://en.wikipedia.org/wiki/Yokkaichi_asthma.
35. This is quoted from a presentation board found at the Gotemba Stratiform, visited by the author May 11, 2014.
36. With the exception of the prototype built in Toyama, with a 60-degree spaceframe, no Stratiform studies that I've seen show any variation from 45 degrees, which would have allowed better adaptation to specific sites.
37. Sorensen, *Making*, 265.
38. Yatsuka, "Nexus," chap. 14-5.
39. See Sorensen, *Making*, 229, 243. Charges of corruption were leveled at Tanaka for tipping off political allies in areas planned for the new transportation, allowing them to buy up cheap land before the specific locations of plans were publicly announced. These charges would lead to his resignation in 1974. See "Kakuei Tanaka," accessed August 28, 2019, http://en.wikipedia.org/wiki/Kakuei_Tanaka#Resignation.
40. This is a characterization provided by Tadatoshi Asano, email exchange with the author, December 28, 2014.
41. The company was privatized in 1987, with its spin-offs taking various names, such as East Japan Railway Company, one of Yotsuya's current operators.
42. Harada, May 15, 2014.
43. Harada, May 15, 2014.
44. According to Harada, the ball joints were eventually discovered to be too expensive, totaling half the cost of the entire primary structure. Harada, May 15, 2014.
45. Harada, May 15, 2014.
46. Asano, December 28, 2014.
47. Harada, May 15, 2014.

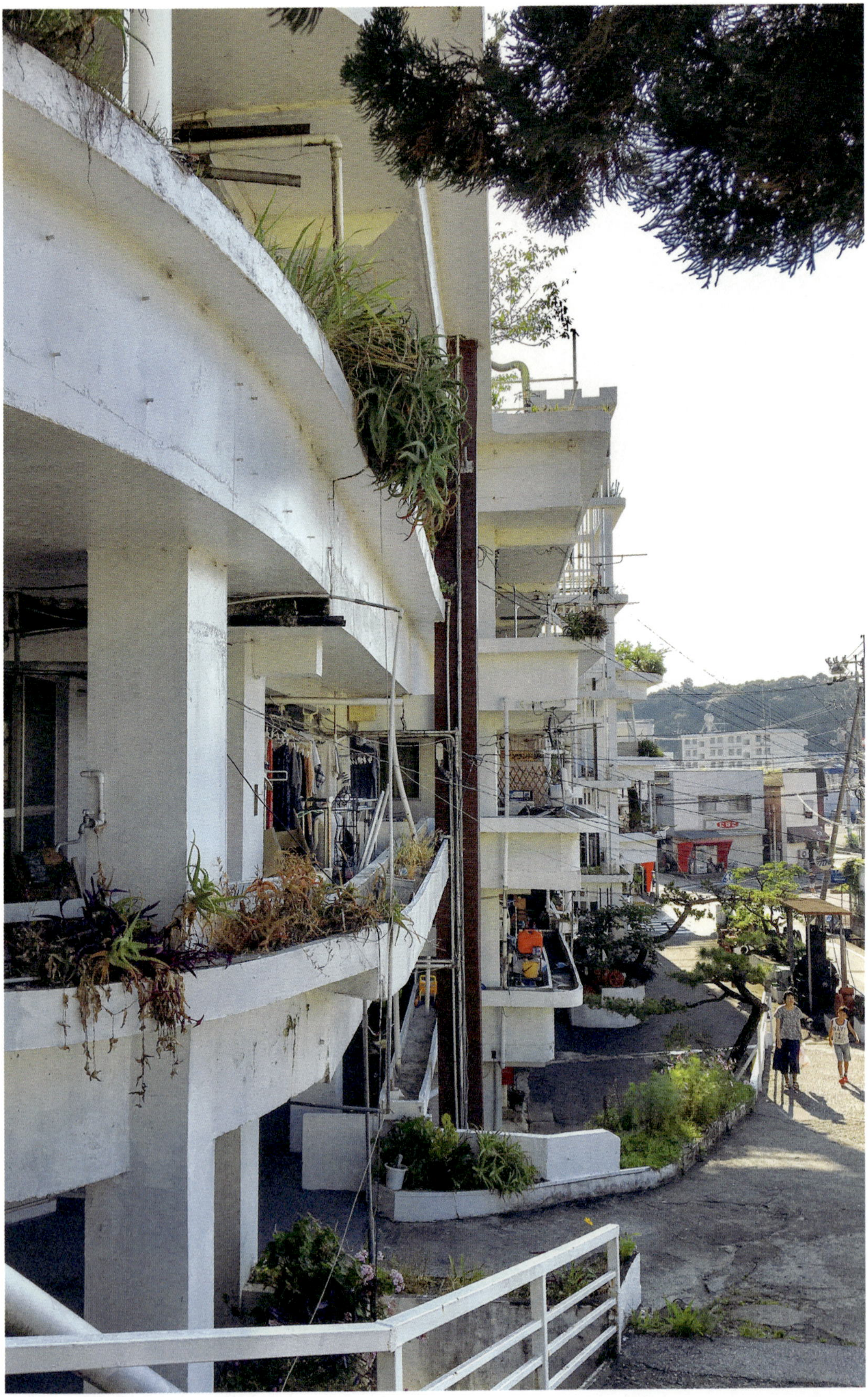

Artificial Land Without Architects:
Sawada Mansion, 1971–

Vernacular architecture tends to be seen as a "timeless way of building" that is natural and correct, or an "applied archaeology" of stylistic imitation.[1] John Habraken's essay "Lives of Systems" avoids this opposition by locating vernacular architecture not in styles but in processes that are, in fact, not timeless. As he observes, a living vernacular is always based on commonly available elements and systems that are understood and used by both experts and laypersons. These materials are almost always industrially produced and subject to ongoing technological improvements, with Habraken noting that "There is no conflict between industrial production and small-scale ad hoc building processes. On the contrary, they thrive on each other."[2]

      This description of vernacular processes links it with informal housing, which is often inhabited without security of tenure to the land it sits on, and usually in violation of zoning and construction codes.[3] Just as Habraken rejects the vernacular's conventional associations with fixed styles and old-fashioned techniques, so he does away with the idea of informal housing as housing built by its occupants. Though this does happen, he claims that more significant are the networks of contractors and construction workers who frequently are the actual builders in the informal sector, moonlighting perhaps from their formal-sector employment. He uses Cairo as an example, where Dom-ino type skeletons built by small local contractors dominate the informal cityscape, showing the degree to which reinforced concrete is firmly entrenched as the preferred building material, as in many other areas of informal urbanization around the world. In Cairo, as just about everywhere, "Anyone can buy cement and steel rods as well as sand and gravel," and "Once the basic principles are understood a simple floor can be constructed by anyone who has seen it done before."[4]

left and following:
Kano and Hiroe Sawada,
Sawada Mansion, Kochi,
1991 (2017)

221

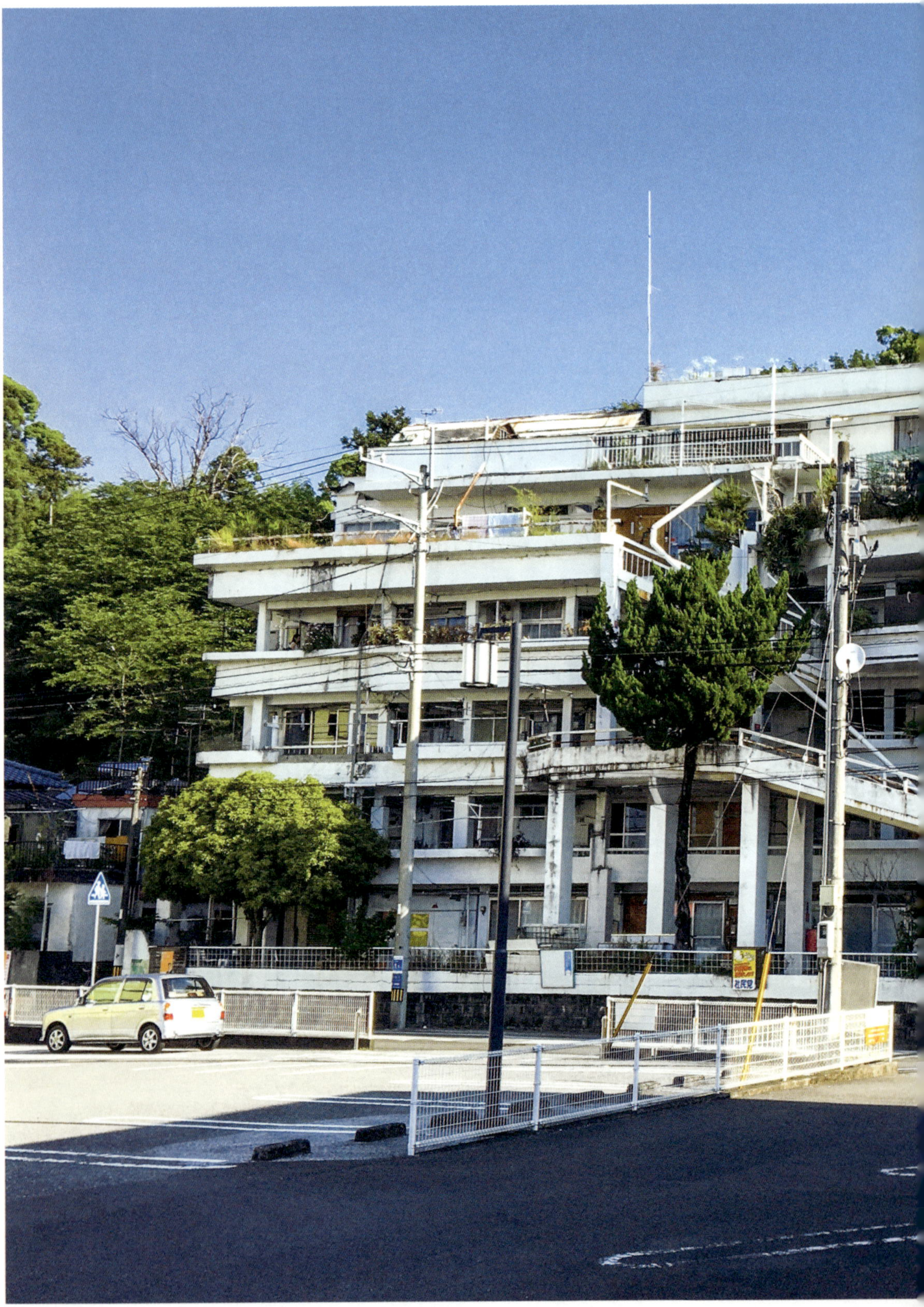

ARTIFICIAL LAND WITHOUT ARCHITECTS: SAWADA MANSION, 1971–

Kano and Hiroe Sawada, 1973

Mom-and-Pop *Zenekon*

While not mentioned in Habraken's essay, Sawada Mansion is another example of his argument, manifested in fantastic form. Affectionately known as "Sawaman" by its residents, the apartment building was built by husband and wife Kano and Hiroe Sawada between 1971 and 1991 in Kochi, on Shikoku Island. It's a stunning specimen of the barrack sensibility that effectively rejects the Metabolist-industrial complex's prefabricated and top-down vision of how to deliver better apartments. Instead, it's a highly expressive use of a concrete skeleton frame, formed and poured by the self-taught builder couple.

Described by some as the Japanese Kowloon Walled City, Sawaman has a fluctuating number of apartments, averaging around sixty, along with a freely interspersed assortment of small businesses. None of the apartments are the same. Six-stories high and served by an open-air elevator, the 70-meter-long building has a ramp winding along it for people, cars, and almost anything else. This connection helps to give each resident what Kano felt to be "a ground-floor experience."[5] There is a large fishpond on the fourth floor, and a lumber mill on the fifth. On the rooftop is an array of solar hot-water panels, a chicken coop, a pig pen, a rabbit hutch, a large vegetable garden and rice paddy, and a home-made construction crane that's as much symbolic as practical for the whole DIY endeavor.

In his famous exhibition and book from 1964, *Architecture Without Architects*, Bernard Rudofsky describes vernacular architecture as "non-pedigreed," a condition that applies to Sawaman's freedom from the influence of Metabolists and ministries.[6] The structure is also free of approval from the Kochi building department.

Yet despite being an outsider, it's one of the most successful demonstrations of artificial land ever built, and proves a point implied by recognized artificial land theorists such as Yosizaka and Kawazoe: the skeleton frame is an accessible, intuitive, and generous way to build, enabling Sunday carpenters and many others.

Sawaman's success is intimately tied to the Sawadas themselves, especially to Kano, who died in 2003 at the age of 75. The architect Tetsuro Kagaya writes in his book *All About Sawada Mansion*—on which I rely for much of this story—that Kano was a lumber dealer before adding design-build developer and property manager to his repertoire of skills. His official education ended after elementary school, where in the fifth grade he chanced across a magazine from an agricultural cooperative that contained an article on apartment building management. From that day forward, he decided that building and managing a big apartment building was his life's calling.[7] With his and Hiroe's roles at Sawaman encompassing design, construction, and management, they created a mom-and-pop version of a giant full-service *zenekon*.[8] What makes this business succeed is their attitude toward management in particular.

People live and work in skeleton frames the world over, but what makes or breaks artificial land's fulfillment is the level of control within a frame. The "hard" side of creating infrastructure is relatively easy, whereas the "soft" side of controlling its usage by a multitude of residents can be much less so. Seen in terms of the artificial land projects so far explored here, this management challenge helps explain the concept's more frequent use in long-term transitions, such as systematic renovations controlled top-down, rather than for maximizing resident participation as an initial and ongoing condition. Participation and diverse build-outs for most architects and managers are too slow and too expensive to be desirable. Yet it's something at which the Sawadas excel, thanks in part, it seems, to their spiritual beliefs.

Buddhist Economics

The Sawadas, now with their adult children's help, are very responsive to individual renters' needs: they renovate and modify apartments to offer a range of units for various lifestyles, and adjust rents to accommodate different financial situations.[9] Rather than profit maximization, this unconventional approach appears to be informed by Kano's devotion to Shintoism and Buddhism, which he learned from his grandmother, who lived with his family when he was a boy.

The pursuit of maximized well-being instead of only personal monetary gain aligns the Sawadas' approach with what economist E. F. Schumacher calls "Buddhist economics." Schumacher established himself as a guru of alternative approaches to development with his 1973 book *Small is Beautiful: Economics as if People Mattered*. He sees capitalism as a conflict between an employer's ideal of "output without employees," and an employee's ideal of "income without employment." To escape this contradiction, he suggests the Buddhist pursuit of "right livelihood." Schumacher writes that right livelihood, a core aspect of Buddhist thought, is the search or practice of work able to "give man a chance to utilise and develop his faculties; to enable him to overcome his ego-centredness by joining with other people in a common task; and to bring forth the goods and services needed for a becoming existence."[10] From this perspective, capitalism's goal of profit maximization fails to achieve the maximum human satisfaction that is the goal of Buddhist economics—as does, Rudofsky notes, most architects' obsession with maximization of prestige instead of problems of living.[11]

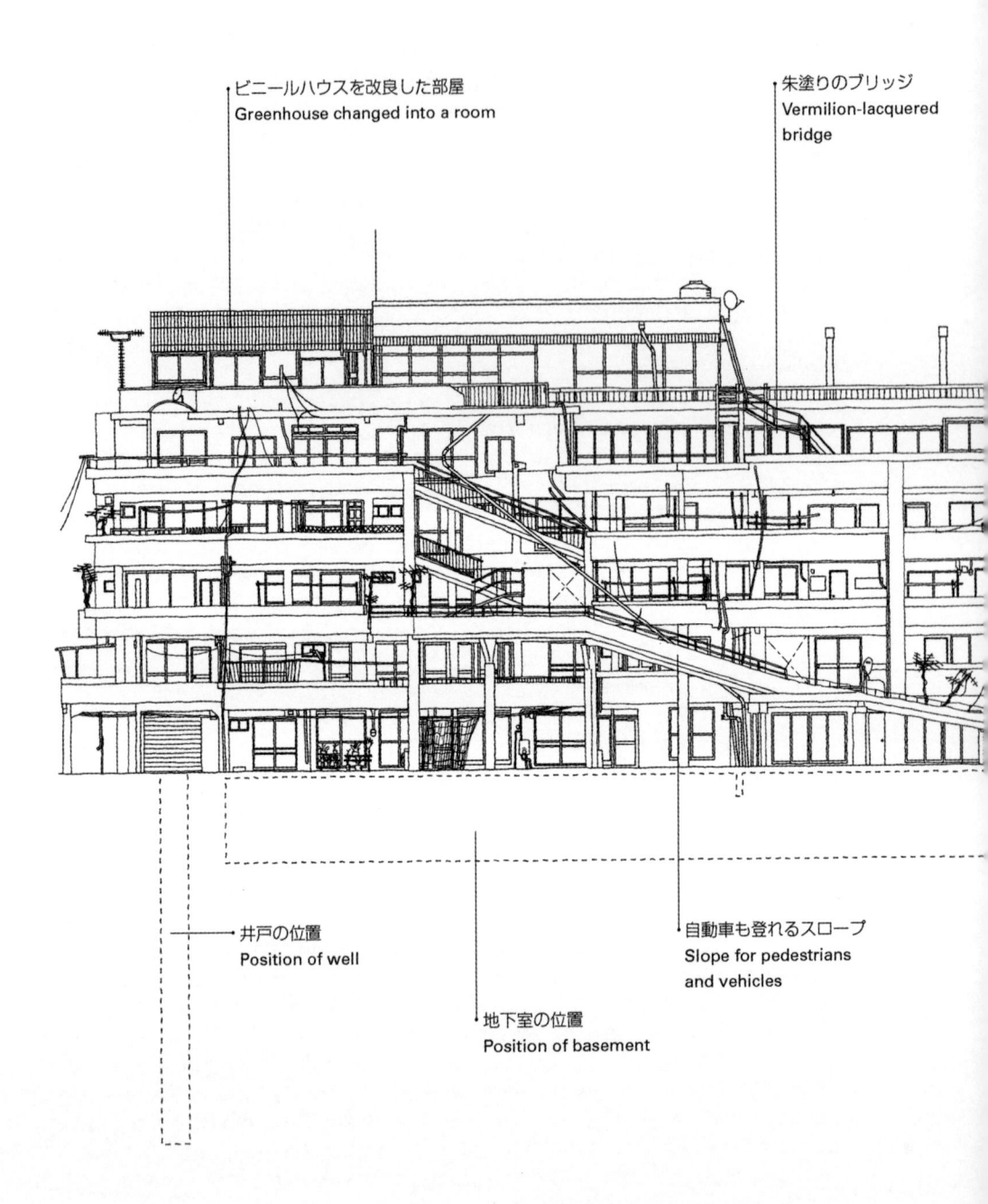

ビニールハウスを改良した部屋
Greenhouse changed into a room

朱塗りのブリッジ
Vermilion-lacquered bridge

井戸の位置
Position of well

地下室の位置
Position of basement

自動車も登れるスロープ
Slope for pedestrians and vehicles

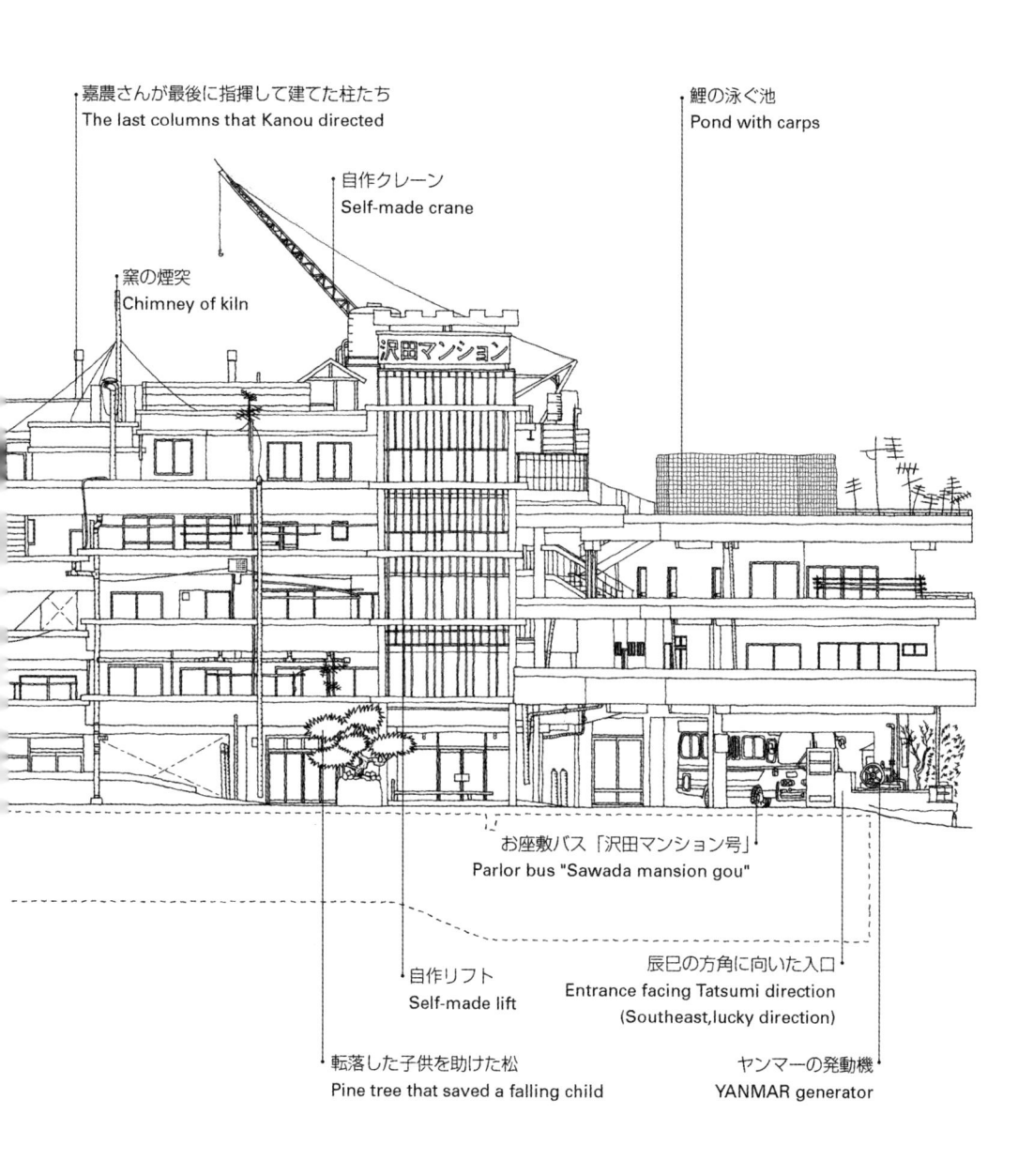

嘉農さんが最後に指揮して建てた柱たち
The last columns that Kanou directed

自作クレーン
Self-made crane

窯の煙突
Chimney of kiln

鯉の泳ぐ池
Pond with carps

お座敷バス「沢田マンション号」
Parlor bus "Sawada mansion gou"

自作リフト
Self-made lift

辰巳の方角に向いた入口
Entrance facing Tatsumi direction
(Southeast, lucky direction)

転落した子供を助けた松
Pine tree that saved a falling child

ヤンマーの発動機
YANMAR generator

Tetsuro Kagaya, Sawada Mansion south elevation survey, 2007

following: Sawada Mansion (2017)

ARTIFICIAL LAND WITHOUT ARCHITECTS: SAWADA MANSION, 1971–

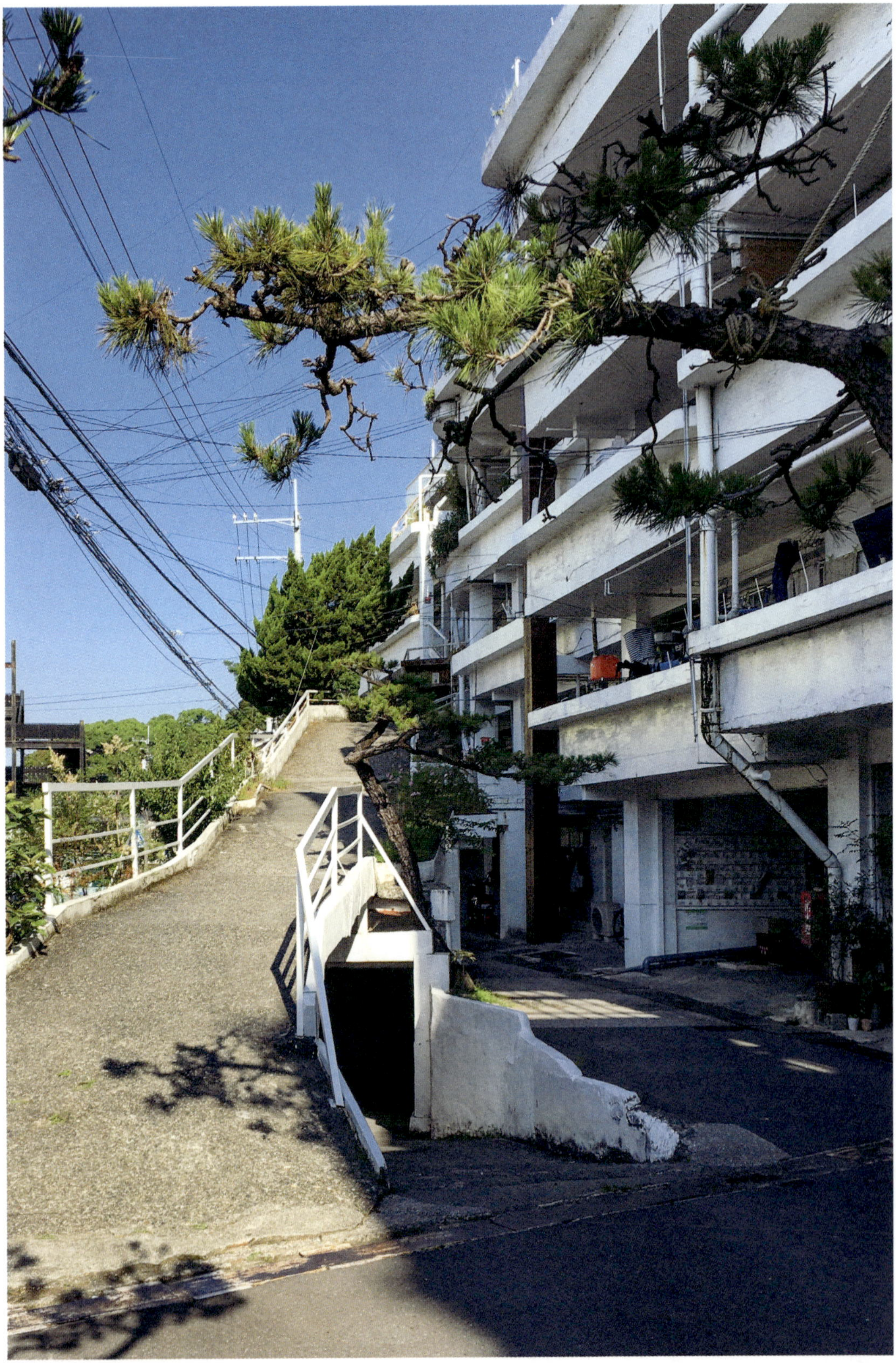

ARTIFICIAL LAND WITHOUT ARCHITECTS: SAWADA MANSION, 1971–

230　　　　　　　　　　　　　　　　　　　　　　　　　2　THE METABOLIST-INDUSTRIAL COMPLEX

ARTIFICIAL LAND WITHOUT ARCHITECTS: SAWADA MANSION, 1971–

Schumacher further writes that a Buddhist approach entails "the systematic study of how to attain given ends with the minimum means," specifically minimal exploitation of human and natural resources, an objective strongly reminiscent of Marx's metabolic vision.[12] In relying on a minimal construction crew of just two people, and building in the service of their own and their diverse tenants' well-being, the Sawadas practice Buddhist property management.

Plans in Heaven

Kano's childhood home was sunless and dank, and this environment helped fuel the other part of his dream: to live in a home flooded with sunlight.[13] The specific form of a large, sunny apartment building began taking shape when he and Hiroe bought a perfect south-facing plot, one in accord with their beliefs on orientation and land features, which were derived from a mixture of geomantic practices.[14]

The couple had been training themselves for the construction project for some time. They had already been operating as design-builders of inexpensive homes in Nakamura and other areas in Kochi Prefecture, a business that started during the period of rapid economic growth in the 1960s. The boom happily coincided with the fame the couple attained through having built a house that was the only structure to survive a massive typhoon in the area. This testament to their skills brought numerous commissions, and they claim to have built over 300 apartments prior to Sawaman.[15] Examples of their work from this period show the couple had a predilection for using a skeleton frame's freedoms to the fullest, with some of their small apartment buildings appearing to be lost relatives of the Yosizaka House, as seen in the varied floorplans and facades. Artificial land appears as pure vernacular, free of theory.[16]

The site for their dream was purchased with the proceeds of the sale of eight apartment buildings in Kochi that the couple had built and managed.[17] Having acquired management experience and a site, they started building on the narrow plot's western end, and moved eastward. Work began in 1971, in three main phases of "horn"-style construction, in which exposed rebar sprouts from the ends of columns and slabs, ready to be spliced into further concrete additions.[18] As soon as each section was complete, they rented it out to fund the rest of the building. Though Kagaya writes in his book that Kano made a rough plan on some graph paper for the first phase, the drawing did not significantly guide the construction. As Hiroe has more recently said, the plans exist only in her husband's head in heaven.[19] Not until Kagaya did survey drawings did she know how big the building in fact was.[20]

Phase 1 consisting of four floors and twenty-four apartments was completed in 1973. The edifice was dubbed a "mansion" in what seems a parody of the aspiration-filled marketing of the banal condominiums then appearing throughout Japan. After the Sawadas moved in, the second phase started the same year. In 1975, Kano brought dirt from one of the forest properties he owned to make a roof garden and provide insulation. The pace of construction then slowed, with the third phase built between 1983 and '85. Kagaya notes that the first and second phase were totally DIY in their engineering and construction, while for the third phase the Sawadas hired a professional to size the structure and build its formwork.[21]

Demonstrating Stewart Brand's observation that "a building is not something you finish" but rather "something you start," Sawaman's construction has not stopped since.[22]

Rehearsals of Sawada Mansion's construction in earlier apartment projects by the Sawadas

following: Sawada Mansion (2017)

ARTIFICIAL LAND WITHOUT ARCHITECTS: SAWADA MANSION, 1971–

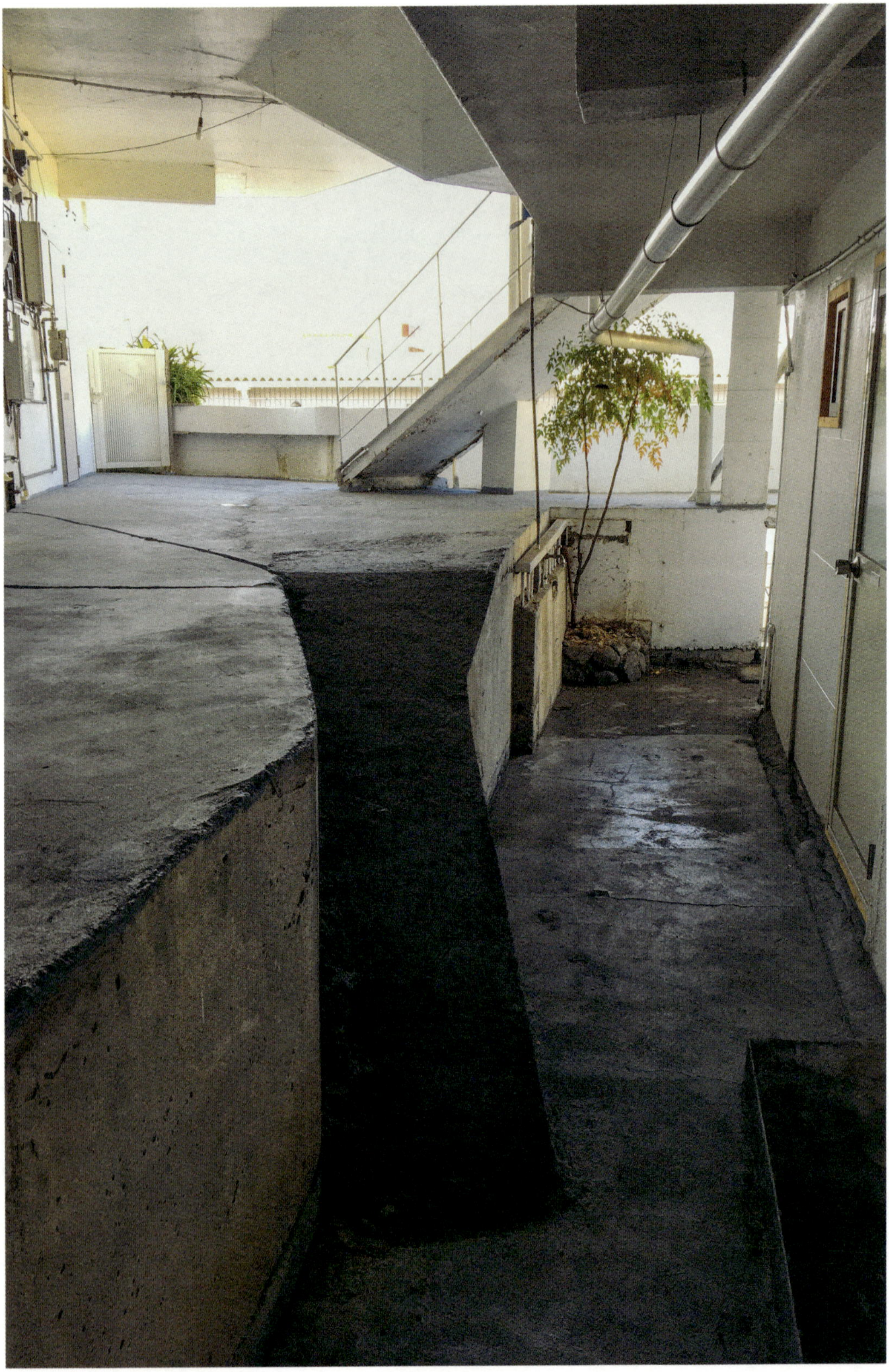

ARTIFICIAL LAND WITHOUT ARCHITECTS: SAWADA MANSION, 1971–

Unlike most buildings, which treat circulation as infrastructure to be built first, stairs and ramps have been added ad hoc, as needs arise. Most dramatically, Kano built the ramp in 1989, and in 1991 added the elevator mainly for bringing wood to and from the lumber mill.

Accommodations

Organizationally, each floor's apartments are grouped into clusters bordered by open-air corridors, with the resulting exposure of the varied units placing Sawaman squarely at the romantic end of artificial land's romantic/realist spectrum. Wide galleries are often located on the opposite sides of units, giving rise to what could be called "double-loaded apartments" rather than the ubiquitous double-loaded corridors found in developer architecture around the globe. The increased exterior surface area improves access to light and air, with some residents relying on cross ventilation instead of air conditioning. But Sawaman doesn't pursue the Stratiform Structure Module's transposition of a suburban lifestyle, aside from perhaps part of the Sawadas' own apartment on the roof, one section of which looks like a cozy gabled cabin. Instead of private front lawns, as Kikutake had imagined, the units usually share the wide pedestrian streets as communal space. Frequently over two meters wide, the corridors exceed architect Christopher Alexander's insistence that balconies, galleries, and the like should be at least that dimension in order to be properly used for socializing.[23] Indeed, occupants use the corridors for outdoor eating, laundry, or displaying wares from their boutiques, living the vibrant street-in-the-sky dream that eluded Western modernists.

above: Sawada Mansion (2017)

right: Ramp creating "a ground-floor experience" on every level

ARTIFICIAL LAND WITHOUT ARCHITECTS: SAWADA MANSION, 1971–

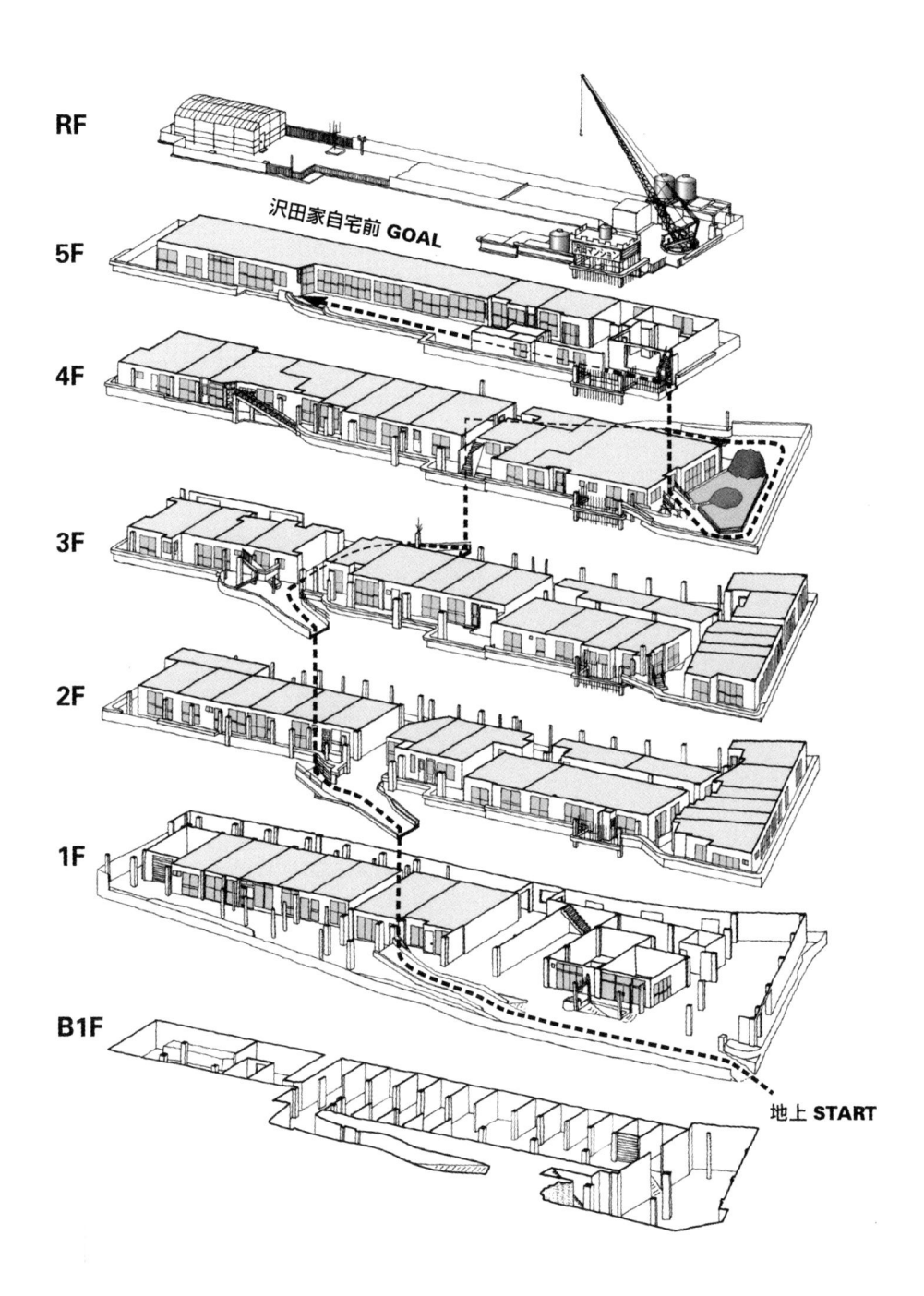

237

Unlike Motomachi and especially Ashiyahama, Sawaman is devoid of large-scale prefabricated components demanding careful coordination, and it thereby avoids what was the bane of Kano's way of working: extensive planning. Instead, the Sawadas' reliance on wieldy materials and basic equipment translates into a responsive, ongoing metabolism. Such transformation is helped by a large stockpile of salvaged doors and windows, as well as by wood from one of the family's forests, milled on the fifth floor to make dimensioned lumber.[24] Now, after Kano's death, his daughter Kazuko performs most of the renovation work, with the changes trending toward larger units.

Thanks to Sawaman's diversity of unit types, it's common for residents to move within the building. Eleven of the twenty-five families interviewed by Kagaya had moved internally, due to needing more or less space, often due to changes in family size.[25] One resident, Meisai Okamoto, who has moved through seven different apartments, says that Kano thought these moves were good for residents to get to know each other.

In addition to the variety the Sawadas offer in what they rent, they are also unusually flexible in how they rent. As Kagaya describes, Sawaman is free of the conventional, and at times challenging, screening process found at most Japanese rental properties, which require guarantors and financial statements. Sawaman's only filter is the Sawadas themselves, and the property has become a refuge for people unable to gain approval for typical rentals. The Sawadas just decide if they trust a potential tenant based on a face-to-face meeting. If so, they require no "key money"—basically a large tip typical of most rentals. Contracts can be flexible in duration, with rent determined on a case-by-case basis depending on what is considered fair.[26]

Today, Sawaman remains an illegal building. When the project was started, it was one of many in Kochi that were erected without approval, as was then common throughout Japan. But Sawaman stands out, making it a particular target for enforcement. The city has asked the Sawadas to be more compliant, though the only concession so far has been the addition of emergency-exit signs. Recently a "Sawaman Expo" has been organized as a festival for generating support and accumulating public affection for the edifice to help defend its existence against threats by the building department. The city increasingly, if begrudgingly, accepts that Sawaman provides for people who don't easily fit in elsewhere.

As Rudofsky writes in *Architecture Without Architects*, people generally consider the "art of living" to be "a form of debauch, little aware that its tenets are frugality, cleanliness, and a general respect for creation, not to mention Creation."[27] Today the truth of this is quite evident and intensified in the promotion of "hedonistic sustainability," a call which adds to the general association of lifestyle with the most spectacle-driven and exclusive ideas of luxury.[28] Sawaman is not exclusive. Not a predefined product, it supports multiple lifestyles by being a tolerant environment. Despite its extreme contrast with the products of the Metabolist-industrial complex, it would be a mistake to see Sawaman as a total outlier from a spirit that can be seen with others in the 1970s. Though it is outside artificial land culture as promulgated by the Metabolists and the ministries, Sawaman's construction coincided with a renewed fascination with vernacular systems then emerging in pedigreed circles.

right and following:
Tetsuro Kagaya, Sawada
Mansion survey plans, 2007

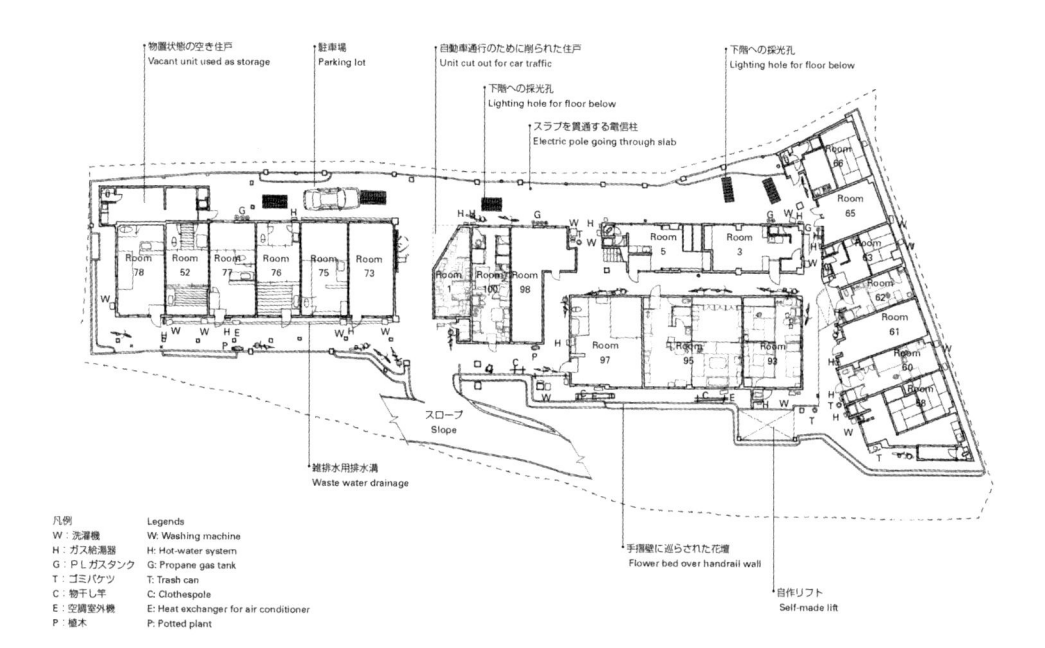

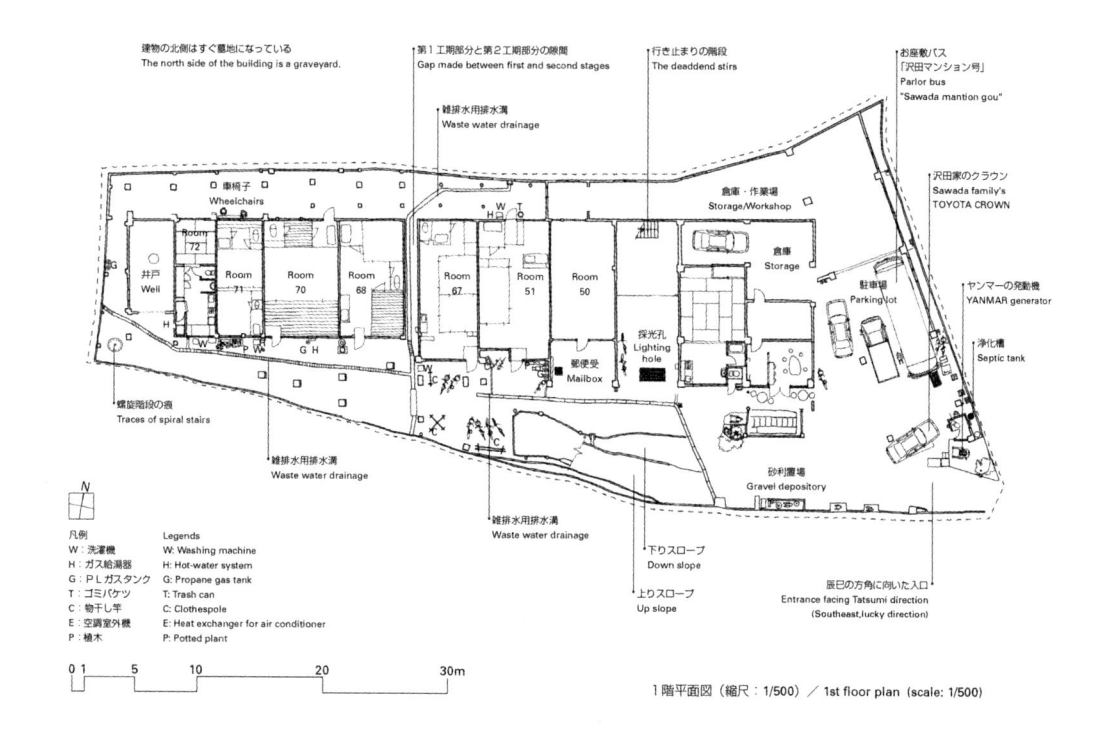

ARTIFICIAL LAND WITHOUT ARCHITECTS: SAWADA MANSION, 1971–

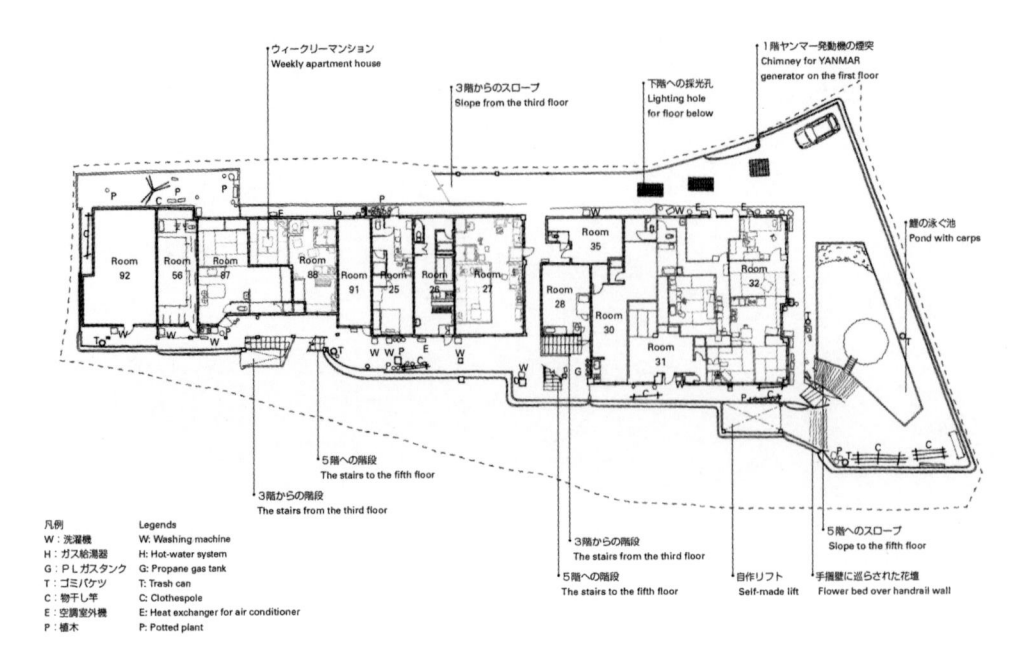

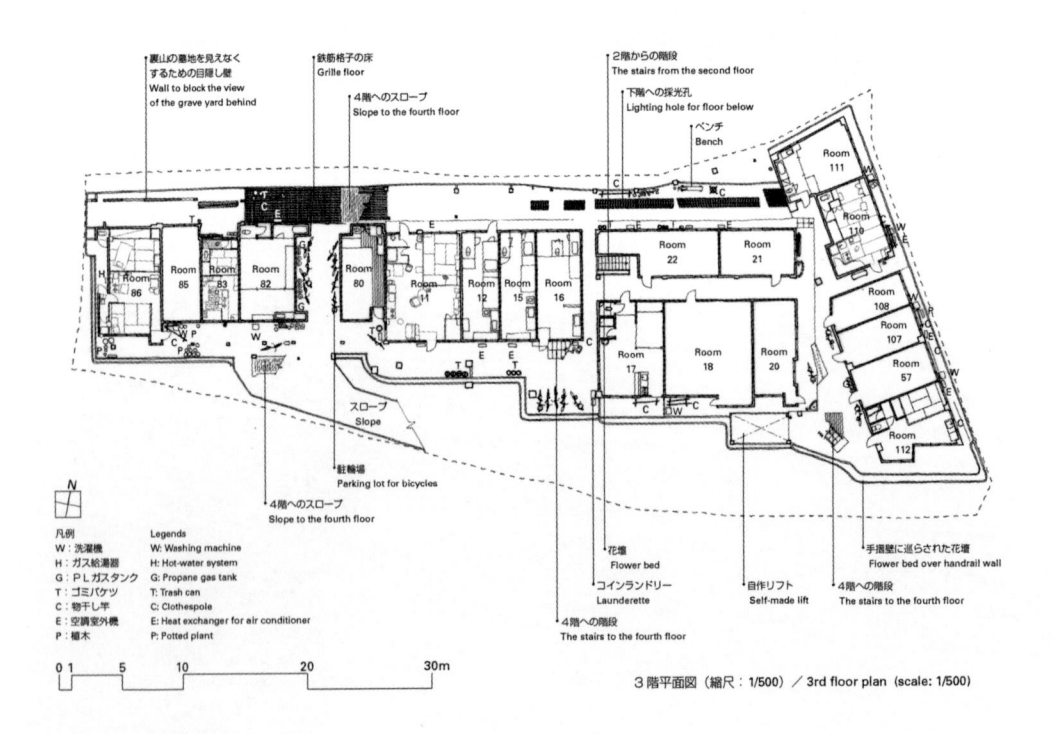

2 THE METABOLIST-INDUSTRIAL COMPLEX

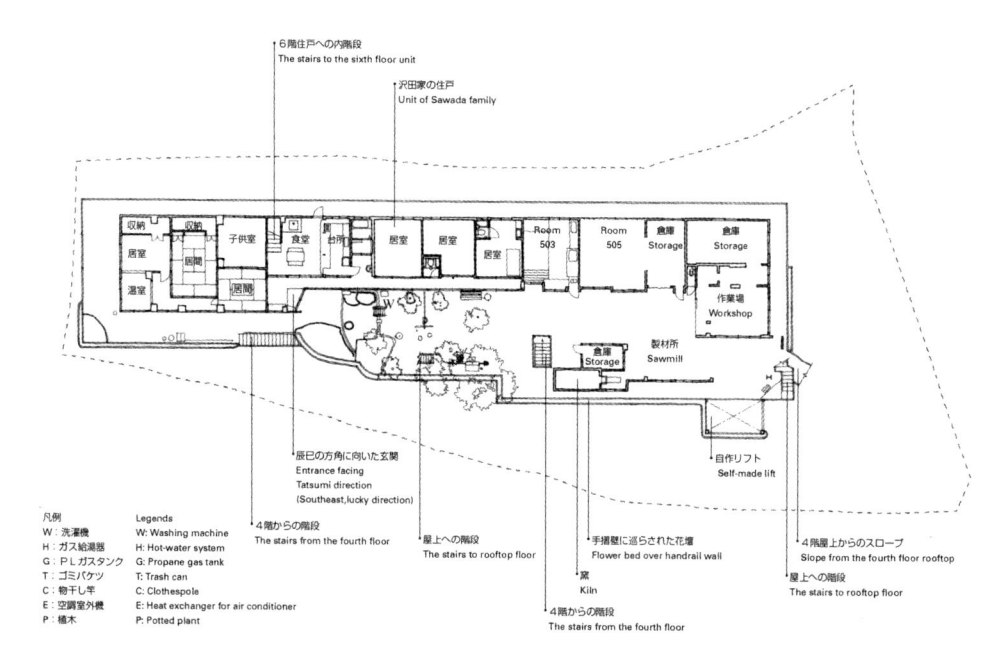

凡例	Legends
W：洗濯機	W: Washing machine
H：ガス給湯器	H: Hot-water system
G：PLガスタンク	G: Propane gas tank
T：ゴミバケツ	T: Trash can
C：物干し竿	C: Clothespole
E：空調室外機	E: Heat exchanger for air conditioner
P：植木	P: Potted plant

5階平面図（縮尺：1/500） / 5th floor plan (scale: 1/500)

沢田マンションの間取りいろいろ

Unit plans

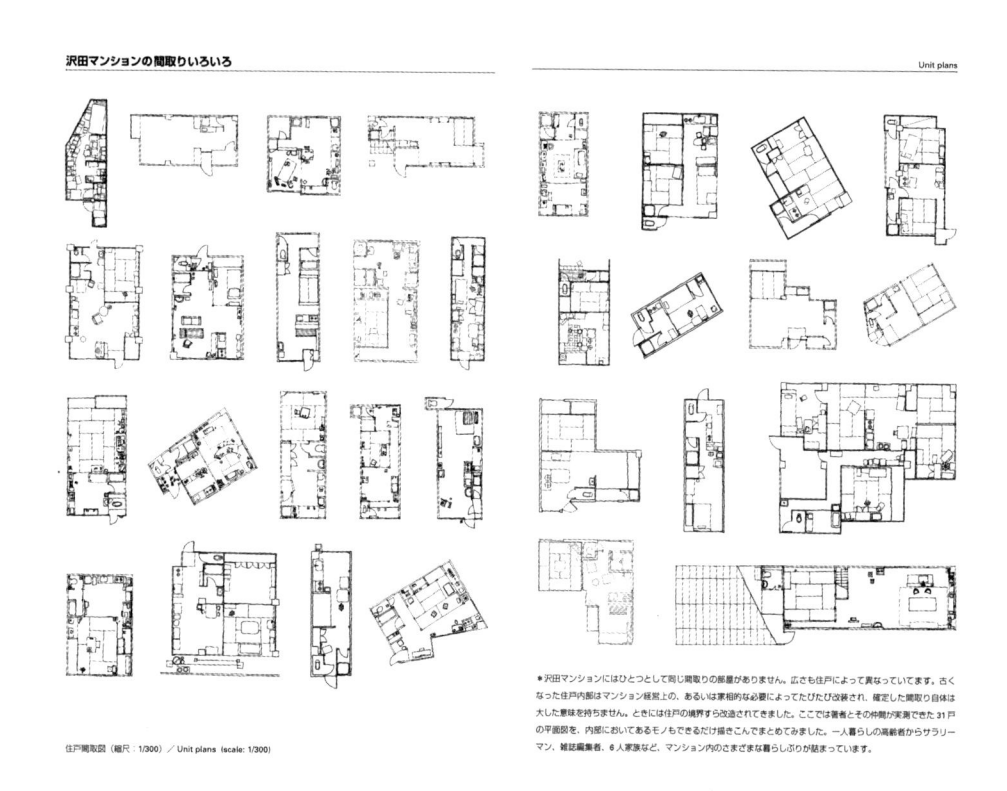

住戸間取り図（縮尺：1/300） / Unit plans (scale: 1/300)

＊沢田マンションにはひとつとして同じ間取りの部屋がありません。広さも住戸によって異なっています。古くなった住戸内部はマンション経営上の、あるいは家相的必要によってたびたび改装され、確定した間取り自体は大した意味を持ちません。ときには住戸の境界すら改装されてきました。ここでは著者とその仲間が実測できた31戸の平面図を、内部においてあるモノもできるだけ描き込んでまとめてみました。一人暮らしの高齢者からサラリーマン、雑誌編集者、6人家族など、マンション内のさまざまな暮らしぶりが詰まっています。

ARTIFICIAL LAND WITHOUT ARCHITECTS: SAWADA MANSION, 1971–

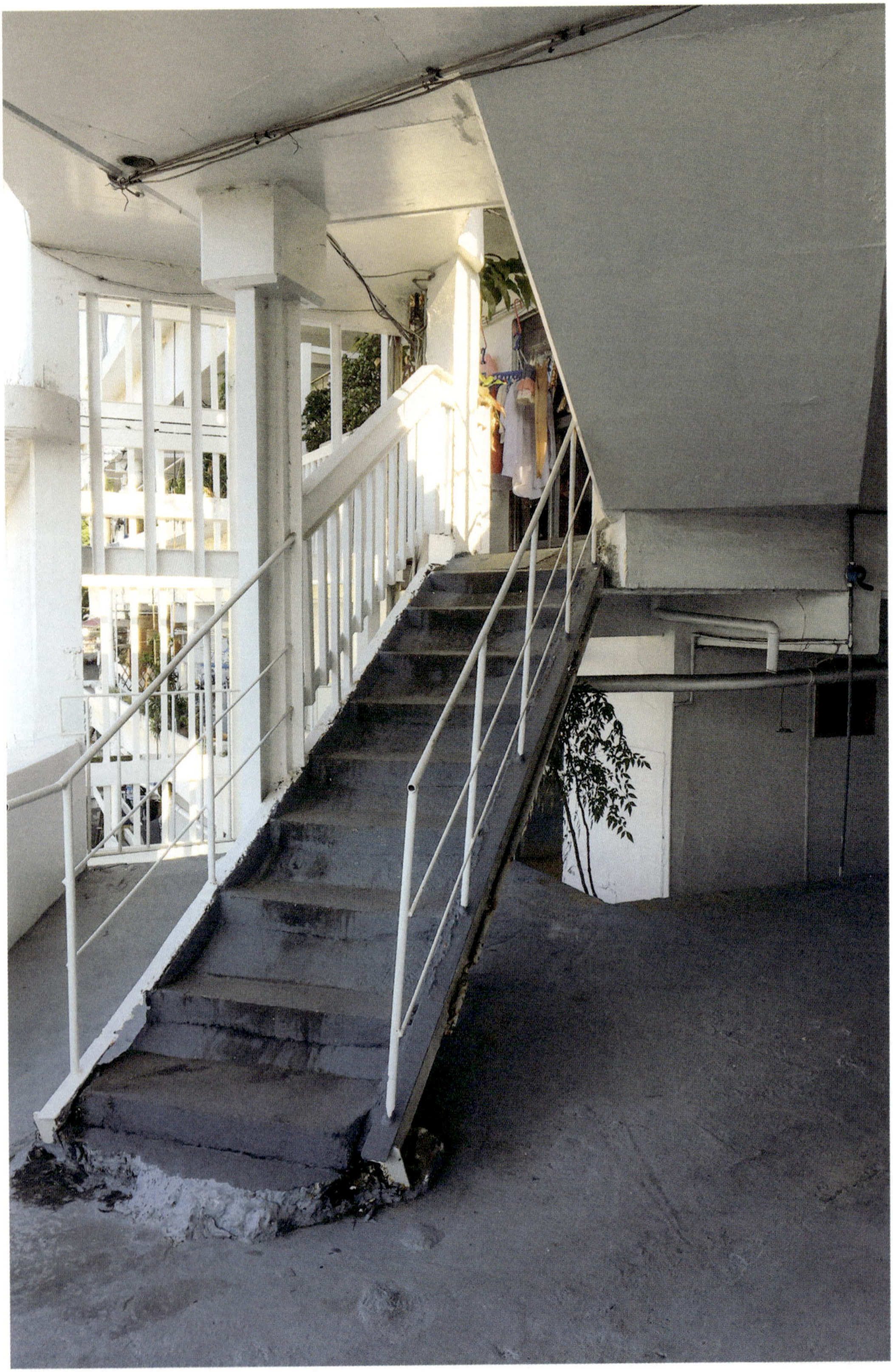

ARTIFICIAL LAND WITHOUT ARCHITECTS: SAWADA MANSION, 1971–

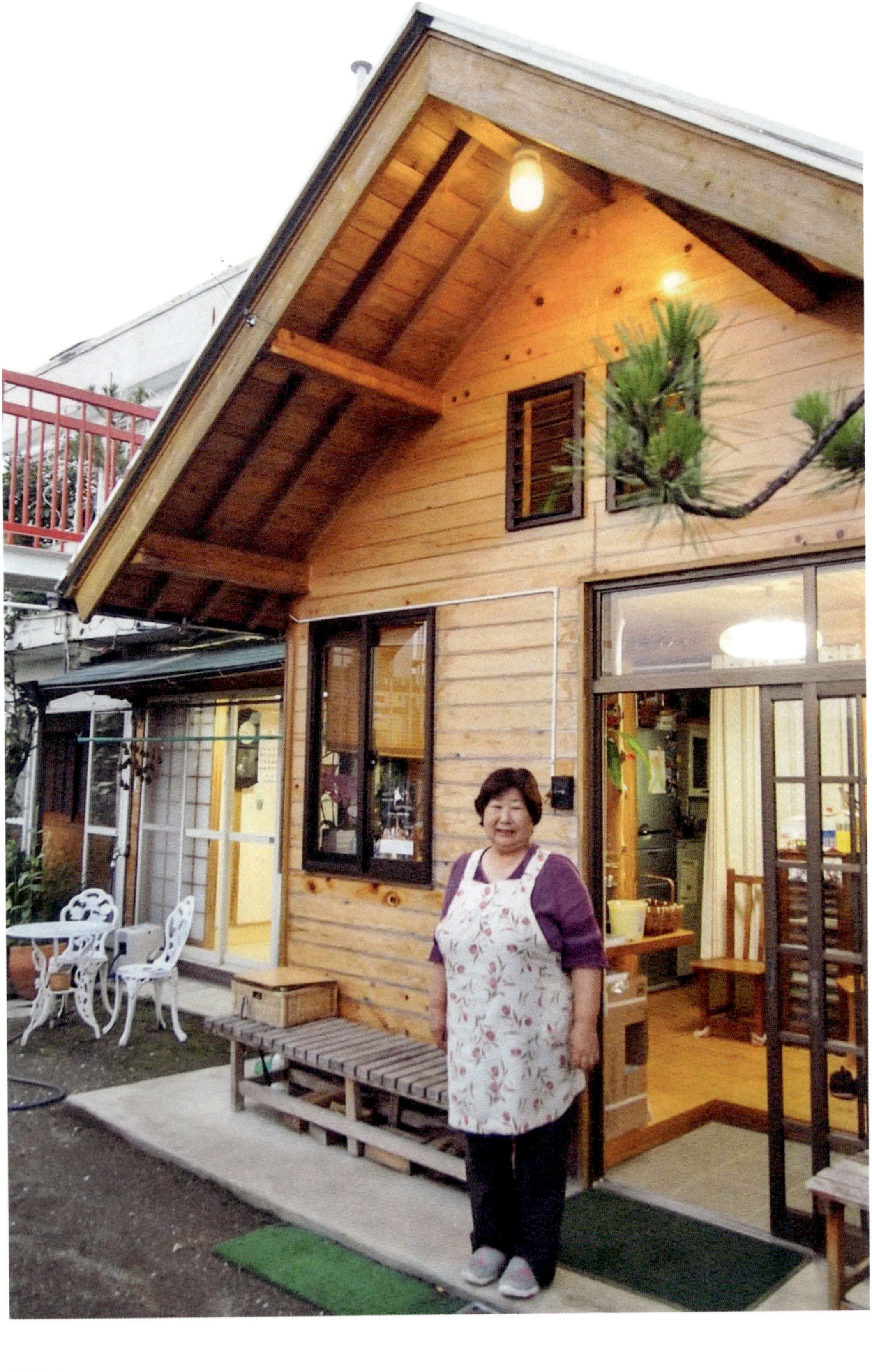

1. These two poles are represented by and quoted from Christopher Alexander and Walter Gropius respectively. See Alexander, *The Timeless Way of Building* (New York: Oxford University Press, 1979); and Gropius, *Scope of Total Architecture* [1943] (New York: Harper & Brothers Publishers, 1955), 72.
2. N. J. Habraken, "Lives of Systems," in *Transformations of the Site* (Cambridge, MA: Atwater Press, 1983), 163–164, 183.
3. This characterization of informal housing is based on its definition found in the United Nations Human Settlements Programme, *The Challenge of Slums: Global Report on Human Settlements 2003* (London: Earthscan, 2003), 196.
4. Habraken, "Lives," 180–182.
5. See Tetsuro Kagaya, *Sawada Mansion chōikkyū shiryō: Sekai saikyō no selfbuild kenchiku tanhō / All About Sawada Mansion: The Most Unique Selfbuild Mansion Tour* (Tokyo: Tsukiji Shokan, 2007), 29. Translation by Riyo Namigata.
6. Bernard Rudofsky, *Architecture Without Architects* (New York: Doubleday, 1964), preface. The exhibition was held at the Museum of Modern Art in New York from November 9, 1964 to February 7, 1965. Interestingly, Rudofsky was at Waseda University as a research professor from 1958 to 1960. It's tempting to think of him befriending Wajiro Kon and Yosizaka while there, two others devoted to the study of lifestyles and architecture without architects.
7. Kagaya, *Sawada Mansion*, 18.
8. *Zenekon* often either directly or through subsidiaries are involved with real-estate development and property management as logical extensions of their design and construction work. Takenaka is one example.
9. Kagaya, *Sawada Mansion*, 147–151.
10. E. F. Schumacher, *Small is Beautiful: Economics as if People Mattered* [1973] (New York: Harper & Row, 1975), 53–55. Right livelihood is one eighth of the Noble Eightfold Path in Buddhism.
11. Rudofsky, *Architecture*, preface.
12. Schumacher, *Small*, 58. It is notable in the convergence here of Buddhism and Marxism that the Dalai Lama is a self-proclaimed Marxist.
13. Kagaya, *Sawada Mansion*, 16.
14. Kagaya, *Sawada Mansion*, 24.
15. Kagaya, *Sawada Mansion*, 23, 33.
16. Vernacular architecture is maybe only theorized after the fact of its construction—or before the fact of it being vernacular.
17. Hiroe Sawada, in conversation with the author, June 16, 2017.
18. Kagaya, *Sawada Mansion*, 46. The "horn" style is one that can be found in informal construction throughout the world. Kagaya notes that while it's very rare in most of Japan, the approach is quite common in Okinawa, where reinforced concrete construction was taught to Okinawans by American military engineers after a major typhoon in 1959. See Kagaya, *Sawada Mansion*, 49.
19. Takaaki Yorimitsu, "Are the Building Plans Up in Heaven? Japan's DIY Apartment with Over 100 Residents," accessed September 19, 2019, https://randomwire.com/wp-content/uploads/Sawada-Mansion.pdf.
20. Tetsuro Kagaya, in conversation with the author, June 16, 2017. Kagaya's wonderful surveys are part of a tradition of what could be called "inhabited" drawings, full of transient signs of life and other anthropological details. They continue the style used by Kon for his *minka* and modernology survey work, and later by Uzo Nishiyama and Yosizaka, among many others. Kagaya's surveys were originally done for his graduate thesis at Tokyo University of Science, where his advisor was a former student of Nishiyama's.
21. Kagaya, June 16, 2017.
22. Stewart Brand, *How Buildings Learn: What Happens After They're Built* (New York: Penguin, 1994), 188.
23. See "Six-Foot Balcony" in Christopher Alexander et al., *A Pattern Language* (New York: Oxford University Press, 1977), 781–784.
24. Kagaya, June 16, 2017.
25. Kagaya, *Sawada Mansion*, 146, 148.
26. Kagaya, *Sawada Mansion*, 150.
27. Rudofsky, *Architecture*, preface.
28. On the concept of hedonistic sustainability, where no one "must give up a portion of their comfortable lifestyle," see Bjarke Ingels, "Hedonistic Sustainability," accessed June 2, 2020, https://www.archdaily.com/203599/tedx-hedonistic-sustainability-bjarke-ingels. While hypothetically attractive, the concept seems to mostly manifest as high-end wellness resorts and condominiums, suggesting that such a form of sustainability will be limited to people who can afford it.

previous: Sawada Mansion (2017)

left: Hiroe Sawada outside her fifth-floor house (2015)

3
Open Systems

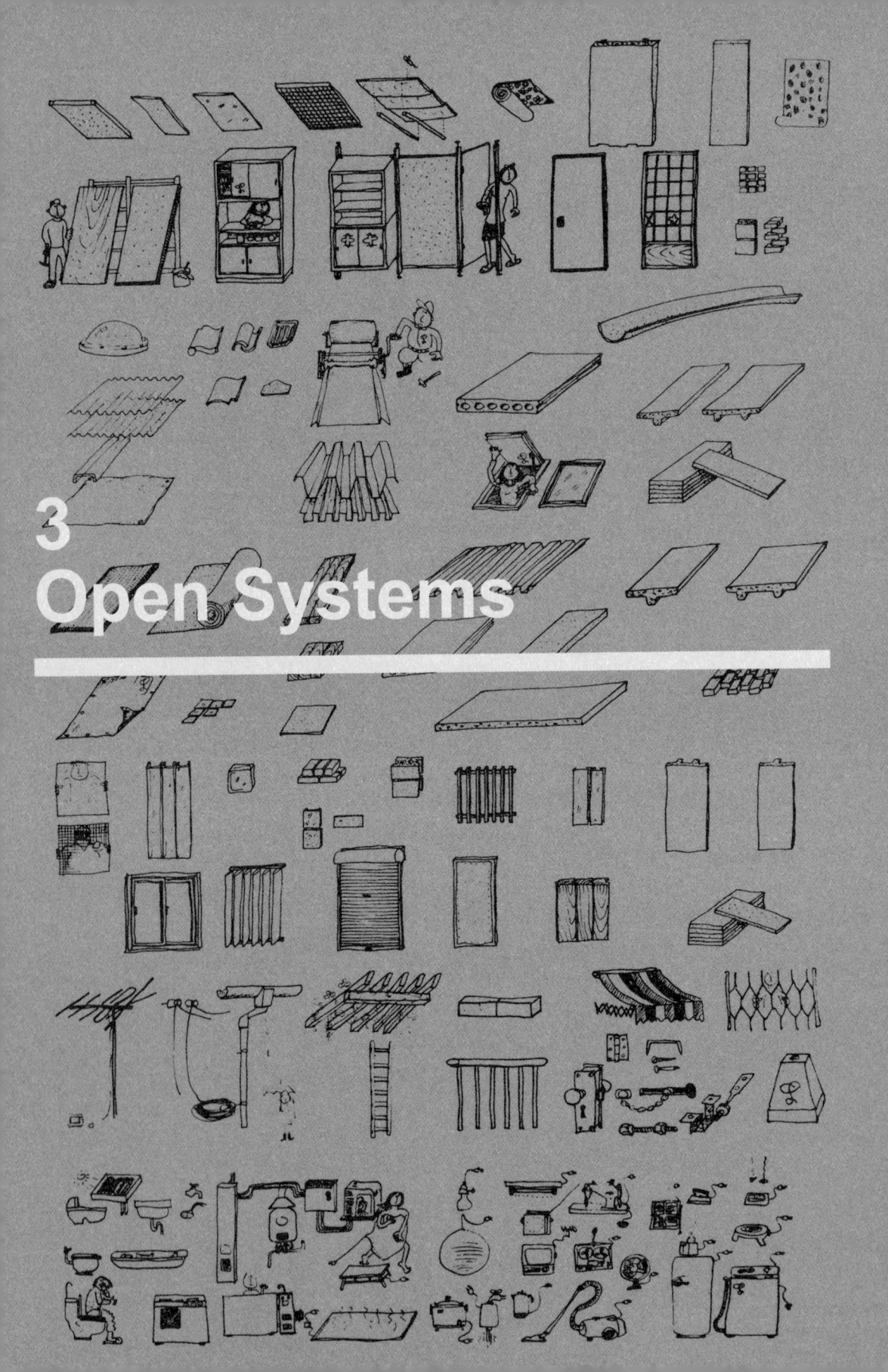

... creation is after all something like a process of digestion.

—Noboru Kawazoe, *Contemporary Japanese Architecture*, 1973[1]

In his 1977 book *Open Systems in Building Production,* Yositika Utida presents a diagram comparing the potentials of prefabricated "large components" and "small parts."[2] The diagram is an implicit critique of Metabolist designs, with mass-produced, big prefab components shown to lead to uniformity, whereas mass-produced small ones lead to diversity. Work from the movement's heyday did emphasize large components, from the unitized capsules of the Nakagin Capsule Tower to big structural frames. Utida, who could be called an "elementalist," focuses instead on the small parts that can articulate multiple lifestyles within a frame.[3] This change makes sense, as by the 1970s the transition from austerity to relative affluence that Harumi anticipated in 1958 had occurred. The transitional concept of artificial land debuted at Harumi had accepted standardized minimum dwellings in a period of crisis. With the passing of that era came an approach more akin to Yosizaka's maximum dwelling, which now seems more responsible and realistic in its embrace of different ways of living. In 1954, Yosizaka was ahead of his time.

The homes on artificial land found in this chapter start to show the bottom-up variety so long hoped-for by knowing architects—Hiroe and Kano Sawada very

Yositika Utida, "Emergence and the current status of open systems," 1977

much excepted. All of the projects are connected directly or in spirit to the thinking of Utida, as well as his Dutch peer, John Habraken. Their work resonates with Metabolism, making it suppler than it had been historically, with the following designs showing the blossoming of thinking over several decades, from the 1970s into the twenty-first century. But before turning to this work, we need to survey the context that drove artificial land's renewed but altered appeal.

Scrap-and-Build

As noted with Ashiyahama, in 1971 MOC housing policy changed from a focus on quantity to quality.[4] Indeed, in 1973 Japan's total number of housing units exceeded the total of households in all of the nation's prefectures.[5] Marking the quantitative triumph over the shortage of the postwar era, this event also inaugurates a problem still alive today, where the construction of new dwellings remains at over one million units per year, despite the country's negative population growth.[6] The problem is the dominance of "scrap-and-build," a phenomenon in Japan's major cities that's particularly acute with housing, where the charge of obsolescence—be it economic, technical, functional, or stylistic—leads to demolition and replacement rather than reuse and renovation.[7]

Though policies shifted toward the promotion of quality, that in itself gave license to a huge quantity of construction. Today, due to scrap-and-build, around 80 percent of Japanese housing was built after 1970, with dwellings having an average life span of only 30 years, compared to an average of 55 in the US and 77 in the UK.[8] The Metabolist-industrial complex—or what's more generally known as the Japanese "construction state"—relies on this continuous destruction of its products in order to keep making more.[9] As historian Eiko Maruko Siniawer describes, when Vance Packard's 1960 bestselling book *The Waste Makers* was released in a Japanese edition in 1961, its indictment of American manufacturers' collusion with Madison Avenue marketing to drive obsolescence was treated by some as an instruction manual rather than damning criticism.[10] Japanese business leaders found in Packard's book American trade sentiments such as "it is not only our privilege to obsolete the minimum home and many home furnishings. It is our obligation. We are obligated to work on obsolescence as our contribution to a healthy, growing society."[11]

Demolition and replacement are not always unwarranted. Japan's high-growth period of the 1960s

top: Yositika Utida, diagram of the implications of production types, 1977

bottom: Vance Packard, *The Waste Makers*, 1960, and Japanese edition, 1961

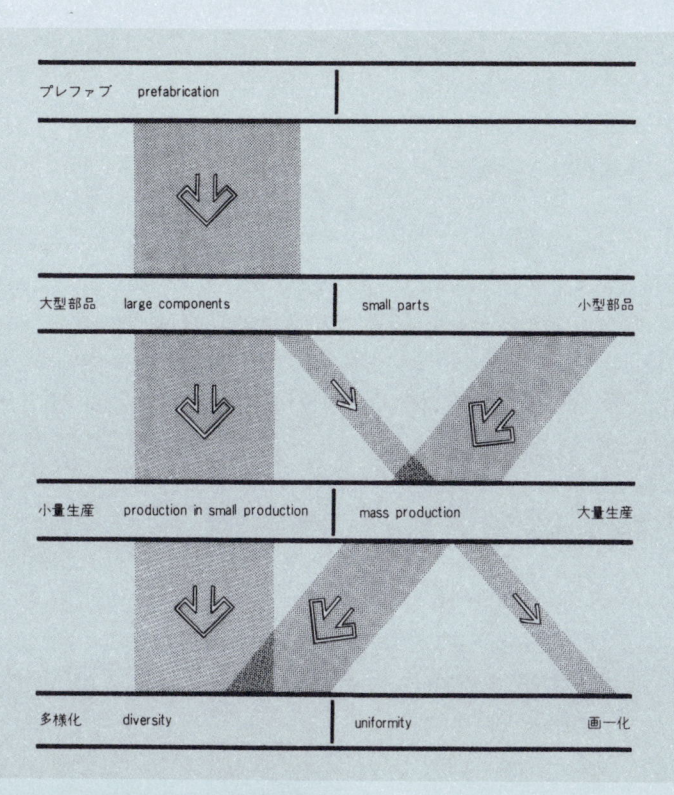

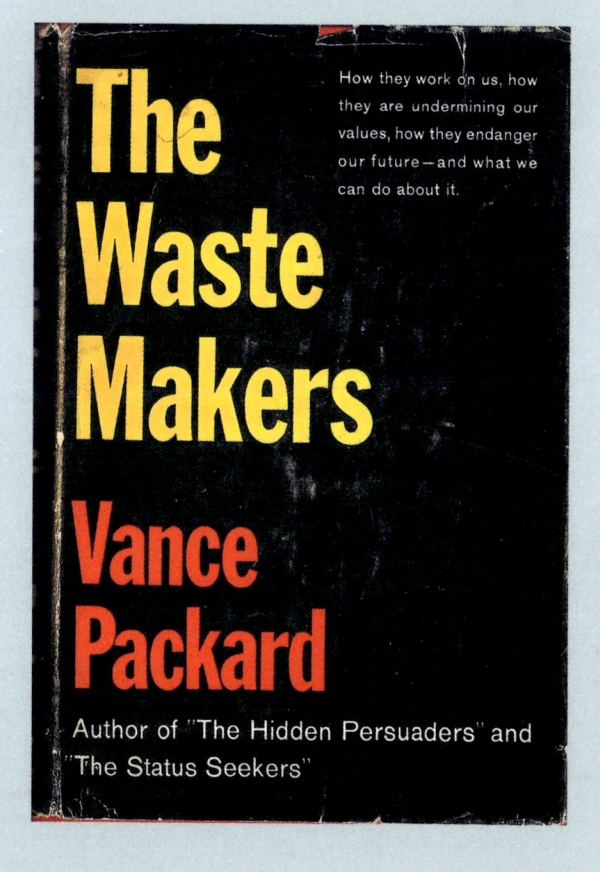

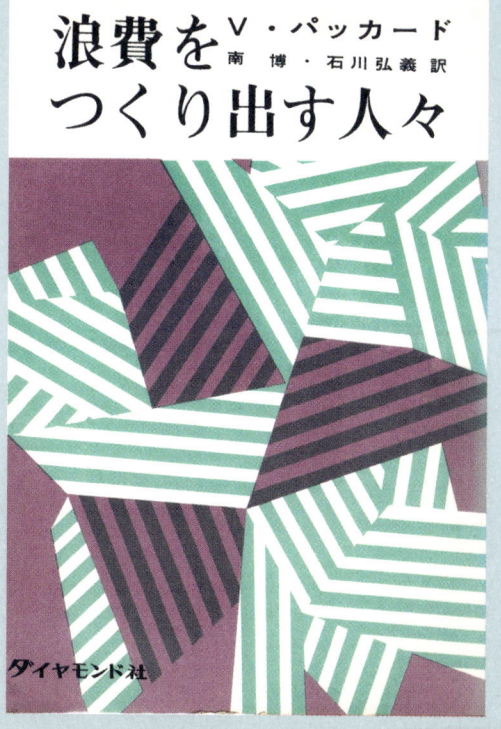

プレファブ	prefabrication		
大型部品	large components	small parts	小型部品
小量生産	production in small production	mass production	大量生産
多様化	diversity	uniformity	画一化

was at least partly due to it being a period of high disposability, with the giant demand for housing promoting speed and low cost, as we've seen.[12] By the 1970s, this had resulted in a large number of poor-quality dwellings that rapidly fell apart. Serious problems of deterioration were abundant, and as the architect Seichi Fukao notes, "we did not know good manners of installing."[13] Pipes and wires were cast into concrete slabs and could not be accessed for repairs, leaks led to mold and structural corrosion, and cramped spaces made maintenance and adaptation often impossible. Entire buildings were demolished due to such problems.[14]

Under the administration of yet another ex-MITI man, Prime Minister Yasuhiro Nakasone, in office from 1982 until 1987, the demolition of such derelict housing accelerated. Following Reagan and Thatcher's leads, the government turned away from public spending toward neoliberal privatization and deregulation. This was in part due to lobbying by private real-estate and construction companies looking to break free from the increased planning controls introduced in the late 1960s.

Nakasone created a win-win opportunity for these companies as well as domestic manufacturers by loosening zoning regulations to allow more high-rise construction. This incentivized the demolition of small and difficult-to-adapt dwellings, which were replaced with bigger apartments that could contain more stuff, namely Japanese-made home electronics and appliances.[15] A washing machine, refrigerator, and vacuum cleaner were the country's so-called "three sacred treasures" of postwar living, and most families had already bought them by the early 1970s.[16] Further purchases required more space. Reconceived as "containers for consumer durables," homes were given a new mission that reinterprets Wajiro Kon's idea of architecture-as-container from a purely consumerist angle.[17] Indicative of the growth Nakasone unleashed, by 1988 the average floor area across all housing types had increased to about 89 square meters, from an average of about 74 square meters in 1968. This expansion was fueled by a housing finance market that had become very profitable, leading to the infamous "bubble economy" of the 1980s.[18]

Despite this growth in profits, spaces, and possessions, it must be noted that the lack of time to enjoy these acquisitions, or to nurture priorities other than their pursuit, has caused much soul-searching in Japan since the 1980s. Studies found many Japanese to crave an "affluence of the heart" over one of material wealth.[19] In this context, in 1991, Prime Minister Miyazawa Kiichi, also ex-MITI, would call for

Japan to become a "lifestyle superpower," acknowledging the real desire for meaningful leisure time, but using the kind of competitive language that had contributed to the problems of an overworked society in the first place.[20] Affluence had brought new anxieties, with some connected to life at home, and including the life of the home itself.

Consequences

Despite the recession and long-lasting stagnation due to the bubble's bursting in the early 1990s, scrap-and-build continues, leading to a peculiar attitude toward architecture. This is seen in Japan's abundance of idiosyncratic freestanding houses, with architects there able to experiment at a level that's rare in the rest of the world. The architect Sou Fujimoto, a paragon of this highly photogenic work that often seems to push the boundaries of habitability, explains in the *Wall Street Journal* that his House NA, completed in Tokyo in 2011, was only possible because "Japanese people don't care about resale value."[21] But this remark is misleading: if Japanese don't care about resale value, it's because they can rarely get it. Even as land on which they sit becomes more valuable, Japanese homes depreciate as rapidly as most cars, with scrap-and-build further pushed by frequent building-code changes that make them obsolete technically. The expectation of lost investment makes clients open to unusual designs, since their homes are semi-disposable. As a result, construction has a corresponding flimsiness, exemplifying that "Buildings are not demolished because they are in poor condition," but rather "buildings are in poor condition so that they can be demolished."[22] Indeed, while Nakasone's administration acted on the problem of old low-quality housing, all too often the replacements were merely new low-quality housing, continuing the cycle of demolition and replacement, a dynamic known as the "scrap-and-build spiral."[23] Even with Japan's improvement in the recycling of building materials, this situation leads to wasted embodied energy and copious amounts of illegal dumping.[24]

Writing in 2008, the economists Richard Koo and Masaya Sasaki have analyzed the negative feedback loop between depreciation and quality of construction. They note that, with the average Japanese home financially worthless after fifteen years, the country has been unable to generate a society with an affluence equivalent to much of the West.[25] Residents are often trapped in devalued homes they can't sell for a profit, can't afford to leave, and can't easily modify to suit changes in their lifestyles.

Koo and Sasaki believe that ending the scrap-and-build spiral and laying the groundwork for growth in personal investment will entail creating a stock of durable housing. This long-lasting stock must be easy to maintain, renovate, and adapt, and must be an appreciating asset—features that recall artificial land's strategic combination of permanent and changeable.[26]

Participation

In a sense, scrap-and-build has hijacked Metabolism. It takes the movement's ideal of durable public platforms supporting private homes and flattens it into sprawl, wherein freestanding houses are easily plugged in and out from the undemanding and comparatively cheap infrastructure of a two-dimensional street plan, exacerbating the wasteful and congested built environment that artificial land was intended to overcome. Within this sprawl, a huge population of architects and construction companies offer their clients what Metabolism never delivered: control over what their homes could be.

At this point, with the call for an adaptable housing stock and the renovations of Motomachi, we can start to see that Metabolism correctly anticipated future needs. Nonetheless, despite changing with the times, Motomachi remains under top-down control, and looking back at Harumi's "variability test," it's clear that even removing the transient minor-structure was a big and dirty job. Heavy construction requires heavy equipment, recalling the architect Günter Nitschke's view that when Metabolism gets "heavier, harder" and "more monstrous in scale," its obsession with flexibility "is just fuss."[27] What proves this sentiment particularly true is that, to be used, the flexibility of the historic projects has indeed relied on large bureaucratic initiatives.

By the start of the 1980s, thanks to neoliberalism, heroic housing by the Metabolists and their followers was no longer being commissioned. Around the same time, "citizen participation-based *machizukuri*" was becoming increasingly visible, a phenomenon in which decisions are driven less by giant agencies or corporations and more by residents. Translated as "community building" or "town making," *machizukuri* is both a practice and an ethos.[28] The term first appeared in the 1950s, often in the context of environmental protest movements, where it expressed people's demand to have a say in what their environment would be.[29] As André Sorensen notes, *machizukuri* is now a vague umbrella term for many groups and things, including government ordinances.[30] But its common denominator is an emphasis on the local and the bottom-up.

Yositika Utida (center), John Habraken (right), and Kiyoshi Miura visiting NEXT21, 1994

Some of Masato Otaka's activities also drew on the grassroots idea. In 1977, he formed a separate office devoted to "soft" planning issues such as developing architectural and urban guidelines with communities to help their revitalization, most notably for his hometown of Miharu, in Fukushima.[31] At the same time, Otaka's colleague Utida developed his concept of "open systems." As we will see, this concept addresses the waste of scrap-and-build and a *machizukuri* spirit found beyond the walls of a single-family house.

Yositika Utida

Though not widely known globally, Utida was from an elite family in Japanese architecture. As noted earlier, he was the son of architect-engineer Yoshikazu Utida, who was director of the Dojunkai housing program, president of the AIJ, and also president of the University of Tokyo. Yoshikazu was also an important formulator of national structural and fire codes, as well as a master planner for colonial Manchuria. Yositika's older brother Yoshifumi was also an architect, and was considered to be Kenzo Tange's main rival in the early 1950s, prior to Yoshifumi's premature death.

At this point, readers will have noticed Yositika Utida's frequent appearances in the background of artificial-land activities at the highest level. While not a Metabolist, for many decades he engaged key themes of the group, such as life cycles and flexibility, long after most of Metabolism's bona fide members abandoned the cause. As an early sign of his commitment to the longevity of buildings, in 1958 he worked on a survey of leaks in JHC apartments.[32] Afterward he was, as we've seen, a member of the Artificial Land Committee with Maki and Otaka, a main juror with Otaka for Ashiyahama, and a chairman for the Stratiform Structure Module research with Kikutake, to list only some of his engagements most directly connected to the movement.

Utida didn't seem to care too much about these Metabolist connections. Stating that he has "always been interested in flexibility as a Japanese," much more significant for him was his long investigation of open systems, pursued through commissions, MOC initiatives, and teaching and research in his influential lab at the University of Tokyo.[33] He proudly stated in 2010 that since the 1977 publication of his book *Open Systems*, he had not changed his philosophy.[34] This may sound close-minded, but perhaps it's a testament to the vitality of flexibility as a topic.

The concept of open systems originates in biology, and describes metabolism in organic life. As the famous biologist Ludwig von Bertalanffy writes, "An open system is defined as a system in exchange of matter with its environment, presenting import and export, building-up and breaking-down of its material components."[35] Always in motion, taking in nutrients and expelling wastes that in turn become nutrients, open systems are the opposite of inorganic closed systems that are stable, existing in equilibrium, such as a rock.

Utida expanded the ecological concept to include inorganic artifacts that extend the human organism's control of the environment, seen with building components, and also clothing.[36] He describes mixing and matching shoes, socks, shirt, and a necktie with a Western suit as an open system, compared to the closed system of an athlete's uniform. Turning to buildings, he gives the example of Japan's prefab house manufacturers: internally, each company is an open system, with all components and subsystems having dimensional or modular coordination, the interrelated sizes and methods of assembly offering flexibility of configuration. Yet each company is itself a closed system, unable to share its elements with those of others.[37] Utida believed that, ultimately, every example of an open system has such a closed system "boundary," both dimensional and cultural, that allows "only inner exchangeability."[38] The question is how and where the closed boundary is defined.

Utida judges the prefab companies in comparison with Japanese wood construction in the Edo period (1603–1868).[39] During this time, techniques and dimensions became increasingly shared, leading to conventions in specific regions. Standardization enabled architectural freedom. While it may sound like an Orwellian contradiction, an example of such freedom is the *kyo-ma ken* method of dimensioning, described in Utida's book.

Kyo-ma ken is translated by the architect Heino Engel as "column distance in metropolis measurement," and is remarkable for being a specifically urban module originating with commoners.[40] Used primarily in the Kansai region, which includes Osaka and Kyoto, the system was a popular rejection of *inaka-ma ken*, or "column distance in countryside measurement," which, despite its name, was prevalent in Tokyo.[41] The unit used by both systems is the *shaku*, a general measurement in Japanese construction equal to 303 millimeters. With *inaka-ma*, the module of 6 *shaku* is the increment for column centerline distances. *Kyo-ma* instead uses a 6.3 *shaku* module that sets distances from column face to column face.[42] This may seem a minor distinction, but the major advantage of *kyo-ma* is that the increment took the form of a tatami mat that became standard in the Kansai region, measuring 6.3 by 3.15 *shaku*. While the regular centerline spacing of *inaka-ma* makes structural layout simpler, when the offset for the thickness of columns is factored in, tatami mats often need to be in varying custom sizes to cover a given floor. As tatami became more prevalent for commoners, not only the well-to-do, the cost of this customization became a problem. A diagram comparing the two methods appears in *Open Systems*, where the same plan configuration is made using each module. While the tatami for the *kyo-ma* version are identical, *inaka-ma* requires five different sizes.[43]

Given the ease of "mass customization" in our parametric age, this tiny difference can seem laughably insignificant. But modularity driven by mats rather than columns improved the input and output of materials, allowing tatami, screens, and other elements to be exchanged between buildings. One outcome of this rationalization was the appearance in the late Edo period of *hadaka-gashi,* or "bare rental," in which landlords would rent *kyo-ma* dimensioned apartments without any interior elements.[44] As these had all become coordinated by the 6.3 *shaku* module, ordinary Kansai residents, who were typically renters, could now afford to raise their level of comfort and domestic choice. They could move and modify dwellings with ease, confident that the space-defining

京間　　　　　　　　　田舎間

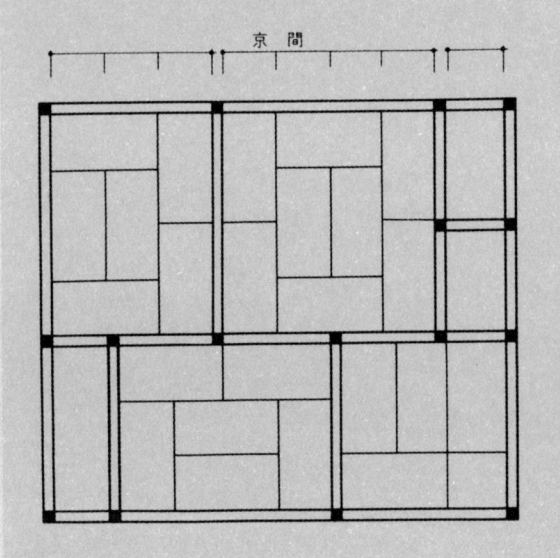

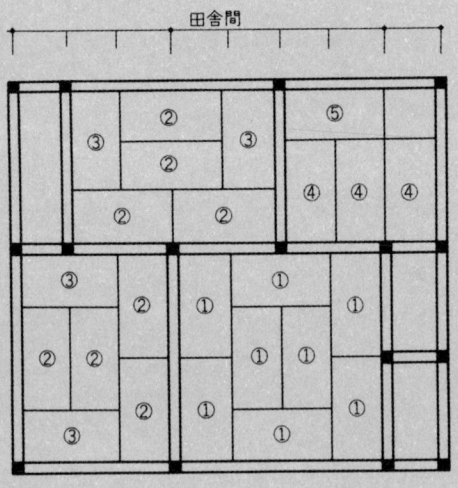

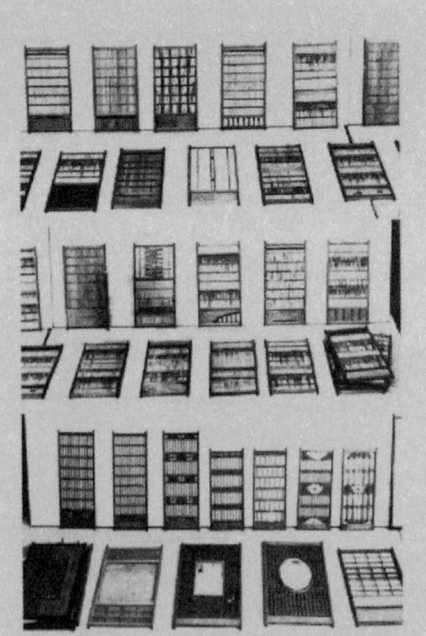

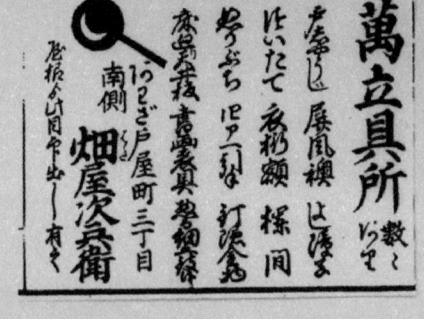

建具　　　大阪市立博物館蔵

components in which they had invested would fit other regional housing. The popularity of *hadaka-gashi* was such that an active market emerged for the sale, repair, and recycling of *kyo-ma* products, which lasted up until World War II. Such might be the reality of an open system.

Like Utida, Kawazoe was also influenced by the *kyo-ma* environment. He refers to it in various writings from the 1960s, envisioning in his essay "The City of the Future" that, "The dwellings of the future will be reduced to 'parts' and attached onto the 'city structural unit,'" with these parts "capable of endless combinations and change by means of standardized systems and joints."[45] Elsewhere he discusses the historical module explicitly, clearly seeing it as a model.[46] Amid the heavy concrete and steel of Metabolism, Kawazoe was inspired by a straw mat.

Given Kawazoe and Utida's shared interests, I asked Utida what he thought of Metabolism. He initially said he was hesitant to criticize the movement because he was unclear about its intentions, which is perhaps a polite way of criticizing its intentions for being unclear. Then he came to the realization that Metabolism's problem is that it's a "totally open system without a boundary."[47] This thought shows how much his idea relies on a closed system within which an open system finds its rationale. Absent that boundary, Metabolism's openness is like that of a scrapheap.

According to Utida, unlike Metabolism, a "system can't be a movement."[48] This position is debatable, though. Looking at *kyo-ma* or 2x4 wood framing, what makes an open system truly open is whether or not it can become a vernacular used by both layperson and expert, which distinguishes it from being merely a modular system.[49] And while a vernacular is not a movement, systems such as reinforced concrete and steel frames provided the form and content for movements intended to create a vernacular. Conversion from the novelty of a movement to the normality of the everyday is, for some movements, the ultimate success, an ambition held by the likes of CIAM and New Urbanism.[50] Many movements fight to make their principles into a new normal.

John Habraken

A de facto movement to make a new normal is found in the work of Habraken, justifiably called a "guru" by Reyner Banham.[51] Born in Indonesia when it was a Dutch colony, Habraken returned with his family to the Netherlands in the 1940s after being in an internment camp during Indonesia's Japanese occupation.

top: Yositika Utida, comparison of same room layout with *kyo-ma* (left) versus *inaka-ma* (right), which requires five tatami sizes, 1977

bottom: Selection of *kyo-ma* fittings, and nineteenth-century advertisements for recycling shops for such products

In 1955, he graduated in architecture from the Delft University of Technology, a time when the Netherlands, like many places, was building mass housing in huge quantities. Witnessing this construction was the trigger for writing his 1961 manifesto-book *Supports: An Alternative to Mass Housing*. The reputation he gained from this small publication led, in 1964, to his being made the first director of the new Stichting Architecten Research (SAR), or Foundation for Architects' Research, based in Eindhoven. Under his leadership until 1975, SAR was a thinktank sponsored by Dutch architects wanting to strengthen their role in housing provision. Its research developed methodologies from ideas outlined in *Supports*.[52]

The book's alternative approach lies in its redistribution of control between those who make mass housing and those who live in it, a situation enabled by what Habraken calls a "support and infill" architecture. Describing supports as "constructions which take over the task of the ground," his coining pre-dates Maki's "megastructure" as an early renaming of artificial land.[53] Unlike megastructure, Habraken emphasizes the issue of territory or boundary implicit in the original term. Like artificial land as first presented in Algiers, a support would be a residential infrastructure provided by the state or public corporation, with infill provided through existing builders and trades reoriented to give residents in mass housing more say. "Don't give me that participation bullshit, man! We want power!" seems to be a sentiment of angry residents that Habraken has internalized, and he avoids describing his goal as participation.[54] Instead he speaks of resident decision-making or "dweller control" to explain a support's reason for being.[55] Supports are for supporting dwellers' desires.

SAR framed issues of decision-making by asking "*who* decides *when* about *what?*"[56] Modular coordination between infill and support was seen as a key to answering this question of sequence and responsibility. Such coordination was not seen as a prescription of proprietary products, but as the adoption of organizational grids that produced a shared language across industries and stakeholders for making and positioning elements such as partition walls. Modularity would empower residents rather than just accelerate industrialized production.[57]

Exchange between the Netherlands and Japan soon followed SAR's founding. Utida was aware of Habraken since the publication of *Supports*, and Seiji Sawada, a former student of Utida's, made a research trip to SAR in the late 1960s. In 1972, the journal *Toshi-Jutaku* published a support/infill special issue. Later, in 1976 and 1977, JHC research staff under Utida made visits to SAR projects in Europe. Also in 1977, Sawada formed a SAR-inspired "Open Housing" study group that included Yujiro Kaneko, who had been part of the Ashiyahama project as head of MOC's Housing Bureau. An unauthorized Japanese translation of Supports was in circulation at the time.[58] Kazunobu Minami, another former student of Utida's, went to study under Habraken at MIT in the early 1980s.[59] Utida and Habraken met through Minami's introduction.

A gauge of Habraken's influence in Japan is that his support/infill terminology has been widely adopted in development and construction as "skeleton/infill," or just "SI." This was helped by two key initiatives that synthesize Habraken and Utida's interests: the Two-Step Housing System and the Century Housing System. These systems effectively carried artificial land into the twenty-first century.

The Two-Step Housing System

A flowchart created by the architects Kazuo Tatsumi and Mitsuo Takada shows how to properly design a skeleton. Through its emphasis on testing a skeleton's capacity for variation, the diagram makes explicit a stage in design methodology that, since Algiers, had been only implied. Academics at Kyoto University and friends of Utida's, Tatsumi and Takada are responsible for introducing the Habraken-inspired language of a public "skeleton" and private "infill" that embody their Two-Step Housing System (TSHS) that the diagram describes.[60] From its earliest research in the late 1970s, TSHS proposed to be a public-private hybrid, or what Takada and Tatsumi call "public-aided housing."[61] Like Yosizaka's 1954 proposal and Supports, the first step is for a skeleton to be constructed by a public agency, then the second step is for plots in the skeleton to be rented to residents who will build the units they own.

What's changed since Yosizaka's context is the culture to support the concept's implementation. Free of the urgency and privations that characterized Japanese housing in the 1950s and '60s, TSHS speaks to a society demanding choices. It also engages the demand for environmental quality and placemaking that's part of the *machizukuri* ethos. Unlike the postwar housing that neglected to provide communal space and basic services, Tatsumi and Takada insisted that skeletons maximize "continuity between dwelling units and the ground," provide "common space with good qualities," and minimize "neighboring environmental impacts." They echo language from *Building a New Japan*, seeing skeletons as a form of "social overhead capital," a necessary investment for the public good.[62] And while residents would decide the

Social part 社会的部分   私的部分 Individual part

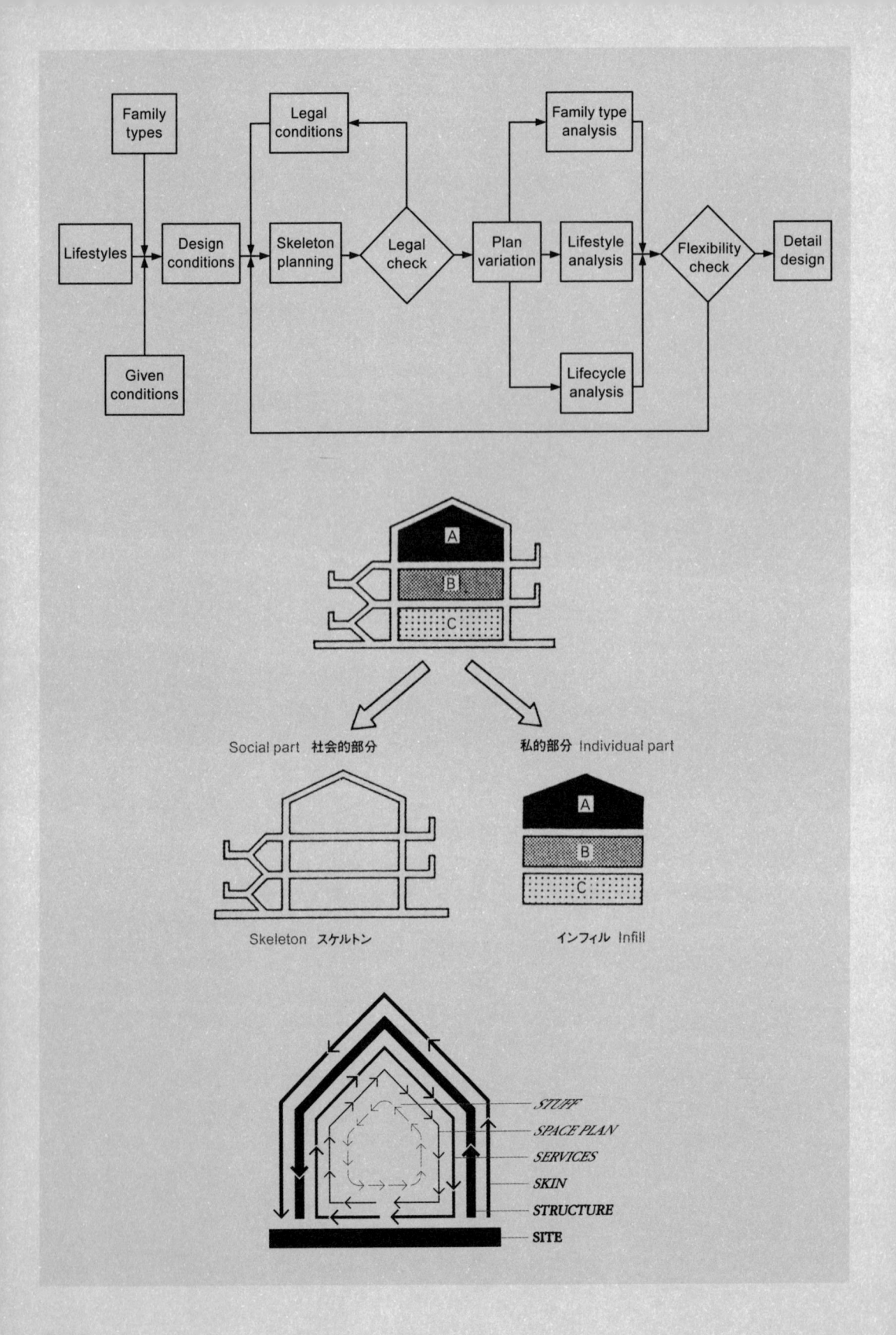

Skeleton スケルトン   インフィル Infill

- *STUFF*
- *SPACE PLAN*
- *SERVICES*
- *SKIN*
- *STRUCTURE*
- *SITE*

design of their units, they would not be abandoned in a DIY situation that might be overwhelming, since consultation with an architect was a key part of the TSHS process.

Another major change from Yosizaka is that Takada and Tatsumi draw inspiration from *hadaka-gashi.* Indeed, they call TSHS a *hadaka-gashi* system for "modern times," with their system promoting similarly modular elements for infill. Such infill would ideally come from small regional construction companies, as was the case with *kyo-ma* components during the Edo period. Standardization and local manufacture would help to remake a culture of flexible and sustainable housing.[63]

The Century Housing System

Fighting against scrap-and-build in its name, the Century Housing System (CHS) promoted a 100-year life span for concrete primary structure, well beyond Japanese housing's typical demolition by age 30. Now defunct, the system was initiated by MOC in 1980 under Utida's leadership. It offered a technical approach that was complimentary to the more social orientation of TSHS. While TSHS is about a method for participation and was spread through the network of Tatsumi and Takada, CHS was a government incentive program that only set specifications that could enable participation. Launched in 1985, it offered condominium buyers favorable loan rates in exchange for builders' compliance with its construction guidelines.[64]

In 1960, Tange had of course called for architecture to combine longer and shorter cycles of time to better meet the future. This was often manifested in dualistic terms through the juxtaposition of permanent and changeable elements. But Utida went far beyond a binary structure, thanks to CHS assigning life spans to every part of a building. The research produced the following table:

3–6 years	Light bulbs
6–12 years	Water heater, home appliances, piping, wiring
12–25 years	Moveable partitions, built-in furniture
25–50 years	Exterior doors and windows, roof
50–100 years	Foundations, main columns, and beams[65]

top: TSHS flowchart

center: Roles of skeleton and infill for TSHS

bottom: Stewart Brand, "Shearing layers of change," 1994

The ambition of this hierarchy was to disentangle all of a building's systems so as to ease repair and renovation, separating and layering them based on respective anticipated life spans to make a temporal "onion" like Stewart Brand's famous diagram.

Overall, the layers codified a relatively conventional sequence of construction, but less conventional was the CHS requirement to use only "dry" mechanical connections, enabling possible disassembly through using bolts, screws, clips, and so on.

The most durable part of the onion, the frame of the primary structure, is typically the part of a building with the highest cost and embodied energy, making it the most crucial to preserve. Despite the robustness to be expected of load-bearing elements, the entanglement of systems had, as noted, often led to entire buildings being scrapped, often due to plumbing-related problems. In response, and likely borrowed from the Stratiform research, raised access floors were made part of CHS to allow easier access to piping and the relocation of bathrooms and kitchens. While moving wet areas may not be urgent, a main complaint by the Hiroshima Housing Authority in renovating Otaka's design was the difficulty of such work.[66] CHS also mandated that no shared plumbing risers could pass through apartments, instead requiring access from shared circulation spaces in order to simplify maintenance and avoid leak damage within units.

Like Japanese wooden architecture, CHS uses the *shaku* as its unit of measurement. The unit used for the *kyo-ma* tatami module, the *shaku* has survived into the present as the standard unit for wood building materials for detached houses, even with the general adoption of metric units. Now the unit for a wood home would determine the dimensions of concrete skeletons holding many homes, thereby optimizing the use of the existing market of wood products for infill elements. Concrete and wood produce a hybrid open system. The Stratiform proposal also relied on the existing, in the form of the prefab industry, but CHS applied this strategy to a much wider range of vernacular elements.

The architectural historian Kenneth Frampton calls Le Corbusier's design approach from the mid-1930s onwards the "monumentalization of the vernacular," a description that can be applied to an extent to the Metabolists.[67] Ideas such as group form and minor-structure found their inspiration in the old traditions of hill towns and *minka*, both attractive for their flexibility. Recalling again Nitschke's comment on flexibility as "fuss," these precedents were indeed interpreted by the Metabolists at giant scales made comparatively rigid by concrete, steel, and bureaucracy. What Utida initiated through CHS is effectively Metabolism's digestion back into a vernacular reality, a demonumentalization to support a democratic urban architecture.[68]

Public Relations

It should be evident at this point that all buildings have a metabolism, whether or not they're Metabolist, and that these metabolisms can vary greatly in their contributions to healthy environments. Despite the importance of Utida's work in consciously addressing this reality in technical detail, no one would see the 2,337 CHS apartments built by 1998 as Metabolism's apotheosis.[69] The same goes for most TSHS projects. All that mattered for these systems was process and logic of assembly, not symbolic expression of change. Yet, despite the justifiable criticism of Metabolism's graphic images from the 1960s, it would be a mistake to see exciting forms in representations or realized buildings as antithetical to the rise of new vernaculars as dreamed of by Utida and others.

As a prime example of this error, Habraken's *Supports* has no illustrations, which contributed to his ideas being misunderstood. Utterly different from Metabolism, with its images of aerial cities and capsules, Habraken, the anti-visionary visionary, in 1961 felt that images would only result in others viewing him as a lone "master" architect, obscuring his focus on mass housing's core problems of control.[70] His insistence that a support is not a skeleton like the Dom-ino House also didn't help, causing much confusion over his precise definition of a support.[71]

For CHS, expression of intentions is hindered due to the system being an incentive program. Unlike previous government sponsorship of specific designs for specific sites, CHS started a trend in Japanese housing initiatives: artificial land's sublimation into guidelines haunted by the ghost of the concept's radicality. The guidelines dictate more than they stimulate.

Kazunobu Minami, now an established figure in housing research and a professor at the Shibaura Institute of Technology, had a doctoral student who researched built CHS units. The student found that the vast majority of residents in those units had never used their architectural freedoms because they had no idea their freedoms existed.[72] By contrast, Metabolism was a movement that knew how to communicate and inspire through dramatic renderings, models, words, and occasionally actual buildings. But it was often only the image of transformation, not a reality, at least as intended. CHS was the reality, or its sober feasibility, without any image. This situation changed with Utida's NEXT21 Experimental Housing Project.

1. Noboru Kawazoe, *Contemporary Japanese Architecture* (Tokyo: Kokusai Koryu Kikin, 1973), 63. Kawazoe paraphrases this sentiment from the poet Paul Valéry.
2. See Yositika Utida, *Kenchiku seisan no open system/Open Systems in Building Production* [1977] (Tokyo: Shokoku-sha, 1995), 23. Translation by Riyo Namigata.
3. The architect Hiroshi Hara, who wrote his University of Tokyo doctoral dissertation under Utida, calls his professor's methodology "elementalism." See Thomas Daniell, *An Anatomy of Influence* (London: AA Publications, 2018), 74.
4. See page 180 of this book and *A Quick Look at Housing in Japan*, eds. The Building Center of Japan et al. (Tokyo: The Building Center of Japan, 2014), 26.
5. *A Quick Look*, 26.
6. See Richard Koo and Masaya Sasaki, "Obstacles to Affluence: Thoughts on Japanese Housing," *NRI Papers*, no. 137 (December 2008): 2, PDF file.
7. As the architect Kazunobu Minami notes, the problem of scrap-and-build is a problem of location, as 13 percent of the country's housing is empty in areas outside the economic pressure of the Pacific Belt. Minami, in conversation with the author, May 14, 2014.
8. Koo and Sasaki, "Obstacles," 3.
9. "Construction state": see Alex Kerr, *Dogs and Demons: Tales from the Dark Side of Japan* (New York: Hill & Wang, 2001), 13–50. Kerr provides a long and compelling description of the ills of the construction state. This vast entity, which is inclusive of the Metabolist-industrial complex, is the network of politicians, ministries, and corporations inadvertently committed to the destruction of the Japanese landscape, through all manner of earthworks, sea walls, land reclamation projects, and so on, fueled by bid rigging, profiteering, and other forms of corruption.
10. See Eiko Maruko Siniawer, *Waste: Consuming Postwar Japan* (Ithaca, NY: Cornell University Press, 2018), 82–83. Packard's book was a best-seller in both the US and Japan.
11. Vance Packard, *The Waste Makers* [1960] (New York: Giant Cardinal, 1963), 46. Packard quotes here from *Retailing Daily*, a trade journal for the home furnishings field.
12. High-growth period as one of high-disposability: see Siniawer, *Waste*, 142.
13. Seiichi Fukao, "Century Housing System: Background and Status Report," *Open House International* 12, no. 2 (1987): 36.
14. Kisho Kurokawa mentions this reality in his *Metabolism in Architecture* (Boulder, CO: Westview Press, 1977), 32. Such problems have also appeared at his Nakagin Capsule Tower, which has been suffering major deterioration due, in part, to inaccessible plumbing.
15. See André Sorensen, *The Making of Urban Japan: Cities and Planning from Edo to the Twenty-First Century* (New York: Routledge, 2002), 274–275.
16. See *A Quick Look*, 15.
17. On "Consumer durables," see Sorensen, *Making*, 274. Durables are typically defined as goods yielding utility that last more than three years.
18. See Eiji Oizumi, "Transformations in Housing Construction and Finance," in *Housing and Social Transition in Japan*, eds. Yosuke Hirayama and Richard Ronald [2007] (New York: Routledge, 2012), 50–51.
19. See Siniawer, *Waste*, 231–237.
20. "Lifestyle superpower": see Siniawer, *Waste*, 238.
21. Fred A. Bernstein, "Architect Sou Fujimoto's Futuristic Spaces," *WSJ Magazine*, November 5, 2014, https://www.wsj.com/articles/architect-sou-fujimotos-futuristic-spaces-1415238522.
22. Holger König et al., *A Life Cycle Approach to Buildings* (Munich: Institut für International Architektur-Dokumentation, 2010), 31.
23. See Oizumi, "Transformations," 57.
24. See Elisabeth Braw, "Japan's Disposable Home Culture is an Environmental and Financial Headache," *The Guardian*, May 2, 2014, https://www.theguardian.com/sustainable-business/disposable-homes-japan-environment-lifespan-sustainability.
25. Koo and Sasaki, "Obstacles," 5–9.
26. Koo and Sasaki, "Obstacles," 13.
27. Günter Nitschke, quoted in Kenneth Frampton, *Modern Architecture: A Critical History* [1980] (New York: Thames and Hudson, 1992), 283.
28. See Sorensen, *Making*, 308–309.
29. See Jordan Sand, *Tokyo Vernacular: Common Spaces, Local Histories, Found Objects* (Los Angeles: University of California Press, 2013), 64.
30. See Sorensen, *Making*, 308.
31. See Akira Nakao, "Urban Design Work," trans. Gen Machida, in *PAU: Uniting Architecture and Society—The Approach of OTAKA Masato* (Tokyo: National Archives of Modern Architecture, 2016), 49.
32. Yositika Utida, *The Construction and Culture of Architecture Today: A View from Japan* (Tokyo: Ichigaya Publishing Co., 2002), 105.
33. Yositika Utida, in conversation with the author, April 23, 2010. Translation by Hajime Yatsuka.
34. Utida, April 23, 2010.
35. Ludwig von Bertalanffy, *General Systems Theory* [1968] (Harmondsworth: Penguin Books, 1973), 149.
36. I'm not aware of Utida making explicit reference to the biological definition of open systems for his own use of the concept, though it may exist.
37. Utida, *Construction*, 95. Note that this book presents in English various ideas from *Open Systems*, which is published in Japanese.
38. Utida, April 23, 2010.
39. Utida, *Construction*, 97, 99.
40. See Heino Engel, *Measure and Construction of the Japanese House* (Rutland, VT: Tuttle, 1985), 25. It should be noted that *kyo-* translates actually as "capital," in reference to Kyoto, thereby indicating *kyo-ma ken*'s regional identity.
41. See Engel, *Measure*, 25–26.
42. See Engel, *Measure*, 36–42.
43. See Utida, *Kenchiku*, 199.
44. No precise dates are in my sources for when exactly *hadaka-gashi* emerged.
45. Noboru Kawazoe, "The City of the Future," *Zodiac* no. 9 (1961): 107.

46. Noboru Kawazoe, "Metabolism," *The Japan Architect* (December 1969): 107–108. Kawazoe also discusses *kyo-ma* dimensioning in "The Ise Shrine and Its Cultural Context," in *Ise: Prototype of Japanese Architecture* [1961] (Cambridge, MA: The MIT Press, 1965), 204–206.
47. Utida, April 23, 2010.
48. Utida, April 23, 2010.
49. In comparison, this vernacular reality is notably missing from the Modulor, Le Corbusier's proportional system meant as a dimensional Esperanto. Illustrative of this shortcoming, the main reference dimensions for the Modulor do not coordinate with any standard sheet material size in either feet or meters. Le Corbusier mentions that standard 1.2-meter sheet widths were used for the interior paneling of the Marseilles Unité to avoid wasted offcut, in lieu of the closest Modulor approximation at 1.13 meters. See Le Corbusier, *The Modulor* [1948] (Basel: Birkhäuser, 2004), 136. It is easy to imagine that this lack of coordination with existing materials was a main reason for the system's failure.
50. The Congress for the New Urbanism, founded in 1994, is directly modelled on CIAM, founded in 1928, adopting its predecessor's policy-oriented methods but not its forms. See Andres Duany et al., *Suburban Nation: The Rise of Sprawl and the Decline of the American Dream* (New York: North Point Press, 2000), 257.
51. Reyner Banham, *Megastructure: Urban Futures of the Recent Past* (New York: Harper & Row, 1976), 10.
52. See Dorine van Hoogstraten, "Between Structure and Form: Habraken and the Alternative to Mass Housing," in Koos Bosma et al., *Housing for the Millions: John Habraken and the SAR (1960–2000)* (Rotterdam: NAI Publishers, 2000), 114–117. It should be noted that Habraken and the SAR's methods gave rise in the 1980s to the "Open Building" movement in the Netherlands, with individuals and groups in various nations soon coming to form a network of Open Building researchers and practitioners. See John Habraken, "Open Building: brief introduction," accessed July 3, 2020, https://www.habraken.com/html/introduction.htm.
53. N. J. Habraken, *Supports: An Alternative to Mass Housing* [1961], trans. B. Valkenburg, ed. Jonathan Teicher (UK: Urban International Press, 2011), 70.
54. This folk saying, apparently from the 1960s or '70s, is "quoted" in David Madden and Peter Marcuse, *In Defense of Housing* (New York: Verso, 2016), 211–212.
55. See N. J. Habraken, "Lives of Systems," in *Transformations of the Site* (Cambridge, MA: Atwater Press, 1983), 176–177; and Habraken, "The Limits of Professionalism," Architectural Association lecture and interview, 1975, https://www.youtube.com/watch?v=RCfxahx9_DY.
56. See Martijn Vos, "The Foundation for Architects' Research (SAR) in Good Times and Bad," in *Housing for the Millions*, 173. Italics in original.
57. See Dorine van Hoogstraten and Martijn Vos, "The SAR Methodology as Applied to Housing Construction, Product Development, and Education," in *Housing for the Millions*, 214–228.
58. Email exchange between John Habraken and the author, April 15, 2016.
59. Habraken went to MIT in 1975, where he was head of the Department of Architecture until 1981, and continued to teach until 1989.
60. Takada graduated from Tatsumi's lab at Kyoto University in 1977, where Tatsumi also attended, having graduated under Uzo Nishiyama in 1953.
61. Kazuo Tatsumi and Mitsuo Takada, "Two Step Housing System," *Open House International* 12, no. 2 (1987): 20.
62. Tatsumi and Takada, "Two Step," 21–23.
63. See Mitsuo Takada and Hidetoshi Yasueda, "Infill (Fit-out) Management System at Flex Court Yoshida," *Open House International* 26, no. 3 (2001): 29–32. Note that earlier than TSHS, in 1959, the *kyo-ma* module was tried in prefab house planning for the Matsushita Type-One by PanaHome. I am not aware of this initiative's results. See Shuichi Matsumura et al., "Technological Developments of Japanese Prefabricated Housing in an Early Stage," *Japan Architectural Review* 2, no. 1 (January 2019): 60.
64. See Robert Schmidt III et al., "Lessons from Japan: A Look at Century Housing System," *12th International Dependency and Structure Modelling Conference* (July 2010): 3, PDF file.
65. Utida, *Construction*, 61. On the goal of a 100-year life span for primary structure, it is highly suggestive that in 1928, Yoshikazu Utida and the engineer Minoru Hamada established an equation showing reinforced concrete's expected service life to be 100 years, due to atmospheric corrosion of reinforcing bars. This life span was of course based on certain assumptions about reinforced concrete specifications. See Lucia Allais and Forrest Meggers, "Concrete is 100 Years Old: The Carbonation Equation and Narratives of Anthropogenic Change" (unpublished manuscript, September 28, 2020), PDF file.
66. Sachiko Komatsu (International Relations Division, Citizens Affairs Bureau, The City of Hiroshima), in conversation with the author, April 8, 2010.
67. Frampton, *Modern Architecture*, 224.
68. This democratic orientation in Utida's work is the focus of an essay by Kengo Kuma, "Yoshichika Uchida: Postwar Democracy," in *Architecture of Defeat* [2002] (New York: Routledge, 2019), 89–96. Note that Kuma's spelling of Utida's name is its standard romanization. To delve into a family tree, Kuma graduated from Hiroshi Hara's lab at the University of Tokyo, and Hara, as mentioned, graduated from Utida's.
69. Utida, *Construction*, 61.
70. Habraken, "The Limits."
71. This confusion was felt by no less than the prolific Team 10 architect Jaap Bakema, a SAR board member, who was perplexed by Habraken's distinction. See van Hoogstraten and Vos, *Housing for the Millions*, 228–229.
72. Minami, May 14, 2014.

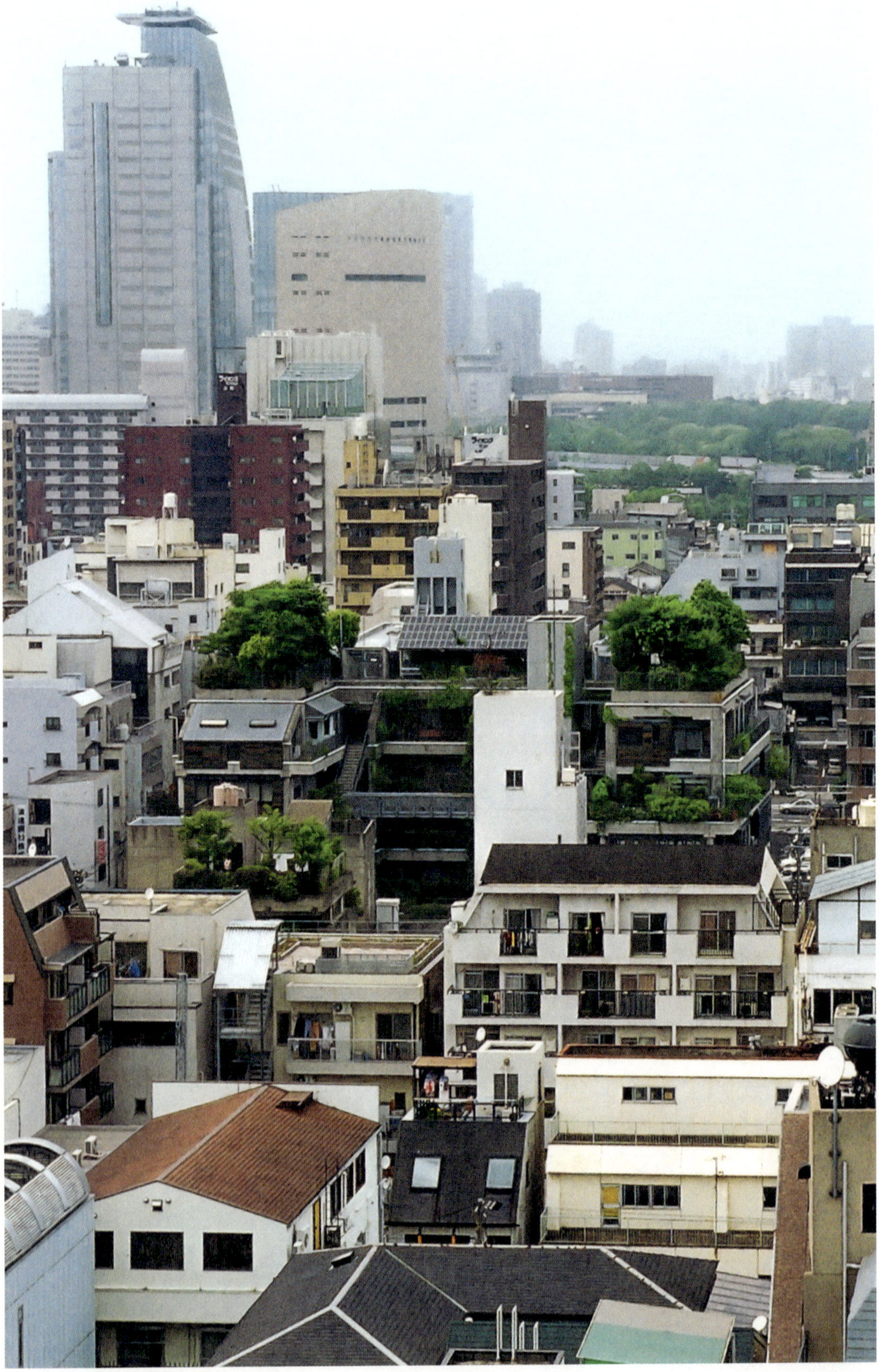

Anti-Speculative Speculation:
NEXT21, 1989–

In the early 1990s, Rem Koolhaas remarked that one finds in Japan "*incredible buildings that are about nothing. They have no program, no social ambition.*"[1] True as this may have been in the bubble era, the story of artificial land suggests that the absence of any fixed program could in fact be a social ambition. Utida recommends we "think of a given building not as a residence... but as space for living that can serve society's shifting needs by transforming into a hospital, a nursing home, a seminar room or an office."[2] Either a tacit or explicit goal in projects from Harumi to the Stratiform Structure Module, such responsiveness also drives Utida's NEXT21 Experimental Housing, built in Osaka and first occupied in 1994. Conceived as model housing for the twenty-first century, the project is a time machine for simulating a host of changes that might otherwise not have happened for decades. Thanks in part to this simulation, NEXT21 presents an exciting and emblematic image of the support/infill concept, which has been so often misunderstood or dismissed.

Started in 1989 by Osaka Gas, a utility provider for over seven million customers in the Kansai region, NEXT21 is a laboratory for the company. It enables research into new approaches to apartments, renovation, and energy, studied in five-year phases, inhabited by Osaka Gas employees as guinea pigs. In 1963, Otaka had in fact proposed that utility companies be the makers and managers of artificial land. Since they already supplied services, it would be logical for them to also supply sites.[3] While it may give one pause to have a negligent company like TEPCO involved, Osaka Gas has used NEXT21 to improve itself, particularly through testing equipment that aims to reduce the need for fossil fuels.[4]

Osaka Gas NEXT21 Committee, NEXT21 Experimental Housing, Osaka, 1993 (2005)

3 OPEN SYSTEMS

NEXT21 in 2013 (left)
and in 2010 (above)

ANTI-SPECULATIVE SPECULATION: NEXT21, 1989–

Soon after Utida's appointment as chairman for NEXT21's development, he took his client team on a tour of Dutch housing led by Habraken. The tour included architect Frans van der Werf's Molenvliet public housing in Papendrecht, a SAR support/infill project from 1978, for which all of the residents had successfully worked with the architect on the design of their own units. Osaka Gas was immediately convinced by the approach.[5]

Beyond adopting support/infill as the model for the future, NEXT21 explicitly equated sustainability with the flexibility that had been artificial land's historical quest. A brochure for the project makes this clear, stating that:

> Along with physical durability, flexibility in remodeling is essential for a dwelling to be lived in for many years. A high degree of flexibility for room arrangement in response to the need of the residents is important for long-term use. Such dwellings become valuable assets of society and contribute to waste reduction. The basic structure of a building functions as an artificial ground and creates a new property value different from the values of land and dwellings.[6]

The indeterminacy of artificial land had previously been seen in Japan as an infrastructural solution to housing economics, but its adaptive capacity is now seen in terms both economic and ecological. This ecological reorientation is partly a response to the wastage of scrap-and-build, but it also indicates a *machizukuri* attitude in which socially sustainable housing needs to be conceived together with the people who will live in it. Indeed, not long before NEXT21 began, cooperative housing with such an approach was embraced in Osaka, and that work can be seen as an inspiration that gives this project a specific critical content. While Utida described NEXT21 as the best building to come out of the bubble, it suggests a model highly at odds with the speculative real estate of that time.[7]

Mini Major-Structure

Utida gathered trusted collaborators for the project, including TSHS inventors Tatsumi and Takada, Seichi Fukao, Shinichi Chikazumi of the Shu-Koh-Sha Architecture and Urban Design Studio, and Toshihiko Kimura. Appropriately enough, Chikazumi had once been an intern in Otaka's office, and had also been one of Utida's students, and after worked with him. Kimura had, of course, worked on Harumi and Chojuen, as well as been a member of the 1962 Artificial Land Committee with Utida. Construction was by Obayashi Corporation, a reputable *zenekon*.

The project's U-shaped massing is an aggregation of six small towers that recall in miniature Kimura's engineering for Chojuen. There, the grouping of the towers as separate elements is only implied, since they have some shared columns. But for NEXT21, each tower is actually independent, not relying on the adjacent towers for seismic stability, and further suggesting an incremental infrastructure adaptable to different types of site. Made from reinforced concrete, each tower skeleton is square in plan, and flares out at the second floor to a larger bay size. The flaring was apparently Utida's idea, and Chikazumi says the design team at first feared it was an old Metabolist cliché, too similar to Sachio Otani's Kawaramachi Housing or the giant A-frames in Tange's 1960 Plan.[8] Yet, transposed to a smaller scale, the flare simply makes space for car parking.

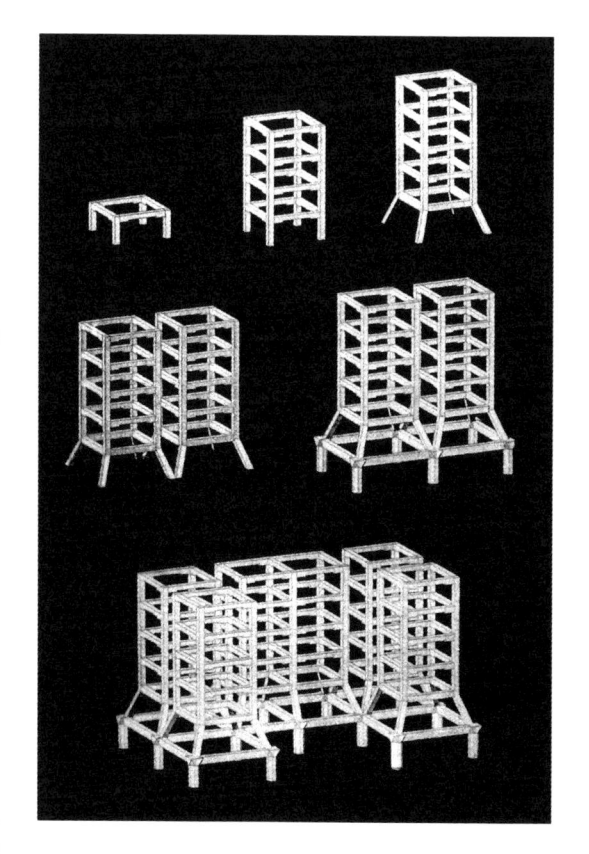

A floor is called a "layer" in NEXT21's official descriptions, and the four upper layers of its group-form skeleton are wrapped by "canals."[9] Basically concrete troughs capped by pavers, the canals link all of the towers as shared circulation. Together with the multiple stairs to the surrounding neighborhood, they form a three-dimensional street network. The canals are free of obstructing transverse beams, resulting in a continuous plenum for supplying services almost anywhere in any possible floor plan, amplifying the freedoms of the raised floors used in more conventional CHS apartments. Reminiscent of the concrete tie holes that characterize the architecture of Tadao Ando, small holes on the faces of the canals act as sleeves to hold scaffolding for doing facade work, thereby turning a renovation method into a tectonic detail. And, as only imagined in the Stratiform research, removing pavers allows the canals to be planted with bushes and small trees. Against the obsession with thinness found in so much post-bubble Japanese architecture, NEXT21's structure demonstrates the generosity of being thick and hollow.

left: Frans van der Werf, Molenvliet, Papendrecht, Netherlands, 1978

right: NEXT21 skeleton as incremental infrastructure

ANTI-SPECULATIVE SPECULATION: NEXT21, 1989–

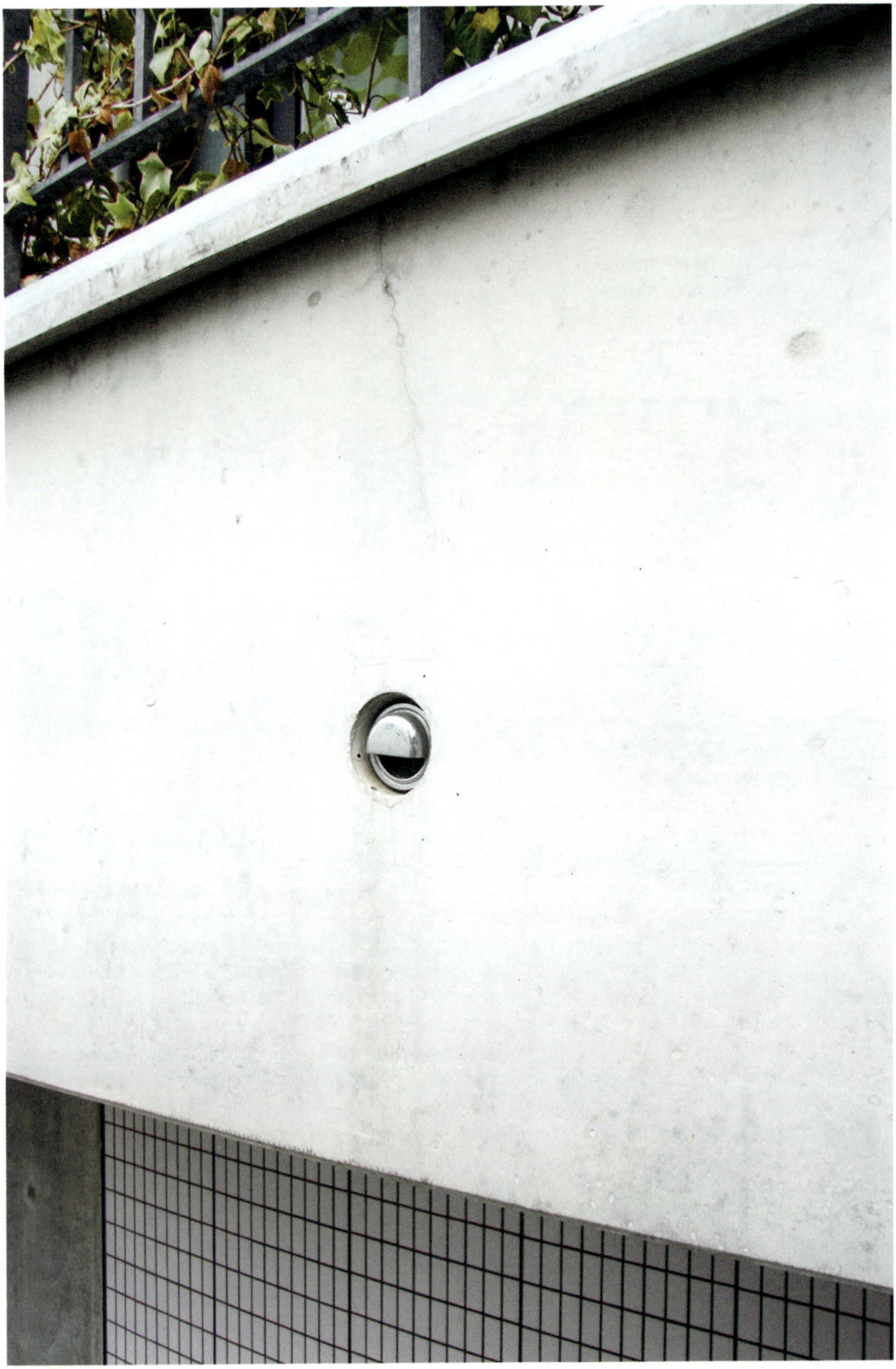

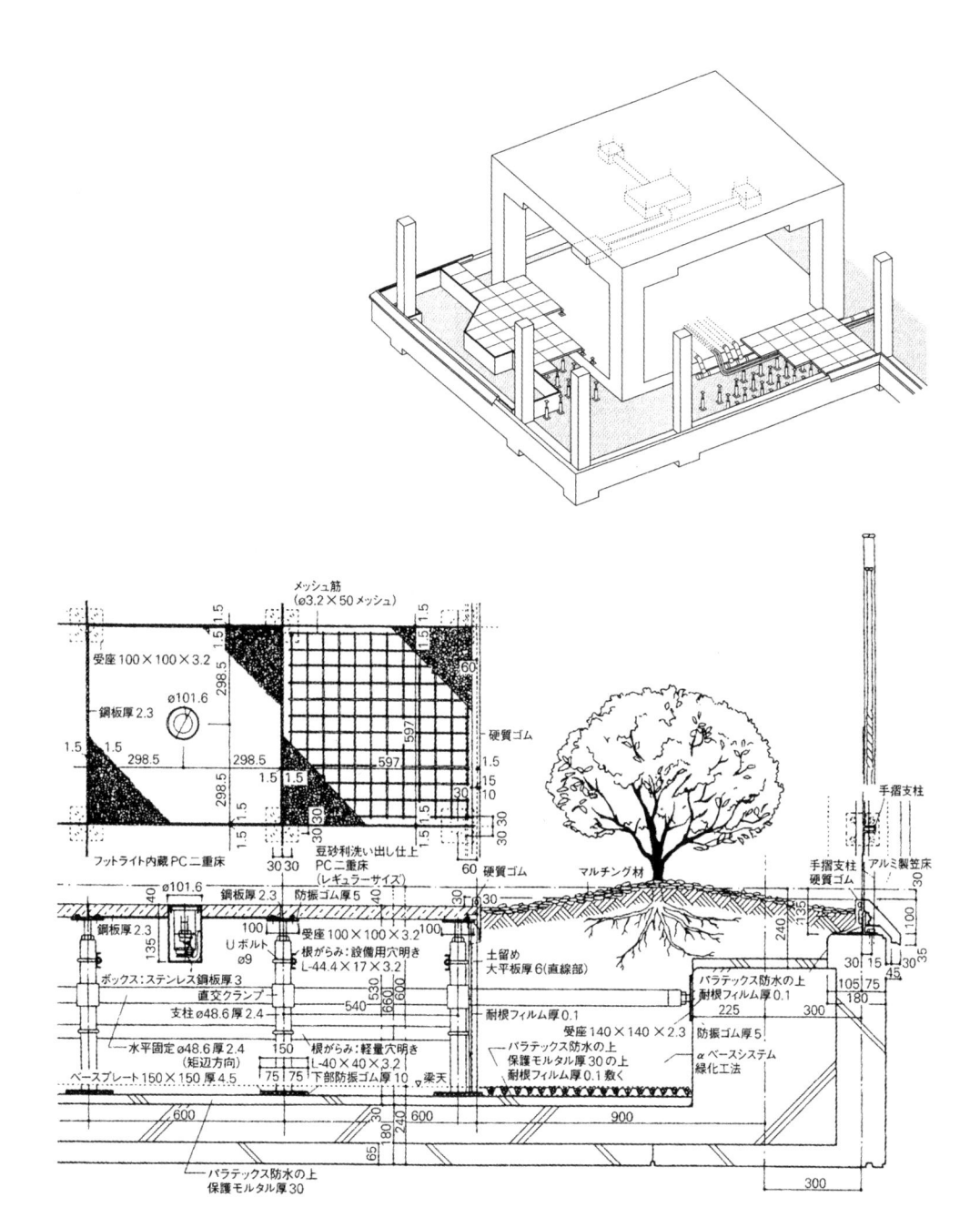

left: Hole in NEXT21's skeleton for holding maintenance scaffolding

above: NEXT21 perimeter "canal" system for plumbing and other services (top) and canal detail (bottom)

ANTI-SPECULATIVE SPECULATION: NEXT21, 1989–

Capacity Planning

The skeleton's flexibility was tested through "capacity planning," a scenario technique identified by Habraken. This method requires first having a schematic design for structure, and then testing its ability to host a range of apartments or other functions to evaluate how this programming works with the provisional structure's ceiling height, floor depth, circulation, and other "found" conditions. As Habraken notes, the iterative testing of design opportunities within conditions outside the architect's control is a basic fact of architectural practice, from interior renovations to urban planning.[10] It's basic to any assessment of a given site's potential. But being so common, iterative testing is rarely embraced for its potential to guide the design of the site itself. What the capacity method creates in this case is a feedback loop wherein the study of infill scenarios acts to adjust or bolster the site-as-skeleton, just as described in the flowchart by Takada and Tatsumi. The process will reveal if a structure is durable through being adaptable, making it an important method for the long-life agenda of CHS, which NEXT21 expresses as never before.

To perform such a test at NEXT21, Utida invited thirteen architects to make designs for a range of lifestyles concocted for eighteen "parcels" in the project.[11] Since the skeleton was already under construction at the time, the test would not remain on paper. Seen together, the scenarios testify to the end of the "housing miracle" that had flooded the country with so many identical apartments. The nuclear family, for which the typical postwar unit was intended, was in decline by the time of the bubble, with Japan's demographics trending toward lower birth rates, fewer marriages, more elderly, and greater affluence. Indicative of these changing conditions and the notion of Japan as a "lifestyle superpower" are the names of the scenarios: Warm, Comfortable House; Young Family House; Independent Family House; Extended Family House; Active Oldsters' House; Garden House; House with Office; House of Harmony; Woody House; Next Generation House; House for Home Party; House with Handicraft Studio; House for Relaxation; House with Fitness Room; House for Time Creation; Changeable House; House for Unmarried City Dweller; and DINKS Apartment.[12]

Infill

The architects interpreted their assigned scenarios within parcels defined only by a property line and height, with the boundary between inside and outside left undetermined. Though the boundary of the envelope was therefore flexible, as was the location of wet services thanks to the canals, the architects had more than a few constraints. For example, the interior infill had to follow the *shaku* dimensioning mandated by CHS, and coordinate with a SAR-inspired planning grid developed by Fukao.

Another constraint was the infill facade system. Control of facades is a touchy subject for adherents and critics of artificial land, as it manifests the collision between issues of waterproofing, insulation, ownership, and a fear that a patchwork appearance may evoke a dilapidated building. One person's lively variety may be another's seeming slum.[13] The compromise at NEXT21 is the requirement to use a custom multi-colored stainless-steel cladding, also based on the *shaku* module, within which window and door openings can be arbitrarily sized and positioned. The facade is not entirely free.

top: NEXT21 House with Handicraft Studio

bottom: NEXT21 Garden House

ANTI-SPECULATIVE SPECULATION: NEXT21, 1989–

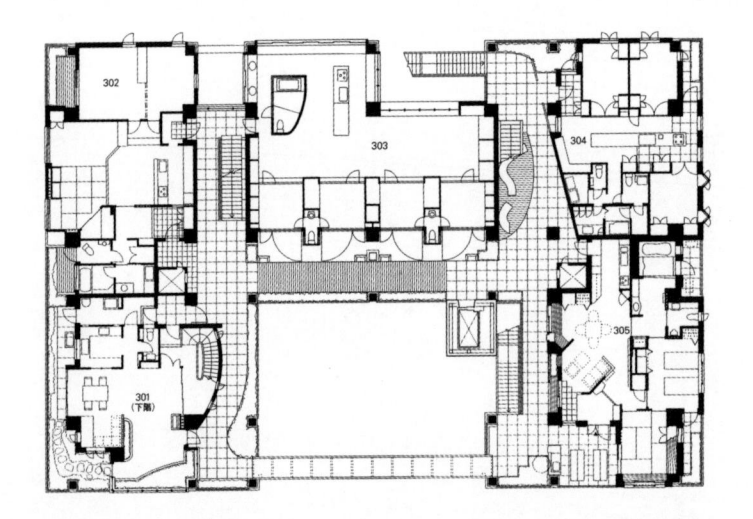

Level 3

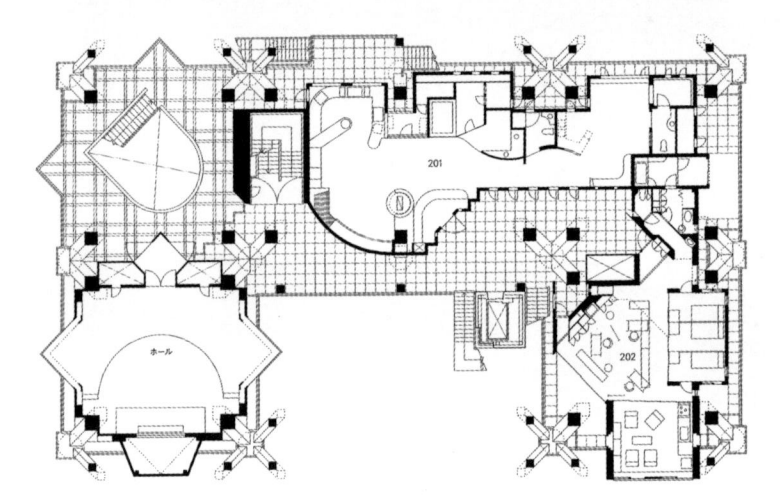

Level 2

202	Warm, Comfortable House	501	House with Fitness Room
		502	House for Home Party
301	Garden House	503	House with Handicraft Studio
302	Young Family House	504	House for Relaxation
303	Independent Family House		
304	Extended Family House	601	House for Time Creation
305	Active Oldsters' House	603	Changeable House
		604	House for Unmarried City Dweller
402	Healthy Child-rearing House		
403	House of Harmony	605	DINKS Apartment
404	Woody House		
405	Next-Generation Family House		

3 OPEN SYSTEMS

Level 6

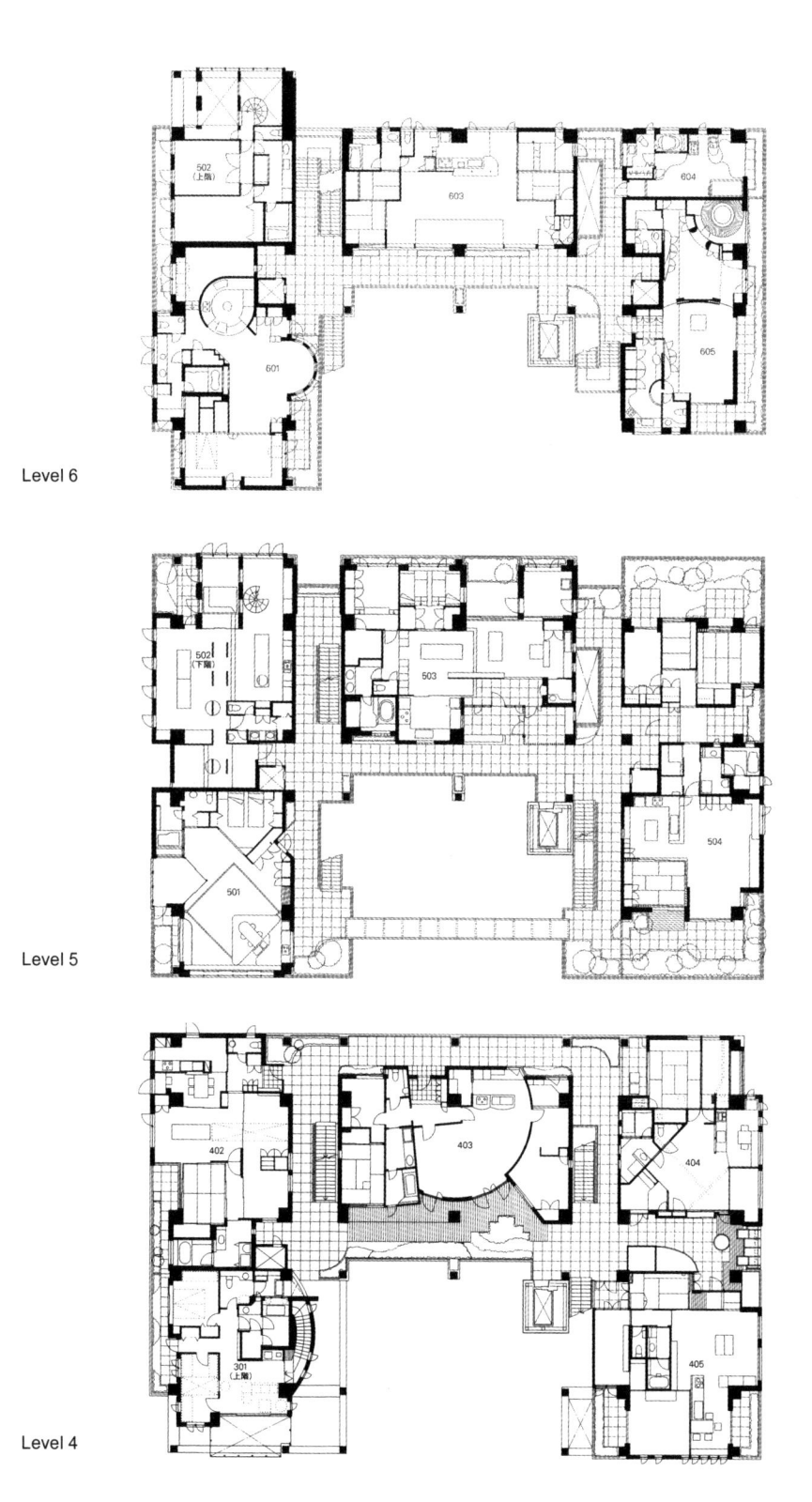

Level 5

Level 4

ANTI-SPECULATIVE SPECULATION: NEXT21, 1989–

Test Phases

In 1994, the Phase 1 residents moved in. They departed in 1999, and Phase 2 residents arrived in 2000. Some units on the structure's fourth layer were modified over these phases, revealing the project's metabolism. First, Unit 402, originally the House with Office, was remodeled in 1996 to convert it into the Healthy Child-rearing House. Unlike the assigned scenarios, this remodeling was done with the full participation of the residents who had been living in the unit since the start of Phase 1. Comparing the plans before and after, we see a small terrace at an outside corner absorbed into the interior and turned into a kitchen, with the kitchen having previously been at the opposite end of the unit. A second existing terrace at the south end was extended north, breaking through the walls of the old kitchen location. A bathroom migrated to the edge of the expanded terrace for a better view, allowing a larger space for the children's room. The unit initially had separate entrances for office and home, but these were combined into a single entry.

In the 1970s, the concept of "long life, loose fit, low energy" became a new environmental goal for architecture, with inspiration coming from adaptable old buildings in tune with their climates.[14] NEXT21 can seem like the idea's apotheosis, yet the insistence on modular control raises doubts about its degree of looseness. Rather than imprecise planning, NEXT21's loose fit partly lies in its dry connections that allow clean disassembly. This CHS feature led to 90 percent of 402's facade being reused for its renovation, thanks also to its modular coordination with the skeleton. As shown with *kyo-ma ken*, sustainability and modularity can work well together.

above: NEXT21, exterior of House for Time Creation (2010)

right: NEXT21, southern courtyard (2010)

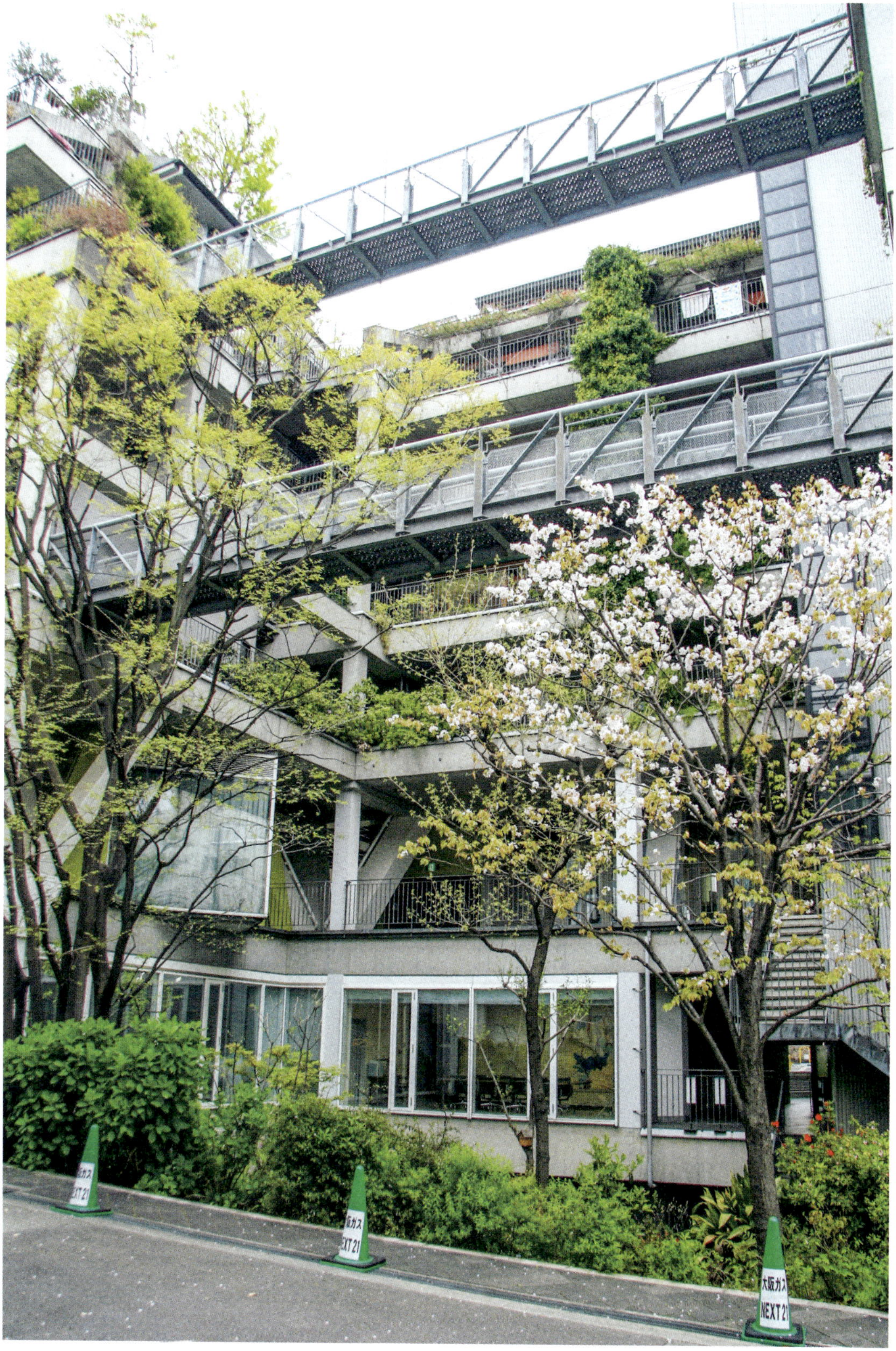
大阪ガス
NEXT21

[写真3] リフォーム前のNEXT21の外観

[写真4] リフォーム工事中のNEXT21

[写真5] リフォーム後のNEXT21の外観

Initial unit:
404 Three-Generation Family House

New units:
404 Woody House (north side)
405 Next-Generation Family House (south side)

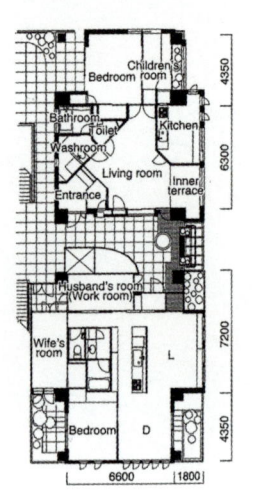

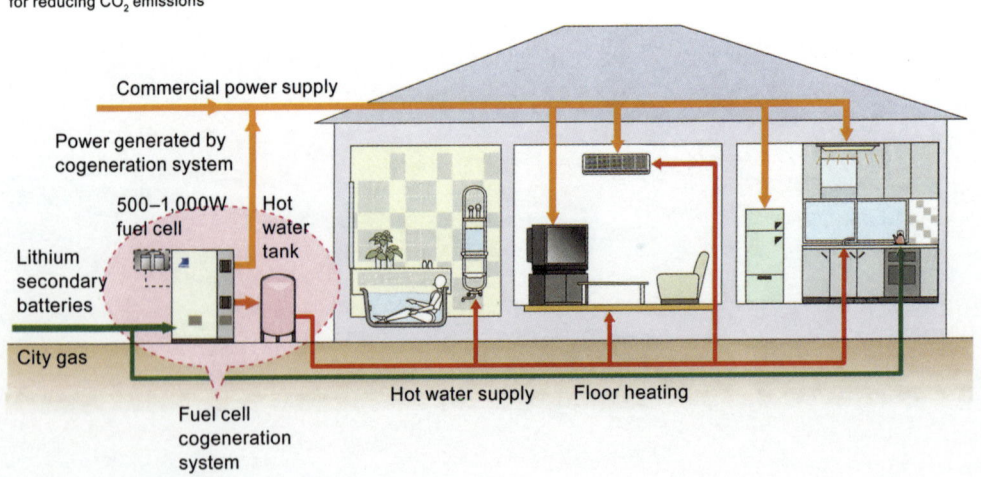

Highly Efficient Power Generation:
Low environmental impact and effective for reducing CO_2 emissions

280

3 OPEN SYSTEMS

Unit 402's neighbor, Unit 403, displays artificial land's touchstone of a freestanding house on an airy platform. Working with the scenario of House of Harmony, the unit is bracketed to the east and west by open public stairways, and is set back from the north and south edges of the skeleton, making it independent in every direction. With two entrances on opposite sides, 403's architect proposed a double-loaded apartment reminiscent of Sawada Mansion. Due to this choice of egress, residents can associate to a greater or lesser degree with neighbors and family—a help for harmonious living.

Later, in 1999 in preparation for Phase 2, Unit 404 underwent a bifurcation that suggests a death in the family. The original Three Generation Family House was split into two separate units by converting the former dining room into an extension of the exterior shared circulation, becoming a tiny pocket park. With the units now reimagined as Woody House and Next Generation House, the latter is made into a model apartment for MOC. The bathroom and kitchen were relocated from the perimeter to the new apartment's center, freeing the outer edges for programs needing better natural light, including a "Wife's Room" that extends out into a terrace from Phase 1.

Throughout these renovations, Osaka Gas was also testing energy systems. The company actively investigated cogeneration engines. Powered by natural gas, the building-wide "cogen" system for Phase 1 used a super-efficient engine that produced electricity supplemented by commercial supply and photovoltaics mounted on the roof. Exhaust heat from the engines was captured to make hot water. Phase 2 tried a micro-cogen approach, in which power production was decentralized through engines sized to suit each apartment. The installation and testing of these services by technicians was greatly assisted by the canals and utility risers being accessible from public spaces.

Post-Occupancy

Overall, NEXT21's attempt to make renovation easier wasn't entirely successful. The architects for the scenarios felt the planning grid had too many rules, making it complicated and confusing to use, which is hardly a way to promote the virtues of modularity.[15] This problem indicates the difference between technical feasibility and social acceptance.

Also on the topic of acceptance, Osaka Gas researcher Midori Kimo notes that most of the Phase 1 units into which the employees moved were based on scenarios developed without their input. One of the first experiments was to see if this potential mismatch mattered. Over the five years of the phase, it was found that residents who had participated in the design of the units they lived in were much happier with their experience than those who had not.[16]

Beyond noise complaints caused by the renovation of Unit 402, living in NEXT21 may have felt like living in a construction site. Like many experiments, the project accelerated the normal passage of time, making changes in tenants, family structures, occupations, and energy systems that elsewhere might take far more than five years, in large part to test flexibility. Though how much do people care about living in a flexible home? While not conducted at NEXT21, a 2002 survey of why owners of CHS apartments had bought them indicated they don't care much. From a list of twenty items, the three things they considered most desirable were size, greenery, and access to sun and air—echoing Le Corbusier's "essential joys." Ranked eleventh was "Easy to change layout."[17]

top: NEXT21, Phase 1 renovation of 402 (left) and Phase 2 renovation of 404 (right)

bottom: NEXT21, Phase 2 test of micro-cogen system

However, returning to Habraken's thinking on capacity planning, a custom home's conception always includes the opportunities inherent to the empty site that precedes it. Choices must be confronted, even if there are few of them. NEXT21's approach to building-as-site amplifies this interpretative condition throughout the fabric of the structure, with its features laying the groundwork for an array of custom homes for people who may have no interest in ongoing flexibility.

Some might see artificial land's emphasis on customization as making it the perfect vehicle for social disassociation, its strong separation of skeleton and infill creating a building that's only a jumble of custom apartments for independent egos with little in common. Yet this doesn't seem to be NEXT21's vision. It may be model housing for the twenty-first century, but exactly what kind of housing?

Co-op of the Future

Mitsuo Takada has said a goal of NEXT21 was "to design a collective housing project," an ambition given significance by the site's location.[18] In the early 1980s, Osaka's Tanimachi neighborhood, just northwest of the project, was Japan's most fertile zone of collective living experiments, in the form of numerous cooperative apartment buildings designed by HEXA, an Osaka architecture office. Unlike speculative developments in which apartments are built before specific residents are known, by starting with the formation of a cooperative, the future residents are known before their apartments are built. Apartments are made to live in, rather than to make a profit. The developments in Tanimachi are examples of this.

Like many urban Japanese in the early 1970s, the architects from HEXA faced a tough choice: have the convenience and excitement of the city center but live in a pricey, tiny, and shoddy apartment, or buy an affordable house in a distant suburb and commute on crowded trains. Instead, several of the architects banded together with friends to buy land unaffordable to any of them individually, and built their own housing. By eliminating the expense that would be entailed by working with an independent developer, they could afford to design and build their own comfortable apartments. This first project's success led HEXA to form a new organization for instigating more co-op developments, dubbed the Association of People Who Wish to Create Their Own Urban Apartment Buildings With Their Own Hands. The name was abbreviated to Tojuso.[19]

By 1987, thirteen Tojuso buildings had been built in Tanimachi, and several hundred families were on a waiting list, eager for the company's services.[20] But even with Tojuso's help, the co-op process was daunting: many aspiring residents lacked the stamina for the negotiations and meetings necessary to reach agreements on everything from land acquisition to financing strategies, and, of course, design. As HEXA architect Osamu Nakasuji noted, while the process could result in an "ideal" apartment building both socially and architecturally, designing was an ordeal of trial-and-error to fit the puzzle pieces of non-standard units within a single volume.[21] Without a more efficient process, co-ops will never be an easy alternative to the speculative housing market's conventionalized product.

In light of the local HEXA phenomenon, NEXT21 seems to test its capacity as the perfect co-op infrastructure. Liberating the relations between above and below, inside and out, the design strives to smooth the frictions caused by combining eclectic units. Supporting this co-op interpretation, it should be noted that the overall organization of NEXT21's apartments is anything but random and antagonistic. Instead, it looks like an intentional community. If the units are read in terms of the specific residents their

HEXA, Tojuso co-ops, Osaka, 1980s (2017)

ANTI-SPECULATIVE SPECULATION: NEXT21, 1989–

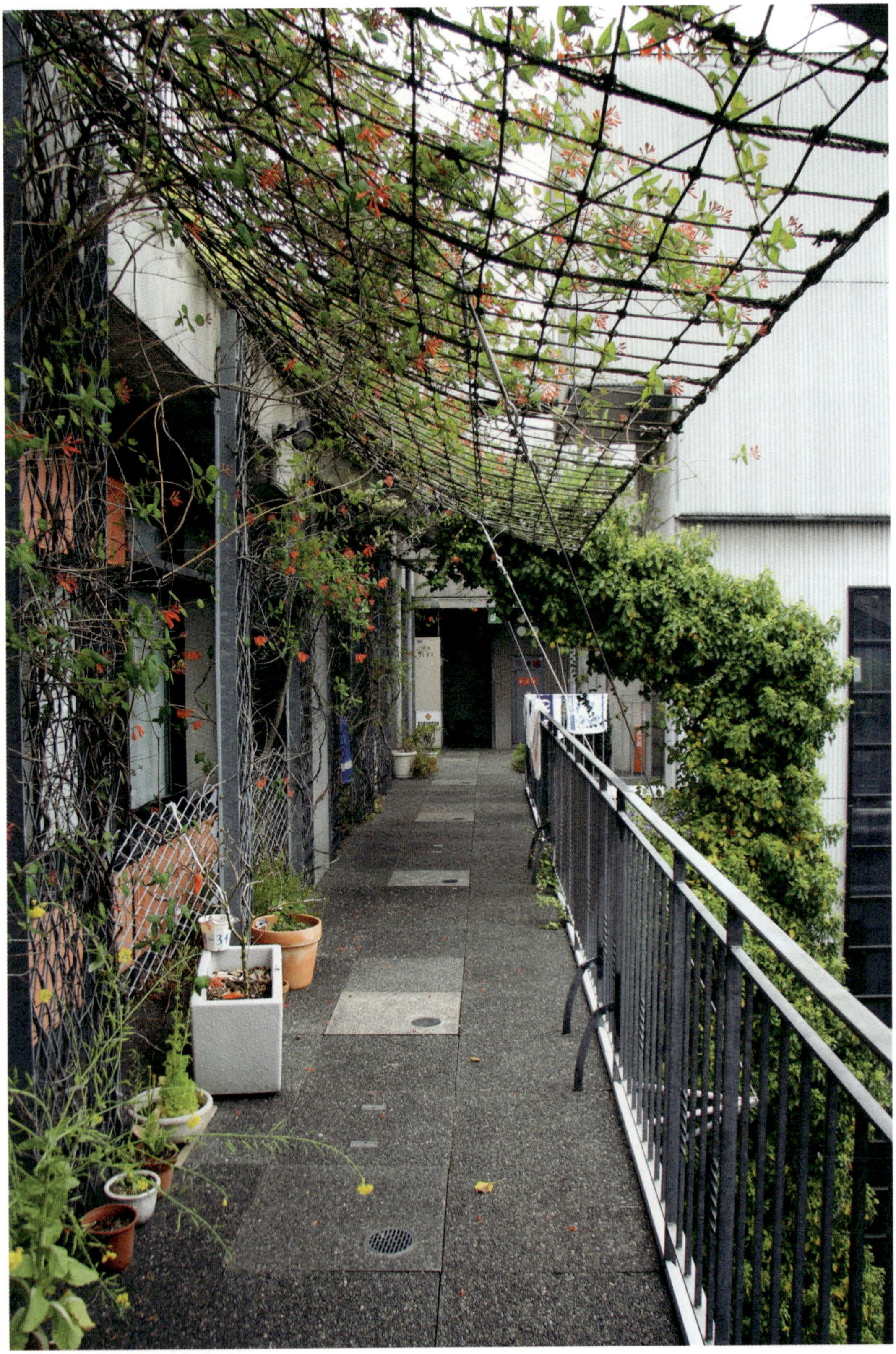

scenarios represent, their distribution is thoughtfully planned: on layers three and four, apartments are for the elderly and families with children, as with the Active Oldsters' House and Healthy Child-rearing House, making for closer proximity to the ground, fewer stairs, and also perhaps better access to childcare from grandparents; above, on layer five, the situation is more child-free, body-conscious, and indulgent, with the House with Fitness Room, House for Relaxation, and the House for Home Party, sitting above the less nocturnal activities of those below; on layer six, the DINKS Apartment is next to the Unmarried City Dweller, perhaps to encourage this lone figure to meet the DINKS' single friends. None of these domestic relationships would last forever, of course. But when they needed to change architecturally, a co-op like NEXT21 would be ready.

1 Rem Koolhaas, "Finding Freedoms: Conversations with Rem Koolhaas," interview by Alejandro Zaera, *El Croquis 53: OMA/ Rem Koolhaas 1987–1993*, ed. Alejandro Zaera (Barcelona: El Croquis Editorial, 1994), 25. Italics in original.
2 Yositika Utida, "NEXT21," *The Japan Architect*, no. 73 (Spring 2009): 35. With the spread of COVID-19 in 2020, this observation gained particular relevance.
3 See Rem Koolhaas and Hans Ulrich Obrist, *Project Japan: Metabolism Talks…* (Cologne: Taschen, 2011), 343.
4 TEPCO (the Tokyo Electric Power Company) is the operator of the Fukushima Daiichi Nuclear Power Plant that disastrously leaked radiation due to the earthquake and tsunami on March 11, 2011. As determined by Japan's national government, the accident was foreseeable and preventable if responsible actions had been taken by TEPCO. See "Fukushima Daiichi nuclear disaster," accessed November 11, 2019, https://en.wikipedia.org/wiki/Fukushima_Daiichi_nuclear_disaster.
5 As described in an email exchange between John Habraken and the author, April 15, 2016.
6 *Osaka Gas Experimental Housing: NEXT21* (Osaka: Osaka Gas Co., 2007), 3.
7 NEXT21 and the bubble: Yositika Utida, in conversation with the author, April 23, 2010. Translation by Hajime Yatsuka.
8 Shinichi Chikazumi, in conversation with the author, May 16, 2014.
9 See NEXT21 Editorial Committee, *NEXT21: All About the NEXT21 Project* (Tokyo: X-Knowledge, 2005), 122.
10 See John Habraken, "Capacity vs. Function," in "Tools of the Trade: Thematic Aspects of Designing" (unpublished manuscript, 1996), 27–28, PDF file.
11 "Parcels" or "parcellation" is a term used in the support/infill context, where it's defined as "the allotment or subdivision of available floor area within a Support" for each infill home to be built on. See Stephen Kendall and Jonathan Teicher, *Residential Open Building* (London: E. & F. N. Spon, 2000), 289. Of course, this language transposes a term typically used for terrestrial land to the artificial.
12 "Lifestyle superpower": see Eiko Maruko Siniawer, *Waste: Consuming Postwar Japan* (Ithaca, NY: Cornell University Press, 2018), 238, and page 248 in this chapter's introduction. Scenarios: see *Osaka Gas*, 24–32.
13 As Chikazumi acknowledges, NEXT21 has what can be interpreted as an "Asian slum" appearance. Chikazumi, May 16, 2014.
14 This objective was promoted by the initiatives of Alexander Gordon, president of the Royal Institute of British Architects from 1971 to 1973. See Alexander Gordon, "Architects and Resource Conservation," *RIBA Journal* (January 1974): 9–10.
15 This complaint was made by Hiroshi Horiba of Coelacanth Architects, designers of the Independent Family House. See Horiba's interview in *NEXT21—An Experiment*. DVD. Directed by Beate Lendt. Amsterdam: x!mage, 2009.
16 See Midori Kimo, interviewed in *NEXT21— An Experiment*.
17 See Robert Schmidt III et al., "Lessons from Japan: A Look at Century Housing System," 12th International Dependency and Structure Modelling Conference (July 2010): 4, PDF file.
18 Mitsuo Takada, interviewed in *NEXT21— An Experiment*.
19 Tojuso translates as "urban housing creation."
20 See Cherie Wendelken and Yoshiyuki Nakabayashi, "Developments in Cooperative Housing in Japan," *Open House International* 12, no. 2 (1987): 58.
21 HEXA Architects and Planners, "Tojuso Tokui-Cho Apartments," *The Japan Architect* 58, no. 8 (August 1983): 66.

NEXT21 (2010)

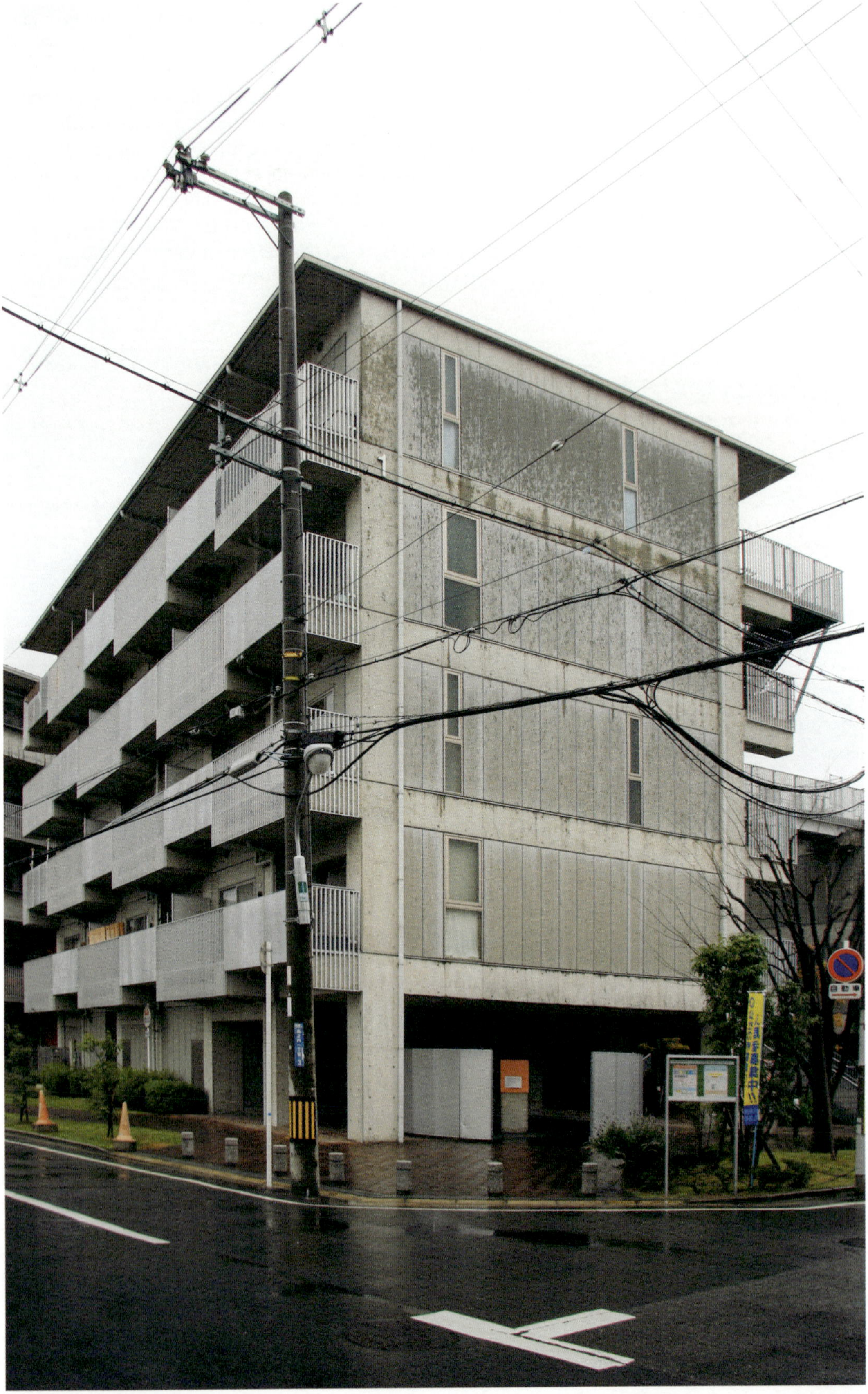

Helping DIY:
Flex Court Yoshida, 1994–

In 1994, MITI launched the Housing Development for Creating Value in Our Lifestyles Project, better known as House Japan. Running until 2001, House Japan was a descendent of lengthy MITI initiatives such as the Stratiform Structure Module. Like Stratiform, this new project assembled an impressive team of collaborators, including Takenaka, along with some forty other companies encompassing multiple disciplines, all aimed at investigating housing based on the concept of skeleton/infill, referred to in the studies by the initials "SI," a most attenuated name for artificial land. Indeed, House Japan was devoid of Stratiform's avant-gardism in name, agenda, and look. It was also unlike its predecessor in that the new research led to SI's widespread adoption by mainstream developers. According to Tadatoshi Asano, House Japan had the effect of normalizing SI construction for new residential towers.[1] Engaging similar issues to those of NEXT21, such as the critical role of durability and life-cycle planning, but with far more architectural restraint, MITI found that SI housing would be 7 percent more expensive to build, but embodied costs would be reduced by 23.5 percent, assuming demolition after one hundred years.[2] The economic argument for SI had never before been so precisely quantified.

Despite the benefits of SI becoming common practice, when implemented by giant developers it has a technical feel, like the rules of CHS. Once again, the value and opportunity of flexibility has been pushed far into the future, beyond the likely experience of an SI building's occupants. Having jettisoned the romance of building houses on aerial plots, the typical SI project at the turn of the millennium also rejected the "soft" side of Habraken and TSHS, which was committed to resident decision-making. A top-down transitional approach to be led by property managers

left and following: Kenchiku Kankyo Kenkyujo and Shu-Koh-Sha, Flex Court Yoshida, Osaka, 1999 (2010)

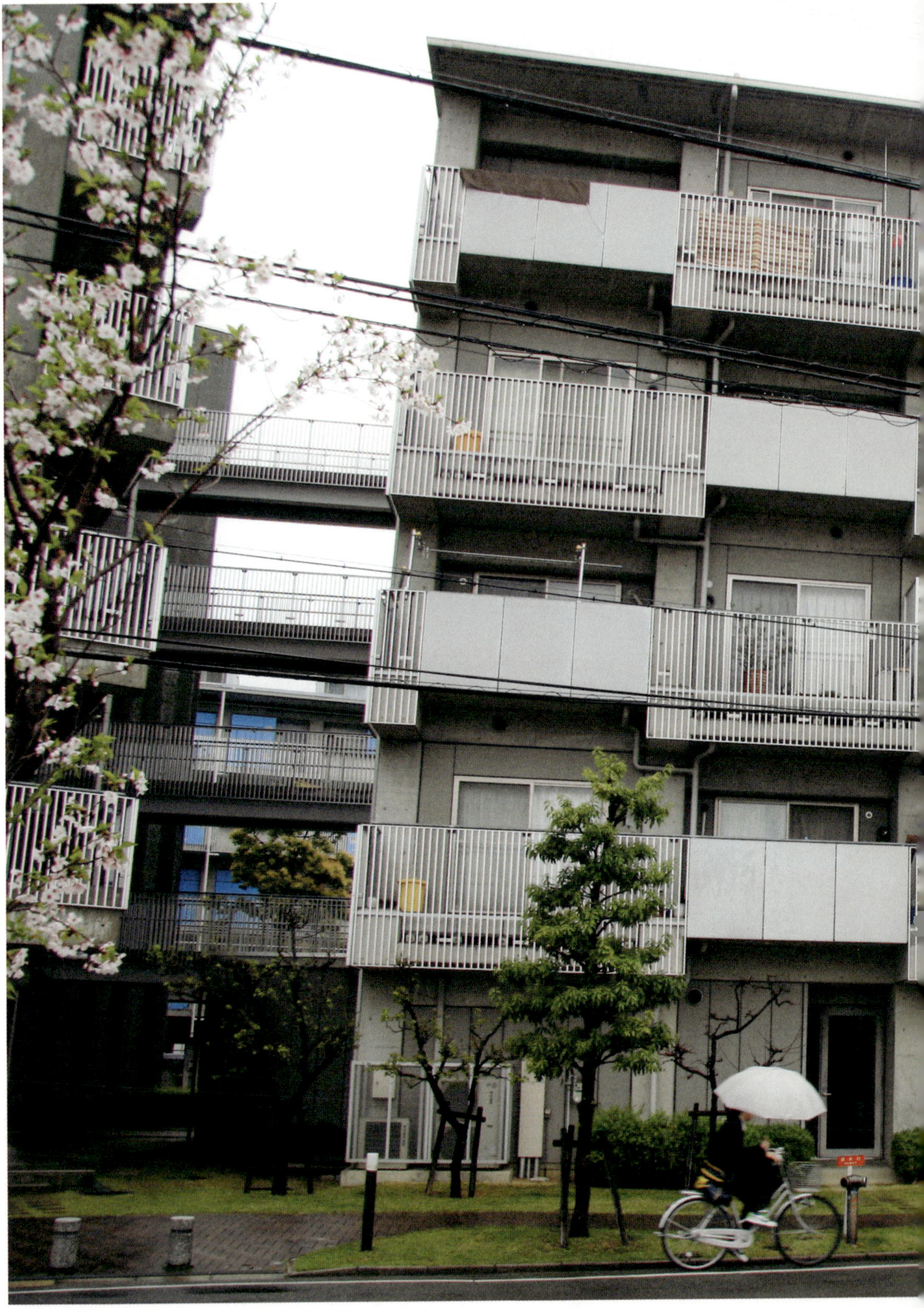

HELPING DIY: FLEX COURT YOSHIDA, 1994–

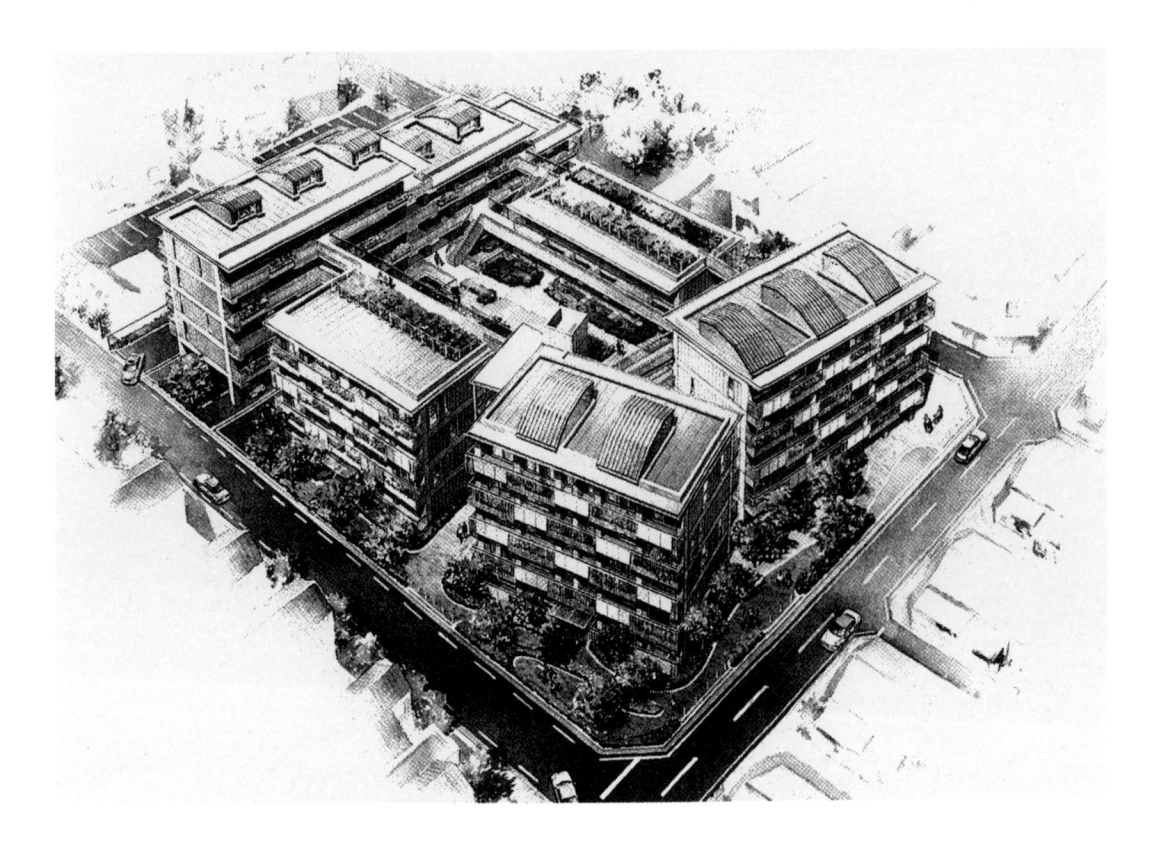

again won out over the engagement of the maximum dwelling. And though we've seen the validity of transitional types, the bandwidth of architectural freedom had become very limited.

However, House Japan did engage resident participation in one area, through developing "interior components for DIY installation."[3] The huge Sumitomo Forestry, a venerable maker of timber building products, provided an infill system of wall partitions and other elements that could be assembled by residents using only a screwdriver, knife, and hammer—three tools that studies found were present in over 80 percent of Japanese homes.[4] Another company, the Dantani Corporation, made floorboards that were affixed with double-sided tape, allowing residents to install their own floors themselves, thus saving labor costs even though the boards cost more than typical wood flooring.[5]

A parallel project to House Japan that also combines SI and DIY is the Flex Court Yoshida project in Osaka. Also initiated in 1994, and led by TSHS inventors Tatsumi and Takada, Flex Court draws on the useful precedent of *hadaka-gashi* for mass DIY living, attempting to spark the re-normalization of such a reality. Aspects of the system had found their way into NEXT21, but Flex Court attempted to resurrect it in the context of rental housing, where it had originally appeared.

Self-build approaches have been criticized as paving the way for an abandonment of responsibility by housing authorities.[6] Yet Flex Court's owner and initial operator, the Osaka Prefectural Housing Supply Corporation, is committed to the long-term support of the experiment. A brochure for the project states its central goal: "Matching the unit to the resident's life, not life to unit."[7] With the help of subsidies from the national government, construction of the

above: Flex Court aerial view

right: Flex Court main staircase, c.1999, and courtyard (2010)

HELPING DIY: FLEX COURT YOSHIDA, 1994–

3 OPEN SYSTEMS

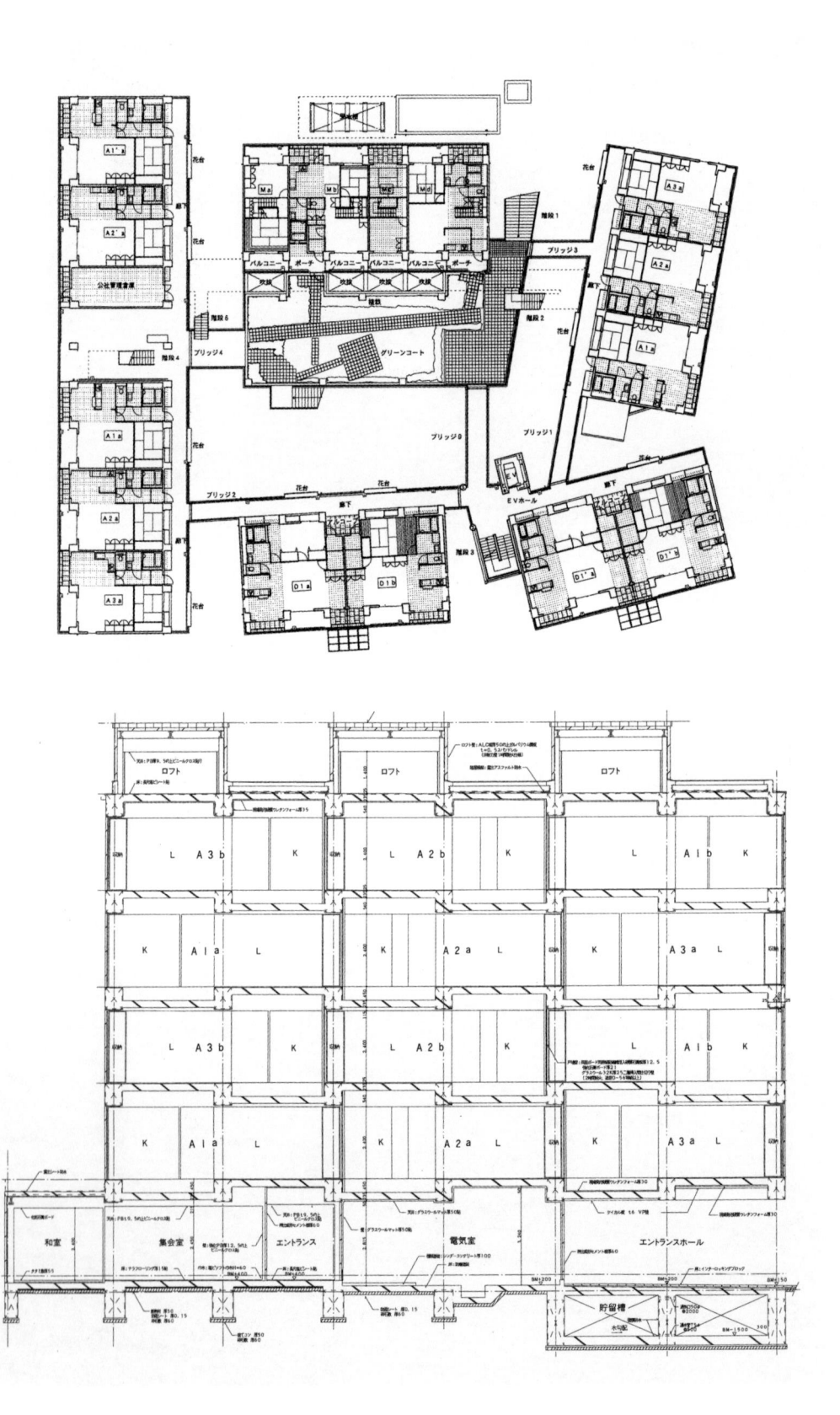

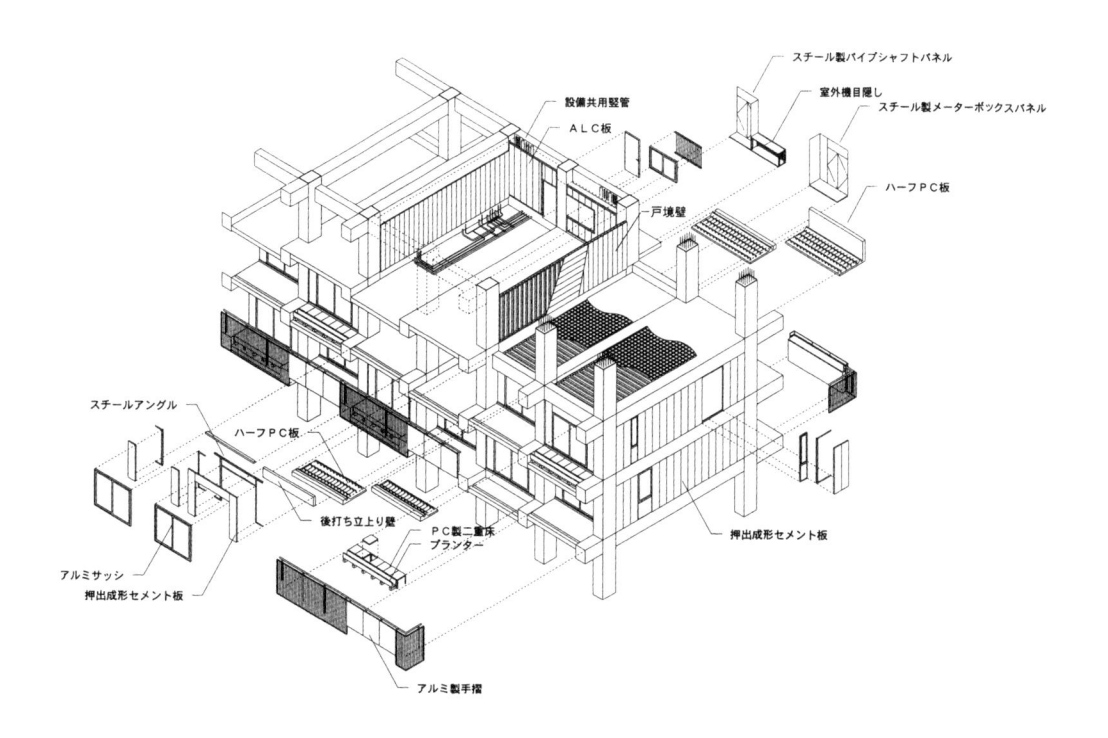

project was completed in 1999, delivering a total of fifty-three apartments for moderate-income households. The units would come to "match" residents' lifestyles by means of a catalog of infill elements newly designed for the project, which took inspiration from the interchangeability of *hadaka-gashi*. Through these coordinated elements, to be bought if and when needed, the hope was to relink DIY space-planning and a rationalized material metabolism. The question was whether or not residents would embrace an open system from the Edo period amid the flood of products, styles, and, of course, home-ownership promotion that have become ubiquitous in Japanese life.

Checkerboard

The skeleton for the experiment was designed by the office Kenchiku Kankyo Kenkyujo. Made from five freestanding blocks arrayed in a broken ring, the site plan is highly porous. Porosity is a feature of Japanese urbanism, with its preponderance of freestanding buildings, and Flex Court's group form extends this connectivity upward through multiple vertical circulation links. These, together with open-air corridors linking all the blocks, tie the project elements together and into the site, similar to NEXT21.

Habraken and his disciples often insist that a support is "not neutral" in its provocations to usage, and at Flex Court positive stimulation comes from the "checkerboard" floors of each block's skeleton.[8] The checkerboard is formed by alternating bands of lowered slabs spanning the depth of each floor, in zones that are staggered from level to level. The lowered areas are for the now-familiar feature of access floors, with the

left: Flex Court, second-floor plan (top) and section (bottom) showing "checkerboard" slabs for services

above: Axonometric of skeleton and infill components

branched plumbing they contain easily connected to risers accessible from the shared corridors. Projecting beyond the envelope to form balconies on the outer perimeter of the blocks, the checkerboard slabs are accentuated by alternating styles of railing that create a weave-like facade. Again similar to NEXT21, the lowered areas can be used as planters. Indoor plumbing contributes to a facade that can green the urban scenery.[9] The structural engineer Robert Le Ricolais said that "the art of structure is where to put the holes," and artificial land increasingly appears to be a related art.[10] Reserves of useful space at various scales make for healthy digestion—from Harumi's triplex frame, to the scaffolding sleeves of NEXT21, to Flex Court's checkerboard. These voids allow systems and programs to be added, expanded, removed, and otherwise changed.

Matchmaking

Tatsumi and Takada focused on the operation of the infill, guiding its design by the companies Daikin, Matsushita, and Panekyo, and also the implementation of its logistics. Instead of variation being an initial condition, as with NEXT21, adaptation to the needs of residents happens through what's called "continuous customization." With this concept, all the units started out relatively standardized, with fixed infill for kitchens and bathrooms. Along with the facade, which was designed by Shinichi Chikazumi, these wet programs are planned to have a thirty-year renewal cycle. Customization may happen around these fixed elements, with "spontaneous modification" enabled by two types of variable infill: mobile storage closets that are part of each lease, and partitions that residents can buy.[11]

above: Flex Court, checkerboard balcony (2010)

right: Flex Court, sample of infill components, c. 1999. Note that lower drawings are of mobile closets that came standard with units.

②収納

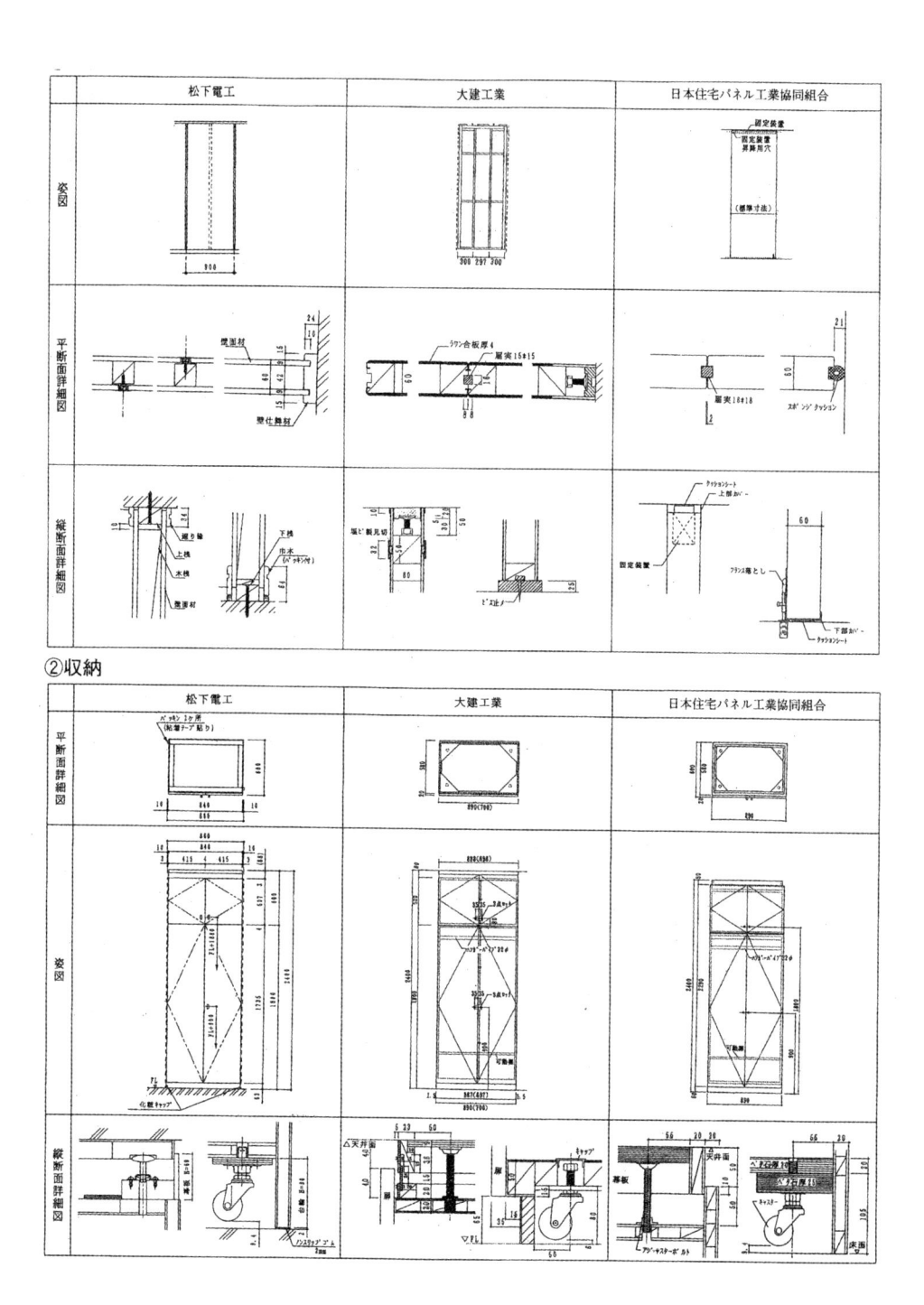

3 OPEN SYSTEMS

Flex Court post-occupancy study of plan changes between 1999 and 2002. Red indicates mobile storage closets.

HELPING DIY: FLEX COURT YOSHIDA, 1994–

With "spontaneous" and "customization" being language found in the project's brochure for prospective renters, we can see how far the marketing of flexibility has come since Harumi, where it was not part of a publicly stated agenda. Now it's openly advertised, and is indeed part of the project's name. In general, advertising these possibilities was a key part of Flex Court's DIY mission, demanded by the larger ambition to persuade producers and consumers to support a *hadaka-gashi* approach. TSHS projects had experimented with resident participation in the past, but they had not tackled this more challenging task of recreating an open marketplace to support that participation.

To that end, Flex Court's designers developed the "Infill Management System." Part of this consisted of software on a CD-ROM, given to each apartment, which educated occupants on the infill opportunities of their units, helping them plan and then purchase appropriate partitions for customization.[12] Another part of the system was an infill manager, a person who mediated between the infill manufacturers and the residents. Recognizing that the residents likely had no experience or knowledge of the original *hadaka-gashi* system, the manager offered guidance on issues of infill purchase, install, change, and resale.[13] Through the figure of the infill manager, Flex Court provides an assistant to the "Sunday carpenter" Kawazoe had imagined in 1961, a bricoleur having only prefabricated modular components to hand, who now reappears like Flex Court's avatar.[14]

To be Continued?

Before the project was built, various infill scenarios were tested in capacity plans, such as a 1LDK becoming a 2LDK or 3DK through progressive subdivision. To see what had actually happened after the project's completion, post-occupancy evaluations were conducted in November 1999, three months after residents moved in, and then again in November 2002.

The realities were found to be quite mundane. In the first survey, five units that had bought variable infill were examined, and five that had not. Perhaps the most significant adaptation found was a 2LDK that had used sliding partitions to create a corridor screening the entrance and bathroom from the living room. For the later survey, forty-nine units were investigated. This time it was clear that there had been little use of purchased infill. Moveable closets, which had been standard equipment, were used much more extensively, as shown by the study of nineteen units that used them to make planning changes. The researchers found the reason was simply that residents wished to avoid the cost of buying partitions. They also discovered that, even after the arrival of newborns, residents tended to prefer the spaciousness of merely visually screening with closets rather than making new, fully enclosed rooms with purchased panels.[15]

As of 2015, architects involved in the project were unaware of further post-occupancy studies.[16] From the two we know, it seems as if the moveable closets short-circuited the arrival of a new *hadaka-gashi* system, even just within the limited ecosystem of Flex Court itself. Certainly the closets were a free and easy option, and perhaps the Infill Management System was too bureaucratic. It would have been interesting to see what post-occupancy studies would have found if all infill elements were supplied free with the lease, thereby further encouraging resident experimentation. Maybe the biggest impediment was that the dream of home ownership looms large for Flex Court's renters, as it does for many Japanese, making it less appealing to purchase partitions for a dwelling that's seen as temporary. In Edo-period Kansai, renting was the norm, while today it's far less common. How much time and money would you put into a home you don't own?

1. Tadatoshi Asano, email exchange with the author, December 28, 2014.
2. Shuichi Matsumura, "Life Cycle Assessment of Support/Infill Housing in House Japan Project": 215. Undated PDF file retrieved from https://www.irbnet.de/daten/iconda/CIB12051.pdf.
3. Matsumura, "Life Cycle," 211.
4. Matsumura, "Life Cycle," 212.
5. Matsumura, "Life Cycle," 212.
6. For arguments against DIY housing methods, see "Illusions of Self-Help," in Mike Davis, *Planet of Slums* (New York: Verso, 2006), 70–94.
7. Osaka Prefectural Housing Supply Corporation, *Flex Court Yoshida hōkokushō* [Flex Court Yoshida Report] (Osaka: Osaka Prefectural Housing Supply Corporation, 2000), 112. This report reprints the bilingual brochure. Note that as of 2015, Mitsubishi Building Maintenance was commissioned by the Osaka Prefectural Housing Supply Corporation to manage Flex Court.
8. "Not neutral": see, for example, Stephen Kendall and Jonathan Teicher, *Residential Open Building* (London: E. & F. N. Spon, 2000), 34. Kendall and Teicher studied with Habraken at MIT, and have been collaborators since then. "Checkerboard": see Hidetoshi Yasueda and Mitsuo Takada, "Construction and Infill Management Systems at Flex Court Yoshida," in *Continuous Customization in Housing*, ed. Tomonari Yashiro (Rotterdam: CIB General Secretariat, 2000), 81.
9. As of my visit to Flex Court in 2010, this greening potential had not notably been taken advantage of.
10. Robert Le Ricolais, quoted in "Visions and Paradox," in *University of Pennsylvania Almanac* 42, no. 19 (February 6, 1996), https://almanac.upenn.edu/archive/v42/n19/ricolais.html.
11. Osaka Prefectural, *Flex Court*, 111.
12. See Yasueda and Takada, "Construction," 83.
13. Mitsuo Takada and Hidetoshi Yasueda, "Infill (Fit-out) Management System at Flex Court Yoshida," *Open House International* 26, no. 3 (2001): 32.
14. "Sunday carpenter": see page 94 of this book and Noboru Kawazoe, "The City of the Future," *Zodiac*, no. 9 (1961): 106–107.
15. All survey information is from Mitsuo Takada, "A Study on the Infill Management System (IMS) in Skeleton Rental Housing: Experimental Study at Flex Court Yoshida" (2003): ix–xi. PDF file retrieved from https://repository.kulib.kyoto-u.ac.jp/dspace/bitstream/2433/84923/1/d423.pdf.
16. Shinichi Chikazumi and Masaki Araki (a supervisor for the project), in email exchanges with the author, March 16, 2015, and April 13, 2015, respectively. The current status of the Infill Management System is also unclear.

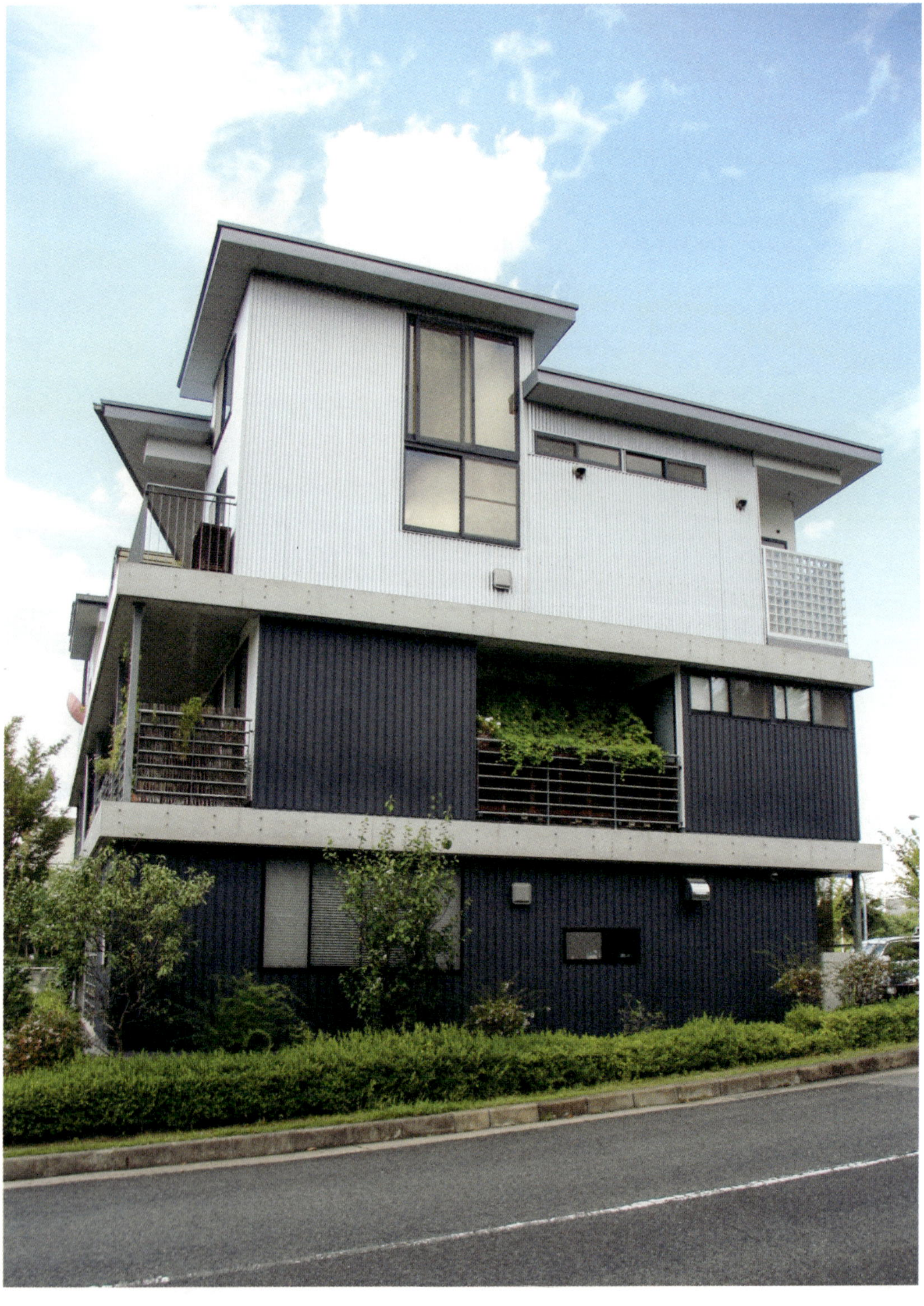

From Promise to Performance:
Tsunane Cooperative House, 1996–

Completed in 2000, the Tsunane Cooperative House in Nara is a realization of NEXT21's simulation of a self-organized community. Like Tojuso's possible influence on NEXT21's concept of housing, artificial land at Tsunane is a strategy to ease the making of a co-op, offering a way to balance the communal and individual that's open to difference and change. In returning to the issue of packing together diverse unit types that had challenged HEXA's architects, we return to the desire for apartments fitted to individual lifestyles and budgets as basic reasons for establishing a co-op. Another reason is to have neighbors you know, with whom you can decide what to create and to share.[1]

First emerging in Japan in the late 1960s, the co-op approach didn't gain larger visibility until the 1970s.[2] An expression of participatory *machizukuri*, the approach came to receive state support through the formation in 1978 of the National Association for the Promotion of Cooperative Housing, which convinced the National Diet and the JHC to give group loans to co-ops that had incorporated as non-profits.[3] Despite this support, co-ops are not common in Japan.[4] Only 10,000 apartments of the type currently exist, a miniscule number compared to other forms, which number in the millions.[5]

But Tsunane is also exceptional as an example of cohousing, a specific kind of co-op that's like a small village. As Kathryn McCamant and Charles Durrett describe in *Cohousing: A Contemporary Approach to Housing Ourselves*, such developments are typically defined by four aspects: participatory process, intentional neighborhood design, common facilities, and self-management by residents.[6] As such, Tsunane's first and foremost motivation is not physical resilience to earthquakes, fires, lifestyle changes, and other forms of obsolescence.

left and following: VANS, Tsunane Cooperative House, Nara, 2000 (2011)

3 OPEN SYSTEMS

FROM PROMISE TO PERFORMANCE: TSUNANE COOPERATIVE HOUSE, 1996–

Rather than the quest for durability that drove the developmental state's use of artificial land as a transitional strategy, from Harumi to CHS, Tsunane's achievement is a verticalization of the cohousing concept that at last delivers custom homes within a skeleton as an initial condition. While prior occupants of flexible skeletons were oblivious or severed from their housing's freedoms, Tsunane is a transparent product of resident self-determination. No longer is variation just a forecast for a distant domestic future.

Back in 1964, Peter Smithson found artificial land lacking "a demonstration of how it is to be done."[7] This "how" is not so much a technical question. While it can be done better or worse, building homes on platforms or in skeletons is less a problem of construction than a challenge for many people to build their homes in such shared conditions while avoiding constant conflict. It's a social question, indeed best answered by an intentional community that works together.

Community Building

The project began in 1996, when two neighbors in a public housing project became dissatisfied with their living situations and found that the housing market lacked acceptable alternatives. Deciding that creating a co-op was their best option, the neighbors asked close friends to join the endeavor, forming an initial group of four households. The members included a university architecture professor as well as an employee of the Urban Renaissance Agency.

A key early decision was to hire an outside architect who, besides providing design services, would also be an impartial project manager and negotiator.[8] The group selected VANS, a Nara-based office led by Toshiaki Ban that had experience with co-ops. VANS helped with site selection, and the one chosen—an empty lot on a west-facing slope next to a train track on Nara's outskirts—required at least twenty-three units in order to be economically viable. This meant VANS in effect had twenty-three clients living side by side. While the initial resident group avoided the middleman cost of a developer, they needed to buy the publicly owned land through a construction contractor, also brought into the process early.

At this point, the group had corporatized as the Tsunane Cooperative Housing Construction Union. "Tsunane" refers to a form of rope binding used in traditional wood construction, making a symbol for the new co-op being bound together, harkening back to the mutual aid between neighbors that had been a norm before the war.[9] It was a kind of reliance many found thwarted by the isolation of *danchi* living.[10]

McCamant and Durrett's research on cohousing communities indicates a range from forty to one-hundred members to be typical and beneficial. This range balances absorption of new members and departing of old ones with a level of familiarity, flexibility in performing collective tasks, and very importantly, the freedom of members not to participate in the community much at all. Smaller communities are more demanding in terms of both time and money.[11] As a case in point, for the few initial members of the union, the burden was entirely on them to find more people. They turned to handing out pamphlets outside the local train station, with interested candidates then invited to a seminar on how the co-op process would work. By 1998, sixteen households were committed, and to find additional members they turned to a new technology: the internet.[12]

VANS had, by then, set the schematic design for the project's massing and structure. Three stories tall and organized into two east-west blocks of skeleton frame defining a central yard, the design adds to artificial land's frequent renaming, with VANS calling the blocks "stages" on which members' lifestyles can be freely

FROM PROMISE TO PERFORMANCE: TSUNANE COOPERATIVE HOUSE, 1996–

North level 2

South level 1

performed—a fitting switch in terminology for a project that was turning a historic promise into a lived demonstration. As hoped, all the households that later joined the union saw the stage strategy as a good idea that kept individual choices open, even while the development of other areas was progressing.

The plot sizes on the stages were adjustable, and finally fixed in direct proportion to each households' budget after a session with VANS at which each was allocated a location within one of the two skeletons.[13] According to the first-hand experience of Yoshitsugu Yamashita, one of Tsunane's founding members, this parcellation was completely amicable, though it could easily be the most contentious part of a collective building project.[14]

With the stages set, VANS began to oversee the infill design. Ban was assisted in this by three other architects from his office, plus one from another company. Floor planning workshops were conducted with the union, starting in March 1998, followed by all the households making their own architectural models. Out of these sessions came the final unit plans.[15] Construction started in June 1999 and completion followed quickly, with residents moving in less than a year later, in April 2000.

82.3 m2

81 m2

99.8 m2

88.7 m2

82.6 m2

57 m2

57.3 m2
44.5 m2

54.4 m2

86.5 m2
39 m2

North level 3

South level 2

Making Rules

Though construction was quick, overall Tsunane's realization was slow, in part because it took time to make the rules necessary in a co-op. Ban is emphatic about this, believing that creating common rules and guidelines beyond existing regulations is "the most important point for co-op housing," and the only way to achieve equality among residents within a participatory design process. He describes a co-op as "a small commune, or a direct, democratically run project without any hierarchy," where residents must define what they collectively value.[16] Tsunane's creation and management of these values is channeled through a periodically elected board of residents, as well as volunteer work groups for architecture, planting, and lifestyle.[17] One thing for which the board created a community policy is outdoor laundry drying, that issue about which Tange had complained.[18]

    Rationalizing the limits of freedom at Tsunane starts with determining who owns what. Joint ownership includes the stages, energy systems, common room with kitchen, garden, and parking, while individual ownership is of the units,

3 OPEN SYSTEMS

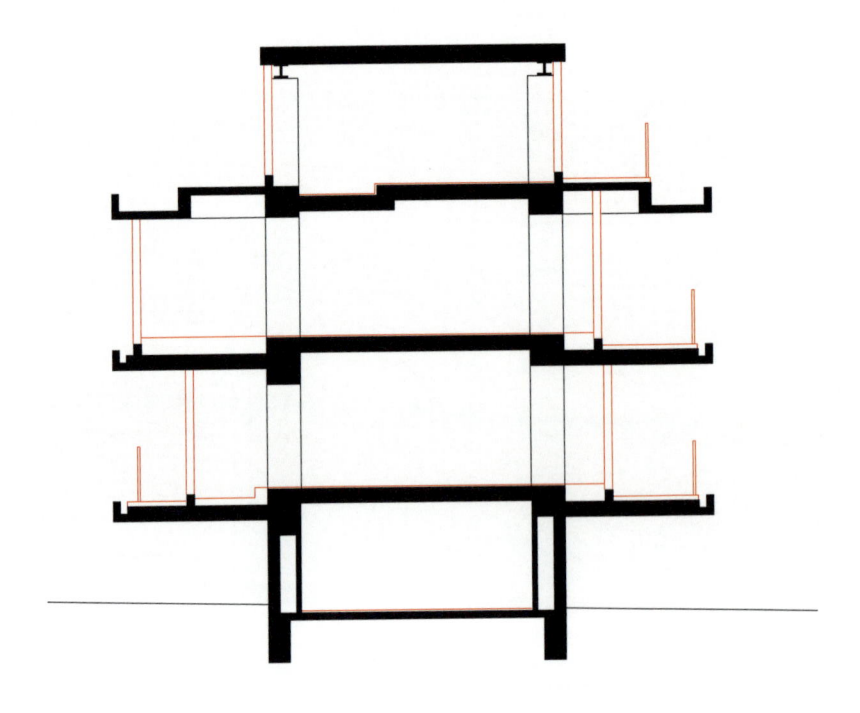

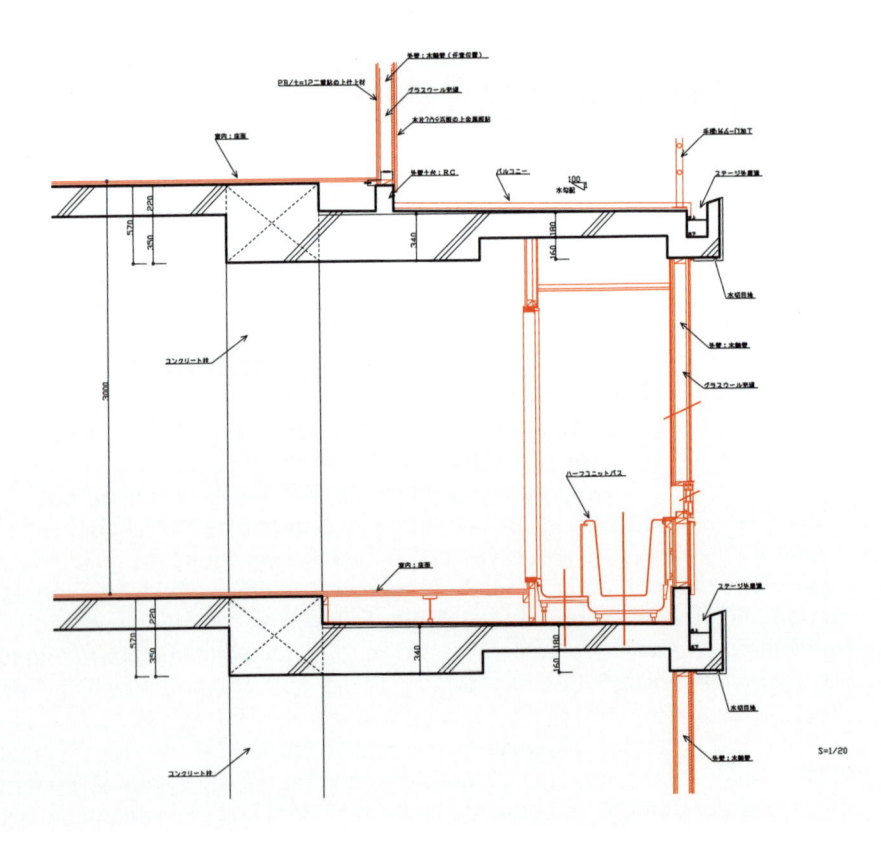

including their exterior envelopes. Control of your own patch of facade is of course an ideal of artificial land, and Ban thinks Tsunane may be the only co-op in the world with such freedom.[19] Though more permissive than NEXT21, the facade still has rules. During development of the unit designs, VANS created a palette of sixteen cladding materials from which residents could choose, ranging from glass block to wood and various types of metal panels. Window and door types and their locations were left open to personal choice.[20]

2x4s

While Tsunane's realization and continued success is fundamentally tied to the shared ethos of its residents, that ethos is supported by the technical realities of the project beyond just the skeleton/infill approach. This interplay between the social and the technical was helped by the site's zoning: according to the building code, the site has a height limit of three stories plus basement, and with Tsunane's focus on low-cost and flexible unit design, an advantage of this is that three-story apartment buildings need to be only semi-fireproof, allowing exterior walls to be wood construction. This led VANS to use 2x4 framing.[21]

It's significant that Tsunane and Sawaman, two of Japan's most vibrant examples of artificial land, both combine wood infill with concrete skeletons. Frei Otto's Ökohaus in Berlin, another exemplary artificial-land project, features this pairing as well.[22] Tsunane's use of wood recalls the fascination with adaptations in the timber-framed *minka* surveyed by Kon and Yosizaka, and in turn the influence of *minka* on modernist designs, as with Harumi. But aside from this rapport with avant-garde history, a reason for the speed with which Tsunane was completed is likely that American-style 2x4 framing has become a conventional method in Japan. Approved by the building code in 1979, the system is, as in America, at once inexpensive, easy to work with, and technically advanced, with all kinds of fasteners and complimentary subsystems.[23]

This freedom is just what the co-op needed. Compared to previous infill approaches discussed in this book, VANS makes refreshing use of a truly vernacular system of off-the-shelf components. As brilliantly pragmatic as Stratiform's piggybacking on the prefab industry may have been, and as fine-scaled as the DIY elements of Flex Court are, neither of them can match the accessibility and responsiveness of the humble 2x4 as a very effective way for artificial land "to be done." To paraphrase Habraken, 2x4 framing dictates very little how it must be deployed in space, even as the logic of its assembly is highly determined. It is a genuine open system.[24]

Stages

Walking around Tsunane, and seeing the outcomes of the many decisions made by residents and architects, the atmosphere is lively and relaxed. There's no impression of an incipient slum or the open lockers of a bathhouse. With a subtly powerful balance between the varied shapes, materials, and plantings of the units and the thick horizontal lines of the slab edges, Tsunane's achievements are partly aesthetic. But unlike Stratiform or SITE's Highrise of Homes, it feels completely unrhetorical. Though clearly displaying diversity, this is realized with simplicity and modesty.

It looks like something you could do yourself with the help of some friends and a few architects—and it is.

Looking at the units "performed" on the project's stages, we find sizes ranging from about 37 to 134 square meters, with

top: Tsunane, section of "stages"

bottom: Section detail

the average around 84. Many are for couples with children, including three-generation families. Some are duplexes. Some have one large south-facing balcony, while others have balconies of various sizes on multiple sides, often with collections of potted plants. One tiny balcony, just off a kitchen, appears to be purpose-built for only a small hibachi. From floor to floor, bathrooms and kitchens take up varying positions too, either centrally located or on the perimeter with windows.

For the design of the stages, VANS uses thick concrete columns typically inset from the slab edges. These "core frames" take the main seismic forces, allowing the perimeter to have only thin columns of solid steel.[25] This lightweight perimeter structure allows much greater freedom in the design of the envelope, avoiding the gridiron elevations found from Harumi to Ashiyahama. Cast-in-place shear walls are also part of the stages, so-called "strong" walls that are usually located on either side of shared access stairs. Distinguished from the "weak" walls of changeable 2x4 framing, the strong walls give a sense of permanent territory as well as acoustic privacy.[26]

Similar to NEXT21's canals, around each core frame is an access floor for plumbing. At the outer edge of these zones, on the exterior, is a gutter-like "ditch." Reminiscent of the drainage ditches often found in small residential streets in Japan, these cast-in-place ditches take rainwater to a shared cistern that gravity feeds hoses for watering greenery. The residents see the system as emblematic of their ecological ideals.[27]

While stairs at first glance appear to be the main form of access, Ban points out that the stages being worked into the slope of the site had a major advantage. The result, in combination with the three-story height limit, is that 16 of the 23 units are accessible without stairs, either through the use of ramps or from ground level. Given Tsunane's elderly residents, and the other residents who won't be young forever, this is an important achievement.

Wanting It

Some might feel that a co-op on three stories of artificial land is too constrained to be a general model for housing in Japan. But Ban is convinced that the country's trend toward extreme high-rise apartments must end, and that three-story co-ops are indeed an alternative.[28] In light of 51 percent of Japanese housing being only one or two stories, Ban's massing may be more applicable than it appears.[29]

The real challenge, though, is the co-op process itself, especially with cohousing. Every such project is a slow process of group formation, financing, design, management, and building construction, all of which must be negotiated. For some people, in particular domineering architects, this raises the prospect of mediocrity thanks to "design by committee." Most developers and architects are very product-oriented, and won't risk the reduced or lost profits of cohousing work.[30] The process is expensive, and while shared among residents-to-be, only so much of an architect's increased expenses for the approach can be charged to them. After all, they're looking for more affordable housing options. Their sweat equity is critical for success. As McCamant and Durrett write, "only people who seek new residential options for themselves will have the motivation to push through the arduous planning and design process without compromising their initial goals."[31]

top: Year-end party with the architect, Toshiaki Ban (tallest, at center), 1997

center: Tsunane groundbreaking ceremony, 1999

bottom: Tsunane common room with kitchen, 2008

FROM PROMISE TO PERFORMANCE: TSUNANE COOPERATIVE HOUSE, 1996–

Tsunane (2011): solid-steel columns (above); private terrace (left); and communal rainwater cistern (right)

FROM PROMISE TO PERFORMANCE: TSUNANE COOPERATIVE HOUSE, 1996–

On the other hand, as Yamashita points out, the slow work makes neighbors get to know each other, which is a big part of forming a co-op in the first place. And while the process is more expensive, the ability of residents to better control where their money is invested makes the cost worthwhile. According to Yamashita, everyone at Tsunane is happy with what they achieved, the architects included.[32] Returning to artificial land's origin in the idea of a vertical Garden City, Ebenezer Howard had advocated cooperative "building societies" as a more equitable way for housing to be constructed.[33] Thinking back to Smithson's desire to know how exactly "each man" will build "his own house" on artificial land, his phrasing sounds quite lonely. As much as it's about individuality, artificial land needs collaboration.

The author at Tsunane with Mrs. and Mr. Yamashita (2011)

1. These reasons are given in Cherie Wendelken and Yoshiyuki Nakabayashi, "Developments in Cooperative Housing in Japan," *Open House International* 12, no. 2 (1987): 56.
2. Wendelken and Nakabayashi, "Developments," 57–58.
3. See "History of Coop Kyo," accessed September 7, 2020, http://coopkyo.gr.jp/about/.
4. Yoshitsugu Yamashita, in conversation with the author, September 19, 2011.
5. See "What is a Cooperative House?," accessed January 17, 2020, http://www.cooperative-funen.jp/owner/.
6. Kathryn McCamant and Charles Durrett, *Cohousing: A Contemporary Approach to Housing Ourselves* [1988] (Berkeley: Ten Speed Press, 1994), 38–43. Unlike many co-ops, cohousing is usually built from scratch with a greater site-planning component and larger shared community facilities, such as a communal kitchen. There remains an emphasis on individual privacy, however, with apartments also having their own private kitchens. As McCamant and Durrett discuss, the concept originated in Denmark in the early 1970s. See *Cohousing*, 12.
7. See Peter Smithson, "Reflections on Kenzo Tange's Tokyo Bay Plan," *Architectural Design* 34 (October 1964): 480, and on page 13 in this book's introduction.
8. Yamashita, September 19, 2011.
9. Tsunane's meaning: Yamashita, September 19, 2011.
10. Isolation of *danchi* living: Wendelken and Nakabayashi, "Developments," 57.
11. McCamant and Durrett, *Cohousing*, 44.
12. Yamashita, September 19, 2011.
13. Email exchange between Toshiaki Ban and the author, July 11, 2013.
14. Yamashita, September 19, 2011.
15. Yamashita, September 19, 2011.
16. Ban, July 11, 2013.
17. Yamashita, September 19, 2011.
18. Regarding laundry and Tange, see page 81 of this book.
19. Yamashita, September 19, 2011. While it's a rental apartment building rather than a co-op, the Hundertwasser House (1985) in Vienna, Austria, grants "window rights" in its lease agreements that give each renter control of their exterior decoration. It's notable that the building's "spiritual" architect, the artist Friedensreich Hundertwasser, first presented his concept for the building in a 1972 sketch model that looks like the Stratiform Structure Module. See "The History of the Hundertwasser House," accessed July 21, 2020, http://www.hundertwasser-haus.info/en/blog/2011/06/21/the-history-of-the-hundertwasser-house/. Thanks to Thomas Daniell for pointing out this Austrian relative.
20. Yamashita, September 19, 2011.
21. Ban, July 11, 2013. The term "2x4" is used in Japan, for members measuring 50 by 100 millimeters.
22. Otto apparently specified wood infill for the self-build co-op in part to reduce weight on the skeleton. See *Dreaming of a Treehouse: Frei Otto's Ecological Building Project in Berlin*. DVD. Directed by Beate Lendt. Amsterdam: x!mage, 2011.
23. See Stephen Kendall and Seiji Sawada, "Changing Patterns in Japanese Housing," *Open House International* 12, no. 2 (1987): 14, and *A Quick Look at Housing in Japan*, eds. The Building Center of Japan et al. (Tokyo: The Building Center of Japan, 2014), 23. Note that while 2x4 construction is not dominant in either the detached or apartment house markets, it is a significant presence.
24. See page 190 of this book, or N. J. Habraken, "Lives of Systems," in *Transformations of the Site* (Cambridge, MA: Atwater Press, 1983), 173.
25. See *SI Jūtaku—Shugojūtaku no skeleton & infill* [SI housing—skeleton & infill for mass housing], *Data File of Architectural Design & Detail*, ed. Kenchiku Sicho Kenkyujo (Tokyo: Kenchiku Siryo Kenkyusha, 2005), 155. Translation by Riyo Namigata.
26. *SI Jūtaku*, 155.
27. *SI Jūtaku*, 155.
28. Email exchange between Toshiaki Ban and the author, September 25, 2011.
29. For figures on Japanese housing by number of stories, see "Dwellings by Type of Building, Stories of Building, Construction Material and Year of Construction (2013)," in *Japan Statistical Yearbook*, 2015, http://www.stat.go.jp/english/data/nenkan/1431-18.htm. Fifty-one percent of Japan's over 53 million houses equals over 27 million houses at one to two stories.
30. Regarding financial risks, see McCamant and Durrett, *Cohousing*, 40, and Wendelken and Nakabayashi, "Developments," 65.
31. McCamant and Durrett, *Cohousing*, 39.
32. Yamashita, September 19, 2011.
33. The Garden City's influence on the idea of artificial land is discussed on pages 31–33 in this book's introduction. Regarding cooperative building societies in the garden-city concept, see Ebenezer Howard, *Garden Cities of To-Morrow* [1898] (Cambridge, MA: The MIT Press, 1970), 107–108.

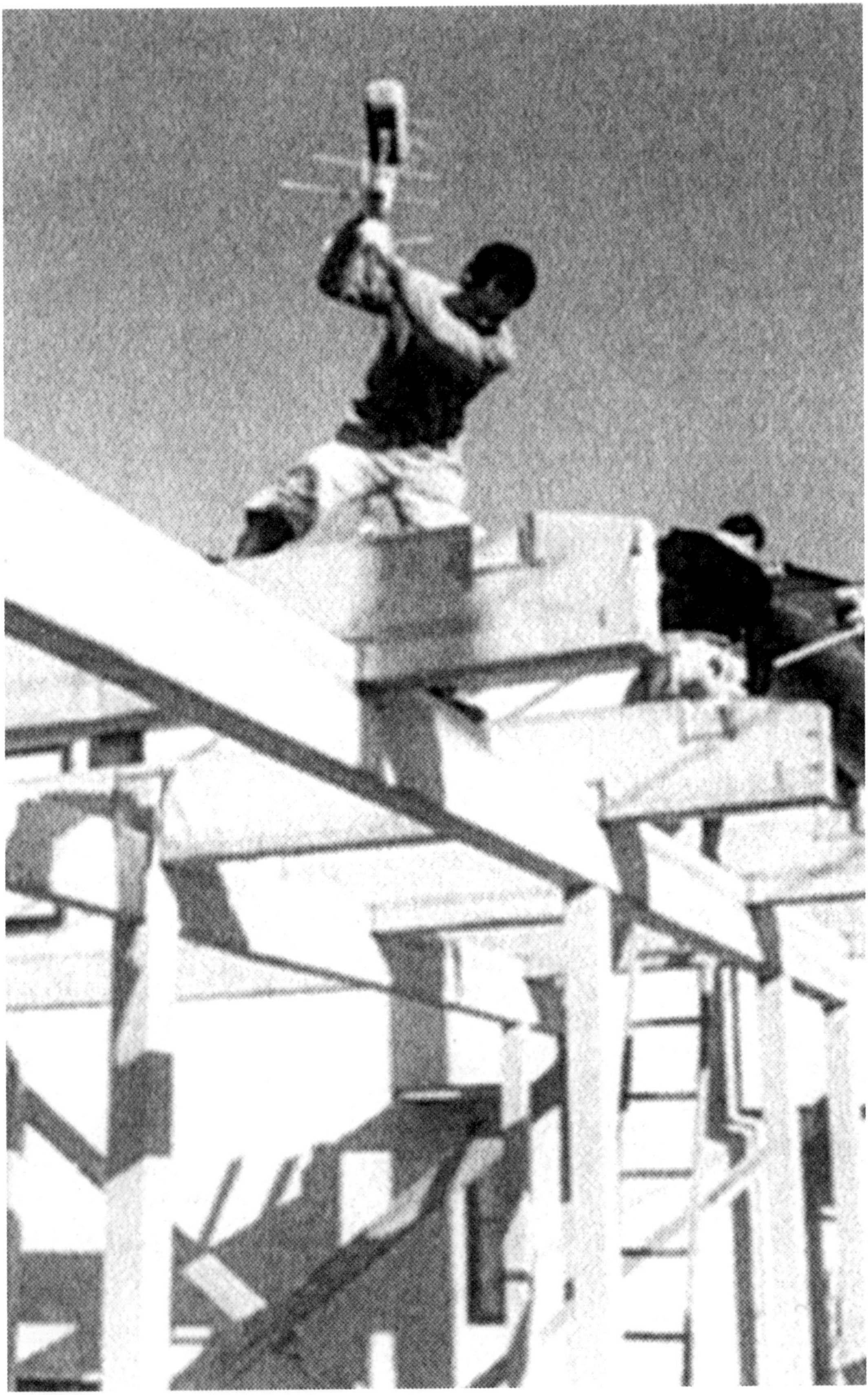

Concrete Timber:
Kugahara House, 1998–2202

The book *Ise: Prototype of Japanese Architecture* appeared in 1961, written by Kenzo Tange and Noburo Kawazoe, with photos by Yoshio Watanabe. Located in Japan's Mie Prefecture, the shrine at Ise is an ancient-yet-new structure, rebuilt out of *hinoki* (Japanese cypress) every 20 years since around 690, except for a few pauses caused by wars and other problems. Given unprecedented access to the cyclic rebuilding in 1953, with a second visit to the complex in 1960, the book's team was able to document the shrine as it had never been before, with the architectural historian Jonathan Reynolds writing that their publication changed perceptions of Ise from a site associated with Shinto nationalism to one of "aesthetic contemplation."[1] Kawazoe's closing essay opened the shrine to ecological contemplation as well. His description of material renewal in traditional Japanese houses and daily life "absorbed into the great stream of Nature" helped inspire interest in Ise in metabolic terms.[2]

But today the shrine's architectural influence as an immaculate "prototype" is debatable. While its rebuilding may appear to be the perfection of sustainability thanks to its reliance on sophisticated silviculture, the periodic replacement can also act as an alibi for the country's supposed predilection for the ephemeral, helping to naturalize the wastage caused by scrap-and-build. On the optimistic side, Yositika Utida believes that "the architectural world must develop a system for recycling materials such as concrete," and that "Ise Shrine shows us one way that problem can be solved."[3]

Utida's hope, expressed in 2002, was not exactly a new one at the time. Kawazoe reflected in 1973 that "the framework of the wooden house and the rigid skeleton of the ferroconcrete

Photo of timber construction used to illustrate the assembly concept for Masato Otaka's 1969 Tochigi Prefectural Council Building, made from precast concrete

following: ARX Architects & Associates, Kugahara House precast skeleton, c. 2002

317

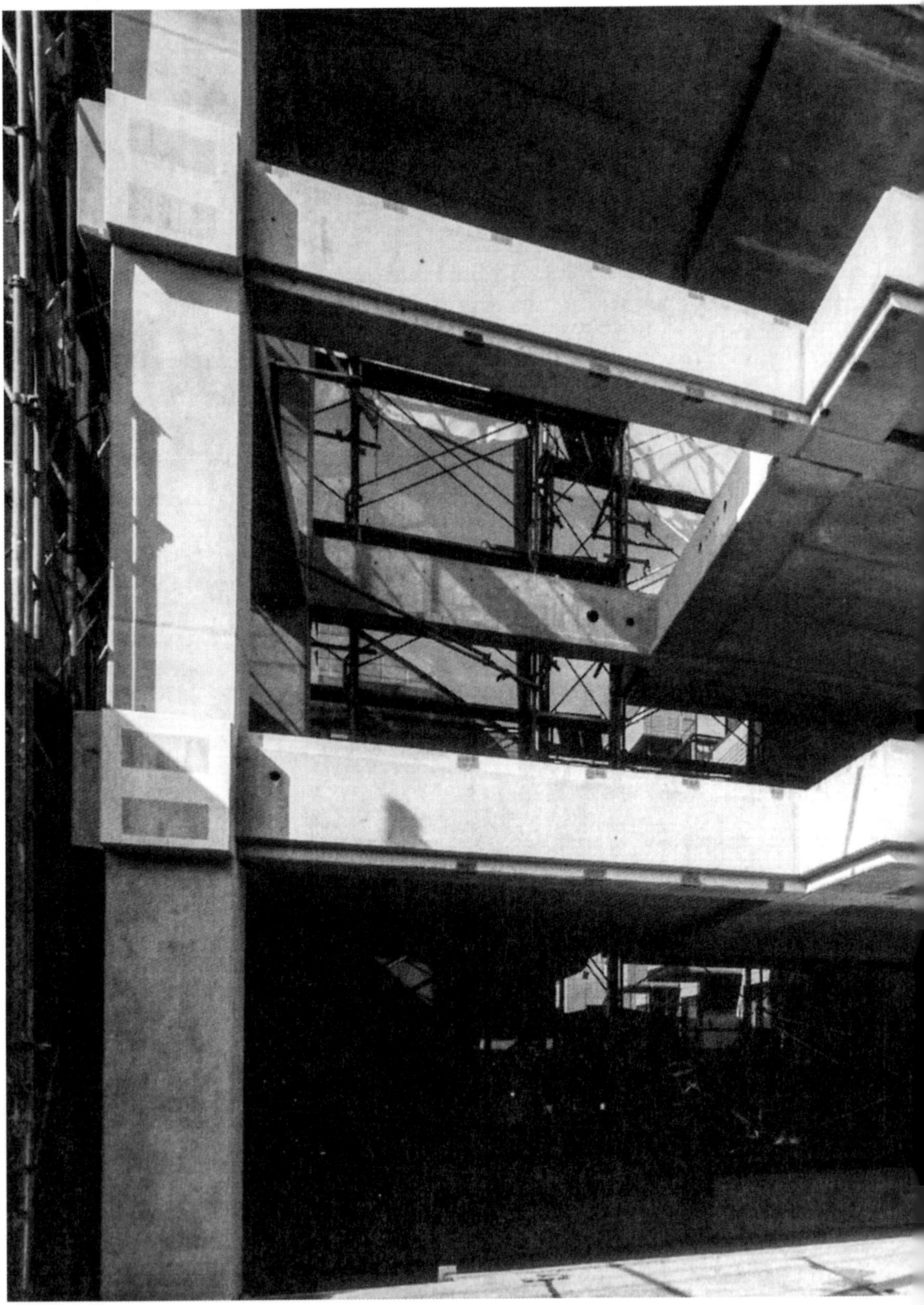

CONCRETE TIMBER: KUGAHARA HOUSE, 1998–2202

building get closer in principle as the site-fabrication of the latter is replaced by the assembly of precast parts," alluding to a sublimation of timber frequently pursued by his fellow Metabolists and their associates: concrete as a new and improved timber.[4] Kiyonori Kikutake, known for his innovative concrete designs in the 1960s, in fact located his awakening to metabolic thinking in his work during the 1950s, reusing old timber trusses from industrial buildings for the Bridgestone tire company.[5]

The transposition of structural logic and assembly process between materials, often only as appearance, has a significant history in architecture. Such a practice was central to architect Gottfried Semper's *Stoffwechsel* theory, articulated in the mid-nineteenth century. Typically understood in English as his theory of "material transformations," *Stoffwechsel* is notably the historical German term for metabolism.[6] Semper saw phenomena such as the translation of timber construction details into the stone metopes and triglyphs of classical Greek architecture as a symbolic perpetuation of the origins of building.

Sigfried Giedion would later attack such translations as demonstrating nineteenth-century architecture's split personality, indicative of technological dishonesty. He saw this split in the way that new building materials, such as cast iron, were used in ways that did not express their inherent nature, but instead imitated the forms of components made of established materials such as wood or stone, a criticism that was foundational for the notion of modernist integrity.[7]

Yet Metabolism's architects and engineers were more Semperian, realizing that handling concrete as if it were wood could synthesize the best of both, fusing cultural transformation with technical performance. Fundamentally part of the quest to reconcile "Japanese spirit with Western knowledge," the pursuit of what could be called "concrete timber" is found in work produced during Metabolism's gestation in the 1950s, its heyday in the '60s, and beyond, with significant evolution seen in concrete's tectonic likeness to timber and the design of environmental life cycles. The syncretic pursuit of concrete timber shares a sensibility with artificial land, a pairing exemplified in the Kugahara House, an experimental project built in 2002. Today the historic fascination with concrete timber appears in a new light, given that in Japan (as in much of the world) timber is becoming the new concrete, now used for building types, such as high-rises, previously beyond its capabilities.

Method as Model
Returning to the inspiration from Ise's cyclic reconstruction, the shrine's Main Sanctuary descends from prehistoric raised granaries, a model in both process and form.[8] In ancient times, protecting the grain harvest against pests and dampness required tight and precise joinery. A large thatched roof, as also used in the Main Sanctuary, acted as a clamp due to increased weight during the rainy season, compressing the stacked *hinoki* members below and thereby keeping them sealed. Periodic reconstruction was critical to prevent deterioration of a structure with such important contents.[9] This inspired the approach to Shinto shrines, not only Ise, and became the means of protecting their sacred artifacts.

The reconstruction of Ise is performed through the *Shikinen Sengu* ceremony, which takes eight years of preparation. First, as many as 10,000 *hinoki* trees are harvested, guided by a meticulous stewardship plan. Forestry plans have existed for the shrine since the seventeenth century, but in 1915 a new plan was introduced that aimed for all wood to be supplied from the shrine's own property within 200 years. As of the 2013 reconstruction, 25 percent of the wood came from this source.[10] The harvested wood is carefully seasoned and cut in the controlled atmosphere of a workshop, to form the multiple jointed elements that will later be assembled on site. Once brought to the shrine, construction happens on an "alternate site," an adjacent plot identical to the one on which the shrine sits. This arrangement means the shrine alternates its location every 20 years, with one plot empty and the other occupied, aside from a relatively brief period of overlap, during which the new shrine is assembled prior to the disassembly of the previous one, so as to keep the shrine continuously in existence. The disassembled wood members are reused and recycled. They are cut up for use in making repairs to torii gates and other elements in the shrine precinct, as well as being distributed to Shinto shrines throughout Japan. Through all of this planning, Ise is an extraordinary rationalization of human-nature metabolism, presenting its architecture as a phase within a regenerative life cycle.[11]

Artificial Wood

Returning to concrete, it of course enabled tall buildings due to its advantages over wood in terms of fire and seismic resistance. But like timber, as Kawazoe observed, precast concrete is prefabricated and then assembled. It can similarly be used without additional surface finishes and coatings, unlike steel, recalling the bare beauty of Ise's *hinoki*. And it can also, like its timber model, be cleanly disassembled thanks to jointed connections.

Several key projects show concrete's attraction and challenges when treated as transformed timber. One forerunner is Tange's Hiroshima Peace Memorial Museum, built in 1955.

Ise Shrine's 2013 reconstruction, prior to dismantling of old shrine

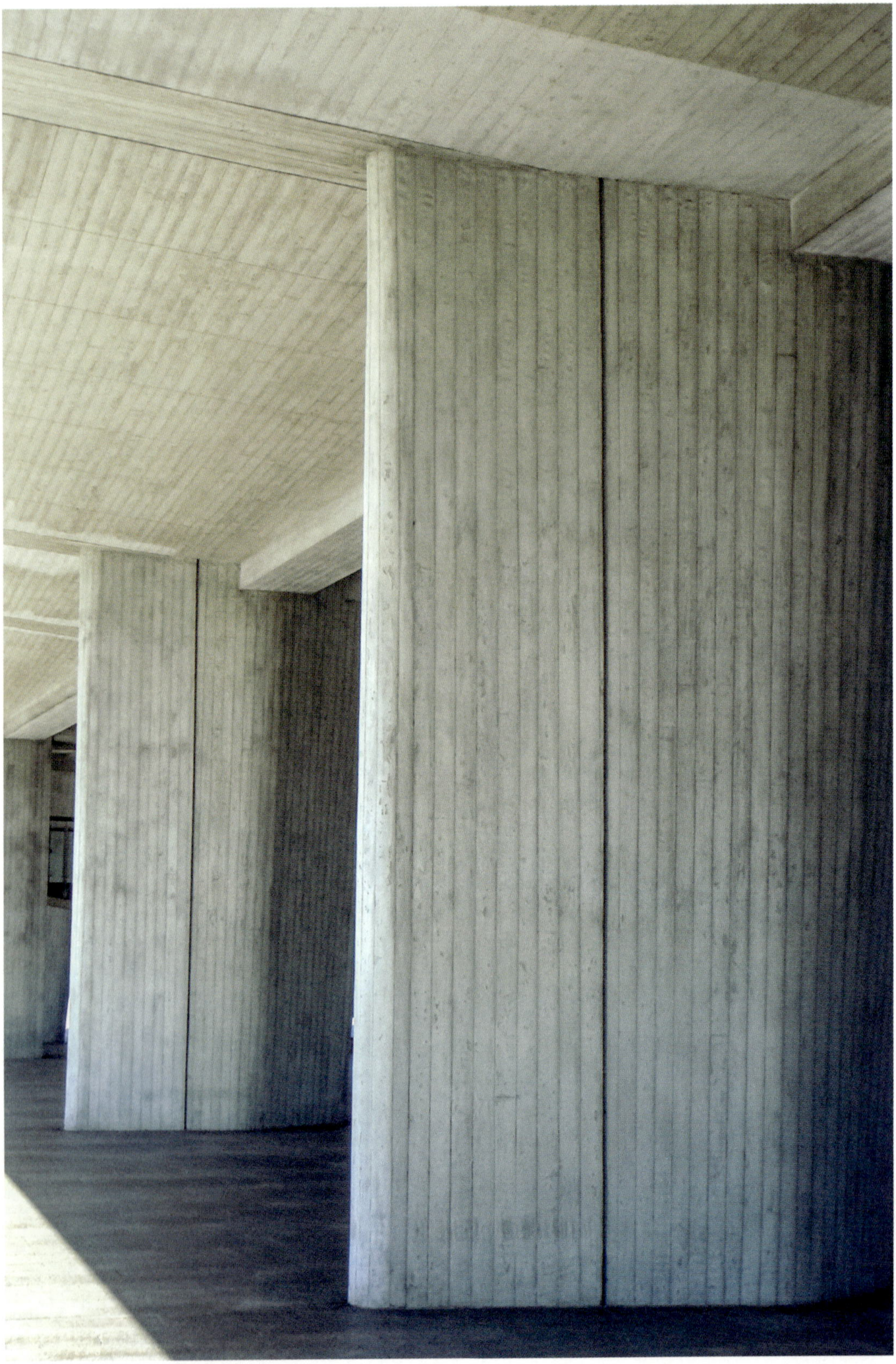

As noted earlier, the structure draws, like Ise, on the form of a storehouse, one to store artifacts from the city's destruction.[12] Though cast-in-place, the museum's *pilotis* show the exquisite appearance that could be achieved with concrete thanks to the skills of Japanese carpenters, with the crisp surfaces of their wooden formwork imprinted into the cast concrete.[13]

With Tange's 1958 Kagawa Prefectural Government Building, concrete timber appears in more graphic form. The building's mimicry of wood is blatant, with thin, rafter-like brackets on the exterior to support balconies. In addition, like the Peace Museum, all of the structure bears the imprint of the wooden formwork. While much celebrated, the building wasn't free from criticism. Otaka and others wondered, "Why should one adopt a form that gives the impression of combining wood and concrete, when concrete is used and cast on site?"[14]

Note that this question doesn't question combining timber and concrete per se. Instead, site-cast versus precast is the critical question in judging the peculiar authenticity of concrete timber, with precast being the "real" thing. Precast is more expensive, however, due to the greater fabrication skills it requires—a constraint that ruled it out for Sakaide. Also, its multiple joints cause lower rigidity, often making it impractical for seismic safety.

Despite these issues, Tange's 1966 Yamanashi Press and Broadcasting Center in Kofu reveals the strong allure of precast. The building is detailed with *kibana*, the timber beam tips found at joints with posts in Japan's traditional wood buildings, and the joint lines overall suggest a dry assembly of parts. However, Yamanashi's project architect Koichiro Okamura states that Tange immediately ruled out the use of precast in

left: Kenzo Tange, Hiroshima Peace Memorial Museum, detail of pilotis, 1955 (2010)

above: Kenzo Tange, Kagawa Prefectural Government Building balconies, Takamatsu, 1958 (2017)

CONCRETE TIMBER: KUGAHARA HOUSE, 1998–2202

323

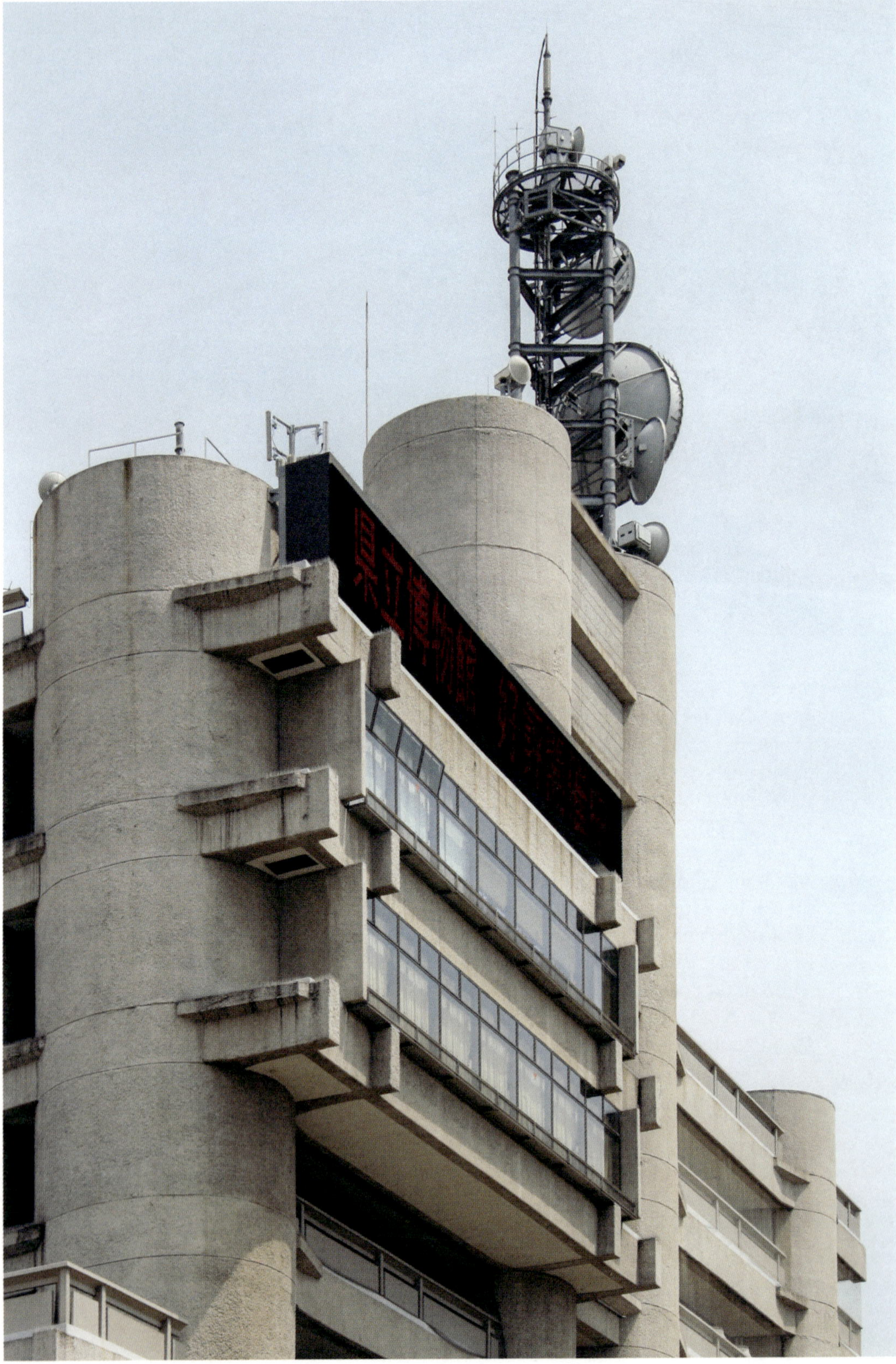
県立博物館

early talks with the engineer, Fugaku Yokoyama, precisely due to its insufficient rigidity.[15] Nonetheless, the detailing persisted as an aesthetic for what is in fact a monolithic site-cast building.

For lower structures, precast was possible. In 1963, Kikutake completed his Izumo Shrine Administration Building, which features 50-meter-long "super beams" to structure a column-free pavilion.[16] Later, Yoshinobu Ashihara's Japanese Pavilion for Montreal's Expo 67 appeared to be a concrete log cabin, built of stacked beams made in Japan and shipped, demonstrating the precision and mobility so hoped for with precast. A final example from Metabolism's golden age is Otaka's Tochigi Prefectural Council Building, completed in 1969. Readable as a critical response to Tange's Kagawa building, Tochigi's "Aerial Frame Method" assembles remarkably timber-like elements supported by a base of massive site-cast "rails." Engineered by Toshihiko Kimura, the design extrapolated the major-structure concept from Harumi to display the height of precast innovation at the time.

Extended Producer Responsibility

Like Harumi before it, Tochigi was demolished in 2007, another victim of scrap-and-build. But in 1997, the year Harumi was destroyed, an association of general contractors known as the Nikkenkei initiated new research to address scrap-and-build's by-products of lost investment, displacement, and increased pollution. The result was the Nikkenkei Open Housing System (NOHS), a precast and post-tensioned skeleton frame that is the peak of the concrete-timber dream.

left: Kenzo Tange, Yamanashi Press and Broadcasting Center *kibana*, Kofu, 1966 (2010)

above: Masato Otaka, Tochigi Prefectural Council Building, Utsunomiya, 1969 (1977)

CONCRETE TIMBER: KUGAHARA HOUSE, 1998–2202

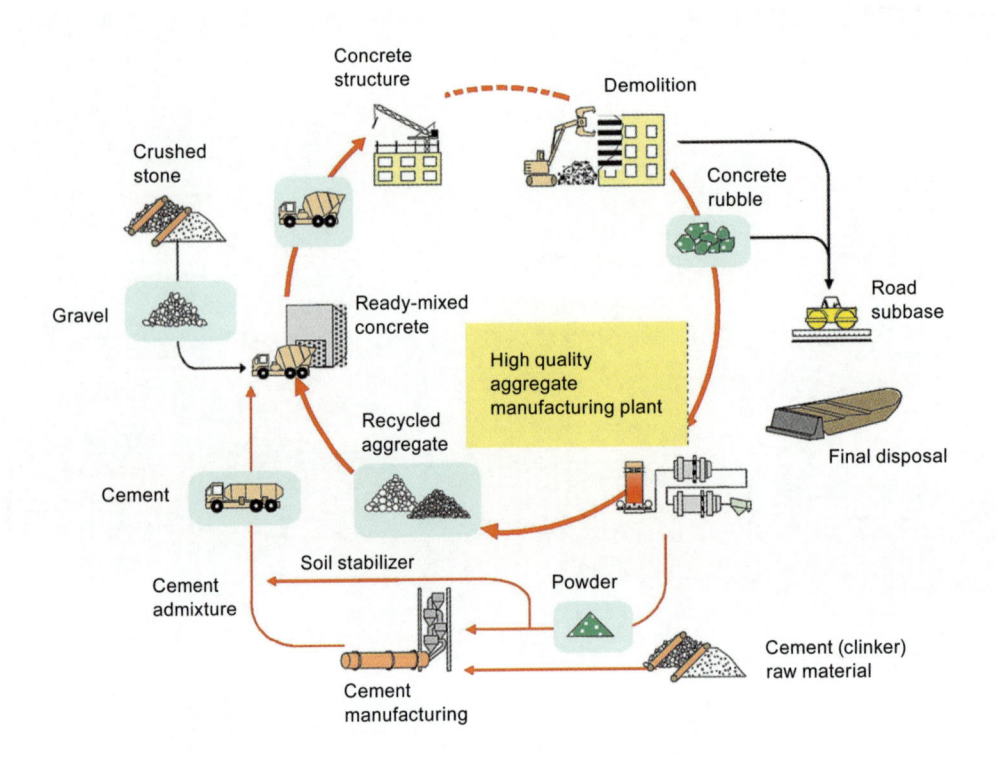

By the late 1990s, it was clear to Japan's construction industry that the way in which concrete buildings were created and destroyed needed to be rationalized. To give a sense of the scale of the national scrap-and-build problem, from 1983 to 1988, about 4,032,000 units of housing were demolished and 7,433,000 constructed. Even after the bubble's bursting, between 1993 and 1998 approximately 2,993,000 units were demolished, and about 7,360,000 were constructed.[17] The concrete involved in this process was estimated to have caused 0.5 percent of the annual carbon-dioxide emissions worldwide.[18] The waste produced was estimated to be 40 percent of all landfills, and 90 percent of all illegal dumping.[19] Illegal dumping had become increasingly common during the 1990s as landfill space became extremely scarce, with the prediction in 1997 of only 3.1 years of proper disposal capacity left in the nation.[20] What was needed was "extended producer responsibility."[21]

Capacity was extended through several initiatives that led to major increases in concrete's recycling.[22] In 2000, the Diet passed the "Fundamental Law for Establishing a Sound Material-Cycle Society," written by the newly formed Ministry of the Environment (MOE). The goal of the law is comprehensive resource management to minimize negative environmental impacts through creating a low-carbon society.[23] Also in 2000, MOC and MOE introduced the "Construction Material Recycling Law" that made contractors responsible for material dismantling, sorting, and recycling.[24]

For the NOHS design team, composed of engineers from the Nikkenkei and Tokyo's ARX Architects & Associates, precast concrete was able to facilitate these processes. The work was led by ARX's Masaru Matsuie in collaboration with Yositika Utida's son, Yoshio Utida, in an impressive

above: Schematic flow of concrete recycling system

right: ARX, NOHS study (top) and base-isolation diagram (bottom)

CONCRETE TIMBER: KUGAHARA HOUSE, 1998–2202

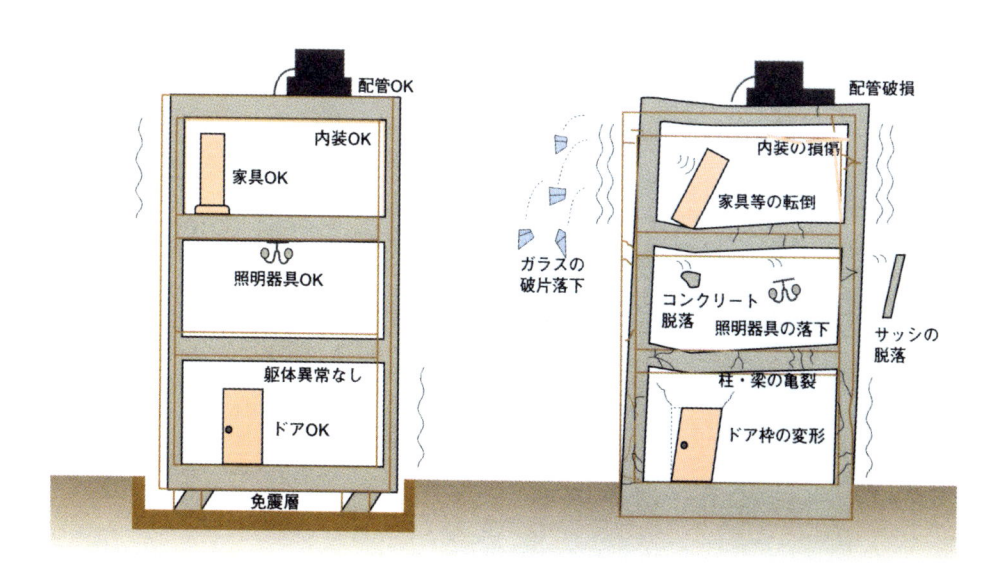

3 OPEN SYSTEMS

lineage of artificial-land activity. Calculating that off-site production of the NOHS precast columns, beams, and floor plates would allow for intense quality and pollution control, the team claimed reductions of 90 percent for industrial waste, 99 percent for forest resources, and 92 percent for carbon dioxide.[25] In the future, should a NOHS building need to be removed, it could be disassembled through de-tensioning and unbolting, and then transported to a concrete-recycling facility. Or it could be reassembled elsewhere, as is sometimes done with *minka*. Like timber frames, tectonics for NOHS is more than the "art of joinings."[26] It's also the art of taking apart.

That said, not needing to take apart and recycle in the first place is often better. Instead of recycling, NOHS strives for reuse. Like CHS before it, the system aims to be a "sustainable element in 'chaotic' Japanese cities."[27] Its biggest environmental savings would come from a greatly reduced use of resources due to its projected 200-year life span, far longer than Japan's 30-year average for housing. Beyond its concrete mix-type and thick rebar cover to resist atmospheric corrosion, this impressive longevity would be enabled by extreme flexibility, with the NOHS team adopting the mantra of "continuous customization," as at Flex Court Yoshida. Speaking about this customization, ARX architect Akihiro Ueda said simply, "We want to build Highrise of Homes," referring to SITE's 1981 vision of artificial land.[28]

Infrastructure in Embryo, Again

The team initially studied NOHS through a hypothetical thirteen-story building. Thanks to the planned use of base isolation, unavailable in Metabolism's heyday, a precast skeleton could now be used for a tall building, with ample double-height floors allowing the insertion of mezzanines. Takenaka had experimented with base isolation in the Stratiform Structure Module, but there the pads had been placed directly underneath houses on the platforms. Now placed below the primary structure at the foundation, base isolation became a fundamental technology for artificial land, disconnecting tremor-prone ground from an ideal ground above.[29]

But the first built test of NOHS is very small: a three-story house with four units in Kugahara, a Tokyo suburb filled with houses that one can imagine won't make it beyond their 30th anniversaries. Completed in 2002, the Kugahara House would not cause passersby to suspect an agenda of domestic satisfaction lasting until 2202. Like Yosizaka's house, it's a tiny project with big ambitions.

Also like its predecessor, the frame is left exposed on every elevation, but the quality of the concrete immediately shows its evolution. Built by the Oriental Shiraishi Corporation, a specialist in concrete bridges and other infrastructure, the finish is devoid of roughness and blotches, achieving the beauty of bare surfaces cherished in wood construction. Junctions of beams and columns are also wood-like, with the *kibana*-type extensions that Tange and others used in reference to timber. Now these extensions are legitimized as anchorages for the post-tension cables that bind the building together, with one anchorage proudly displayed as metabolic engineering behind little windows.

Due to the frame's columns and beams taking all horizontal loads, precast floorplates dropped into the frame have considerable freedom. Capped by removable access flooring, the precast floorplates themselves can also be removed to vary spaces, resulting in what the design team describes as an "artificial land [...] composed of open frame."[30] The team's embrace of artificial land through a kind of artificial timber leads to the potential for "vertical voids," augmenting the free plan with the free section.

Kugahara House, cable anchorage (2010)

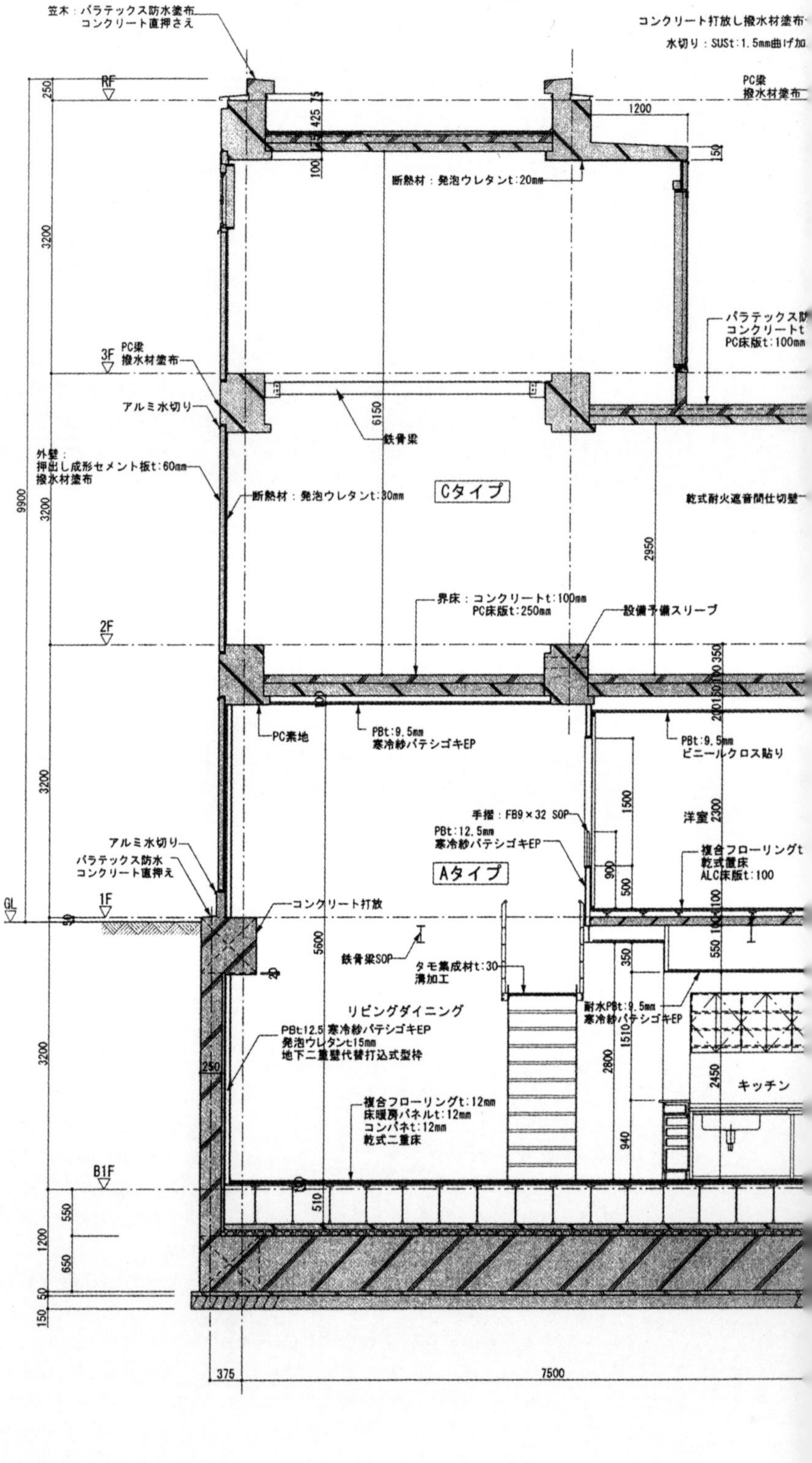
笠木：パラテックス防水塗布
コンクリート直押さえ
コンクリート打放し撥水材塗布
水切り：SUSt:1.5mm曲げ加
PC梁
撥水材塗布
断熱材：発泡ウレタンt:20mm
パラテックス防
コンクリートt
PC床版t:100mm
PC梁
撥水材塗布
アルミ水切り
鉄骨梁
外壁：
押出し成形セメント板t:60mm
撥水材塗布
断熱材：発泡ウレタンt:30mm
Cタイプ
乾式耐火遮音間仕切壁
界床：コンクリートt:100mm
PC床版t:250mm
設備予備スリーブ
PC素地
PBt:9.5mm
寒冷紗パテシゴキEP
PBt:9.5mm
ビニールクロス貼り
手摺：FB9×32 SOP
PBt:12.5mm
寒冷紗パテシゴキEP
洋室
複合フローリングt
乾式置床
ALC床版t:100
アルミ水切り
パラテックス防水
コンクリート直押え
Aタイプ
コンクリート打放
鉄骨梁SOP
タモ集成材t:30
溝加工
リビングダイニング
耐水PBt:9.5mm
寒冷紗パテシゴキEP
PBt12.5 寒冷紗パテシゴキEP
発泡ウレタンt15mm
地下二重壁代替打込式型枠
キッチン
複合フローリングt:12mm
床暖房パネルt:12mm
コンパネt:12mm
乾式二重床
RF
3F
2F
1F
GL
B1F
9900
3200
375
7500

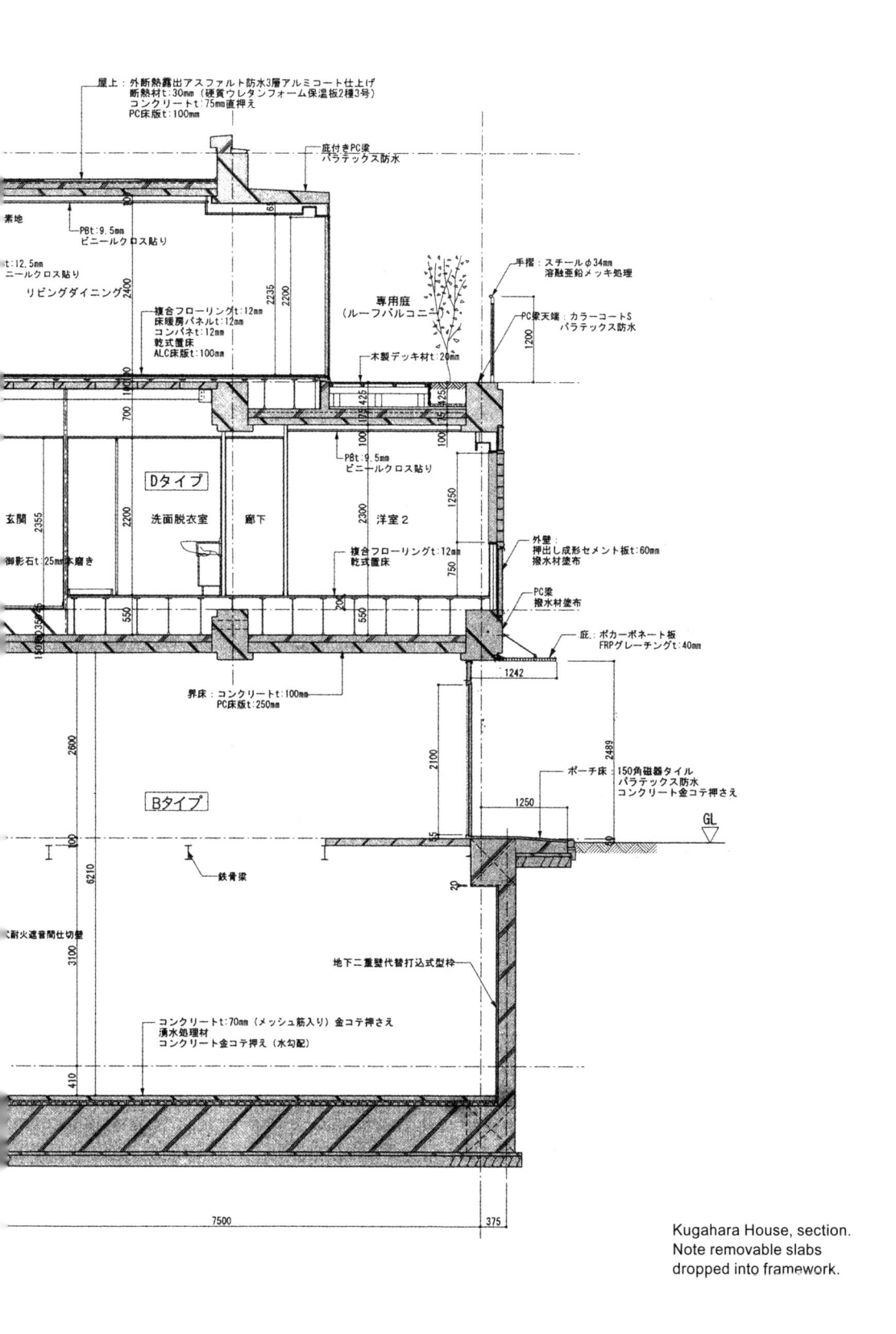

Kugahara House, section.
Note removable slabs
dropped into framework.

CONCRETE TIMBER: KUGAHARA HOUSE, 1998–2202

Menu Planning

In terms of infill, the team decided to make the first-ever private sector Two-Step skeleton, bringing the experiment somewhat closer to the historic reality of *hadaka-gashi* than the publicly subsidized Flex Court. Whether the system could be successful without such support was a major question.[31] In adopting the TSHS concept, the project had to confront various thorny issues in combining the restrictions of renting with the freedoms of owning, issues exacerbated by the increase in regulations and building systems since the *hadaka-gashi* era.

To simplify, an initial decision was made to treat the envelope as part of the skeleton, unlike at Tsunane, thus placing it under the control of the building owner. With variation thereby limited to interiors, three approaches to infill were offered: a "free plan" option where residents would be entirely responsible for organizing unit design and build-out; a "menu plan" option with three choices per plot, created by ARX; and as a last resort, build-out by the building owner into a rental unit if no takers were found for a given plot.[32] Unlike Flex Court, no infill system was specified.

To rationalize the investment in owned infill on a rented plot, a twenty-year minimum lease was set, which included provisions for transferring or selling infill to the building owner if the lease was broken or not renewed. Clearly this timeframe made for a significant commitment to avoid lost investment in infill, making Kugahara attractive to residents with a high level of stability in life and work.[33]

The project team faced further procedural issues in terms of the actual infill build-out. One question was whether the work should be centralized through a single contactor mandated by the building owner, or should residents instead be free to hire ones of their

Kugahara House, skeleton with infill for four different units, c. 2002

332

3 OPEN SYSTEMS

choosing. Due to Kugahara's size, it was decided to allow residents to hire their own.[34] But more of a challenge to build-out was building code. With the ideal being the "free plan" option—the best exemplar of artificial land's potential—the skeleton had to be filed for code approval with provisional unit plans showing "tentative use," since approvals can only be given for complete designs. Later, once the skeleton was built and units had been designed or selected for actual residents, the plans were refiled as an amendment.[35]

As it turns out, three of Kugahara's four plots are occupied by architects. Mr. U designed infill for plots A and B, and uses B as his studio. Mr. N, an architect apparently known for his housing design, designed the infill for his apartment on plot C. The last, plot D, is occupied by a couple who moved back to Japan after many years living in America and learned of the project through an online advertisement. Their design was selected from the plan menu.[36]

Wishful Thinking?

Despite its innovations, the Kugahara House is the only built example of NOHS. Part of the reason it will likely remain so is that it instantiated the Metabolist dream of concrete timber just as timber was becoming the new concrete. Japan, in part due to government support, now has an obsession with mass timber.[37] With two-thirds of the country forested, and strong interest in greater self-sufficiency and renewable, carbon-sequestering building materials, the government has been encouraging mass timber's use since 2010. In particular, it encourages the use of Cross-Laminated Timber, or CLT—a kind of super plywood that, among other things, has improved resistance to fire—with government support ranging from subsidies of up to 50 percent of the cost of starting a CLT factory, to changes in the building code.

While CLT and other forms of mass timber such as glulam are being used for types of construction that would previously have been concrete, they could take more inspiration from the expressiveness and freedom of concrete timber, as seen in the 1950s and '60s. Indeed, CLT construction often needs large shear walls to resist horizontal loads, producing the kinds of obstructions to space planning that earlier concrete projects had worked hard to avoid.

As a result of such limitations, an all mass-timber building isn't always practical, especially as a high-rise. Addressing this shortcoming, research by Skidmore, Owings & Merrill has created a genuine hybrid where timber and concrete work together, with each used in those places where they best perform. This approach was studied by the firm for a reimagining of its 1965 Dewitt Chestnut apartment tower in Chicago, which introduced architect-engineer Fazlur Khan's concept of the "framed tube." The study transformed the concrete tube into a "concrete jointed timber frame," with concrete used for girders and beams that make connections between mass-timber columns and floor slabs that constitute the majority of the redesign's material.[38]

It would be interesting to perform a similar transformation on Kagawa, Harumi, Tochigi, or Kugahara. These buildings, unlike the original Dewitt Chestnut tower, already engage wood in sublimated form. They suggest a long-term project to keep wood construction alive even in the absence of the actual material, making reference to wood to perpetuate an ethic of life-cycle consciousness. That today they could be wood feels more like a realization of a wish inherent to Metabolism rather than its contradiction—that "Each epoch dreams the one to follow" is sometimes true.[39] A wooden model of Harumi displayed at the Urban Renaissance Agency's museum fulfills this Metabolist dream in miniature.

But Metabolism's quest for material durability in the form of skeletons and platforms has a possible drawback. In 2013, a writer on Ise's reconstruction ceremony that year remarked that the reason for the shrine's longevity "isn't heroic engineering or structural overkill, but rather cultural continuity."[40] The ceremony is a sharing of knowledge and spirit dedicated to renewal. On the other hand, Kugahara's structure is heroic in performance, if not size, with its 200-year life span threatening to negate anything similar to the cultural practice that Ise maintains through its 20-year rebuilding cycle. Indeed, the NOHS team prepared an instruction manual for the frame's proper care, indicating a loss of direct human communication over its life.[41] Some seem to accept this discontinuity as inevitable, as the low maintenance required for durable SI structures can be seen to respond to a shrinking population, particularly of construction workers, a loss which also underlies Japan's development of construction robots.[42] For now, the robots aren't ready to take over. Yet what might Kugahara's cultural context be in 2202, the year of its expiration?

1 Jonathan M. Reynolds, "Ise Shrine and a Modernist Construction of Japanese Tradition," *Art Bulletin* 83, no. 2 (June 2001): 316.

2 Kenzo Tange and Noboru Kawazoe, *Ise: Prototype of Japanese Architecture* [1961] (Cambridge, MA: The MIT Press, 1965), 206. The original 1961 Japanese edition was published by the newspaper *Asahi Shimbun*.

3 Yositika Utida, *The Construction and Culture of Architecture Today: A View from Japan* (Tokyo: Ichigaya Publishing Co., 2002), 119.

4 Noboru Kawazoe, *Contemporary Japanese Architecture* (Tokyo: Kokusai Koryu Kikin, 1973), 61.

5 See Kiyonori Kikutake, "When Metabolism was Born of Renovation," *The Japan Architect*, no. 73 (Spring 2009): 12–15.

6 See Harry Francis Mallgrave, *Gottfried Semper: Architect of the Nineteenth Century* (New Haven, CT: Yale University Press, 1996), 284.

7 See Sigfried Giedion, *Building in France, Building in Iron, Building in Ferroconcrete* [1928], trans. J. Duncan Berry (Santa Monica, CA: The Getty Center for the History of Art and the Humanities, 1995), 104.

8 While my focus here is on the Main Sanctuary, other areas of the shrine are also part of the cyclic reconstruction, and also draw on the granary model.

9 Here and following, I am indebted to Junko Edahiro's description of the 2013 *sengu* process and the shrine's typological origins. See Junko Edahiro, "Rebuilding Every 20 Years Renders Sanctuaries Eternal—the Sengu Ceremony at Jingu Shrine in Ise," *JFS Newsletter*, no. 132 (August 2013), http://www.japanfs.org/en/news/archives/news_id034293.html.

10 See Edahiro, "Rebuilding." Note that *Ise: Prototype of Japanese Architecture* barely touches on the specific preparations for the rebuilding.

11 But not a cheap phase: as of 2013, the cost to replace was ¥55 billion, raised through donations by citizens. See "Ise Donates Cypress Logs to Fix Tohoku Shrines," *Japan Times*, January 12, 2013, https://www.japantimes.co.jp/news/2013/01/12/%25news_category%25/ise-donates-cypress-logs-to-fix-tohoku-shrines/.

12 See page 153 of this book and Hajime Yatsuka, "The Social Ambition of the Architect and the Rising Nation," in *Kenzō Tange: Architecture for the World*, eds. Seng Kuan and Yukio Lippit (Zurich: Lars Müller Publishers, 2012), 47.

13 Historian Adrian Forty notes that the pilotis of the museum, after they had deteriorated, had their surfaces meticulously removed and recast, true to the original precision. See Forty, *Concrete and Culture: A Material History* (London: Reaktion Books, 2012), 137.

14 Kawazoe, *Contemporary Japanese Architecture*, 71.

15 Email exchange between Koichiro Okamura and the author, Dec 10, 2009.

16 Super beams: see *Metabolism—The City of the Future: Dreams and Visions of Reconstruction in Postwar and Present-Day Japan*, ed. Mami Hirose et al. (Tokyo: Mori Art Museum, 2011), 109.

17 Eiji Oizumi, "Transformations in Housing Construction and Finance," in *Housing and Social Transition in Japan*, eds. Yosuke Hirayama and Richard Ronald (New York: Routledge, 2007), 57. A unit equals one household, be it an apartment or freestanding house.

18 Tomonari Yashiro et al., "Development of Open Building System as Sustainable Urban Element," in *International Symposium on Integrated Life-Cycle Design of Materials and Structures*, ed. A. Sarja (Paris: RILEM Publications, 2000), 260.

19. See Chia-Liang Weng and Tomonari Yashiro, "The Benefit of Open Building System to Recycled Use of Resources," in *Proceedings of Continuous Customization in Housing, 16–18 October 2000, Tokyo, Japan*, ed. Tomonari Yashiro (2000): 208, PDF file.
20. See Tsuyoshi Fujita et al., "Regional Management of Waste Circulation and Eco-industrial Networks," in *Establishing a Resource-Circulating Society in Asia: Challenges and Opportunities*, ed. Tohru Morioka et al. (Tokyo: United Nations University Press, 2011), 125.
21. See Tohru Morioka, "Introduction: Asian Perspectives of Resource-Circulating Society—Sound Material Metabolism, Resource Efficiency and Lifestyle for Sustainable Consumption," in *Establishing a Resource-Circulating Society in Asia*, 3.
22. See Yoshio Kasai, "Recent Trends in Recycling of Concrete Waste and Use of Recycled Aggregate Concrete in Japan," in *SP-219: Recycling Concrete and Other Materials for Sustainable Development*, eds. Tony Liu and Christian Meyer (March 1, 2004): 12, PDF file.
23. See Keishiro Hara, "Indicator Systems as an Instrument for Establishing Sustainable Resource-Circulating Societies," in *Establishing a Resource-Circulating Society in Asia*, 58.
24. See Ministry of the Environment, "Solid Waste Management and Recycling Technology of Japan: Toward a Sustainable Society" (February 2012): 28, PDF file.
25. Shin Okamoto et al., "Design and Construction of First Skeleton-Rent Apartment in the Private Sector," in *Building for the Future: The 16th CIB World Building Congress 2004* (2004): 2, PDF file.
26. Adolf Heinrich Borbein, quoted in Kenneth Frampton, *Studies in Tectonic Culture* (Cambridge, MA: The MIT Press, 1995), 4.
27. Tomonari Yashiro, "Development," 260. "Chaotic" has become a well-established if not clichéd descriptor for Japanese cities, perhaps explaining the quotation marks here, with such chaos perceived by many avant-garde architects and cultural observers, at least historically in the 1970s and '80s, as a source of inspiration, foreboding, or both.
28. Akihiro Ueda in conversation with the author, April 20, 2010. See Highrise of Homes on page 18 of this book.
29. As noted on page 211 of this book, Tadatoshi Asano believes base isolation has played a fundamental role in enabling SI high-rise construction. Email exchange between Asano and the author, December 28, 2014.
30. Okamoto, "Design," 2.
31. Shin Okamoto et al., "Trial of 'Skeleton Rent System' in Private Sector Using Nikkenkei Open Housing System," in *Proceedings of Continuous Customization in Housing*, 71.
32. Okamoto, "Design," 5.
33. Okamoto, "Trial," 76.
34. Okamoto, "Trial," 76.
35. Okamoto, "Design," 7. In comparison at least to New York City, the process described here is like a "Post-Approval Amendment," which also addresses changes to an initial approved design as it adapts to more specific conditions, often after construction has started.
36. Okamoto, "Design," 7.
37. As of 2021, this obsession is found in much of the architectural world.
38. See Skidmore, Owings & Merrill LLP, "Timber Tower Research Project: Final Report," Executive Summary (May 6, 2013), PDF file.
39. Jules Michelet, quoted in Tyrus Miller, "'Glass Before Its Time, Premature Iron': Architecture, Temporality and Dream in Benjamin's *Arcades Project*," in *Walter Benjamin and the Arcades Project*, ed. Beatrice Hanssen (London: Continuum, 2006), 241.
40. See Austin Brown, "Alexander Rose Visits Ise Shrine Reconstruction Ceremony," (October 3, 2013), http://blog.longnow.org/02013/10/03/alexander-rose-visits-ise-shrine-reconstruction-ceremony/.
41. Yashiro, "Development," 261.
42. These demographic and robotic connections to SI are raised in Kazunobu Minami, "Japanese Innovation in Adaptable Homes," in *Loose-Fit Architecture: Designing Buildings for Change*, ed. Alex Lifschutz (Oxford: John Wiley & Sons, 2017): 45.

SHARAKU
elements 祭

4
Neo Edo

東洲齋寫樂画

The 200th anniversary of SHARAKU 1794–1994 The Mainichi Newspapers

Looking back over the past thirty years, I am keenly impressed by how many things have been done, but I still cannot help feeling that it is only in the future that Metabolism will be able to display its true worth.

—Noboru Kawazoe[1]

This reflection, made in 1991, identifies Metabolism's main problem: to prove its value, on its own terms, requires the passage of time. It would have been much easier for the young architects who launched the movement in 1960 if they'd been content to "just make it beautiful."[2] But Kenzo Tange's call at the World Design Conference for an architecture that combined longer and shorter life spans was, by the 1990s, clearly prescient, despite its typical realization in SI high-rises having a banality that Tange, circa 1960, would likely find disappointing. Writing in 2002, Yositika Utida calls for "a technology that enables us to accept and accommodate other, endlessly changing technologies," echoing Tange and showing the remarkable persistence of an abstracted artificial land that, through so many challenges over decades, has been seen as the way to balance the fixed and the changeable.[3]

One reason for this persistence may be a phenomenon that Japanologist Alex Kerr summarizes as "once a concept, always a concept."[4] This alludes to the tendency of ministries like MOC and MITI to receive initial funding for a given project, such as research into flexible housing, and then incorporate that money into their annual budget requests for decades. Old concepts endure because money is allocated for them

Kiyoshi Awazu, "Sharaku Elements" poster celebrating the 200th anniversary of artist Toshusai Sharaku, 1794–1994 to be investigated again and again. The phenomenon is perhaps a partial cause of the Metabolist-industrial complex's longevity. Less cynically though, artificial land has legitimately, if not always successfully, engaged real needs in times of both growth and shrinkage, from the diversification of lifestyles and aging of the population, to the economic and environmental impact of scrap-and-build. And, like Fort l'Empereur's combination of skeleton frame and Algerian vernacular, artificial land in Japan has, with varying degrees of explicitness, long offered a way to reconcile Western techniques with Japanese identity—a cultural challenge that has existed since Japan opened to the West in 1868, the start of the Meiji era. What follows is, by way of a conclusion, a sketch of these persistent forces of bureaucratic inertia and cultural adaptation, with a particular focus on Meiji's predecessor, the Edo period. Edo is an era to which Japan often returns, not merely as nostalgia but as a guide for the future, just as it returns to artificial land for the same purpose.

The 200-year Housing Plan

In 2010, I asked Utida what he thought of the Century Housing System thirty years after its introduction. He replied with a laugh, "Well, now it's obsolete!"[5] Indeed, in 2008 the Diet passed the "Act for the Promotion of Long-Life Quality Housing," better known as the "200-year housing plan." With the goal of making housing able to last 200 years, the plan expands to a national scale the bicentennial ambitions of the tiny Kugahara House. Commenting on the plan's presentation by then–Prime Minister Yasuo Fukuda in 2007, the journalist Philip Brasor wrote in the *Japan Times* that "Fukuda explained something everybody knew at least intuitively: Japanese homes were not made to last."[6]

The biggest difference between CHS and the 200-year plan, besides an additional century, is the prominence of the new plan at a national level. While making 200-year housing sounds extreme, there are large quantities of dwellings in the world in active service that are as old, and even older—just not in Japan. As the sociologist Robert D. Leighninger Jr. points out, Harold Ickes, the head administrator of America's Public Works Administration in the 1930s and '40s, was criticized for his "mania for durability" in the construction of public housing.[7] And yet, Leighninger observed that these are "structures that are, for the most part, still in use today almost three-quarters of a century later," even after decades of minimal maintenance budgets.[8] Durability can be a good investment.

Unsurprisingly, the 200-year plan's development, like CHS, is connected to MOC, which as of 2001 has the unwieldy name Ministry of Land, Infrastructure, Transport and Tourism, or MLIT.[9] The plan's nine chapters have many now familiar topics, from "Durability of Material and Deterioration Measures," to "Adaptability," to "Unit Floor Space Standards," and "Long-Term Maintenance Planning."[10] Like CHS, high-quality concrete with additional rebar coverage is specified. Access floors are encouraged too, with the new plan requiring slab-to-ceiling heights of 2.65 meters or greater to facilitate this access.[11]

The plan is also financially similar to CHS, in being an incentive program offered to occupants of housing certified under the guidelines. While CHS offered home buyers preferential loans, building to the new guidelines will reduce occupants' income tax.[12] As in the past, the assumption is that developers will pursue certification due to units being made more financially attractive to buyers. And, as with its predecessor, no resident participation in unit design is required.

Unfortunately, housing developers are major critics of the plan. Many don't see long life as a sufficiently appealing attribute to promote sales.[13] As a result, applications for multi-unit housing have been small, far exceeded by detached houses: as of 2012, of the 199,720 applications made for certification, only 3,847 have been for apartment buildings.[14] For now, the biggest certified projects have been built by Haseko Corporation, since the late 1960s one of Japan's largest *zenekon* specializing in condominiums. Haseko's 69-unit Branchera Urawa in Tokyo and 114-unit Branchera Suita Katayamakoen in Osaka, both completed in 2011, have flexible features such as access floors and facade systems that are replaceable from inside the units.[15] They raise the question, however, of whether they're the kind of buildings one wants to be part of the cityscape for the next two centuries.

The Final Scrap-and-Build
A further criticism of the plan is that it's merely another sop to the construction state through contributing to what the economist Eiji Oizumi has called "a final 'scrap and build.'" An idea that sounds more ominous than optimistic, the concept has been substantiated by a host of new laws and policies for improved building safety and ecological planning, in which the 200-year plan is paradigmatic. The promotion of mass timber is part of it, too. It is, as the name suggests, a final round of demolition and replacement of all buildings that are of substandard and inflexible construction. As one example of a possible target, in 2007

about a third of Japan's more than 50 million housing units were estimated by MLIT not to meet safety standards established in 1981. In principle, all of these will need to be replaced with acceptable future stock.[16]

Philip Brasor may have provided the bluntest assessment of the 200-year plan and its "final" relatives. He writes, "In the long run, these policies will make little difference. According to the Population Research Center, if the current birth rate persists, 100 years from now there will be 45 million people in Japan, which is fewer persons than there are houses right now. It's impossible to say whether the quality of those houses in 2108 will be good or bad, but they sure will be cheap."[17] Oizumi partly echoes this sentiment, noting that the overall consumer demand for housing in Japan is diminishing, thanks to a shrinking and aging population, economic uncertainty, and lack of job security. He suggests the final scrap-and-build will only happen in a piecemeal fashion, with an inevitable bias toward the long-established hot places of Tokyo, Nagoya, and Osaka, where demolishing substandard housing may displace and exclude lower-income people who cannot afford the replacements. Affordability is not a component of the new policies, and so the cheap homes of the future will more likely be in cities and towns that have been largely abandoned.[18]

From Forecasting to Backcasting

Kazunobu Minami, Utida and John Habraken's former student and a contributor to the development of the 200-year plan, quite reasonably says that it's too early to say if the plan is a success or failure.[19] In light of this, and the legitimate criticisms of the plan, it's important to identify some criteria by which we might judge its success—or what some people might want such criteria to be.

Like Metabolism, the plan draws on prediction: events are anticipated and designs are intended as appropriate responses. The science of climate change is also of course reliant on prediction, with collected data extrapolated to forecast what will happen in the future. Essential as prediction is, in the past few decades climate researchers and others have increasingly come to realize the limitations of such forecasting, and have turned to the complementary practice of "backcasting": scenarios describing attractive futures, used to test our ability to reach them. Such futures are reverse engineered to determine what technologies, communities, and policies are needed for their realization. This should be contrasted with the pioneer futurist Herman Kahn, specialist in nuclear deterrence and later the Japanese economy, who took the pursuit of ICBMs and high GNPs as given metrics for national strength, rather than asking what other measures people might use in closer correlation with their desired health.[20] Environmental researcher John B. Robinson, who coined the term backcasting, writes, "To the extent that the most likely future is not the most desirable, then what we want are not simply good predictions, but indications of what alternative futures seem available and what their characteristics are."[21] Scientists in a publication from the United Nations echo this, writing that while "the Japanese government defines the concept of a sustainable society as a combination of a low-carbon society, a resource circulating society and naturally symbiotic society," a "holistic vision integrating these three societal visions has not yet been presented or fully clarified."[22] Backcasting produces such holistic visions, where, as the scientists say, "Scenarios are stories about the future [...] to help make better decisions in the present."[23]

Architects specialize in designing attractive futures and showing how to reach them, partly through their ability as storytellers. From this perspective, it's more charitable and perhaps accurate to see the Stratiform Structure Module less as an example of solutionism than of backcasting: here is a future we'd like—how do we get there?

Haseko Corporation, Branchera Suita Katayamakoen, Osaka, 2011

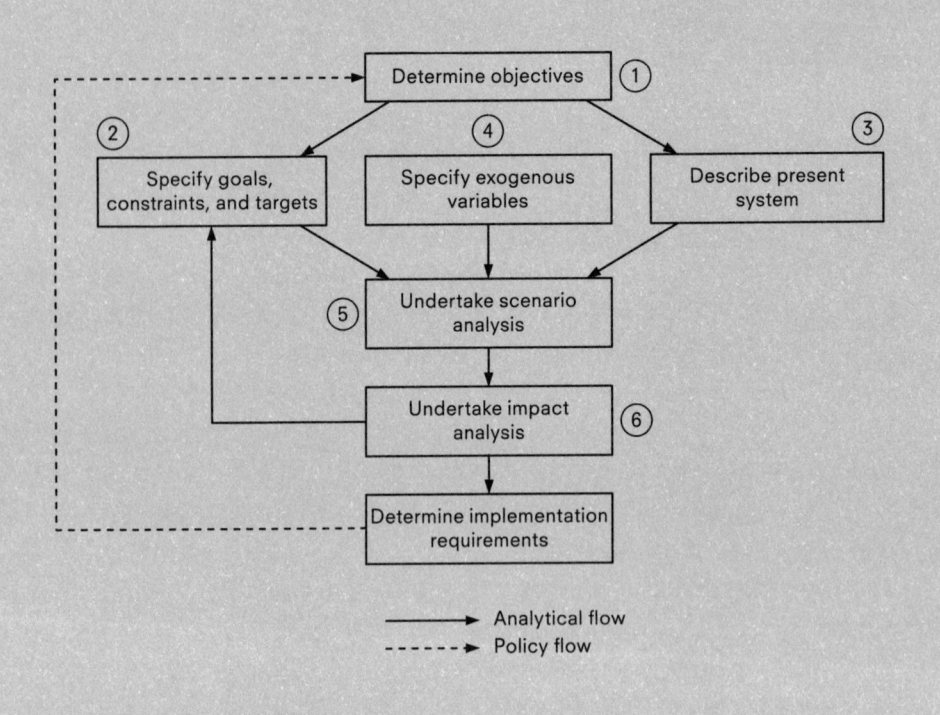

```
                    ┌─────────────────────┐
         ┌──────────│ Determine objectives │ ①
         │          └─────────────────────┘
      ②  │           ↙         ④  ↓       ↘  ③
  ┌──────────────┐  ┌──────────────┐  ┌──────────────┐
  │Specify goals,│  │   Specify    │  │Describe present│
  │constraints,  │  │  exogenous   │  │    system     │
  │ and targets  │  │  variables   │  │               │
  └──────────────┘  └──────────────┘  └──────────────┘
```

(Diagram: Backcasting method flow chart, steps 1–6: Determine objectives → Specify goals, constraints, and targets / Specify exogenous variables / Describe present system → Undertake scenario analysis ⑤ → Undertake impact analysis ⑥ → Determine implementation requirements. Legend: solid arrow = Analytical flow; dashed arrow = Policy flow.)

One professional storyteller, novelist Eisuke Ishikawa, believes a pivotal node occurred in Japan exactly at the moment of Metabolism's emergence. He writes:

> Many feel that Japan had changed significantly after the 1964 Tokyo Olympics, but as I recall, by 1960 the life of the Japanese was sufficiently affluent and was more comfortable than its prewar days in almost every respect with lavish supply of food. Moreover, natural land was plentiful with well-maintained forests and yet an abundance of farmland.
>
> Looking back, that period was the *exact crossroad* where Japan would either become an environmentally conscious country or an environmental wasteland. Had more than half the Japanese in 1960 felt that their economic wealth was sufficient, Japan would not have become the world's second economic power alongside America and the EU. Yet had the entire country refined its culture-based lifestyle and not increased its consumption of fossil fuels, it would have by now become a unique nation of environmental consciousness effortlessly living off its revenues in tourism, hailing curious visitors from all over the world.[24]

John B. Robinson, diagram of generic backcasting method, 1990

This is a stunning suggestion of an alternate Japan, in part because the node Ishikawa describes so strongly alludes to the metabolic rift that seems to have struck Kawazoe. To Ishikawa, it seems this node has reappeared in the early twenty-first century as a second chance, around the time of MOC starting to oversee national tourism. His "curious visitors" could be the future incarnation of aspiring culturati travelling to Japan instead of Italy for the essential education of a Grand Tour, one now ecological as much as aesthetic.

Ishikawa has for some time been a speculative historian of the Edo period, the era of Tokugawa rulers who chose to shut Japan off from foreign influences almost entirely. Lasting from 1603 to 1868, the period saw the seat of government move from Kyoto to Edo (today's Tokyo). He describes the missed early 1960s crossroad in his 2000 book *Japan in the Edo Period—An Ecologically-Conscious Society*, in which he delves into the period's many hints for crafting scenarios for a sustainable nation, since by contemporary material-culture standards, premodern Japan achieved high levels of physical well-being.[25] He observes that "it might be far more realistic to know about a nearly perfect circulation type society which thirty million ancestors were actually managing than to dream of a revolution which aims at a fictitious ideal society."[26] Prefiguring the "Sound Material-Cycle Society" sought today, Edo has the pragmatic value of being a holistic model thanks to an abundant and vivid historical record covering all aspects of Japanese life. Despite this pragmatism, Ishikawa is very aware his topic opens him to charges of nostalgia. Yet it's important to recall that in Europe there was also a concentrated study of the distant past that produced great innovation: the Renaissance.[27]

Seeds

Ishikawa is not alone in his fascination with the Edo period. The era has indeed captivated to varying degrees since it ended, from literary reflections in the late nineteenth century by those who had experienced it, to the appearance of *Edogaku*, or "Edo studies," in the 1970s as a recognized vocation.[28] This lingering influence is shown in Edward Seidensticker's classic history of Tokyo, *Low City, High City*, which chronicles the lag time between the era's nominal demise in 1868 and its much later physical and cultural demise with the Great Kanto Earthquake of 1923, which destroyed most remnants of Edo urban fabric.[29] While the study of Edo can often be nostalgic and mournful, a significant part of it can instead be characterized,

4 NEO EDO

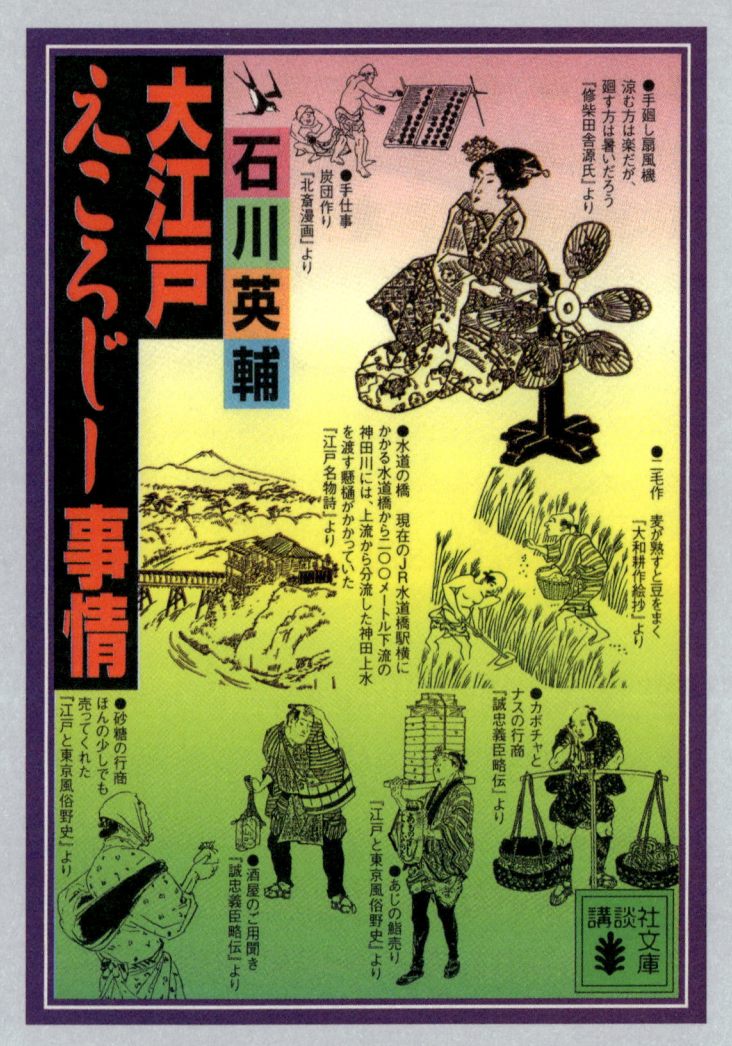

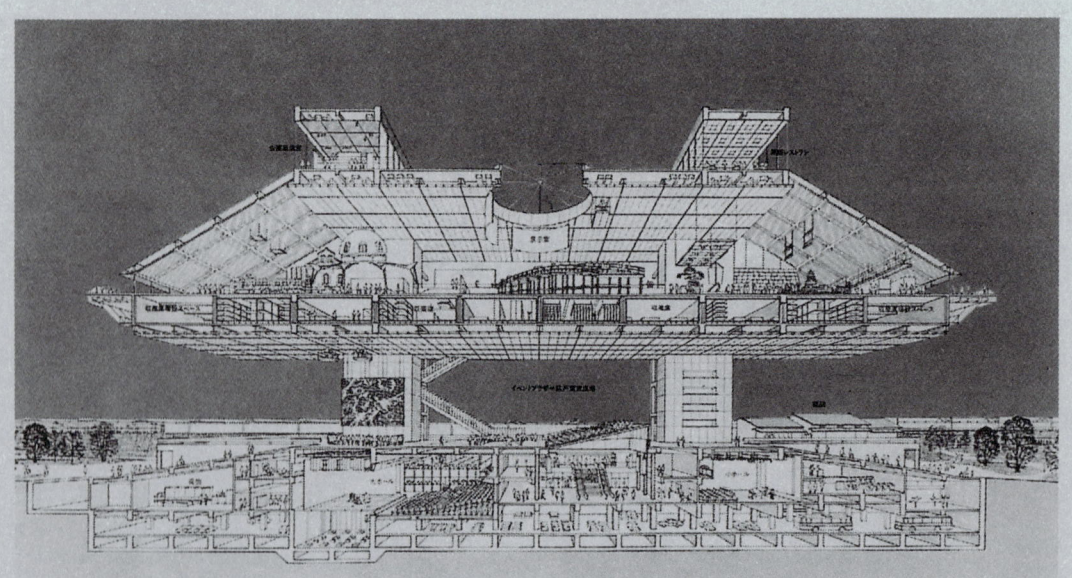

like Ishikawa's attitude, as a "future-oriented nostalgia."[30] At this end of the spectrum, Utida says, "We have much to learn from our [Edo] predecessors" in how we build.[31] The Edo-Tokyo Museum, designed by Kiyonori Kikutake and completed in 1993, is a giant elevated platform of artificial land on which is built, among other things, full-scale reconstructions of Edo-era shops and houses, offered up for study.[32]

What's not appealing is that the era had strong class boundaries: it was stratified into nobility, warriors, farmers, artisans, merchants, and untouchables. But out of this strong social order came effective ecological planning that was enforced at the national level, with regulations that came to operate culturally throughout society. Forestry planning was the most important of these ecological initiatives. As Conrad Totman writes in *The Green Archipelago: Forestry in Preindustrial Japan*, the country's "abundant verdure is not a monument to nature's benevolence and Japanese aesthetic sensibilities but the hard-earned result of generations of human toil that have converted the archipelago into one great forest preserve."[33] This toil was a response to vast deforestation that threatened all aspects of the country's health. Though large-scale loss of forests was not unique to the Edo period, such destruction was raised to a new level by the population and building booms engendered by the peace under Tokugawa rule. A ruinous trajectory that would impact soil stability and farmland was averted by regulations introduced nationally in the 1660s.[34] These led to the "Era of Man-made Forests" that included the first initiatives to guarantee replacement *hinoki* for the Ise Shrine's periodic rebuilding.[35]

With cities being the main wood consumers, forest regulations were part of the urban ecology, and that the period saw large-scale urbanization is a major part of its current appeal. By the early 1700s, Tokyo's population was approximately one million people, making it possibly then the world's largest city. Yet at the same time, it was one half-forested due to trees in places such as the gardens of temples, shrines, and well-to-do houses.[36] Urban building became much more standardized and resourceful, with secondary growth and sawn timber coming to predominate over old-growth logs. Rapidly renewable materials such as soft rush straw came to be used for tatami.

Recalling influences on NEXT21 and Flex Court Yoshida, it's illuminating that *kyo-ma ken* and *hadaka-gashi* are both Edo developments. These vernacular

top: Eisuke Ishikawa, *Japan in the Edo Period—An Ecologically-Conscious Society*, 2000

bottom: Kiyonori Kikutake, Edo-Tokyo Museum, perspectival section, 1988. Note that this section differs somewhat from the museum as built, which opened in 1993.

systems, which rearticulated artificial-land thinking from the 1970s onward, need to be seen in the historical context of a drive to create systems for a self-isolated country with limited natural resources. The market for repair and resale of standardized *kyo-ma* infill that arose is indeed only one example of a widespread culture of life-cycle consciousness. While *daiku* and related artisans took care of buildings, thousands of different repair and recycling businesses took care of everything else, serving all segments of society.[37] As for buildings, when they were demolished, their organic debris was dumped in government-designated areas of swamp, thereby also initiating the practice of land reclamation. By the late eighteenth century, over 1.2 million square meters had been reclaimed.[38]

The planning or consciousness of how materials and products would be made, used, and then digested for new purposes pervaded everyday life. It can be summarized in the attitude of *mottainai*, a word that encapsulates the ethos of the Edo period. The word for the Buddhist concept of intrinsic worth or dignity, *mottai*, when given the suffix *-nai*, implies a lack of respect for that worth.[39] To be *mottainai* was to be avoided, yet the term also signifies the philosophy and awareness of avoiding waste. In post-bubble Japan, the idea has come to signify a search for "affluence of the heart" that suggests the economic stagnation of the "Lost Decade" of the 1990s (and beyond) has in some ways been a positive time of rediscovery.[40] Ishikawa illustrates the proper Edo *mottainai* spirit with the life cycle of a traditional *yukata* robe: loose fitting, it could be handed down to multiple family members, going from a public robe to private pajamas once its cotton was sufficiently softened through use, later cut up to make diapers, then rags for cleaning floors, and at the end of its life, being tossed in the fire to heat bathwater.[41] An era with such a spirit may sound dour. But Edo coincided with a blossoming of the arts, from kabuki theater to the popularization of ikebana and woodblock prints to name a few, all best expressed in *ukiyo*, the decadent urban culture of the "floating world" in which Edo's classes mixed. Hedonism and sustainability can sometimes go together.

Japanologist Susan B. Hanley writes in *Everyday Things in Premodern Japan* that, in the mid-nineteenth century, Japanese life expectancy was higher than that of Western countries just before they experienced industrialization.[42] A balance was found between rising incomes that allowed greater consumption, and hence improved living conditions, and limitations so that there was no significant rise in pollution and disease as a consequence of unhealthy lifestyles due to overconsumption.[43] A key part of this physical health was also related to sanitation. As with the disposal of building scrap in designated areas, the collection of human sewage ("night soil") was also systematized. Trade in night soil for use as fertilizer, sold or bartered between urban landlords and rural farmers, provided organic nutrients for agriculture and also led, through its removal from the city, to extremely low levels of illness from cholera and other diseases caused by human sewage.[44]

The loss of the nutrient cycle between city and country is of course precisely what provoked Marx's description of a "rift in the interdependent process of social metabolism" in the part of *Capital* that we know Kawazoe read frequently.[45] Japan's night-soil trade, though dying at the time thanks to industrial synthetic fertilizers, could still be found in suburban areas of 1960s Tokyo and other cities, when the Metabolist movement was born.[46] This makes it tempting to speculate that Kawazoe, a historian deeply engaged in the politics of everyday life, knew that this Edo practice continued in some alleys, with it perhaps suggesting a combination of old and new societal models that might help heal the growing rifts in Japan's metabolism.[47] Turning to a Japanese approach to sewage appearing in the early twenty-first century, we find residues left after its treatment being used to make cement for concrete.[48] Night soil has been reconnected to the city as an ingredient for its construction.

Past as Policy

This metabolic sewage cycle is described in a 2008 report by MOE entitled *The World in Transition, and Japan's Efforts to Establish a Sound Material-Cycle Society.* Here we find a government ministry directly bringing Edo practices into the service of the present, with the authors writing that "Evidence from the Edo era strongly suggests that a sustainable society can be established," with the period seen to offer a "primitive" sound material-cycle (or SMC) ripe for adaptive reuse.[49] Another 2008 publication from MOE contains a manga in which the famous Edo-period artist Katsushika Hokusai takes people of the present day on a tour of the ecological intelligence of his era, introducing the ethic of *mottainai* and other approaches fit for a new SMC.

Also in 2008, the Diet passed the "Revision to the Fundamental Plan for Establishing an SMC," developed by MOE to further the law introduced in 2000 to systematically develop a low-carbon society.

The 200-year plan passed in 2008 is a facet of this objective. Calling for the creation of a durable "stock-based society"—a phrase at the center of the *hadaka-gashi* research that became the Two-Step Housing System and often heard in the SI context—MOE's revision assumes the widespread construction of 200-year housing, along with an increased use of mass timber in multistory buildings.[50] Through such measures, MOE strives for a revival of Edo environmental culture, including the wood that had historically supported it. The 200-year plan is a path toward Neo Edo.

A Futurist Vernacular

For sure, old Edo is hardly a perfect model. Its ecological success was dependent on a high level of social control, raising the threat of an ecofascism in which a selective sustainability is enforced by authoritarianism. But the value of backcasting, according to the environmental strategist Karl H. Dreborg, lies in the promotion of exploration and creative thinking in the present rather than total justification of a given scenario as a future solution.[51] Neo Edo is a renovation—not a restoration. Now sustainability, both environmental and social, needs to happen through democracy and collaboration. Looking to the grassroots culture of *machizukuri*, which grew out of citizen protests against pollution, bottom-up organization in Japan is already a significant force positively influencing local and national government. This influence should grow further, in Japan and beyond.

The architect John F. C. Turner observes that, similar to the way that Ise's longevity is rooted in culture more than construction, human institutions have more to do with the longevity of housing than building technologies.[52] He notes that the will of residents is crucial to the long-term success of any housing: residents need to be able to find fulfillment on their own terms. Housing therefore has to offer structures and environments that are receptive, leading to commitments to physical places.[53] Despite the truth of Turner's observation, construction techniques exist in inescapable feedback with the people they support, either well or poorly.

After the experience gained during its travels through Japan, the imported idea of artificial land has taken on new ideas that may be exported. There are various ways it may be "done," with some interpretations far more receptive than others. Without question, in its most full-blown, participatory form—as tested by Yosizaka in his yard, "found" at Sawaman, rehearsed by NEXT21, and realized at Tsunane—artificial land is a demanding endeavor that isn't for everyone. Kugahara's menu approach acknowledges this reality: maximizing the concept won't always be the right answer. Yet, as Gregory Bateson writes, in the complex environment of cities "We try to prohibit certain encroachments, but it might be more effective to encourage people to know their freedoms and flexibilities and to use them more often." He compares this effort to developing ourselves through physical exercise.[54] Architects and others can help create this awareness of freedoms in housing that stimulates rather than dictates, offering agency. This stimulation could also be called education. Whether enacted freedoms will have a lively result visible in a building's facades is negotiable rather than a requirement. Artificial land gives encouragement by suggesting ways to extend the Earth, now no longer wholly natural.

1 Noboru Kawazoe, "The Thirty Years of Metabolists," *Thesis, Wissenschaftliche Zeitschrift der Bauhaus-Universität Weimar* 6 (1997): 150. This essay was first published in Takenaka's journal *Approach* 116 (1991).

2 This is a folk quote of a command commonly received by myself and my colleagues while working at offices that appear in *El Croquis*.

3 Yositika Utida, *The Construction and Culture of Architecture Today: A View from Japan* (Tokyo: Ichigaya Publishing Co., 2002), 129.

4 Alex Kerr, *Dogs and Demons: Tales from the Dark Side of Japan* (New York: Hill & Wang, 2001), 227.

5 Yositika Utida, in conversation with the author, April 23, 2010. Translation by Hajime Yatsuka.

6 Philip Brasor, "The Japanese Art of Useless Homes," *Japan Times*, December 21, 2008, http://www.japantimes.co.jp/news/2008/12/21/national/media-national/the-japanese-art-of-useless-homes/#.VkteeL9terh.

7 Miles Colean, research director of the Federal Housing Administration, quoted in Robert D. Leighninger Jr., *Long-Range Public Investment: The Forgotten Legacy of the New Deal* (Columbia, SC: The University of South Carolina Press, 2007), 128.

8 Leighninger Jr., *Long-Range*, 128.

9 MLIT is a merger of MOC with several preexisting ministries: the Ministry of Transport, the Hokkaido Development Agency, and the National Land Agency.

10 See Kazunobu Minami, "The New Japanese Housing Policy and Research and Development to Promote the Longer Life of Housing," in *CIB W104 16th International Conference: Open and Sustainable Buildings* (2010): 2–3, PDF file.

11 While I'm uncertain of their status as 200-year certified, it's encouraging to see access floors in many of the recent housing projects featured in the "Living Together" issue of *The Japan Architect*, no. 111 (Autumn 2018).

12 Minami, "New Japanese," 5.

13 Minami, "New Japanese," 5.

14 See Kazunobu Minami, "The Development of Infill System for Long Life Housing in Japan," in *Proceedings of the 9th International Symposium on Architectural Interchanges in Asia* (2012): 1, PDF file.

15 Minami, "The Development," 2.

16 See Eiji Oizumi, "Transformations in Housing Construction and Finance," in *Housing and Social Transition in Japan*, eds. Yosuke Hirayama and Richard Ronald [2007] (New York: Routledge, 2012), 67.

17 Brasor, "Japanese Art."

18 Oizumi, "Transformations," 62, 68, 69.

19 Kazunobu Minami, in conversation with the author, May 14, 2014.

20 See Herman Kahn, *The Emerging Japanese Superstate: Challenge and Response* (Englewood Cliffs, NJ: Prentice-Hall, 1971).

21 John B. Robinson, "Futures Under Glass: A Recipe for People Who Hate to Predict," *Futures* 22, issue 8 (October 1990): 821. As Karl H. Dreborg notes, Robinson in fact credits the backcasting method (if not the term) to the physicist Amory Lovins. See Dreborg, "Essence of Backcasting," *Futures* 28, no. 9 (1996): 827.

22 Yasushi Umeda, Yusuke Kishita, and Tohru Morioka, "Framework of Future Vision, Scenario, and Roadmap," in *Establishing a Resource-Circulating Society in Asia: Challenges and Opportunities*, ed. Tohru Morioka et al. (Tokyo: United Nations University Press, 2011), 22.

23 Umeda, Kishita, and Morioka, "Framework of Future Vision," 23.
24 Eisuke Ishikawa, Ō-edo ecology jijō [Japan in the Edo-period—an ecologically-conscious society] (Tokyo: Kodansha Publishing, 2000), chap. 14. Note that this authorized English translation, by "Mr. Oki" and anonymous volunteers, appeared under "Sustainability in Edo (1603–1867)" (May 30, 2005), https://www.japanfs.org/en/edo/index.html. Italics added.
25 I am indebted to Susan B. Hanley for the idea of "physical well-being" as opposed to the more conventional economic metric of "standard of living." As Hanley describes in her book *Everyday Things in Premodern Japan*, physical well-being is more of a qualitative description based on physical historical evidence, while standard of living is usually gross domestic product divided by population, an approach that ignores issues like income distribution and quantity of unpaid labor. However, she also points out that physical well-being makes no claim to people's inner lives. See Susan B. Hanley, *Everyday Things in Premodern Japan: The Hidden Legacy of Material Culture* [1997] (Berkeley: University of California Press, 1999), 5–8.
26 Ishikawa, *Ō-edo ecology jijō*, chap. 1.
27 Habraken discusses this Renaissance drive to fresh creation with the elements of classical architecture particularly in the work of Palladio, who he sees as the archetype of the modern architect. See N. J. Habraken, *Palladio's Children* (New York: Taylor & Francis, 2005), 24–26.
28 See Jordan Sand's discussion of *Edogaku* in his *Tokyo Vernacular: Common Spaces, Local Histories, Found Objects* (Los Angeles: University of California Press, 2013), 21–22.
29 See Edward Seidensticker, *Low City, High City: Tokyo from Edo to the Earthquake* (New York: Alfred A. Knopf, 1983).
30 "Future-oriented nostalgia": see Eiko Maruko Siniawer, *Waste: Consuming Postwar Japan* (Ithaca, NY: Cornell University Press, 2018), 278.
31 Utida, *Construction*, 99.
32 Kikutake compared the museum to the Stratiform Structure Module, and it was in fact built on former property of Japanese National Railways. His desire for extensive glazing, a feature ultimately rejected by the exhibition planners, made schematic iterations of the design much more expressive of the artificial land concept than what was built. See Kiyonori Kikutake, *Edo Tōkyō Hakubutsukan* [Edo-Tokyo Museum] (Tokyo: Kajima Institute Publishing Co., Ltd., 1989), 135.
33 Conrad Totman, *The Green Archipelago: Forestry in Preindustrial Japan* (Berkeley: University of California Press, 1989), 1.
34 See Jared Diamond, *Collapse: How Societies Choose to Fail or Succeed* (New York: Penguin, 2006), 294–306.
35 Ishikawa, *Ō-edo ecology jijō*, chap. 5.
36 Ishikawa, *Ō-edo ecology jijō*, chap. 5.
37 See Ministry of the Environment, *The World in Transition and Japan's Efforts to Establish a Sound Material-Cycle Society* (2008), 33–34, PDF file.
38 See Ministry of the Environment, *World in Transition*, 31.
39 See Shuichi Yamamoto and Victor S. Kuwahara, "Influence of Nature, Policy and Thoughts on Environmental Ethics in Japan: Maintenance of the Forest and the Ecosystem in the Edo Period," *The Journal of Oriental Studies* 24 (2014): 64. Siniawer writes that *mottainai* has had multiple definitions over time, however, and cannot be reduced to a Buddhist origin. See Siniawer, *Waste*, 292.
40 "Affluence of the heart" and *mottainai*: see Siniawer, *Waste*, 278. As Siniawer points out, the former Prime Minister Junichiro Koizumi (in office 2001–2006) saw *mottainai* as a facet of national identity suited to the post-bubble period. See Siniawer, *Waste*, 298.
41 Ishikawa, *Ō-edo ecology jijō*, chap. 9.
42 Hanley, *Everyday Things*, 2.
43 Hanley, *Everyday Things*, 8.
44 See Ministry of the Environment, *World in Transition*, 24, 27.
45 "Rift": see page 93 of this book regarding Marx and Kawazoe, or Marx as quoted in John Bellamy Foster, *Marx's Ecology: Materialism and Nature* (New York: Monthly Review Press, 2000), 155.
46 See André Sorensen, *The Making of Urban Japan: Cities and Planning from Edo to the Twenty-First Century* (New York: Routledge, 2002), 41.
47 Regarding Kawazoe's engagement of the politics of everyday life, see Sand, *Tokyo Vernacular*, 117.
48 See Ministry of the Environment, *World in Transition*, 51.
49 See Ministry of the Environment, *World in Transition*, 1, 5.
50 "Stock-based society": see Ministry of the Environment, *World in Transition*, 14; 200-year housing and mass timber: see Ministry of the Environment, *Building a Low Carbon Society* (December 2007), 7, PDF file.
51 See Karl H. Dreborg, "Essence of Backcasting," *Futures* 28, no. 9 (1996): 819.
52 See John F. C. Turner, *Housing by People: Towards Autonomy in Building Environments* [1976] (London: Marion Boyars, 1991), 47.
53 Turner, *Housing by People*, 39.
54 Gregory Bateson, "Ecology and Flexibility in Urban Civilization," in *Steps to an Ecology of Mind* [1972] (Chicago: The University of Chicago Press, 2000), 511.

Appendix:
Mottainai Metabolism—
A New Artificial Land

This proposal layers a new artificial land on top of Sakaide's Phase 1 platform from 1968. The project makes use of the flexibility engineered into the original platform, which was designed to allow additional loading for future expansions, testing this engineering's capacity to help attract new residents and enhance urban vitality, both of which are aims of the *machizukuri* plan of Sakaide City. Another challenge for the city is sea-level rise, with safe land area in Sakaide anticipated to shrink over the coming decades. Against the dominant tendency in Japan of scrap-and-build, the new proposal embraces a *mottainai* attitude: it reuses and conserves Otaka's design as much as possible, both as a physical infrastructure and a social ambition. How can a new artificial land knit with the old to support density and diversity in a condition of population and land shrinkage? Should Otaka's artificial land be reconceived as an artificial island? Facing the necessity of adaptation, what would we like the future to look like?

Objectives:
1. Maximize use of the existing artificial land platform, testing the original Metabolist planning.
2. Minimize demolition of the existing concrete housing, partly through using some housing as "columns" to support a new publicly-owned skeleton structure above.
3. Attract new residents per the city's *machizukuri* plan by offering low-interest loans for building custom homes within the new skeleton.
4. Use mass-timber construction as much as reasonable.
5. Improve the existing apartments by renovating and combining to enlarge.
6. Offer existing residents impacted by the addition the choice of either relocating to renovated apartments or moving into new apartments in the addition, with the new units designed based on their needs and desires.
7. Selectively convert some existing apartments into commercial space to offer live/work opportunities, with priority for commercial rental given to residents within the project.
8. Plan for aging-in-place: add elevator access for all apartments and commercial spaces within or adjacent to the proposal.
9. Build a demonstration project for the national government's 200-year housing plan by making the addition durable and highly adaptable.
10. Extend Kagawa Prefecture's tradition of promoting creative culture, as seen with Tange, Noguchi, and Otaka in the 1950s and '60s, and today's Art Setouchi Triennale.

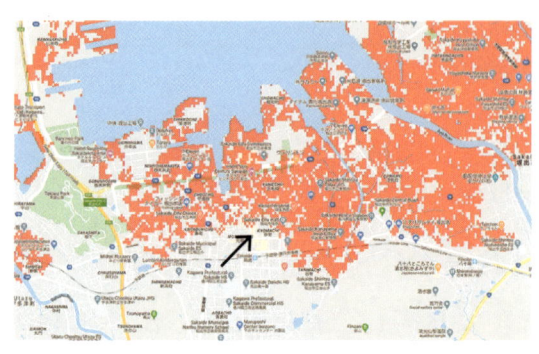

2030

2050

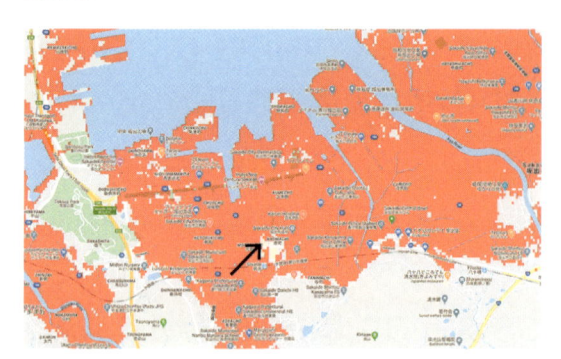

2070

■ Sakaide's projected sea-level rise + annual flooding, assuming moderate pollution cuts

Projection source: Kopp et al. 2014
Map source: www.climatecentral.org

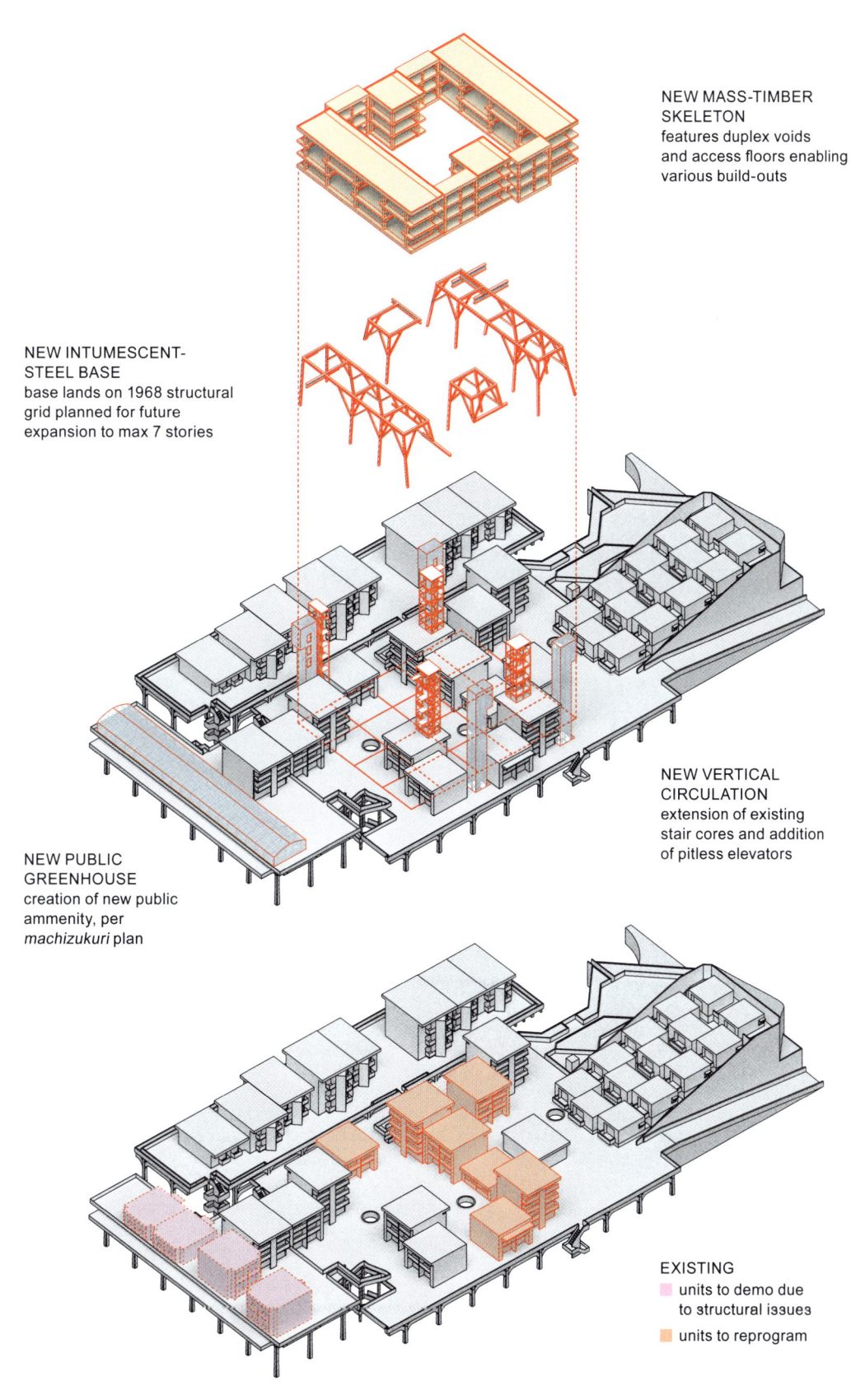

NEW MASS-TIMBER SKELETON
features duplex voids and access floors enabling various build-outs

NEW INTUMESCENT-STEEL BASE
base lands on 1968 structural grid planned for future expansion to max 7 stories

NEW VERTICAL CIRCULATION
extension of existing stair cores and addition of pitless elevators

NEW PUBLIC GREENHOUSE
creation of new public ammenity, per *machizukuri* plan

EXISTING
- units to demo due to structural issues
- units to reprogram

355

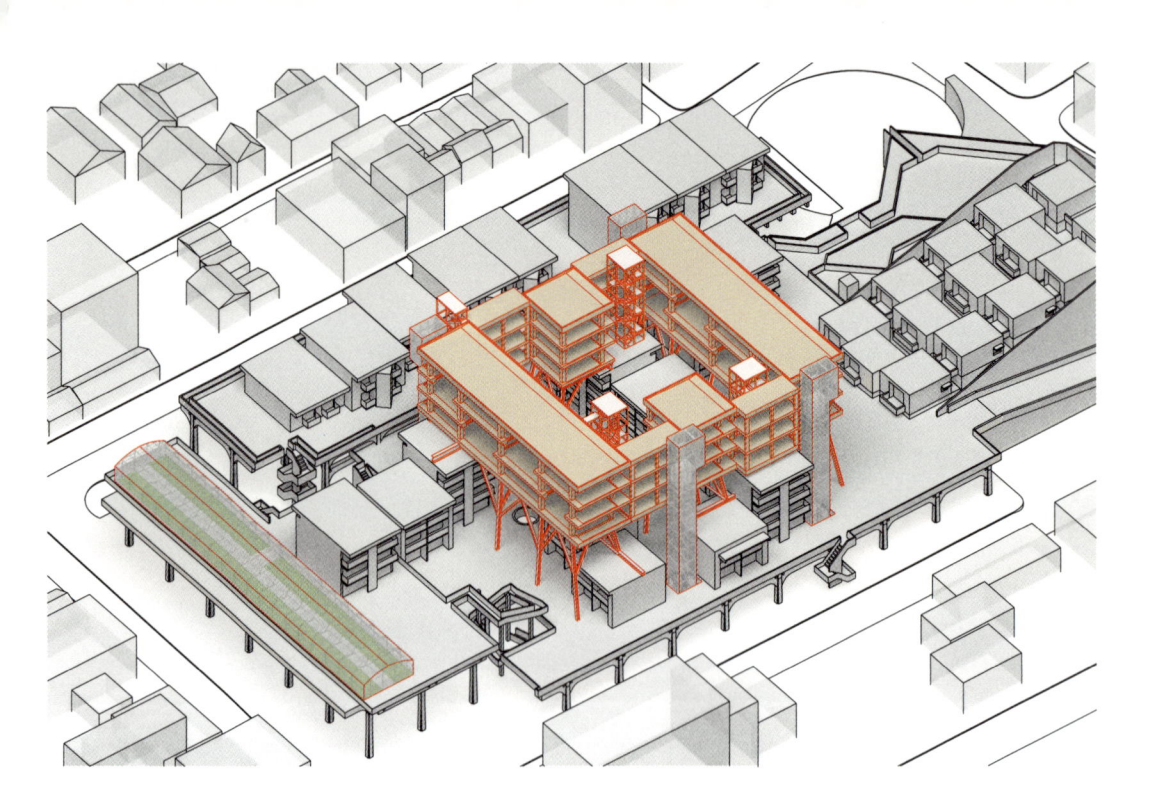

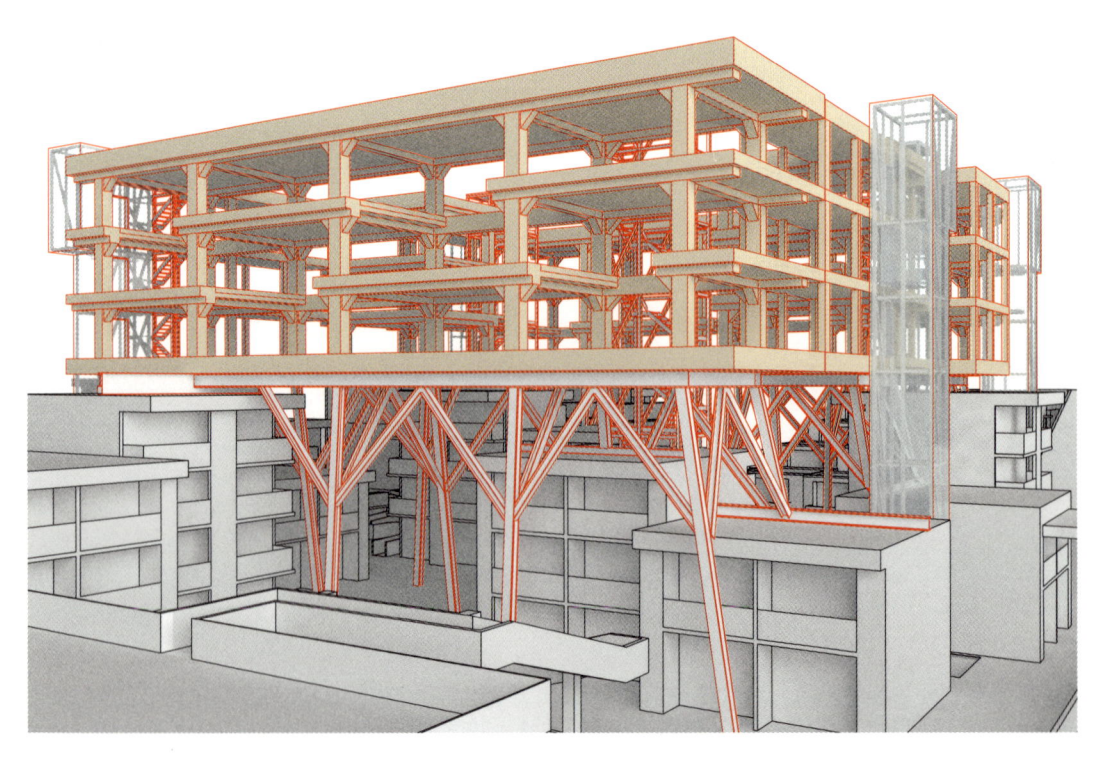

New skeleton, circulation, and greenhouse

356 APPENDIX: MOTTAINAI METABOLISM—A NEW ARTIFICIAL LAND

8

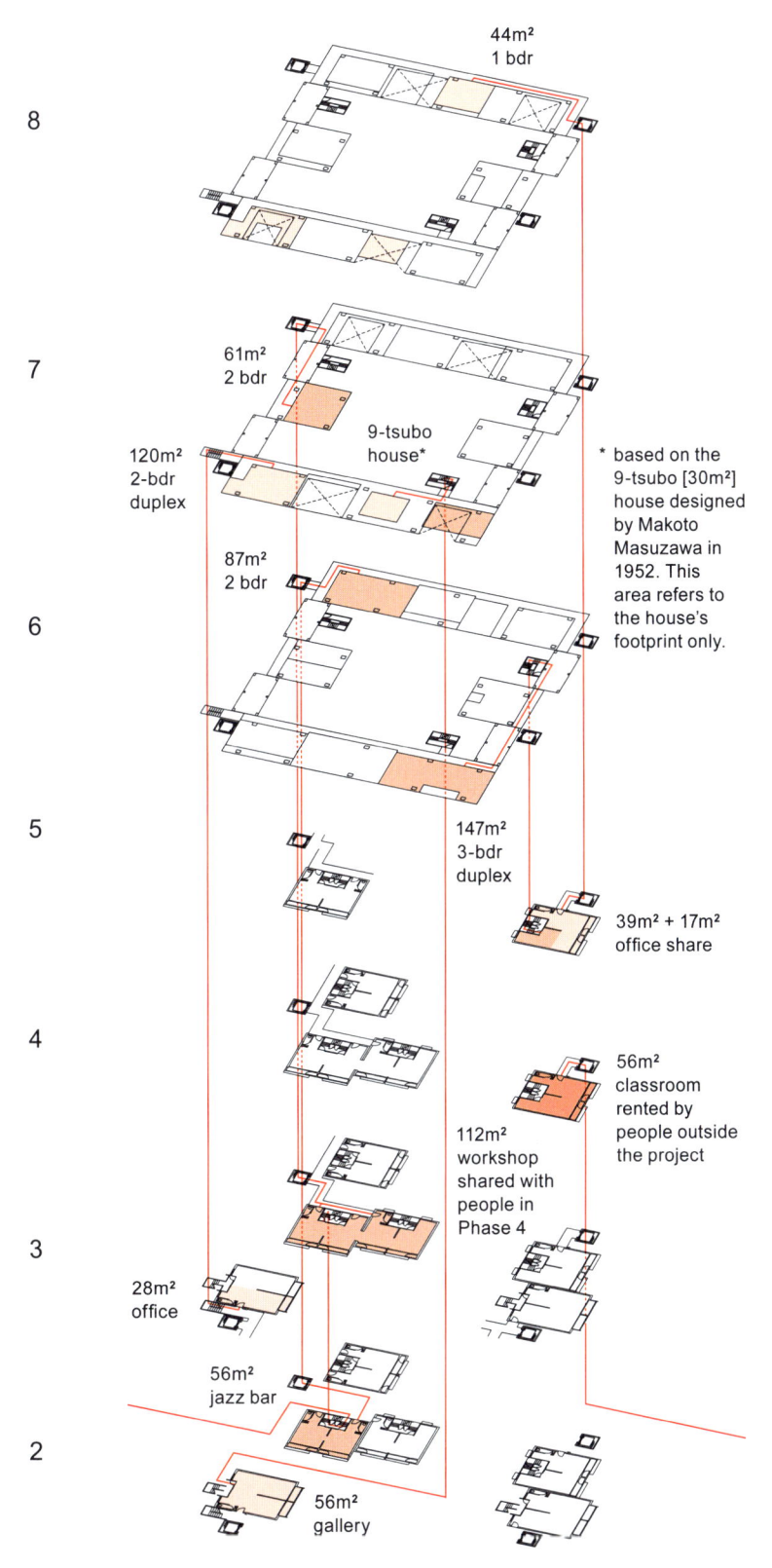

44m²
1 bdr

7

61m²
2 bdr

9-tsubo
house*

120m²
2-bdr
duplex

* based on the
9-tsubo [30m²]
house designed
by Makoto
Masuzawa in
1952. This
area refers to
the house's
footprint only.

87m²
2 bdr

6

5

147m²
3-bdr
duplex

39m² + 17m²
office share

4

56m²
classroom
rented by
people outside
the project

112m²
workshop
shared with
people in
Phase 4

3

28m²
office

56m²
jazz bar

2

56m²
gallery

Possible live/work scenarios

357

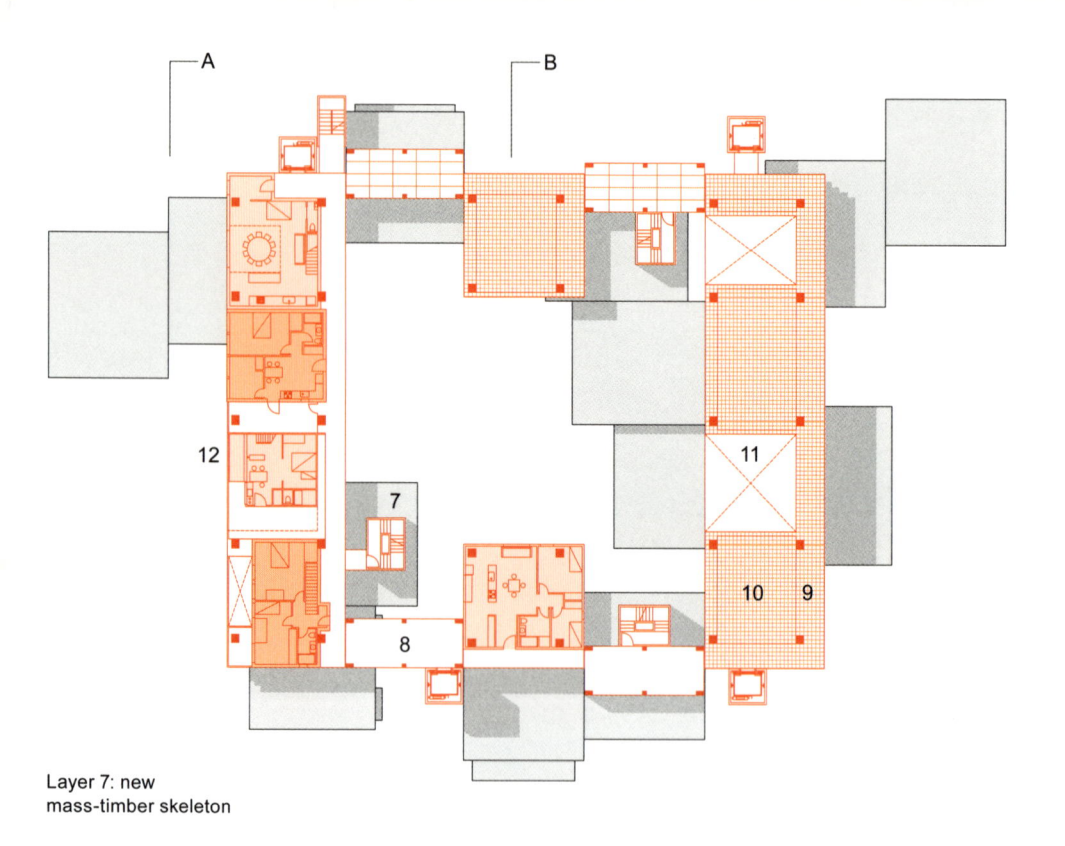

Layer 7: new
mass-timber skeleton

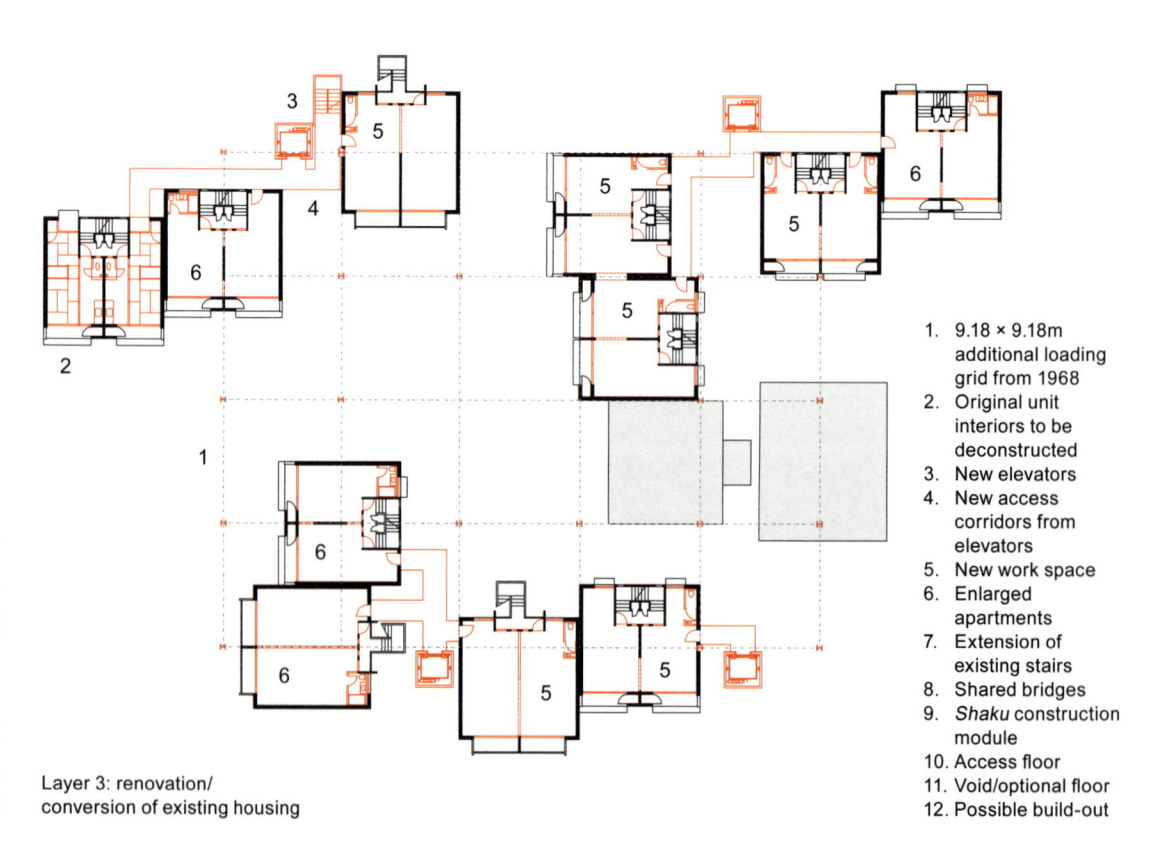

Layer 3: renovation/
conversion of existing housing

1. 9.18 × 9.18m additional loading grid from 1968
2. Original unit interiors to be deconstructed
3. New elevators
4. New access corridors from elevators
5. New work space
6. Enlarged apartments
7. Extension of existing stairs
8. Shared bridges
9. *Shaku* construction module
10. Access floor
11. Void/optional floor
12. Possible build-out

358　　　　　　　　　　　　APPENDIX: MOTTAINAI METABOLISM—A NEW ARTIFICIAL LAND

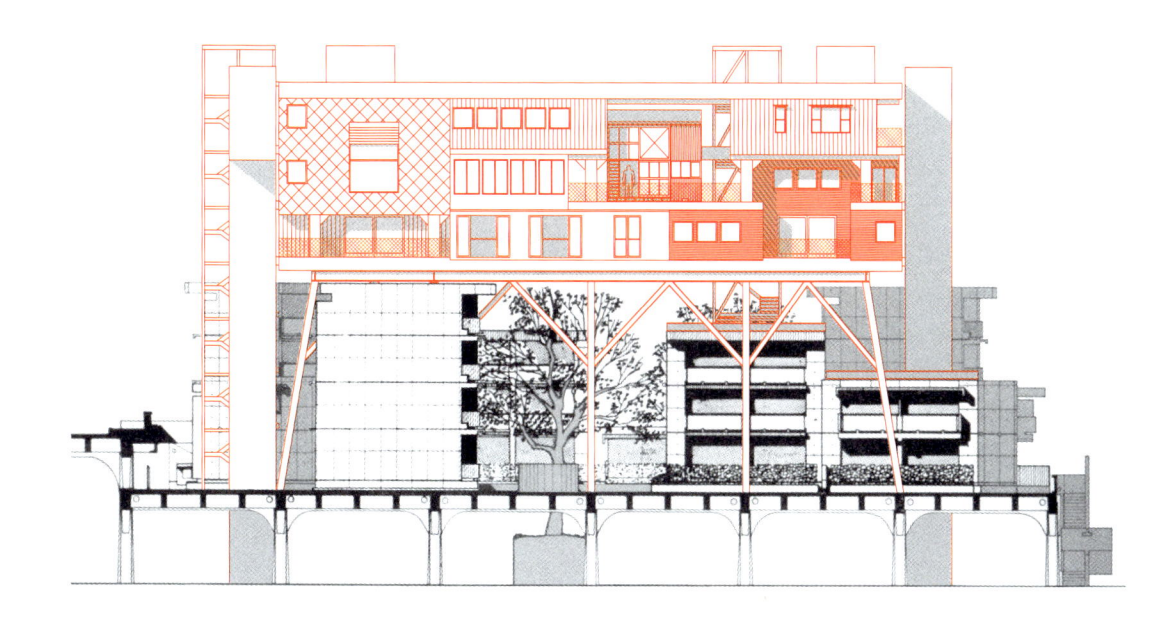

Elevation 'A' with
possible build-out

Section-elevation 'B'
with possible build-out

Team: Casey Mack,
Tomoyo Nakamura,
Anne Ketterer, Jun Sato
(structural advisor)

Index

Page numbers in italics indicate captions

A

A-Bomb Slum, *143*, 149, 156, *156*, 165
access floors, 199–200, *200*, 211, 218n14, 218n15, 262, 293, 310, 329, 339, 349n11, 358
ACROS Fukuoka Prefectural International Hall, *see* Ambasz, Emilio
Act for the Promotion of Long-Life Quality Housing, 338
adaptive reuse, 347
affordable housing, affordability, 52, 56, 69n10, 109, 208, 282, 310, 340
aging (of population), 166, 338, 340, 354
air rights, *see* New York City Zoning Resolution
Alexander, Christopher, 236, 245n1
Algiers (Algeria), 10–11, 13, 26–29, 200, 258–259
All About Sawada Mansion (Kagaya), 225–227, 232, 237–241, 245n18, 245n20
Allied (American) occupation, 43, *43*, 49, 91, 109, 153
Ambasz, Emilio, 211, *211*
Anderson, Chris, 39n38
Ando, Tadao, 204, 271
Antarctic base (Japanese), *see* Takenaka Corporation
Aoki, Shigeru (Lab), 115, 117, 159
Arcades des Anglais, *27–28*, *28–29*
Archigram, 23
Architectural Institute of Japan (AIJ), 108, 128n12, 253
Architecture Without Architects (Rudofsky), 224–225, 238, 245n6
artificial land, confusion caused by, 16, 20, 39n31, 263; definition of, 13, 19, 108, 117; megastructure, relationship to, 19, 119–125; skeleton/infill and support/infill, relationship to, 258–259, 287; sublimation of, 83, 263, 320. *See also* Artificial Land Committee; Le Corbusier; Metabolism (movement); *and* Yosizaka, Takamasa
Artificial Land Committee (ALC), 22, 108–113, 115, 117, 119–120, 128n12, 128n13, 138, 141n12, 180, 254, 271
Artificial Stone, 27, 38n23. *See also* concrete
ARX Architects, *317*, 326, *326*, 329, 332. *See also* Kugahara House
Asada, Takashi, 22, 83, *92*, 108, 111, 128n12, 156, 200
Asahi Shimbun, The, 177, 334n2
Asano, Tadatoshi, 183, 189, 211, 219n40, 287, 335n29
Ashihara, Yoshinobu, 325
Ashiyahama Seaside Town, *see* Ashiyahama Shin'nittetsu Takenaka Matsushita

Ashiyahama Shin'nittetsu Takenaka Matsushita (ASTM), *131*, 175n21, 177, *177*, 180, 183, 186, 189, 193; Ashiyahama Seaside Town, *131*, 175n21, 177, *177*, 180, *180*, 189–190, 193n2, 193n12, 193n13, 193n14, 193n22, 195, 208, 238, 248, 254, 259, 310
Aspdin, Joseph, 38n23
asthma (from pollution), 135, 219n34
Atlas Portland Cement Company, 27, 38n23
atomic bomb, 132, *143*, 149, 153, 156, 165, 174n1, 174n2, 174n8
Awazu, Kiyoshi, 22, 83, *92*, *337*

B

backcasting, 341, *342*, 348, 349n21
Bakema, Jaap, 265n71
Ball, Stuart S., 108, 127n8
Ban, Toshiaki, 304, 306–307, 309–310, *310*, 315n21
Banham, Reyner, 19, 25, 36, 38n22, 38n23, 125, 127, 129n46, 257
barracks (improvised housing), 43, *43*, 44, 46, *46*, 48, 56, 174n1
Bateson, Gregory, 349
Bertalanffy, Ludwig von, 254
Big Five (general contractors), 137, 141n26
Bing, Francis C., 103n53, 123
birth rates, 166, 274, 340
Branchera Suita Katayamakoen and Branchera Urawa, *see* Haseko Corporation
Brand, Stewart, 232, 261, *261*
Brasor, Philip, 338, 340
Breuer, Marcel, 94
Brutalism, 37
bubble economy, 94, 141n26, 250–251, 267, 270–271, 274, 326, 346, 350n40
Buchli, Victor, 77
Buddhism, 20, 245n12, 346, 350n39
Buddhist economics, 225, 232, 245n10
Building Center of Japan (BCJ), 180, 193n14, 315n23
Building in France, Building in Iron, Building in Ferroconcrete (Giedion), 320
Building a New Japan (Tanaka), 136, *136*, 141n21, 195, 198, 208, 259

C

Cairo (Egypt), 221
capacity planning, 274, 282
Century Housing System (CHS), 259, 261–263, 271, 274, 278, 281, 287, 304, 329, 338–339
Chikazumi, Shinichi, 271, 285n13, 294, 299n16
Chojuen Apartments, *see* Otaka, Masato
City in the Air, *see* Isozaki, Arata

Congrès Internationaux d'Architecture Moderne (CIAM), 25, 55, 82, 102n28, 257, 265n50
Charter of Athens, 25, 38n16
cooperative (co-op) housing, 270, 282, *282*, 285, 301, *301*, 304, 307, 309–310, 314, 315n6, 315n19, 315n22, 315n33
closed system, 254, 257
Code Napoléon, 108, 127n5, 127n6
cogeneration, cogen, 281, *281*
cohousing, 301, 304, 310, 315n6
Cohousing: A Contemporary Approach to Housing Ourselves (McCamant and Durrett), 301, 304, 310, 315n6
"Collective Form—Three Paradigms" (Maki and Ohtaka), see *Investigations in Collective Form* under Maki, Fumihiko
Commissioners' Plan (Manhattan), 33
concrete, 38n22, 45, 55–56, 58, *58*, 71, 74–75, 78, 81, 109, 111, 117, 190, 257, 261–262, 271, 309, 326, *326*, 347; monolithic (site-cast, cast-in-place), 36, 139, 173, 199, 224, 250, 310, 323, 325, 334n13; and Portland cement, 27, 38n23; precast, 159, 173, 183, 186, 190, 193n16, 199, *317*, 320–321, 323, 325–326, 329; reinforced concrete (ferroconcrete), 27, 38n23, 74, *96*, 221, 232, 245n18, 257, 265n65, 271, 317, 339; steel-reinforced concrete (SRC), 74, *75*; wood, comparison to, 78, 317, 320–321, 323, 325, 329, 333
Concrete Atlantis, A (Banham), 38n22, 38n23
construction state, 248, 264n9, 339
continuous customization, 294, 329
cross-laminated timber (CLT), see timber (wood) construction

D
Daikin, 294
daiku (carpenter), 45, 56, 139, 323, 346
danchi (group land), 51, 135, 198, 304
developmental state, 132–133, 136, 138, 159, 304
Debate on Tradition, 77, 83
decision-making (by residents), 190, 193, 258, 287, 309
Deconstructivism, 37
Delany, Samuel R., 20
Delft University of Technology, 258
Delirious New York (Koolhaas), 16, 20
Department of Defense (US), 137
design-build, 37, 56, 137, 200, 225, 232
Dewitt Chestnut Apartments, see Skidmore, Owings & Merrill
Dialectics of Nature (Engels), 83
digestion (and Metabolism), 37, 247, 262, 294, 346

Disney World, 205
Dobbins, Michael, 205, 219n30
Docomomo, 119, 128n36, 218n21
do-it-yourself (DIY), 94, 103n66, 139, 224, 232, 261, 290, 293, 298, 299n6, 309
Dojunkai, 71, 74, 108, 253
Dom-ino House, see Le Corbusier
Dower, John, 91
Dreborg, Karl H., 348, 349n21
Durrett, Charles, see *Cohousing*

E
Edo (era), 255, 261, 293, 298, 338, 343–348, *345*, 350n24
Edogaku (Edo studies), 343
Edo-Tokyo Museum, see Kikutake, Kiyonori
Eisenhower, Dwight D., 140
Ekuan, Kenji, 22, 83
embodied energy, 200, 251, 262, 287
Embracing Defeat (Dower), 91
Endo, Shokan, 69n20
Engel, Heino, 255, 264n40
Engels, Friedrich, 83, 91, 93, 103n55
Enterprises Rationalization Promotion Law, 132, 137
Everyday Things in Premodern Japan (Hanley), 346, 350n25
Expo '70, 131, 138, *139*, 141n28, 177
Expo 67, 325

F
Ferriss, Hugh, 127n4
firebombing (of Tokyo), 43, *43*, 45
Flex Court Yoshida, 287, 290, *290*, 293–294, *293*, *294*, *297*, 298, 299n7, 299n8, 299n9, 299n16, 329, 332, 345
flexibility, 23, 75, 111, 115, 117, 125, 173, 199–200, 252, 254, 262, 270, 274, 281–282, 287, 298, 304, 329; and parametricism, 26, 117, 128n32, 255; and polyvalency, 25–26, 38n21
Floor Area Ratio (FAR), see New York City Zoning Resolution
Ford, Edward R., 36
forecasting, 304, 341
Fort l'Empereur, see Le Corbusier
Foster, John Bellamy, 91, 103n53, 103n55
Frampton, Kenneth, 218n25, 262
Friedman, Yona, 16, *16*
Fuji, Mount, 205, 211
Fujimoto, Masaya, 115, 128n31, 153, 159, 162, 165, 173, 174n1
Fujimoto, Sou, 251
Fukao, Seichi, 250, 271, 274
Fukuda, Yasuo, 338
Fukushima, 253, 285n4
Fuller, Buckminster, 94, 208; livingry, idea of, 138–139, *140*, 153, 159, 173; Wichita House, 138–139, *140*
Future City on the Sea (Satoh), 189

G
ganko (flying geese) formation, 162, *162*
Garden City, see Howard, Ebenezer
Giedion, Sigfried, 125, 129n47, 320
Gilbert, Cass, 105, 109, 127n1
Ginzburg, Moisei, 71, 77, *77*. See also transitional type
Good Fast Cheap triangle, 186
Gotemba (Japan), *195*, 205, 211, *211*, 219n35
Government Housing Loan Corporation (GHLC), 56, 58, 66, 203
Gordon, Alexander, 285n14
Gottmann, Jean, 123, 136
Graham Foundation for Advanced Studies in the Fine Arts, 83
Grand Central Terminal, 109, 127, 128n13
Great Kanto Earthquake, 44, 45–46, *46*, 71, 74, 343
Green Archipelago, The (Totman), 345
group form, 22, 90, 103n42, 120, 162, 165, 262, 271, 293

H
Habitat 67, see Safdie, Moshe
Habraken, John, 16, 190, 221, 224, 257–258, 263, 265n52, 265n55, 265n59, 265n71, 274, 282, 287, 293, 299n8, 309, 341, 350n27; Japan, influence in, 248, *253*, 258–259, 270
Hachinohe, Yasuke, see Aoki, Shigeru
Hachioji (Japan), 97
hadaka-gashi (bare rental), 255, 261, 264n44, 265n63, 290, 293, 298, 332, 345, 348
Hanley, Susan B., 346, 350n25
Hara, Hiroshi, 264n3, 265n68
Harada, Shizuo, 69n16, 198, 200, 208, 211, 218, 218n1, 219n44
Harumi Apartments, see Maekawa, Kunio
Harumi Island, 71, 74, 86
Harvard University, 83, 123
Haseko Corporation, 339, *341*
Hertzberger, Herman, 25, 38n21
HEXA Architects, 282, *282*, 301
hibakusha (explosion-suffering people), 149, 174n1
Hillside Terrace, see Maki, Fumihiko
Highrise of Homes, see SITE
Higuchi, Kenji, *135*
hinoki (Japanese cypress), 317, 320–321, 345
Hirayama, Yosuke, 38n15, 117
Hiroshima (Japan), *143*, 149, *149*, 153, 156, 159, 162, *165*, 173, 174n1, 174n2, 174n8, 175n18, 175n28, 183, 321, *323*
Hiroshima Housing Authority (HHA), 173, 175n27, 175n28

361

Hokusai, Katsushika, 347
home ownership, 38n15, 56–57, 108–109, 115, 127, 127n5, 135, 203, 274, 293, 298, 307
Hong Kong (China), 119
Howard, Ebenezer, 31, 39n30, 39n31, 57, 103n55, 314, 315n33
Housing Development for Creating Value in Our Lifestyles Project (House Japan), 287
Housing in Postwar Japan (Waswo), 53n15, 141n5
housing shortage (in postwar Japan), 43, 55, 66, 74, 156, 248
Hudson Yards, 119, 218n13
Hundertwasser House, 315n19
Hyogo Prefecture (Japan), 177, 183

I
IBM, 199
Ickes, Harold, 338
Ikeda, Hayato, 94, 132, 136, 141n20
imperialism (Japanese), 91, 159
inaka-ma ken (column distance in countryside measurement), 255, *257*
incentive zoning, see New York City Zoning Resolution
Income Doubling Plan, 94, 131, 139
informal (bottom-up), 165, 193n28, 221, 245n3, 245n18
International Design Conference (Aspen, Colorado), 82
Investigations in Collective Form, see Maki, Fumihiko
Ise Shrine, 175n10, 317, 320–321, *321*, 323, 334, 334n9, 334n10, 334n11, 345, 348
Ise: Prototype of Japanese Architecture (Tange and Kawazoe), 265n46, 317, 334n2, 334n10
Isomura, Eiichi, 123
Isozaki, Arata, 37, 137, 175n16, 175n18, 218n25; City in the Air, 153, 174n7; Joint Core System, 180, *180*
Ishikawa, Eisuke, 342–343, 345–346, *345*, 350n24
Italy, 343
Ito, Toyo, 204, 219n26
Itoh, Teiji, 38n5, 78, 162

J
Japan Architect, The, 77, 89. See also *Shinkenchiku*
Japan in the Edo Period—An Ecologically-Conscious Society (Ishikawa), 343, *345*, 350n24
Japan Housing Corporation (JHC), 51, 56, 71, 74, 97, 131–132, 135, 141n5, 141n13, 183, 198, 254, 258, 301
Japan Sinks (Komatsu), 131, 140n1
Japan Times, The, 338
Japanese National Railways, 208, 219n41, 350n32

Jencks, Charles, 177, 193n1
Johnson, Chalmers, 132, 137, 141n7, 141n8, 141n20, 141n33
Joint Core System, see Isozaki, Arata
jinko tochi (artificial land), 20, 117, 125
jukyo-gaku (dwelling studies), 51

K
Kagaya, Tetsuro, 225, *227*, 232, 238, *238*, 245n18, 245n20
Kahn, Herman, 341
Kahn, Louis, 82
Kaneko, Masanori, 111, 128n24
Kaneko, Yujiro, 259
Kano, Hisaakira, 71, 74, 82, 86, 102n4
Kansai region, 255, 267, 298
Katsura Imperial Villa, 162, *162*, 175n16
Kawakami, Hidemitsu, 108–109, 127n10, 128n12
Kawaramachi Housing, see Otani, Sachio
Kawazoe, Noboru, 22, 43, 53n10, 77, 115, 225, 247, 257, 264n1, 265n46, 317, 321, 334n2, 337, 349n1; Debate on Tradition, 77, 83; Expo '70 planning, 131; Harumi Apartments, review of, 71, 81, 97; Marxist influence on, 83, 91, 93–94, 343, 347, 350n45, 350n47; Metabolism, formation of, 82–83, *92*, 102n31, 103n63; as operative critic, 23, 38n12; *Shinkenchiku* editorship, 77, 83, 102n29; Sunday carpenter, idea of, 94, 103n66, 298; at Waseda University, 91, 103n51. See also *Ise: Prototype of Japanese Architecture* and Metabolic rift
Kenchiku bunka, 86
Kenchiku Kankyo Kenkyujo, *287*, 293. See also Flex Court Yoshida
Kenmochi, Isamu, 82
Kenzo Tange and the Metabolist Movement (Lin), 102n31, 141n28, 174n3
Kepes, Gygöry, 125
Kerr, Alex, 218n1, 264n9, 337
Khan, Fazlur, 333
Khrushchev, Nikita, 75
khrushchevka (housing type), 75
Kiichi, Miyazawa, 250
Kikutake, Kiyonori, 57, 69n20, 137–138, 195, *195*, 198, 200, 208, 211, *211*, 218, 219n26, 236, 254; Bridgestone, work with, 320; Edo-Tokyo Museum, 345, *345*, 350n32; Izumi Shrine Administration Building, 325; Metabolism, formation of, 22, 83, *92*; Sky House, 23, 38n10, 69n18, 83, 162; Stratiform Structure Module, 195, *195*, 198–200, *199–200*, 204–205, 208, 211, *211*, 218, 218n15, 219n35, 219n36, 236, 254, 262, 267, 271, 287, 309, 315n19, 329, 341, 350n32;

Tower-Shaped Community, 89, 102n28; at Waseda University, 91, 103n51
Kimo, Midori, 281, 285n16
Kimura, Toshihiko, 125; Artificial Land Committee, participation in, 108, 111, 115; Chojuen Apartments, 159; Harumi Apartments, 74–75, 123; Kunio Maekawa, work with, 74, *75*; NEXT21, 271; Tochigi Prefectural Council Building, 325. See also major-structure and minor-structure
Klein, Alexander, 49, *51*, 61
Kochi (Japan), *221*, 224, 232, 238
Kofu (Japan), 323, *325*
Kokusai kenchiku, 55, 66
Komatsu, Sachiko, 175n28
Komatsu, Sakyo, 131, 140n1
Kon, Wajiro, 43, 46, *46*, 48, 51–52, 53n8, 53n10, 53n18, 94, 245n6, 245n20, 250, 309
Koo, Richard, 251–252
Koolhaas, Rem, 16, 20, 91, 93, 102n27, 102n31, 129n48, 141n21, 141n30, 174n3, 218n3, 267
Korea, Koreans, 43, 53n8, 149, 174n1
Kowloon Walled City, *7*, 224
K-Project, see Maki, Fumihiko
Kurakata, Shunsuke, 61
Kure Naval Arsenal, 159
Kurokawa, Kisho, 83, *92*, 102n28, 138; Agricultural City, 89; Helix City, 153; Metabolism, formation of, 22–23; Nakagin Capsule Tower, 23, *25*, 89, 190, 247, 264n14; Toshiba IHI Pavilion, *139*, 141n28
kyo-ma ken, 255, 257, *257*, 261–262, 264n40, 265n46, 265n63, 278, 345–346
Kyoto (Japan), 162, 255, 264n40, 343
Kyoto University, 259, 265n60
Kugahara House, 317, *317*, 320, 329, *329*, *331–332*, 332–334, 338, 349
Kumagai Gumi, 141n26, 153

L
Land Readjustment (LR), 109
land reclamation, 16, 74, 180, 264n9, 346
Language of Post-Modern Architecture, The (Jencks), 177, 193n1
Le Corbusier, 45, 51, 53n19, 74, 94, 109, 117, 175n27, 262, 281; Algiers, influence of, 28–29, *28*; artificial land concept, origins of, *11*, 22, 27, 38n23, 128n13; Centrosoyuz, 77; Chandigarh, 52; Dom-ino House, 28, 58, 221, 263; Fort l'Empereur, *11*, 13, 16, 19, 27, 29, 31, *31–32*, 33, *35*, 36, 57, 77, 108, 125, 166, 200, 204, 338; Ebenezer Howard, influence of, 31, 39n30, 57, 103n55, 314; Masions Jaoul, 52; *Le Modulor*, 53n19, 265n49; Narkomfin Communal

House, influence of, 71, 77, 102n10, 102n11; National Museum of Western Art, 69n26; *Radiant City, The*, 11, 33, 38n23, 56, 69n4; "sun, space, and greenery," pursuit of, 31, 39n30, 281; Tokyo visit, 66, 67; Unité d'Habitation Marseilles, 32, 35, 36, 52, 52, 71, 77, 102n3, 265n49; Unité d'Habitation Nantes-Rezé, 52; vertical garden city, as critique of Howard, 31, 31, 117, 314. See also artificial land; Maekawa, Kunio; Sakakura, Junzo; and Yosizaka, Takamasa

Leighninger Jr., Robert D., 338
Le Ricolais, Robert, 294
Liebig, Ludwig von, 91–94, 103n55
life cycle, 23, 25, 83, 115, 190, 254, 261, 320–321, 346
life span (of buildings), 248, 261, 265n65, 329, 334, 337
life span (of humans), 166
Lin, Zhongjie, 102n31, 141n28, 174n3
Lingotto Fiat factory, 28
Lissitzky, El, 109
"Lives of Systems" (Habraken), 190, 193n29, 221, 224
livingry, 138–139, 153, 173, 205
long life, loose fit, low energy (motto), 278
long tail, 36–37, 37, 39n38
Lost Decade, 94, 346
Low City, High City (Seidensticker), 343
Lower Manhattan Expressway plan, 205, 208

M

machiya (townhouse), 77–78
machizukuri (town-making), 252–253, 259, 270, 301, 348, 353–354
Maekawa, Kunio, 69n26, 74, 75, 125, 159; "elastic space," search for, 74; Harumi Apartments, 71, 71, 74–75, 81–83, 81–82, 86, 93–94, 95, 97, 97, 102n3, 115, 119, 123, 128n23, 132, 137, 159, 162, 165–166, 180, 189–190, 195, 208, 247, 252, 267, 271, 294, 298, 304, 309–310, 325, 333; Le Corbusier, work with, 77; Metabolism, opinion on, 91, 94; Narkomfin Communal House, comparison to Harumi, 77, 77. *See also* Otaka, Masato; Kimura, Toshihiko; major-structure; *and* minor-structure
major-structure, 74–75, 97, 123, 159, 159, 173, 183, 271, 325. *See also* megastructure *and* minor-structure
Maki, Fumihiko, 22, 102n28, 128n35, 218n25; Artificial Land Committee, participation in, 108, 111, 119, 129n38, 254; Ashiyahama Seaside Town, advice on, 180; Graham Foundation Fellowship, 83; and group form, 90, 103n42, 120, 162; Hillside Terrace, 119; *Investigations in Collective Form*, 19, 120, 120, 125, 137, 141n25, 162; K-Project, 125; Metabolism, formation of, 83, 90, 90, 92, 103n42; Masato Otaka, collaborations with, 90, 90, 103n42, 129n48, 162, 180; megastructure, defintion of, 120, 123, 125, 129n49, 258; in *Megastructure* (Banham), 19, 125; in *Space, Time and Architecture* (Giedion), 125; Shinjuku Station proposal, 90, 90; Takenaka family, marriage into, 137, 141n25. *See also* group form *and* megastructure
Making of Urban Japan, The (Sorensen), 135, 140n3, 141n12, 193n10, 218n2, 219n39, 264n17
mansion (condominium), 208, 232
Marx, Karl, 245n12; *Capital*, 93, 347; Japan, postwar influence in, 91; Ludwig von Liebig, influence of, 91–92, 103n55; on metabolism, 91–94, 232; work day, shortening of, 94. *See also* Kawazoe, Noboru; Marx's Ecology; *and* metabolic rift
Marx's Ecology: Materialism and Nature (Foster), 91, 103n53, 103n55, 350n45
Massachusetts Institute of Technology (MIT), 16, 83, 86, 89, 259, 265n59, 299n8
mass customization, 203, 255, 282
mass timber, *see* timber (wood) construction
Matsuie, Masaru, 326
Matsushita, 177, 186, 265n63, 294
Matta-Clark, Gordon, 97
Matté-Trucco, Giacomo, 28
maximum dwelling, 55, 57, 69n10, 71, 81, 247, 290
McCamant, Kathryn, see *Cohousing*
Mechanical Social Systems Foundation, 195, 208
megalopolis, 123, 198
Megalopolis: The Urbanized Northeastern Seaboard of the United States (Gottmann), 123, 136
megastructure, 16, 19–20, 22, 120, 123, 125, 127, 129n49, 180, 189–190, 258
Megastructure (Banham), 19, 36, 38n22, 125, 129n46
Meiji (era), 127n6, 338
metabolic rift, 91, 93–94, 103n55, 140, 343, 347, 350n45
metabolism (biological and social/technical), 83, 91–94, 103n53, 123, 173, 173, 190, 238, 254, 278, 293, 320–321, 347. See also *Marx's Ecology*
Metabolism (movement), 38n9, 43, 69n18, 77, 108, 127, 136, 149, 153, 193, 200, 204–205, 218n25, 219n26, 224, 238, 247–248, 252–254, 257, 262–263, 264n9, 264n14, 265n46, 271, 320, 325, 329, 333–334, 337, 341, 349n1; Archigram and Team 10, comparison to, 23; and artficial land, 22–23, 86, 89–90; long tail of, 37, 37; and Marxism, 91, 93–94; members, 22, 36–37; members, differences, 91, 119, 205; *Metabolism/1960* book, 89, 91, 103n42; origin of name, 83; formation and debut, 71, 82–83, 85, 86, 89–91, 92, 102n27, 120, 342, 347; "swan song" of the movement, 138, 141n28, 177, 180; and two cycles of change, 23, 25, 83, 97, 115, 117, 140, 190. See also metabolic rift *and* metabolism (biological and social/technical)
Metabolism—The City of the Future (exhibition and catalog), 103n41, 129n47
Metabolist-industrial complex, 139–140, 177, 189, 200, 224, 238, 248, 264n9, 338
Middleton, Robin, 127
Mie Prefecture (Japan), 317
Mies van der Rohe, Ludwig, 26, 105, 127n4
military-industrial complex (US), 140
Minami, Kazunobu, 259, 263, 264n7, 335n42, 341
minimum dwelling, 25, 48–49, 56–57, 66, 69n10, 69n13, 247–248
Ministry of Construction (MOC), 37, 108, 132, 138, 141n8, 180, 193, 200, 203, 208, 248, 259, 261, 281, 326, 337, 339, 343, 349n9
Ministry of the Environment (MOE), 326, 347–348
Ministry of International Trade and Industry (MITI), 37, 82, 132, 136–138, 141n7, 141n8, 141n20, 141n21, 141n33, 195, 198–200, 203, 208, 211, 218n2, 218n3, 250, 287, 337
Ministry of Land, Infrastructure, Transportation, and Tourism (MLIT), 339–340, 349n9
minka (houses of the people), 46, 48, 78, 78, 94, 245n20, 262, 309, 329
minor-structure, 74–75, 77, 78, 83, 97, 125, 173, 252, 262
Misawa Homes, 200, 203, 218n20
MITI and the Japanese Miracle (Johnson), 132, 141n7, 141n8, 141n20, 141n33
Mitsubishi, 138, 299n7
Miyagi Prefecture (Japan), 218
Miyazaki, Motoo, 66
modernology, 53n10, 245n20
modular coordination, 203, 254, 258, 278
modularity, 149, 255, 258, 278, 281
Molenvliet (housing), 270, 271
moment frame, 159
Montreal (Canada), 26, 325
Mori, Minoru, 117, 119, 128n35

363

Mori Museum, *85*, 119, 129n47
Motomachi Apartments, see Otaka, Masato
mottainai (disrespect of worth), 346–347, 350n39, 350n40, 352
Munitions Ministry, 132

N
Nagoya (Japan), 133, 340
Nakagin Capsule Tower, see Kurokawa, Kisho
Nakasone, Yasuhiro, 250–251
Nakasuji, Osamu, 282
Nara Prefecture (Japan), 301, *301*, 304
Narkomfin Communal House, see Ginzburg, Moisei
National Association for the Promotion of Cooperative Housing, 301
National Diet, 78, 141n20, 301, 326, 338, 347
Neoliberalism, 25, 38n15, 250, 252
New City Planning Law, 136
New Urbanism, 257, 265n50
New Wave (Japanese architects), 204, 218n25
New York City Zoning Resolution (1961), 105, 108, 109; air rights, 109, 128n12; Floor Area Ratio (FAR), 105, 128n12, 128n23; incentive zoning, 105, 127n4
NEXT21 Experimental Housing, see Osaka Gas
Nieuwenhuys, Constant, 16, *16*
night soil (human sewage), 92, 103n55, 347
Nikkenkei Open Housing System (NOHS), 325–326, *326*, 329, 333–334
Nishiyama, Uzo, 48–49, 51, 53n17, 53n18, 245n20, 265n60
Nitschke, Günter, 252, 262
nLDK system, 48, 53n17
Noguchi, Isamu, 111, 128n24, 354
noka (farmhouse), 77–78

O
OAPEC, 138, 177
Obayashi Corporation, 141n26, 271
Obrist, Hans Ulrich, 91, 93, 102n27, 102n31, 129n48, 141n21, 141n30, 174n3, 218n3
obsolescence, 23, 83, 140, 180, 248, 251, 301, 338
Ohno, Katsuhiko, 203, *203*
oil embargo (1973), 138, 177
Oizumi, Eiji, 339–340
Okamura, Koichiro, 323
Ökohaus, see Otto, Frei
Olympics, Tokyo (1964), 135, 342
Open Building, 265n52
open systems (biological), 254, 264n36
open systems (architectural), *247*, 253–254, 257, 262, 264n36, 293, 309

Open Systems in Building Production (Utida), 247, 254–255, 264n37
oppressive house (phenomenon), 69n10
Oriental Shiraishi Corporation, 329
Osaka (Japan), 131, 133, 135, *135*, 137–138, *139*, 255, 267, *267*, 270, 282, *282*, *287*, 290, 339–340, *341*. See also Expo '70
Osaka Gas, 267, 270, 281; NEXT21 Experimental Housing, *253*, 263, 267, *267*, 269, 270–271, *271*, *273*, 274, *274*, 278, *278*, 281–282, *281*, 285, *285*, 285n2, 285n15, 287, 290, 293–294, 301, 309–310
Osaka Prefectural Housing Supply Corporation, 290, 299n7
Otaka, Masato, 129n47, 138, 141n13, 180, 183, 267, 271, 323, 353, 354; Artificial Land Committee, participation in, 108, 111; Chojuen Apartments, 149, *152*, 153, 156, *156*, 159, 174n1, 174n3, 175n33, 180, 189, 262, 271; Harumi Apartments, 77, 82–83, 86, 123, 162, 165–166; *machizukuri* work in Fukushima, 253; Kunio Maekawa, work with, 77; Fumihiko Maki, collaborations with, 90, *90*, *92*, 103n42, 119–120, 123, 125, 129n48, 129n49; Metabolism, criticism of, 136; Metabolism, formation of, 22–23, 82–83, 90, *90*, 103n42; Motomachi Apartments, 149, *149*, *152*, 153, 156, *156*, 159, *159*, 162, *162*, 165–166, *165–166*, 173, *173*, 174n1, 174n3, 175n18, 175n21, 175n27, 190, 238, 252, 262; Otemachi proposal, 111, *113*; PAU methodology, 149, 153, 159, 173; Sakaide Artificial Land Platform, 38n9, *105*, 113, *113*, 115, *115*, 117, *117*, 119, *119*, *120*, 123, 127, *127*; Tochigi Prefectural Council Building, *317*, 325, *325*; Tokyo Bay proposal, 86, *87*
Otani, Sachio, 103n42, 175n21, *204*, 205, 208, 271
Otto, Frei, 309, 315n22

P
Pacific Belt (of Japan), 135, 195, 198, 264n7
Packard, Vance, 248, *248*, 264n10, 264n11
Palladio's Children (Habraken), 350n27
Panasonic, 177, 203. See also Matsushita
Panekyo, 294
parametric(ism), 26, 37, 117, 128n32, 255
parcels, parcellation, 109, 274, 285n11, 306
Paris (France), 33, 51–52, 55, 77, 205, *208*
Pepsi, 138

pollution, 94, 135–136, 198, 208, 218, 325, 329, 347–348
polyvalency, 25–26, 38n21
post-occupancy evaluation, 22, 281, *297*, 298
prefabrication, prefab, 36, 83, 129n47, 186, 193n16, 200, 203–205, 224, 238, 247, 254, 262, 265n63, 298, 309, 321
Prefabrication, Art and Architecture, Urbanism (PAU), 149, 153, 159, 173
Project Japan (Koolhaas and Obrist), 91, 93–94, 102n27, 102n31, 129n48, 141n21, 141n30, 174n3, 218n3
private development, 25, 51, 56–57, 71, 111, 129n51, 131–132, 135, 198, 218, 250, 252, 332
Prouvé, Jean, 82
Pruitt-Igoe, 166, 175n25, 177, 193n1, 193n2
public housing, 25, 55–57, 66, 102n4, 111, 127, 131, 205, 270, 304, 338
Public Works Administration, 338
Purism, 37

R
Renaissance (European), 29, 343, 350n27
renovation, 20, 81, 173, 175n27, 175n33, 225, 238, 248, 252, 261, 267, 271, 274, 278, 281, *281*, 334n5, 348
rental housing, 25, 38n15, 56–57, 66, 109, 113, 173, 180, 203, 238, 255, 290, 315n19, 332
Reynolds, Jonathan, 141n24, 317
Rikuzentakata City, 218
Robinson, John B., 341, *342*, 349n21
Roppongi Hills, 117, 119, 127, 128n35
Rudofsky, Bernard, 224–225, 238, 245n6
Rudolph, Paul, 82, *208*
Rue des Amiraux Apartments, see Sauvage, Henri

S
Safdie, Moshe, 26
Sakakura, Junzo, 69n26, 82
Sand, Jordan, 38n5
Sankei Newspaper, 81
Sano, Toshikata, 45, 74
Sasaki, Masaya, 251–252
Sato, Jun, 359
Satoh, Sanae, 189
Sauvage, Henri, 205, *208*
Sawada family, 225, 232, *232*, 236, 238; Hiroe, *221*, 224–225, *224*, 232, *245*, 247; Kano, *221*, 224–225, *224*, 232, 236, 238, 247; Kazuko, 238; Sawada Mansion, Sawaman, *221*, *221*, 224–225, *227*, 232, *232*, 236, *236*, 238, *238*, 245n18, *245*, 281, 309, 348
Sawada Mansion, Sawaman, see Sawada family
Sawada, Seiji, 258–259

scenarios, *117*, 186, 200, 274, 278, 281, 285, 298, 341, 343, 348, *357*
Schumacher, E. F., 225, 232, 245n10
Schumacher, Patrik, 128n32
Schwann, Theodor, 91
scrap-and-build, 248, 251–253, 261, 264n7, 270, 317, 325–326, 338–340, 353
scrap-and-build spiral, 251–252
Seagram Building, *see* Mies van der Rohe, Ludwig
Seidensticker, Edward, 343
seikatsu-gaku (lifeology), 46, 53n10, 53n18
seismic base isolation, 211, 329, 335n29
Sekisui Chemical Company, 203
Sekisui Heim M1, 203, *203*
Semper, Gottfried, 320
Senri New Town, 135, *135*, 138, 175n21
Seto Inland Sea, 111
shaku, 255, 262, 274
Shibaura Institute of Technology, 263
Shikinen Sengu (for Ise Shrine), 320
Shikoku Island (Japan), 111, 224
Shimizu Corporation, 137
Shinkansen, 198
Shinkenchiku, 57, 77, 83, 102n29
Shinohara, Kazuo, 138, 141n29, 204, 219n26
Shinto(ism), 225, 317, 320–321
Showa Yokkaichi Oil, 135, *135*, 136
shrinkage, shrinking (cities), 198, 334, 338, 340, 353
Shu-Koh-Sha Architecture and Urban Design Studio, 271, *287*. *See also* Chikazumi, Shinichi
silviculture, 317
Siniawer, Eiko Maruko, 248, 350n39, 350n40
SITE, 16, *19*, 309, 329, 335n28
skeleton frame, 19–20, 26–28, 58, 200, 221, 224–225, 232, 263
skeleton/infill (SI), 259, *261*, 271, *271*, *273*, 274, 278, 281–282, 287, 290, 293–294, *293–294*, 298, 304, 306, 309, 315n22, 317, *317*, 325, 329, 332–334, *332*, 338, 346, 348, 354, *355–356*, *358*. *See also* support/infill
Skidmore, Owings & Merrill, 333
Sky House, 23, 38n10, 69n18, 83, 162
Small is Beautiful (Schumacher), 225
Smithson, Alison, 82
Smithson, Peter, 13, 16, 23, 25, 58, 82, 89, 304, 314
social overhead capital, 137, 141n22, 180, 198, 259
solutionism, 195, 205, 208, 218, 219n30, 341
Sound Material-Cycle (SMC), Sound Material-Cycle Society, 326, 343, 347

Sorensen, André, 135, 140n3, 141n12, 193n10, 218n2, 219n33, 219n37, 252, 264n17
Space, Time and Architecture (Giedion), 125, 129n47
sprawl, 56, 135–136, 140, 198, 208, 252
Starrett-Lehigh Building, 16, *19*
steel, *35*, 36, 74, *75*, 81, 138–139, 159, *159*, 173, 177, 183, 186, 199, 221, 257, 262, 274, 310, *312*, 321, 355
steel-reinforced concrete (SRC), 74, *75*
Stichting Architecten Research (SAR) (Foundation for Architects' Research), 258, 265n52, 265n71, 270, 274
stock-based society, 348
Stoffwechsel (metabolism, or theory of material transformations), 320
Stratiform Structure Module, *see* Kikutake, Kiyonori
Structure in Art and Science (Kepes), 125, 129n49
Sunday carpenter, 94, 103n66, 225, 298
sunshine rights, 183, *183*, 193n10, 208, 219n33
Supports (Habraken), 16, 258–259, 263
support/infill, 258–259, 263, 267, 270, 285n11
supportive shack (concept), 69n10
sustainability, 238, 245n28, 270, 278, 317, 346, 348, 350n24
Suzuki, Shigebumi, 51, 53n17
symbolic planning, 162

T
Tafuri, Manfredo, 38n12, 105, 204
Takada, Mitsuo, 259, 261, 265n60, 271, 274, 282, 290, 294, 299n15
Takenaka Corporation, 141n24, 177, 186, 189, 193n13, 211, 245n8, 329; Antarctic base (Japanese), 200, *200*; Metabolists, connections to, 137–138, 141n25, 153, 180, 183, 195, 349n1. *See also* Ashiyahama Shin'nittetsu Takenaka Matsushita
Tama New Town, 135, 141n13
Tamura, Akira, 108–109
Tanaka, Kakuei, 136, *136*, 141n21, 180, 195, 198–199, 208, 219n39
Tange, Kenzo, 57, 77, 102n28, 111, 123, 135, 175n10, 200, 253, 307, 315n18, 317, 329, 354; A Plan for Tokyo, 13, *13*, *15*, 16, 125, 175n21, 205, 271; Boston Bay project, 16, *16*, 83, 153; Debate on Tradition, role in, 81; Hiroshima Peace Memorial Museum and Park, 153, 156, 162, 165, 321, *323*; Japanese commissions, loss of, 138, 177; Kagawa Prefectural Government Building, 128n24, 323, 325; at MIT, 83, 86; Metabolism, formation of,

22, 37, 82–83; Tange Lab at the University of Tokyo, 38n11, 141n21; WoDeCo, two-cycles speech, 23, 25, 83, 261, 337; Yamanashi Press and Broadcasting Center, 162, 323, *325*; Yoyogi National Stadium, 137
Tanimachi neighborhood, 282
tatami mats, 49, 51, 255, *257*, 262, 345
Tatsumi, Kazuo, 259, 261, 265n60, 271, 274, 290, 294
Team 10, 23, 82, 102n28, 265n71
terrain artificiel (artificial land), 13, *32*, 36, 39n23, 52, 125
timber (wood) construction, 36, 45, 49, 56–57, 63, 74, 78, 236, 238, 255, 262, 290, 304, 309, 315n22, 317, *317*, 320–321, 323, 325, 329, 333, 335n38, 345; mass timber (CLT), 333, 339, 348, 350n50, 354; 2x4 framing, 190, 257, 309–310, 315n21, 315n23
Tohoku earthquake and tsunami (March 11, 2011), 71, 218, 285n4
To-morrow: A Peaceful Path to Real Reform (Howard), 31
Tojuso co-ops, 282, *282*, 285n19, 301
Tokaido Megalopolis, *133*, 135, 141n11, 198
Tokaido Road, 135, 141n11
Tokugawa (rule), 343, 345
Tokyo (Japan), 22–23, 27, *43*, 52, 53n17, 69n26, 82–83, 86, 90, 93–94, 97, 103n63, 108, 111, *111*, 117, 119, 133, 135, 153, *180*, 198, *204*, 208, 251, 255, 285n4, 326, 329, 339–340, 342; and Edo era, 343, *345*, 345–347, *345*, 350n32; height limits for construction, 71, 128n23, 174n7; night-soil trade, 347; reconstruction after the Great Kanto Earthquake, 45–46, 71, 74; reconstruction after World War II, 43, 45, 55–57, 66; scrap-and-build, dominance of, 264n7, 340. *See also* Tokyo Bay proposal *under* Otaka, Masato; A Plan for Tokyo *under* Tange, Kenzo; *and* University of Tokyo
Torre David, 20, *20*, 190, 193n28
Toshiba, 138, *139*, 141n28
Toshi-Jutaku, 258
Totman, Conrad, 345
Toyota Home, 203, 218n20
transitional type, 77, 81, 94, 97, 115, 159, 173, 180, 247, 290, 304
Truman, Harry, 174n8
Tsunane Cooperative House, 301, *301*, 304, 306–307, 309–310, *309–310*, *312*, 314, *314*, 332, 348
Turner, John F. C., 69n10, 348
2x4 framing, *see* timber (wood) construction
2DK, 48–49, *49*, 51, 53n17, 56–57, 61, 71, 74, *78*, 159, 180
200-year housing plan, 338–341, 348, 349n11, 350n50, 354

365

Two-Step Housing System (TSHS), 259, 261, *261*, 263, 265n63, 271, 287, 290, 298, 332, 348

U

Ueda, Akihiro, 329
ukiyo (floating world), 346
University of Tokyo, The, 38n11, 51, 83, 103n42, 108, 127n10, 203, 253–254, 264n3, 265n68
Urban Renaissance Agency, 97, *97, 99*, 304, 333
Ushimi, Akira, 66
USSR, 75
Utida, Yoshifumi, 253
Utida, Yoshikazu, 74, 108, 253, 265n65
Utida, Yoshio, 329
Utida, Yositika, 203, 264n3, 265n68, 267, 317, 326, 337, 341, 345; Artificial Land Committee, participation in, 108, 254; Ashiyahama Seaside Town competition, 180, 186, 189, 254; John Habraken, relation with, 248, *253*, 258–259; Metabolism, opinion of, 257; on open systems, *247–248*, 254–255, *257*, 264n36, 264n37; Stratiform Structure Module, involvement with, 195, 211, 254. See also Century Housing System; *Open Systems in Building Production*; and NEXT21 *under* Osaka Gas

V

VANS Architects, *301*, 304, 306, 309–310
vernacular construction, 16, 23, 29, 33, 46, 77, 90, 190, 200, 221, 224, 232, 238, 245n16, 257, 262–263, 265n49, 309, 338, 345, 348
vertical garden city, 29, 31, *31*, 117, 314
Ville Spatiale, 16, *16*

W

Wall Street Journal, The, 251
War Reconstruction Institute, 132
Waseda University, 46, 69n20, 91, 94, 245n6
Washington University in St. Louis, 83
Waste: Consuming Postwar Japan (Siniawer), 264n10, 350n39, 350n40
Waste Makers, The (Packard), 248, *248*, 264n10, 264n11
Waswo, Ann, 53n15, 132, 141n5
Watanabe, Yoshio, 317
Wendelken, Cherie, 153, 315n1
Werf, Frans van der, 270, *271*
Wilgus, William J., 109
wood, *see* timber (wood) construction
Woolworth Building, 127n1
World Design Conference (WoDeCo), 23, 82–83, *85*, 89, *92*, 102n27, 120, 138, 261, 337
World War II, 20, 36, 257

Y

Yale Law Journal, The, 108
Yamasaki, Minoru, 175n25
Yamashita, Yoshitsugu, 306, 311, 314, *314*
Yamato (battleship), 159, 175n13
Yanagi, Sori, 82
Yatsuka, Hajime, 23, 38n9, 38n11, 45, 53n9, 127n10, 128n12, 128n23, 175n10, 205, 208
Yokkaichi, *135*, 135–136,
Yokoyama, Fugaku, 74–75, 325
Yoshitake, Yasumi, 51, 53n17
Yosizaka, Takamasa, 43, *43, 44*, 53n9, 74, 245n20; artificial land, Yosizaka's interpretation of, 55–58, *55*, 69n4, 81, 93, 109, 125, 131, 139, 225, 259, 261; criticism of Yosizaka's interpretation, 66; Japan Pavilion, Venice, 36; *jukyo-gaku* (dwelling studies), 51; and Wajiro Kon, 46, 53n10, 309; Le Corbusier, work with, 36, 45, 51–52, *52*, 53n19, 69n26; maximum dwelling, idea of, 57, 69n10, 71, 247; standardization, criticism of, 52; Ura House, 69n18; at Waseda University, 46, 69n20, 91, 94, 103n51, 245n6; Yosizaka House, 58, *58*, 61, *61*, 63, *63, 64*, 66, *67, 69*, 69n20, 193, 232, 329, 348; Masakuni Yosizaka, 61, *64*, 69n16; Masamitsu Yosizaka, *64*
Yotsuya Station, Tokyo, 208

Z

zenekon (design-build general contractor), 137–139, 153, 177, 186, 225, 245n8, 271, 339
Zevi, Bruno, 38n12
Zodiac, 38n12
zoning, 105, 108, 117, 127n4, 128n12, 128n13, 135, 198, 208, 211, 221, 250, 309

Image credits

Every effort has been made to trace copyright holders and to obtain their permission for the use of copyrighted material. The author apologizes for any errors or omissions in the list below and would be grateful if notified of any corrections that should be incorporated in any future editions of this book.

Photo: Ian Lambot, 6–7; ©F.L.C./ADAGP, Paris/Artists Rights Society (ARS), New York 2021, 10–11, 28, 30, 32–33, 35; Courtesy Tange Associates/photo: Akio Kawasumi, 12; Courtesy Tange Associates, 14–15; Yona Friedman, *Toward a Scientific Architecture* (Cambridge, MA: The MIT Press, 1975), 17 top; Kenzo Tange Archive/Gift of Mrs. Takako Tange, 2011/Courtesy Frances Loeb Library, Harvard University Graduate School of Design, 17 center; Photo: Tom Haartsen ©Constant/Fondation Constant c/o ARS New York 2020, 17 bottom; Courtesy SITE, 18 top left; Russell G. and Walter M. Cory with Yasuo Matsui, 18 top right; Photo composite: Filip Dujardin, 18 bottom; A.B. Walker, 21 top; Photo: Iwan Baan, 21 bottom; Photos: Casey Mack, 24, 84–85, 97–101, 121–124, 126, 167–171, 174, 178–179, 191, 192, 194, 212–217, 220, 222–223, 228–231, 234–236, 242, 243, 269, 272, 278, 279, 283, 284, 286, 2–289, 291 bottom, 294, 300, 302–303, 305, 312, 313, 324, 328; Public Domain, 27, 44 top, 142, 143; Popular Architecture, 34, 37, 41, 76, 79, 116, 187, 355–359; Universal Images Group via Getty Images, 42; Courtesy Masakuni Yosizaka, 43, 44 bottom, 52, 54, 58–63, 67; Courtesy Kogakuin University Library, 47; Uzo Nishiyama, *Sumai no kokongaku: gendai Nihon jutakushi* (Tokyo: Shokokusha, 1989), 49; Catherine Bauer, *Modern Housing* [1934](University of Minnesota Press, 2020), 50; © National Archives of Modern Architecture, Agency for Cultural Affairs, 64–65, 90, 113, 154–155, 156, 164; © National Archives of Modern Architecture, Agency for Cultural Affairs/Courtesy Mutsuko Smith/Yuki Kikutake and Mitsunori Kikutake, 88; Photos: Eiji Kitada, 68, 266, 275; Courtesy Urban Renaissance Agency, 70, 75 bottom, 95, 96, 134 top; Photo: Chuji Hirayama, 72–73; Courtesy Maekawa Associates, Architects & Engineers, 75 top, 78; Photos: Richard Langendorf, 80, 81; Photo: Yukio Futagawa, 82; Courtesy Makiko Otaka, 86, 87, 106–107, 118, 119, 163; Photo: Eitaro Torihata, 89; Courtesy Mari Asada, 92 left; ©Yaeko Awazu/Courtesy Ken Awazu, 92 right; ©Yaeko Awazu/Courtesy 21st Century Museum of Contemporary Art, Kanazawa, 336; *Shinkenchiku*, 104, 114; Courtesy Atelier Bow-Wow, 110 top; Courtesy Architectural Institute of Japan, 110 bottom, 112 top and center; Courtesy Hikaru Kinoshita and Hiroaki Kondou, 112 bottom; Courtesy Maki and Associates, 120; Courtesy Takenaka Corporation, 130, 176, 181 bottom, 182, 183, 184–185, 187, 1, 201 bottom; Takashi Doi/*Ekistics*, 133; Photo: Kenji Higuchi, 134 bottom; Fair use, 136, 249 bottom left and right, 344 top; Takato Marui/Creative Commons, 139; Courtesy The Estate of R. Buckminster Fuller, 140; Photos: Larry Rosensweig, 144–147; Photos: Tomio Ohashi, 148, 152, 158; Photo: Addison Godel, 150–151; Courtesy Hiroshima Municipal Archives, 157, 160–161; Sutemi Horiguchi, 163; Photo: Junko Kimura/Getty Images News/Getty Images, 165; Courtesy Adam Staniland, 166; Courtesy Hiroshima Housing Authority, 172–173; ©Isozaki, Arata/Gift of The Howard Gilman Foundation/Digital Image ©The Museum of Modern Art/Licensed by SCALA/Art Resource, NY, 181 top; Courtesy Joho Kenchiku Co., Ltd./Mutsuko Smith/Yuki Kikutake and Mitsunori Kikutake, 196–197, 344 bottom; Courtesy Mechanical Social Systems Foundation, 199, 201 top, 210 top; Courtesy Sekisui Chemical Co., Ltd. Housing Company, 202, 203; Creative Commons, 204–205; Yoshio Higashikata, *In-fill with Capsules Architectures* (Tokyo: Ohmsha, 2007), 206; Paul Rudolph/Courtesy Library of Congress, 209 top; Maurice Culot, Robert L. Delevoy, and Lise Grenier, *Henri Sauvage 1873–1932* (Brussels: Archives d'Architecture Moderne, 1978), 209 bottom; Photo: Hiromi Watanabe, 210 bottom; Courtesy Sawaman Youth Group, 224; Courtesy Hiroe Sawada, 244; Tetsuro Kagaya, *Sawada Mansion chōikkyū shiryō: Sekai saikyō no selfbuild kenchiku tanhō* (Tokyo: Tsukiji Shokan, 2007), 226–227, 233, 237, 239–241; Courtesy Yositika Utida, 246, 249 top, 256 top; ©Osaka Gas Co., Ltd., 253, 268, 280; Courtesy Mitsuo Takada/Osaka City Museum, 256 bottom; Courtesy Mitsuo Takada, 260 top (redrawn by Popular Architecture), 296–297; Donald Ryan in Stewart Brand, *How Buildings Learn: What Happens After They're Built* (New York: Viking, 1994), 260 bottom; Courtesy Frans van der Werf, 270; Courtesy Shu-Koh-Sha Architecture and Urban Design Studio, 271, 273, 276, 277, 295; Courtesy Tokuichi Yoshimura, 290, 291 top, 292, 293; Courtesy VANS Architects, 306, 307, 308 (redrawn by Popular Architecture), 311, 314; *Kenchiku Chishiki*, 316; Courtesy ARX Architects and Associates, 318–319, 327, 330–331, 332; *The Yomiuri Shimbun* via AP Images, 321; Photo: Alice Chung, 322; Ida-10/Flickr, 323; Photo: Botond Bognar, 325; Hirokazu Shima et al., 326; Courtesy Haseko Corporation, 340; Courtesy John B. Robinson, 342 (redrawn by Popular Architecture); Courtesy Climate Central, 354

© 2022 Hatje Cantz Verlag, Berlin,
and
© 2022 Casey Mack
www.populararchitecture.com

All rights reserved. Requests for permission to reproduce material from this work should be sent to the author.

Published by
Hatje Cantz Verlag GmbH
Mommsenstraße 27
10629 Berlin
www.hatjecantz.com
A Ganske Publishing Group Company

ISBN 978-3-7757-4642-7

Project management:
Claire Cichy, Hatje Cantz
Adam Jackman, Hatje Cantz

Copy editor:
Thomas Daniell

Translations:
Riyo Namigata
Shohei Kawanaka
Tomoyo Nakamura

Design:
Alice Chung, Omnivore

Production:
Thomas Lemaître, Hatje Cantz

Reproduction:
DLG Graphic, Paris

Printing and binding:
Livonia Print

This book has been composed in Arial on Munken Polar, 130 gsm.

Printed in Europe.

Cover: Le Corbusier with Takamasa Yosizaka, visiting Yosizaka's house in Tokyo, 1955

Digesting Metabolism: Artificial Land in Japan 1954–2202 is made possible by grants from the Graham Foundation for Advanced Studies in the Fine Arts and the New York State Council on the Arts with the support of the Office of the Governor and the New York State Legislature, and with additional support from the Takenaka Corporation.

Graham Foundation

NEW YORK STATE OF OPPORTUNITY. | Council on the Arts

TAKENAKA